Princes of Ireland, Planters of Maryland

Princes of Ireland,
Planters of Maryland

A Carroll Saga, 1500–1782

Ronald Hoffman

in Collaboration with Sally D. Mason

Published for the
Omohundro Institute of
Early American History and Culture,
Williamsburg, Virginia, by the
University of North Carolina Press,
Chapel Hill and London

The Omohundro Institute of Early American History and Culture
is sponsored jointly by the College of William and Mary and the
Colonial Williamsburg Foundation.
On November 15, 1996, the Institute adopted the present name
in honor of a bequest from Malvern H. Omohundro, Jr.

Set in Minion type by G&S Typesetters
Manufactured in the United States of America

Library of Congress Cataloging-in-Publication Data
Hoffman, Ronald, 1941–
Princes of Ireland, planters of Maryland : a Carroll saga, 1500–1782 /
Ronald Hoffman, in collaboration with Sally D. Mason.
p.   cm.
Includes index.
ISBN 978-0-8078-2556-3 (cloth: alk. paper)
ISBN 978-0-8078-5347-4 (pbk.: alk. paper)
1. Carroll, Charles, 1702–1782. 2. Carroll, Charles, 1737–1832. 3. Carroll family.
4. Plantation owners—Maryland—Biography. 5. Statesmen—Maryland—
Biography. 6. Catholics—Maryland—Biography. 7. Irish Americans—
Maryland—Biography. 8. Elite (Social sciences)—Maryland—Biography.
9. Maryland—History—Colonial period, ca. 1600–1775. 10. Maryland—
History—Revolution, 1775–1783. I. Mason, Sally D. II. Title.
F184.C37 H64   2000
975.2'02'0922—dc21
[B]   99-052475

The paper in this book meets the guidelines for permanence and durability
of the Committee on Production Guidelines for Book Longevity of the
Council on Library Resources.

Publication of this book has been made possible in part by grants from the
L. J. Skaggs and Mary C. Skaggs Foundation to the Omohundro Institute of Early
American History and Culture and to the University of North Carolina Press.

cloth   06 05 04 03 02   6 5 4 3 2
paper   11 10 09 08 07   7 6 5 4 3

In memory of my mother,

Ethel Lubin Hoffman,

who, like the ghosts of the

Slieve Bloom Mountains,

loved a good story

PLATE 1. Litterluna Abbey.
Photograph by Simon Marsden, The Marsden Archive

Preface

This book evolved from the persistence in my mind of a place — Ireland. More than fourteen years ago I sat down to record my thoughts regarding the Carroll family of colonial Maryland as a way of clarifying my understanding of their fascinating history. By then I was well into editing their papers, a substantial collection of eighteenth- and nineteenth-century manuscripts located primarily at the Maryland Historical Society in Baltimore. At the time, I thought I knew the broad outlines of the story fairly well. My first encounter with the Carroll materials had occurred in the late 1960s, during the writing of my doctoral dissertation, when I drew on them extensively for my account of Maryland in the period of the American Revolution. My dissertation adviser, the late Merrill Jensen, found the human drama contained in the Carroll documents exciting, and he suggested that at some future time I consider preparing an edition of them. Several years later Jack P. Greene read my manuscript on Revolutionary Maryland and urged me to embark on such a project. Other pushes in that direction came from my good friend Edward C. Papenfuse, Archivist of the State of Maryland, and, most insistently, from a research associate, Sally D. Mason.

An initial grant from the National Endowment for the Humanities and longer-term support from the National Historical Publications and Records Commission allowed the work to commence. Time passed, and, as the story of the Carrolls unfolded in growing complexity before me, I judged it appropriate to distill my impressions. The strategy also had an ulterior motive — I thought such a piece might make a good article. Perhaps even the *William and Mary Quarterly* would accept it. Hope springs eternal.

I envisioned the pivotal relationship between Charles Carroll of Carrollton and his father, Charles Carroll of Annapolis, as the narrative's central dynamic. The story would open in the 1740s with the son's boyhood, continue through the American Revolution, and end with the father's death just before the close of that conflict in 1782. After a series of false starts I decided to pursue what I perceived as a faint refrain in the Carroll letters — the echoes of Ireland that I occasionally heard in them. I reasoned that, before portraying the lives of these eighteenth-century, Maryland-born Carrolls, whose correspondence I had read and reread, I should know something about their Irish forebears. I would begin with the first member of the family to emigrate from Ireland, Charles Carroll the Settler, grandfather of Charles Carroll of Carrollton, who arrived at St. Mary's City in

1688. I did not anticipate an extensive investigation — just a quick sketch of this Carroll's background, why he came to Maryland, and perhaps how the experience of Ireland influenced his conduct and the raising of his family.

Live and learn — that short excursion into Irish history took nearly seven years. And, as I peeled back layer after layer and generation after generation, I came to see the saga of the family in a wholly different light — as a story informed not only by the harsh realities of eighteenth-century Maryland but also by the powerful sway of the conscious memory and the subconscious influence of Ireland. Although written about people of another religion in a much different time and context, words from Elie Wiesel's novel *The Forgotten* effectively capture the essence of what I learned about the Carrolls during my journey into their Irish past:

> For a Jew, nothing is more important than memory. He is bound to his origins by memory. It is memory that connects him to Abraham, Moses and Rabbi Akiba. If he denies memory he will have denied his own honor.

Acknowledgments

One of the consequences of laboring so long on this project has been the exponential mounting of debts. When I presented part of this story to the University of Maryland's Early American Seminar, my colleagues had much to say, and not all of it was pleasant to hear. Ira Berlin has been a hard taskmaster since our days together in graduate school, and his comments over the years have significantly influenced my conceptual framework. I have known David Grimsted for only a slightly shorter period, and his astute judgments always weigh heavily on my mind. Emory Evans and James Henretta provided valuable suggestions on a number of occasions, and John McCusker helped enormously in two separate areas — trade, for which his scholarship is impeccable, and Roman Catholic doctrine and practice, a body of knowledge that he knows well and generously shared with me. Alison Olson supplied useful leads on questions involving imperial background, and other seminar members, especially Lois Green Carr and Lorena S. Walsh, made their invaluable research available. I am especially beholden to Lorena for access to her files on mortgage accounts and for our many conversations on tenantry.

As my journey to understand the Carrolls moved back to a land and time when they were the O'Carrolls, I needed even more guidance. My earliest forays into Irish historical research were greatly facilitated by Louis Cullen of Trinity College, Dublin, Donal Begley, the former Chief Herald of Ireland, and James Carroll, an Irish diplomat with a keen curiosity about his clan's past. About a year into my Irish quest, I met Gerald Carroll, a London-based investor and developer whose passion for the family saga matched my own. Our adventures together were memorable. Scholars of Irish history are indebted to Gerald for endowing at Hertford College, Oxford, England's first chair in Irish history, now held by Roy Foster, and for his creation of the Carroll Institute. The financial support afforded my research by Gerald Carroll and the array of talent he recruited for the Carroll Institute constituted extraordinary resources. The staff of the Carroll Institute — the late Peter Davies, Elizabeth FitzPatrick, Aoife Leonard, and Tim Venning — were marvelous colleagues with whom to work. Through the Carroll Institute I also came to know Simon Marsden. Several of his haunting photographs of the O'Carroll territory, among them his brilliant portrait of Leap Castle, are contained in this volume. Not far from Leap sits Birr Castle, once a Carroll fortification and now occupied by the earl and countess of

Rosse, whose generous hospitality matches the splendid manuscripts housed in their muniments room. Finally — and most importantly for this book — I met, by way of the Carroll Institute, Rolf and Magda Loeber, whose scholarly investigations of early modern Irish history truly merit the definition of pathbreaking. The Loebers' remarkable use of land records enabled me to achieve a perspective on the O'Carrolls that has been invaluable.

In my rambles through Ireland I met wonderful people everywhere. Where else but in Roscrea would the officers of a local historical society open up their doors for me at 10:00 P.M. on a Sunday night, set before me a bottle of Irish whiskey, and tell me to go at it? I did — at both the manuscripts and the whiskey. And where else but in Offaly could I meet a local historian like Patrick Heany, whose knowledge of Ely O'Carroll and the Slieve Bloom Mountains is spellbinding? Were I an anthropologist, Paddy would be my subject — because I am a historian, he is my esteemed colleague. I also benefited from my visits with Canon Thomas Ryan at Lorrha and from my conversations and correspondence with Nicholas Canny, whose observations on my manuscript's introductory section were very helpful. Tracey Coughlan of Ely O'Carroll Tourism graciously helped me acquire photographs of the O'Carrolls' country in County Offaly. In Great Britain, I want to thank Father Geoffrey Holt at Farm Street for a discussion of St. Omers, the earl of Lytton for making available John Baker's diary, and the staff of Holkham Hall for facilitating my research of its archive. For his gracious friendship, invaluable research assistance, and incomparable knowledge of Jesuit education from its beginnings through the eighteenth century, I am deeply grateful to Maurice Whitehead of the University of Hull.

Repositories for research, seminars for testing out of ideas, and financial support for the time to explore, think, and write are the infrastructure of the historian's craft. I have benefited greatly from all of these. At the Maryland Historical Society, manuscript librarians Donna Ellis, Karen Stuart, and Jennifer Bryan were invariably patient and accommodating. Ed Papenfuse's incomparable organizational talents as an archivist made my work at the Maryland State Archives enormously productive. There Susan Cummings never tired in fulfilling my requests, and I had the considerable privilege of many informative conversations with Phebe Jacobsen. Besides the Early American Seminar at the University of Maryland, I learned much from presentations at the Columbia Seminar, the Cushwa Center at the University of Notre Dame, where I had several meaningful talks with Phillip Gleason, the McNeil Center for Early American Studies at the University of Pennsylvania, and the Omohundro Institute of Early American History and Culture. On a trip to Catholic University I spent little more than an hour with Father John Lynch, then chair of the Department of

Canon Law. Although our visit was short by most standards, he provided indispensable information. Finally, when I most needed time to organize, reflect, and write, the University of Maryland's General Research Board provided support that allowed for completion of a first draft.

But, as authors know — especially those who work with the Omohundro Institute of Early American History and Culture — a first draft is just that, a beginning. Trading on friendship, I persuaded Jon Sensbach and Mechal Sobel to read the manuscript at that stage, and, as they will see, their suggestions were taken to heart. Richard Dunn and Thad Tate also completed useful evaluations that persuaded me of the need to be concise. Just before I signed off on the manuscript, Kenneth Lockridge gave it an extremely penetrating reading, and his critique assumed considerable significance when I subsequently reconceptualized important aspects of my interpretation. Once the work became an official submission to the Institute, my editor, colleague, and friend Fredrika J. Teute sent it out to John Murrin and Peter Onuf, who provided marvelous — and manageable — suggestions for revision. Building on their analyses, Fredrika wrote a lengthy — I should say staggering — assessment that cut to the core of my argument and set out a formidable agenda. And so I have revised and revised, and the vastly improved result attests the skill and strength of her editorship. When at last the revised version had been completed, my irrepressible former student, Beatriz Betancourt Hardy, read every word with care. Bea's knowledge of Maryland's colonial Catholic population has served more than once to correct an assumption or modify a conclusion. My colleague Philip D. Morgan performed a similar service by providing a critique that forced me to weigh carefully and sharpen my analysis of the Carrolls as slaveowners and the actions of the persons they enslaved. And finally, Gil Kelly, the managing editor of the Institute's publication program, brought his formidable skills to bear in seeing the manuscript through to publication. Gil's absolute dedication to perfection in the art of copyediting has made his reputation a legend among Institute authors.

Two individuals made indispensable contributions to moving my work on the Carrolls forward. Although each is a person of considerable accomplishment, both — the Honorable Benjamin L. Cardin of Maryland's Third Congressional District and Hays T. Watkins, former chairman and chief executive of CSX and a member of the Institute's Executive Board (1993–1999) — agreed that I could recognize them here only if I did so modestly. So I will simply say that their support allowed me to shape this monograph and structure the documentary edition of the Charles Carroll of Carrollton Papers according to my best judgment and that I greatly appreciate their help.

Of all the debts I have accumulated, none is greater than those I owe to my two associates on the Carroll papers, Eleanor S. Darcy and Sally D. Mason. Eleanor's incisive research in Irish history and finely honed genealogical skills provided essential information for creating the framework and perspective of the book. Having Eleanor as my colleague for many years has been a stroke of good fortune indeed. As for Sally D. Mason, my indebtedness is so profound that I could not live with myself if her name did not appear on the title page with mine. Over the years my knowledge of the Carrolls expanded through a relentless thrashing out of ideas and lines of analysis with her. When it came to the women of the Carroll story, her graceful pen recreated their portrait with little help from me. Conversely, there is not a line in the rest of the book that she did not in some way shape. Her love of the Carroll story is only matched by the tenacity of her intellect — I am immensely pleased to have written this saga with her.

Contents

Preface   vii

Acknowledgments   ix

List of Illustrations and Tables   xv

List of Abbreviations   xvii

Introduction   xix

Prologue. Fields of Hunger: Faith and War   1

Chapter 1. "Anywhere so long as There Be Freedom"   36

Chapter 2. "Marylando-Hibernus"   61

Chapter 3. "A Well-Regulated Œconomy"   98

Chapter 4. "Sound & Strong": A Worthy Heir   131

Chapter 5. Affairs of the Heart: 1765–1773   184

Chapter 6. "A Prudent Management"   218

Chapter 7. "The Occupation of Agriculture"   235

Chapter 8. "There Is the 1st: Citizen": Political Beginnings   265

Chapter 9. A Broader Allegiance: The American Revolution   303

Chapter 10. The Family Economy: 1777–1782   334

Chapter 11. Scenes from a Marriage: Charley and Molly, 1776–1782   351

Epilogue   389

Appendix 1. A Poem about the O'Carroll Forces after the
Battle of Aughrim   393

Appendix 2. Ely-Éile   395

Appendix 3. Incomes of the Wealthy in Early Maryland   396

Appendix 4. Nineteenth-Century Accounts of Charles Carroll
of Carrollton's Birth   398

Appendix 5. Carroll Real Estate Transactions, Baltimore Town,
1745–1763   402

Appendix 6. Genealogical Charts   404

Index   415

Illustrations and Tables

MAPS

1. The Four Provinces of Ireland, Ely O'Carroll, and
   O'Carroll Castles, 1200–1650   2
2. Ely O'Carroll, by Boazio   4
3. The O'Carrolls' Irish World, c. 1500–1700   6
4. Ely O'Carroll, by Lythe   9
5. Land Owned by Catholics, 1641–1703   50
6. The Carrolls' Maryland World, 1765–1782   188
7. Plan of the Harbour and City of Annapolis   381

PLATES

1. Litterluna Abbey   vi
2. Slieve Bloom Mountains   xxviii
3. Leap Castle   17
4. O'Neill's Well   18
5. Ballymooney Castle   24
6. Carroll Coats of Arms   45
7. Bookplate of Charles Carroll the Settler   55
8. Charles Carroll the Settler   60
9. Mary Darnall Carroll   69
10. Charles Carroll of Annapolis as a Boy   96
11. The Carrolls' Annapolis Residence   106
12. Elizabeth Brooke Carroll   133
13. Charles Carroll of Annapolis   134
14. Perspective View of St. Omers   145
15. Exercise Book of Charles Carroll of Carrollton   148
16. Charles Carroll of Carrollton   171

17. Daniel Carroll II of Rock Creek   190

18. Doohoragen Manor   236

FIGURE

1. Population Pyramid of Carroll Slaves, 1773   251

TABLES

1. Building a Landed Estate: Charles Carroll the Settler's
   Land Transactions   68

2. Charles Carroll the Settler: Land Acquisitions, 1693–1720   71

3. Distribution of Carroll Slaves, 1773–1774   252

4. Carroll Loans Outstanding in 1776   263

Abbreviations

BL	British Library, London
Cal. S.P.	Great Britain, Public Record Office, *Calendar of State Papers,* Colonial Series (London, 1860–)
CC	Charles Carroll (son of Charles Carroll of Annapolis) (until 1765)
CCA	Charles Carroll of Annapolis
CCC	Charles Carroll of Carrollton (son of Charles Carroll of Annapolis) (after 1765)
CCS	Charles Carroll the Settler
DLC	Library of Congress, Washington, D.C.
EB	Elizabeth Brooke
EBC	Elizabeth Brooke Carroll
DNB	*Dictionary of National Biography*
HMC	Great Britain, Historical Manuscripts Commission
HSP	Historical Society of Pennsylvania, Philadelphia
MDC	Mary Darnall Carroll (Molly)
MdHi	Maryland Historical Society, Baltimore
MdAA	Maryland State Archives, Annapolis
NLI	National Library of Ireland, Dublin
PRO	Public Record Office, London
PROI	Public Record Office, Ireland (Dublin)
PRONI	Public Record Office of Northern Ireland, Belfast
RD	Registry of Deeds, Dublin
TCD	Trinity College, Dublin
WMQ	*William and Mary Quarterly*

Introduction

Charles Carroll of Carrollton is most often remembered as the only Roman Catholic to affix his name to the Declaration of Independence and, following the deaths of John Adams and Thomas Jefferson on July 4, 1826, as the sole surviving signer of that seminal document. During the last years of Carroll's life, Daniel Webster lauded him as the nation's "venerable old relic," children, towns, and counties were named after him, and poets and composers created works in his honor. Astute to the end of his days, Carroll loved the adulation.[1]

Carroll's long life rather surprised him, for, as a young man, he had predicted that his "thin & puny habit of body" would consign him to an early grave. By middle age his robustness had markedly improved, a circumstance he attributed to the strict physical regimen he followed and that he urged, to no avail, on other members of his family: "due exercise of body and mind . . . going to bed at nine o'clock and rising by five o'clock in the morning," followed by a cold bath, a brisk horseback ride, and prayers or mass — all of this before breakfast.[2] Although some benefits undoubtedly accrued to Carroll from this vigorous schedule, his living to the age of ninety-five was a happy outcome to some extent beyond his control. The magnitude of his good fortune should not be underestimated: his world was not only beset by a variety of pestilences but was also bedeviled by medical practices so rudimentary that the treatments endangered life as much as the diseases.

By contrast, Carroll's Catholicism was deliberate, the latest in a series of conscious choices made by him and by two generations of his American forebears and many more generations of his Irish ancestors. A statement attributed to Carroll late in his life — that in signing the Declaration of Independence he "had in view not only our independence of England but the toleration of all sects professing the Christian religion and communicating to them all equal rights" —

1. For example, *The Carrolton March, Performed at the Ceremony of Commencing the Baltimore and Ohio Railroad, on the Fourth of July 1828*, dedicated by permission to the Hon. Charles Carroll of Carrollton, by A. Clifton (Baltimore, 1828), and a poem "To Hon. Charles Carroll, the Only Survivor of Those Who Signed the Declaration of Independence," *Hampshire Gazette* (Northampton, Mass.), July 16, 1828.

2. CC to CCA, May 1, 1764, Carroll Papers, MS 206, MdHi; CCC to Charles Carroll of Homewood, July 1, 1809, CCC's Correspondence with His Son, MdHi.

cannot be confirmed.[3] Neither do his Revolutionary war papers demonstrate an overriding concern with such issues. Nonetheless, his signature can be interpreted within the context of his family's history as a dramatic vindication of an unwavering, sorely tested commitment to freedom of conscience.

Because of the Carrolls' unbending adherence to their Catholic faith, their story provides a unique perspective on early America. Despite great wealth, their religion cast them as outsiders, persons stripped of all political and most civil rights by Protestant authority. Generally, historians have described the Chesapeake gentry from the vantage of the *insiders,* the Protestant elite whose security and status were grounded in English law and practice and who enjoyed as the most fundamental of their civil guarantees the right of property. But Maryland's wealthy Catholics — ten of the colony's twenty largest fortunes belonged to people derisively known as "papists" — found life far more insecure. Although Catholics constituted less than 10 percent of Maryland's population, the economic success of the Catholic gentry loomed disproportionally in the consciousness of the colony's non-Catholic majority and periodically became a focus for both local discontent and official jealousy. Nor did the legal system protect them; indeed, it imperiled their existence. Since the enactment of the Elizabethan penal codes during the last half of the sixteenth century, English law had been used to destroy Catholic wealth. Most of Ireland's great Catholic landholding families and many of England's as well had been broken, their estates confiscated and redistributed to Protestants. Spared from the threat of this legislation until 1689, Maryland's Catholics lived from that date until the eve of the American Revolution with the very real possibility that their lands would be taken. For those economically menaced and politically marginalized families, Chesapeake society assumed a capricious and arbitrary reality that separated their experience from that of the broader, occasionally militant Protestant gentry.

The Carrolls' position as Catholic outsiders in Protestant Maryland and their conscious memory of their family's long, bitter, and ultimately futile struggle against conquest and dispossession in Ireland provide more than a different perspective on early American society. Such experiences also reveal something important about how people who endured thought about themselves, how they structured themselves internally, how they developed a sense of self, and how memory and powerful social forces, working in tandem over sweeps of time, shaped the identity and behavior of successive generations. Threatened relent-

---

3. Quoted in Joseph Gurn, *Charles Carroll of Carrollton, 1737–1832* (New York, 1932), 51. No manuscript copy of this letter has been found.

lessly between 1500 and 1782, first by the territorial ambitions of rival clans, then because of their stubborn attachment to their Gaelic heritage, and finally for their defiant adherence to Catholicism — both in Ireland and in Maryland — the Carrolls consistently developed strategies comparable to those used by their ancestors, confronting each peril with compromise, cunning, implacable will, and a tenacious determination to survive. Memory explains part of the family's parallel reactions over centuries of time, but the deeper continuity in their behavior stretches well beyond that. As if in response to an inexorable nudge from conscious and subconscious cultural forces, each generation seemed to live out the unfinished lives and carry on the unfinished business of its predecessor. Thus, the story of the Carrolls reveals a remarkable paradigm of reassertion in the face of conquest and devastation. Formed by an uncanny ability not merely to survive but to prevail and control, the fierce working of this drive for dynastic power suggests that generations are molded and conditioned by historical time that extends far beyond memory.

Moving backward through Carroll history, from eighteenth-century Maryland to sixteenth-century Ireland, exposes this continuity of motive and experience. Menaced, often simultaneously, by the powerful dynasties of Anglo-Norman descent poised on the borders of their ancestral territory in the Irish midlands, by the unremitting pressure of English expansion, and by bloody internal battles over clan leadership, the O'Carrolls confronted, challenged, resisted, and manipulated a seemingly endless array of hostile opponents intent on vanquishing them. The confiscation of land that followed Cromwell's 1649 invasion, in the aftermath of the second English Civil War, dealt a severe blow to O'Carroll holdings and prospects; but, although the ancestors of the Maryland Carrolls were greatly reduced by the effects of the conquest, they escaped the total destruction visited upon other branches of the clan. That fate caught up with them later, during the Williamite confiscation after the Battle of the Boyne in 1690. In the early eighteenth century, the Irish stem of the Maryland Carrolls' family tree was, in the words of its colonial kin, "extirpated."

By the time of that denouement, however, the person destined to carry the traditions of the family forward and rebuild its wealth in colonial Maryland had migrated to the Chesapeake. Born and raised in Ireland in the wake of Cromwell's destruction of the great Catholic landowning families, the Charles Carroll referred to in this study as Charles Carroll the Settler (1661–1720) nevertheless acquired an excellent education in France, largely through the good offices of a kinsman, Richard Grace, whose devotion to the Royalist cause during the 1650s served him well after the Restoration. Unwilling to accept the prospects that English conquest allotted to Catholics, Carroll secured the midlevel post of attorney general in Maryland through a series of fortuitous links to the colony's proprietors, the Calverts, Lords Baltimore. An English Roman Catholic family with Irish connections, the Calverts' motives in founding and governing their New World settlement included toleration for adherents of their faith.

Charles Carroll the Settler arrived in the provincial capital, St. Mary's City, in the fall of 1688, expecting to find a less hostile environment, within which a well-educated, ambitious Roman Catholic could, like other men on the make at the margins of empire, advance himself politically and economically. He had scarcely landed, however, when events precipitated by the Glorious Revolution transferred control of the provincial government from the Roman Catholic proprietor to the crown, thereby depriving the Settler of his official post and inspiring the solidly Protestant general assembly to enact laws denying Catholics the right to hold public office, practice law, worship publicly, and provide religious educations for their children.

Confronted in colonial Maryland with the same kind of disabling restrictions that had thwarted his forebears in Ireland, the Settler responded in ways that expose the strength of the forces that shaped his lineage: an atavistic obsession with ancient wrongs, a tenacious determination to survive without compromising his Irish Catholic heritage, and a rapacious desire to reconstitute a dynasty founded on vast wealth. Disdaining to solve his problems by changing his religion, he seized the economic opportunities still available to him and built a handsome fortune based on land, slaves, moneylending, and mercantile pursuits. Despite his achievements, the Settler was unable to set aside his desire for political power commensurate with his wealth, and he at length challenged Maryland's Protestant governor in an ill-advised and unequal contest, whose outcome confirmed the defiant ambition that had spurred his ancestors — and the virulence of the religious intolerance that had helped vanquish them. Ultimately unsuccessful, the Settler's bid to reclaim a share of public authority and reestablish Catholics' right to hold public office provoked the general assembly to enact legislation that denied to his coreligionists the last of their civil liberties: the right to vote.

Charles Carroll the Settler's eldest son, Charles Carroll of Annapolis (1702– 1782), inherited both his father's wealth and his bitter legacy of political impotence. Assuming control of the family fortune after the Settler's death in 1720, this second-generation Maryland Carroll periodically faced the legislative threat of the penal laws, the legal restrictions that the English used against Catholic landowners in England and Ireland. The possibility that these statutes would be implemented in Maryland hung over the province's Catholic population for nearly fifty years. Thus, instead of enjoying the legal guarantees of property that

Introduction

were the birthright of the Protestant gentry, Catholics who asserted the cultural identity of their religious faith remained vulnerable to threats of confiscation and dispossession. As had preceding generations of Carrolls, Charles Carroll of Annapolis perceived the world as an unfriendly place and the men who held power within it as foes never to be relied upon or trusted.

Juxtaposed with the memory of past injustices, the reality of being Catholic in an often militantly Protestant society shaped Charles Carroll of Annapolis and his son, Charles Carroll of Carrollton (1737–1832), in interesting ways. Driven, as his father had been, to restore the Carrolls' wealth and acutely aware of the bitter social and economic reduction of his Irish kin, Charles Carroll of Annapolis steadily developed and expanded the assets left by the Settler. In the other great undertaking of his life, he set himself to mold an heir worthy of his Carroll ancestry, to fashion a son able to carry on the unfinished business of the generations that preceded him. To accomplish this goal, Charles Carroll of Annapolis devised some extraordinary strategies, among them delaying marriage to his son's mother for two decades until the lad had proved himself. His purpose in this instance was plain: he would not legitimate and make an heir of his only child until the young man had shown himself capable of preserving a great Catholic estate within a society frequently marked by combative Protestantism.

Sent to Europe for sixteen years to pursue a rigorous regimen of study, Charles Carroll of Carrollton became an intellectually able, coolly competent, emotionally distant man whose distaste for intimacy would ultimately take its unhappiest toll upon his marriage. In the decade preceding the break with England, however, he proved exceptionally adroit, not only at managing his family's vast finances but also at navigating skillfully within Maryland's gentry culture. He put these attributes to good use in the mid-1770s, when, despite his Catholic faith, he maneuvered himself into the colony's Revolutionary leadership. During the American Revolution, Carroll's mental acuity and emotional self-control similarly enabled him to confront the dangers to his family's property and status posed by the war while capitalizing upon its political and economic opportunities. Far less Irish in the way he defined himself than either his father or his grandfather, Charles Carroll of Carrollton's behavior in times of crisis echoed the ancestral willingness to use whatever tactics were most likely to assure the unchanging goals — survival and dominance.

Several explicit markers suggest how these Maryland Carrolls transmitted their complex heritage of conscious and subconscious cultural memory, tradition, and legend from one generation to the next. The strongest mode of transmission by far was their adamant refusal to change their religion. For the Settler, religious fealty interwove with Jacobite loyalties to produce an arrogant man no more willing to abjure the Stuarts than to deny the doctrines of his church, a combination that rendered him entirely obnoxious to the colony's Protestant power structure. Although lacking his father's Jacobite overtones, the atavistic piety through which Charles Carroll of Annapolis expressed his connection to his Irish past was equally uncompromising. In his lexicon, intermarriage with Protestants and the expedient ruse of partial conversion — whereby a man gained the franchise and access to public office while his wife and children remained Catholic — were unthinkable. As with the Settler, Charles Carroll of Annapolis's defiant assertions of his Roman Catholic identity involved him in dangerous confrontations with governmental authority.

Although the extended course of European study prescribed by his father removed Charles Carroll of Carrollton from Maryland's climate of religious hostility, he nevertheless remained aware of the vulnerability inherent in his Catholicism. Despite his ability, thanks to the Carroll wealth, to live the comfortable life of an English gentleman while he dabbled at legal studies at the Inns of Court, the young man knew that his Catholicism, however enlightened and cosmopolitan, created barriers that neither money nor gentility could bridge. Free to study law, he could not practice it, because the penal statutes forbade his being called to the bar. On one occasion, the reports he received from his father about the Maryland legislature's anti-Catholic actions moved him to acknowledge explicitly the cultural and religious sources of his identity: "I cant conceive," he wrote in late 1759, "how any Roman Catholick especially an Irish Roman Catholick can consent to Live in England or any the British dominions, if he is able to do otherwise." Even if Catholics were presently "quiet and unmolested," he continued, the "most tyrannical laws" remained on the books, ready to be enforced whenever the king asked Parliament to activate them. "The parliament," he concluded with the wariness and distrust bred into him by his family's history, "wou'd allways readily comply with such a demand."[4]

The continuity between the Carrolls' Irish past and their Maryland ambitions is expressed in the names the Settler gave to the largest tracts of land he acquired in the colony — Ely O'Carroll, Litterluna, Clinmalira — each a place in Ireland intimately connected to his forebears. Equally symbolic, the Settler is known to have brought with him into Maryland in 1688 a "little Irish Manuscript Book" containing the genealogies of the O'Carrolls. When he realized, more than three decades later, that he would die before his heir, Charles Carroll of Annapolis, finished his education abroad and came home, the Settler "strictly" charged his wife with the responsibility of delivering the record of the

4. CC to CCA, Dec. 10, 1759, Carroll Papers, MS 206.

Introduction

Carroll lineage to their son upon his return to Maryland. Lacking his father's presumed ability to decipher the Gaelic in which the genealogy was inscribed, Charles Carroll of Annapolis eventually verified the document's importance by having it translated into English during a visit to Paris in 1757. Thereafter, he used the translation, with the Gaelic and English scripts on facing pages, to substantiate his claim to his son that although "our Family is not now Decked wth. Titles . . . we derive our Descent from Princes," and he added to its pages the marriages, births, and deaths of his Catholic Maryland kin.[5] In the early 1760s, Charles Carroll of Annapolis insisted that his son, then studying in England, hire a genealogist to explore the family's lineage more fully, but the younger Carroll responded with only limited enthusiasm and gleaned no reliable information about "our extirpated family." Yet, when the time came for Charles Carroll of Carrollton, the third-generation Maryland Carroll, to record the names and dates of the woman he married and the children he sired, he chose to enter them in the Gaelic-English version of the Settler's book.

Today, the "little Irish Manuscript Book" remains in the hands of a descendant who lives on the manor the Settler patented in 1707 and named Doohoragen, recalling Déuiche Uéı Riagéain, the ancestral territory of a sept located on the northeastern boundary of the O'Carroll patrimony in the Irish midlands.[6] This twentieth-century Carroll has often told me that he knows little about and is not particularly interested in his family's Irish past. But once, when I casually mentioned that on a recent research trip to Ireland I had met the current scion of a family of English Protestants whose possession of a Carroll castle and ancestral lands had been confirmed by Cromwellian policy in 1652, he glared at me and said, with unaccustomed warmth, "Those people are on our land."

Nearly 175 years before my conversation occurred, the behavior of another

5. Notes by CCA included in "Genealogy of O Carroll," MS, Carroll-O'Carroll Genealogies, MdHi; CCA to CC, Sept. 1, 1762, Carroll Papers, MS 206.

6. The Cotton Map of Leix and Offaly, c. 1565 (British Library, Cotton MS Augustus, I, ii, 40), and consultations with Elizabeth FitzPatrick, National University of Ireland, Galway. Local tradition in the foothills of the Slieve Bloom Mountains maintains that a small valley of approximately three hundred acres located at Letter Cross Roads is also known as the Doohoragen Valley. Although that place-name does not appear on any map of the region, the area is said to have been frequently contested by the O'Carrolls and the O'Dunnes, the sept that held sway over Déuiche Uéı Riagéain. The poem passed down in the Slieve Bloom Mountains (printed in Appendix 1, below) lends support to this claim. Conversations with Paddy Heaney and Paddy Lowry of Cadamstown, County Offaly. The spelling of Doohoragen is that used by the family during the eighteenth century. By the beginning of the nineteenth century, the spelling had been changed to Doughoragen.

Carroll, a first cousin three times removed of the gentleman with whom I spoke, echoed a similar sentiment. Her name was Mary Ann Caton, she was a granddaughter of Charles Carroll of Carrollton, and in her life she brought the story of this family of early modern Carrolls full circle. In 1825, after a series of adventures worthy of her ancestors, Mary Ann married Richard Colley Wellesley, a former governor-general of India, foreign secretary during the Peninsular war, and the elder brother of the duke of Wellington. Beyond being one of the first notable unions of New World money with Old World titles, the event resonates within the Carroll saga, because at the time of the marriage Lord Wellesley held the post of viceroy of Ireland; and, until he resigned in 1828, Mary Ann presided with him in Dublin as vicereine. Although the Catholic disability statutes remained in effect and even enjoyed the support of Wellington, her powerful brother-in-law, Mary Ann went openly to Mass, much to the scandal of polite English society, and she assiduously undertook to verify and complete the Irish pedigree of the Carroll family that had eluded both her great-grandfather, Charles Carroll of Annapolis, and her beloved "Grand Papa," Charles Carroll of Carrollton. In taking such actions in the land her great-great-grandfather, Charles Carroll the Settler, had fled a century before her birth, Mary Ann affirmed a Gaelic past and a defiant heritage whose shaping force she might have only dimly understood. Thus are succeeding generations moved, unawares, to complete the unfinished agenda of those who preceded them.

Princes of Ireland, Planters of Maryland

PLATE 2. Slieve Bloom Mountains.
Photograph by Redmond of Roscrea

Fields of Hunger: Faith and War

The Slieve Bloom Mountains meander for a distance of some fifteen miles along the southeastern border of County Offaly in the Irish midlands. West of the range, the land is remote and sparsely populated, separated by the line of hills from the more populous and prosperous Dublin hinterland. The forests that once covered the slopes have been gone for centuries, but the ubiquitous peat still gives the ground a dark and somber hue. The terrain that is not bog is more suitable for pasture than for cultivation, and widely scattered herds of sheep and cattle graze peacefully on the hillsides. Yet, the present-day tranquillity of this nearly deserted landscape belies its history, for from Tudor times until the beginning of the eighteenth century the Slieve Bloom was a battleground in the fierce struggle between the Gaelic Irish and the English for control of the destiny of Ireland. And it was in those hills and valleys, in the midst of that bitter conflict, that this story of the Maryland Carrolls began.

From ancient times four provinces have demarcated Ireland: Ulster in the north, Leinster in the east, Munster in the south, and Connacht in the west. Ely O'Carroll, the territory over which the O'Carroll clan (or sept) held sway, originally lay in Munster and in medieval times encompassed parts of the modern counties of Offaly, northern Tipperary, and Laois.[1] The progenitor of the branch of the O'Carroll sept that produced Charles Carroll of Carrollton was a "Chief of Ely" named Daniel O'Carroll, who had, by the end of the twelfth century, settled at Litterluna, a parish in the northeast corner of the barony of Ballybritt, on the outskirts of his clan's domain. Although the records indicate that this Daniel was "killed by the English" about 1227, the clashes in which he and the next three

1. The shiring of the Irish midlands by the English in 1605 placed the O'Carroll patrimony in Leinster. On the word *Ely,* see Appendix 2, below.

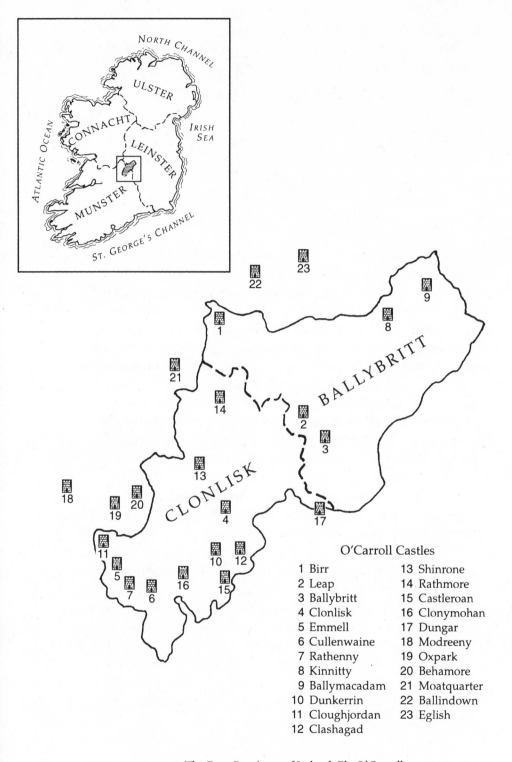

O'Carroll Castles

1 Birr	13 Shinrone
2 Leap	14 Rathmore
3 Ballybritt	15 Castleroan
4 Clonlisk	16 Clonymohan
5 Emmell	17 Dungar
6 Cullenwaine	18 Modreeny
7 Rathenny	19 Oxpark
8 Kinnitty	20 Behamore
9 Ballymacadam	21 Moatquarter
10 Dunkerrin	22 Ballindown
11 Cloughjordan	23 Eglish
12 Clashagad	

MAP 1. The Four Provinces of Ireland, Ely O'Carroll,
and O'Carroll Castles, 1200–1650.
Compiled by Tim Venning and Elizabeth FitzPatrick, 1990. Drawn by Richard Stinely

generations of his descendants participated were primarily internal rivalries for clan dominance rather than battles against foreign invaders. Daniel's successors apparently failed in their quest: his great-grandson who died in 1377 was the last of the Litterluna Carrolls to be recorded as a "chief of Ely," a designation that then passed on to a branch of the sept centered to the southwest at Birr. Until the late sixteenth century, the O'Carrolls of Litterluna probably lived in Bally-macadam Castle, a fortified dwelling set on a hill that commanded the strategic northern route into the substantial lands their sept controlled in the heart of Ireland (Maps 1 and 2).[2]

"LAND OF PEACE, LAND OF WAR"

Moving beyond this bare outline to recapture the experience of the Litterluna O'Carrolls in late-medieval and early modern Ireland requires three levels of historical reconstruction, beginning with the broad sweep of the Irish past, narrowing the focus to the experience of the entire O'Carroll clan, and finally converging on the family within that sept whose descendants emigrated to Maryland in the late seventeenth century. A general survey of this period properly begins in 1169, when the Anglo-Norman forces of King Henry II invaded and established his country's claim to the island the English came to call the "land of peace" and the "land of war." As the newcomers took root in Ireland, they gradually solidified their control over some of the best land, founded a number of dynasties, and underscored the power of their presence in the architecture of their imposing castles. Although the Anglo-Normans had become so acculturated within a few generations that they thought of themselves as "Irish," the Gaelic chiefs over whom they meant to prevail saw them as invaders and tenaciously resisted their advance. Thus, armed conflict in Ireland between 1200 and approximately 1530 primarily involved Gaelic septs fighting to preserve their an-

2. Frederick John O'Carroll, "Stemmata Carrollana, Being the True Version of the Pedigree of Carroll of Carrollton, and Correcting That Erroneously Traced by Sir William Betham, Late Ulster King-of-Arms," *Journal of the Royal Historical and Archaeological Association of Ireland*, 4th Ser., VI (October 1883), chart; Simon O'Carroll, "The Genealogy and Rulers of Éile O Cearbhaill," *Éile: Journal of the Roscrea Heritage Society*, no. 2 (1983–1984), 14–15; "Genealogy of O Carroll," MS, Carroll-O'Carroll Genealogies, MdHi; Steven G. Ellis, *Tudor Ireland: Crown, Community, and the Conflict of Cultures, 1470–1603* (New York, 1985), 14; Brian Mac Cuarta, "Newcomers in the Irish Midlands, 1540–1641" (master's thesis, University College, Galway, 1980), 6.

MAP 2. Ely O'Carroll. *Detail from* Map of Irelande, *by Baptist Boazio, 1599. Permission of the British Library, Maps, C.2.cc.1*

cestral territories from Anglo-Norman incursions and simultaneously battling each other and vying with members of their own families for clan leadership.[3]

Upon these violent contests the English crown exerted little meaningful influence. Confined to a thirty-square-mile area on the coast between Dublin and Dundalk known as the Pale, England's authority over its Irish "lordship" was, before the reign of Henry VIII, a matter of form rather than substance — a government composed of a lord lieutenant, a council, a parliament, and law courts modeled on the English system, but without the power to impose its will upon

3. James Lydon, "A Land of War," in Art Cosgrove, ed., *Medieval Ireland, 1169–1534* (Oxford, 1987), vol. II of T. W. Moody, F. X. Martin, and F. J. Byrne, eds., *A New History of Ireland,* 240. The description "land of peace" first appeared, according to Lydon, in 1248, and "land of war" in 1272. With regard to acculturation, J. C. Beckett asserts that, by the end of the fourteenth century, their adoption of "native names and customs" had made the Anglo-Normans "hardly distinguishable from their Irish neighbors" (*The Making of Modern Ireland, 1603–1923,* 2d ed. [London, 1981], 14). See also Colm Lennon, *Sixteenth-Century Ireland: The Incomplete Conquest* (Dublin, 1994), 10–18.

Prologue

the rest of the island's fractious inhabitants. Moreover, the civil strife that attended Henry VII's seizure of the English throne in 1485 further impaired England's ability to extend its control and forced the king to rely upon the most powerful of the Anglo-Norman (or Anglo-Irish, as they had come to be known) magnate families, the Fitzgeralds, earls of Kildare, to govern Ireland.[4]

The Kildare hegemony did not go unchallenged, and by the end of the fifteenth century a second great Anglo-Irish family, the Butlers, earls of Ormond, had become the Fitzgeralds' most formidable rival. Between them, the houses of Kildare and Ormond struggled for control over large portions of Leinster and Munster, west and south of the Pale, drawing less powerful Anglo-Irish and Gaelic families into their respective orbits by means of factional alliances that advanced their interests and those of their supporters. Kildare lands covered large sections of eastern and east-central Ireland and bordered the Pale, and the earls of Ormond controlled much of the southern and south-central portions of the country. Between those contending forces lay the territories of several Irish clans — the O'Mores, O'Dempseys, O'Dunnes, and O'Carrolls — whose leaders continually shifted their allegiances to gain advantage and security. To preserve their territories from each other as well as from the rival Anglo-Irish lordships, the Gaelic chiefs employed a range of strategies — the payment of tribute, dynastic marriages, and military alliances.

ENGLISH POLICIES

Before 1513, the O'Carrolls generally regarded the Fitzgeralds as the greater threat and therefore assiduously nurtured their ties to the Butlers, a strategy similar to that employed by Henry VIII, who began his reign by seeking to counter the power of the Kildares by favoring the Ormonds. Dissatisfied with that effort and increasingly wary of the ability of his Spanish enemies to make trouble for him in Ireland, the second Tudor king moved in the 1530s to break Kildare control. A decade of warfare accomplished that end, and in the 1540s the

4. Ellis, *Tudor Ireland,* chaps. 4, 5; Beckett, *Modern Ireland,* 16–19; David Beers Quinn and Kenneth W. Nicholls, "Ireland in 1534," in T. W. Moody, F. X. Martin, and F. J. Byrne, eds., *Early Modern Ireland, 1534–1691* (Oxford, 1976), vol. III of Moody, Martin, and Byrne, eds., *A New History of Ireland,* 1–9, 20–27, 34–35. The pope made Henry II "lord of Ireland," and the island was considered an English lordship until 1541, when the Irish parliament made it a kingdom by conferring the title "King of Ireland" on Henry VIII (Lennon, *Sixteenth-Century Ireland,* 18).

MAP 3. The O'Carrolls' Irish World, c. 1500–1700: Ely O'Carroll
and Neighboring Lordships.
Drawn by Richard Stinely

English monarch began consolidating his gains through a policy known as surrender and regrant. Designed to force a formal acknowledgment of the supremacy of crown authority in Ireland, surrender and regrant demanded that both the Gaelic chiefs and the semiautonomous Anglo-Irish lords yield their lands to the king, who would then return them under the conditions of feudal vassalage. As intended, the transaction gave the English crown a lawful basis for laying claim to Irish lands. For the next two centuries, all English seizures, from the first plantations initiated by Mary Tudor (r. 1553–1558) in King's and Queen's

Prologue

Counties until the Williamite settlement in 1703, looked for their legal justification to the vesting of title provided for by surrender and regrant.[5]

The policy affected the two groups that composed Ireland's population in vastly different ways. Notwithstanding their acculturated Irishness, the Anglo-Irish lords regarded the transaction as nothing more than a reaffirmation of familiar principles; but, for the Gaelic chiefs, participation in surrender and regrant demanded the abrogation of the beliefs and practices that structured their society. To gain the promised benefits — noble titles, increased personal power, the right to establish a patrimony by primogeniture — the chiefs must relinquish ancient birthrights to ancestral territories that belonged by tradition and custom to themselves and to the members of their clans. Nevertheless, the possibility of manipulating the crown's program to serve their immediate interests induced many clan leaders to take the fateful step. Even the most prescient among them could hardly have grasped how profoundly their decision would affect the succeeding generations. For Ely O'Carroll the policy would ultimately bring destruction.[6]

ELY O'CARROLL

When the sixteenth-century surveyor Robert Lythe prepared his map of Ireland, he left Ely O'Carroll and adjacent sections of Tipperary and south Offaly (King's County) blank, noting, "The perambulation of thys lordshype is not traversed."

5. Beckett, *Modern Ireland*, 16, 18–19. Gerald, eighth earl of Kildare, who began his career as lord deputy of Ireland in 1477 and represented the zenith of the Kildare ascendancy, died in 1513. The new mode of land tenure imposed by the English constituted a major assault on gavelkind, the Gaelic cultural system that vested property in lineage groups of clans.

6. Mary O'Dowd, "Gaelic Economy and Society," in Ciaran Brady and Raymond Gillespie, eds., *Natives and Newcomers: Essays on the Making of Irish Colonial Society, 1534–1641* (Dublin, 1986), 134–139; Colm Lennon, "The Counter-Reformation in Ireland, 1542–1641," in Brady and Gillespie, eds., *Natives and Newcomers*, 82–83 (and see also Bernadette Cunningham, "Native Culture and Political Change in Ireland, 1580–1640," 148–170). For a case study of one of the first Gaelic chiefs who sought to manipulate Tudor policies to preserve his autonomy and that of his clan, see David Edwards, "Collaboration without Anglicisation: The Persistence of Gaelic Government in the Lordship of Upper Ossory during the Sixteenth Century," in Patrick Duffy, David Edwards, and Elizabeth FitzPatrick, eds., *Essays in Settlement and Landscape in Gaelic Ireland, c. 1350 – c. 1600* (Dublin, forthcoming). Edwards's study is representative of the new and developing historiography that emphasizes agency among the Gaelic lords.

One of the few cartographers of his day who actually went to Ireland, Lythe knew that the Gaelic clans, with no tradition of mapmaking, did not hesitate to kill the men who came to chart their lands, and he deemed the country of the O'Carrolls too dangerous to enter (Map 4). The savage reputation of the midlands in general and Ely O'Carroll in particular had been well established long before Lythe's day. In 1306, an official in the Court of Common Pleas recorded the unlikely possibility of apprehending some of the area's unlawful residents who were in "a strong march at Kenwath in the cantred of Elicarwell, where no serjeant dare to go to levy the debt," nor even "dare do his office, on account of the Irish of Sliefblame."[7] Another English writer, perhaps a resident of the Pale, penned a similar description of the Gaelic clans in the early sixteenth century:

> They are for the most part good and hardy men of war and can hard[i]ly suffer great misery, and will adventure themselves greatly against their enemies. . . . These men hate the King's laws, and, notwithstanding any gifts, will on occasion do their best for their own advantage. They make themselves strong and take the goods of other subjects when they please, as their own proper goods.
>
> When the lord dies the strongest succeeds: and the son seldom succeeds the father. "They get many children besides their lawfully begotten, whereof all be gentlemen." Their father's lands, purchases and farms are divided equally between them. They teach their sons to be men of war from the age of 16 and "continually practised in feats thereof." They provide for them benefices from Rome, though they can scarce read: ["]the profit whereof they spend among us; but God sendeth constantly dissension among them."[8]

Mathew de Renzi, an early-seventeenth-century Flemish settler in the area, recounted the deep-seated feelings of cultural superiority toward outsiders that formed the core of Gaelic midland life and observed that the Irish believed all newcomers could be subdued through either murder or assimilation. He considered the people violent and remarkably hardy; he went so far as to urge that English standards of housing be introduced to erode the physical vigor of the population. De Renzi further deplored the Gaelic obsession with genealogy and

7. Robert Lythe, *Map of Ireland,* 1571, Petworth House Archives 9681, West Sussex Records Office, Chichester, U.K.; J. H. Andrews, *Irish Maps,* Irish Heritage Series, no. 18 (Dublin, 1978), n.p.; PROI, *Calendar of the Justiciary Rolls . . . , of Edward I,* II, *1305–1307,* ed. James Mills (London, 1914), 193–194, quoted in Tim Venning, "The Central Middle Ages, 1169–c. 1377," Carroll Institute, Report, December 1991, 30.

8. PRO, *Cal. S.P., Relating to Ireland, of the Reigns of Henry VII, Edward VI, Mary, and Elizabeth* (London, 1860–1912), *1601–1603, and Addenda, 1565–1654,* 666.

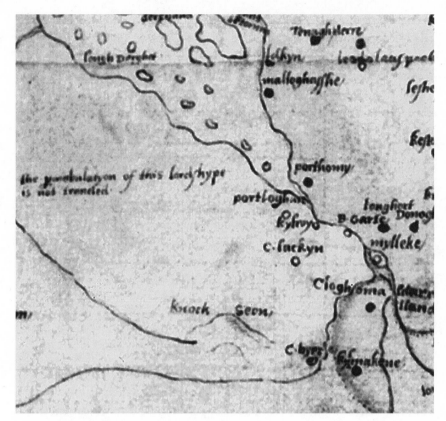

MAP 4. Ely O'Carroll. *Detail from* Map of Ireland, *by Robert Lythe, c. 1571.*
Petworth House Archives, courtesy Lord Egremont and West Sussex Record Office

family pride evoked by bards as they recalled the illustrious deeds of their countless ancestors. Theobald Butler, of the Anglo-Irish Ormond family, recorded
similar impressions: "May it therefore pleas your lordship thus to understand
the country of Ealy is pleasant, but verry wast & waunteth the manurance of industrious inhabitants for these that liue ther are (unles they haue store of cattle
hidden in woods) voyd of civillity both in howses, apparell, & all other good
manners." [9]

9. Mac Cuarta, "Newcomers in the Irish Midlands," 53, 69; Theobald Butler, Viscount, to [Chichester], Oct. 11, 1610, in HMC, *Fourth Report* (London, 1874), 566. More
information on de Renzi and his ideas regarding the civilizing of the Irish can be found
in Rolf Loeber, "Civilization through Plantation: The Projects of Mathew De Renzi," in
Harman Murtagh, ed., *Irish Midland Studies: Essays in Commemoration of N. W. English*

The borders of sixteenth-century Ely O'Carroll fluctuated according to the relative strengths of the clan and the earls of Ormond, and at various times between 1540 and 1600 the O'Carrolls extended their control along their violent frontier into the baronies of Upper and Lower Ormond, in modern County Tipperary, which the Butlers claimed as part of their medieval palatinate. However, the core of Ely O'Carroll in this period remained the baronies of Ballybritt and Clonlisk, an area that spanned slightly more than twenty miles on its north-south axis and twelve miles from east to west. A landscape of flat and gently rolling fields, framed to the east by the Slieve Bloom Mountains and on the west by the Little Brosnagh River and the territories of other clans (like the O'Kennedys who were allied with the Anglo-Irish Butlers), Ely O'Carroll was home to some six or seven thousand people by the early seventeenth century. Cattle, one of the most important measures of wealth, grazed everywhere throughout the O'Carroll domain, their numbers ranging roughly from two to three thousand. Although the soil ran to bog, particularly in the north, the primitively tilled fields produced sufficient grain to satisfy the needs of the inhabitants and livestock.[10]

SURRENDER AND REGRANT

For the O'Carroll sept, the new strategic opportunities offered by surrender and regrant came at a particularly critical time. By the 1540s, a series of bloody suc-

---

(Athlone, 1980), 121–135; see also Ciaran F. Brady, "The O'Reillys of East Breifne and the Problem of 'Surrender and Regrant,'" *Breifne: Journal of Cumann Seanchais Breifne* (1985), 233–262.

10. During the Middle Ages, Ely O'Carroll also included the baronies of Eliogarty and Ikerrin in modern County Tipperary. Rolf Loeber, "The Changing Borders of the Ely O'Carroll Lordship," in William Nolan and Timothy P. O'Neill, eds., *Offaly History and Society: Interdisciplinary Essays on the History of an Irish County* (Dublin, 1998), 289.

My estimates of the cattle present in Ely O'Carroll are derived from the records of livestock confiscation in the region during the early years of the 1641 rebellion (see William Parsons, diary, Oct. 18, 1641–Jan. 20, 1642/3, Rosse Papers, A/9, Birr Castle, Birr, Co. Offaly). I am indebted to the earl and countess of Rosse, the present owners of Birr Castle, for making the diary of William Parsons available. Scholars wishing to explore the seventeenth-century holdings in the Rosse Papers should also consult the excellent guide to the collection, "The Rosse Papers: A Calendar of the Papers of The Earl of Rosse, Birr Castle, Co. Offaly," prepared by PRONI, and the work of Aoife Leonard for the Carroll Institute, London.

cession struggles had fractured the clan and seriously weakened its ability to maneuver advantageously against Gaelic and Anglo-Irish adversaries. The feuding O'Carrolls recognized that a faction leader who successfully negotiated surrender and regrant with the crown would gain support for his claims and that the titles conferred by the English king promised to secure O'Carroll lands against the external threats and ambitions of the Butlers. Accordingly, between 1552 and 1600, three O'Carroll chiefs from the branch of the family seated at Birr sought to exploit royal policy to their advantage while joining other clans in resisting English pressure against their native holdings.

Teige O'Carroll (d. 1553), the first of this group of O'Carroll chiefs, defeated his rivals and received grants of land in Ely O'Carroll and the title lord baron of Ely from Edward VI in 1552. Having savored his triumph for barely a year, Teige died, without issue, at the hands of another family challenger, and another round of internecine fighting ensued. Before the end of the decade, Teige's brother, William Odher, had prevailed, and by 1567 he had proved himself sufficiently useful to the crown to persuade Elizabeth I to make him "a Baron, as his brother was," to allow him to hold his lands *"in capite,"* and even to entertain a proposal to grant him a hereditary peerage. Pressure from the Butlers ultimately prevented his gaining the peerage, but Sir William nevertheless solidified his position, alternately assisting the English and making trouble for them as best suited his primary aims of preserving — and even extending — the borders of Ely O'Carroll and thwarting the plots of his intraclan rivals. His skill and tenacity triumphed between 1576 and 1578, when he secured his dominance and that of his descendants in Ely by negotiating the formal surrender and regrant of the O'Carroll lands.[11]

11. Tim Venning, "The O'Carrolls of Offaly: Their Relations with the Dublin Authorities in the Sixteenth Century," in Nolan and O'Neill, eds., *Offaly History*, 191. Mr. Venning's very fine study, first prepared for the Carroll Institute, illustrates the possibilities for reconstructing the experience of the Gaelic clans in sixteenth-century Ireland. See also F. J. O'Carroll, "Stemmata Carrollana," *Jour. Royal Hist. and Arch. Ass.*, 4th Ser., VI (October 1883), chart.

On William Odher: Carroll, "Stemmata Carrollana," chart; Venning, "The O'Carrolls of Offaly," in Nolan and O'Neill, eds., *Offaly History*, 195, and Loeber, "The Changing Borders," 193, 291, 309. Sir Henry Sidney (1529–1586), lord deputy of Ireland, wrote Queen Elizabeth in April 1567 in support of William's desire to "have some Title of Nobilitie, as to be called a Baron," a request "wherein I can see no Hurte to com to your Highnesses Service, but rather Good." William evidently traveled to London with Sidney in October 1567; see Lord Deputy Sir Henry Sidney to Queen Elizabeth, Apr. 20, 1567, in

Sir William's success in abrogating the claims of his collateral relatives by ac-knowledging English jurisdiction over their ancestral lands did not bring an end to the strife in Ely. Indeed, a good deal of bloodletting was subsequently required to enforce on the ground the rights of possession and primogeniture he had ac-quired on paper. In 1581 Sir William was murdered in a plot that implicated his son John, who was in turn dispatched by a wing of the family allied with the But-lers. Another of Sir William's sons, Charles, then killed off two other Carroll contenders and seized power. Having eliminated, at least for the moment, any sustained opposition, Charles set about reinforcing his position, acquiring a knighthood in 1585 and journeying to London in 1591 to pledge his loyalty to the crown.[12]

The attempts by these O'Carroll chiefs to manipulate the triangulated struggle among the native Irish, Anglo-Irish, and the English attest the increas-ingly desperate character of the contests in which they and their Gaelic contem-poraries were engaged. During the fratricidal strife that culminated in Sir Charles O'Carroll's assumption of power, pressure against O'Carroll lands arose both from English expansion into Leix-Offaly, a center of Gaelic resistance be-tween Ely O'Carroll and the Pale, and from the Ormonds, whose strength had supplanted that of the Kildares. In response to the marauding forays conducted against the Pale by bands operating out of Leix-Offaly, Mary Tudor's Privy Council garrisoned the territory and in 1557 shired it as King's and Queen's Counties. With the goal of establishing royal authority by planting the area with English settlers, the crown then began to implement a plan of land redistribu-

---

Arthur Collins, ed., *Letters and Memorials of State* . . . (London, 1746), I, 18–19, quoted in Rolf Loeber to Peter Davies and Elizabeth FitzPatrick, May 25, 1992, a copy of which Dr. Loeber generously shared with me. For other invaluable contributions made by Dr. Loe-ber and his wife, Dr. Magda Stouthamer-Loeber, to the study of medieval and early mod-ern Ireland, see n. 20, below.

12. Venning, "The O'Carrolls of Offaly," in Nolan and O'Neill, eds., *Offaly History*, 195–196; F. J. O'Carroll, "Stemmata Carrollana," *Jour. Royal Hist. and Arch. Ass.*, 4th Ser., VI (October 1883), chart. That Sir William's rightful heir should have been involved in his murder is the final twist in a remarkable chain of events. In recommending William to Queen Elizabeth I in 1567, Sir Henry Sidney had strongly praised the character of his el-dest son. Describing him as "a yonge Man of vearie great Hope, of much Honestie, and manny good Partyes, nerelie addicted to the *English* Order," the lord deputy evidently saw John as a reliable future ally. Sidney had a firm basis for this opinion, having taken William's son into his household in 1557, probably as a hostage to assure the O'Carroll chief's obedience, and keeping him there for a decade. Lord Deputy Sir Henry Sidney to Queen Elizabeth, Apr. 20, 1567, in Collins, ed., *Letters and Memorials of State,* I, 18–19, quoted in Loeber to Davies and FitzPatrick, May 25, 1992.

tion that enticed native chiefs to comply by offering them the right to retain the westernmost third of their holdings. Problems elsewhere diverted Elizabeth I's attention from Ireland at the beginning of her reign. With resources required in other parts of the kingdom, Elizabeth relied on surrender and regrant, enforced by periodic impositions of martial law, to erode the power of defiant chieftains. As a result, lands within traditional Gaelic domains became available to both English and Irish tenants of the crown.[13]

Although Ely O'Carroll lay outside the areas immediately affected by these policies, the O'Carroll chiefs — Teige, Sir William, and Sir Charles — joined their Gaelic neighbors in resisting English incursion, even as they tried to gain English support by manipulating surrender and regrant. Mounting a series of revolts, the clan leaders thwarted temporarily the plantation of Leix-Offaly, but at the price of brutal military reprisals. At the same time, steady encroachment upon O'Carroll lands by the earls of Ormond strained the sept's resources even further. By 1589 the threat from that quarter had grown so severe that Sir Charles O'Carroll petitioned the Privy Council to include Ely O'Carroll within the bounds of King's County.[14]

Notwithstanding his negotiations with the crown for the titles and support he needed to counter the forces that opposed him in Ireland, Sir Charles, like other Gaelic chiefs, apprehended the potential of such arrangements for undermining their cultural and religious heritage. That he continued to play the dangerous game despite his distrust of his putative allies and the ultimate aims of their policies attests his ambition and his determination to retain power. Undeterred by the rejection of his petition to have Ely O'Carroll incorporated into King's County, Sir Charles worked assiduously to secure his position and his borders through traditional means like marriages and clan alliances and in the courts to which he recurred in the 1590s to combat a blitz of territorial challenges introduced by the earl of Ormond.[15] Characterized as one of the "subtle papists"

---

13. Ellis, *Tudor Ireland*, 234–235, 250–251. Simultaneous threats against the Pale arose in other sections of Gaelic Ireland during the Tudor period, most notably from Munster and Ulster (228–274). See also David Edwards, "Martial Law and the Tudor Reconquest of Ireland," *History Ireland*, V, no. 2 (Summer 1997), 16–21.

14. Ellis, *Tudor Ireland*, 235; Sir Charles O'Carrol to the Privy Council [June] 1589, *Cal. S.P., Ire., 1588–1592*, 213.

15. Venning, "The O'Carrolls of Offaly," in Nolan and O'Neill, eds., *Offaly History*, 196–197. In 1598 Sir Charles checked the ambitions of his Ormond rivals by arranging to have a long-standing boundary dispute between them heard in the Pale's courts rather than in courts within the jurisdiction of the earl's palatinate of Tipperary. The ruling reversed the situation existing in 1595, when the earl's influence at court led the queen to

by the Anglican archbishop of Cashel, Milerus McGrath, Sir Charles made repeated trips to London to pledge his loyalty to the crown. In July 1597, an anonymous royal official grasped the essence of his strategy:[16]

> Sir Charles O'Carroll and Sir John Mac Coghlan both are lords of great coun-
> tries; both have been rebels, and more rebellious minds are not in Ireland, yet
> both are subjects; but why? They have rivals. There be others have more right
> to their lands than themselves. . . . Their surrender to Her Majesty is their
> only security. These and others are commended for good subjects for their
> cutting of the heads of some of their name and nation; but those heads which
> they send in are better pledges of their own security than any kind of assur-
> ance of their loyalties.[17]

THE NINE YEARS' WAR

In 1594, consistent with his strategy for survival, Sir Charles chose to remain
loyal to the crown when Hugh O'Neill, the earl of Tyrone and a leader of one of
the North's most powerful families, raised his banner in Ulster and began a campaign to drive the English from Ireland. Inflaming Gaelic resentment of Elizabethan policies into a religious crusade by identifying the Catholic religion with
the defense of the Irish nation, Tyrone's rising — the Nine Years' War (1594 –
1603) — changed the character of violence in Ireland from internal clan rivalry
and tribal conflict to a polarity anchored by the external threat posed by the English. In fusing religion and country to oppose a common enemy, Tyrone offered a powerfully unifying call to arms that neither required Gaelic chiefs to relinquish their clan identities nor prevented gaelicized Anglo-Irish lords from
joining with them in what became the most formidable rebellion ever mounted
against the English presence. Many Gaelic chiefs rallied to the cause, but others,
who believed that Tyrone's true intention was simply to make himself overlord
of Ireland, made a different — and in the case of Sir Charles O'Carroll, a fatal —
choice.

---

order Sir Charles "to submitte hymselfe to the Erles own arbitrament." Loeber, "The
Changing Borders," in Nolan and O'Neill, eds., *Offaly History*, 305, 308.

16. Milerus McGrath to Patrick Crosby, 1591, *Cal. S.P., Ire., 1588–1592*, 447.

17. "Paper Recommending Improvements the Queen Can Make in Ireland," quoted
in Venning, "The O'Carrolls of Offaly," in Nolan and O'Neill, eds., *Offaly History*, 199;
Cal. S.P., Ire., 1596–1597, 398.

When the hostilities began, Sir Charles, "a man whom the enemies greatly fear," hoped to keep the O'Carrolls out of the conflict, but he compromised his neutrality by continuing to maintain a company of Irish foot in royal service and reiterating to Tyrone loyalists his support of Elizabethan policies. When he savagely attacked a force of Tyrone mercenaries that threatened Ely O'Carroll, Sir Charles sealed his fate. An enraged Tyrone ordered the O'Carroll territory destroyed: "Nothing was left of it but ashes instead of its dwellings," recounted one chronicle. Tyrone then set up a rival O'Carroll chief, who had Sir Charles murdered in July 1600. Sir George Carew, the principal English official in charge of Munster, observed: "This last week . . . Sir Charles O'Carroll (a good servant of Her Majesty's) was murdered by one of his kinsmen. Four of the O'Carrolls are in competition for the lordship of that country. Before that question is settled it will cost much blood, but therein the State is nothing indemnified."[18]

As Carew reported, four rivals emerged as contestants for the O'Carroll chieftainship out of the chaos of Tyrone's rebellion. The identities of only two are known: John, the deceased Charles's four-year-old great-nephew, who became the designated heir under the entail secured by Sir William in 1578, and Maolroona, Sir Charles's older brother, whose name also appeared in the 1578 list of Sir William's sons. The rivalry continued until 1605, two years after the war ended with the English victory over Tyrone at the battle of Kinsale. In the establishment of a new O'Carroll chief, English influence was everywhere. Maolroona received a knighthood in 1603 for his service as commander of a crown regiment of one hundred foot. At the same time, the crown knighted Sir Thomas Ashe, a loyal Protestant Ely O'Carroll settler, and made him John's guardian. In rapid succession the royal authorities recognized the boy as Sir Charles's rightful heir and, in 1605, shired his inheritance, Ely O'Carroll, as part of King's County. The final subordination of the O'Carrolls to the crown came with John's betrothal and marriage, before he reached his majority in 1617, to the earl of Ormond's great-niece Eleanor, and the nearly simultaneous opening up of the O'Carroll lands to plantation. These events marked the death of the O'Carroll lordship — the era of the Ely chieftains had ended.[19]

18. Venning, "The O'Carrolls of Offaly," in Nolan and O'Neill, eds., *Offaly History,* 200–201.

19. Theobald Butler to the lord deputy [Sir Arthur Chichester], Oct. 11, 1610, in HMC, *Fourth Report,* 566–567; Venning, "The O'Carrolls of Offaly," in Nolan and O'Neill, eds., *Offaly History,* 201; F. J. O'Carroll, "Stemmata Carrollana," *Jour. Royal Hist. and Arch. Ass.,* 4th Ser., VI (October 1883), chart.

Situating the Littterluna O'Carrolls, the branch of the sept from which Charles Carroll of Carrollton's family descended, within the strife that characterized late-medieval and early modern Ireland is a challenging proposition. To begin, they must be located. Some twenty rude castles, most of them tower houses built between 1420 and 1500, delimited the bounds of sixteenth-century Ely O'Carroll and marked the holdings of the clan's various families. The principal strong-holds among these structures were the Black Tower at Birr and the menacing stone fortress at Leap, where bloody murders occurred with unnerving frequency. Seven castles ranging along the southern and eastern borders of the barony of Clonlisk defended against Ormond incursions. Ballymacadam, the castle built by the Litterluna O'Carrolls near the holy well and church of Litterluna parish, commanded the region's northeastern reaches, close to the lands of the Kildares to whom these O'Carrolls paid tribute in the early sixteenth century (see Map 1).[20]

A tempting target by virtue of its exposed location, Ballymacadam fell to English troops in the mid-sixteenth century. Determined to end the incessant Gaelic raids staged from Leix-Offaly and adjacent territories, the crown sent Sir Edward Bellingham to Ireland in 1547 with orders to establish a screen of English garrisons that would secure the Pale's outer zone and impose stability on the midlands. Ranging deep into Ely O'Carroll, Bellingham's men occupied O'Carroll strongholds at Ballymacadam, Nenagh, and Athlone. The conduct of Edmund Fahy, an English commander in the field, attests the savagery of the conflict. To celebrate his conquest over the O'Carrolls' northern neighbors, the clan of MacCoghlan, Fahy (known as the Red Captain) had their heads taken to "Baile-Mic-Adam, in Kinel-Fearga, in Ely O'Carroll, and elevated on sharp

---

20. "Distribution of O'Carroll Castles 1200–1650," map compiled by Tim Venning and Elizabeth FitzPatrick, Car. Inst. Report, September 1990, 103; "Therll of Kyldare's du-ties upon Irrishmen" [rental of Gerald, earl of Kildare], in HMC, *Ninth Report* (London, 1883–1884), part 2, 275. For this information on Ballymacadam Castle and for much more, I am deeply appreciative of the cooperation extended to the Carroll Papers staff by Dr. Rolf Loeber and Dr. Magda Stouthamer-Loeber. All students of early modern Irish history are well aware of the remarkable scholarship accomplished by the Loebers in their painstaking analyses of local Irish sources, especially land records. Their work sug-gests that the remarkably rich social histories of discrete places that have been completed during the past thirty years for early modern Europe and British North America can also be prepared for Ireland and that, as a consequence, our knowledge of Irish history would be enormously advanced.

PLATE 3. Leap Castle.
Photographs by Simon Marsden, The Marsden Archive

PLATE 4. O'Neill's Well.
Photograph by Michael McGrath

poles as trophies of victory." Fahy held Ballymacadam for nearly two years as he raided widely throughout the midlands. When the O'Carrolls reclaimed the castle in 1550, the annalists memorialized their victory: "Baile-Mic-Adam was taken from Edmond a Faii, and the O'Carrolls returned to it again; in consequence of which there was great rejoicing and exultation in Ely."[21]

There are no records linking the Litterluna O'Carrolls to the struggles for clan dominance that occupied their kinsmen Teige, Sir William, and Sir Charles during the last half of the sixteenth century. However, a series of pardons confirms the persistent local legend that this branch of the sept broke with Sir Charles to side with the forces of the earl of Tyrone in the Nine Years' War, thereby escaping the punishment Tyrone inflicted upon the parts of Ely whose inhabitants allied with the English. On his march through the midlands to Kinsale, the site of the struggle's epic battle, the earl, having received assurances of local support, bivouacked his army in the area known in local tradition as the

21. Ellis, *Tudor Ireland,* 229–230; John O'Donovan, ed., *Annals of the Kingdom of Ireland, by the Four Masters, from the Earliest Period to the Year 1616,* V (Dublin, 1851), 1509, 1517; see also [John Wright], *The King's County* (Parsonstown, 1890), 84, 89.

Doohoragen Valley. O'Neill's Well, located near the center of the valley, recalls his passage.[22]

CHURCH AND PLANTATION

England's victory in the Nine Years' War, together with the devastation of large sections of the Irish countryside and population, gave the crown a good opportunity to consolidate and extend its power.[23] Two policies, initiated under James I (r. 1603–1625) and continued until midcentury by Charles I (r. 1625–1649), provided the principal means for accomplishing this end. One plan was the first systematic attempt to make economic, social, and political status contingent upon conformity to the Anglican Church, and the other would confiscate and redistribute land in the most intensely Gaelic sections of the country.

Initially subtle, the first program, begun in 1605, caused considerable disagreement among royal officials under both James I and Charles I over how vigorous a campaign should be mounted against the Roman Catholics, the vast majority of Ireland's population.[24] Convinced that the most reliable and least in-

22. Local historian Patrick Heaney, of Cadamstown, County Offaly, first made me aware of the legend. Subsequent research into the granting of pardons for those who bore arms for O'Neill suggests that Mr. Heaney's information is correct. See general pardons to Donell Dorogh McTeige ower O'Carroll of Kenechane, gent., 12 Dec. 3 James I [1605], and to Donell Dirogh McTeige Oureokearole of Keanechane, gent., 27 May 4 James I [1606], Irish Manuscripts Commission, *Irish Patent Rolls of James I* (Dublin, 1966), 87, 99.

23. The Nine Years' War exacted an enormous toll from Gaelic Ireland. Besides bringing a defeat so bitter that the revolt's principal leaders quit the country in 1607, the struggle ravaged the lands and livelihoods of the people in large sections of the country. With livestock slaughtered, crops destroyed, and commercial networks and towns in shambles, the specter of famine haunted the countryside, and many areas of Ireland were in a more primitive condition at the end of the Tudor era than at its beginning. Ellis, *Tudor Ireland*, 50, 315; R. A. Butlin, "Land and People, *c.* 1600," in Moody, Martin, and Byrne, eds., *Early Modern Ireland*, 146–147.

24. Aiden Clarke and R. Dudley Edwards, "Pacification, Plantation, and the Catholic Question, 1603–23," in Moody, Martin, and Byrne, eds., *Early Modern Ireland*, 190–192. According to Butlin, ("Land and People, *c.* 1600," 147), no "reliable population figures" exist for Ireland at the beginning of the reign of James I, although he estimates the total to be less than 1,000,000, of which Roman Catholics were the majority. By 1685 at the beginning of James II's reign, J. H. Andrews in a similar essay ("Land and People, c. 1685," 466) estimates that, as a consequence of England's seventeenth-century Irish policies, the country's total population equaled 1,100,000, of which some 300,000 — slightly more than one-quarter — were Protestants.

cendiary means of strengthening the Anglo-Protestant interest lay in planting English settlers on Irish land, James I proceeded with caution in religious matters. Accordingly, he directed his more militant administrators in Dublin to avoid openly antagonistic actions against recusants. A significant division in Irish society persuaded the king of the wisdom of this course.

Within Ireland, Roman Catholics belonged to two distinct groups: the Gaelic Irish like the O'Carrolls, whose grievances against the English were territorial and cultural as well as religious, and the Old English, as the Anglo-Normans or Anglo-Irish preferred to call themselves after the Nine Years' War. Descended from the invaders who settled in Ireland in the twelfth century, the Old English defined themselves as "natives" and for centuries had intermarried with the Gaelic Irish. At the same time, they regarded their cultural traditions and interests as compatible with those of their Anglo-Protestant rulers — the New English. Unlike their Gaelic coreligionists, the Old English did not resist the imposition of English legal and political systems, and by the end of the Tudor era they had firmly entrenched themselves in local government and formed a majority in the Irish parliament.[25]

The Old English were eager to demonstrate that their political loyalty to the crown and their religious loyalty to Rome were not mutually contradictory. Though inherently suspicious of this divided allegiance, Elizabethan officials, whose military resources were frequently straitened, had no choice but to rely upon it during their protracted efforts to subdue Ireland. That task having been successfully accomplished by 1603, James I and his advisers found it imperative to address the political ramifications of recusancy.[26]

At the outset of James I's reign, Old English recusants, anticipating a favorable response from the king, moved quickly to restore Catholic services in the churches of several principal towns. Certain that another rebellion was imminent, the Dublin government marshaled troops to invade the offending cities in

25. Ellis, *Tudor Ireland*, 246–249; T. W. Moody, "Early Modern Ireland," in Moody, Martin, and Byrne, eds., *Early Modern Ireland*, xliii; Beckett, *Modern Ireland*, 40–53. Other signs of Anglo-Norman gaelicization include their commissioning of bardic poems and assumption of Gaelic election practices. Elizabeth FitzPatrick, "Gaelicisation and Inauguration: The De Béurca Assembly Sites," in Duffy, Edwards, and FitzPatrick, eds., *Essays in Settlement and Landscape.*

For an incisive discussion of the New English, see Nicholas Canny, "Identity Formation in Ireland: The Emergence of the Anglo-Irish," in Nicholas Canny and Anthony Pagden, eds., *Colonial Identity in the Atlantic World, 1500–1800* (Princeton, N.J., 1987), 159–212.

26. Beckett, *Modern Ireland*, 40–53.

violation of ancient charter rights. James's response, which satisfied neither side, was to temporize. Lacking sufficient funds and troops to garrison all of Ireland, the king had no desire to persecute Catholics to the extent that the Old English and Gaelic Irish would unite against him. At the same time, he wished to avoid antagonizing Irish Protestants by authorizing a policy of open toleration.

At length, James crafted a compromise. He ordered that the anti-Catholic penal laws enacted under Elizabeth I be enforced in such matters as the attendance of prominent recusants at Anglican services and the expulsion of Catholic priests and seminarians from Ireland, but he refused to sanction a general and sustained harassment of papists. As a result, Old English recusants knew that the royal ear was attentive to their complaints and that they could generally protect themselves from the most ominous kinds of abuse, even when the persecutorial zeal of the English administration in Dublin burst the bonds of official restraint to attack Catholics. Beset by increasingly serious financial difficulties and an uncooperative Parliament, Charles I continued his father's policy of practical toleration in hopes that sizable revenues as well as political and military support could be raised in Ireland. Among the concessions he extended to recusants was the relaxation of the requirement that Roman Catholics swear the oath of supremacy, which denied the pope's spiritual and temporal authority, in order to practice law and exercise certain rights involving inheritance.[27]

The early Stuarts balanced that modest religious sufferance with land policies that were unwaveringly favorable to the Protestant interest. The period of peace that followed England's military victory in 1603 permitted James I to implement his plantation schemes without the Gaelic interference that had impeded previous Tudor efforts. The first and best-known plantation was initiated in Ulster in 1610 and was well under way by 1619, when James turned his attention to the midlands. There he ordered that one-quarter of the acreage held by Gaelic Irish landowners be regranted to Anglo-Protestant settlers.[28]

"ENGLISH WAYES"

Protestant plantation was far more complex than this apparently arbitrary rationale suggests. Among the midland territories specified for plantation, the English evaluated Ely O'Carroll as open to the introduction of civilized ways, pre-

27. Ibid., 40–53, 60.
28. Ibid., 54; Clarke and Edwards, "Pacification, Plantation, and the Catholic Question," in Moody, Martin, and Byrne, eds., *Early Modern Ireland*, 221–222.

sumably because most branches of the clan supported the English during the Nine Years' War. "As for the county of Longford and O'Carroll's country," observed one English report, "it is very fit, for the reformation of them in religion, and of some defects in their manners and course of life, that some Britaines be planted amongst them." Moreover, once an English presence had been firmly established, the writer continued, a spread of civility would probably follow, because "the nature of th' Irish is to bargain, chop, and sell to Britaines that are once brought in amongst them, but never to suffer the bringing in of any, if they can keep them out."[29]

In pacifying the midlands and subordinating the power of the Irish lords, the English attempted to balance the two countervailing tendencies that underlay their policies. By planting "natives" as well as English in Longford, Ely O'Carroll, and "th' other baronies of O'Moyloy, McGoghlan, O'Dunne, McGeoghegan, Foxe, and O'Meolaghlan," reported one official, "the chief regard will be to break the dependency of the subjects from th' Irish Lords, and to bring them to hold immediately from the Crown, by giving to every of them, that be of any fitness, parcels of land within their own countries." At the same time, crown authorities recognized the chiefs' power to cause costly and bloody disturbances and wished to avoid any action that might incite clan leaders to call for popular resistance. Accordingly, great care was taken not to offend the leading Gaelic families. As the lords commissioners charged with devising the plans for plantation advised the king and Privy Council: "Your Deputy and Commissioners [are] to be required to have a special care to give contentment to the best gentlemen and chiefs of several septs, by making good provision for them, that the clamours of the multitude may be restrained."[30]

This cautious mode of plantation permitted the development of what seemed to be reasonably civil relationships between planters and natives. For example, in 1620, Birr Castle, an O'Carroll stronghold sold to the Butlers by Teige McCallagh O'Carroll in 1595, was granted to Sir Laurence Parsons, the brother of William Parsons, his majesty's surveyor-general of lands in Ireland. Subsequent correspondence between Teige McCallagh and the Parsons indicates cordial connections, with Laurence writing to Teige of "My brother who remains your constant fre[nd]," and William referring to Teige as "His Trew and loving neighbour." Out of mutual interest the families collaborated in the securing of land

29. HMC, [Fifteenth Report], *Report on the Manuscripts of the Duke of Buccleuch and Queensberry, K.G., K.T., Preserved at Montagu House, Whitehall*, I (London, 1899), 77.

30. Ibid.; J. S. Brewer and William Bullen, eds., *Calendar of the Carew Manuscripts...*, VI (London, 1873), 378.

titles and the collection of rents. Even more significantly, their sons sat together in Birr Castle, where they learned "to write a fayre sett."[31]

The experience of the Litterluna O'Carrolls was similar in many respects to that of their clansmen at Birr. Relocating, for reasons unknown, from the parish of Litter to that of Seirkieran, some nine miles to the southwest, early in the seventeenth century, Charles Carroll of Carrollton's ancestors reestablished themselves as a family of substance. Having previously sought security and advancement through marital ties with the Fitzgeralds and the more distant Butlers, they now concentrated on forging the same kinds of alliances with other Old English families — the Dillons, the Condons, and the Graces. The last connection would prove especially important in shaping the destiny of these O'Carrolls through the rest of the seventeenth century.[32]

The land that Donnell McTeige Oure O'Carroll of Ballymacadam acquired at Seirkieran in 1605 consisted of 858 acres of "good rich pasture" land and 82 acres of wood and bog. His patent specified that he was to adopt English practices in the handling of his estate and forbade him "to grant or demise any of the aforesaid premises to any person but according to the laws of England." To assure that neat English settlements would replace the unruly sprawl of Irish agriculture, Donnell's grant instructed him to take care that his tenants "erect their dwelling-houses contiguous to each other, in 'town reeds,' and not scattered or single, as well for the mutual defence and safety of the said O'Carroll, and of his tenants, as for the erection of several villages for the public good and service of the kingdom of Ireland." Other stipulations directed that he grow hemp, that he eschew the Irish inheritance "custom of Gavelkind," and that he not enter into

31. William Parsons to Teige O'Carroll, Jan. 12, [1626], Rosse Papers, A/5/19(B); Laurence Parsons to Teige O'Carroll, n.d., Rosse Papers, A/5/18; Laurence Parsons, accounts, 1627–1628, Rosse Papers, A/8. See also Teige McCallagh O'Carroll to the king, petition [1622], Rosse Papers, A/4, fol. 31.

32. For the marriage of Teige Carroll of Aghagurty and Ann Dillon, see Garrett Dillon and Daniel Carroll, agreement, Nov. 3, 1638, Thrift Abstract 5072, PROI. For the relationship between Col. Richard Grace and Daniel Carroll of Ballymooney, see Colonel Grace to Secretary Bennett, petition, July 1, 1663, S.P. 63/314/1–2, PRO; "The State of Colonel Grace His Case" [1674], Stowe MSS 205, fol. 306r, BL; and Colonel Richard Grace's Case, July 3, 1674, described in Charles McNeill, "Reports on the Rawlinson Collection of Manuscripts Preserved in the Bodleian Library, Oxford," *Analecta Hibernica,* I (1930), 158. It may be that the connection between the Carrolls and the Graces was through the family of Eleanor Condon, Richard Grace's mother. See J. J. Kelly, "Colonel Richard Grace, Governor of Athlone," *Irish Ecclesiastical Record,* 4th Ser., XXVI (1909), 42.

PLATE 5. Ballymooney Castle.
Photograph by Simon Marsden, The Marsden Archive

long-term leases with any "'mere Irish'" who were "not of the English race and name." Finally, if Donnell committed rebellion or took "the stile, name, or title of 'the great O'Carroll'" or used such a reference in any of his dealings, his lands were liable for reversion to the crown.[33]

Having secured himself a considerable estate, Donnell embarked on an extensive building program. At the junction of a series of connecting roads that facilitated market transportation for his ever-expanding pool of tenants, he con-

33. References supplied by Rolf Loeber regarding the property Donnell McTeige Oure O'Carroll acquired at Seirkieran show that it was confiscated from Augustinian monks during the reign of Edward VI (1547–1553) and subsequently leased to Sir William O'Carroll and then to the Old English family of Lucas Dillon for sixty years; see Aubrey Gwynn and R. Neville Hadcock, *Medieval Religious Houses: Ireland* [Blackrock, 1988], 195; lease to Sir William Carrell, knt., 3 Aug., XX [1578], *Fiants, Ireland, Elizabeth*, no. 3399, *Thirteenth Report of the Deputy Keeper of the Public Records* (Dublin, 1881); the king to Donell McTeig Oure O'Carroll, grant, 10 Jan. 17th [1620], *Cal. Pat. Rolls, Ire., James I*, 450. For a description of the quality of the acreage, see "A Book of Postings and Sale of the Forfeited and Other Estates and Interests in Ireland, 1703," MS 2578, fol. 37, PRONI.

According to the custom of gavelkind the land of the deceased was placed in a common pool and distributed among the sept.

Prologue

structed a handsome, four-story residence designed for both security and comfort. Reflecting the steady erosion of the Gaelic world, he acquiesced in the crown's demand that the prefix O be dropped from native surnames and styled himself Daniel Carroll of Ballymooney, after one of his townlands. By the time his son Daniel had succeeded him in the 1640s, the property had grown to more than seventeen hundred acres, and the village where the tenants and other settlers lived was the second most populous settlement in the barony of Ballybritt: In moving from Ballymacadam to Seirkieran and accommodating themselves to "English wayes," Daniel and his father had achieved a measure of prosperity and propelled themselves along the road to membership in the Jacobean gentry.[34]

The progress made by the first two Carrolls of Ballymooney confirmed the apparent success of the careful, pragmatic approach adopted by the English in the planting of the midlands.[35] Similarly, the family's acceding to the English program suggests that some segments of the native population were willing to live with the moderate religious strictures imposed by the Stuarts. Nonetheless, neither the Gaelic nor the Old English found any basis for long-term optimism or reassurance in the policies of the first two Stuart kings. In reality, the quiescence those policies bought in Ireland during the first forty years of the seventeenth century was only a thin veneer, beneath which seethed a potent mixture of Gaelic resentment, especially in Ulster, over the loss of land, and the dread suspicion of the Old English that their Catholicism would eventually render them vulnerable to displacement and dispossession.

34. Rolf Loeber, Magda Stouthamer-Loeber, and Harman Murtagh, "A Survey of the O'Carroll Castle at Ballymooney, Co. Offaly, and Its Immediate Vicinity," MS (1991); Books of Survey and Distribution, King's County, fols. 59, 60, 77; Dillon and Carroll, agreement, 3 Nov. 1638, TA 5072; William Petty, *Hiberniae Delineatio* . . . ([London?], 1685).

Baile an Mhéoinéin, of which Ballymooney is the anglicized rendering, means "a grassy area in bogland," an apt description of the site of the fortified house and its hinterland. Conversation with Elizabeth FitzPatrick.

The father-son lineage given here for Donell McTeige Oure O'Carroll and Daniel Carroll of Ballymooney is taken from the genealogical table prepared for the Carrolls before 1688 and brought to Maryland by Charles Carroll the Settler. The lack of corroborating evidence in other contemporary sources has led Elizabeth FitzPatrick to conclude that these men are, not father and son, but the same person.

35. Nicholas Canny has made some suggestive observations in this regard in his essay "The Marginal Kingdom: Ireland as a Problem in the First British Empire," in Bernard Bailyn and Philip D. Morgan, eds., *Strangers within the Realm: Cultural Margins of the First British Empire* (Chapel Hill, N.C., 1991), 35–66. See also Nicholas Canny, *Kingdom and Colony: Ireland in the Atlantic World, 1560–1800* (Baltimore, 1988), esp. chap. 2.

In October 1641 the tenuous balance of competing interests fashioned by the Stuart monarchs disintegrated as Gaelic anger erupted in a violent rebellion. A midland chief named Rory O'More persuaded the bitterly disaffected Ulster gentry that support from the Old English as well as from abroad would be forthcoming, and so began a "rising" in the recently planted northern counties, where dispossessed Gaelic landowners unleashed their vengeance against the Protestant settlers who had displaced them. Although contemporary accounts of massacres of Protestants by Catholics appear to have been exaggerated for propaganda purposes, it is nonetheless true that "in the first months of the rising the insurgents committed many murders often savagely . . . because of lack of discipline, for private vengeance, or out of religious fanaticism." In addition to the casualties caused by direct attacks, thousands of Protestants who were driven from their homes perished for want of food and shelter.[36] Rallying from the unexpected blows of their enemies, Protestants retaliated in kind. In less than a year the revolt had spread across the entire country, but, almost from the outset, its leadership was fractured by internal dissension that foretold the failure of the cause.

To the Old English population of Ireland, the 1641 rising presented a crisis of allegiance. Menaced on the one hand by the Ulster rebels and their confederates and threatened on the other by a hostile Dublin government, the Old English reluctantly abandoned their hopes for a mutually beneficial relationship with the Protestants and joined their fate to that of their Gaelic coreligionists. The Protestant power structure in Ireland saw the Gaelic–Old English cooperation as unassailable proof of its long-standing contention that adherence to Roman Catholicism was inherently treasonous. Moreover, Charles I, despite his earlier leniency toward recusants and their insistence that they remained loyal to him in the face of rebellion, assented in March 1642 to the Adventurers' Act, stipulating that the lands of papist rebels would be confiscated and regranted to persons who contributed money toward crushing the revolt.

By August 1642, however, Protestants in Ireland as well as in England were facing their own crisis of allegiance as the dispute between Charles I and Parliament deepened into civil war. With both sides in this contest — the king's men (also known as Royalists or Cavaliers) and the parliamentarians (or Roundheads) — intriguing for soldiers and support in Ireland, yet another divisive

36. Patrick J. Corish, "The Rising of 1641 and the Catholic Confederacy, 1641–5," in Moody, Marin, and Byrne, eds., *Early Modern Ireland*, 291–292.

force beset that already fragmented country. As the decade ground on, the Irish situation grew progressively chaotic. The confederation formed by the insurgents to provide unity and leadership for their cause splintered under the pressure of traditional Gaelic–Old English rivalries, military ineptitude, and lack of materiel, and by 1648 the rebellion had disintegrated into a multiplicity of local clashes, each with its own commander and agenda. Irish Protestants, whose interests and loyalties were closely linked with developments in England, also found themselves in factional disarray, which persisted even as the impending triumph of the Roundheads over the Royalists became apparent.[37]

Once they had executed the king and further consolidated their victory at home, the parliamentarians turned their attention to Ireland. On August 15, 1649, Oliver Cromwell and an army of three thousand men landed in Dublin. Welcomed with great fanfare by the city's Protestant population, Cromwell lost no time in making an indelible impression upon Ireland's Catholics. When he left the country, ten months and two massacres later, he had shattered both the remaining structure of the rebellion and most vestiges of Royalist support. Pressing beyond military subjugation, Cromwell and the English Parliament enacted and implemented, between 1650 and 1658, a series of laws designed to build a Protestant community capable of deterring any future challenges like the 1641 rising. As generally provided by the earlier Adventurers' Act and spelled out more specifically by the Act for the Settlement of Ireland, passed by Parliament in August 1652, lands were to be confiscated from rebellious papists and any other persons, Protestants included, found to have helped or encouraged them. The government would then use those properties to satisfy its obligations to the investors who had "adventured" their money toward putting down the revolt and to pay the army.

Those penalties fell most severely upon Catholic landowners, depriving the Gaelic Irish and Old English recusants alike of anywhere from one-fifth to all of their estates. Moreover, those allowed to retain a portion of their acreage could be forced to yield their current holdings for lands of supposedly equal value west of the Shannon River in the province of Connacht. Based on surveys made in 1654–1655 by army physician and surveyor Sir William Petty (1623–1687), the redistribution of land known as the Cromwellian settlement reduced Catholic ownership from nearly 60 percent to less than 25 percent, thereby establishing a firm basis for Protestant domination of Ireland. To reinforce the Protestant hegemony created on the land, Cromwell's government enacted civil and religious policies that deprived Catholics of all status in the body politic, forbade

37. Beckett, *Making of Modern Ireland*, 99–101.

them to exercise their religion publicly, and severely punished priests and Catholic schoolmasters for performing sacramental or instructional duties. Yet, even in the face of these debilitating pressures, the vast majority of Catholics clung tenaciously to their faith, and conversion to Protestantism was extremely rare.[38]

The restoration of the Stuarts to the English throne in the spring of 1660 raised hope among dispossessed Irish Catholics that the harsh treatment meted out to them by Cromwell might be mitigated or reversed. On November 30, 1660, scarcely seven months after his return, Charles II encouraged those aspirations by issuing a declaration that affirmed the claims of adventurers and soldiers to tracts they had already been awarded and promised equitable treatment to "innocent papists" and Irish Royalists whose lands had been confiscated. Many of the latter had lost their estates when they followed the king into exile.

It soon became apparent, however, that the king's obligations and the expectations kindled by his declaration greatly exceeded the amount of land available for distribution. In the ensuing clash of competing claims, Protestants consistently fared better than their Catholic opponents. Thus, the various actions taken during the reign of Charles II, 1660–1685, known collectively as the "restoration settlement," did little to modify the severity of previous measures and never seriously jeopardized the Protestant domination established under Cromwell. Although some Catholics regained some land, the basic configuration of ownership set in the 1650s did not change, a reality that became increasingly clear to Ireland's dispossessed and nutured among them a thirst for revenge.

In the summer of 1662, Parliament enacted legislation to implement the royal policy enunciated in November 1660. The Act of Settlement, introduced by an intensely anti-Catholic preface, provided for a seven-member court of claims empowered to hear cases and resolve conflicts and disputes involving the disposition of confiscated lands. For the eight months it was in session, however, the court of claims concentrated exclusively on petitioners seeking to obtain "decrees of innocence" that would absolve them from the penalties attached to participation in the 1641 rebellion. Any Protestant or Catholic who satisfied the strict eligibility requirements and received a decree of innocence was, theoretically, enabled to recover his lands or be compensated with tracts in another place. Besides the shortage of available land, the commissioners' brief tenure allowed them to consider the pleas of only a fraction of the claimants clamoring

38. Patrick J. Corish, "The Cromwellian Regime, 1650–60," in Moody, Martin, and Byrne, eds., *Early Modern Ireland*, 358, 375–376; J. G. Simms, *The Williamite Confiscation in Ireland, 1690–1703* (London, 1956), 196. See also Map 5, below.

for their attention, and their decisions pleased neither side. Not surprisingly, Protestants charged that Catholics had been indulged at their expense, and Catholics asserted that they had been severely injured by the numerous cases left unheard.[39]

THE GRACE OF SURVIVAL

The experience of Daniel Carroll of Ballymooney and his progeny within chaotic Cromwellian Ireland became an important part of the remembered past that shaped succeeding generations. A letter written in Maryland in 1762 by Charles Carroll of Annapolis recalls: "Notwithstanding Our Sufferings under Elizabeth & Cromwell We were in Affluent Circumstances & Respected & we intermarryed wth the best Families in the Kingdom of Ireland." The documents that detail the Irish land confiscation give a more forceful and explicit account of the harsh circumstances the family endured in those years. Like the majority of Catholic landowners in the midlands, Daniel Carroll of Ballymooney was forced to forfeit the bulk of his estate to Protestants. Specifically, the records of the Cromwellian settlement for Seirkieran parish in King's County show that three-quarters of the acreage that belonged to him in 1641 had, by 1662, been distributed to new owners. Family members who managed to remain in the area did so as head tenants on far smaller tracts.[40]

The story of the Ballymooney Carrolls' survival can be reconstructed in even

39. By 1665 mounting dissatisfaction with the shortcomings of the court of claims' actions forced Parliament to enact an additional measure known as the Act of Explanation. In an attempt to resolve the most pressing difficulties associated with confiscated Irish land, this law directed adventurers and soldiers to yield one-third of the acreage they had been granted in order to create a pool from which the claims of other Protestants and a limited number of Catholics could be appeased. As with the Act of Settlement three years earlier, the Act of Explanation proved incapable of meeting Catholic demands, and its provisions made Protestants acutely unhappy. Moreover, the execution of the law became enormously time-consuming and complicated, especially in cases where Protestant proprietors were to be ousted in favor of Catholic claimants. J. G. Simms, "The Restoration, 1660–85," in Moody, Martin, and Byrne, eds., *Early Modern Ireland,* 425–426.

40. CCA to CCC, Sept. 1, 1762, Carroll Papers, MS 206, MdHi; Books of Survey and Distribution, King's County, fols. 59, 60, 77; Petty, *Hiberniae Delineatio.* J. G. Simms estimates that, in the provinces of Leinster and Munster, Catholics who had owned two-thirds of the land before the 1641 rising retained only one-fifth after the Cromwellian settlement. See "The Restoration, 1660–85," in Moody, Martin, and Byrne, eds., *Early Modern Ireland,* 427.

greater detail. As the mid-eighteenth-century Maryland Carrolls descended from this branch knew and recounted on other occasions, one of Daniel Carroll of Ballymooney's grandsons, Charles, born in Ireland in 1661, received a fine education in Europe, undertook legal studies at the Inner Temple in London, and secured an appointment as attorney general for the province of Maryland.[41] Although the particulars are not part of the records left by their Maryland kin, Irish documents suggest that what saved the Carrolls of Ballymooney amid the turmoil of the Cromwellian era and eventually gave Charles his chance was precisely their ability to forge marital alliances with well-placed Irish families. For most of the seventeenth century, the Ballymooney Carrolls' most critical ties were those that connected them to the Old English family of Richard Grace, a man with remarkable access to the highest circles of the Stuart court.

Born into a wealthy Kilkenny family that held extensive lands in King's County as well, Richard Grace was the essence of the Irish-Jacobite Cavalier — handsome, courageous in battle, and absolutely unequivocal in his loyalty to the House of Stuart. When the 1641 rebellion erupted, Grace and his uncle, Daniel Carroll of Ballymooney, pursued similar paths.[42] Because of his loyalty to the Stuarts, Grace refused to support the initial rising, and his lands were plundered by Gaelic partisans in King's County. Eager to demonstrate his loyalty to Charles I, Grace, then a man of twenty-five, left Ireland carrying a letter of recommendation from a relative, the duke of Ormond, and entered the king's army, serving with distinction until the Royalists surrendered at Oxford in 1646. With the fighting over in England, Grace returned to Ireland, recruited a regiment, and entered the confederate wars — the continuing rebellion in Ireland against English control. Like many of the Old English, he bound his fate to that of the Stuarts, recognizing, as did many of the Old English, that the crown afforded them the better protection against the Protestants — the New English.[43]

Daniel Carroll of Ballymooney followed a similar course. Judged correctly by

41. See CCC to the Countess d'Auzouer, Sept. 20, 1771, CCC, letterbook 1770–1774, MdHi.

42. Richard Grace's relationship to Daniel Carroll of Ballymooney is documented in a number of instances. The most important manuscripts that emphasize the ties between the two men are [the king to the lords justices], 24 Sept., 13th [1661], S.O. 1/5/33, PRO; Grace to Bennett, petition, July 1, 1663, S.P. 63/314/1–2; "State of Col. Grace" [1674], Stowe MSS 205, fols. 306r, 306v; Col. Grace's Case, July 3, 1674, Rawl. B.492, in McNeill, "Rawlinson Collection," *Analecta Hibernica*, I (1930), 158.

43. "State of Col. Grace" [1674], Stowe MSS 205, fol. 306r; *DNB*, s.v. "Grace, Richard;" Foster, *Modern Ireland*, 51–52.

a later commission to have remained loyal to Charles I in 1641, Daniel temporized when the rising erupted. Holding back in the first flush of rebellion, he sought to protect the local crown authorities, including the governor of Birr, William Parsons. As Parsons recorded in his diary: "John Carroll of Leape and Donnell Carroll of Ballamoneine in the King's County Esquires came to me to Parsonstowne and told me that they were sworne to deliver me a message from John Carroll of Clonliske, and Luke Delahoyd Esquires which was this, that they desired me to leave the Castle of Parsonstowne and Countrey, and that they would see me safely conveyed to Dublin with all my ffamilye." John and Daniel promised further that in Parsons's absence they would protect not only his home and properties but those of the other planters as well.[44]

By the spring of 1642, many Carrolls had joined the rebellion. Noted Parsons in March, "The Carrolls Campe lay an Ambush, for my Troops, and had like to have shott my Lieutenante." Parsons's policy of beheading his opponents — in February he had brought home the head of one of the Carroll captains, "which I caused to be sett upon the Sessions house" — certainly contributed to the spreading violence. Even then Daniel remained unprovoked, and in April Parsons gratefully recorded that he had just "bought 5 barrells of wheat from Donnell Carroll of Ballamoneyne," food that he and his dependents required. The governor's position in Birr grew increasingly serious, however, and on April 13 he recorded the destruction of his town. At "about 10 a clocke att night," according to his diary, the Carrolls, Molloys, Coghlans, and Ormonds "burnt my Towne almost every house to the ground, And when they saw the Towne on fire, they blew upp their Baggpipes, and beat upp their Drums, and fell a Dauncinge on the Hills." Still, Parsons held his castle until January 1643, when it fell after an intense, five-day siege. Allowed to withdraw, he joined the English army in Dublin, leaving his stronghold at Birr in the hands of his Catholic opponents, who garrisoned and later burned it as the war turned against them in the late 1640s and early 1650s.[45]

With civil strife engulfing both England and Ireland, Daniel Carroll of Ballymooney took up arms for the Catholic cause as a captain in the confederate army. His vision of what he might gain from the conflict seems to have stretched, perhaps wryly, well beyond the shores of Ireland. When Rory O'More, the rebel

44. Parsons, diary, Dec. 23, 1641, Rosse Papers, A/9; Philip Dwyer, *The Diocese of Killaloe, from the Reformation to the Close of the Eighteenth Century* (London, 1878), 239.

45. Parsons, diary, Feb. 23, Mar. 23, 1641/2, Apr. 11, 13, 1642, Rosse Papers, A/9; PRONI, "Rosse Papers," 3.

Irish commander, held out the prospect that the Carrolls might receive more Irish land because of their services, Daniel responded that he "hoped (ere it were long) to have his proportion of land within five myles of London." [46]

Throughout the confusing intervals of conflict and negotiation in the late 1640s, Daniel remained active in the confederate struggle. Even after Cromwell's devastating conquest and the surrender of the main Catholic command, he and Richard Grace refused to submit, choosing instead to fight on with the partisans who still controlled the mountains and bogs of the midlands. Both men were elevated in rank — Grace to colonel, Daniel to lieutenant colonel — and their troops attacked and successfully destroyed English outposts at Birr, Kildare, and Roscrea. The English acknowledged their tenacity by placing a bounty on their heads: three hundred pounds for Grace, two hundred pounds for Carroll. Grace responded by swearing his commanders to undying resistance in May 1652.[47]

Nevertheless, the fight could not be won. Daniel Carroll surrendered in mid-June. Grace, though initially outraged by what he termed Carroll's "impious and ungodly staine of publicke periurie," followed suit in August. The terms negotiated by Grace, the last of the Irish commanders to submit, allowed him to take twelve hundred men to Spain, where he continued to serve Charles II and the duke of York. Daniel Carroll was similarly forced to leave Ireland.[48] His descendants endured the range of fates characteristic of the Gaelic experience in post-Cromwellian times. A few ultimately conformed to the Church of Ireland and enjoyed the opportunities for advancement that generally resulted from that decision. Others were transplanted to Connacht or chose to emigrate, but most elected to stay in Ireland and hold fast to their faith. By the end of the century, that act of loyalty had impoverished them and brought them to the brink of extinction.

Through the branch of Daniel of Ballymooney's family descended from his son Anthony, the compelling force of these choices and their consequences reached far beyond the times and places of mid-seventeenth-century Ireland to

46. George Stockdale, deposition, 1643, MS 810, fol. 14, TCD.

47. Dan Bryan, "Colonel Richard Grace, 1651–1652," *Irish Sword,* I (1951–1952), 43–51; Diarmuid Murtagh, "Colonel Richard Grace," *Irish Sword,* I (1951–1952), 173; *DNB,* s.v. "Grace, Richard." For an overview of Richard Grace, see the six articles by J. J. Kelly, "Col. Richard Grace," *Irish Eccl. Rec.,* 4th Ser., XXVI (1909), XXXII (1912), 5th Ser., II (1913).

48. John T. Gilbert, ed., *A Contemporary History of Affairs in Ireland from 1641 to 1652* (Dublin, 1879–1880), III, 130–132, 392; Diarmuid Murtagh, "Colonel Richard Grace," *Irish Sword,* I (1951–1952), 173; *DNB,* s.v. "Grace, Richard."

Prologue

shape Carroll lives in the very heart of the American Revolution. Little is known of Anthony's life, but his death had enormous significance for future generations of his family, because he died soldiering for Richard Grace in the Stuarts' European campaigns of the 1650s. Anthony's loyalty and that of men like him helped Grace forge enduring ties to Charles and James, the heirs apparent of England's deposed royal family. From 1654 until 1658, Grace fought regularly with the Stuart brothers in behalf of their interests in France and Spain. In 1658, he served under James, the duke of York, at the Battle of the Dunes, and later became his chamberlain.[49] Accompanying James on his return to England for Charles II's Restoration to the throne in 1660, Grace had achieved a position that allowed him to ask for whatever he desired. He chose his lands in Ireland, and within a year all his properties had been restored.[50]

Correspondence concerning Grace reflects the nature of his relationships with the most powerful figures of his time. From the mid-1650s Charles II wrote of the "more than ordinary assurance of his devotion" to Grace and throughout the 1660s continued to recall his "loyal services." Matching his rhetoric with action, the king granted Grace a series of handsome gifts. Until all the arrangements for the restoration of his Irish lands had been completed, Grace received a pension of one hundred pounds per month. In 1675, the crown awarded him an annual pension of three hundred pounds, to continue during his life and that of his son-in-law as well, and remitted forever all quitrents on his properties. Although the precise amount of land Grace reacquired and purchased cannot be determined, the recorded transactions indicate that he accumulated a

49. Grace to Bennett, petition, July 1, 1663, S.P. 63/314/1–2. Kelly, "Col. Richard Grace," *Irish Eccl. Rec.*, 4th Ser., XXVI (1909), 255–258, relates Grace's record on the Continent in the 1650s.

50. Kelly, "Col. Richard Grace," *Irish Eccl. Rec.*, 4th Ser., XXXII (1912), 400–401; the king to the lord justices of Ireland, Feb. 7 [1660/1], S.O. 1/4/232. Grace had other influential friends, although he might not have needed them. The most important of these, his kinsman James Butler (1610–?1688), the twelfth earl of Ormond, chose to join Charles Stuart in exile in 1651. Created duke of Ormond by his grateful king in 1661, he gained two terms as lord lieutenant of Ireland, a post to which Charles I had appointed him in 1644. During his initial post-Restoration tenure, 1661–1669, Ormond supervised the redistribution of land under the Acts of Settlement and Explanation, and his second, which began in 1677, gave him a reasonably firm hold on Ireland through the accession of James II in 1685 (Foster, *Modern Ireland*, 88).

Richard Grace's brother, John Grace of Courtstown, also supported the royal cause and reportedly donated one thousand gold pieces to the Stuart treasury in 1658. Kelly, "Col. Richard Grace," *Irish Eccl. Rec.*, 4th Ser., XXVI (1909), 258.

minimum of five to six thousand acres during the 1660s and probably added considerably more acreage during the next thirty years. He also gained lucrative rights to establish manors and to hold fairs and weekly markets.[51]

Thus, Richard Grace had the resources and influence to provide for whomever he wished, and among those he supported were the descendants of Daniel Carroll of Ballymooney. Daniel had been his uncle and a comrade in arms, and one of his sons had died under Grace's command. Before leaving Ireland to join Charles I in 1641, Grace had made a bequest of his townland of Moyelly and other assets to his uncle Daniel Carroll, perhaps in an effort to secure this property from retaliation. Whatever his motive, the transaction demonstrated a bond of trust between nephew and uncle that was neither weakened nor forgotten during the ensuing two decades.[52] By the time the crown restored Moyelly to Grace in 1661, the Old English Cavalier had already assumed the responsibility of caring for two wards, one of them the grandson of Daniel Carroll of Ballymooney, and in 1663 he petitioned the king in their behalf.

Writing to Henry Bennett, principal secretary to Charles II, Grace explained the situation that prompted his appeal: "I am now become a suitor to you on behalf of a couple of infants, cousins german of my own, their fathers having died in the King's service under my command, the one beyond seas, the other here. When I came here I found one of these poor things keeping calves, the other in

51. The king to Don Juan [October 1656], in O. Ogle et al., eds., *Calendar of the Clarendon State Papers . . .* (Oxford, 1869–1970), III, 194; the king to the lords justices, Mar. 5, 1662, *Cal. S.P., Ire., 1660–1662,* 514; the king to the lord lieutenant, June 20, 1669, *Cal. S.P., Ire., 1669–1670,* 163–164; "State of Col. Grace," [1674], Stowe MSS 205, fol. 306v; the king to the lord lieutenant, warrant, Nov. 12, 1675, *Cal. S.P., Ire., 1675–1676,* 401; Kelly, "Col. Richard Grace," *Irish Eccl. Rec.,* 4th Ser., XXVI (1909), 259, 5th Ser., II (1913), 51; the king to the lord lieutenant, Jan. 2, 1673/4, S.O. 1/9/33–34; the king to the lord lieutenant and the lord deputy, Mar. 31, 1665, the king to [the lord lieutenant and the lord deputy], draft, Mar. 31, 1665, *Cal. S.P., Ire., 1663–1665,* 560–561; the king to the lord lieutenant, Aug. 30, 1672, *Cal. S.P., Domestic Series, 1672,* 542; duke of Ormond, warrant, July 25, 1663, E. Edwards, "Calendar of the Carte Papers," XXXVI, fol. 472, Bodleian Library, Oxford. See also Col. Grace to Lane, Sept. 5, 1663, Edwards, "Calendar of Carte Papers," XXXVII, fol. 145.

52. Chancery bill, Apr. 23, 1640, TA 3164; Richard Grace to Daniel Carroll, deed to Moyelly, May 2, 1640, TA 5072; Col. Grace's Case, July 3, 1674, in McNeill, "Rawlinson Collection," Rawlinson B. 492, *Analecta Hibernica,* I (1930), 158; "State of Col. Grace," [1674], Stowe MSS 205, fol. 306r. Moyelly was eventually confiscated by a Cromwellian, John Eyre. The lord lieutenant to Secretary Bennett, Dec. 18, 1663, and draft of the king to the lord lieutenant, 1663, *Cal. S.P., Ire., 1663–1665,* 318, 345.

no better condition."[53] Stating his wish to provide for the youths, Grace asked that the king restore to them their fathers' lands. No record of the crown's reply has been found, but many of Daniel Carroll of Ballymooney's tracts were returned — to Richard Grace. Among them was the 136-acre townland of Aghagurty, where Daniel of Ballymooney's grandson settled and added to his name, Daniel Carroll, the distinguishing appellation "of Aghagurty." Translated from the Gaelic, *Aghagurty* means "field of hunger or starvation," an appropriate residence for a young man who had survived by "keeping calves."[54]

53. Grace to Bennett, July 1, 1663, *Cal. S.P., Ire., 1663–1665,* 156. "Infants" designates persons who have not reached twenty-one, the age of majority. "Cousins german" means close kin, usually first cousins.

54. Books of Survey and Distribution, King's County, fol. 60; "Ordnance Survey Field Name Books of the King's County, 1837–1840," II, typescript, Offaly County Library, Tullamore.

CHAPTER 1

"Anywhere so long as There Be Freedom"

Daniel Carroll of Aghagurty (or Daniel Carroll of Litterluna, as later generations preferred to call him in remembrance of his family's earlier holdings in Ely O'Carroll) fathered four sons — Anthony, Charles, John, and Thomas. Anthony and most of his descendants would remain in Ireland and fall into poverty and obscurity. Thomas would die fighting against William of Orange in 1690, leaving two sons who were placed with and raised by Protestant families. Setting a new course, Charles and John would emigrate to Maryland, where John died a man of modest means. By contrast, Charles achieved remarkable success, establishing a new Carroll fortune and founding a vital and impressive family. His grandson would be Charles Carroll of Carrollton.

Until the final decade of the seventeenth century, Daniel Carroll of Aghagurty and his family continued to benefit from their ties to Richard Grace. Grace's reacquisition of his lands in the early 1660s coincided with a posthumous grant of a decree of innocence to his kinsman Anthony Carroll of Aghagurty. That Anthony and his half brother Owen were among the 566 Catholics so favored from the thousands who applied can reasonably be ascribed to the colonel's influence. The dispensation enabled Daniel Carroll of Aghagurty (Anthony's son and Grace's "cousin german") to gain the title of head tenant on the 136-acre townland of Aghagurty. Grace might also have set aside for his ward's use other properties that had belonged to Daniel Carroll of Ballymooney but were now in his possession. Hence, although the great hopes the Stuart restoration engendered among the Irish Catholics ended in disappointment, the descendants of Daniel Carroll of Ballymooney retained some access to property and enough financial resources to survive the worst of the sufferings of the Cromwellian confiscations and their aftermath.[1]

1. Catholics judged to be "innocent Papists" by the court of claims — the seven commissioners charged with executing the Act of Settlement that redistributed Irish lands

Beyond this outline of the circumstances into which Charles Carroll was born in 1661 (the year after the Stuart restoration), nothing is known about his early life. One can only speculate about the substance of his youth, a boyhood shadowed by the mountains that had sheltered his defiant ancestors and by reminders of the religious, cultural, and economic threats visited upon them. The ruins of the stone dwelling that can be seen at Aghagurty today certainly do not suggest a pretentious place, but Charles, as a younger son, might have been fostered out, a common custom of the time, to the more substantial home of his kinsman Richard Grace, who did not have a son.

Two facts of Charles's personal history point strongly in this direction. First, Charles underwent a course of intensive schooling, but his older brother, Anthony, remained illiterate. Second, Charles not only attended institutions in France that ostensibly demanded far greater resources than those available to a head tenant, studying humanities and philosophy at Lille and civil and canon law at the University of Douai, but he also enrolled exclusively in institutions operated by the Society of Jesus. Here Grace's influence is unmistakable, since the Old English strongly preferred the Jesuits, whereas the Gaelic Irish favored Dominicans and Franciscans.[2] The Carroll brothers' lives exemplified this sharp divergence, with Charles and his descendants maintaining a firm attachment to the Jesuits, and Anthony and his son Daniel choosing to be buried in the churchyard of the Dominican chapel at Lorrha in County Tipperary.[3] Both An-

---

confiscated as a result of the 1641 rebellion — were either reinstated on their former property or compensated with equivalent land elsewhere. "Inrolments of Decrees of Innocents passed under the Act of Settlement; preserved in the Office of the Chief Remembrancer of the Exchequer, Dublin," in Great Britain, Commissioners of the Public Records of Ireland, *Reports from the Commissioners Appointed by His Majesty to Execute the Measures Recommended in an Address of the House of Commons Respecting the Public Records of Ireland, Eleventh, Twelfth, and Thirteenth, Fourteenth, and Fifteenth Reports* (London, 1824–1825), 528, 538; J. G. Simms, "The Restoration, 1660–85," in T. W. Moody, F. X. Martin, and F. J. Byrne, eds., *Early Modern Ireland, 1534–1691* (Oxford, 1976), vol. III of Moody, Martin, and Byrne, eds., *A New History of Ireland, 422–425.*

2. R. F. Foster, *Modern Ireland, 1600–1972* (London, 1988), 47. Evidence of Anthony Carroll of Lisheenboy's illiteracy is suggested by his use of a mark to sign a 1719 deed (William Worth to Anthony Carroll, Sept. 1, 1719, lease of Killcrogane, Lower Ormond, Co. Tip., D3249/1/2, PRONI). Charles Carroll's education was described by his son Charles Carroll of Annapolis in notes appended to the family pedigree in "Genealogy of O Carroll," MS, Carroll-O'Carroll Genalogies, MdHi, and in CCC to Countess d'Auzouer, Sept. 20, 1771, CCC, letterbook 1770–1774, MdHi.

3. Anthony Carroll of Lisheenboy, May 21, 1724, and Daniel Carroll of Killecregane, March 1723, prerogative wills, Irwin Abstracts, fols. 475–476, Genealogical Office,

thony and Charles remained strong in their Catholic faith and absolutely loyal to the Stuarts. Neither man ever bent or compromised his commitment to family, church, or the heritage of the O'Carrolls, but it was Charles's strategy of survival that brought the family to renewed power, wealth, and glory.

In May 1685, Charles Carroll, age twenty-five, registered in London for the study of the common law. After paying fees amounting to £3.7.8 and entering "into Bond for Discharge of his Duties to the house," the second son of "Daniel Carroll of Aghagurton," as he styled himself, gained admission into the society and commons of the Inner Temple.[4] For an Irishman of his background, London in the spring of 1685 must have seemed a hopeful place. James II, who had converted to Catholicism in the early 1670s, became king upon the death of his brother in February. Making no secret of his religious allegiance, the new monarch went openly to Mass and heartened his coreligionists by setting free numerous Catholics and other Nonconformists who had been incarcerated on religious grounds. Further encouragement came in May, when the infamous Titus Oates, whose allegations of a conspiracy to murder Charles II and establish Roman Catholicism in England had created the Popish Plot and brought hardship, imprisonment, and even death to a number of priests and innocent laymen, was finally brought to trial for perjury. For Catholics, Oates's conviction and subsequent punishment — he was to be whipped publicly and pilloried — signaled the end of a dismal period of anxiety and fear that the troublemaker's accusations had initiated in 1678 and kept alive for nearly seven years.

Less than a month after Oates's sentencing, James II's illegitimate Protestant nephew, the duke of Monmouth, mounted a rebellion that the king quelled, with what many regarded as excessive brutality, in about six weeks. Thereafter, James began to move with increasing boldness to install Catholics in positions of influence within his government and in 1686 appointed Catholic peers — and, a year later, a Jesuit priest — to the Privy Council. Developments in Ireland during the early months of James's reign also suggested the dawning of a better day for Catholics. Although disappointed at the king's selection of "a high-tory Anglican," the second earl of Clarendon, as viceroy over the "popish champion," Richard Talbot, whom James had recently created earl of Tyrconnell,

---

Dublin. The fact that Anthony's grandsons had become Jesuit priests by the mid-eighteenth century can be attributed to the influence of Charles on Anthony's son James, who also emigrated to Maryland and in the end provided the money that educated his brothers' sons.

4. Charles Carroll [the Settler], May 7, 1685, certificate of admission to the Inner Temple, Carroll Papers, MS 206, MdHi.

"Anywhere so long as There Be Freedom"

Irish Catholics could still point to the restructuring of the army to admit Catholic recruits and officers and a relaxation of oath-taking requirements as signs that other long-desired improvements in their status were to come.[5]

Yet, however promising the accession of an avowed Catholic to the English throne might have seemed, leading members of the English Catholic community, both laymen and ecclesiastics, harbored no illusions about the possibility of restoring the Roman church to its former glory. Even among James II's inner circle of advisers the two Catholic peers (both of whom proved important to Charles Carroll's future) distrusted both the durability of the king's changes and the viability of his more aggressive plans for the future. Accused by Oates of complicity in the Popish Plot, these men — William Herbert, Lord Powis (1617–1696), and Henry, third Lord Arundell of Wardour (1606?–1694) — had been imprisoned in the Tower of London from October 1678 until granted bail in February 1684, and it was not until Oates's conviction for perjury more than a year later that the House of Lords ordered all charges against them dropped. Although Powis and Arundell had benefited from James's actions — appointment to the Privy Council in 1686 — they urged the king to pursue a moderate course that allowed Catholics to consolidate their gains, instead of attempting a more radical restoration of Catholic power and influence that would inevitably threaten and alarm England's Protestant majority.[6]

James II rejected the cause of moderation, a decision that had important consequences for young Charles Carroll, whose decision to emigrate to Maryland might have been directly attributable to Powis's pessimistic assessment of Catholic prospects in England. Several factors make this theory plausible. Although undocumented, Carroll family tradition maintains that, during the mid-1680s, Charles Carroll, perhaps with the help of Richard Grace, secured a position as Powis's clerk. Such employment not only would have exposed him to that gentleman's opinions but also would have brought him into contact with other prominent Catholics, like Lord Arundell of Wardour and Arundell's first cousin Charles Calvert, third Lord Baltimore and proprietor of Maryland, a colony conceived in part as a safe haven for Catholics.[7] According to the family account,

5. J. G. Simms, *Jacobite Ireland, 1685–91* (London, 1969), 19–22. William Herbert, Lord Powis, and Henry Arundell were the peers; Edward Petre, the Jesuit.

6. John Bossy, *The English Catholic Community, 1570–1850* (New York, 1976), 71.

7. This information was originally published in John Carroll Brent's anecdotal *Biographical Sketch of the Most Rev. John Carroll, First Archbishop of Baltimore: With Select Portions of His Writings* (Baltimore, 1843), 16, and repeated in Kate Mason Rowland's generally reliable biography of Charles Carroll of Carrollton (*The Life of Charles Carroll*

Powis, dismayed by the future he foresaw, urged his young clerk to "go out to Maryland" and offered to recommend him to Lord Baltimore. One thing is certain: Charles Carroll left London in a considerable hurry, not bothering to pay his remaining fees to the Temple, a prerequisite of being called to the bar. Whatever the precise configuration of events, Charles Carroll did receive a commission as attorney general of Maryland from Lord Baltimore on July 18, 1688, and he arrived in the colony on October 1.[8]

In view of events in England during the last six months of 1688, the timing of Charles Carroll's departure can only be described as fortunate. Months before he left, ominous trends were already evident as James II's aggressively pro-Catholic policies increasingly challenged Protestant civil and religious hegemony openly and directly. Alarmed by the king's boldness and the warm approval of his actions by France's Catholic monarch, Louis XIV, a group of Protestant peers entered discussions in April 1688 with James's Dutch son-in-law, William of Orange, concerning the role they might persuade him to play in preventing a resurgence of Catholic power. The birth of a son to James's queen on June 10 made a Catholic succession an urgent possibility, and in late September seven of the negotiators invited William to mount an expedition to England.[9]

Defections to William's banner began immediately upon his landing at Torbay on November 5, and on December 22, three days after the Dutchman entered London, James II escaped to France, where the queen and their infant son,

---

of Carrollton, 1737–1832, with His Correspondence and Public Papers [New York, 1898], I, 3–4) with a citation to Brent. The story as related by Brent is supposed to have been told by Charles Carroll of Carrollton late in his life. Powis also had a family tie to the Calverts: his wife was Elizabeth Somerset, whose uncle John Somerset was married to Mary Arundell, aunt of Charles Calvert, third Lord Baltimore and proprietor of Maryland. Genealogical Files, Charles Carroll of Carrollton Papers, MdHi.

8. Rowland, Life of Charles Carroll of Carrollton, I, 3; Bench Table Orders, Nov. 10, 1692, in Inner Temple, London, A Calendar of the Inner Temple Records, ed. F. A. Inderwick, III (London, 1901), 292; interview with W. W. S. Breem, librarian and keeper of manuscripts at the Inner Temple, Sept. 23, 1986; Notes by CCA in "Genealogy of O Carroll," MS, Carroll-O'Carroll Genealogies.

9. William had no apparent desire to become king of England, but he very much wanted to bring that country's military resources into an alliance with those of the Dutch and other European states — Catholic as well as Protestant — to curb France's expanding power. Dale Hoak, "The Anglo-Dutch Revolution of 1688–89," in Hoak and Mordechai Reingold, eds., The World of William and Mary: Anglo-Dutch Perspectives on the Revolution of 1688–89 (Stanford, Calif., 1996), 20–21.

"Anywhere so long as There Be Freedom"

taken out of England in secret by Lady Powis, awaited him. A month later the Convention Parliament declared the throne vacant, stated its opposition to a Catholic monarch, and offered the crown jointly to William of Orange and his wife, Mary, James's older daughter from his first marriage, whom he had allowed to be raised a Protestant. Charles Carroll's presumed mentor, Lord Powis, followed the king into exile, to remain a loyal and trusted adviser until his death in 1696. As a consequence, English authorities attainted Powis in July 1689, outlawed him in October, and confiscated his estates.[10]

As the first rumors of the events in England in the fall of 1688 did not reach Maryland until mid-December, Carroll's career in the colony began agreeably enough. On October 13, 1688, two weeks after his arrival, the new attorney general presented his commission from Lord Baltimore to the council, the select group of proprietary appointees who advised the governor. The spare account of the proceedings on that day gives no hint that major trouble lay in the immediate future. Indeed, the council's attention since the end of September had been largely focused on orders from Lord Baltimore and the Privy Council directing that the people of Maryland celebrate the birth of James II's son. Thus, the four councillors present (of eleven) that day received Carroll's credentials without comment and turned to other business.[11]

The basic framework of the government of which Carroll's commission made him a part had been set down in the Maryland charter awarded to the Calverts by Charles I in 1632. By its terms, Lord Baltimore, the proprietor, owned all the land in the colony and possessed supreme governing authority over its inhabitants. Those powers the proprietor delegated to an array of appointed officials — governors, secretaries, councillors, magistrates, legal officials (such as the attorney general), and clerks — who resided in Maryland and assumed the immediate responsibility for governing it. Equally important, those officials were expected to protect and advance their patron's interests in the colony, specifically in the matter of collecting and transmitting to him the various fees, duties, rents, and taxes that constituted the proprietary revenue. And because their own salaries were also paid out of those moneys, proprietary officeholders

10. Lady Powis had witnessed the birth of the Prince of Wales on June 10, 1688, and on the same day was appointed governess to James II's children. Lord Arundell, Powis's former prison mate, fared better than Powis; withdrawing entirely from public affairs, he lived in retirement at his estate in Hampshire.

11. William Hand Browne et al., eds., *Archives of Maryland* (Baltimore, 1883–), VIII, 39–47.

had a special incentive to be diligent. As a counterweight to the proprietor's extensive powers, the Maryland charter provided three safeguards: every colonist would possess all the rights of native-born Englishmen; all provincial statutes must be conformable to those of the mother country; and an assembly of free men or their deputies could pass laws for the colony, though all such measures would require the proprietor's assent. The first recorded meeting of such an assembly took place in St. Mary's City in 1635, scarcely a year after the first settlers landed on St. Clement's Island (Blakiston Island).[12]

By the time of Charles Carroll's arrival in Maryland half a century later, both the proprietary governing establishment and the assembly of free men had acquired distinctive and adversarial characteristics. The assembly of free men had evolved into a bicameral legislature composed of a lower house elected by men possessing fifty acres of land or visible property worth forty pounds — perhaps as many as two-thirds of the colonial population — and an upper house whose members were the proprietary appointees who also sat on the governor's council. The lower house, which contained during the 1686–1688 proprietary assembly twenty-two delegates (two from each of Maryland's ten counties and its capital, St. Mary's City) represented interests that were frequently at odds with those of the proprietor and the upper house. The composition of the lower house and Maryland's general population of some twenty-five thousand souls reinforced this confrontation: both were overwhelmingly Protestant, but only Roman Catholics had been appointed to the upper house since 1682. Always a distinct minority, Maryland's Catholics lived primarily in the Western Shore counties of Charles and St. Mary's and were linked by the missions and priests that served them. Like their Protestant neighbors, most Catholics were modest landowners, but an elite group of a few highly visible and quite wealthy men headed their community.[13]

12. Lois Green Carr and David William Jordan, *Maryland's Revolution of Government, 1689–1692* (Ithaca, N.Y., 1974), 5. In addition to Lord Baltimore's revenues, certain levies known as the "plantation duty" were payable to the crown. These funds were collected by royal officials who were also responsible for enforcing the navigation laws, which regulated trade. Donnell MacClure Owings, *His Lordship's Patronage: Offices of Profit in Colonial Maryland* (Baltimore, 1953), 8–10, 92.

13. David W. Jordan, *Foundations of Representative Government in Maryland, 1632–1715* (Cambridge, 1987), esp. part 2; Edward C. Papenfuse et al., eds., *A Biographical Dictionary of the Maryland Legislature, 1635–1789* (Baltimore, 1979–1985), I, 30; Carr and Jordan, *Maryland's Revolution of Government*, 33nn.

Carr and Jordan (*Maryland's Revolution of Government*, 6n) point out that no study of how many persons could vote in Maryland for the period 1670–1689 has been com-

"Anywhere so long as There Be Freedom"

Notwithstanding their majority in the lower house and their dominance of county and local offices, ambitious Maryland Protestants recognized that the proprietary patronage had concentrated the most powerful and lucrative positions in a very select group of Catholic gentlemen, most of whom were relatives of the proprietor. Of the eight men serving as councillors and members of the upper house in 1688, six — Henry Darnall, Clement Hill, William Joseph, Vincent Lowe, Edward Pye, and Nicholas Sewall — were Roman Catholics, and all of the Catholics except Joseph were kin to Lord Baltimore. In addition, Darnall's and Hill's wives were sisters. Moreover, William Digges, one of the two Protestant councillors, was married to the proprietor's stepdaughter, a union that also related him to Hill, Lowe, Pye, and Sewall.[14]

The Catholic monopoly of high offices rankled a number of ambitious Protestants who considered their domination of the lower house of assembly as well as of county and local offices insufficient compensation for a policy that denied them access to the top echelons of provincial power. In the spring of 1689 the uncertainties generated in Maryland by the triumph of a Protestant succession in England provided those men with an opportunity to redress the balance in their favor. Led by a habitual troublemaker named John Coode, they concocted a "rising in armes" that wrested the authority to govern Maryland from Lord Baltimore and transferred it to the English crown.[15]

For the next several years the situation in Maryland remained confused, as a series of ad hoc conventions under Coode's authority assumed control and colonial administrators in London struggled to devise a comprehensive settlement. Sympathetic to Protestant interests but uncertain about the legal implications of accepting the rebels' challenge to Lord Baltimore's charter rights, English officials examined contradictory petitions from Maryland regarding past and present conditions and weighed personal appearances before the Lords of Trade by Charles Calvert, John Coode, and other witnesses from both sides. Unable to find a satisfactory resolution, Whitehall finally referred the issue to the Privy Council.

At this juncture, Calvert, emboldened by the official stalemate and a show of support from a delegation of prominent Maryland Protestants, adopted a rigid

---

pleted. The suggestion that two-thirds of the population qualified for the franchise is based on Lois Green Carr's analyses of Prince George's County, in "County Government in Maryland, 1689–1709" (Ph.D. diss., Harvard University, 1968), 597–599, 601–602.

14. Carr and Jordan, *Maryland's Revolution of Government,* 13n, table 2, 66–70.

15. The definitive account of the 1689 rebellion in Maryland is Carr and Jordan, *Maryland's Revolution of Government.*

stance and refused to relinquish any of his charter rights to administer Maryland, including the power to appoint the governor. His sole concession was a promise to choose a Protestant for that post. The Privy Council ultimately dismissed this proposition and in January 1691 issued a final decision: Lord Baltimore would continue to own the land of Maryland and to receive certain revenues from the colony, but his authority in governmental affairs was "negated." Henceforth, the provincial government would derive its authority from and be exclusively responsible to the crown.[16]

Two distinct administrative structures were thus created: a proprietary establishment of personnel responsible to Lord Baltimore for the management of his landed and financial interests, and a provincial establishment of officials authorized by the crown to govern the colony. Under this regime, Roman Catholics who refused to qualify themselves for government positions by swearing oaths of allegiance, abhorrence, and abjuration and receiving the Anglican communion could continue to serve the proprietor within his reduced private organization. The power to make political appointments resided exclusively in the crown, which immediately installed a new set of Protestant officials in the colony. Although Lord Baltimore occasionally protested, Maryland continued under this arrangement until 1715, when the Calvert family, having converted to Protestantism, reacquired its control over the provincial government.

To an Irish Catholic like Charles Carroll, the developments in Maryland during the early 1690s were depressingly familiar. The enactment in the colony of the Elizabethan-era oaths used to bar Catholics in England and Ireland from holding public office carried an unmistakable message: their religion would now make them as vulnerable in their new environment as it had in the old to penalties that could constrict and confine them and, at worst, lead to their destruction. Deeply angered by the events that had so rudely thwarted his expectations, Carroll did not accept the proprietor's overthrow gracefully, and his open contempt for those who led the rebellion earned him two stays in jail. For a man whose hopes, upon emigration, had led him to change the motto on his family crest from the tenacious and unyielding watchword of the O'Carroll past, "In fide et in bello forte" ("Strong in faith and war"), to the ringing declaration, "Ubicumque cum libertate" ("Anywhere so long as there be freedom"), these confinements must have been especially galling.[17]

16. Ibid., 155–161.

17. Ibid., 212–213; see also Carr, "County Government," 163–164. In 1704 other penal statues were enacted that forbade Catholics from worshiping publicly or educating their children under "Popish" schoolmasters. Browne et al., eds., *Archives of Maryland,* XXVI,

PLATE 6. Carroll Coats of Arms.
Courtesy Carroll Institute; courtesy the present owner

The attack on Lord Baltimore's government coincided with Carroll's slow recovery from a period of acclimatization to Maryland's environment, and his characterization of the latter as a "hard seasoning" was an apt description of both ordeals. But if his physical strength had temporarily waned, his mind and spirit remained vigorous and undaunted. Writing to the proprietor in September 1689, Carroll castigated the "profligate wretches and men of scandalous lives" who had brought about the "grate calamity," and asserted his confidence that Calvert possessed the legal means to counter the Protestant rebels in their quest for legitimacy and royal favor. The familiar tone of the letter, smuggled out of the colony and conveyed to England by Colonel Henry Darnall, Calvert's cousin and Maryland's most powerful Catholic, suggests that its author and the proprietor were well acquainted.[18]

Carroll's loyalty did not waver when Lord Baltimore failed to recover his authority to govern the province, and his disdainful gibes at the new regime, combined with his Catholicism, shortly made him thoroughly unpopular with Maryland's Protestant power structure. His first incarceration, for unspecified "high misdemeanors" in the spring of 1691, did not intimidate him. Two years later, Carroll's behavior so infuriated Governor Lionel Copley that he ordered the sheriff of St. Mary's County to place him in custody for

340–341. For the change of motto, see CCC to Countess d'Auzouer, Sept. 20, 1771, CCC, letterbook 1770–1774.

18. Charles Carroll to Lord Baltimore, Sept. 25, 1689, in Browne et al., eds., *Archives of Maryland,* VIII, 125.

uttering several mutinous & seditious speeches in derogation to the present Government scandalously reflecting upon affronting and abusing the same and the Authority thereof in their most legal & Iudicious proceedgs in the Administration of Justice . . . to the Breach of their Majestys Peace and the disturbance of the quiet Rule and Government of this their Province.[19]

Carroll immediately requested bail, and Copley put the question to his council, asking whether he should "set the said Carrol to Bayle thereby giving him further opportunity of doing mischief or Confine him till further orders." Rejecting Carroll's petition, those gentlemen acerbically observed that by breaching previous bonds for "good Behaviour" the offender had shown his contempt for such instruments. Indeed, Carroll had publicly characterized them as worth no more than a "pottle of Cyder." Moreover, the colony's disquietude made it especially important to keep a malcontent of Carroll's reputation under arrest. Stating that "through the instigation of the said Carroll & such like Persons as himself a Generall defection througout the Province is threatned and likely to grow if not timely prevented to a greater heighth," the council "advised resolved & Ordered that the said Carroll be closely Confined till further order from this Board."[20]

Although Carroll eventually secured a release from jail, his career in Maryland had clearly not taken the direction he intended. Nonetheless, his aggressive public stands in behalf of the proprietor and the legal skills he had to offer allowed him to carve out a key role for himself in Lord Baltimore's private establishment. The offices he accrued within that organization during the period of royal government in Maryland (1690–1715) attest to his ability and his ambition — and to the growing esteem in which Charles Calvert held his services.

The fates proved far less kind to the Carrolls in Ireland and to their kinsman Richard Grace. Sensitive at first to the tension his Catholicism kindled in English politics, James II had begun his reign by continuing his brother's practice of placing Protestants in the highest echelons of Ireland's governing structure. Then in 1687 the king reversed his earlier action and appointed Richard Talbot, earl of Tyrconnell, a defiant advocate of irredentist Catholic claims, lord deputy in Ireland. A rush of other major Catholic appointments ensued at all levels of government, and the lines of the Irish Parliament were redrawn to ensure a Catholic majority. Most threatening to Protestants, however, was a series of lim-

19. Browne et al., eds., *Archives of Maryland*, VIII, 259, 496.
20. Ibid., 508–509.

ited but unsettling moves initiated later in the year by Tyrconnell, with the apparent backing of James, that portended redressing, if not completely reversing, the Cromwellian land settlement.

The feverish hopes those actions ignited in Catholic Ireland quickly cooled with James II's flight from England in December 1688, only to flame again in March 1689 when the Stuart king arrived triumphantly in Dublin with the promise of vigorous backing from Louis XIV of France.[21] An Irish Parliament summoned by James and composed overwhelmingly of Catholics repealed the Cromwellian land settlement and prepared the way for restoring to Catholic families the lands they had possessed in 1641. Much to the dismay of his Irish admirers, James reacted ambivalently to the measure and finally acquiesced to it with noticeable reluctance. Far more cautious than his Irish subjects, James recognized that the move would be widely unpopular in England and create additional obstacles to his reacquiring the English crown — his foremost objective, and that of his sponsor, Louis XIV. His leadership appeared indecisive in other quarters as well, especially on the battlefield. Assuming command of the army, he failed to achieve a victory over the towns of Derry and Enniskillen, two Protestant strongholds in the north that had blunted the Jacobite advance.

At the same time that a military stalemate was taking hold in Ireland, bringing with it a corresponding decline in Catholic morale, William III concluded that, despite pressing problems on the Continent, he would have to mount and lead a major expedition against the Irish Jacobites. On June 30, 1690, after months of careful preparation, he met his father-in-law at the river Boyne, setting the stage for what is arguably the epic battle of Irish history. William commanded thirty-six thousand men; James, twenty-five thousand. The fighting commenced during the early morning of July 1. Smartly outmaneuvered by William's forces, the Jacobites resisted sharply for several hours before their lines collapsed into a disordered retreat. No one fled more rapidly than James, who raced to the coast and sailed for France on July 4.[22]

William's victory at the Boyne did not end the Catholic resistance, nor did it

21. The following account of conditions in Ireland from 1685 to 1704 is drawn largely from J. G. Simms, "The War of Two Kings, 1685–91," in Moody, Martin, and Byrne, eds., *Early Modern Ireland,* 478–508; and Simms, "The Establishment of Protestant Ascendancy, 1691–1714," in T. W. Moody and W. E. Vaughan, eds., *Eighteenth-Century Ireland, 1691–1800* (Oxford, 1986), vol. IV of Moody, Martin, and Byrne, eds., *A New History of Ireland,* 1–30.

22. For a judicious account of the most famous of all Irish military engagements, see Simms, *Jacobite Ireland,* esp. chap. 8.

destroy the Jacobite army. Losses on both sides were relatively light, and the Irish, although seriously shaken by James's departure, rallied strongly under the leadership of Patrick Sarsfield to defeat William's attack on the city of Limerick in August. At the end of the month, with his ammunition running out, William lifted the siege and returned to England, turning the war over to his Dutch general, Godard van Reede, baron von Ginkel. A cautious soldier, Ginkel succeeded, if just barely, in bringing the fighting to a close in 1691 with his victory at Aughrim and the surrender of the Irish garrisons at Galway in July and Limerick in October. With both sides eager to arrange a settlement, the final articles negotiated at Limerick in October were benign, promising free transportation to all Irish officers and soldiers who wished to go to France. Equally important, rebellious Irish Catholics who now swore allegiance to William were to be granted full pardons and allowed the freedoms they had enjoyed under Charles II, among them being religious liberty, the right to bear arms, and the privilege of practicing their professions. Moreover, persons dispossessed of their estates because of their opposition to William could have their lands restored by presenting a claim before September 1699.[23]

What actually happened to Ireland's Catholics was far different. The moderate articles of Limerick had scarcely been agreed to, when the situation of Catholics began to deteriorate, and within a few years Ireland's Protestants moved to consolidate their power by ending all toleration of Catholics. The shape of things to come was evident by 1695, when a reconstituted Irish Parliament controlled exclusively by Protestants took steps to disallow a number of measures agreed to under the Limerick treaty. Arguing that its interpretation of past arrangements did not prohibit the passage of statutes detrimental to Catholic recusants, the Parliament enacted harsh anti-Catholic laws that renewed and extended the penal code developed under Elizabeth I.[24] The most severe measures forbade Catholic education at home or abroad and directed that Catholics be disarmed. Legislation banning all Catholic bishops and clergy followed in 1697, and in 1704 the Irish Parliament instituted statutes relegating Catholic recusants to permanent political, social, and economic inferiority. The most stringent and debilitating provisions involved land: Catholics were not allowed to buy it, to receive

23. J. G. Simms, *The Treaty of Limerick* (Dublin, 1961), 19–24.
24. J. C. Beckett, *The Making of Modern Ireland, 1603–1923,* 2d ed. (London, 1981), 151–152, 157–159. Under the Elizabethan laws, which continued to be enforced and added to during the eighteenth century, Catholics could not "vote or sit in Parliament," bear arms, own a horse worth more than five pounds, convert a Protestant, or celebrate Mass. The priesthood was outlawed, and Catholics were "compelled to attend the Anglican service."

"Anywhere so long as There Be Freedom"

it from Protestants either by inheritance or marital alliances, to lease it for periods longer than thirty-one years, or to devise any they already owned except by an equal division among all sons — unless the eldest son was a Protestant, in which event he acquired the entire estate. Those measures completed the destruction of most of Ireland's landed Catholic families, reducing their holdings from 59 percent in 1641, to 22 percent in 1688, and 14 percent in 1703 (Map 5). By the time of the American Revolution, Irish Catholics owned only 5 percent of their country's land.[25]

Militantly Jacobite Old English families like the Graces suffered along with their Gaelic coreligionists. Joining James II soon after he landed in Ireland, Richard Grace's nephew John outfitted a regiment of foot and served as Sarsfield's aide-de-camp. James appointed Richard governor of the strategic fortress of Athlone, located in the center of Ireland on the river Shannon and judged from "a military point of view the most important place in the Island." A principal English target, Athlone was first besieged after the Boyne, when Lieutenant General James Douglas attacked the fortress with twelve thousand men. Before commencing action, Douglas requested Grace to state his terms for surrender. The old Cavalier is supposed to have responded "that these were his terms that he would defend his post to the very last even if he had to eat his boots." Grace held true to his word: as one of James II's earliest biographers who worked closely with the king's memoirs recorded, "The great towns indeed before which the Enemie apear'd, made little resistance . . . but Athlone where Colonel Grace commanded, did not only stand a formal Siege, but forced the Enemie to rais it after a considerable loss."[26]

Grace died defending his post during the final siege of Athlone in June 1691. He left an only child, a daughter, who retained some of his lands; but, after his

25. Peter Roebuck, "The Irish Registry of Deeds: A Comparative Study," *Irish Historical Studies*, XVIII (1972–1973), 62, 64–65; J. G. Simms, *The Williamite Confiscation in Ireland, 1690–1703* (London, 1956), 158. Although Ireland's landed Catholic families functioned under exceptionally difficult circumstances in the eighteenth century, some managed to retain their gentry status. See Karen J. Harvey, *The Bellews of Mount Bellew: A Catholic Gentry Family in Eighteenth-Century Ireland* (Dublin, 1998). Other works that challenge the all-determinative influence of the penal laws in eighteenth-century Ireland include T. P. Power and Kevin Whelan, eds., *Endurance and Emergence: Catholics in Ireland in the Eighteenth Century* (Dublin, 1990); and S. J. Connolly, *Religion, Law, and Power: The Making of Protestant Ireland, 1660–1760* (Oxford, 1992).

26. J. J. Kelly, "Colonel Richard Grace, Governor of Athlone," *Irish Ecclesiastical Record*, 4th Ser., XXXII (1912), 494, 496; J. S. Clarke, *The Life of James the Second* (London, 1816), II, 414.

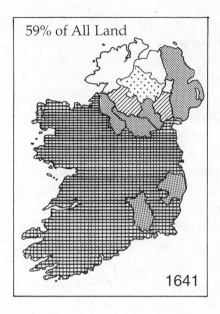

59% of All Land

1641

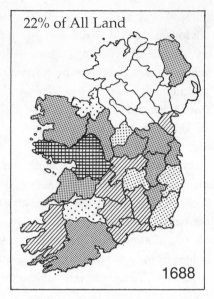

22% of All Land

1688

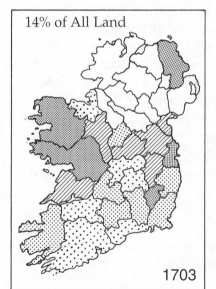

14% of All Land

1703

LAND OWNED BY CATHOLICS,
1641, 1688, 1703,
by County

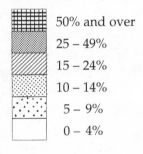

50% and over
25 – 49%
15 – 24%
10 – 14%
5 – 9%
0 – 4%

MAP 5. Land Owned by Catholics, 1641–1703, by County. *After J. G. Simms,*
The Williamite Confiscation in Ireland, 1690–1703 *(London, 1956), 196.*
By permission of Faber and Faber Ltd. Drawn by Richard Stinely

line was attainted for treason, a branch of the Grace family that had converted to the Protestant Church of Ireland acquired most of his property. His epitaph caught this bitter twist: "For valour and fidelity we may look to the example of Colonel Grace — for success and fortune to the history of others."[27]

Richard Grace's Carroll kin fared no better. His cousin, Daniel Carroll of Aghagurty, died in 1688, leaving three sons in Ireland — Anthony, the eldest, Thomas, and presumably John — and another, Charles, either in Maryland or on his way there. All of Daniel's sons were staunch Jacobites, and Anthony and Thomas fought gallantly with the Irish forces. A fierce fighter whose exploits are recounted to this day by the people of the Slieve Bloom Mountains, Thomas Carroll held the rank of lieutenant colonel in the Royal Irish Dragoons. Known as Black Tom, he commanded an Irish cavalry unit at the Boyne, died on the battlefield, and became a legend. Anthony Carroll and his son Daniel survived the Battle of the Boyne and continued to serve as officers until the bitter end of the Jacobite cause. Both men were part of the garrison at Limerick that surrendered when the articles ending the war were signed. Nothing is known of the wartime activities of the third brother, John.[28]

According to one family tradition, Thomas Carroll's two sons, Thomas and John, were taken to Northern Ireland following the defeat at the Boyne and placed under the care of Protestants, one in the home of a Presbyterian, the other of a member of the Church of Ireland. During this same period, Daniel of Aghagurty's youngest son, John, emigrated to Maryland, settled near his brother Charles, and became a small planter. He died childless in 1720, leaving his widow, Mary, an estate of £160.1.2.[29]

27. Kelly, "Col. Richard Grace," *Irish Eccl. Rec.*, 5th Ser., II (1913), 50–52. According to the *London Gazette*, July 13, 1691, Grace "fell during the siege, defending himself with heroic spirit" (quoted ibid.).

28. "A List of the adjudications at the Council boord," MS 744, formerly MS N.1.3, fol. 125, TCD; J. G. Simms, "Irish Jacobites, Lists from TCD MS N.1.3," *Analecta Hibernica*, XXII (1960), 13–14, 108. Because the exact date of Daniel Carroll of Aghagurty's death is unknown, it cannot be determined whether Charles knew of his father's passing when he embarked for Maryland in midsummer 1688.

Patrick Heaney of Cadamstown, County Offaly, has shared with me the oral traditions of the Slieve Bloom Mountains concerning Black Tom. I am enormously grateful for our many hours of conversation.

29. Provincial Court, Testamentary Proceedings, liber 24, fol. 392, MdAA; letters sent by Robert W. Carroll to Joseph Hatton Carroll, 1878–1893, in the possession of David Carroll, Leeds, posted on the Worldwide Web, http://dsocarroll.future.easyspace.com/ohio.htm. Another unverified tradition holds that Thomas Carroll's widow, Jane Macnemara, and their two sons, Thomas and John, joined the "wild geese" — the officers,

Thus, only Anthony, the eldest of Daniel of Aghagurty's four sons, remained in Ireland. There he endured a life of mounting hardship. Before he responded to James II's call to arms, his prospects seem to have been at least modestly hopeful, despite his being unschooled and probably illiterate. Leaving his native Seirkieran parish as a young man, he moved some fifteen miles west into the barony of Lower Ormond in northern Tipperary, where, by the early 1680s, he held the townland of Ballyvolvassy in Aglishcloghane parish and was styled a "gentleman." Marrying into the branch of the Carroll family centered at Kilfadda, a tract that joined Ballyvolvassy on the north, Anthony fathered a large family, of whom four sons and three daughters can be identified. In 1683 he secured a seventeen-year lease for the lands of Lackagh, in a neighboring parish, from the duke and duchess of Ormond, relatives and close associates of his family's mentor Richard Grace. Upon the death of his father, Daniel, at Aghagurty in 1688, a few assets in the form of goods and chattels might have fallen into his hands, although their value was perhaps outweighed by the debts that came with them.[30]

James II's landing in Ireland in 1689 fatefully linked Anthony's future to Catholic Ireland's struggle for sovereignty. Both Anthony and his eldest son, Daniel, served in James's army, Anthony as a captain, until the surrender of the Limerick garrison. As provided by the terms of the articles of capitulation, they applied for confirmation of their prewar holdings, and, upon their adjudication for treason in 1699, they gained validation of their claim to Lisheenboy, a tract near Kilfadda, from which Anthony took the appellation he used until the end of his life.

---

soldiers, and families that followed James the former king into exile at St. Germain, in France. Shortly after the turn of the century, the sons, perhaps because of the exile community's impoverishment, are alleged to have returned to live in Cork. They later conformed to the Church of Ireland and married into modestly comfortable families.

These traditions, which have descended in different branches of the Carroll family that are unaware of each other's existence, have certain intriguing elements in common: Thomas O'Carroll's death at the Battle of the Boyne and the eventual relocation of his two sons, both converted to Protestantism, to Cork. Thomas O'Carroll's rank and his death at the Boyne are mentioned in John O'Hart, *Irish Pedigrees; or, The Origin and Stem of the Irish Nation*, 5th ed. (Dublin 1892; rpt. Baltimore, 1876), I, 77. John D'Alton, *Illustrations Historical and Genealogical of King James's Irish Army List — 1689*, 2d ed. (Dublin, 1861), 435, identifies Thomas Carroll as "appointed *first* Lieutenant-Colonel" of Carroll's Dragoons.

30. James, duke of Ormond, Lady Elizabeth his wife, and Anthony Carroll of Ballynvolvassy, Apr. 17, 1683, indenture, D.5091, NLI; Donagh Carroll v. Daniel Carroll and Anthony Carroll, Nov. 15, 1693, exchequer bill, Thrift Abstracts 3360, PROI.

The precariousness of Catholics' postwar position and the specter of steadily diminishing opportunities, especially with respect to land, had by this time already persuaded at least two of Anthony's younger sons, James and Charles, to emigrate to Maryland. There James associated himself with his uncle Charles and, prospering under that tutelage, faithfully sent money to aid the family he had left in Ireland. By 1715, all of Anthony of Lisheenboy's daughters — Joyce, Margaret, and Joanna — had also come to the Chesapeake.[31]

The experience of Anthony's cousin Keane Carroll underscores the wisdom of emigration. In 1686 he secured a lease for Aghagurty from Richard Grace. Outlawed for high treason for accepting a captaincy in James II's army, he filed his claim under the Limerick articles in 1694 and was permitted to retain access to the land. Six years later, the trustees of forfeited estates, who controlled the disposition of property formerly owned by unredeemed Jacobites like Grace, refused to confirm the ruling, despite Keane's prior payment of £450 to secure it. In 1703 the trustees sold Aghagurty to the Corporation of Hollow Sword Blades, an English joint stock company. Neither Keane's name nor that of any Carroll figured in the transaction; the tenant on Aghagurty was a man named Edward White. Nothing is known of Keane's subsequent activities in Ireland, but by 1717 his twenty-one-year-old son Daniel had settled in Maryland, where, with the assistance of his kinsman Charles, he became the Prince George's County merchant known as Daniel Carroll I of Upper Marlboro (1696–1751).[32]

Two sons of Anthony Carroll of Lisheenboy, Daniel and Michael, stayed with their father in Ireland. Michael remained a farmer at Lisheenboy, but Daniel

31. "List of adjudications," MS 744, fol. 125; Simms, "Irish Jacobites," *Analecta Hibernica,* XXII (1960), 13–14, 108. Evidence of the payments is found in James Carroll's day book, Special Collections Division, Georgetown University Library, Washington, D.C. Chart A, "Irish Ancestry of the Carrolls," showing Charles Carroll's network of Irish kin, appears in Appendix 6, below.

32. "A List of the Claims As they are Entred with the Trustees as Chichester-House . . . ," 1700, MS 2548, fol. 198, PROI; Simms, "Irish Jacobites," *Analecta Hibernica,* XXII (1960), 64, 92; "List of adjudications," MS 744, fols. 46v, 104v; "List of Claims," 1700, MS 2548, fol. 198; "A Book of Posting and Sale of the Forfeited and Other Estates and Interests in Ireland," 1703, MS 2578, fol. 37, PROI; Rent Rolls, Calvert Papers, 1–125, MdHi. On May 13, 1717, Daniel Carroll and Daniel Herne bought 203 acres of land in Anne Arundel County from Charles Carroll. Both surviving sons of Daniel Carroll I of Upper Marlboro achieved distinction: in 1787, the elder, Daniel Carroll II of Rock Creek (1730–1790), became one of Maryland's three signers of the United States Constitution. Two years later, the Vatican appointed the younger, John (1735–1815), the first Roman Catholic bishop in the United States.

pursued a career in the law. The date of his admission to Gray's Inn (April 13, 1704) coincides with the end of an extended visit that Charles Carroll made to Lord Baltimore. A reunion between uncle and nephew, likely though undocumented, would have acquainted Charles with his family's worsening condition in Ireland and the loss of his father's old tract, Aghagurty. The bookplate he had printed for himself while in London certainly suggests a recognition of these changes of fortune. Styling himself the "second son of Daniell Carroll of Litterlouna," Charles replaced the Aghagurty he had known in his youth with a mythical reference to a locale his family had controlled before 1600, many years before his birth.[33]

The forces arrayed against Daniel's promising beginning quickly undercut his dreams. In 1704 the entirely Protestant Irish Parliament enacted statutes that categorically prohibited Catholics from entering any professions, the law included. With this avenue summarily closed to him, Daniel came back to Ireland to farm the tract at Lisheenboy with his father and brother. Before long, the number of people living on Lisheenboy — what was left of Anthony's family, Daniel, and Michael and his wife's growing brood — exceeded the land's ability to support them. Anthony's acquisition of an annually renewable lease to an additional townland called Ballyspellane offered only temporary assistance, with no guarantees for the future. Determined to provide for both of his sons, Anthony in 1718 sublet Ballyspellane to his kinsman Alexander Carroll of Kilfadda and left Tipperary to seek work as a stonecutter in Dublin, where a building boom had already begun. The following year he secured a future for his oldest son by obtaining a three-lives' lease from William Worth, Esquire, of Dublin, for one hundred acres of a tract called Killecregane in the parish of Lorrha, approximately three miles north of Michael's farm at Lisheenboy.[34] The tenure, slated to run for the lives of Daniel, his wife Mary Browne, and his nephew Anthony (Michael's oldest son) — Daniel and Mary had no children as yet — represented the best Anthony Carroll of Lisheenboy, stonecutter, could do. Although he

33. Joseph Foster, ed., *Register of Admissions to Gray's Inn, 1512–1889*, Collectanea Genealogica, II, no. 1 (London, 1889), 135, 354. Charles Carroll was in England from August 1702 through the spring of 1704. Browne et al., eds., *Archives of Maryland*, XXV, 130; Land Office (Patents), liber DD no. 5, fols. 711–712, MdAA.

See the reproduction of Charles Carroll's bookplate below, Plate 7, and in Ann C. Van Devanter, ed., *"Anywhere so long as There Be Freedom": Charles Carroll of Carrollton, His Family, and His Maryland* (Baltimore, 1975), i.

34. Chancery Bills, Feb. 9, 1721, TA 3146, TA 3201; Worth to Carroll, Sept. 1, 1719, lease, D3249/1/2, PRONI.

PLATE 7. Bookplate of Charles Carroll the Settler.
Courtesy Maryland State Archives, MSA SC 1262-6

might have surmounted his Jacobite politics (the 1715 rebellion of Stuart loyalists in England and Scotland rallied no Irish Catholics to its cause), he would not forsake his religion or the proud Irish heritage of his family. And so his life began a downward trajectory of dispossession and displacement that reflected the crushing constriction of opportunity imposed upon Catholics who refused to conform.

"Anywhere so long as There Be Freedom"

A 1721 court suit involving Anthony and his son Daniel, now called "of Kielliecregane," underscores their desperate condition. The plaintiff, Alexander Carroll of Kilfadda, acting as executor for his father, filed a bill in chancery against his kinsmen Anthony and Daniel to collect a ten-pound debt they owed the estate. While the case was muddled with conflicting accounts, the court documents confirm the differing status of the parties: the word "Esq." followed Alexander's name and "Gent." his father's, but Anthony Carroll of Lisheenboy and Daniel Carroll of Killecregane were identified as farmers. The particulars of the chancery bill also reveal related suits against Anthony and Daniel for debts they owed to other parties.[35]

Both Anthony Carroll of Lisheenboy and Daniel Carroll of Killecregane died of unknown causes in 1724, the son predeceasing the father by six weeks. Their wills, of which only abstracts exist, suggest the material dimensions of their lives. The most valuable asset that remained to Daniel's widow and three minor children was the lease for Killecregane, and by the end of the year in which her husband died she had renewed the agreement, replacing Daniel, whom she proudly styled a "gentleman," with their two-year-old son Anthony. Anthony Carroll of Lisheenboy had more people to provide for and less to give. Lisheenboy went to Michael, and to his parish priest the valiant old stonecutter left "the best of my two coults." The inheritance he received from his father did little to improve life for Michael Carroll of Lisheenboy. Unable to help his five sons make their way in the world, Michael relied upon his brother James in Maryland. James, who never married, did not disappoint him, educating two of the boys for the priesthood and welcoming a third, Dominick Carroll, to the Chesapeake. James shouldered similar responsibilities for his brother Daniel's son, Anthony, who, with his uncle's assistance, became a Jesuit.[36]

35. The details of the dispute between Alexander Carroll of Kilfadda and Anthony Carroll of Lisheenboy appear in the following chancery bills, all dated Feb. 9, 1721: TA 3142, TA 3144, TA 3146.

36. Daniel Carroll of Killecregane, Mar. 10, 1723, prerogative will, Irwin Abstracts, fol. 475, Genealogical Office, Dublin; Daniel Carroll of Killecregane, Mar. 10, 1723, prerogative will, Betham's Will Abstracts, XI, fol. 96, no. 294, PROI; Edward Worth to Thomas Ridge, Dec. 17, 1724, lease of Killcrogane, 47/9/29314, RD; Anthony Carroll of Lisheenboy, May 21, 1724, prerogative will, Irwin Abstracts, fols. 475–476; Anthony Carroll of Lisheenboy, May 21, 1724, will, Cunningham MSS, X, fol. 12, St. Kieran's College, Kilkenny. The Irwin Abstract of Daniel's will also mentions the tracts Ballynoe and Rodeene, townlands located north of Killecregane in the united parishes of Durra and Bonocum. Daniel might have had some sort of access to these lands as well. Un-

"Anywhere so long as There Be Freedom"

The downward spiral of the Lisheenboy Carrolls because they refused to conform differs markedly from the rise of their kin who chose the other course. Owen Carroll of Kilmaine and his son, Barnaby, illustrate both the resilience required of and the price to be paid by Catholics who remained in Ireland and aspired to a life of means. Born early in the 1650s, before his father, Daniel Carroll of Ballymooney, left Ireland under the command of Richard Grace, Owen's education culminated with legal studies at the Middle Temple in London and then at King's Inn in Dublin. While practicing law in Dublin in the late 1670s, he began to accumulate land in King's County, and in 1682 he married into the Coghlan family, old allies of the Carrolls. When the Irish rose to support James II in 1689, Owen joined them as had his father half a century before; winning the rank of lieutenant colonel, again like his father, he participated in a second taking of Birr Castle. Described as a "cunning lawyer," and the pretended friend of Sir Laurence Parsons, to whom he owed a good deal of money, Owen drew up the articles for the surrender of the fortress and later supervised the seizing and disposal of the property. Possibly one of his sweetest moments occurred when he had cypress trees, tulips, and other flowers uprooted from Laurence Parsons's garden and replanted on the grounds of his home, Kilmaine House.[37]

Outlawed by the English in 1690, Owen was forced to forfeit his lands in 1703. Because he was educated and resourceful, he still managed to live in comfort without repudiating Catholicism, and at his death in 1723 he left a bequest

---

fortunately, those who abstracted the wills were more interested in genealogy than in property.

Anthony of Lisheenboy's horse could not have been worth much, since Catholics, according to the penal law of 1695, were not allowed to own horses valued in excess of five pounds.

Although Anthony the Jesuit spent most of his life teaching in Europe, he was deeply involved with his Maryland kin. He served as tutor to his young second cousin Charles Carroll (later of Carrollton) in the late 1740s and early 1750s. Anthony was murdered in London in 1794.

37. Edward Keane, P. Beryl Phair, and Thomas U. Sadlier, *King's Inns Admission Papers, 1607–1867* (Dublin, 1982), 78; the king to Owen Carroll, grant for letters patent, 26 Jan. 1676/7, Stowe MSS 211, fol. 61; the king to the lord lieutenant, warrant for Owen Carroll, 26 Jan. 1676/7, S.O. 1/10/82–84; Kenneth Nicholls, "The MacCoghlans," *Irish Genealogist*, VI (1983), 454; Edward Whitten to CC, May 28, 1763, Carroll Papers, MS 206; Narrative of the events of 1689, Rosse Papers, A/24, fols. 11, 12, 87–88, 108; book of taxes levied, 1689–1690, Rosse Papers, A/19.

of one thousand pounds to be divided among his four grandchildren. Owen's adherence to his faith nevertheless had limited the heights to which he could aspire, and his son, Barnaby, chose another path. Educated at the University of Utrecht in Leyden, where he earned a doctorate of civil and canon law in 1712, and at the Middle Temple in London, Barnaby conformed to the Church of Ireland in the early 1720s and successfully sued to reacquire his family lands. He flourished during the Protestant ascendancy: by the 1730s, his earnings exceeded twelve hundred pounds per annum.[38] The descendants of Black Tom (Anthony Carroll of Lisheenboy's brother who died at the Boyne) and even the Kilfadda Carrolls (the family into which Anthony had married) also decided they preferred the opportunities of the new era to the struggles of the past. By the 1720s, some Carrolls had clearly forsaken their Catholic faith to make full use of the civil and economic benefits that change of allegiance offered: landownership, the franchise, and protection rather than persecution by the arbitrary power of government.

In sharp contrast, Michael Carroll of Lisheenboy, Anthony's third son, remained an iron witness to the heritage of the O'Carrolls. Tempted neither by the material improvements available to his newly Protestant relatives nor by the opportunities open to his kin who had emigrated to the Chesapeake — nor even by the grandchildren born in Maryland whom he had never seen — Michael Carroll stubbornly lived out his life in Lower Ormond, County Tipperary. In 1762, the year that Michael died, his nephew Father Anthony Carroll, Daniel of Killecregane's son, received a letter from his Maryland relatives asking for details about the lineage and fate of the family. Although the priest seemed to be a living link with the Carroll past, he had been scarcely two years old in 1724, when his father and grandfather died, and he knew little of the family saga. His response to his Chesapeake kin constituted an epitaph and a lament:

> I shall do all in my power to procure the information both you and your father desire tho' it seems pretty certai[n] I can not do much considering how matters stand at this time: the last letter I had from Ireland gave an account of the death of Mr. Alexander Carroll, Cæsar's father; Mr. John Carroll, the Colonel's brother; & uncle Micha[el] I scarce know any one that I can expect intelligence from. When I was a boy we had Dr. Keaten's Irish history in MS

38. Simms, "Irish Jacobites," *Analecta Hibernica,* XXII (1960), 33; "Book of Postings and Sale," 1703, MS 2578, fol. 37; Owen Carroll, prerogative will, 1723, TA 1624; Barnaby Carroll v. Richard Viccars, Apr. 2, 1731, Add. MSS, 36, 150, fols. 281, 284, BL.

in which I remember to have heared say that our genealogy was preserved but that as well as other things disappeared before I left the kingdom. This I mention to let you see how hard it will be to get any satisfactory account of our extirpated family.[39]

39. CC to CCA, Aug. 6, 1762, Outerbridge Horsey Collection of Lee, Horsey, and Carroll Family Papers, MdHi. Geoffrey Keating's genealogy of the O'Carrolls, compiled about 1620, can be found in P. S. Dineen, ed., *Foras Feasa ar Éirinn,* Irish Texts Society, XV (Dublin, 1913), 115–118. The source Keating cites for his information, Donnghalach Ó Réioghbhradéain, the *"ollamh* or chief learned man of the O'Carrolls and other Munster septs," also appears in the genealogical record of his family that Charles Carroll the Settler brought with him to Maryland. Elizabeth FitzPatrick to author, Nov. 20, 1998, and "Genealogy of O Carroll," MS, Carroll-O'Carroll Genealogies.

PLATE 8. Charles Carroll the Settler. By Justus Engelhardt Kühn. C. 1712.
Courtesy the Maryland Historical Society

CHAPTER 2

"Marylando-Hibernus"

In 1771 Charles Carroll of Carrollton recounted to a European correspondent the circumstances that inspired his grandfather's coming to Maryland:

> The family estate being greatly impaired by the iniquity of the times, which had stripped the most ancient Irish families of their property, he resolved to seek his fortune far distant from the scene of such oppressions. Being a Roman Catholick he pitched on Maryd where the free exercise of that religion & equal priveleges were granted to its professors by a royal Charter, after wards confirmed by a perpetual law of this Province.[1]

Driven by the harshness of Old World realities, this Charles Carroll, Charles Carroll the Settler, carried with him a determination to reconstitute his family's economic and political fortunes in the Chesapeake without betraying either his religious traditions or his proud cultural heritage. His striving for this goal over thirty-two years brought him both stunning success and bitter, ironic failure. Charles Carroll the Settler went to his grave a Catholic in 1720. The wealthiest man of any religion in Maryland, he was also disenfranchised and without political power. This remarkable juxtaposition of outcomes was in great measure of Carroll's own making, forged out of his Irish past and his reckless, implacable ambition.

A full appreciation of the expectations that Charles Carroll the Settler brought to Maryland and what it meant to him to be deprived of them by the rebellion of 1689 requires an understanding of the character of the provincial society upon whose opportunities he intended to capitalize. At the time of his arrival the

---

1. CCC to the Countess d'Auzouer, Sept. 20, 1771, CCC, letterbook 1770–1774, MdHi. An earlier version of this chapter appeared in *WMQ*, 3d Ser., XLV (1988), 207–236.

colony's heavily forested land gave way only intermittently to human habitation, in the form of a scraggly patchwork of settlements that clung to the shores of the Chesapeake Bay and its tributary rivers and creeks. There were no towns of any size; the capital, though called St. Mary's City, was merely a collection of generally rude structures. To this setting Carroll brought two distinct personal advantages: he was a free man rather than an indentured servant, and he came with the middle-level post of attorney general in the proprietary government, from which he could expect a return of some £50 sterling a year. In a society where the annual income of ordinary planters ranged from £10 to £15, and frequently fell below, the Settler could count upon a modest measure of comfort from his legal duties alone. But, even if events had not robbed Carroll of his official position, a man of his ambition would never have confined himself solely to that pursuit. Great planters in what was still a frontier society annually grossed £200–£250 from their tobacco.[2] Moreover, by virtue of their other activities as merchants, creditors, lawyers, and local or provincial officeholders, the wealthiest of those men could expect to make an additional £200–£350 a year, and, if they were placemen in the highest echelons of the governing establishment, they often increased their annual earnings by £500 or more. The Settler's behavior in Maryland unmistakably indicates that it was to these heights that he aspired.[3]

Despite the substantial incomes of Maryland's wealthiest men, traditional distinctions of rank were just beginning to emerge. By the 1680s the crystallization of a propertied elite, encouraged by proprietary policy, was clearly under way, and the colony already contained distinguishable groups of wealthy, middling, and poor planters. Such divisions were nevertheless rudimentary, for virtually all planters shared a style of life that can be described only as crude, and even the richest of them preferred capital investments in land, slaves, livestock, and mercantile goods to expenditures for refinements or improving their creature comforts. Most affluent late-seventeenth-century Maryland planters resided in timber houses containing six modestly sized rooms, and their poorer neighbors inhabited one- or two-room structures. Members of the fledgling gentry expressed their economic success by acquiring feather beds and a variety

2. Lois Green Carr, "'The Metropolis of Maryland': A Comment on Town Development along the Tobacco Coast," *Maryland Historical Magazine,* LXIX (1974), 124–125; Donnell MacClure Owings, *His Lordship's Patronage: Offices of Profit in Colonial Maryland* (Baltimore, 1953), 43–44; Paul G. E. Clemens, *The Atlantic Economy and Colonial Maryland's Eastern Shore: From Tobacco to Grain* (Ithaca, N.Y., 1980), 87–89; Gloria L. Main, *Tobacco Colony: Life in Early Maryland, 1650–1720* (Princeton, N.J., 1982), 84.

3. For an explanation of how incomes were arrived at, see Appendix 3, below.

of chairs (rarely found in the homes of poor and middling planters) rather than through such objects as looking glasses, plate, clocks, pictures, and books that became badges of status among the elite during the "consumer revolution" of the eighteenth century.[4]

Moreover, the religious and economic tensions expressed in the political turmoil of the early years of royal government, 1689–1692, tended to blur class distinctions. Thus, although the coming to power of the Protestants, combined with the spread of slavery, ultimately created a society with recognizable lines of division between the upper, middling, and meaner sort, the Maryland of the late 1680s remained in flux. Nor had the colony's system of proprietary governance hardened into a pattern of hierarchical authority. Even in the depressed economy of the 1680s, political, socioeconomic, and geographic mobility retarded the development of deferential relationships. The coterie of Catholic officeholders attached to the proprietary family had used their ties to considerable personal advantage, but they had not produced an intergenerational ruling elite, and their tenuous hold on power allowed Coode's Protestant rabble-rousers to displace them with little difficulty.[5]

4. Lois Green Carr and Lorena S. Walsh, "Changing Lifestyles and Consumer Behavior in the Colonial Chesapeake," in Cary Carson, Ronald Hoffman, and Peter J. Albert, eds., *Of Consuming Interests: The Style of Life in the Eighteenth Century* (Charlottesville, Va., 1994), 59–167; Main, *Tobacco Colony*, chaps. 4–7; and see also Lois Green Carr, Russell R. Menard, and Lorena S. Walsh, *Robert Cole's World: Agriculture and Society in Early Maryland* (Chapel Hill, N.C., 1991), 97–107.

For an able description and analysis of the Upper South, see John J. McCusker and Russell R. Menard, *The Economy of British America, 1607–1789* (Chapel Hill, N.C., 1985), esp. chap. 6. The strength of their material on colonial Maryland rests in large measure on the fine work of a generation of scholars who have remarkably enriched our understanding: Lois Green Carr, Paul G. E. Clemens, Carville V. Earle, James P. P. Horn, Allan Kulikoff, Gloria L. Main, Russell R. Menard, Edward C. Papenfuse, Jean B. Russo, Anita H. Rutman, Darrett B. Rutman, Gregory A. Stiverson, and Lorena S. Walsh.

5. For a suggestive treatment of the patterns of officeholding in Maryland from 1660 to 1715 and the emergence of a governing elite, see David W. Jordan, "Political Stability and the Emergence of a Native Elite in Maryland," in Thad W. Tate and David L. Ammerman, eds., *The Chesapeake in the Seventeenth Century: Essays on Anglo-American Society* (Chapel Hill, N.C., 1979), 243–273.

Although I agree with Allan Kulikoff's general conclusion in *Tobacco and Slaves: The Development of Southern Cultures in the Chesapeake, 1680–1800* (Chapel Hill, N.C., 1986) that a mature intergenerational gentry class did not blossom in Maryland until sometime after the first quarter of the eighteenth century, he ascribes to that class a uniformity that did not exist. First, in the 1680s, and even before, there were elitist individuals of recognizable power who conceived of themselves as gentlemen and thus superior to the com-

The relative openness of that society offered ample opportunities to a young man on the make like Charles Carroll the Settler, and he devised a simple and effective strategy for advancing himself: he made a habit of marrying well. Following the several months of "hard seasoning" that coincided with the overthrow of the proprietary government, Carroll cushioned the blows dealt his original prospects by contracting a marriage in November 1689 with a wealthy widow named Martha Ridgely Underwood. Several years his senior and the mother of four young children, Martha had come to Maryland as an indentured servant, but by 1671 she had married the man to whom she was bound — Robert Ridgely, a Protestant, prominent attorney, and holder of several provincial offices.[6] Upon Ridgely's death in 1681, Martha inherited a sizable estate consisting of two plantations (a dwelling plantation of ninety-four acres on St. Inigoe's Creek in St. Mary's County and a twelve-hundred-acre tobacco plantation on Wicomico River in Somerset County) along with all of her husband's personal property, including household goods, plate, servants and slaves, livestock, and debts owed to him, totaling in value five hundred pounds.[7]

Sometime after 1683 Martha Ridgely married Anthony Underwood, a former

_____

mon folk. The most powerful of them were wealthy, had close personal ties to the proprietor, and were Roman Catholics. They were deeply resented and, as Lois Green Carr and David William Jordan have shown in *Maryland's Revolution of Government, 1689– 1692* (Ithaca, N.Y., 1974), they were replaced in the turmoil of Coode's Rebellion. Second, religious enmity continued to divide Maryland's nascent gentry as Protestants and Catholics vied for dominance during the period of royal government, 1690–1715. Even after the Protestants won their decisive political victory in 1718, religion persisted in influencing the development and character of the colony's gentry until the eve of the American Revolution. While the wealthiest of Maryland's Roman Catholics were economically qualified for membership in the provincial elite, their religion and highly self-conscious ideology sharply differentiated them from their Protestant counterparts. For further treatment of this topic see Chapter 8, below, and the excellent doctoral dissertation of Beatriz Betancourt Hardy, "Papists in a Protestant Age: The Catholic Gentry and Community in Colonial Maryland, 1689–1776" (University of Maryland, 1993). I am indebted to Dr. Hardy for her nuanced understanding of the internal dynamics of Maryland's Catholic gentry families.

6. William Hand Browne et al., eds., *Archives of Maryland* (Baltimore, 1883–), VIII, 126. For evidence of Martha Ridgely's servitude, see Land Office, Patents, liber 16, fols. 400–401, MdAA. Robert Ridgely served as clerk of the council, 1664–1674, clerk of the lower house, 1671–1681, and clerk of the secretary's office and provincial court, 1670/1– 1673, and acted as deputy secretary, 1671–1673. Owings, *His Lordship's Patronage,* 126, 128, 136, 138, 140.

7. Will of Robert Ridgely, St. Mary's County, Wills, liber 2, fols. 162–166, and Prerogative Court, Inventories and Accounts, liber 8, fols. 295–302, MdAA.

bound servant and law clerk of her first husband. A prime example of the fluid socioeconomic conditions that still prevailed in Maryland, Underwood, who had some legal training and had worked as a clerk in England, began to practice law upon completing his servitude and by March 1682 had gained admission to the provincial court. In 1685, now a planter whose ownership of a brigantine suggested that he also had mercantile interests, he secured the position of alderman in St. Mary's City, and the following year he gained a seat in the lower house of the Maryland assembly. When his upward career ended with his death at age thirty in 1689, Underwood left a personal estate — composed almost entirely of the property his wife had inherited from her first husband — worth nearly £550 sterling and about two thousand acres of land.[8]

Into this convenient breech stepped the enterprising and ambitious Charles Carroll the Settler, who happened to be the executor of Anthony Underwood's estate. On November 9, 1689, no more than six months after Underwood's demise, Carroll wed the well-provisioned Martha and carefully noted in his administrative accounts that the sum of £11.0.0 was due Underwood's estate "from Self being released in law by intermarrying with the Executrix." The union was short. In November 1690, Martha Ridgely Underwood Carroll, who had borne Anthony Underwood no children, died in childbirth, followed three days later by the infant, a son who had been christened Anthony. Notwithstanding his responsibilities to Martha's children who were still minors, Carroll, barely two years after his arrival in Maryland and despite the obstacles resulting from the Glorious Revolution, had by means of his marriage positioned himself to take immediate advantage of Maryland's agricultural and mercantile opportunities.[9]

Although the bulk of the Ridgely-Underwood inheritance went to Martha's

8. By 1687 Underwood had also been admitted to the St. Mary's and Calvert County courts and the prerogative court. The 700 acres he patented on his own, plus the 1,294 acres Martha received by the will of Robert Ridgely, composed his total landed estate. Edward C. Papenfuse et al., eds., *A Biographical Dictionary of the Maryland Legislature, 1635–1789* (Baltimore, 1979–1985), II, 846.

9. Prerogative Court, Inventories and Accounts, liber 10, fols. 320, 329; Charles Carroll, Bible Records, #48735, Filing Case A, MdHi. Martha Ridgley Underwood Carroll's religion is nowhere specified but assumed to be Protestant like that of her children by Robert Ridgley. However, the Settler's recording the christening of their short-lived son in his family Bible suggests that the infant received Catholic baptism.

The Settler acknowledged his responsibilities to Martha's children when he appealed to Governor Copley to release him from jail in the spring of 1693 because of "the great detriment which my present Confinement brings not only upon my self but likewise the Orphans whose Concerns I have in charge." Browne et al., eds., *Archives of Maryland,* VIII, 508.

surviving children, the legacy was central to Carroll's rise to power and wealth. Capitalizing as administrator upon the assets of his wife's estate, the Settler acted quickly to establish himself in trade: records of a suit filed against him in February 1692 for illegally importing a sizable quantity of "Strong beer" and wine show that he operated a warehouse on St. Inigoe's Creek, the site of the Ridgely-Underwood dwelling plantation.[10] Although it is unclear whether he also made similar use of Little Bellean, Martha's twelve-hundred-acre Somerset County plantation, he certainly continued to occupy her St. Mary's County house. Anthony Underwood's inventory, filed by Carroll in 1692, evaluates the contents of that seven-room residence, including £11.01.06 of possessions ("Beds & furniture, Chairs, Tables &c") in a chamber the administrator referred to as "my roome."[11]

10. Carroll's obligations to his deceased wife's minor children appear to have been largely fulfilled by the turn of the century. By the terms of Robert Ridgely's will, Robert, Charles, William, and Martha Ridgely, all of age by 1701, received specific bequests separate from the provisions that made their mother the principal heir. Mrs. Ridgely was charged, however, with the children's maintenance and schooling until they reached the age of majority, and from all indications Carroll assumed these responsibilities upon his wife's death. A law passed by the Maryland assembly in June 1692 stipulating that orphans could not be placed in "the hands of any person of different Judgement in Religion to that of the deceased parents of the said Orphans" caused the youngest child, his stepdaughter Martha, to be removed from his care and placed with a Protestant guardian. He nevertheless readily agreed to continue to support her from the estate until she became twenty-one (Browne et al., eds., *Archives of Maryland*, XIII, 433; Prerogative Court, Testamentary Proceedings, liber 15, fol. 24, MdAA). In March 1705 Carroll paid £6.6.8 to his stepdaughter, who had married a merchant named Lewis Duvall, and the same sum to one Thomas Underwood, "part heir" of William Ridgely, as "the filial portions" of their father's estate. Robert Ridgely, Jr., and his brother Charles had died in 1702 and 1705, respectively, and William's whereabouts were unknown; he had apparently left Maryland in 1698. Martha Ridgely Duvall died in 1709. Prerogative Court, Testamentary Proceedings, liber 19B, fols. 14, 90–91.

The Settler won the lawsuit on appeal in 1697. Carroll T. Bond, ed., *Proceedings of the Maryland Court of Appeals, 1695–1729* (Washington, D.C., 1933), I, 31.

11. In addition to the main house, the Ridgely-Underwood plantation included at least three outbuildings — a kitchen, a milkhouse that seems to have become a washhouse by 1692, and a quarter that presumably housed Underwood's four servants and two slaves. A "store," usually a structure used for storage of new goods, appears in Ridgely's inventory but not in Underwood's, replaced perhaps by the Settler's warehouse on St. Inigoe's Creek (Prerogative Court, Inventories and Accounts, liber 10A, fol. 1, liber 8, fols. 295–302; Papenfuse et al., eds., *Biographical Dictionary*, II, 846; Main, *Tobacco Colony*, 294). By 1704, Martha's twelve-hundred-acre Somerset County tract, Little Bellean, had been broken up and sold (Land Office, Somerset County Rent Rolls, liber 9, fol. 32, MdAA).

The Settler's access to this inheritance — it is impossible to verify whether he ever permanently acquired any of Martha's property — shielded him from the most harmful practical effects of Protestant ascendance in Maryland. But, like other Catholics, he faced new proscriptions that limited his opportunities. His unwillingness to compromise his religious beliefs made his legal career vulnerable to the kinds of anti-Catholic restrictions long common in England. Clients continued to seek his services in the immediate aftermath of the overthrow of proprietary government, but Carroll and other attorneys of his faith were permitted to practice only in the chancery and prerogative courts following the formal institution of royal government in 1692. Such restrictions did not prevent him from continuing to provide astute legal advice not only to the proprietor, Charles Calvert, but also to Calvert's cousin, Colonel Henry Darnall, who oversaw Lord Baltimore's interests in Maryland.[12]

Whether Carroll received any financial reward from the proprietor for his loyalty and counsel is unknown, and none of the legal maneuvers he suggested enabled Calvert to regain control of the government of Maryland. But his fearless efforts to protect proprietary interests brought him two enormously important benefits: the third Lord Baltimore's gratitude and, perhaps even more significant, the approbation and patronage of Darnall. Once again Carroll had positioned himself to the utmost advantage, and in February 1693/4 he moved decisively to consolidate his gains by marrying the colonel's fifteen-year-old daughter, Mary, a girl less than half his age.

The opportunities this alliance brought Carroll can scarcely be exaggerated. Until the overthrow of the proprietary government, Darnall sat on the council, the colony's most powerful political body, served on the board of deputy governors and the land council, was the proprietor's rent roll keeper, and held the two extremely lucrative offices of Lord Baltimore's agent and receiver general, and keeper of the great seal. Most significantly, Darnall, though deprived, like all nonconforming Catholics, of his political posts after 1689, had retained all his positions within the proprietor's private establishment, and the power and wealth that continued to flow from these posts made him indisputably one of the colony's dominant personalities.[13]

12. Browne et al., eds., *Archives of Maryland*, VIII, 408, 508; Carr and Jordan, *Maryland's Revolution of Government*, 60n, 150.

13. As noted in the preceding chapter, Charles Calvert, third Lord Baltimore, retained ownership of the land and rights to specific revenues after he lost political control of Maryland in 1691.

TABLE 1. Building a Landed Estate: Charles Carroll the Settler's Land Transactions (in Acres)

	Methods of Land Acquisition				
County[a]	Marriage and Inheritance[b]	Patent	Purchase (Sale)	Fore-closure	Total in 1720
Anne Arundel/ Baltimore[c]		19,403	6,857 (3,573)	8,138	30,825
Calvert			1,380	1,240	2,620
Cecil		2,304	2,330 (3,109)	666	2,191
Dorchester		1,500			1,500
Kent				100	100
Prince George's	3,507	1,806	1,850 (236)	1,105	8,032
Queen Anne's		1,000	500 (500)		1,000
St. Mary's		400	109		509
Talbot				1,000	1,000
Overall	3,507	26,413	13,026 (7,418)	12,249	47,777

Sources: County land records (warrants, certificates of survey, and patents), MdAA.

Note: Not included in this table are three large manors upon which Carroll acquired the right to collect rents. Bashford Manor (1,500 acres) and St. Clement's Manor (11,000 acres) were located in St. Mary's County; Westwood Manor (1,600 acres) was in Charles County. The records available do not indicate whether the Settler ever realized any income from these properties. By midcentury, lawsuits in which his descendants were engaged over these lands indicated a long history of tenant refusal to acknowledge the Carroll family's claim to any rents. The tenants insisted up to the American Revolution that they held their properties as freeholds from owners previous to the Carrolls (Chancery Court Records, liber I.R. no. 4, 100–131, MdAA; "Answers of Tenants," Carroll-McTavish Papers, MdHi). The Settler's will also mentions 20,000 acres of unpatented land in Prince George's County. Charles Carroll of Annapolis laid part of this tract out as Carrollton, 10,000 acres, in 1723. (The Settler's will specified that the other 10,000 acres go to his daughters.)

[a] The county boundaries are those in existence at the Settler's death.

[b] Carroll received four tracts of land from his father-in-law, Henry Darnall. Two parcels, totaling 1,381 acres, were part of the Settler's marriage settlement with Darnall's

PLATE 9. Mary Darnall Carroll. By Justus Engelhardt Kühn. 1708.
Courtesy the present owner

---

daughter in 1693/4. Darnall willed him the other two in 1711. Warrants, liber A-C, 373, and Anne Arundel Wills, liber 13, 223, MdAA.

ᶜ Because the boundary between western Anne Arundel County and western Baltimore County remained somewhat indefinite at the time of the Settler's death, his holdings in those counties have been grouped together. For example, Doohoragen Manor, the 7,000-acre tract at Elk Ridge that became the family's principal dwelling plantation, appears as part of Carroll's Baltimore County lands in his will, drawn in 1718, but was within the next decade recorded within the bounds of Anne Arundel County.

Carroll had hardly recited his wedding vows, when his fortunes took still another turn for the better. Darnall bestowed on his new son-in-law two Prince George's County tracts totaling 1,381 acres. Far more important, when Maryland's land office reopened in May 1694, the colonel appointed Carroll clerk, a position that carried a salary of approximately £100 a year and placed him at the center of all land transactions.[14] This was precisely where Darnall needed an ally whom he could trust to protect not only the proprietor's interests but also those of Maryland's beleaguered Catholic gentry. In all, Henry Darnall had two sons, five stepsons, and six sons-in-law, but from the mid-1690s to the end of his life in 1711 his principal protégé was Charles Carroll.

Carroll's career exemplifies the classic pattern of broadly diversified Chesapeake entrepreneurs who built fortunes by combining strategic marriages with the activities of a planter, banker, lawyer, merchant, and proprietary officeholder. Land constituted the foundation of his wealth: when he died in 1720, he owned 47,777 acres and was the largest landholder in the province. He also possessed a warrant for 20,000 additional acres, 10,000 of which were patented by his son Charles Carroll of Annapolis in 1723. Conservatively, the Settler's acreage was worth twenty thousand pounds.[15] He accumulated this estate by several methods. Nearly three-fifths of the land he held at the time of his death (26,413 acres) he had acquired by patent. He also had purchased 13,026 acres and had obtained

14. Land Office, Warrants, liber A.C., fol. 373, MdAA; Owings, *His Lordship's Patronage*, 169–170. Land acquisition in Maryland began with the payment of "caution money" (120 pounds of tobacco per 100 acres) to the proprietor's agent and receiver general, who in 1694 was Henry Darnall. The agent then directed the clerk of the land office (in this case, Darnall's son-in-law Charles Carroll) to forward a warrant to the deputy surveyor for a tract to be laid out in a particular county. Following the survey and the approval of the certificate of the examiner general, the clerk of the land office drew up a patent confirming the tract. The patent then went to the keeper of the great seal (again, Henry Darnall), who affixed the proprietor's stamp and returned the document to the land office to be picked up by the patentee. Ibid., 80–81; Carr and Jordan, *Maryland's Revolution of Government*, 36.

15. The portrait of the diversified Chesapeake planter was first suggested by Aubrey C. Land, "Economic Base and Social Structure: The Northern Chesapeake in the Eighteenth Century," *Journal of Economic History*, XXV (1965), 639–654. The ten-thousand-acre tract patented as Carrollton by the Settler's son lay in western Prince George's, later Frederick County, between the Potomac and Monocacy Rivers. The worth of the Settler's acreage was calculated on the basis of Paul Clemens's evaluation of the Lloyd family lands in 1733 (*Atlantic Economy*, 135n).

TABLE 2. Charles Carroll the Settler: Land Acquisitions, 1693–1720

Year	Increase (Decrease)	Cumulative Total	Year	Increase (Decrease)	Cumulative Total
1693	1,381	1,381	1707	4,210	20,044
1694	2,000	3,381	1708	2,415	22,459
1695	0	3,381	1709	800	23,259
1696	1,000	4,381	1710	638	23,897
1697	0	4,381	1711	11,218	35,115
1698	900	5,281	1712	(2,575)	32,540
1699	0	5,281	1713	5,276	37,816
1700	0	5,281	1714	500	38,316
1701	2	5,283	1715	3,913	42,229
1702	8,000	13,283	1716	3,080	45,309
1703	0	13,283	1717	980	46,289
1704	969	14,252	1718	2,067	48,356
1705	282	14,534	1719	(917)	47,439
1706	1,300	15,834	1720	338	47,777

Sources: County land records (warrants, certificates of survey, and patents), MdAA.
Note: This table includes all of Carroll's land acquisitions, whether by marriage settlement, inheritance, patent, purchase, or foreclosure. Although Carroll acquired no lands during his first five years in Maryland, 1688–1692, he had access to and benefited from the real and personal property of his first wife, Martha Ridgely Underwood Carroll.

another 12,249 through mortgage foreclosures. Additionally, during his lifetime Carroll sold 7,418 acres that he had either bought or acquired by foreclosure (see Table 2).

From the outset the Settler concentrated his land acquisitions in the Western Shore counties readily accessible to Annapolis, the Severn River village that became the colony's capital in 1695. Although he lived in the environs of St. Mary's City for several years, he never acquired any large southern Maryland holdings, perhaps realizing early on that the major zone of future expansion would be farther up the bay. In December 1695, he purchased Geffes Increase, a 180-acre plantation, with "dwelling houses, barns, stables, gardens, orchards," located about three miles from Annapolis, and its proximity to the new seat of government allowed him to continue to represent the proprietor's interests before the legislature.[16] The Settler began to buy property within the town's borders in 1701, and in 1706 he commenced assembling lots on the point where a wide stream, known subsequently as Carrol's Creek, flowed into the Severn. Within a decade, according to a "Plan of Annapolis" prepared in 1718, he owned most of the western portion of the peninsula. At some point between 1706 and 1718, the year he drew his will, the Settler relegated Geffes Increase, later known as the Farm or Annapolis quarter, to the status of a supply plantation and moved his family into a commodious, eleven-room frame structure situated on his waterfront property.[17]

Chronologically, the Settler's land acquisitions were clearly related to the improved prospects brought by his second marriage and show his ambition to build a landed estate. Beginning in 1696, two years after he wed Mary Darnall, Carroll commenced purchasing warrants, the first step in securing title to land. By 1700 he had bought warrants for about 12,000–13,000 acres, although during those four years he patented only 3,900, including a 1,500-acre Eastern Shore property. The first significant increase in accumulation was in 1702, when he patented 7,000 acres at Elk Ridge on the border of Baltimore and Anne Arundel Counties, the nucleus of what was to become the family's principal dwelling plantation, Doohoragen Manor. Its acquisition shows how Carroll used his powerful connections to advance his interests. He purchased a warrant for 7,000 acres in 1699 but did not secure a patent until July 2, 1702. The next month he left Maryland for his extended trip to England, where it appears he so favorably impressed the proprietor that he returned home with a remarkable dispensation. In a document issued on March 9, 1704, Lord Baltimore extended to Car-

---

16. The Ridgely/Underwood property on Van Sweringen's Point consisted of only 94 acres. The only major St. Mary's County holdings in which the Settler acquired an interest were St. Clement's and Bashford manors. For a discussion of the Carrolls' sixty-three years of difficulty with these tracts, see below, Chapter 6.

On Geffes Increase, see William Voss Elder III, "The Carroll House in Annapolis and Doughoregan Manor," in Ann C. Van Devanter, ed., *"Anywhere so long as There Be Freedom": Charles Carroll of Carrollton, His Family, and His Maryland* (Baltimore, 1975), 59. The Maryland assembly first convened in the province's new capital, formerly called Anne Arundel Town, in February 1695. Elihu S. Riley, *"The Ancient City": A History of Annapolis, in Maryland, 1649–1887* (Annapolis, Md., 1887), 62–63.

17. Anne Arundel County Deeds, liber W.D., fol. 663, and liber W.T. no. 2, fols. 372–373, MdAA; James Stoddert, "Plan of Annapolis, 24 July 1718," copied by Harry A. H. Ewald, Apr. 16, 1956, in Morris L. Radoff, *The State House at Annapolis* (Annapolis, Md., 1972); Elder, "The Carroll House in Annapolis," in Van Devanter, ed., *"Anywhere so long as There Be Freedom,"* 60.

roll the unique privilege of paying no quitrents on his 7,000-acre tract until his infant son Charles, for whom the land was intended, reached his majority some twenty years hence. Further, even if the child died before his twenty-first birthday, the dispensation would remain in effect until the date when the boy would have come of age.[18]

The next quantum leap in the Settler's accumulation of land occurred in 1711, the year his father-in-law, Henry Darnall, died. Once again, Carroll's personal loss was compensated by a distinct improvement in his economic position. He immediately assumed both of Darnall's important offices in the proprietor's private establishment, becoming agent and receiver general as well as keeper of the great seal, and he acted in those posts for more than a year until his official appointment to them in the fall of 1712. Collectively, they enhanced his potential income by £500–£900 sterling annually and allowed him to expand his planting and mercantile activities. In the decade between Darnall's death and his own, he doubled the acreage he had acquired during his first two decades in the colony (Table 2). Although a similar chronological calculation for Carroll's investment in slaves cannot be made, at his death he owned 112, half of whom were working hands. Valued at £1,931, Carroll's slaves resided on the quarters of his five plantations, where they produced tobacco, wheat, and corn, and tended livestock worth more than £600.[19]

Like his rate of land acquisition, Carroll's banking activities increased markedly after he assumed his father-in-law's offices in 1711. In a society where liquid capital was always scarce, those who could provide credit performed a vital and extremely profitable service. After 1704 the interest rate on such transactions was regulated by law in Maryland at 8 percent per hundredweight when the loan was based on the colony's prime staple, tobacco, and 6 percent per hundred pounds sterling for cash. Carroll was involved in the mortgage loan market as early as 1700, with a marked increase occurring after 1705, and by 1711 he had more mortgage loans outstanding than anyone else in Maryland — a total of thirty. His nearest competitor was one of his most important legal clients, the English merchant John Hyde. During the period 1700–1711, Hyde contracted only fourteen

18. Browne et al., eds., *Archives of Maryland*, XXV, 130; Land Office, Patents, liber D.D. no. 5, fols. 711–712.

19. "Working hands" means male and female slaves sixteen years old or older, the age at which they were counted as part of the taxable property of their owners.

Value of slaves: analysis of inventories of CCS by Victoria Allan, MdAA, for the Charles Carroll of Carrollton Papers. The inventories are contained in ledger X, Carroll-McTavish Papers, MdHi.

mortgages, although the cumulative value of his fewer loans totaled more than Carroll's many —£4,615 to £2,514.[20] It should be emphasized, however, that since many of these loans were repaid or foreclosed — most had a life of one to three years — neither lender had his entire cumulative total out at one time.

Within two years of assuming Darnall's high proprietary offices, Carroll replaced Hyde as the colony's largest lender. In 1712 and 1713 Hyde made substantial loans totaling £1,704, but the provincial court deeds record no further activity on his part. By contrast, between 1711 and 1720 the Settler made twenty-four loans worth £4,464. Conceivably, since Hyde continued to be active in the Maryland tobacco trade, he might have lent money to Carroll, who in turn re-lent it at a higher rate.[21] The prospects for such an arrangement perhaps suggested themselves to Hyde as early as 1710, when the depression in the tobacco economy resulting from Queen Anne's War intimidated lenders. Creditors might well have been further deterred in 1714, when the Maryland assembly restricted suits for the collection of debts worth up to £20 sterling or two thousand pounds of tobacco exclusively to the county courts. Although Hyde's mortgage loans were much larger, the legislation combined with severe economic depression to create an unpropitious climate for creditors. In this situation Carroll's positions both as an accomplished lawyer well versed in representing mercantile interests — one court petition in 1714 referred to him as an "Attorny in fact for divers Merchants and others in Great Britain" — and as a high proprietary official would have offered Hyde considerable security. In a letter to a Maryland correspondent several years later, Hyde indicated that Carroll was already extremely familiar with his operations in the colony. Explaining his refusal to advance further credit, Hyde wrote: "But Mr Carroll knows very well that I have such Sumes of money allready due to me in Maryland which I cannot gett in that I am not willing to runn any further."[22] Whatever the case, it is clear that, while Carroll's income from proprietary offices increased markedly after 1711, his sub-

20. Browne et al., eds., *Archives of Maryland,* XXVI, 352; Provincial Court, Deeds, libers T.L. no. 2, P.L. no. 3, P.L. no. 6, T.P. no. 4, P.L. no. 5, MdAA. I wish to thank Dr. Lorena S. Walsh for making her research into these records available to me.

21. Aubrey C. Land believes that such practices had developed in Maryland by the 1730s; see *The Dulanys of Maryland: A Biographical Study of Daniel Dulany, the Elder (1685–1753), and Daniel Dulany, the Younger (1722–1797)* (Baltimore, 1955), 103.

22. Browne et al., eds., *Archives of Maryland,* XXIV, 439–442, XXIX, 368; Alan Frederick Day, "A Social Study of Lawyers in Maryland, 1660–1775" (Ph.D. diss., Johns Hopkins University, 1977), 205–206; John Hyde to Lewis Duvall [London], Mar. 25, 1710, in John M. Hemphill II, "Documents Relating to the Colonial Tobacco Trade," *Md. Hist. Mag.,* LII (1957), 156.

stantial mortgage activities show that he found access to an even greater source of capital.

Besides lending money on mortgages, Carroll extended numerous loans. Although his personal accounts have not survived, the extent of the credit he advanced is revealed by his frequent recourse to the provincial courts in efforts to collect debts that ranged from £20 to £280 sterling. From 1699 to 1718, Carroll brought sixty suits and received awards totaling £1,712 sterling, more than twenty-three hundred pounds of tobacco, and £100 current money. In addition, in eight of those cases the records specify that he was allowed to collect more than eight thousand pounds of tobacco for his expense in bringing suit. (Similar costs were also granted in his other cases, but the exact amounts were not recorded.) Equally significant, in 1721, the first year after his death, Carroll's administrators brought suit in behalf of his estate for debts amounting to £2,200 sterling.[23]

Although Carroll was prohibited from practicing law in the provincial court, he remained very active in the chancery court and also practiced, though much less frequently, in the prerogative court. Undoubtedly, he concentrated his efforts on chancery cases because the fees were higher. In 1708 the Maryland assembly standardized the amount that lawyers could charge in chancery at six hundred pounds of tobacco per case but allowed only four hundred pounds in the prerogative court. In that year Carroll carried his heaviest case load — forty clients — and thus earned a minimum of one hundred pounds sterling. Presumably, Maryland's most able lawyers, Carroll among them, worked out private arrangements for higher fees despite the law. One thing is clear: his legal practice was exceptionally lucrative. As an envious adversary noted in 1718, Carroll acquired "a vast estate in this Province, by the Offices he formerly Employed, and his Practice in the Law."[24]

Carroll's mercantile activities proved similarly prosperous. The inventory of the goods in his Annapolis store at the time of his death included an exten-

<hr>

23. Provincial Court Judgments, libers W.T. no. 3, T.L. no. 3, T.B. no. 2, P.L. nos. 1–4, I.O. no. 1, V.D. no. 2, T.P. no. 2, W.G. no. 1, MdAA.

24. Day, "Social Study of Lawyers," 203; Browne et al., eds., *Archives of Maryland,* XXXIII, 120. Owings states that twelve thousand pounds of tobacco equaled fifty pounds sterling a year (*His Lordship's Patronage,* 44). Beyond court appearances, there was a host of other services for which lawyers earned handsome fees not regulated by law. For example, they were paid retainers for drawing mortgages and bonds, drafting and recording legal forms, and giving advice (Day, "Social Study of Lawyers," 223–225). Day's study provides a rich analysis of Maryland's colonial legal profession.

sive selection of dry goods, pewter, brass, hosiery, stays, bodices, upholstery, saddlery, jewelry, guns, glass, earthenware, sugar, stationery, cutlery, groceries, ironware, wigs, harnesses, spices, and rum, with a total value of £3,144 current money. By comparison, Samuel Chew, a wealthy merchant-planter who died in 1718, possessed an inventory of "new goods" worth only £545, and Amos Garrett, who succeeded Carroll as Annapolis's major merchant, left a mercantile inventory valued at £3,570 in 1727. Moreover, Carroll's nephew James (d. 1729), a son of Anthony Carroll of Lisheenboy, is known to have invested profitably in the slave trade. As James had benefited from his uncle's sponsorship and worked closely with him from the time he arrived in Maryland in the 1690s, it is likely that the Settler invested with him in such ventures.[25]

By 1715 or thereabouts Charles Carroll had become one of Maryland's most powerful men, and the inventory of his possessions at his death vividly portrays his status. The total appraised value of his assets, excluding land, amounted to £7,535, the largest personal estate ever probated in the colony to that time. The total value of the Settler's estate, both landed and personal, was between £20,000 and £30,000.[26]

25. Ledger X, Carroll-McTavish Papers, and Allan, analysis of CCS's inventory, Charles Carroll of Carrollton Papers; Main, *Tobacco Colony*, 236; analysis of the Inventory of Amos Garrett, courtesy of Dr. Jean B. Russo, Historic Annapolis, Inc.; James Carroll, day book, Special Collections Division, Georgetown University Library, Washington, D.C.

26. Although Charles Carroll the Settler's dates fall within the time span covered by Gloria L. Main's excellent study, *Tobacco Colony*, his inventory is not on file at the MdAA and thus escaped her notice.

Two testamentary bonds, the instruments used to ensure that administrators did not steal from the legacies entrusted to them and usually calculated at twice the value of the estate, were taken out to secure the administration of the Settler's personal estate. The first was drawn in August 1720 in the amount of £60,000 sterling. The second, recorded in January 1720/1 when the eldest of Carroll's "Executors in Chief," his son Charles, had returned to Maryland from his studies abroad, reduced the amount to £40,000. The difference between the total appraised value of the Settler's personal estate and the £20,000 indicated by the bond apparently represented the debts owed the estate (Prerogative Court, Testamentary Proceedings, liber 24, fols. 283, 385). The appraisals of the various sectors of Charles Carroll the Settler's estate took place over five years, beginning in November 1721 with his Baltimore County quarter and ending in December 1726 with the inventory of his goods and chattels on Poplar Island. The evaluation of the Settler's Annapolis estate, by far his most substantial property in 1720, is dated May 2, 1723, a month to the day after the twenty-first birthday of his elder son, Charles Carroll of Annapolis. The inventory of his Prince George's County quarters, Western Branch and Enfield Chace, was completed on Dec. 20, 1721, immediately after that of his Baltimore County

The variety and riches of the Settler's wearing apparel, the size of his house, and its elaborate furnishings indicate even more dramatically than the value of his estate the kind of presence he projected in Annapolis and provincial society. His wardrobe, worth £114, included eight suits, one of which was a splendid garment of "fine Cloath trimmed wth gold" worth £16, five wigs, and a variety of breeches and waistcoats, among them a scarlet coat and pants. Appropriately costumed for all seasons and settings, the Settler owned Holland shirts, silk stockings, a great coat, a "drab coat," a cloak, several pairs of shoes, half a dozen hats, a scabbard, and four nightgowns. The eleven well-appointed rooms that composed his house made similarly strong assertions about the status and identity he claimed for himself and his family. Besides such marks of gentility as feather beds and chairs, the domicile boasted an array of refinements that signified a style of living virtually unequaled in Maryland at that period. His kin could behold their likenesses in looking glasses or in the eight family portraits that, with five other pictures, adorned the walls. There were clocks to measure the hours of their days; their dining table displayed silver and fine linen, and the separate tea service, kept in a bedchamber where such entertaining generally took place before 1720, marked the Carrolls as one of the few families in the early Chesapeake whose resources permitted them to engage regularly in that genteel ritual. The kitchen, equipped with an assortment of kettles, pans, skillets, chafing dishes, and cooking utensils, bespoke the preparation and presentation of far more elegant, sophisticated meals than those that sustained the vast majority of their contemporaries. Yet, the Settler's dwelling also housed a well-furnished chapel that probably served Annapolis Catholics of all social ranks as well as the members of his immediate household.[27]

By the middle of the eighteenth century's second decade, Charles Carroll's climb to the economic pinnacle of his society had made him Maryland's most influential and visible Catholic, a man whose wealth and proprietary connections were not to be taken lightly by the officials of the government to which his religion

---

establishment. A fifth appraisal, untitled, undated, and possibly incomplete, was probably for the supply plantation, later referred to as Annapolis quarter. Ledger X, Carroll-McTavish Papers.

27. Kevin M. Sweeney, "High-Style Vernacular: Lifestyles of the Colonial Elite," in Cary Carson, Ronald Hoffman, and Peter J. Albert, eds., *Of Consuming Interests: The Style of Life in the Eighteenth Century* (Charlottesville, Va., 1994), 8–10, and Carr and Walsh, "Changing Lifestyles and Consumer Behavior in the Colonial Chesapeake," 128; Ledger X, Carroll-McTavish Papers.

denied him access. He had built a great fortune from scratch and reestablished the pride of the Carroll name, but the course of action he chose during the last five years of his life reveals that these triumphs had not quenched his thirst for political power. In 1715, a quarter-century after he had been deprived of his appointment as attorney general, Charles Carroll the Settler perceived in the rapid turnover of the proprietorship and the return of the government of Maryland to the Lords Baltimore an opportunity to reclaim for Roman Catholics a share of the colony's public offices — and to install himself on an equal footing with the governor. His chief opponent in carrying out this bold plan was Maryland's governor, John Hart. A Protestant Irishman and former captain in the British army, Hart was as implacable a foe of Catholic ambitions as Carroll was their champion. Thus the stage was set to play out in Maryland the same bitter conflicts that during the seventeenth century had destroyed Ireland's great Catholic landowners and driven the Settler to the New World.

The unusually fluid political conditions both in England and in Maryland between 1714 and 1716 seemed to augur well for Carroll's strategy. Within two months of Queen Anne's death on August 1, 1714, the accession of her Hanoverian cousin George I to the British throne assured the Protestant succession. Stuart hopes were not entirely vanquished, however, and sentiment favoring the return of the Old Pretender, who aspired to become James III, began to mount in the West and North of England and in Scotland during the spring and summer of 1715. Encouraged by the disaffection of principal Tory leaders Henry Saint-John, Viscount Bolingbroke, and James Butler, duke of Ormond, both of whom fled to France in 1715 to escape impeachment, the Old Pretender's supporters in France joined with Scottish highlanders to foment the Fifteen Rebellion, which broke out in September 1715. Although the threat of the uprising was contained in England within about six months, the Jacobite–anti-Jacobite passions it aroused persisted for some time and particularly unsettled politics in Maryland.

During the same period, problems of succession also kept the Maryland proprietorship in flux and the colony's government in some uncertainty. Those difficulties began in 1713 when the Board of Trade renewed a drive, first initiated in 1701, to put an end to proprietary colonies. In response to this pressure, Charles Calvert, third Lord Baltimore, sought to negotiate with Queen Anne's most powerful minister, Robert Harley, earl of Oxford and lord high treasurer, "an Equivalent for the government of the province of Maryland." [28] Dismayed by Lord Baltimore's apparent readiness to bargain away the Calvert patrimony

28. Lord Baltimore to Robert Harley, n.d., printed in Michael G. Hall, "Some Letters of Benedict Leonard Calvert," WMQ, 3d Ser., XVII (1960), 360.

and more than a little suspicious that the eighty-three-year-old proprietor intended to make his fourth wife — to whom he had been married scarcely a year — the principal beneficiary of any such arrangements, Benedict Leonard Calvert, Charles Calvert's eldest son and heir apparent, took matters into his own hands. Calculating that the proprietary family's Catholicism constituted the chief impediment to any improvement of their fortunes with regard to Maryland, Benedict Leonard simply decided to change his religion, gambling that he could offset his father's intense displeasure over such an act with the crown's approbation.

It was a risky business, but it worked. In a series of letters written to Harley during the fall of 1713, Benedict Leonard portrayed himself as having been long inclined "to embrace the Protestant religion" and as hesitating only for fear that his father "would withdraw my Subsistence." Of course, that is precisely what the irate Charles Calvert did. As soon as rumors of his son's impending apostasy reached his ears, he cut off Benedict Leonard's annual allowance of £450, and he refused to continue paying for the education and maintenance of his grandchildren once their father had removed them from the "Popish communion." Forced "by the unkindness of his Father . . . to live upon his marriage settlement," a paltry £600 yearly, £200 of which was set aside for the maintenance of his estranged wife, Benedict Leonard prevailed upon the crown to allow him a compensatory £300 per annum. In addition, Queen Anne acceded to his wish to have Captain John Hart commissioned as governor of Maryland, an appointment that further enriched Benedict Leonard, since Hart had agreed to pay his patron £500 a year out of the profits of the governor's office. However wounded he was by his son's "forsaking the Religion you were brought up in," Charles Calvert, unable for some four years to get a governor of his own choosing appointed, recognized clearly that Benedict Leonard was "endeavoring to get his Father's Inheritance (the Government of Maryland)," but he was powerless to do anything about it. By November 1713, Benedict Leonard had "publicly renounced the Romish Errors, and received from the hands of the Bishop of Hereford the Blessed Sacrament of the Lord's Supper, in the Church of St. Anne Westminster." [29]

The return of political control of Maryland to the Calverts was to require an-

29. Benedict Leonard Calvert to Robert Harley, [Oct. 20, 1713], Charles Calvert to Benedict Leonard Calvert, [Aug. 7, 1713], and Charles Calvert to Robert Harley, Dec.(?) 31, 1713, ibid., 361, 362, 366; memorial of Benedict Leonard Calvert to George I, Feb. 2, 1715, printed in J. Thomas Scharf, *History of Maryland from the Earliest Times to the Present Day* (Baltimore, 1879), I, 379; Owings, *His Lordship's Patronage*, 113–114.

other year and a half of patience and negotiation. Sometime between April and June 1714, Queen Anne, ostensibly at Benedict Leonard's request, appointed Thomas Beake, a Protestant living in London, to the post of principal secretary of Maryland. As with Governor Hart, there seems to have been a quid pro quo — someone, undoubtedly Benedict Leonard, promised Thomas Beake the post for life if he managed to obtain "the restoration of the government of Maryland to the Lords Baltimore." Six months after Queen Anne's death, Benedict Leonard reaffirmed his Anglican faith and his loyalty to the crown in a memorial that he presented to the new monarch, George I, on February 2, 1715.[30] Two weeks later, Charles Calvert died, and Benedict Leonard, fourth Lord Baltimore and Maryland's third proprietor, immediately petitioned the king to return governing authority over Maryland to the Protestant Calverts. The master schemer was not destined to enjoy the final result of his carefully crafted plan, however. Benedict Leonard followed his father to the grave a scant eight weeks after succeeding to the proprietorship, leaving his title and the disposition of Maryland in the hands of his sixteen-year-old son, Charles.

As he was a minor at the time of his father's death, it was necessary for the fifth Lord Baltimore to select a guardian to handle his affairs until he came of age. The person he chose, Francis North, second Baron Guilford, a prominent Tory and a member of the Board of Trade, was also a man of unsavory reputation and questionable politics — "a Jacobite of debauched habits, whose example corrupted Baltimore's character." Within a month after young Charles Calvert succeeded to his titles, on May 15, 1715, the government of Maryland was officially restored to the proprietary family, an event proclaimed in the colony on December 27, 1715.[31]

30. Owings, *His Lordship's Patronage,* 127. Although Owings does not say who made the deal with Beake, it is hard to imagine who besides Benedict Leonard Calvert would have done so. Benedict Leonard's memorial, which relates the progress of his apostasy, is printed in Scharf, *History of Maryland,* I, 379.

31. Papenfuse et al., eds., *Biographical Dictionary,* I, 186; Owings, *His Lordship's Patronage,* 114. It is difficult to see how Guilford's "example" could have proved any more harmful to young Charles Calvert than that set for him by his own father, Benedict Leonard Calvert. According to the diarist Thomas Hearne, an intimate friend of Charles's younger brothers, Benedict Leonard was not "contented with [his wife], but lay much with (generally more than with his Lady) a fine, beautifull young Girl, one Mrs. Grove . . . to the great discomposure of his Lady, whom he used very barbarously, and would often (when he came late home a-nights) force out of her Bed quite, as it were naked, &, for fear, she would hide herself, & sometimes run up to the top of the House, & at other times apply to a Friend, not far off, for Cloaths in that condition to hide her Nakedness" ("Hearne's Remarks and Collections," IX, Oxford Historical Society, LXV, reprinted in "Calvert

For Charles Carroll the Settler this combination of events — the accession of George I, the sentiments exposed by the Fifteen Rebellion, the rapid turnover of the proprietorship, and the restoration of the government of Maryland to the Calverts — posed enormously tempting opportunities and equally grave dangers. While onerous, the laws that circumscribed Catholics in Maryland under crown rule were far less disabling than the penal statutes invoked against their English and Irish coreligionists in the sixteenth and seventeenth centuries. To the strictures enacted in Maryland during the 1690s barring Catholics from practicing law and holding office, the colony's general assembly had by 1704 passed statutes that forbade them to maintain schools for their children and to worship publicly, although a specific dispensation of the legislature allowed priests to say Mass in private houses. Beyond the periodic passage of laws limiting the numbers of Irish Catholic servants that could enter the colony, the assembly took no other overt actions to harass Catholics between 1704 and 1716. Moreover, Catholics retained the franchise, provided they could meet the property requirements that applied to all male residents.[32]

From the perspective of Maryland's Protestant majority, the Catholic minority was treated quite well and owed the governing powers a debt of gratitude, a view that Charles Carroll the Settler manifestly did not share. Even though he must have known that his situation in Maryland was far better than the desperate circumstances his brother Anthony faced in Ireland, Carroll was, as the official record of his behavior between 1716 and 1720 attests, neither grateful nor

---

Memorabilia," *Md. Hist. Mag.,* X [1915], 373). Married to Benedict Leonard in 1699, Charlotte Lee Calvert had borne him seven children by 1705, when the couple separated (Mrs. Russel Hastings, "Calvert and Darnall Gleanings from English Wills," *Md. Hist. Mag.,* XXII [1927], 334–336n). In 1713 Charles Calvert, third Lord Baltimore, reported to Robert Harley that his son "has for his housekeeper, to take care of his four sons, his one Groves, a woman by whom he has two Bastards, who live with him, and has kept him company ever since his separation from his wife, and was the chief instrument of his parting with the Lady Charlott" (Charles Calvert to Robert Harley, Dec. [?] 31, 1713, printed in Hall, "Some Letters," *WMQ,* 3d Ser., XVII [1960], 366). A decade after Benedict Leonard's death, Hearne recorded, "I am told the present Lord Baltimore (who is unmarried) keeps the said Mrs. Grove company, as his father did" ("Hearne's Remarks and Collections," in "Calvert Memorabilia," *Md. Hist. Mag.,* X [1915], 373).

32. Browne et al., eds., *Archives of Maryland,* XXVI, 340–341, 431–432, 630–631. The law passed by the April–June 1715 session of the assembly requiring officeholders to swear their abjuration of the Old Pretender did not further deprive Catholics, as they were already barred from public posts by the oath of abhorrence and the test.

As of 1670, men possessing a fifty-acre freehold or a visible estate worth forty pounds could vote. Carr and Jordan, *Maryland's Revolution of Government,* 16.

content. His actions in those years persuasively demonstrate his conviction that the restoration of Maryland's government to the Calverts offered Catholics a chance to reclaim the civil and political rights they had enjoyed under proprietary rule before 1690. His ambitions for himself assumed an equally obvious and even grander scale. Counting his quarter-century of protecting and advancing the proprietary family's interests as an unassailable asset, he made a strong bid to continue this work, with increased powers, as an official in Lord Baltimore's newly restored government. If he succeeded, as he fully expected to do, his Protestant counterparts would be forced to acknowledge his authority. The records kept by those who opposed him strongly suggest that Carroll both acted for himself and his coreligionists and that he enjoyed the support of a coterie of prominent men derisively known as the "Catholic faction." When called to account for their behavior in 1720, that group's members included the heads of most of Maryland's Catholic gentry families, many of whom were wealthy and, in varying degrees, the Settler's kin.[33]

The first hint that something was afoot surfaced early in 1716 when Carroll informed Governor Hart that he intended to present his views on restoring office-holding privileges to Catholics to the proprietor. For both personal and professional reasons Hart did not welcome this news. From the governor's arrival in the colony in May 1714, his encounters with Carroll had been testy. Recognizing the Settler as a troublemaker and a potential rival, Hart used the opportunity afforded him by the return of proprietary government to underscore the considerable authority that his office possessed. On the day that the restoration was formally proclaimed in Maryland, December 27, 1715, Hart required Carroll to surrender to him the proprietor's great seal, which, during the period of royal government, had been in the Settler's keeping as Lord Baltimore's chief agent in the colony.[34] Hart might have enjoyed that moment, but he reacted quite differently upon learning of Carroll's plan to travel to England to see the proprietor. As the governor later recounted to the Maryland assembly, Carroll "shewed me

33. Browne et al., eds., *Archives of Maryland*, XXXIII, 620–623. The sole account of the Settler's conduct between 1716 and 1720 is found in the proceedings of the Maryland general assembly. None of his personal papers has survived, and none of the records pertaining to the proprietary family contains any information on this subject.

34. Ibid., 120. During the period of royal government two great seals were used in Maryland — a crown seal for the government and the Calvert seal for all land transactions that fell within the domain of the proprietor's private establishment. With the restoration of the colony's government to the proprietor, the crown seal was discarded, and the proprietor's emblem once again became Maryland's official seal. For earlier incidents of tension between Hart and Carroll, see ibid., XXIX, 360, 374, XXX, 345.

a Representation, which was to be presented to their Lordships on behalf of the Roman Catholicks of this Province Importing that they Prayed to be Restored to what they alledged was their Right of being Qualifyed for Offices in the Government, as they formerly had been." Hart responded bluntly: "I plainly told Mr Carroll that It was against the Laws of Great Britain & the Acts of Assembly of this Province, & that I would Oppose it to the Utmost of my Power." According to Hart — and it must be noted that this is his recollection set down two years after the event — the "Surprise & Indignation" with which he greeted Carroll's proposal persuaded that gentleman not to deliver the appeal to the proprietor, on condition that Hart keep what had passed between them confidential.[35]

Shortly after this incident, Carroll embarked on his voyage to England, where he met on several occasions with proprietary officials, among them Lord Guilford, the young proprietor's guardian, and Charles Lowe, the colony's coprincipal secretary along with his brother-in-law, Thomas Beake. During these discussions, Carroll, in direct violation of his alleged agreement with Hart, urged restoring the rights to public office to Maryland Catholics.[36] Subsequent events indicate that his appeal fell on receptive ears. Carroll left England with a new commission from Lord Baltimore confirming him in all his former proprietary posts and giving him public powers that challenged the governor's authority in two critical areas — control of the revenues for the support of the government and local patronage. A major confrontation with Hart thus became inevitable, as the Settler must have known, and the ways he chose to unveil his new commission intensified the drama of the clash.

Reentering Maryland without fanfare, Carroll made no fuss about the fact that William Bladen, a Protestant, had assumed, along with the office of provincial attorney general, the duties of proprietary attorney general that had formerly been his. If this apparent acquiescence lulled Hart, his peace of mind was to be short-lived. On June 10, 1716, while the governor was absent from the capital, a couple of Irish servants fired two of Annapolis's "Great Guns on the Court House Hill" in honor of the Old Pretender's birthday, and other Jacobites drank openly to his health and spoke "contemptibly of the King." Upon his return to

---

35. Ibid., XXXIII, 120, 121.

36. Owings, *His Lordship's Patronage*, 127. Accused by Hart some months later of "unfaithful Dealing on this Account," the Settler justified his behavior by maintaining he had not asked "that the Roman Catholicks might be Qualified for Imploymts but that they might not be Unqualifyed for them." Unimpressed by this fine distinction, the governor reported to the legislature, "So poor & Jesuiticall an Evasion wants no Remark." Browne et al., eds., *Archives of Maryland*, XXXIII, 121.

Annapolis on June 15, Hart, horrified by the affront, issued a proclamation calling for the apprehension and punishment of the perpetrators of the "Traiterous Wicked Audacious & Insolent Action" and offering a reward of twenty pounds sterling to anyone who discovered the culprits. In less than a month one of the offenders came forward with evidence, probably in order to claim the reward. His collaborator was taken into custody, tried, and convicted by a specially summoned court of oyer and terminer. For his crime he was whipped and pilloried, and two others who had toasted the Pretender and denigrated the king — one of whom happened to be a kinsman of Carroll's named William Fitzredmond — were fined one hundred pounds sterling for this and other offenses and committed to jail until they satisfied the penalty. On July 10, 1716, Charles Carroll thrust himself into the center of this agitated situation by informing the governor that "He had a Commission from the Lord Proprietary and his Guardian under the Lord Proprietary's Great Seal And that He would discharge those Fines which the Sherriff of Ann Arundel County was directed to receive." [37]

Outraged, Hart immediately demanded to know by what authority Carroll — a professed Catholic — intended to act in a public capacity. The Settler answered by revealing the text of his new commission, which specifically continued him in his position as the proprietor's agent and receiver general and empowered him to act as escheator and naval officer, and to receive all fines and forfeitures. Moreover, as the commission stipulated, the proprietor had given Carroll the authority "to inspect into[,] Order[,] Manage & Account for all & every other Branch or Branches of our Revenue within our said Province." In short, Carroll was to have control of both the proprietor's private revenues and all public moneys intended for the support of government, including Hart's own salary! [38]

For a man like Hart, whose pride and tenderness of ego equaled Carroll's, the situation was intolerable. Several years later, his sense of being grossly insulted unsoothed by the passage of time, Hart charged, "I should have been by so Servile a Complyance Reduced to the Despicable Circumstance of Applying to him for my bread by Craving of him that Appointment their Lordships were pleased to nominate for my maintenance." Besides perceiving Carroll's new powers as a calculated assault on duly constituted Protestant authority in Maryland, Hart was furious at the diminution of his own status that the granting of those powers implied. Unable to deny the validity of the commission, the governor countered with a demand that the Settler qualify himself for his public po-

37. Ibid., XXX, 373–374.
38. Ibid., 375–376.

sitions by swearing the oaths of allegiance and abjuration required by the act of the assembly of all Maryland officeholders. Though apparently willing to swear allegiance, Carroll refused to take the oath of abjuration that denied all present and future Stuart claims to the English throne and affirmed the Protestant succession. Yet, in spite of the fact that he had not sworn, Carroll proceeded to receive the fines and to order the release of the Annapolis prisoners.[39]

Scarcely able to contain his rage at this audacity, Hart on July 17 placed the entire matter before the upper house of the assembly, informing that body that he considered the granting of this kind of authority "to any other Person but himself, especially to a Papist," to be "such a lessening of his Power & Dishonour to his Character that He has desired to be recalled unless He can be Restored to the full Authority he held under the Crown." Accusing Carroll of having "deceived the Lord Proprietary in his tender age & also his Guardian" in order to obtain his expanded appointment, Hart reported that Carroll, "by virtue of his s[ai]d commission," had already required of him an accounting of the moneys appropriated for the colony's defense, a request to which "his Excellency" had retorted that "He would as soon give him up his Hearts Blood."[40]

Hart then launched a two-pronged counterattack. First, he sought to discredit his opponent's character by asking whether the upper house did not agree with him that Carroll had "imposed upon the Lord Proprietary and his Guardian in obtaining such Commission." Of the eight gentlemen present, only one, Philemon Lloyd, dissented from the governor's interpretation. It was Hart's second thrust, however, that held the potential for bringing the Settler down: was Carroll, asked the governor, capable of holding public office in Maryland without swearing the oath of abjuration? To this question the members of the upper house responded unanimously: Having refused to swear one of the oaths "Enjoined by the Laws of Great Brittain and this Province," Mr. Carroll "is absolutely incapable of holding or Executing the af[oresai]d Commission as to any the powers therein Which do or may Concern the publick Affairs or Interest of this Province."[41]

A little more than a week later the upper house summoned Carroll and put to him a series of questions prepared by Hart concerning precisely how the new commission had been obtained. Essentially, the inquiries asked the Settler to address three points: Had he informed the proprietor of certain existing statutes that governed appointments? How did he expect to qualify for the posts

39. Ibid., 376, 517, XXXIII, 481.
40. Ibid., XXX, 377, 379.
41. Ibid., 378, 379.

awarded him given his allegiance to the Church of Rome? And, finally, did not Carroll consider it necessary to take all the required oaths, including the oath of abjuration repudiating the Old Pretender's claim to the British throne, in order to assume the positions to which he had been appointed?

Carroll's replies, delivered on August 1, were deemed by the governor and both houses of the assembly to be evasive and entirely unsatisfactory, but they constitute the Settler's only recorded rationale for his behavior. Basically, Carroll acknowledged that he had not discussed with Lord Guilford any of the statutes cited by the queries as impinged upon by his new commission nor had he specified to any of the officials with whom he dealt in England precisely what steps he intended to take to assure that he was qualified for the posts granted to him. In the first instance, Carroll explained that, as he was "very well Satisfied that there was nothing in them that would hinder the said Lord Propr[ietar]y as hereditary Governour of Maryland from granting the Commission," he saw no need to raise such questions with Lord Guilford. Likewise, as he was not asked to specify how he planned to qualify himself for office upon his return to Maryland, he deemed it needless to state that he would "doe what was necessary." He was not required "to make a profession of his faith" and thus believed "it would be look't upon as Impertinent in him" to do so. With regard to the oaths of allegiance and abjuration that Maryland law had required of all public officeholders since 1704, the Settler advanced an interesting argument. Stating that he had served the proprietor for twenty-five years under the crown without having to take any objectionable oaths, he saw no reason why he should not continue that service now that the government of the province had been restored to his lordship. He further maintained that, at the time the authority to govern Maryland was reinvested in the proprietor, Lord Baltimore had not agreed to require the oath of abjuration of officeholders and, therefore, the Settler's refusal to swear that oath could not prevent him from executing his commission. Dismissing Carroll's reasoning as "purely a panegerick upon his own deserts," the upper house was not persuaded.[42]

Beyond Carroll's stated reasons, a number of factors presumably induced him to believe that he could successfully challenge the governor and council. Aside from the professional services he had rendered Charles Calvert, third Lord Baltimore, and his family, the Settler's personal ties to the old proprietor had been quite strong. His youngest child Eleanor was born at the Calvert country estate Woodcote, located at Epsom in Surrey, in 1712. Moreover, his sons attended the College of the English Jesuits at St. Omer, the institution in French

42. Ibid., 544–548.

Flanders that was Charles Calvert's alma mater and the school where his grand-sons were also enrolled before their father became an Anglican. And Charles Calvert apparently found the Settler's company sufficiently agreeable to wish him for a neighbor when visiting Maryland, writing on one occasion that Car-roll should be granted a tract of land "as near as possible to one of the propri-etor's manors, for the benefit of his society."[43]

Carroll had further cemented his ties to the Calvert family by performing legal services for intimate relations. In 1709, he served as the administrator of the estate of Edward Maria Somerset, the proprietor's son-in-law, and he also appears to have assisted the widows of the third and fourth Lords Balti-more, Margaret Calvert and Charlotte Lee Calvert. The latter was the estranged wife of Benedict Leonard and enjoyed important connections with the Stuarts, since she was the granddaughter of Barbara Villiers, the favorite mistress of Charles II.[44] Motives far more compelling than his association with Charlotte

43. On Settler's ties to Calvert: Kate Mason Rowland, *The Life of Charles Carroll of Carrollton, 1737–1832, with His Correspondence and Public Papers* (New York, 1898), II, 437. Carroll and his wife were in England in the summer of 1712. The Settler's purpose was to secure from the proprietor an official commission appointing him to Darnall's posts. He returned to Maryland in February 1712/3 with the document, signed by Charles Calvert, in hand.

On St. Omers: Geoffrey Holt, *St. Omers and Bruges Colleges, 1593–1773: A Biographi-cal Dictionary,* Catholic Record Society, LXIX (London, 1979), 56–59. (From a very early date following its founding in 1593, the English Jesuit College at St. Omer was known in the English-speaking world as St. Omers. That name has been retained in this study.) While the records show that Henry and Charles Carroll, the Settler's two older sons, were enrolled at St. Omers by 1713, the year that Benedict Leonard Calvert withdrew his sons from the school, it cannot be firmly documented that the boys were there at the same time.

The quote from Charles Calvert appears in Rowland, *Life of Charles Carroll of Car-rollton,* I, 6, without citation. Although Charles Calvert, third Lord Baltimore, left Mary-land to reside permanently in England in 1684, four years before the Settler's arrival in the colony, his sentiment, inadvertently, or by design, eventually became reality: the ten-thousand-acre Baltimore County tract My Lady's Manor, surveyed as a gift from Charles Calvert to his fourth wife, Margaret, in 1713, adjoined the five-thousand-acre parcel Clin-malira, patented by the Settler in 1711. Gregory A. Stiverson, *Poverty in a Land of Plenty: Tenancy in Eighteenth-Century Maryland* (Baltimore, 1977), 151; Thomas D. Penniman and Malcolm W. Waring, "Some Baltimore County Land Grants," reproduction of a plat of My Lady's Manor, with adjacent tracts, Prints and Photographs Department, MdHi.

44. Provincial Court, Judgments, liber P.L. no. 2, fol. 596, no. 3, fol. 17; Rowland, *Life of Charles Carroll of Carrollton,* I, 6; Hastings, "Calvert and Darnall Gleanings from En-glish Wills," *Md. Hist. Mag.,* XXII (1927), 334–335n.

Lee might have led the Settler to remain loyal to the Stuarts while serving the Calverts. His family's ties to the Jacobite cause through their connection with Richard Grace, arguably one of Ireland's most militant Stuart champions, undoubtedly constituted a vivid force in the Settler's memory. Aware that Grace had willingly sacrificed his life in the Jacobites' ill-fated defense of the Irish midlands against the Williamite armies and that he, of all the Carrolls, had benefited the most from Grace's access to the Stuarts, the Settler perhaps could not bring himself to abjure one of the principal legacies that had defined his life.

Nor did he think it was necessary to, given his stellar performance in Lord Baltimore's private establishment, particularly after Darnall's death in 1711. Quite simply, Carroll had every reason to believe that Charles Calvert's successors would continue to rely upon his proven abilities, a supposition that was reinforced by a letter from Benedict Leonard shortly after his father's death confirming the Settler in all his proprietary posts. As Carroll explained when discussing the proprietor's motive for increasing his powers, "his faithful services and the Justness of his accounts with his Lordship's Ancestors was the only Inducement his Lordship had to Committ the receipt of the revenue of this Province rather to his care then to others who p[er]haps were not so well known in the family." [45]

Carroll's assessment of his prospects for augmented personal authority and restoration of officeholding rights to Catholics might also have been encouraged by the fact that English papists perceived a relaxation of the enforcement of the restrictions against them and assumed the same policy would extend to the colonies. The basis for this belief was the relatively mild punishment that George I meted out to participants in the Fifteen Rebellion — a number of whom were transported to the Chesapeake — as well as the overt encouragement given Catholic office seekers in Maryland by the colony's coprincipal secretary in England, Charles Lowe, one of the chief proprietary officials with whom the Settler dealt in acquiring his expanded commission. [46]

45. Browne et al., eds., *Archives of Maryland*, XXX, 546. Although Benedict Leonard Calvert's actual letter of confirmation has not been found, its existence and contents are referred to in the proceedings of the upper house (ibid., 377).

46. Writing to his son Richard in Maryland, Richard Rudyard, a London Catholic, "Signifyed to his son that Mr. Lowe one of the Secretarys of this Province had promised him that he & the other Secretary of this Province would write to Mr. Lloyd the Deputy Secretary to prefer him to a County Clerks place upon the first Vacancy." Noting that "the King has Shewn a great deal of mercy in pardoning several of the Rebels which endears him much to the people," and that "all come in & take the Oaths voluntarily," including "several Romans of note," Rudyard advised his son "that if this Office should happen to be offered to you I would not have you lose it on Account of not qualifying yourself for that nicety is all over in England." Ibid., 421.

Although Carroll's general evaluation of the religious and political climate in Great Britain and Maryland might have had some basis in fact and his goals been at least within the realm of possibility, he made two serious miscalculations. First, he failed to take into account the sustained and vigorous opposition Hart was prepared to mount against him, a campaign fueled by the governor's deep personal animosity. Second, the Settler seems not to have suspected that proprietary support for his plan might be exceedingly shallow. Once Hart, with the assembly's backing, focused on Carroll's refusal to swear all of the oaths required of public officeholders, the challenger's downfall became inevitable: the governor had struck at the Achilles' heel of the newly Protestant proprietorship.[47] There was little chance that Lord Guilford and his minions, having held the reins of Maryland's government for scarcely a year, would risk what they had gained in behalf of a stubborn Irish Catholic Jacobite, no matter how much his loyal and diligent service had benefited the proprietary family in the past.

Unable or unwilling to acknowledge those realities, Carroll continued to conduct himself in a manner designed to challenge and provoke the governor. Early in August 1716, he instructed Hart to forward him the revenues due the proprietor from one of the major tonnage assessments, with the exception of one thousand pounds, which he gave the governor leave to deduct "for your Excellency's Sallary." He also advised Hart to use "Caution . . . in assenting to some Laws which I understand are prepared And whereby his Lordship's Interest will evidently suffer detriment," and "humbly" recommended that, "till his Lordship's pleasure be known," the laws not be put into effect.[48] Outraged, the governor, who was just recovering from "several violent fitts of sickness," immediately sent the offensive letter off to the assembly with a note that vividly conveyed the poisonous nature of his confrontation with the Settler: "I Just now received the Inclosed Insnareing and Insolent letter and Considering the circumstance of my health it is very Inhumane in Mr. Carroll. As to what that Gent. speaks of my Sallary I know not what he means, the word Sallary being a Terme too mean and base to accept from a Subject by a person who has had the honour to serve the Crown in so many Imployments." With regard to Carroll's claim to control, by virtue of his new commission, the revenues from which the governor was to be paid, Hart declared that he held those instructions to be contrary to law; but, even if they were not, he would still "disdain as a protestant Governour to goe to a Virulent Papist to know when my family may have leave

47. Provincial Court, Judgments, liber V.D. no. 2, fol. 139.
48. Browne et al., eds., *Archives of Maryland*, XXX, 466.

to Eat. Upon the whole," the governor concluded, "I cann[o]t see what this Insolent man would be at. . . . Pray Gent. give him your Opinion."[49]

Responding immediately, the assembly appointed a joint committee to consider Carroll's letter. Reporting the following afternoon, the committee strongly castigated the Settler for his behavior and advised that no governmental revenues "ought to be given up Especially into the hands of Mr. Carroll or any other Disaffected to his Ma[jes]tys Governm[en]t or the Protestant interest." Carroll's recommendation that Hart be cautious in assenting to certain laws was an affront, and the Settler had "used a very indecent freedome with his Ex[celle]ncy . . . a ffreedome wee have never heared used before by any Subject to a Govr." Carroll was "guilty therein of great arrogance unless he has some Superior authority which (if he has) ought to be made publick." So strongly did the upper house endorse the committee's conclusions that it urged the lower house to send for "the said Mr. Carroll" and to "shew your Just resentm[en]ts by reprimanding him after such manner as you shall see fitt."[50]

Whether the lower house acted on this recommendation is unknown, but as a direct result of Carroll's behavior the assembly passed in August near the end of its 1716 session a bill entitled "An Act for the Better Security of the Peace and Safety of his Lordship's Government, and the Protestant Interest within This Province." This legislation made unmistakably clear just where Catholics stood. Not only did the law reiterate that all prospective officeholders must qualify themselves by swearing the oaths of allegiance, abhorrence, and abjuration and publicly denying the doctrine of transubstantiation, but also that even after installation they must be willing to swear again at any time if so requested. Any individual who executed an office without properly qualifying himself would, if discovered, forfeit the position and pay a fine of £250 sterling, half of which sum would be given to the informer. Finally, if "any Person who holds any Office or Trust within this Province, and has taken the Oaths appointed by this Law" should subsequently attend "any Popish Assembly, Conventicle or Meeting," participate in Mass, or take the Sacrament, he would be forced to relinquish his office, pay the fine, and be held "incapable of taking, holding, or executing any Commission or Place of Trust within this Province, until he shall be fully reconciled to the Church of England, and receive the Communion therein."[51]

With the assembly firmly behind him, Hart sat back to await a response from the proprietor, to whom he had sent a detailed account. He was not disap-

49. Ibid., 599.
50. Ibid., 602, 603.
51. Ibid., 617.

pointed. On February 20, 1717, notwithstanding nearly twenty-nine years of loyal service, Charles Carroll was cast aside. The proprietor revoked his commission and bestowed his office on a Protestant Calvert relative. There can be no doubt that Governor Hart took special pleasure in reading his lordship's letter to the assembly when it convened on April 22:

> As we Cannot Enough commend the Loyalty & Zeal you have shewn for his Majesty & the Succession in the Illustrious house of Hanover so none of those Laws to which we have Assented met with a more ready Confirmacon of them than that, which makes it penall for men to Act in Imployments without takeing the Oaths to our Dread Sovereign King George Whereby Protestants & Papists may Clearly Perceive that your Lord & Propr[ietar]y is not as has been Maliciously suggested by some A Papist in Masquerade but a true Protestant of the Church of England in which faith he is Resolved to live & Die.[52]

To Hart's chagrin, however, his vanquished opponent had no intention of being a graceful loser. The Settler did not accept the governor's view that, having been defeated, "the Gentlemen of the Romish Comunion" should "prudently consider their own Interest & Content themselves with the Lenity of the Governmts they live under who admitts them in this Province to an Equal share of Priviledges with the rest of their fellow Subjects the bearing of Offices alone Excepted."[53] Perhaps Carroll, having had his "Interest" so rudely thwarted in a way that left him bereft of any official recourse, saw no reason to count his blessings and behave in a prudent manner. Perhaps his disappointment was too bitter for a man of his pride to stomach without some form of retaliation. Perhaps his sense of outrage at what he perceived to be the injustice of his treatment was too great to be checked by reason. Whatever the motive, or combination of motives, the Settler reacted to his defeat by embarking on a course of action that ultimately deprived Maryland Catholics of the last of their civil "Priviledges" — the franchise — for the next half-century.

The only record of Carroll's activities during 1717 and early 1718 is contained in the report Hart presented to the legislature on April 23, 1718. According to the governor, Maryland's Roman Catholics, under Carroll's direction, had mounted a concerted campaign

> to Calumniate my Conduct, and by heaping of Indignities upon me, used their Utmost Efforts, thereby to Remove me from this Station.

52. Ibid., XXXIII, 4.
53. Ibid., 7.

... I am informed that a very large sume of money, was Subscribed for, by the Leading men of the Romish Community and some of them went as Emissaries to London And were very Active there against me, and Exclaimed in bitter Terms of my prosecuteing the Papists in this Province and how Cruel a manner they were Treated in.[54]

Not only had Hart, who perceived himself the defender of "the Protestant Constitution," been forced to contend with "popish Mallice," but he had also found public order threatened in an equally outrageous fashion by Charles Carroll's lawyer and kinsman, a nominal Anglican named Thomas Macnemara. Almost from the day of his arrival in the colony, Thomas Macnemara had been a disruptive force in Maryland. If ever a man merited the term "a wild Irishman," it was he — indeed, his behavior makes the actions of his fellow countrymen Hart and Carroll seem almost decorous. A former Catholic, Macnemara entered Maryland as a redemptioner shortly before the turn of the century and bound himself to Charles Carroll the Settler. Retained as a law clerk in the Settler's household, he took advantage of the hospitality by impregnating Carroll's niece, whom he married upon being released from his obligatory service. By 1707 Margaret Macnemara had fled from him, apparently in fear of her life, and appealed to the council to sanction the separation because of the "cruel, barbarous inhuman treatment of an unnatural husband towards her," including a "Tyrranicall haughty Domineering Carriage too Severe to be used even to Slaves." Sympathetic to her plight, the council noted that "not long since the said Margaret" had appeared before them "So battered bruised and Inhumanly beaten in most parts of her body that had She not been of a Constitution more than ordinary Strong She Could hardly have recovered it." They ordered Macnemara to pay his battered spouse fifteen pounds sterling a year alimony.[55]

Thomas Macnemara's public behavior did not improve upon his private conduct. At various times charges were brought against him for a wide range of offenses, including extortion, impertinence and disrespect to duly constituted authorities, buggery, assault, and murder. To the last infraction Macnemara pleaded "homicide by chance medley" — that is, death by accident. After several acquittals by petit jurors, the provincial justices raised the charges to manslaughter and ordered his right hand branded. Attempts to disbar him because of his actions were frequent, but, to the consternation of Maryland's constantly offended officials, Thomas Macnemara, for reasons unknown, retained the un-

54. Ibid., 121.
55. Land, *Dulanys of Maryland,* 15; Chancery Court Records, liber T.C., fol. 579.

"Marylando-Hibernus"

wavering support of both the proprietor and the crown and always managed to get himself readmitted to the practice of law in the time it took for mail to cross and recross the Atlantic. He was less successful in Pennsylvania. Having, by his "Insolent Carriage and Behaviour . . . Rendered himself . . . obnoxious to the Country in Generall," not to mention the courts, Macnemara lost the right to practice law in Pennsylvania in 1709.[56]

A series of highly unpleasant public confrontations between Hart and Macnemara, all involving Charles Carroll, led the governor to suspect the two men were in league against him. In July 1716, Macnemara disputed the authority of the specially convened court of oyer and terminer to try the men accused of firing the great guns and other Jacobite activities, maintaining that the case should be heard in the provincial court. "He said," Hart later recalled, indignantly, in a report to the upper house, "lett me see who dare to try them by this Commission or words to that Purpose." The next recorded confrontation occurred in October 1717, before the chancery court, where Macnemara, who was representing Carroll, rudely interrupted the governor's interrogation of the Settler and advised his client not to answer any more questions. Macnemara's demeanor — in Hart's words, his "Intolerable Insolence" — and his frequent recourse to "Indecent & Contumacious Tones and Gestures" so provoked the governor that he completely lost his temper. Declaring Macnemara "a Rogue & a Rascall," Hart ordered him prosecuted for "his Obstinate and Contemptuous manner of Treating this Court."[57]

With his authority thus under siege on two fronts, Hart readily concluded that Macnemara had joined forces with Carroll and the "Popish faction" in an effort to blacken his character, undermine his credibility, and secure his removal from office. Their principal goal was clear: "It is Obvious to all (who are not willfully blind)," the governor told the legislature on April 23, 1718, "what Steps the Roman Catholicks were takeing to Introduce themselves Again into the Administration of this Governm[en]t." Moreover, his excellency had proof of the collusion:

I am Authentically Informed that Mr. Carroll and Mr. Macnamara have made fresh Complaints to their L[or]d[shi]ps against me. And as these two

56. Land, *Dulanys of Maryland*, 7–10, 15–17; Browne et al., eds., *Archives of Maryland*, XXXIII, 143. I am indebted to Professor C. Ashley Ellefson for clarifying the charges brought against Thomas Macnemara and the sequence of legal action associated with them.

57. Browne et al., eds., *Archives of Maryland*, XXXIII, 181, 128–130.

persons are both named Togeather, I shall Speak of their behaviour in this publick Manner as being the most Candid and open method to set their misconduct in a true light to their L[or]d[shi]ps And to take of those artful & false Insinuations with which they Endeavour to amuse and poyson the minds of the Good People, as if there was neither Law nor Justice to be had under my Administration."[58]

Recalling the events of 1717–1718 in another address to the legislature in 1720, shortly after Macnemara's death, Hart could only shudder at the fate he believed would have befallen the "Protestant Interest" had Carroll and his deceased collaborator succeeded. "If their fury had been so outragious to the p[er]son of your Governour, what must the People have Expected from men of such Virulent and implacable Spirits, Could they gain their Ends on those they Esteem Hereticks." Lest they forget that the danger had been real, Hart reminded his audience:

> So sure was the Faction of their game that my Ruin was Openly threatened and one of their accomplices (whom the Pleasure of Providence has since removed to another Life) went down on his Knees and with horrid Execrations said, he did not Doubt to see me as fast in Prison as ever he was (who had been so for murder and other Crimes) and my Innocent Children set a begging[.] Truly this unhappy man Aided by the Faction did all that a base mind could perpetuate to Destroy my Character and Fortune."[59]

If, in the end, Hart and Macnemara proved to be beyond each other's reach, Charles Carroll the Settler and his Catholic allies were less fortunate. The governor and his supporters in the 1718 session of the general assembly consolidated their power by putting Carroll and the Catholic faction down hard. Specifically, the delegates enacted two laws. An Act Repealing an Act to Prevent the Growth of Popery rescinded a range of provisions passed in 1704 that protected Maryland Catholics from the harsher restrictions against religious observance contained in the English penal laws. The second measure, adopted on April 29, 1718, deprived Catholics of the right to vote. In a memorial to the proprietor praying his assent to the legislation, the assembly stated that the most immediate justification for the bill was the organized effort in Annapolis by Carroll and his associates to elect a representative sympathetic to their cause to the lower

58. Ibid., 120–121.
59. Ibid., 482. Not to be outdone in invective, Macnemara once compared the proceedings of the governor and council to the Spanish Inquisition. Ibid., 181.

house.[60] The proprietor assented, the bill became law, and Roman Catholics remained disenfranchised until the end of proprietary government in 1774.

The final scene in the political reduction of Maryland's Catholics occurred in April 1720. Hart, who continued to be annoyed by their repeated complaints to the proprietor of unremitting persecution under his administration, challenged a dozen of the faction's most prominent leaders to justify their accusations in public, before the assembly. He was particularly interested in hearing them defend their claim that Maryland's charter guaranteed to Catholics privileges equal to those of all other inhabitants, since, in his view, "the Papists" did not "derive any Privileges here beyond what the Connivance of the Government may indulge them in." The spokesmen summoned included Charles Carroll and his principal supporters: James Carroll, Henry Darnall, Jr., his son, Henry III, William Digges, Benjamin Hall, Clement Hill, William Fitzredmond, Henry Wharton, Charles Digges, Major Nicholas Sewall, Richard Bennett, and Father Peter Atwood, a Jesuit priest. All were duly served with sheriff's warrants ordering them to appear before the assembly by April 16, 1720, but none of them did so, even though the majority were known to be in Annapolis.[61] Their failure to present themselves completed Hart's victory. The assembly proceedings for April 19 record his triumph:

> His Excellency and this House Observe on the foregoing proceedings That Although the most Eminent of the Papists were in Town at the time appointed Them to make good their pretentions, yet they have not thought fitt to appear then or at any time Since to offer any thing in Vindication of their pretended Rights, and therefore take this their Demeanour as a Tacit Acknowledgment that their Pretentions are Groundless and their Exclamations most unreasonable.[62]

The battle was over. In May 1720 Hart, replaced as governor, sailed for England. On July 1, 1720, Charles Carroll died, leaving his coreligionists and his descendants an ironic and compelling legacy. To the former, Carroll left the political disabilities that would bind Maryland Catholics until the coming of the American Revolution. To his heirs he bequeathed the most substantial estate ever created in Maryland to that time, a fierce tribal loyalty, and a tenacious memory. The Settler's personality and perception of the world bore the indelible imprint

60. Ibid., 279.
61. Ibid., 484, 503–504, 516, 620–623.
62. Ibid., 532–533, 622–623.

PLATE 10. Charles Carroll of Annapolis as a Boy. By Justus Engelhardt Kühn. C. 1712.
Courtesy the Maryland Historical Society

of the ruthless struggle over land and culture waged by his Gaelic forebears and the English and Irish Protestants intent on displacing them. Raised in the crucible of that conflict, he had traveled to Maryland on an inflexible quest to reconstitute the Carroll fortune and lay the foundations of a renewed dynasty.

The year before he died, the Settler bound his second son Charles to the task of extending the family's prowess through an unrelenting pride of lineage and a determination to work its will upon the world. The death in April 1719 of the Settler's eldest son, Henry, had made Charles his family's principal link to the future. In the only personal letter of the Settler's that has been found, he wrote to his remaining sons, Charles, seventeen, and Daniel, twelve—both abroad in school—about the duties now incumbent upon them as a result of their brother's grievous demise. Carroll's sorrow reinforced the stern message he directed to the older boy. As heir apparent, Charles was to bend firmly to the task of becoming his father's successor, remembering always who he was, from whence he came, and the burden of history he carried. Thus Carroll instructed his son to pray for his dead brother, visit his mother when she came to Europe, and "Vigorously prepare for the defense of your Universall Philosophy," dedicating the performance to him, as Henry had done. The Settler ended his letter with a command to Charles that fused the remembrance of the family's Irish past with a commitment to forging its future in Maryland: "I would have you Stile your Self in your Thesis Marylando-Hibernus."[63]

63. CCS to Charles and Daniel Carroll, July 7, 1719, Carroll-McTavish Papers.

CHAPTER 3

"A Well-Regulated Œconomy"

When Charles Carroll the Settler died on July 1, 1720, he bequeathed to his heirs a substantial estate, an inhertitance that his eldest surviving son, Charles Carroll of Annapolis, would expand into one of the great fortunes of colonial America. But although they were similarly successful in achieving their economic goals, father and son nevertheless functioned within markedly different contexts. Throughout most of his career the Settler benefited from his close personal relationship with the Calvert family and the access to proprietary office that association guaranteed. By taking skillful advantage of a network of professional and personal patronage, he acquired land, slaves, a mercantile and banking business, and an active legal practice. Then he overreached, and, in consequence, his defeat by Governor John Hart redefined, to their sharp disadvantage, the world the Settler's descendants would inhabit.

Charles Carroll of Annapolis thus received a double-edged legacy from the Settler. He had inherited a solid foundation for building an even greater fortune, but he had no access to the advantages that had been the cornerstone of the Settler's success. Denied the powerful connections and public influence that his father had manipulated so effectively and bitterly resentful of the treatment accorded the Settler by Maryland's proprietary family, eighteen-year-old Charles Carroll of Annapolis returned from school at Douai to a capricious and frequently hostile colonial environment. Wary and distrustful, his sense of alienation and anger did not weaken his resolve but instead honed his determination to shape the circumstances in which he found himself to serve his own interests. Half a century later, his son Charles Carroll of Carrollton summarized the principles that drove Charles Carroll of Annapolis in his expansion of the Carroll assets: an unshakable commitment to accruing the "sweets of independence" and, as the "necessary means of attaining" that goal, "a well-regulated œconomy." [1]

The fortune-building career of Charles Carroll of Annapolis falls into two distinct chronological periods, the first differentiated from the second by his role as the executor and adminstrator of the Settler's estate. From 1721 to 1757, Charles Carroll of Annapolis managed the legacies bequeathed to the various heirs collectively, in a manner he steadfastly maintained was mutually beneficial. In 1757 he initiated a final settlement of his father's will, and from that time until his life ended in 1782, he concentrated solely — and without any pretense to the contrary — upon the protection and advancement of his own interests.

The Settler's will provided the assets and dictated the terms with which Charles Carroll of Annapolis began. To his widow, whose family connections had served him so well, the Settler left a life estate in his sixteen-hundred-acre Prince George's County tract called Enfield Chace and "fifteen able negroe Slaves" as compensation for "her Dower of my Real Estate and *rationabile parti bonorum* of my personall estate." Additional bequests to Madam Carroll included her lifetime use of the Settler's substantial dwelling house in Annapolis and its contents; his chariot, horses, and equipage; and one thousand pounds sterling "to do therewith as she shall think fitt." Finally, Mrs. Carroll was granted, for as long as she remained a widow, the rental income from the Settler's lots in Annapolis, a sum her son Charles later estimated to have been one hundred pounds Maryland gold per year at the time of his father's death.[2]

The Settler also provided generously for his four surviving children. To each of his daughters, Mary, nine, and Eleanor, eight, he left a lot in Annapolis, a five-thousand-acre portion of the unsurveyed twenty-thousand-acre tract "intended to be laid out for me on Potomack," and one thousand pounds sterling to be

---

1. CCC to the countess d'Auzouer, Sept. 20, 1771, Charles Carroll of Carrollton, letterbook 1770–1774, fol. 13, MdHi.

2. CCS, Dec. 1, 1718, will, Prerogative Court Wills, liber 16, fol. 176, MdAA (a printed transcription appears in Kate Mason Rowland, *The Life of Charles Carroll of Carrollton, 1737–1832, with His Correspondence and Public Papers* [New York, 1898], II, 375); CCA, Apr. [27?], 1761, "As to their Answer to my Remarks," in CCA, letterbook 1757–1761, fols. 56–57, MdHi. "Maryland gold" refers to the colony's hard currency (John J. McCusker, *Money and Exchange in Europe and America, 1600–1775: A Handbook* [Chapel Hill, N.C., 1978], 191). According to McCusker's tables for converting "gold" or paper currency to equivalent sterling values (197), Mrs. Carroll's Annapolis rental income was worth about seventy-five pounds sterling.

paid at age sixteen or upon marriage, whichever occurred first, with the interest to be used in the meantime for the young women's support and maintenance. A stern caveat accompanied these bequests: should the recipients "not prove dutiful to their Mother" or to the Settler's trustees with regard to marriage, decisions concerning their inheritances would be left "to the discretion of their said Mother and my said trustees."[3]

The Settler's devises to his sons were more briefly stated and far more substantial. When the Settler drew his will in December 1718, his eldest son, Henry Carroll, was studying law at Gray's Inn in London.[4] As the Settler's "heir at law," Henry would automatically inherit all lands not specifically given to others as well as all the real and personal property bequeathed to his mother during her life. In addition, Henry was to receive all of the "altar plate," one-third of the household plate, and the residue of his father's personal estate. The remaining two-thirds of the household plate and the bulk of the landed estate — some 30,825 acres in Baltimore County — the Settler bequeathed to his two

3. CCS, will, Dec. 1, 1718, Prerogative Court Wills, liber 16, fol. 176. The children of CCS and Mary Darnall Carroll were Charles (b., d. 1695), Charles (b., d. 1696), Henry (1697–1719), Eleanor (b., d. 1699), Bridget (b., d. 1701), Charles (1702–1782), Anthony (b., d. 1705), Daniel (1707–1734), Mary (1711–1739), and Eleanor (1712–1730). Genealogical Files, Charles Carroll of Carrollton Papers, MdHi. See genealogical chart C, "Descendants of Charles Carroll the Settler: Charles Carroll of Annapolis's Line," Appendix 6, below.

4. Before his matriculation at Gray's Inn in Sept. 1718, Henry had studied at the College of the English Jesuits at St. Omer from at least 1713 to 1716 and then at Douai. See Joseph Foster, ed., *Register of Admissions to Gray's Inn, 1521–1889*, Collectanea Genealogica, II, no. 1 ([London], 1889), 135, 363; Geoffrey Holt, *St. Omers and Bruges Colleges, 1593–1773: A Biographical Dictionary*, Catholic Record Society, LXIX ([London], 1979), 59; Geoffrey Holt, ed., *The Letter Book of Lewis Sabran, S.J. (Rector of St. Omers College), October 1713 to October 1715*, Catholic Record Society, LXII ([London], 1971), 65–66; *Records of the Scots Colleges at Douai, Rome, Madrid, Vallodolid, and Ratisbon, I, Register of Students* ([Aberdeen], 1906), 69.

During the eighteenth century, Catholics were permitted to enter the Inns of Court but could not be called to the bar. A similar situation prevailed at Cambridge University. Catholics could attend the institution but were not allowed to graduate unless they subscribed to the Church of England's Thirty-nine Articles, which denied major principles of Catholicism. At Oxford subscription to the articles had to occur before enrolling. Colin Haydon, *Anti-Catholicism in Eighteenth-Century England, c. 1714–80* (Manchester, 1993), 204.

"A Well-Regulated Œconomy"

younger sons, Charles and Daniel, "to be equally divided share and share alike."[5]

The death of Henry Carroll in the spring of 1719, on board the ship that was returning him to Maryland from his studies abroad, altered the personnel but not the intent of the Settler's plans. He did not revise his will during the fifteen months between Henry's death and his own, the news of which reached his younger sons Charles, now "heir at law," and Daniel at Douai in the summer of 1720. Forced by the Settler's demise to put aside his dream of studying law at the Inns of Court, Charles departed for Maryland, leaving Daniel behind to complete his education. Arriving in Annapolis at some time before January 1721, he joined his mother's household and placed himself under the guidance of his first cousin and godfather, James Carroll, the active trustee of the Settler's estate.[6]

With the Settler's help, James had set out to make a fortune of his own in Maryland. His success did not match his uncle's but was nonetheless considerable, and, by the time of his death in 1729, he possessed more than seven thousand acres of land and a personal estate worth at least three thousand pounds sterling. Like the Settler, James did not restrict himself to planting; he also took advantage of other opportunities, serving as rent roll keeper for both the Eastern and Western Shores from 1707 until 1729. His salary from this relatively minor proprietary post amounted to about forty pounds sterling a year, and,

5. CCS, Dec. 1, 1718, will, Prerogative Court Wills, liber 16, fol. 176. Among the Baltimore County lands was Doohoragen Manor (later in Anne Arundel County) as well as the tracts of Ely O'Carroll, Litterluna, and Clinmalira. The Settler also gave each of his younger sons a lot in Annapolis.

6. CCA to CC, July 14, 1760, Carroll-McTavish Papers, MdHi; CCA to Clement Hill, Dec. 24, 1761, CCA, letterbook 1757–1761, fol. 98; *Records of the Scots Colleges,* I, *Students,* 69. Although *Records of Scots Colleges* suggests that Daniel left with his brother in August 1720, accounts kept by Charles Carroll of Annapolis show that Daniel did not return to Maryland until the spring of 1726. CCA's arrival in Maryland is deduced from the first entry, which is dated Jan. 3, 1720/1. Charles Carroll, "An Old Cash Book and Accots: raised in 1749 with People indebted to John Digges whose Bonds are assigned to C: Carroll," fols. 1, 9, Manuscripts Division, DLC. I am grateful to Lorena S. Walsh for bringing the existence of this account book to my attention.

In addition to his sons, who were to be the executors of his estate, the Settler appointed four "overseers and trustees": his brothers-in-law Henry Darnall II (1682–1759) and Benjamin Hall (1667–1721) and his "kinsmen" Daniel Carroll I of Upper Marlboro (1696–1751) and James Carroll. CCS, Dec. 1, 1718, will, Prerogative Court Wills, liber 16, fol. 176.

though he was not always able to collect the cash owed him, James did receive two sizable grants of land — approximately ten thousand acres, most of which he sold. Among his most lucrative ventures were his mercantile pursuits: he served as a factor for English tobacco firms, conducted moneylending operations, was active in the dry goods business, and invested profitably in the slave trade.[7]

Upon the Settler's death, James assumed control of his estate, and during Charles's minority he continued to make the important financial decisions while he schooled the inexperienced young man in the methods of Chesapeake commerce and agriculture. For his part, Charles willingly accepted his godfather's patient and careful guidance and made his gratitude for it abundantly clear. In June 1723, shortly after his twenty-first birthday, Charles gave James a prime lot in Annapolis to "Acknowledge," as he stated in the deed, the "Naturall Love and Affection he Doth beare unto him the said James Carroll."[8] In addition to dispensing the lessons in frugality that produced in his godson a lifelong commitment to a "well-regulated œconomy," James also influenced Charles by the strength of his personal conduct in ways that were more subtle but equally enduring. Dedicated to the service of the family as his foremost ideal, James pursued tenaciously, though without the Settler's flamboyance, the wealth that enabled him to provide for his relatives, particularly his nephews in Ireland. In 1761, more than thirty years after James's death, Charles would describe his own life in very similar terms: "I have since the time I came from School in 1720 to the year 1757 been a constant Servant to my family."[9] In his single-minded quest, James never married, setting an example that Charles took to heart and ultimately interpreted in a remarkable way.

7. Testamentary Papers, 1730–1736, box 35, folder 39, MdAA; Donnell MacClure Owings, *His Lordship's Patronage: Offices of Profit in Colonial Maryland* (Baltimore, 1953), 88–89, 176. I am indebted to Lorena S. Walsh for alerting me to James Carroll's service as a factor for Thomas Colmore. Carroll's other pursuits are noted in James Carroll's day book, Special Collections Division, Georgetown University Library, Washington, D.C.

8. Anne Arundel County Deeds, liber R.C.W. no. 2, fol. 177, MdAA. The property, number 33 on the 1718 Stoddert map, was located on the corner of Market and South East Streets (James Stoddert, "Plan of Annapolis, 24 July 1718," copied by Harry A. H. Ewald, Apr. 10, 1956, reproduced in Morris L. Radoff, *The State House at Annapolis* [Annapolis, Md., 1972], 13). At the time, lots in Annapolis regularly sold for more than twenty pounds sterling.

9. James Carroll, Feb. 12, 1728, will, Prerogative Court Wills, box C, folder 13 (a printed version appears in Rowland, *Life of Charles Carroll*, II, 382–385); CCA to Clement Hill, Dec. 24, 1761, CCA, letterbook 1757–1761, fol. 98.

"A Well-Regulated Œconomy"

The sole surviving record of the years Charles spent under James's tutelage is a cashbook in which the younger man recorded various kinds of disbursements over a twenty-one-year period beginning in 1721. The earliest entries, 1721–1724, indicate that Charles initially concentrated on his father's mercantile business in Annapolis, which brought him into contact with the capital's elite, including Governor Charles Calvert, upon whose store account he received a payment in August 1723.[10] Other notations show that he participated in the West Indian trade: in June 1724, he settled with ship's captain Clement Brooke for "the freight of goods from Barbadoes," and the following October he paid Brooke £19 to make purchases upon returning to that island. The cashbook also offers several glimpses of Charles's service to his family. Early in 1723 he recorded that he had spent £2.12.0 on a "new years gift" for his sisters, a present that might have marked their departure, under the care of their uncle Henry Darnall II, for a school at Liège run by the English Canonesses of the Holy Sepulchre. "When it was proper to bring them home," he recalled many years later, "I could not prudently trust them to strangers, I went for them & bore my own Expences." The cost of the trip — £194.0.10 ¾, which Charles's entry notes as being taken "out of the scrutore" on May 11, 1725 — represented his largest single expenditure during the 1720s.[11] By the middle of that decade, however, he had commenced an endeavor that would entail, by the time he completed it in the 1730s, considerably more expense, namely, the construction of a house of his own adjacent to the Settler's frame dwelling where his mother resided.

In a very real sense, the residence Charles Carroll of Annapolis erected served as an accurate indicator of his maturing personality. A story and a half on the north, where its main entrance looked out from beneath a gambrel roof onto Duke of Gloucester Street, the dwelling presented its most imposing facade to its southern, waterfront side. There the slope of the terrain made possible an-

10. Carroll, "Old Cash Book," fol. 3. Charles Calvert (d. 1733/4), the proprietor's cousin, succeeded John Hart as governor in 1720 and held the office until 1727, when Lord Baltimore's brother Benedict Leonard Calvert (1700–1732) replaced him. Edward C. Papenfuse et al., eds., *A Biographical Dictionary of the Maryland Legislature, 1635–1789* (Baltimore, 1979–1985), I, 185, 188; Owings, *His Lordship's Patronage,* 120–121.

11. Carroll, "Old Cash Book," fols. 5, 6, 7, 8; CCA to Hill, Dec. 24, 1761, CCA, letterbook 1757–1761, fol. 98. The "two Miss Carols" attended the school for perhaps two and a half years beginning Apr. 5, 1723, and two misses Darnall were there from 1721/2 until at least 1723/4. "Records of the English Canonesses of the Holy Sepulchre at Liège, now at New Hall, Essex, 1652–1793," in Richard Trappes-Lomax, ed., *Miscellanea,* X, Catholic Record Society, XVII (London, 1915), 208–209.

other story at ground level, assuring that no one approaching Annapolis by ship would fail to notice the presence of an edifice far more substantial and impressive than most of the structures that composed the little town's scraggly landscape. One of the few brick buildings in the capital, Carroll's plain, solidly built, four-bay house unmistakably asserted that its occupant did not mean to be overlooked.[12]

Some of Charles Carroll's ledger notations for the early 1720s hint that he briefly toyed with the idea of becoming a dandy — in May and June 1723 he spent nearly £6 on fencing lessons, and in June of the following year he paid a Mr. Thomson £1.13.0 "for Musick." If so, he put any such proclivities aside forever once he, along with his mother, had brought his sisters and his younger brother, Daniel, safely home from Europe at the beginning of 1726. Indeed, Daniel's presence in Maryland might well have offered Charles the opportunity to forgo a social role he did not really desire in favor of immersing himself in the management of his family's affairs, a task for which he was both well prepared and temperamentally better suited. Few as they are, the cashbook entries for 1726 lend credence to such a speculation: the expenditures recorded for nineteen-year-old Daniel include payments for a loss at cards and "raffling at the fair" and the remarkable sum of £23 spent to buy him a horse. It is conceivable that, in seeing Daniel so well mounted, Charles intended to enhance his brother's marriageability. If so, the investment certainly paid off, for in 1728, the year he turned twenty-one, Daniel wed eighteen-year-old Ann Rozer (1710–1764), a well-provisioned heiress. The only offspring of Notley Rozer (1673–1727) and his first wife, Jane Digges Rozer, and an orphan by the time of her marriage, Ann brought her husband considerable property, most notably the 1,326-acre tract of Prince George's County land called Duddington Manor that is today the location of the United States Capitol.[13]

12. Although the Settler's frame house had been destroyed by the mid-nineteenth century, his son's extensively remodeled residence remains part of present-day Annapolis. Dendrochronological tests performed on the building in 1989, as part of its continuing restoration, indicate that the wood in the oldest part of the structure came from trees felled in 1721. Ledger entries listing disbursements for building supplies for "C.C. Brick House" cover the period 1723–1735 and further reveal that, by the early 1730s, a passageway connecting the brick house and the frame dwelling had been constructed. The original appearance of Charles Carroll's brick house probably resembled the c. 1730 residence on Prince George Street, known as the John Brice II house. Charles Carroll, Sr., of Annapolis and Doughoregan, account book, c. 1730–1757, MdHi.

13. Carroll, "Old Cash Book," fols. 4, 5, 8, 9. The cost of the horse included ferriage from Kent County to Annapolis. Even so, the price still seems excessive, especially when

During their short union of six years — Daniel died in April 1734 at the age of twenty-seven — the young couple lived graciously as well as comfortably. Duddington Manor, from which Daniel took the appellation "of Duddington" that subsequently distinguished succeeding generations of his family, was divided into eight quarters housing a total of ninety-three slaves, a third of whom were working hands. The Home House, attended by five adult slaves, contained all of the items that marked great wealth. The family slept on feather beds covered with fine Holland sheets, sat at their walnut desk and tea and dining tables in an assortment of leather chairs, and enjoyed meals well above the common fare from their well-equipped kitchen. Daniel's ownership of a spinet, a violin, and a library of some one hundred books, a third of them in French, suggests he led a cultured life that reflected his European education. He dressed fashionably in expensive coats and britches, silk vests, and silver-buckled shoes, with a "Silver hilted Sword" to complete his sartorial splendor. Besides these material blessings, Daniel's brief marriage also produced three children. A son, Charles, was born in 1729, followed in 1732 and 1733 by daughters Eleanor and Mary, to whom their uncle's cashbook refers fondly as "Miss Nelly" and "Miss Molly."[14]

What we can glean of the elder Carroll brother during the late 1720s reveals a man of serious purpose, intent on minding his family's business rather than on partaking of social pleasures. To begin with, the names by which he came to be known — Charles Carroll of Annapolis and Charles Carroll, Esquire — suggest a no-nonsense practicality and lack the manorial grandeur associated with the appellation Daniel chose. An incident during the late 1720s reinforces the impression of a young man intensely devoted to the protection of his own interests. In 1726, the Maryland assembly, to arrest an alarming decline in the price of the tobacco, proposed a bill to curtail its production: all tobacco judged to be of an inferior quality would be burned. Since this method of supply control

___

compared to the £7.3.0 spent in 1732 for a horse for Mrs. Carroll. Ibid., fol. 40.

Devised to Notley Rozer by his godfather Thomas Notley (1634–1679), Duddington Manor was originally known as Cerne Abbey Manor, a tract that incorporated three parcels — New Troy, Duddington Pasture, and Duddington Manor. In addition to her property, Ann Rozer also possessed impeccable genealogical credentials. Both her maternal grandmother and her paternal step-grandmother were stepdaughters of Charles Calvert, third Lord Baltimore. CCA to Henry Darnall and William Digges, Apr. 13, 1733, Provincial Court, Deeds, liber P.L. no. 8, fol. 140, MdAA; Papenfuse et al., eds., *Biographical Dictionary*, I, 271–272, II, 707–724.

14. Inventory, Daniel Carroll of Duddington, ledger X, Carroll-McTavish Papers; Carroll, "Old Cash Book," fol. 49. In March 1733, Charles recorded an expenditure of twelve shillings for "a childs Cradel for my B." "Old Cash Book," fol. 40.

Charles Carroll's Residence

PLATE 11. The Carrolls' Annapolis Residence. *Detail from [Edward] Sachse,*
View of Annapolis *(Baltimore, c. 1850).*
Courtesy Maryland State Archives, MSA SC 1195

would inevitably assist the colony's wealthier planters at the expense of their poorer counterparts, the lower house sought to mitigate the latter's distress by insisting that the law also provide for a one-third reduction in all tobacco debts. The attempt to placate a variety of contending interests pleased none of them and instead provoked considerable anger and unrest throughout the colony. After a two-year deadlock, the upper and lower houses finally managed to pass a tobacco law in 1728, but it was never enforced, and in 1730 the proprietor's objections forced its repeal.[15]

Charles Carroll of Annapolis became publicly immersed in the heated controversy while the bill was before the legislature in July 1726 — and he did so in

15. Vertrees J. Wyckoff, *Tobacco Regulation in Colonial Maryland,* Johns Hopkins University Studies in Historical and Political Science, N.S., XX (Baltimore, 1936), 140–147.

"A Well-Regulated Œconomy"

a style worthy of the Settler. So strongly did he favor raising the price of tobacco, even at the expense of a one-third reduction in the tobacco debts owed to him, that he challenged James Hollyday of Talbot County, a delegate who opposed a tobacco law, to a duel. Equally exercised, Hollyday accepted the challenge, but, before they came to blows, the assembly intervened and chastised both men for their intemperate conduct. Reprimanded for breaching the security of the house by challenging a sitting member to a duel, Carroll was ordered to apologize and directed to guarantee his future good behavior by posting security bonds of two thousand pounds sterling. And, until such time as he fulfilled these conditions, he was remanded to the custody of the sergeant at arms! The assembly proceedings recorded Carroll's response: he would apologize for offending the house, but, rather than post the bonds, he would remain in custody.[16]

Carroll's behavior in this instance hightlights the traits that dominated his personality throughout the rest of his life: a fierce determination to defend his interests, a defiant refusal to bow to any man or group of men, and a congenital distaste for parting with any of his money. A fourth characteristic — tenacity — is readily apparent in his actions during the same period with regard to the tenants on St. Clement's and Bashford Manors, two large St. Mary's County tracts purchased by his father encompassing some 13,500 acres. In acquiring these properties, the Settler had gained the right, as lord of the manor, to collect perpetual fixed-fee rents on all freeholds within the bounds of the purchase and to sell or rent any parcels not already granted. By 1728, however, income from these manors had virtually stopped; when Charles Carroll of Annapolis tried to reinstate a regular system of collecting rents, the tenants not only refused to pay but also disputed the legitimacy of the demand. A report from Carroll's steward Joshua Doyne in February 1729 reveals the tactics of their resistance: "I have called the Tenants of St. Clement's Manor to the Manor House four Severall times of which this day is the last butt really very few have as yett brought any Corne, tho' Severall have promised, other's again grumble, butt none as yett doe absolutely refuse beside Mr. Forbes & the rest Chiseldynes heirs butt Severall have never appear'd upon notice given att the Manor house."[17] Undeterred by

---

16. Browne et al., eds., *Archives of Maryland*, XXXV, 557. Carroll's actions clearly made a lasting impression. In October 1728, a deposition taken from Edward Harris of Queen Anne's County regarding a barroom brawl between supporters and opponents of tobacco legislation stated that one of the instigators of the melee had reminded the other participants of how "Mr. Carroll bullied and Scared Mr. Holliday some time ago about a Tobacco Law." Ibid., XXXVI, 144–146.

17. Joshua Doyne to CCA, Feb. 7, 1728/9, Carroll-Maccubbin Papers, MdHi.

such recalcitrance, Carroll persisted, making several trips to St. Mary's County himself and ordering Doyne to continue his efforts to collect the corn and tobacco due. Gradually, threats of distraint sales and evictions brought about a grudging resumption of payments; and, although the sums involved, thirty-eight to forty-seven pounds a year, never constituted a major source of revenue, Carroll continued his battle to extract them into the 1760s. Clearly, this was a man who intended to derive the maximum benefit from his possessions.

During the 1730s Charles Carroll of Annapolis began to develop strategies to build his fortune, and by the end of the decade he had constructed the economic framework he used for the rest of his life. As in his father's case, Charles's career shows that a series of personal losses ultimately benefited his endeavors. The first of these was the death of James Carroll in June 1729. Then, between 1730 and 1742, Charles's two sisters, his brother Daniel, and his mother also died, leaving him the sole survivor among the Settler's original heirs and the administrator of their estates in behalf of Daniel's children. Family mortality shaped Charles's activities in several ways. While it is true that the administration of the Settler's estate had legally devolved upon him when he reached the age of twenty-one in 1723, his mentor James's demise probably prompted him to reassess both the obligations and the opportunities associated with his administrative responsibilities. At any rate, subsequent records indicate that he employed two different methods in dealing with the legacies of the Settler's heirs. With regard to the property left to his mother and sisters, he confined himself to acting as an agent, accepting the rents, debts, and interest due to them and making for them whatever payments were required for their living and other expenses. For these services, he charged commissions against their estate accounts as provided by law — 5 percent for receiving and remitting. By contrast, he handled the devises to himself and his brother Daniel like capital investments, opting for judicious development designed to produce solid, long-term gains. He had, with Daniel's obvious concurrence, treated their inheritances as a unit, and he considered himself authorized to continue this practice after 1734 as trustee of his brother's estate and after 1750 by the specific request of the heir at law.[18] When he finally initiated a settlement with Daniel's heirs in 1757, however, Charles Carroll of An-

18. "Charles Carroll, Jr. [of Annapolis], Draft of a Reply to Complainant his Uncle Charles Carroll re Properties from the Estates of Daniel Carroll, deceased [brother of Complainant] and Mary Carroll, deceased [mother of Complainant]," [c. 1767], Daniel Carroll of Duddington Papers, Manuscripts Division, DLC. Although the Library of Congress identifies Charles Carroll, Jr., as "of Annapolis," the author of this draft was Charles Carroll of Duddington and not CCA.

"A Well-Regulated Œconomy"

napolis became embroiled in an exceedingly bitter dispute over the motives as well as the methods of his long stewardship. It is safe to say that the former would not have been called into question if the latter had not been so blatantly successful.

From the six different occupations upon which the Settler had focused his efforts — land speculation, moneylending, mercantile activities, officeholding, the practice of law, and planting — Charles Carroll of Annapolis pursued only two, agriculture and banking. Unlike officeholding and the practice of law, which were beyond the reach of Roman Catholics, Carroll's decision to discontinue his father's mercantile operations at the end of the 1720s and to refrain from land speculation, except on a very limited basis, appears to have been calculated. In their place, he added an entirely new economic venture: on October 1, 1731, he and Daniel joined their Irish kinsman Dr. Charles Carroll (1691–1755) and two of Maryland's wealthiest and most powerful men, Benjamin Tasker, Sr. (1690–1768), and Daniel Dulany, Sr. (1685–1753), in capitalizing the province's second ironworks, the Baltimore Company.[19]

Each partner made an initial investment of seven hundred pounds sterling. The source of the Carroll brothers' funds is unknown; their contribution presumably was drawn from their inheritances and perhaps from the liquidation of the Settler's mercantile assets, which were more than sufficient to cover the required advance. Far clearer is the motivation of the Carrolls and of their partners for investing in the ironworks: the tobacco trade had been locked in an acute depression since the mid-1720s, and by the early 1730s the stagnation's corrosive effect on Maryland's economy was painfully evident. Attributing "the exceeding Poverty of the People in general" to low tobacco prices, a visitor to the colony in 1732 noted that "the Makers" of the staple "have been brought to the want of many of the Necessarys of Life, & by their neglecting other things, & Trusting solely to that, in hopes of an Amendm[en]t in its Value, They seem now almost reduced to an Incapacity of Carrying on any considerable Trade Whatsoever."[20]

19. Benjamin Tasker, CCA, Daniel Dulany, Daniel Carroll of Duddington, and Dr. Charles Carroll, Oct. 1, 1731, partnership agreement, Colonial Collection, oversize, MdHi. The Principio Company, Maryland's first ironworks, was in operation in Cecil County by 1720, but, unlike the Baltimore Company, its financing came from abroad. Michael Warren Robbins, "The Principio Company: Ironmaking in Colonial Maryland, 1780–1781" (Ph.D. diss., George Washington University, 1972), 2–3, 24, 26.

20. Browne et al., eds., *Archives of Maryland*, XXXVII, 588–589. This assessment was made by William Janssen, Lord Baltimore's brother-in-law.

More enterprising than the general run of planters in contending with these circumstances, the prospective partners thoroughly explored the various dimensions of organizing and operating an ironworks before launching their project. In the spring of 1731, six months before the venture was incorporated, Charles Carroll of Annapolis traveled to Virginia to consult with Colonel Alexander Spotswood (1676–1740), a former governor of that colony and the highly successful proprietor of several ironworks. Maryland's former governor Charles Calvert accompanied Carroll on the trip and provided his entrée to Spotswood.[21]

From its first sales in 1734 the Baltimore Company proved a sound investment, and by 1736 the partners were sanguine enough to increase their initial commitment of £3,500 sterling to approximately £11,200. The Carroll brothers' share of the additional £7,700 amounted to £3,080. To meet the capital requirements of their expanding enterprise, the partners reinvested all profits received from sales, a practice they continued until about 1750. With profits surging by the middle of that decade, Charles Carroll of Annapolis began drawing annual revenues of more than £300 sterling; by the mid-1760s, his portion averaged £400 per year.[22]

Charles Carroll of Annapolis initiated a similarly adventurous and profitable

21. For Spotswood's career and his importance to the founding of the Baltimore Company, see Keach Johnson, "The Genesis of the Baltimore Ironworks," *Journal of Southern History*, XIX (1953), 177–178, and Johnson, "The Baltimore Company Seeks English Markets: A Study of the Anglo-American Iron Trade, 1731–1755," *WMQ*, 3d Ser., XVI (1959), 35, 41; Lester J. Cappon, *Iron Works at Tuball: Terms and Conditions for Their Lease as Stated by Alexander Spotswood on the Twentieth Day of July 1739* (Charlottesville, Va., 1945), 10. Calvert's presence on the trip is confirmed by entries in Carroll, "Old Cash Book," fol. 40.

22. The commitment of the five investors as recorded in the Baltimore Company's 1736 stock account was £14,385.4.0 3/4 gold and £2,873 currency (Carroll, "Old Cash Book"). Carroll attributed the company's improving profits in part to the hiring of his cousin Richard Croxall as manager. "Our disbursements were very great and our profits very small," he wrote in the late 1750s, "untill Mr. Croxall had the management which was in 1746 or 1747" (Remarks appended to CCA to Clement Hill and Basil Waring, Oct. 19, 1761, CCA, letterbook 1757–1761, fol. 65). For the partners' method of financing the company's growth, see Johnson, "The Baltimore Company Seeks English Markets," *WMQ*, 3d Ser., XVI (1959), 51, 52n; Baltimore Company, Jan. 24, 1731–Mar. 18, 1774 minute book, Carroll-Maccubbin Papers; Clement Hill and Basil Waring, "Answer to Mr. Carroll's Bill," [ca. 1763], Clement Hill Papers, MdHi; and the Baltimore Company accounts in Carroll, "Old Cash Book." For CCA's Baltimore Company income in the mid-1760s, see CCA to CC, Jan. 9, 1764, Carroll Papers, MS 206, MdHi.

"A Well-Regulated Œconomy"

system in cultivating the landed portion of the Settler's estate. The provisions of his father's will enabled him to begin his career as a Chesapeake planter as the master of four agricultural establishments, all in rudimentary stages of development. The largest of these, both in acreage and labor force, was the 10,000-acre Doohoragen Manor, where almost half of the Settler's slaves (46 of 112) resided. Twenty were probably working hands. The other large tracts of land — Poplar Island in the Chesapeake Bay (1,000 acres), and Western Branch (800 acres) and Enfield Chace (1,600 acres) in Prince George's County — contained the remaining 66 slaves.[23] None of these tracts was primarily devoted to tobacco culture, but instead produced a mix of that staple, grains, and livestock. The weak tobacco market of the 1720s compared to the strength of the West Indies provisioning trade probably accounted for this pattern.

There is no evidence during the 1720s that Charles Carroll of Annapolis altered the form of agricultural operations established by his father, but in the mid-1730s he initiated an innovative strategy to bring more of his vast landed inheritance into cultivation. Rather than increasing his slave work force, the means preferred by expanding planters, Carroll recruited tenant labor from Ireland and Germany.[24]

Several precedents within Carroll's experience might have influenced his decision. James Carroll, as rent roll keeper, was well aware of the tenanting of the proprietary manors that began in Maryland early in the eighteenth century. By then, the idea of manorial tenantry was nearly as old as the colony, the Lords Baltimore and a few other investors having started to reserve lands for such a possibility in the 1600s. Although these efforts initially made little headway, the proprietary establishment had begun to realize some success by the 1730s, when Carroll commenced renting land. As of 1733, the first year for which a complete list of proprietary tenants survives, more than 24,369 acres on fifteen propri-

23. Patented in 1702 as seven thousand acres, Doohoragen was resurveyed in 1707 as ten thousand. Land Office, Warrants, liber A.A., fol. 43, MdAA. CCA's mother, Madam Mary Carroll, received an income from the crops of corn, wheat, tobacco, and livestock produced on Enfield Chace until her death in 1742. What role, if any, the tract subsequently played in CCA's overall agricultural scheme is unknown; in 1759 he sold the plantation to Benjamin Tasker for £1,327 sterling. Account Book of Charles Carroll, Sr., of Annapolis and Doughoregan, c. 1730–1757, n.p., MdHi; CCA to Clement Hill, Aug. 5, 1761, CCA, letterbook 1757–1761, fols. 13–14; Provincial Court, Deeds, liber B.T. no. 1, fols. 401–407.

24. CCA, remarks addressed to Clement Hill and Basil Waring, Mar. 11, 1761, CCA, letterbook 1757–1761, fol. 27.

etary manors had been leased to 148 tenants. Similarly, Virginia's Governor Spotswood, whom Carroll consulted about ironworks, had tenanted slightly fewer than 15,000 acres with 104 renters by the early 1730s.[25] The Jesuits also had farmed their 3,500-acre tract, Cedar Point Neck, near Portobacco in Prince George's County, with tenants since 1652, and, by the fourth decade of the eighteenth century, the estate contained twenty tenements of 200 acres or fewer leased to renters on long-term leases. Whatever his inspiration, Charles Carroll's scheme proved enormously successful as a way of developing land quickly while conserving capital. Over the next twenty years, he negotiated nearly 200 leases and brought more than 19,000 acres into production.[26]

Carroll began with a ten-thousand-acre frontier tract lying between the Potomac and Monocacy Rivers that he had patented as Carrollton in 1723. By December 1733, he was drawing up leases for some fifty-two prospective tenants. Seven of these agreements survive, all for twenty-one years. The terms specified cash rents that doubled every seven years, beginning with an annual levy of 8s 4d sterling a year for the initial period and rising to 16s 8d sterling for the second and £1.13.4 for the third, excluding quitrents. If a tenant fell more than forty days behind in his payments, his delinquency entitled Carroll to distrain — to sell his possessions and keep from the proceeds the amount due. The leases also obligated tenants to plant an orchard and to keep their dwellings and tobacco barns in good repair. However, contracts for renting land on Carrollton did not restrict the number of laborers that could be employed on the tenements, an op-

25. Gregory A. Stiverson, *Poverty in a Land of Plenty: Tenancy in Eighteenth-Century Maryland* (Baltimore, 1977), 3–9; Leonidas Dodson, *Alexander Spotswood Governor of Colonial Virginia, 1710–1722* (Philadelphia, 1932), 299. Spotswood's interest in tenantry was evident as early as 1714, when he seated some forty Germans, abandoned by their original benefactor, at Germanna on the Rappahannock River (277).

26. Long-term leases extended through three lives — those of the original lessee, his wife, and a child (Lorena S. Walsh, "Land, Landlord, and Leaseholder: Estate Management and Tenant Fortunes in Southern Maryland, 1642–1820," *Agricultural History*, LIX [1985], 374–375). Dr. Walsh is responsible for the definitive scholarship on tenancy in the Chesapeake. I have also relied on her essay "Plantation Management in the Chesapeake, 1620–1820," *Journal of Economic History*, XLIX (1989), 393–406, and "'To Labour for Profit': Plantation Management in the Chesapeake, 1620–1820," MS, which she generously made available. Also useful are Lois Green Carr, "County Government in Maryland, 1689–1709" (Ph.D. diss., Harvard University, 1968), chap. 7; Edward C. Papenfuse, Jr., "Planter Behavior and Economic Opportunity in a Staple Economy," *Ag. Hist.*, XLVI (1972), 297–312. Willard F. Bliss's essay "The Rise of Tenancy in Virginia," *Virginia Magazine of History and Biography*, LVIII (1950), 429–441, is less helpful for the period before 1770, as it focuses primarily on tenancy during the final quarter of the eighteenth century.

"A Well-Regulated Œconomy"

tion unique to that frontier settlement. As a result, some Carrollton tenants acquired slaves, and by the late 1750s several renters owned as many as eight.[27]

Having begun settling his remote "Monocasi" property, Charles Carroll of Annapolis turned next to his quarter on the Western Branch of the Patuxent River, in Prince George's County. Removing the slaves and livestock from this underdeveloped tract, he had by the end of 1734 rented the tract's eight hundred acres of prime tobacco land to eight tenants, all of whom received twenty-one-year leases. Not surprisingly, the Carrolls' arrangements with these leaseholders differed from those with the renters who undertook the more formidable task of carving farmsteads out of Carrollton's frontier wilderness. Carroll's Western Branch tenants contracted to pay their rents in "clean and merchantable tobacco" rather than in cash, varying from eight hundred to twelve hundred pounds per one-hundred-acre tenement, delivered "in a Convenient Cask" to the landing on the Eastern Branch of the Potomac River. During the next four years, Carroll used similar agreements to tenant three more Prince George's County tracts.[28]

27. Land Office, Patents, liber P.L. no. 5, fols. 566–567, MdAA; Carroll, "Old Cash Book," fol. 48. For Carrollton leases, see Prince George's County, Land Records, liber T., fols. 161–173, MdAA. Tenants on proprietary manors and manors belonging to the Jesuits were required to pay for and erect their dwellings and outbuildings. Entries in Carroll's cashbook for the 1730s indicate that he bore this cost on some of his tenanted properties, but there is no specific information on whether he did so on Carrollton Manor. Stiverson, *Poverty in a Land of Plenty,* 11; Walsh, "Land, Landlord, and Leaseholder," *Ag. Hist.,* LIX (1985), 375; "Old Cash Book," fols. 56, 58–60, 68; CCA to Clement Hill, Dec. 24, 1761, CCA, letterbook 1757–1761, fol. 87; Mary C. Jeske, "Autonomy and Opportunity: Carrollton Manor Tenants, 1734–1790" (Ph.D. diss., University of Maryland, 1999), chaps. 1, 2. I am deeply indebted to Dr. Jeske for the information on tenant slaveholding.

28. Prince George's County, Land Records, liber T., fols. 260–270. As Lois Carr has pointed out, the fertile soil in the Western Branch watershed still produces tobacco today. "County Government in Maryland," 566–570.

The foregoing chronology of development is based upon entries in CCA's cashbook combined with recorded leases in the county land records. The vast majority of these agreements were for twenty-one years, although two tenants on the Girles Portion secured leases for three lives. Because not all leases were recorded — recording being by the choice and at the expense of the tenant (Walsh, "Land, Landlord, and Leaseholder," *Ag. Hist.,* LIX [1985], 387n) — the information from the sources may not always appear to coincide. For example, CCA paid two pounds to have agreements prepared for Eastern Branch (Clouen Couse) on Mar. 24, 1735 ("Old Cash Book," fol. 54), but the first recorded lease on that tract bears the date June 25, 1740 (Prince George's County, Land Records, liber Y., fols. 214–215). For recorded leases on Clouen Couse, the Girles Portion, and Darnall's Goodwill, see Prince George's County, Land Records, liber Y., fols. 139–140,

Daniel Carroll's death on April 15, 1734, shortly after the initial Carrollton leases were signed, gave a broader scope as well as an additional impetus to Charles Carroll of Annapolis's agricultural schemes. Besides his twenty-four-year-old wife Ann, Daniel left three children, all under the age of six, for whose support his will made Charles, as trustee of the estate, responsible. The youthful widow remarried quickly: by 1736 she had not only taken a second husband, Benjamin Young (d. 1754), but had also begun another family by bearing him a son.[29] Ann's new status did not affect Charles's role with regard to her Carroll children, however, nor did it mitigate the expense of maintaining them. Fortunately, the steady increase in income required to raise and educate Daniel's children properly meshed neatly with Charles's own ambitions, and, notwithstanding his view of himself as his family's servant, he fulfilled his obligations to his nephew and nieces in ways that were mutually beneficial.

Daniel's instructions regarding the disposition of his smaller tracts of land and his personal estate were straightforward: his wife was to retain their home, Duddington Manor, and its contents, except for his half of the Settler's plate, which was to go to their son. The rest of his goods and chattels together with all tracts of five hundred acres or fewer were to be sold and the proceeds invested in funds or stocks in England. The interest thus garnered, plus Daniel's share of the Baltimore Company's profits, would then be used to meet the children's needs. Convinced that he knew more advantageous ways of serving his brother's children, Charles Carroll of Annapolis chose not to follow those instructions to the letter. Although he did sell most of Daniel's smaller parcels of land over the next twenty to twenty-five years, he did not put the money received into English stocks, but instead lent it out in Maryland at higher rates. In defending his decision many years later, Carroll acknowledged that, had he done as his brother specified, "I might have saved myself much trouble." "But," he continued, "I knew their Money Kept at Interest here would be more beneficial to them," a contention he maintained that his records proved, even allowing for his carefully noted commissions for receiving and remitting.[30]

With regard to the greatest portion of his landed estate—his share of the

---

196–202, 214–215, 260–261, 398–400, 592–594, 602–603, 669–670, liber E.E., fol. 53, liber B.B. no. 1, fols. 318–319.

29. Ann Rozer Carroll's marriage to Benjamin Young produced a son (Notley [1736/7–1802]) and at least two daughters. Papenfuse et al., eds., *Biographical Dictionary*, II, 929.

30. Will of Daniel Carroll of Duddington, Apr. 12, 1734, Wills, Prince George's County, box 4, folder 50, MdAA; CCA to Hill, Dec. 24, 1761, CCA, letterbook 1757–1761, fol. 98.

"A Well-Regulated Œconomy"

more than thirty thousand acres that he and Charles had jointly inherited —
Daniel left no directions, an omission that suggests the brothers had already
agreed to continue their long-standing arrangement whereby Charles managed
these properties as a unit. At any rate, that is the course Charles pursued, and
within a year of Daniel's death he had taken steps to improve the largest — and
in his long-range plans the most important — of these tracts, Doohoragen. In
this instance, he relied upon a combination of slavery and tenantry, adding the
slaves he had removed from Western Branch in the fall of 1734 to the black population established at Doohoragen by his father, and agreeing in April 1735 with
thirteen tenants to whom he offered the same terms he had concluded with his
Western Branch leaseholders. At the same time, Carroll began the construction
of a one-and-a-half-story brick house, flanked on one side by a separate structure containing a kitchen, buttery, and storerooms, and on the other by a
matching "T-shaped" chapel, buildings that clearly indicated the significant future he had in mind for this plantation. By November 1737 he had initiated the
division of Doohoragen into quarters (eventually there were ten) and commenced distributing his increasing number of slaves among them.[31]

From the Baltimore County parcels whose ownership he shared with Daniel's
heirs, Charles Carroll of Annapolis selected three to bring under cultivation
through tenancy. He began in 1742 by leasing 100-acre tenements on Clinmalira,
the 5,000-acre tract that adjoined the proprietary family's manor Lord Baltimore's Gift, or My Lady's Manor. The six recorded leases surviving for 1742–
1745 differ from the agreements with the majority of tenants on his other tracts
in that all of them were long-term contracts for three lives rather than the
shorter variety he generally employed. His decision in this instance was most

31. Carroll, "Old Cash Book," fols. 55–56, 61; Anne Arundel County, Land Records,
liber R.B. no. 3, fols 137–141. Before the passage of Maryland's first tobacco inspection law
in 1747, Doohoragen tenants delivered their tobacco to Charles Carroll of Annapolis in
bulk to be prized in casks that he provided. CCA to Hill, Dec. 24, 1761, CCA, letterbook
1757–1761, fol. 87.

The house CCA built at Doohoragen is described in William Voss Elder III, "The Carroll House in Annapolis and Doughoregan Manor," in Ann C. Van Devanter, ed., "Anywhere so long as There Be Freedom": Charles Carroll of Carrollton, His Family, and His
Maryland (Baltimore, 1975), 74–78. The core of this dwelling is a four-room structure
that family tradition dates from 1717.

Payments for a midwife's attendance to slaves named Fanny and Grace in the spring
and fall of 1733 suggest the growth of Doohoragen's black population, as do disbursements in late November of that year for making a total of 117 children's shifts. Carroll,
"Old Cash Book," fols. 44, 48.

likely a response to the policies adopted on the neighboring proprietary manor to accommodate prospective renters. Aside from differences in length, the Clinmalira contracts were similar to the Prince George County leases, as were those Carroll drew up for two other Baltimore County tracts, Ely O'Carroll (1,000 acres) and Litterluna (1,300 acres).[32]

One aspect of Carroll's leases deserves particular comment: the decisive steps he took to preserve the fertility of his lands. Although his leasing practices were obviously motivated by a desire to secure a good return, Carroll's restrictions probably decreased his rental income in the short run but guaranteed the long-term productivity of his acreage by preventing its abuse. Provisions protecting timber and requiring the planting of orchards were common to most rental agreements, but Carroll's leases were unique in limiting, except on Carrollton, the amount of labor that could be employed on the tenement to the wives and children of the leaseholder, or, if wives and children could not work, to one additional hand. The sixty-three leases entered in county court records confirm Carroll's consistent use of such arrangements, and presumably the unrecorded agreements with the more than two hundred other tenants whose names appear in his ledgers embodied the same stipulations.

Nor did Carroll hesitate to enforce those regulations rigorously. Upon learning in the mid-1760s that several of his Carrollton tenants had ignored the restrictions concerning timber and cleared their acreage extensively in order to plant more crops, he added fifty acres to and increased the rent sharply for the affected tenements, with strict orders that henceforth trees could be taken only when needed for firewood and fencing. His explanation underscores his appre-

32. Carroll was certainly aware of the system of development employed on My Lady's Manor. Thomas Brerewood, Sr., the father-in-law of the fifth Lord Baltimore's sister Charlotte, began tenanting this tract with artisans and agricultural renters in 1734, offering both long- and short-term leases at annual rents of ten shillings per one hundred acres, the standard rate on proprietary manors (*Maryland Gazette* [Annapolis], July 19, 1734; Stiverson, *Poverty in a Land of Plenty,* 13). Robert Nelson Turner and Elmer Hutchins's well-researched, though unfootnoted, volume, *St. James of My Lady's Manor, 1750–1950* (Baltimore, 1950), is the most detailed history of this proprietary tract currently available.

The Clinmalira leases also required tenants to allow open access to any springs on their tenements, granted them the use of a gristmill if Carroll decided to build one, and directed them to supply Carroll with two capons annually, a stipulation that also applied to his Carrollton tenants by the mid-1760s. (Baltimore County, Land Records, liber T.B. no. C, fols. 371, 392, 418–420, 457–461, no. D, fol. 425, MdAA; CCA, Account Book and Index, 1754–1784, MdHi). For leases on Ely O'Carroll and Litterluna, see Baltimore County, Land Records, liber B.B. no. 1, fol. 640.

ciation for both the land's capacity and its vulnerability: "Had they [the trans-gressing tenants] acted honestly and used my land as they would have used it had it been their own, they would not have been under the necessity of adding 50 a[cres] to their old tenements, but as they destroyed my timber by deadening it and over running their tenements[,] common prudence obliges me not to suffer them to do so again." When informed that some tenants found his policy harsh, he tersely averred, "I might with reason and justice have turned of[f] such tenants and made two tenements out of one by granting the 50 a[cres] of cleared land to one tenant and 50 to another, adding to each 50 a[cres] of wood land, so that instead of complaining they ought to be thankful they are not turned of[f]." [33]

How well did Carroll's system of land development work? Measured either by the amount of acreage brought into production or by the revenues thereby generated, the answer is exceedingly well. In addition to the 12,553 acres that Carrollton comprised by 1746, Carroll targeted 21,286 acres of the Settler's landed estate for development. [34] By 1756 he had tenanted just more than half of this property (56 percent): 9,942 acres of the 16,709 belonging solely to him, and 8,900 acres of the 17,130 he chose for improvement from the acreage he held in common with Daniel's heirs. Moreover, he initiated and encouraged cultivation using leases of twenty-one years or less. Of the 195 tenants on Carroll lands by 1765, only 14 (7 percent) can be identified as holders of leases for lives. By comparison, other Chesapeake landlords found themselves locked into the "life lease system" until the late 1750s, when the death of tenants finally allowed them to employ more immediately lucrative rental strategies. [35] By that time, most of the

33. CCA's responses to notes on tenants, [c. Sept. 1766], Carroll Papers, MS 216, MdHi.

34. A resurvey of Carrollton conducted in the mid-1740s added 2,553 acres to the original 10,000-acre tract. Thos. Gittens, Dec. 1, 1744, plat of pretensions on Charles Carroll of Annapolis's land, Carrollton; Josa. Beal, 1744, field notes for Carrollton; field notes for the resurvey of Carrollton, Mar. 26, 1745, all in Carroll-McTavish Papers; certificate of the Addition to Carrollton, Oct. 5, 1746, Carroll-Maccubbin Papers.

35. Walsh, "Land, Landlord, and Leaseholder," Ag. Hist., LIX (1985), 375, 386. Unlike short-term leases, which served the landlord's interests by guaranteeing opportunities to renew at higher rents as development progressed, leases for lives benefited the tenant by providing several important advantages — "long term security, a salable asset, an inheritance for at least one child, and the same political privileges afforded to freeholders" (ibid., 375–376). In other respects, the fourteen three-lives leases are identical to the agreements recorded by other Carroll renters on the same tracts. Not all of Carroll's tenants went to the trouble and expense of recording their leases. Walsh surmises that leaseholders who were willing to bear the cost of that transaction probably did so because they

leases Carroll had executed in the 1730s had already expired, and he had relet the majority of his tenements "at will" (that is, on annually renewable leases) and at higher rents. Notwithstanding his unabashedly self-interested approach, Carroll never lacked for tenants, both because of the quality of the land offered and, as he vigorously emphasized, his aggressive recruiting via "printed and written Advertisements & many long letters writ to Several parts of Europe with conditions on which the Lands were to be let, describing the Lands, beside very many Inland Letters."[36]

The fragmentary records of the tracts Charles Carroll of Annapolis tenanted for himself and his brother's heirs preclude determining precisely their annual income. The leases and accounts that are available, however, yield a rough estimate for the period from 1750, when the vast majority of the tenants had been settled on the land, to 1756, the last year Carroll managed the jointly held tracts as a unit. Of the 195 tenants Carroll had procured by midcentury, 150 owed rents directly to him. Of those leaseholders — specifically, those on his Prince George's County lands, excluding Carrollton, plus half the tenants on the shared tracts — 85 were obligated to pay tobacco rents at rates eqivalent to at least 55,200 pounds of the staple a year. At the mean tobacco price of 1.13 pence sterling for the years 1750–1756, Carroll could expect an annual income of at least £260 from those properties. Carrollton's potential, on the other hand, did not begin to be realized fully until after 1755, when the original leases expired and Carroll switched his tenants from cash to tobacco rents at the rate of one thousand pounds of tobacco per one-hundred-acre tenement.[37] This change, which

---

had "rights they wanted to protect" (387n). Between 1734 and 1752, sixty-two Carroll tenants took that step. The total number of Carroll tenants has been compiled from county land records, entries in Carroll's cash and account books, and his letterbook for the years 1757–1761. The figure does not include approximately fifty-five St. Mary's County tenants whose status remained ambivalent and from whom rents were received only sporadically, if at all.

36. CCA to CC, Apr. 10, 1764, Carroll Papers, MS 206; CCA to Hill, Dec. 24, 1761, CCA, letterbook 1757–1761, fol. 87. Unfortunately, none of these "Advertisements" or letters of solicitation has been found.

37. Tobacco prices have been computed from "Prices of Maryland Tobacco: 1711–1775" (Ser. Z 578–582) in U.S., Bureau of the Census, *The Statistical History of the United States from Colonial Times to the Present*, ed. Ben J. Wattenberg (New York, 1976), 1198. The first evidence of the change from cash to tobacco rents on Carrollton is found in the account of Thomas Brashears, transferred from ledger T, which has not survived, into ledger MT (CCA, Account Book and Index, 1754–1784, fol. 64) in 1754. Brashears's rent is stated as one thousand pounds of tobacco and two capons. The last recorded lease for Carrollton, executed in 1751, specified a cash rent for a term of 11½ years. Frederick County, Land Records, liber B, fols. 181–184, MdAA.

"A Well-Regulated Œconomy"

included all Carrollton leaseholders by 1762, brought about a considerable growth in revenue. In 1755 the cash rents owed by 65 Monocacy tenants could have generated about £109 sterling a year, giving Carroll a gross annual return from all his agricultural renters of at least £369. By 1764, however, he reported that Carrollton, with approximately half its acreage now "let to Tenants at Will," was currently "Producing Annually £250 Sterling," or £3.16.11 per tenant, a substantial increase over the £1.13.4 due each year of the last seven on most of the old cash rent leases.[38]

It was not all profit, of course, and the extent to which the cost of doing business could be charged against the returns became a bitter point of contention when Charles Carroll of Annapolis sought to settle accounts with his brother's heirs. Aside from the initial outlays involved in procuring tenants, making out leases, and the surveying, laying out, and constructing of tenements, there were recurring expenses to be met every year. When the hiring of stewards became necessary, Carroll paid them 2s 6d sterling for every 950 pounds of tobacco they received, and he also noted the expense he had been put to in "entertaining them & settling with them . . . beside other Mony frequently lent them in small Sums to encourage them." The theft of hogsheads from rolling houses, losses in weight, and the cost of retaining clerks to assist him in keeping tenants' accounts certainly reduced his intake, as he steadfastly maintained, and some tenants appear to have been chronically in arrears. Nevertheless, even if all Carroll's claims are allowed, it is still clear that his scheme of agricultural development through tenantry yielded him a tidy sum.[39]

38. Thirteen leases for cash rents on Carrollton were recorded between 1742 and 1751. With tenures that decreased from a maximum of 19 years on the 1742 lease to 11½ years on the 1751 contract, all would have expired by 1762, with the exception of Carroll's 1749 agreement with John Darnall, Esq., for 240 acres at twenty-four shillings sterling a year for three lives. Nevertheless, Darnall's son, who took over 100 acres of the tenement upon his father's death in 1768, subsequently paid his rent in tobacco. Prince George's County, Land Records, liber B.B. no. 1, fols. 179–190, 196–197, 264–265, 379; Frederick County, Land Records, liber B., fols. 91–92, 181–184; John Darnall, 1768, will, Frederick County Wills, box 4, folder 4, MdAA; account of John Darnall, CCA, Account Book and Index, 1754–1784, fol. 5.

Income by 1764: CCA to CC, Apr. 10, 1764, Carroll Papers, MS 206. For an analysis of Carroll's agricultural income based on a different reading of the data, see Edward C. Papenfuse, "Charles Carroll of Carrollton: English Aristocrat in an American Setting," in Van Devanter, ed., *"Anywhere so long as There Be Freedom,"* 48.

39. CCA, Mar. 11, 1761, "Remarks on the Accounts sent me by Messrs. Hill & Waring," CCA, letterbook 1757–1761, fol. 27, CCA to Hill, Dec. 24, 1761, fols. 87–88. Jeske's analy-

With records pertaining to Carroll's use of slave labor before 1757 virtually nonexistent, his activities in this regard can only be inferred from later developments. By 1764 he owned 285 slaves, whose total worth he placed at £8,550 sterling. His move toward consolidation of his labor force in the 1730s, when he transferred his Western Branch slaves to Doohoragen, suggests (as slave inventories compiled in 1773–1774 confirm) that the vast majority of these blacks lived and worked on Doohoragen Manor. His principal crops, produced primarily at Doohoragen and Poplar Island under white overseers, continued to be tobacco, corn, and, increasingly, wheat, supplemented by the raising of cattle, swine, and sheep. In calculating his net worth in January 1764, Charles Carroll of Annapolis gave the agricultural tools and livestock at all his plantations a combined value of £1,000 sterling, more than twice the total value of £459 sterling placed on the much smaller number of such items contained in his father's inventories.[40]

In addition to the revenues from the Baltimore Company and from agriculture, Charles Carroll of Annapolis profited from a range of real estate transactions, especially in Annapolis and Baltimore, although he did not speculate in land as his father had. Certainly the most enduring of these projects involved the 550-acre tract Coles Harbour, on the northwest branch of the Patapsco River. Acquired by the Settler in 1701 and subsequently rented to several tenants, Coles Harbour became part of Charles and Daniel's joint inheritance and remained under cultivation until 1729, when the Carroll brothers joined other local property owners in petitioning the upper house of the Maryland assembly, "Praying leave to Erect a Town" on the site.[41]

Signed into law on August 8, 1729, the legislation authorizing the erection of the settlement designated "Baltemore Town" appointed seven Baltimore County justices, all of whom owned property in the locale, to serve as commissioners with responsibility for acquiring sixty acres of Coles Harbour "as lies most convenient to the Water" and dividing it into sixty one-acre lots intersected by "convenient Streets, Lanes, and Allies." As "Owners of the said Land," the Carrolls were to "have their first choice of one Lot." With typical acumen, Charles Carroll of Annapolis selected lot 49, a waterfront property next to the only ex-

---

sis of Carrollton Manor shows that most of those tenants prospered and that a few did well enough to leave substantial estates ("Autonomy and Opportunity," chaps. 2, 4, 6).

40. CCA to CC, Jan. 4, 1764, Carroll Papers, MS 206; Victoria Allan, Analysis of CCS's inventories, Charles Carroll of Carrollton Papers.

41. Browne et al., eds., *Archives of Maryland*, XXXVI, 396–397.

isting wharf. In 1773, after collecting more than one hundred pounds sterling in rents for a period of twenty years, Carroll sold lot 49 to Baltimore merchant Thomas Harrison for two hundred pounds sterling. An agreement concluded between the Carrolls and the commissioners on December 1, 1729, provided for the sale of the other fifty-nine parcels at the price of 40 shillings current money apiece, or the equivalent in tobacco at the rate of one penny per pound.[42]

Although the Carrolls eventually reaped a respectable return from the venture, Baltimore Town initially developed slowly.[43] Part of the problem seems to have been that in 1732, just as the Carrolls and their neighbors were seeking to promote Baltimore Town, another group of local property owners secured the legislature's permission to erect a second town, on the east side of the Jones Falls directly opposite. Settlement at this location, named Jones' Town, progressed no faster than at Baltimore, however, and in 1745 the assembly agreed to combine the two, specifying that the newly incorporated entity should be "for the future called and known by the name of Baltimore-Town and by no other Name."[44] The merger coincided with the rapid expansion of the wheat trade that began in the 1740s as a result of the increasing settlement of the backcountry. Unlike the region's tobacco trade, which had not been sufficient to stimulate town growth, wheat production provided a strong commercial impetus, and, within two years of the incorporation, Baltimore Town's promoters began to press for its enlargement.[45]

Not surprisingly, the sale of Carroll property in Baltimore mirrored the town's fortunes. From 1729 until 1744 the family earned meager sums from the sale of lots, but a period of steady sales at decent prices began in 1745. In all, Charles Carroll of Annapolis, acting in behalf of his brother's heirs, earned

42. Wilbur F. Coyle, *First Records of Baltimore Town and James' Town, 1729–1797* (Baltimore, 1905), x, xi; Provincial Court, Deeds, liber D.D. no. 5, fols. 444–445.

43. The commissioners' records indicate that only thirty-three of the original sixty lots were ever taken up; of these, five were forfeited once, three twice, another five three times, and one four times for failure to develop within the specified time period. Twenty-seven were never taken up at all and reverted to Carroll ownership after seven years. Coyle, *First Records*, 1–9.

44. Browne et al., eds., *Archives of Maryland*, XXXVII, 533–536, XLIV, 215.

45. In 1747, 1750, and again in 1753, the Maryland assembly authorized additions to Baltimore of eighteen, twenty-five, and thirty-two acres respectively (ibid., XLIV, 653–655, XLVI, 463–464, L, 301–302). For the effect of wheat production on urban development, see Carville Earle and Ronald Hoffman, "Urban Development in the Eighteenth-Century South," *Perspectives in American History*, X (Cambridge, Mass., 1976), 48–50.

£591.04.01 ½ sterling from the sale of thirty-one lots, totaling 222 ¾ acres, and of two tracts of unspecified size.[46]

Carroll's aggressive fortune building gave him a distinctive reputation in the Protestant society with which he alternately coexisted and contended. By 1756, he could confidently assert, "There is but one Man in the Province whose Fortune equals mine." Eight years later in compiling "a short Abstract of the Value of my Estate," he calculated his net worth at £88,380.9.7 sterling and noted, "I have a clear Revenue of at least £1800 per Annum." Moreover, with his wealth "Annually increasing by the Increase in the Value of my Lands," he reckoned that his possession of many tracts that were as yet "unimproved" enhanced the valuation of his holdings well beyond the amount his figures indicated.[47]

Notwithstanding his assertions, Charles Carroll of Annapolis's economic reach is most accurately indicated, not by the increasing value of his lands, but by the value of the debts that were owed to him. With more than twenty-four thousand pounds sterling out at interest, his involvement in credit transactions can be described as pervasive, and by the 1760s he was undoubtedly Maryland's premier lender. Since most loans were renewable annually, at which time the interest, set by Maryland law at 6 percent, was also due, Carroll must have been a constant presence in the lives of many of his contemporaries, for whom the distasteful reality of being in his debt was further accentuated by his practice of adding any unpaid interest to the principal of their notes. Undeterred though intermittently irritated by complaints that he charged compound interest, Carroll defended his method as entirely legal and just: "Money is Supposed to Carry an Interest in whatever hand it lays & Does not the Borrower who makes an Interest . . . by not paying it to the lender Cheat the Lender of that Interest?" As long as a lender did not "take more than 6 pr Ct on Money lent" per year, he

46. In comparison, CCA calculated the value of his Annapolis real estate, consisting of twenty lots and the houses upon them that he had acquired by purchase and default on mortgages as well as reversion at his mother's death, at four thousand pounds sterling in 1764 (CCA to CC, Jan. 9, 1764, Carroll Papers, MS 206). For the Carrolls' Baltimore Town sales, see Appendix 5, below.

47. CCA to CC, July 26, 1756, Carroll-McTavish Papers; CCA to CCC, Jan. 9, 1764, Carroll Papers, MS 206. As recorded in the proprietary Debt Books, Carroll's holdings by 1764 included 17,352 acres in Frederick County (12,553 of which composed Carrollton), 14,943 acres in Anne Arundel County (with Doohoragen accounting for 11,339), 2,026 acres in Prince George's County, the 1,000 acres of Poplar Island in Talbot County, and 2,475 acres in St. Mary's County, for a total of 37,796 acres. Debt Books, liber 24, 1763, fol. 28, liber 3, 1764, fol. 9, liber 34, 1763–1764, fol. 21, liber 38, 1763, fol. 17, liber 40, 1764, fol. 36, MdAA.

"A Well-Regulated Œconomy"

could not be prosecuted for charging compound interest, although, were a lender to add unpaid interest to the principal *every month*, he would certainly be violating the law.[48]

Notwithstanding this rather curious rationale, none of Carroll's critics took issue with his system of levying interest in court, although some were well able to, including Daniel and Walter Dulany, his Baltimore Company partners and holders of high office in Maryland's government.[49] Without legal action, Carroll had no incentive to change his obviously successful ways of doing business: his determination to build a great fortune far outweighed any desire to curry favor with minions of the proprietary power structure like the Dulanys, or to gain the approval of any of his other contemporaries, for that matter. By midcentury, Charles Carroll of Annapolis was the sole survivor among his father's original heirs and the only one of his mother's ten children to outlive her. Through skill, shrewdness, and hard work, he had accumulated the wealth that made him a man to be reckoned with, even in a Protestant society that continued to discriminate against Roman Catholics, and what people thought of him or whether they liked him was largely irrelevant. It is thus particularly ironic that, when the challenge came, it came, not from disgruntled debtors or members of the Protestant establishment provoked by Carroll's abrasiveness, but from a member of his own family — Charles Carroll of Duddington, his brother Daniel's son.

The seeds of conflict sprouted in the spring of 1757, when Charles Carroll of Annapolis began setting his affairs in order in preparation for a trip abroad that he expected to keep him away from Maryland for at least a year.[50] An important part of his arrangements was concluding a final settlement of the family inheritances with his nephew, which he decided to accomplish in two separate transactions: one that divided up the jointly held lands and another that balanced

48. CCA to CC, Dec. 24, 1762, Carroll Papers, MS 206.

49. Upon the death of their father in 1753, Daniel Dulany (1722–1797) and his brother Walter (d. 1773) each inherited a one-tenth share in the ironworks. A lawyer by trade, Daniel capped a career that included multiple terms in both houses of assembly with his appointment as secretary of Maryland in 1761. Although somewhat less distinguished, Walter also served in the assembly and from 1767 until his death held the lucrative post of commissary general. Like his father, Daniel cultivated close ties with the proprietary family. See Papenfuse et al., eds., *Biographical Dictionary*, I, 286–289. An excellent study of the Dulany family is Aubrey C. Land, *The Dulanys of Maryland: A Biographical Study of Daniel Dulany, the Elder (1685–1753), and Daniel Dulany, the Younger (1722–1797)* (Baltimore, 1955).

50. For a discussion of the reasons behind this trip, see Chapter 8, below.

and closed out the cash accounts. In addition, Carroll wanted to devise a way of terminating his long stewardship that would continue to protect the principal of Charles Carroll of Duddington's estate from being dissipated by the potentially disastrous combination of Duddington's personal extravagance and reluctance — or inability — to pay serious attention to conducting business. Accordingly, Carroll asked Duddington's brothers-in-law, Daniel Carroll II (1730–1796) and Ignatius Digges (d. 1785), to take over the management of the young man's affairs; but only Daniel, who was married to Duddington's sister, Eleanor, was willing. Ignatius Digges, Mary's husband and head of the household in which Duddington had resided since 1752, not only refused, for reasons unknown, to act as a trustee but also declined even to be present on the day the new arrangements were formalized. When neither Daniel's best efforts nor Carroll's could persuade Digges to change his mind, they decided to proceed without him, and on March 21, 1757, the three men met at Carroll's house in Annapolis to bring matters to a conclusion. By March 25 they had finished, evidently to the satisfaction of all concerned, and Charles Carroll of Duddington rode back to Mellwood, the Diggeses' plantation near Upper Marlboro in Prince George's County.[51]

Three days later, having consulted with several local relatives, including his maternal uncle Henry Rozer (1726–1802), his cousin Clement Hill (1707–1782), and Digges, Charles of Duddington began to have second thoughts.[52] The disposition of the real estate was apparently not the problem. By the terms of that agreement, signed and recorded on March 25, 1757, Charles Carroll of Duddington had accepted a total of 7,715 acres in Baltimore, Frederick, and Prince George's Counties from his uncle in return for conveying to him his share of Doohoragen and an adjacent tract called Chance, 5,380 acres in all. However, the cash settlement and the way Charles Carroll of Annapolis had tied it to Daniel's trusteeship provoked serious criticism from those relatives. Basically, Carroll of Annapolis had given his nephew £995.7.6 sterling and £218.4.0 current money by placing the sums in Daniel's hands for investment. To retain these sums and re-

51. Ignatius Digges to CCA, Mar. 19, 1757, CCA to Ignatius Digges, Mar. 22, 1757, Carroll-Maccubbin Papers. The dates of the meeting are assumed from those of the documents signed ("Money I give my Nephew conditionally" and "Articles entred into By him"), Mar. 21, 1757, ibid., and the indenture dividing the real estate, Provincial Court, Deeds, liber B.T. no. 1, fols. 72–82.

52. Clement Hill and Charles Carroll of Duddington were actually first cousins once removed: Hill's mother, Ann Darnall Hill, was Charles's grandmother's sister. Genealogical Files, Charles Carroll of Carrollton Papers.

ceive interest on them, Duddington had agreed to fulfill certain "Conditions," chief among them the relinquishment of all authority over his affairs to Daniel and the promise that neither he nor any of his representatives "shall pretend to call the Accots. my Uncle has this day Setled with me into Question" without first returning the money with interest.[53]

On March 28, just a week after he had assented to this arrangement, Charles Carroll of Duddington wrote to Charles Carroll of Annapolis asking that it be rescinded on the grounds that his advisers found it detrimental to his interests. Not surprisingly, the matter quickly became a topic of public discussion, and this unwelcome development, along with the advice of other family members, persuaded Carroll of Annapolis to release his nephew from their financial agreement upon the return of the funds already deposited with Daniel. Confident that an impartial inspection of his records would verify the fairness and generosity of the settlement Duddington had rejected, Carroll of Annapolis then informed Clement Hill, in a letter of May 3, 1757, that he was "willing to Submit the Accots I have Setled with Charly to the examination and Decision of any indifferent Friends and Relations." Anxious to have a means of settling their affairs in place before his uncle left for Europe, Duddington readily accepted this suggestion, and, before Carroll sailed on June 2, the two had agreed to place their dispute in the hands of their mutual Roman Catholic kinsmen Clement Hill and Basil Waring (1711–1793), by whose "determination" they promised to abide.[54]

Matters moved slowly, however, even after Carroll's return in June 1758, and it was not until October 25, 1759, that formal action began, with uncle and nephew executing bonds of four thousand pounds sterling to guarantee that they would accept whatever decision the arbitrators reached.[55] Having delivered his accounts to Messrs. Hill and Waring, Carroll then watched what he had expected to be a routine inspection and an amiable confirmation of his position turn instead into an exceedingly uncomplimentary interpretation of his service to his family, which impugned his motives and forced him to defend in tedious detail his methods of doing business and managing inheritances. Themselves

53. CCA and CC, Jr., Mar. 25, 1757, indenture, Provincial Court Deeds, Liber B.T. no. 1, fols. 72–82; "Money I give my Nephew conditionally," Carroll-Maccubbin Papers.

54. CCA to Charles Carroll [of Duddington], Mar. 31, May 24, 1757, Henry Carroll to CCA, May 2, 1757, Clement Hill to CCA, May 2, 1757, [CCA] to Clement Hill, May 3, 1757, Carroll-Maccubbin Papers. Waring, like Hill, was a Prince George's County planter and a Roman Catholic. He was Charles Carroll of Duddington's first cousin and CCA's first cousin once removed. Genealogical Files, Charles Carroll of Carrollton Papers.

55. Text of this bond in CCA, letterbook 1757–1761, fol. 1.

substantial planters with mercantile interests (though their wealth did not approach Carroll's), Hill and Waring found the records alternately mystifying, devious, and self-serving, and they reacted with shock to Carroll's documented practice of charging his relatives commissions — in their view, exorbitant ones — for transacting their business.

For his part, Carroll could not understand how the arbitrators, or anyone else, could expect a man to manage another person's affairs without charging for all the fees the law allowed. His charging 5 percent for receiving and remitting as the administrator of a trust or estate was common practice. What set him apart from his contemporaries was the relending of those moneys at interest and charging his relatives a commission for that service as well. Although consistent with the most advanced mercantile business methods, his actions diverged sharply from the behavior of less astute planters and thereby exposed him to charges of misconduct.[56] The idea that his rates were so high that they diminished the profits of the undertakings struck him as outrageous: "I never heard before that 5 per Cent was judged a high Commission for any business transacted in this Country," he protested on one occasion, adding, "It's a very poor business that will not bear a Commission of 5 per Cent." That "all men who do business require to be paid not only for the charges attending the business they do, but for the time & Labour they employ in doing the business," was, for Charles Carroll of Annapolis, a well-established practice in the world he inhabited, and he saw no reason why he should be "an Exception to the general Rule." The fact that some of the people for whom he acted might also be his relatives — his mother, his sisters, his brother, and his brother's children — was simply irrelevant, as he made quite clear in defending his management of his sister Mary's money: "The trouble of Receiving her Debts was certainly as great as the trouble of Receiving any other Debts," he wrote irritably to Hill and Waring in the spring of 1761. "She was my Sister & what then. Is not 5 per Cent a very low Commission for Receiving & Remitting?"[57]

Carroll's increasingly antagonistic responses to the questions Hill and Waring put to him over the two years they spent studying his accounts suggest that he foresaw a somewhat less favorable resolution than had seemed likely in May 1757, when Mr. Hill wrote to him admiringly of his frequent wish that "all Guardians would Act the Generous part I think you have done." As rendered on October 28, 1761, the arbitrators' decision disallowed a considerable portion of

---

56. As on numerous occasions, I am indebted to Lorena S. Walsh for her perspective.

57. CCA, remarks to John Darnall appended to CCA to Clement Hill and Basil Waring, Apr. [27?], 1761, CCA, letterbook 1757–1761, fol. 54.

"A Well-Regulated Œconomy"

the expenses, interest, and commissions Carroll of Annapolis had charged against his nephew's estate and ordered him to pay Carroll of Duddington £992.4.3 sterling, £493.7.6 gold currency, and 33,859 ½ pounds of tobacco.[58]

Whatever he might have anticipated, Carroll of Annapolis had no intention of obeying such an order, despite the fact that he and Duddington had renewed their performance bonds the previous spring. In mid-October, Carroll of Annapolis made his position clear in a blistering letter to Mr. Hill: the decision was nothing more than proof of the arbitrators' own appalling ignorance of standard business procedures and bookkeeping practice and of their partiality to Duddington. "You no sooner had my Accounts in your Custody than you Damned them. You did not understand them & therefore concluded they were wrong." Beyond that, the arbitrators had sought to conceal their ineptitude by widely discussing his records: "You made them the common object of your Conversation, it was how could he reconcile that, how can he clear up this?" As he acidly reminded Hill: "Your reflections before my Neice Carroll [Daniel's wife] in her own house were such as to oblige her to leave the Company after she had told you she was sure her Uncle Carroll was an honest man. . . . I have not heard what you said," he continued, "but it must have been something very gross to oblige a Woman of her Meekness to such a reply & to quit her Company."[59]

With overtones of righteous indignation, Carroll of Annapolis pointed to Hill's acceptance of a pipe of wine from Duddington as evidence of how the relationship between the arbitrators and his nephew had compromised their impartiality and corrupted the integrity of the proceedings, remarking caustically,

58. Clement Hill to CCA, May 1757, Carroll-Maccubbin Papers. No copy of the Hill and Waring decision has been found. The amounts are recorded in Provincial Court, Deeds, liber D.D. no. 6, fols. 65–77.

59. Provincial Court, Judgments, liber D.D. no. 6, fols. 65–77, MdAA; Charles Carroll, Jr., "Draft of a Reply," [c. 1767], Daniel Carroll of Duddington Papers; CCA, remarks appended to CCA to Clement Hill, Oct. 19, 1761, CCA, letterbook 1757–1761, fols. 69, 71. There is some evidence to corroborate Carroll's criticism of Hill and Waring's competence with regard to accounting procedures. In her MS "'To Labour for Profit': Plantation Management in the Chesapeake, 1620–1820," Lorena S. Walsh concludes that both men used "exceedingly haphazard methods for keeping track of their affairs." They kept careful accounts of relatively insignificant items from "small sums of money lent to relatives and neighbors; wagers on shooting matches, card games, cock fights and horse races; minor local purchases; and borrowing back and forth of goods used such as tools, leather, rum, coffee, candles, cheese, salt, flour, bread, sugar, soap, vinegar, molasses, and even of fruit and vegetables," but "they kept records of all important tobacco sales . . . simply by filing the annual accounts and invoices the merchants sent in pigeonholes in their desks" (16–17). Carroll would probably not have been surprised.

"Some men perhaps would chuse to drink Water all their Lives rather than accept a Pipe of Wine on such an Occasion." But no aspect of the decision rankled Carroll of Annapolis more than what he saw as the arbitrators' effort to extract from him concessions he had already generously incorporated in the rejected offer of March 1757. Recalling that in the original settlement he had written off all his commissions as well as a number of Duddington's other expenses, he pithily stated his view of the current situation: "Believe me, Sir," he told Hill, "my Nephew shall not owe to your scandalous partial Behaviour, what he was not suffered to owe to my Affection & Bounty." [60]

Vowing to take whatever steps were necessary to set aside the award without forfeiting his bond, Carroll of Annapolis pursued the matter privately and through the courts for another dozen years. Compounding his anger and frustration, Ignatius and Mary Digges filed a similar suit against him in 1761 over interest Mr. Digges deemed due his wife on money from her father's estate that had been lent to William Clifton of Stafford County, Virginia.[61] Although greatly displeased by the public exposure to which these proceedings increasingly subjected him, Carroll remained unalterably convinced of the rightness of his "cause," and neither the passage of time nor the continuing estrangement within his family swayed that conviction or soothed the deep sense of personal injury associated with it. Indeed, the extent of his ego involvement prevented any progress toward resolving the points at issue until the late 1760s, when he finally yielded the legal protection of his interests to cooler, more practical defenders.

In the end, however, even the skills of two of Maryland's most able young lawyers, Thomas Johnson, Jr., and his associate, William Cooke, failed to produce the sweeping public vindication Carroll desired, leaving both suits to be concluded privately in the mid-1770s. Moreover, the final settlements unmis-

---

60. CCA, remarks appended to CCA to Clement Hill, Oct. 19, 1761, CCA to Clement Hill, Dec. 24, 1761, CCA, letterbook 1757–1761, fols. 76, 95. Duddington maintained that the wine he gave Hill was, not a bribe, but a "present" to show his appreciation of Hill's hospitality. Waring, however, when offered a similar gift, refused it (Charles Carroll, Jr., "Draft of a Reply," [c. 1767], Duddington Papers, fol. 16). It is also interesting to note that in 1763 Charles Carroll of Duddington married Clement Hill's niece Mary Hill (1744– 1822). Regarding this step, Charles Carroll of Annapolis remarked caustically, "My Nephew who is not capable of doing a wise thing has lately done the foolishest thing he ever did, for he has taken to himself a Wife, the Daughter of Mr. Hen: Hill." CCA to CCC, [Apr. 28], 1763, Carroll-Harper Papers, MdHi.

61. The first official record of the Digges suit is found in Chancery Court (Records), liber D.D. no. 1, fol. 15, MdAA.

"A Well-Regulated Œconomy"

takably embodied financial concessions on Carroll's part, particularly in the case of Ignatius Digges whose "Pride" and "Obstinacy" brought, not the punishment his opponent wished upon him, but the "Moiety of Cliftons Bond & Interest thereon" for which he had originally sued, a sum that, by the date of settlement in the spring of 1773, totaled £1,411.15.11 sterling.[62] Carroll fared better with regard to his nephew, perhaps because Charles Carroll of Duddington's demise in late 1771 facilitated resolution of the suit. By February 1774, Duddington's widow, Mary Hill Carroll, had accepted bond for £1,500 sterling from Carroll of Annapolis to be held in trust, with interest, for her three minor sons until each boy reached his twenty-first year. In return, Mrs. Carroll "remised, released, and forever quitted Claim" to "all actions suits claims and demands whatsoever in law and in equity" that her late husband had brought against his uncle. According to the calculations of an unknown adviser to Mrs. Carroll, the bond fell £1,400 short of the value that the original Hill and Waring award, plus interest to November 1772, would have yielded Charles Carroll of Duddington's estate.[63]

Did Charles Carroll of Annapolis cheat his relatives, or at the least shortchange them, as the widow Carroll's adviser seems to imply? Many of his contemporaries who regarded him as a shrewd and ambitious fortune-builder, keenly and unabashedly (if not unscrupulously) committed to his own interests, believed him capable of both. His view of himself as revealed through his own records of those conflicts is far more complicated. A product, like his father, of complex and compelling forces and shaped by a past that the present would not allow him to transcend, Charles Carroll of Annapolis did not regard his pragmatic be-

62. CCA to CCC, May 15, 1771, Carroll Papers, MS 206; Charles Carroll of Annapolis, Account Book, Liber A, Manuscripts Division, DLC; Charles Carroll of Carrollton's bond with Ignatius Digges, Mar. 16, 1773, Carroll-McTavish Papers, MdHi.

63. A "Coppy of the release Mrs. Carroll signed on haveing the Bond of £1,500-Sterl for the use of her Children" can be found on reel 1 of the microfilm edition of the Daniel Carroll of Duddington Papers, Manuscripts Division, DLC. To guarantee performance of the agreement, Charles Carroll of Annapolis bound himself to Notley Young, half-uncle to Charles Carroll of Duddington's sons, in the amount of three thousand pounds sterling.

Reel 5 of the microfilm edition of the Daniel Carroll of Duddington Papers contains an account showing that, by the terms of the 1761 Hill and Waring award, Charles Carroll of Annapolis would have owed Charles Carroll of Duddington £2,725.18.6 plus interest, for a total of £3,925.6.4 ¼, in November 1772. An appended note states that the interest has been calculated by "allowing Tobo at the under price of 20/ p C," that is, twenty shillings per hundredweight.

havior in matters of business as a contradiction of family loyalty and affection. From the time of his brother's death in 1734, Carroll believed he had acted as "a Father to his Children" and that he had "managed their fortunes as if they were his own," and he saw the consistent support he received from his niece Eleanor, her husband Daniel, and other relatives for his administration of estates in which they shared an interest equal to that of his antagonists as confirmation of that assessment. And, despite his long and obdurate display of tough practicality, Carroll held no grudges. The bond of fifteen hundred pounds sterling marked the beginning of genuine interest and involvement in the upbringing and education of Charles Carroll of Duddington's sons, particularly Daniel, the eldest, and in October 1774 Mary Carroll Digges, wife of the troublesome Ignatius and party to his suit, traveled from Mellwood, their Charles County plantation, to the home of relatives at Rock Creek in Prince George's County, for the express purpose of making peace with her uncle. It was, Carroll noted, "a tender Meeting"; together with his characterization of his niece as "a good tender Hearted Girl," it signaled the resumption of a warm and enduring family relationship.[64]

Although the breaches within the Carroll family caused by the Duddington and Digges lawsuits were eventually healed, Charles Carroll of Annapolis did not forget the bitterness exposed by the decades of rancor and confrontation. That his kinsmen Hill and Waring and Ignatius Digges, fellow Catholics and men he had presumed to be honorable, would construe his long stewardship in a way that suggested he had depleted the fortunes of his brother's heirs in order to increase his own reinforced his wariness of the world by showing him that a man's enemies might be dangerously close to, if not within, his own household. Even more important, Carroll's conflict with his nephew starkly reaffirmed the truth of his perception that Charles Carroll of Duddington possessed character flaws of the most serious nature, deficiencies that placed the young man's fortune and the future of his family in the gravest jeopardy. Already well into the second great work of his life — the creation of an heir intellectually, morally, and temperamentally worthy of receiving the grand legacy he was building — Charles Carroll of Annapolis saw in the failures of his brother's son a confirmation of the course he had chosen to pursue in molding his own. His success and the means he used to achieve it constitute one of early American history's most remarkable human dramas.

64. CCA to Clement Hill, Dec. 24, 1761, CCA, letterbook 1757–61, fol. 98; CCA to CCC, Oct. 14, 1774, Carroll Papers, MS 206.

"A Well-Regulated Œconomy"

CHAPTER 4

"Sound & Strong": A Worthy Heir

As no personal writings by Charles Carroll of Annapolis have survived from the 1730s, his reasons for embarking upon fatherhood remain a matter of speculation. The timing — his only child was born in 1737 — suggests that the motivation might have developed after the death of his brother Daniel in April 1734, which made the perpetuation of their line of Carrolls entirely dependent upon the health and progress of one five-year-old boy, Daniel's son Charles. Unwilling, perhaps, to bind the future of the family to a single, slender reed — after all, Henry Carroll, the Settler's other son, had survived the diseases and accidents of childhood only to be claimed by an unknown malady at the age of twenty-two — Charles Carroll of Annapolis might well have concluded that he, too, must now assume parental responsibilities. Or perhaps he simply fell in love. Whatever the combination of calculation and sentiment, Charles Carroll of Annapolis began, at some point during the 1730s, an intimate relationship with his first cousin Elizabeth Brooke, a woman seven years his junior and one of the nine children of Prince George's County planter Clement Brooke, Sr. (1676– 1737), and his wife Jane Sewall Brooke (by 1685–1761). Probably born on her father's one-thousand-acre plantation on Piscattaway Creek, near Upper Marlboro, Elizabeth, about whose early life and schooling nothing is known, came to live in Annapolis in the mid-1720s. She resided either in Charles Carroll's house or his mother's, which adjoined it, and quite likely acted as a companion to Charles's sisters Mary and Eleanor, only two and three years younger and recently returned to Maryland from schooling abroad. Indeed, Charles Carroll's earliest surviving acknowledgment of Elizabeth Brooke's existence occurred at Eleanor Carroll's death in 1730: among the costs of his sister's funeral in his account book, Charles noted the expenditure of £20.14 "paid my sister Mary for her own & Betty Brooke's use." Elizabeth's signature, along with that of her brother, Nicholas (perhaps serving as their cousin's clerk), on several leases executed by Charles Carroll of Annapolis in the mid-1730s indicates that she continued to reside with the Carrolls after Eleanor's death. Her witnessing of Daniel Carroll of Duddington's will on April 12, 1734, suggests an even closer involvement in the family's affairs.[1]

If the times and places of Charles Carroll and Elizabeth Brooke's initial encounters remain elusive, the birth of their son, Charles, on September 19, 1737 (New Style), provides irrefutable proof of the relationship that had developed between them. Because no marriage had taken place, the child born to these parents was illegitimate, according to both common and canon law. Nevertheless, Charles Carroll and Elizabeth Brooke lived openly together without benefit of clergy until February 15, 1757, when a Jesuit priest named Mathias Maners joined them in holy matrimony in the presence of two witnesses, one of them being the bride's mother.[2] By the time his parents married, "Charley," as Charles and Elizabeth called their cherished only child, was almost halfway through the twentieth year of his life.

Besides the marriage certificate, duly signed by the officiating clergyman, Jane Sewall Brooke, and John Ireland, the principal overseer at the Carroll dwelling plantation, Doohoragen Manor, several other documents corroborate the familial situation. Most explicit is the marriage settlement signed by Elizabeth Brooke on November 7, 1756, by which she waived her dower right to a third of her prospective husband's real and personal estate in exchange for an annual stipend of one hundred pounds sterling should she outlive him. Equally pointed is the congratulatory message penned to the bridegroom on November 17, 1757, by his old friend Onorio Rozolini, a Protestant convert who had served as armorer of the province of Maryland from June 1734 until he returned to his native Italy in August 1741. Having received news of the nuptials from Charles Carroll of Annapolis, Rozolini's warm good wishes confirmed his full knowledge of the Carrolls' prior circumstances: "I am glad that Miss Brook that was, is now

1. Account Book of Charles Carroll, Sr., of Annapolis and Doughoregan, c. 1730–1757, MdHi. Elizabeth was also called Betsy by members of the family. See Michael Macnemara to CCA, Feb. 10, 1761, Carroll Papers, MS 216, MdHi, in which greetings are conveyed to "Cousin Betsy."

Among the documents signed by Elizabeth and Nicholas were the original leases for tenements on Carrollton Manor. Prince George's County Land Records, liber T, fols. 161–164, 269–270, 491–492, 518–519; Anne Arundel County Deeds, liber R.D. no. 2, fol. 197, MdAA. Daniel Carroll of Duddington's will: Prince George's County Wills, liber 21, fol. 37, MdAA.

2. CCA and EB, marriage articles, Feb. 15, 1757, Carroll-McTavish Papers, MdHi.

"Sound & Strong"

PLATE 12. Elizabeth Brooke Carroll. By John Wollaston. 1753–1754.
Founders Society Purchase, Mr. and Mrs. Walter Buhl Ford, II Fund.
By permission The Detroit Institute of Arts. Photograph © The Detroit Institute of Arts

PLATE 13. Charles Carroll of Annapolis. By John Wollaston. 1753–1754.
Courtesy the present owner

Mrs. Carrill, & beg of you to wish ioy [joy] from us, as we wish you the same; If you remember I told you that your Son would answer all your expectations." Nor had the common law relationship been a secret to the couple's contemporaries, at home or abroad. Writing to a friend in Maryland in 1743, a former proprietary official who had returned to England remarked, "I find Mr. Carroll was of your party to St. Mary's, is he in great esteem among you, because the contrary is asserted here, but perhaps his admired Cousin is now his Wife, and then all's well." [3]

Most telling of all, however, is the care both Charles Carroll of Annapolis and Elizabeth Brooke exercised to dispel any supposition that a valid marriage existed between them. Every document to which Charley's mother affixed her name until the day of her wedding in 1757, including all of her letters to him, bears the bold signature "Elizabeth Brooke." In witnessing the will of John Carr of Anne Arundel County on September 7, 1754, she signed herself "Elizabeth Brooke," but at probate on October 7, 1759, nearly three years after she married, she identified herself as "Elizabeth Carroll, late Elizabeth Brooke." With similar precision, she closed her premarital correspondence to her son with "Yrs Affecly" or "Mo: Affec Yrs, Eliza. Brooke." Not until after February 15, 1757, did she write to Charley as "Yr Affect Mother Eliza. Carroll." With only one exception — a letter written in September 1756 when the decision to legalize the union had apparently been made — Charles Carroll of Annapolis behaved in the same manner, signing his letters to Charley "Mo: Affly Yrs, Chars. Carroll," a designation he abandoned forever after his wedding in favor of "Yr Mo: Afft: Father Cha: Carroll." [4] By contrast, Charley always wrote to his parents as "Mama" and "Papa," except on one occasion when he used the formal salutation "Hon: Father."

3. CCA and EB, marriage settlement, Nov. 7, 1756, Colonial Collection, oversize, MdHi; Donnell MacClure Owings, *His Lordship's Patronage: Offices of Profit in Colonial Maryland* (Baltimore, 1953), 48, 49n; Onorio Rozolini to CCA, Nov. 17, 1757, Carroll Papers, MS 206, MdHi; John Gibson to John Ross, c. 1743, Gibson-Maynadier Papers, MdHi, quoted in Sally D. Mason, "Mama, Rachel, and Molly: Three Generations of Carroll Women," in Ronald Hoffman and Peter J. Albert, eds., *Women in the Age of the American Revolution* (Charlottesville, Va., 1989), 255, with thanks to Shirley V. Baltz.

4. Anne Arundel County Wills, liber 30, fol. 766, MdAA; EB to CC, Sept. 30, 1754, Colonial Collection, MdHi; EB to CC, Sept. 8, 1756, and EBC to CC, Nov. 30, 1757, Carroll Papers, MS 206. CCA's letter of Sept. 14, 1756, signed "Yr Mo: Afft: Father Cha: Carroll," enclosed one from Charley's mother dated Sept. 8 in which she hinted broadly that marriage was in the offing. CCA to CC, Sept. 14, 1756, Carroll Papers, MS 216, and EB to CC, Sept. 8, 1756, MS 206.

Efforts to explain, account for, and even deny the existence of this unusual domestic arrangement have produced interpretations that are almost as interesting as the situation itself. Early Carroll biographers, notably Kate Mason Rowland, whose two-volume study based on the family's papers appeared in 1898, and Ellen Hart Smith, author of a life of Charles Carroll of Carrollton published in 1942, ignored, or else did not comprehend, the evidence of Charley's out-of-wedlock birth and upbringing. During the 1970s, Thomas O'Brien Hanley, a biographer hagiographically committed to Charles Carroll of Carrollton as the only Roman Catholic signer of the Declaration of Independence, broke his silence on the subject to castigate historians who had begun to discuss it in print. Decrying what he considered an undue emphasis on the circumstances of Charley's nativity, Hanley argued that Charles Carroll and Elizabeth Brooke had, before their son arrived, been properly joined in wedlock by means of a sacramental marriage, "which needed no sanction from a corrupt provincial government as far as a proud Irish breed was concerned." A more general assumption that also prevailed held that an official union might have been difficult to come by because of a shortage of priests in militantly Protestant colonial Maryland.[5]

The latter contention is easily dispensed with: the catalog of the Maryland mission of the Society of Jesus shows that there were never fewer than eight priests in the province between 1730 and 1760. The assertion that Charles Carroll and Elizabeth Brooke brought their son into the world after entering a sacramental marriage — a union recognized as valid by the church — merited a more extensive investigation. The Roman Catholic Church's laws on marriage, especially as they applied to Protestant countries during the seventeenth and eighteenth centuries, were complex. Although one of the church's seven sacraments, marriage differs from the other six in that it is conferred by the participants upon each other rather than administered to them by a priest. Believing that the form of the sacrament had been divinely instituted and that no earthly

5. Kate Mason Rowland, *The Life of Charles Carroll of Carrollton, 1737–1832, with His Correspondence and Public Papers,* 2 vols. (New York, 1898); Ellen Hart Smith, *Charles Carroll of Carrollton* (Cambridge, Mass., 1942). In *Charles Carroll of Carrollton: The Making of a Revolutionary Gentleman* (Washington, D.C., 1970), 13–14, Thomas O'Brien Hanley states, "True to the Catholic gentry code of marrying its own kind, with leniency toward prohibitions of consanguinity, he [Charles Carroll of Annapolis] courted and married Elizabeth Brooke." He does not mention that the wedding took place in February 1757, six months after their son's nineteenth birthday. Five years later, however, Hanley took "historians . . . weighted . . . to economic history and curiosity (e.g., about the semblance of bastardy . . .)" to task in "Carroll Did More Than Sign, But Who Knows It?" Clippings file, Charles Carroll of Carrollton Papers.

power could alter it, the church, until the middle of the sixteenth century, accepted as authentic those unions that men and women contracted with each other without the presence or blessing of an ordained cleric. Parties to such arrangements, known as "clandestine marriages," were held in canon law to be committed to each other for life, their children were considered legitimate, and attempts by either party to discard the other in favor of a new partner were condemned as bigamous. Potential for abuse was ingrained in the system: the absence of readily verifiable proof of a clandestine marriage deprived a woman of any legal right to her husband's estate and made it difficult to assign responsibility for the care and maintenance of offspring. Nevertheless, the church continued to allow the practice for centuries, periodically reiterating its preference that marriages be solemnized in the presence of a priest but refusing to invalidate those that were not. Finally, the Council of Trent, during its deliberations in 1545–1563, acted to regularize nuptial practices by ruling that, in order to be valid marriages, conjugal unions must be contracted before a priest and two other witnesses.[6]

The council's action did not entirely solve the problem, however, because the new decree, known as *Tametsi*, could not go into effect until publicly announced within a formal ecclesiastical establishment. Thus, while each parish in almost all Catholic countries published *Tametsi*, with the consent of the civil authority, shortly after the closing of the council, the decree could not be proclaimed in Protestant countries like England and, later, her North American colonies, where no formal Catholic organization existed. As a result, marriages of Catholics in Maryland technically continued to depend upon the mutual consent of the parties.

That being so, the relationship that existed between Charles Carroll of Annapolis and Elizabeth Brooke for at least twenty years might theoretically have fallen within the pre-Tridentine definition of a valid marriage, thereby making their son legitimate, at least in the eyes of the church.[7] However, the text of the

6. Catalog of the Members of the Maryland Mission, Special Collections Division, Georgetown University Library, Washington, D.C.; George Hayward Joyce, *Christian Marriage: An Historical and Doctrinal Study* (London, 1933), 103–116. According to Joyce, the medieval church considered clandestine marriage "a grave breach of ecclesiastical law" but did not treat "the union itself . . . as immoral" (106). Whether the church had the power to make such reforms as regulating nuptial practices was a question of dogma debated by the bishops before being decided in the affirmative (ibid., 124–130).

7. Joyce, *Christian Marriage*, 127. I am indebted to Father Joseph White of the University of Notre Dame for suggesting that I explore the explanatory possibilities of

Carrolls' 1757 marriage certificate, which bears the signature of the officiating priest, Mathias Maners, refutes this seemingly plausible explanation:

> I Mathias Maners a Priest of the Society of Jesus do hereby certify that I did on the 15th day of February in the year of our Lord 1757 marry Charles Carroll Esq: and Elizabeth Brooke Daughter of Clement Brooke Esq. late of Prince Georges county deceased.
>
> In testimony whereof I have hereunto set my hand, and affixed my Seal the day and year first above mentioned.
> testeth
>
> Jane Brooke   Mathias Maners
> John Ireland   S.J.[8]

Authorities on canon law unequivocally confirm that Maners could not have administered the marriage and signed the document if an earlier sacramental marriage had taken place.[9] And, notwithstanding the unpublished status of *Tametsi*, the form of the ceremony, with a priest and two witnesses present, conforms precisely to the Tridentine definition of a valid union.

Anecdotal nineteenth-century explanations that attempt to account for Charles and Elizabeth's ménage (representative samples are included in Appendix 4) reveal more about that era's attitudes concerning class and gender than they do about the motives of the two people involved. The claims range from assertions that Elizabeth Brooke was "a woman of the lowest class" who served as Charles's housekeeper (implying that she seduced her wealthy cousin), the fanciful story of a foundling baby whose return to his mother forced Charles Carroll of Annapolis to acknowledge paternity, to the equally unsubstantiated notion that the son had pressured his father into wedlock as a condition of his returning to Maryland from his studies in Europe. Concern about lineage was nonetheless real and persistent, as confirmed by a report from an unimpeachable source that, in the early decades of the twentieth century, the shadow of the

---

Tametsi. It should also be noted that sacramental, or clandestine, marriage persisted widely in Ireland well into the sixteenth century. Kenneth Nicholls, *Gaelic and Gaelicised Ireland in the Middle Ages* (Dublin, 1972), 73–77; Colm Lennon, "The Counter-Reformation in Ireland, 1542–1641," in Ciaran Brady and Raymond Gillespie, eds., *Natives and Newcomers: Essays on the Making of Irish Colonial Society, 1534–1641* (Dublin, 1986), 78, 91.

8. CCA and EB, marriage articles, Carroll-McTavish Papers.

9. I am indebted to Father John Lynch of the Department of Canon Law at the Catholic University of America for verifying this conclusion.

bar sinister upon the Carroll escutcheon led certain patriotic societies to deny membership to women who based their eligibility on descent through Charles Carroll of Carrollton's line.[10]

Notwithstanding fables to the contrary, there were no inherent defects to deter "Papa," as Charles Carroll of Annapolis was affectionately known to his son, from marrying the boy's beloved "Mama." It is true that Elizabeth Brooke had little of material value to offer — her father's will, probated in May 1737, left her no legacy from an estate worth some £350 net — but she was by no means "a woman of the lowest class." She possessed impeccable religious and genealogical credentials. Her mother's family was solidly Catholic, and her maternal grandfather, Major Nicholas Sewall (1655–1737), of Mattapany in St. Mary's County, was the stepson of Charles Calvert, third Lord Baltimore, in whose behalf he had fought vigorously during Coode's rebellion.[11] Elizabeth's paternal grandfather, Major Thomas Brooke (1632–1676) of Calvert County, had been raised a Protestant, but at the time of his marriage, or shortly thereafter, he converted to Catholicism and raised his family in that faith. His eldest son ultimately returned to the Anglican Church, but three others became Jesuit priests. Literate and intelligent, Elizabeth was also physically attractive, at least as depicted by the portrait John Wollaston painted of her about the time of her marriage; and, according to everything Papa and Charley ever said about her, she consistently displayed a sweet and agreeable temperament.[12] Clearly, the forces that impelled Charles Carroll of Annapolis to forgo wedlock, thereby keeping his son illegitimate and the woman who bore him in social, and perhaps emotional, limbo, had little to do with her qualifications. His single-mindedness and resolve in this matter attest that he moved in response to far more compelling considerations.

Charles Carroll of Annapolis's behavior becomes comprehensible only within the context of his family's Irish past and his father's subsequent career in

10. I am grateful to Miss Minnie Hill of Washington, D.C., a direct descendant of Daniel Carroll of Duddington, for giving me this information.

11. Mason, "Mama, Rachel, and Molly," in Hoffman and Albert, eds., *Women in the Age of the American Revolution,* 251–252. For a detailed account of Sewall's activities, see Lois Green Carr and David William Jordan, *Maryland's Revolution of Government, 1689–1692* (Ithaca, N.Y., 1974), 59–61, 93–94, 143, 152.

12. Mason, "Mama, Rachel, and Molly," in Hoffman and Albert, eds., *Women in the Age of the American Revolution,* 251. On Wollaston's portrait, see Ann C. Van Devanter, ed., *"Anywhere so long as There Be Freedom": Charles Carroll of Carrollton, His Family, and His Maryland* (Baltimore, 1975), 130–131.

Maryland. The influence of this remembered knowledge upon his view of the world is the reality that shaped him, that differentiates him from the rest of the Chesapeake gentry — and even from many of his English Catholic counterparts — and that informed his conduct toward Elizabeth Brooke and their son. As a colonial, Charles Carroll of Annapolis undoubtedly shared with other members of Maryland's elite the anxieties inherent in trying to fashion a genteel persona while living on the outermost rim of the British Empire. Ambitious provincials like William Byrd II, Thomas Jefferson, and Robert Bolling recognized that their best efforts to achieve gentility would always be regarded as hopelessly inferior by the movers and shakers in the metropolis on the other side of the Atlantic. That awareness could ratchet psychic tensions to a level that found expression in distinctive behavior and otherwise inexplicable personality traits, misogyny among them.[13] To this crisis of self-construction the Carrolls brought another critical dimension — the experience of further marginalization as Roman Catholics relegated to the fringe of *provincial* society.

In the letters he wrote to his son during the boy's formative years, Charles Carroll of Annapolis regularly reiterated his deep resentment at being denied the place in society to which he believed his family's wealth, lineage, education, and loyal service to the proprietor entitled him. Additionally deprived of the privilege and protection inherent in civic rights and political participation, he nevertheless adamantly refused to mitigate his situation by making, as did many of his English coreligionists, the strategic compromise whereby men conformed to the Anglican Church while their wives and children remained in the Church of Rome. Nor did he elect, as did others of his faith like his niece's husband Ignatius Digges, to accumulate wealth and live quietly without challenging the Protestant system that excluded him. Explicitly aware of how his father had surmounted his family's marginalization in Ireland by prospering in Maryland, only to be disavowed and disenfranchised by a Protestant government supported by the apostatizing Calverts, Charles Carroll of Annapolis neither tempered his religious allegiance nor forgot past injustices. And he did not hesitate to assert his identity as he strove to prevail in an environment where discrimination against un-

13. This pattern of behavior is compellingly delineated in Kenneth A. Lockridge, *On the Sources of Patriarchal Rage: The Commonplace Books of William Byrd and Thomas Jefferson and the Gendering of Power in the Eighteenth Century* (New York, 1992), and "Colonial Self-Fashioning: Paradoxes and Pathologies in the Construction of Genteel Identity in Eighteenth-Century America," in Ronald Hoffman, Mechal Sobel, and Fredrika J. Teute, eds., *Through a Glass Darkly: Reflections on Personal Identity in Early America* (Chapel Hill, N.C., 1997), 274–339.

yielding papists enjoyed legal sanction. There is no truer affirmation of these essential aspects of his character than the method he devised for molding his son into a man worthy of inheriting the Carroll fortune and capable of preserving it in a grasping and treacherous colonial world.

His common law relationship with Elizabeth Brooke and Charley's illegitimacy served Charles Carroll of Annapolis's purposes in two critical ways by offering a measure of protection for his fortune and an effective means of compelling the behavior he desired from his son. In Papa's view, the vicissitudes of the penal laws as they applied to Catholic inheritances and the Maryland statutes regarding rights of dower and guardianship posed real and present dangers to the wealth he had striven so single-mindedly to accumulate. In the first instance, he surely knew that the law — then in effect in England although not in Maryland — currently required all persons to swear "the oaths of allegiance and supremacy and subscribe the declaration against transubstantiation" within six months of reaching eighteen years of age or be rendered "incapable of either inheriting or purchasing land." More immediately, he must contend with the dower right, which entitled a widow to one-third of her husband's estate, and the guardianship right, which could put her in charge of the other two-thirds in behalf of minor children. A widow with access to a fortune as large as his would truly be irresistible and upon remarriage might carry the Carroll legacy into "a strange Family" — perhaps even a Protestant one. That possibility was a danger against which Papa explicitly warned Charley when the young man approached marriageable age. By contrast, a common law relationship conferred no dower rights upon the female partner, nor did it entitle her to "claim administration of his goods as his widow" upon the male participant's death.[14]

As the prenuptial settlement Charles Carroll of Annapolis and Elizabeth Brooke signed in November 1756 attests, the right of dower could be effectively and legally countered if the woman agreed to another arrangement for her jointure in its stead. Although this course was always open to him, Papa did not intend to utilize it until his son reached his majority and had satisfied all paternal demands. New anti-Catholic legislation enacted in Maryland in May 1756 upset

---

14. Robert Blackey, "A War of Words: The Significance of the Propaganda Conflict between English Catholics and Protestants, 1715–1745," *Catholic Historical Review*, LVIII (1972–1973), 535n; CCA to CC, Sept. 1, 1762, Carroll Papers, MS 206; Joyce, *Christian Marriage*, 139. Kenneth Lockridge has suggested in several conversations with the author that the possibility of women's carrying financial resources from one family to another constituted a major concern for male members of the colonial gentry.

the elder Carroll's timetable by driving him to concoct a plan to abandon the province for Catholic Louisiana. Securing comparable property in the French colony required that he negotiate with highly placed officials in Paris, to which he planned to embark in June 1757. Such an undertaking could not be pursued unless his affairs in Maryland were in order, and that necessity accounts for the timing of his prenuptial agreement and his wedding as well as for his attempts between March and May 1757 to reach a settlement with his nephew, Charles Carroll of Duddington.

For the first nineteen and a half years of his life Charley's legal status was just as precarious as his mother's. A son born out of wedlock was deemed a bastard with, according to Blackstone, very few rights besides "such as he can *acquire,* for he can inherit nothing, being looked upon as the son of nobody." More explicitly: "The incapacity of a bastard consists principally in this, that he cannot be heir to any one, neither can he have heirs, but of his own body; for, being *nullius filius,* he is therefore of kin to nobody, and has no ancestor from whom any inheritable blood can be derived." Within the bounds of canon law, the stigma of bastardy and its consequences could easily be removed: the subsequent marriage of the parents automatically legitimated any previously begotten child. Far less compassionate, the common law's sole mechanism for legitimating the illegitimate, thereby rendering a man born a bastard "capable of inheriting," lay in "the transcendent power of an act of parliament, and not otherwise."[15] Therefore, the marriage into which Papa and Mama finally entered in February 1757 legitimated their son's birth only in the eyes of the church and left the ability to inherit entirely dependent upon Papa's willingness to make Charley his legal heir by so designating him in a duly drawn, properly witnessed will. That action Papa intended to take only when Charley had incontestably proved himself.

There is no question that Charley clearly understood his situation: having received in October 1761 his first copy of his father's will, he responded in a way that confirms his knowledge of his position. "The sending a copy of yr. will, tho' it proves how much you love me, was an unnecessary step if with an intent to remove any apprehensions or disquiet I might feel on that subject. I have been all along per[sua]ded, that yr. good sense, steady conduct, & our mutual love were a sufficient security against any disposition of yr estate that might greatly prejudice me." But, as Charles Carroll of Annapolis's childrearing practices confirm, what ultimately qualified Charley in his father's judgment was, not filial

15. William Blackstone, *Commentaries on the Laws of England: A Facsimile of the First Edition of 1765–1769* (Chicago, 1979), I, 447.

affection, but his meeting, in Onorio Rozolini's revealing phrase, all of Papa's "expectations." [16]

Papa began to implement his plan for Charley in August 1748, about six weeks before the boy's eleventh birthday, when he was sent to school in France. The educational odyssey he thereby commenced would keep him away from home for the next sixteen years. As no adequate schools existed for Catholic children in Maryland, Papa, like other members of the Roman Catholic gentry, chose to educate Charley abroad, initially at the English Jesuit College at St. Omer in Flanders, an institution founded during the reign of Elizabeth I to circumvent penal statutes that prevented the establishment of Catholic schools in England.[17] Since Maryland law forbade Catholics to send their children away to study in "popish" academies, Papa's decision involved an element of risk, albeit a calculated one, since the general assembly had never followed its periodic complaints about breaches of the measure with action against individuals suspected of violating it.

16. CC to CCA, Oct. 13, 1761, Carroll Papers, MS 206. No copy of this will has been found. It replaced an earlier will, undated but probably drawn in late 1759, based on Papa's reference in it to "my Son Charles Carroll now a Student in the Temple in London." There is no evidence that Papa ever sent Charley a copy of the earlier document (Carroll Papers, MS 206), which made Mama administrator of the estate in Charley's behalf.

Legally, in fact, Charley remained a bastard until 1788, when a new law of descents enacted by the Maryland assembly in 1786 took effect. Deeming the former "law of descents, which originated with the feudal system and military tenures . . . contrary to justice," the legislature abolished it and replaced it with An Act to Direct Descents, thereby bringing common law into conformity with canon law. Section 7 of the new statute provided "that if any man shall have one or more children by any woman, whom he shall afterwards marry, such child or children, if acknowledged by the man, shall in virtue of such marriage and acknowledgment be hereby legitimated, and capable in law to inherit and transmit inheritance as if born in wedlock" (*Laws of Maryland, Made and Passed at a Session of Assembly, Begun and Held at the City of Annapolis, on Monday the Sixth of November, in the Year of Our Lord One Thousand Seven Hundred and Eighty-six* [Annapolis, (1787)]). That the law did not deem Charles Carroll of Carrollton automatically legitimated by his parents' marriage was first pointed out by Pauline Maier in her essay on Carroll in *The Old Revolutionaries: Political Lives in the Age of Samuel Adams* (New York, 1980), 237–238.

17. Founded as a boarding school in 1593 by Father Ralph Persons and initially attached to the Walloon College, which served a local clientele, the English Jesuit College at St. Omer became a separate entity staffed entirely by English Jesuits in 1614. The school continues today as Stonyhurst College in Lancashire, England. John Gerard, *Stonyhurst College: Its Life beyond the Seas, 1592–1794, and on English Soil, 1794–1894* (Belfast, 1894), 2; Thomas E. Muir, *Stonyhurst College, 1593–1992* (London, 1991), 15–33.

For Charley, the risk inherent in leaving Maryland was undoubtedly a good deal more personal. Having two cousins, Watty Hoxton and Jacky Carroll, among the group destined with him for St. Omers might have been of some comfort, but their presence could not possibly have compensated for the harsh reality of being wrenched from his mother's side and abruptly thrust into a strange foreign world filled with stern, black-robed priests intent on making him into a classical scholar by means of a rigorous curriculum known as the *Ratio Studiorum*. Perhaps the knowledge that he was following in the footsteps of his father, who had also been sent away to St. Omers at the age of ten, stiffened his spine and helped make him brave.[18] But, however Charley felt and whatever he was able to understand as he stood on the deck of the ship and watched Annapolis slowly disappear, his embarkation meant that his childhood, full of secluded hours spent with Mama at Doohoragen, was lost to him forever. Small wonder that, later in his life, images of such times formed his most cherished memories. "Those happy days spent at Elkridge in her sweet company, our lonely retirement and mutual fondness pass in remembrance before me," he wrote after Mama's death in 1761. "I shall never see such days again."[19]

Nor did his mother. If time eased somewhat the painful loss of her only child's departure, her poignant evocation of their warm and nurturing relationship in a letter she wrote to Charley in 1760, a dozen years after she had last seen him, reveals that she, too, found solace in memories: "Yr tender concern for my we[l]fare & health often puts me in minde of what you used to tell me, when a little Boy lolling & fondling a bout me, that you loved me dearly & always shou'd have the same fondness & affection for me during Life, yr behaviour & the regard you have shewn me, hitherto, convinces me of the truth of those words, which I assure my de[ar g]ives me no small Comforte."[20]

The human drama, often interlaced with pathos, revealed in the letters exchanged by parents and son during the long separation that Charley sometimes called his "banishment" belies the apparent confidence concerning Papa's intentions that Charley expressed upon receiving a copy of the elder Carroll's will in October 1761.[21] Increasingly aware of his total dependence upon his father and

18. CCA entered St. Omers in 1713. Geoffrey Holt, *St. Omers and Bruges Colleges, 1593–1773: A Biographical Dictionary,* Catholic Record Society, LXIX (London, 1979), 59.

19. CC to CCA, June 10, 1761, Carroll Papers, MS 206. As their dwelling plantation, Doohoragen Manor, was located at Elk Ridge in Anne Arundel County, the Carrolls habitually used the two names interchangeably.

20. EBC to CC, Sept. 10, 1760, Harper-Pennington Papers, MdHi.

21. Quoted in CCA to CC, July 14, 1760, Carroll Papers, MS 206.

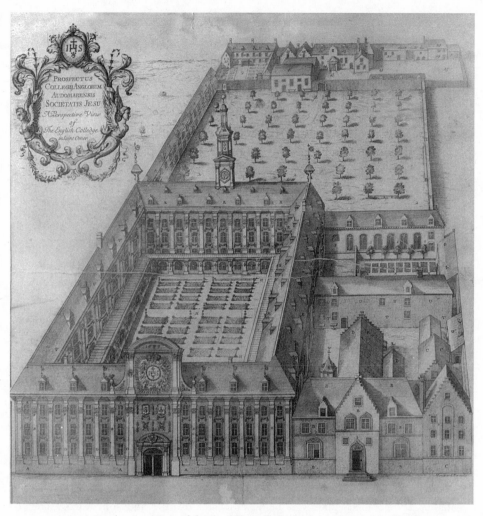

PLATE 14. A Perspective View of the English Colledge in Saint Omer. Montbard, 1689.
Courtesy Stonyhurst College, Lancashire, England

consequently of the importance of heeding all paternal directions, Charley—
first as a little boy, then as an adolescent, and finally as a young man—sought
above all else to please. And Papa, unwavering in his determination to mold a
son who would meet all his expectations, proved an unstinting taskmaster. So
indomitable was his will upon the condition of vulnerability he had deliberately
created that he could compel obedience to his wishes across three thousand
miles of ocean. Tirelessly dictating his expectations through his letters, the elder

Carroll concerned himself with every aspect of Charley's mental, moral, social, religious, and even physical development.

And how did Charley's mother figure in his father's scheme of separation? Perhaps, given her position as an unwed mother, Mama had no choice except to acquiesce in Papa's wishes, but her letters to Charley convey a different sense of reality. Although she sorely missed her son, she loyally supported Papa's decision to send him away, and she faithfully encouraged him to fulfill his father's expectations.[22] Dutiful and uncomplaining, she also seemed secure in the intimate and loving bond that bound the three of them together. Nor was Papa insensitive to her feelings. "You have not begun your Letters *Dr. Papa & Mama*, as I formerly [dir]ected, nor Wrote to your Mother this Year," he chastised Charley in the fall of 1754. "Althô She is not, She has reason to be displeased. I attribute it to inattention, but for the future be more Considerate." For her part, Mama rose graciously to the challenge of long-distance mothering. With typical maternal solicitude, she wrote her small, slight child to ask whether he had grown — "Tel me your Hight" — and reminded him, "Take care of yr Teeth." The news that he had been "seized with . . . a Severe fit of the Cholick" while on a journey made her deeply anxious and led her to urge, "Be carefull of yr Self my dr Charly & avoid every thing that you find disagrees with you or that may impair yr health for our greatest happyness, yr Papas & mine I mean depends upon yr welfare." Not content with firsthand reports from Marylanders who had seen her son, she insisted in 1754 on "having yr Picture & imagine you wonte meet with any difficulty in geting it drawn where you are." Writing to Charley after the likeness arrived two years later, she averred that she "set great Store by it for I think it has a great resemblance of you when y[ou] was here." Although she agreed with the general opinion of friends and acquaintances that he favored his father, she recalled Charley as being much handsomer and concluded, "The Limner has not done you justice."[23]

Mama had no such reservations about the glowing reports Papa brought her when he returned from his trip abroad in the summer of 1758: "I cannot express my dear Child the Joy I felt at meeting with yr Papa nor the Satisfaction & Com-

22. For my discussion of the familial relationship of Papa, Mama, and Charley during Charley's absence from Maryland, I have drawn extensively from Sally D. Mason's graceful essay "Mama, Rachel, and Molly," in Hoffman and Albert, eds., *Women in the Age of the American Revolution*, 244–289.

23. CCA to CC, Sept. 30, 1754, Carroll-McTavish Papers; EB to CC, Sept. 30, 1754, Colonial Coll.; EB to CC, Sept. 8, 1756, Carroll Papers, MS 206. The portrait has not survived.

fort I recd. from his Conversation concerning you," she wrote Charley in August. Everything Papa told her pleased her immensely: "I find his Opinion of you just to my wishes," noting that she had perused "all yr letters to yr Papa & those to me with the utmost pleasure, they are so full of tenderness & affection for us that they cou'd not fail to delight & at the same time to draw Tears from me. . . . You are always at heart my dear Charly & I am never tired of asking yr Papa questions about you some times to tease, he answers me that you are a good for no thing Ugly little fellow, but when he Speaks his Real Sentiments of you there is not any thing that can give me greater Comfort."[24]

Deprived, though she bore it gracefully, of her son, Mama found things to sustain her. Letters from Charley provided special joy — "I wish we cou'd hear from you every Month" — as did Papa's apparent satisfaction with the boy's progress. "Yr Papa's love for you is so great & he is so well pleas[e]d with yr diligence improvement and good dispositions [that h]e is inclined to do every thing for yr Satisfaction [& a]dvantage," she told Charley in the fall of 1754.[25] Unlike Mama's letters, filled with the warmth, encouragement, and news of home that provided Charley with an emotional bridge between the world he had once lived in and the one he now inhabited, Papa's sterner correspondence reflected his didactic commitment to shaping his son. It was not that he had no feelings. "Had I listened to nature & been only guided by Inclination & a mistaken love," he told Charley in July 1760, "I should never have parted with you."[26] Rather than yielding to false sentiments, Papa declared that his "sincere love guided by Reason" had prompted him to make the rest of Charley's life "happy, easy & Ornamental by giving you the best Education in my power."[27]

The quality of Charley's life might have figured peripherally in Papa's calculations, but a stronger motive underlay the elaborate educational enterprise he fashioned for his son — his belief that a Catholic must master a variety of skills to survive and prosper in a society governed by men of such "Malice that they

24. EBC to CC, [Aug. 29, 1758], Carroll-McTavish Papers.

25. EC to CC, Mar. 4, 1759, ibid.; EB to CC, Sept. 30, 1754, Colonial Coll.

26. CCA to CC, July 14, 1760, Carroll-McTavish Papers. The last four words of the quote are obliterated in the manuscript copy of the letter and have been supplied by Thomas Meagher Field's early-twentieth-century edition of Carroll correspondence, *Unpublished Letters of Charles Carroll of Carrollton and His Father, Charles Carroll of Doughoregan* (New York, 1902), 45. Although Field's transcriptions are seriously flawed by silent omissions, misreadings, and other inaccuracies, these words fit the context and appear to be correct.

27. CCA to CC, July 14, 1760, Carroll-McTavish Papers.

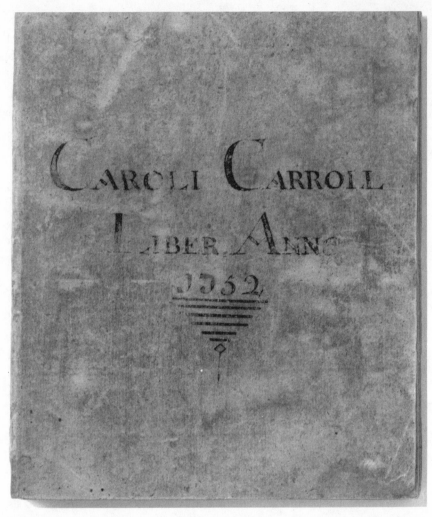

PLATE 15. Exercise Book of Charles Carroll of Carrollton. Cover, leaf 48.
Courtesy The Gilder Lehrman Collection on deposit at the Pierpont Morgan Library,
New York. GLC 600

would not only deprive us of our Property but our lives." [28] This reality sharpened the urgency of his insistence that Charley come to understand and be able to use the law, be able to conduct and monitor extensive financial ventures, comprehend the management of an estate (including all aspects of surveying), and possess the refined social graces required to move with ease among the powerful members of genteel society.

28. Ibid., July 14, 1760.

"Sound & Strong"

In laudem Sancti ___ Poema.

The force that compelled Charley to conform strictly to this demanding agenda was the unbreakable connection his father had forged between performance and reward. Writing to the fifteen-year-old boy on October 9, 1752, near the end of his course at St. Omers, Papa made the link unmistakably clear:

All the Letters I have or shall write to you or concerning you to any o[ne] are carefully entred in a Book so that in case you should be so unfortunate [as to] return not improved in proportion to the Money Time and Care laid out on you [they] will at least be undeniable Testimonies of my Attention to your Welfare and a Cons[tant] Reproach to you for not corresponding on your part to that attention.[29]

Moreover, Papa presumed that the boy kept his letters and periodically referred to the instructions they contained. Having "never Wrote to you as a Child," he expected Charley would repeatedly "reap some advantage" from serious perusals of his correspondence.[30]

Between 1748 and September 1759, Charley studied at four different institutions in France. He remained at the English Jesuit College at St. Omer from 1748 through 1754 and then devoted a year to poetry at the college of the French Jesuits at Rheims. The next two years he spent at the Collège Louis-le-Grand in Paris, where he presented his thesis, written in Latin on conclusions from universal philosophy, and received his degree in July 1757. The following December he moved to Bourges to begin the legal studies that Papa considered the centerpiece of his education. After fourteen months of mingling with provincial society and trying, with mixed success, to unravel the intricacies of civil law, he quit Bourges and returned to Paris, where he hoped to bring his endeavors to a satisfactory conclusion. Completing that course ended his sojourn in France, and for the next five years, 1759–1764, he wrestled with the common law in London.

What went on with the son outside these classrooms mattered just as much to the father as what took place within them. Throughout the entire sixteen-year period he spent abroad, nothing Charley did, thought, or contemplated doing escaped Papa's attention. Had he broken himself of the unfortunate habit of "Stooping & pokeing out yr: head?" If not, "Correct it," Papa ordered; "it is absolutely inconsistent with the Cariage I recommend." Had Charley heeded Mama's advice on dental care? If the "good hair" he had enjoyed as a child continued, "pray wear it, it will become you better than a Wig and beside you will be more in the fashion." And he must dress well; if "worked ruffles" were indeed necessary for "going in company," then Charley must have them.[31] Achieving the proper social deportment required that he perceive correctly and perform

29. Ibid., Oct. 9, 1752.

30. Ibid., Sept. 30, 1754.

31. Ibid., Sept. 30, 1754, Aug. 30, 1758, CC to CCA, Dec. 19, 1757, Carroll Papers, MS 206. Writing to Papa again on Dec. 28, Charley reported that he had acquired six pair of "worked ruffles" at a cost of 60 livres tournois — approximately £2.10.0 sterling (CC to CCA, Dec. 28, 1757, ibid.). Currency equivalents are found in John M. McCusker's *Money and Exchange in Europe and America, 1600–1775: A Handbook* (Chapel Hill, N.C., 1978), 87, 97.

"Sound & Strong"

accordingly. Beginning with a keen, though covert, observation of "the behaviour of all about you," since "what may become a Man in One Country may be very ridiculous in another," Charley must then take care never to seem "so Servile an Im[itator] as to let it be seen you Copy." In all situations, he must make sure that his "Actions be your Own, Natural, and Set easy o[n] you." Moreover, while he must always associate with only the best people, he must at the same time be wary about forming relationships: "A return of Civilities is to be paid to all, an intimacy is not to be Contracted with any, untill You are well acquainted with their Characters, Manners & untill you are Convinced they are in the esteem of good Men."[32]

Finally, Papa expected Charley to accomplish those goals without resorting to extravagant expenditures. He was not to appear "mean," but neither was he to be ostentatious. A "neat" and "genteel" style should be aimed for, a tasteful median between frugality and conspicuous consumption. Achieving this happy equilibrium depended upon three inextricably linked factors: judgment, discretion, and the keeping of regular accounts. Ignoring this triad invited disaster, for living genteelly could be a very tricky business. The generosity required of Charley in one set of circumstances must be prudently balanced with "œconomy" in others; yet he must constantly be aware that his acquaintances would closely scrutinize his habits. Indeed, Papa warned, "a very trifle either spent or saved on particular occasions may make you be esteemed generous or stingy." "In short," the elder Carroll told his son in August 1758, "yr: Judgment & discretion must direct your Expences & you cannot Regulate yr: Expences with Judgment & Discretion without keeping a Regular Acct of them." This meant that Charley must keep accurate records and review them periodically, in order to discern "what Articles of Expence may be avoided" and to acquire "an early habit" of knowing exactly where his finances stood. Such practices would, Papa guaranteed, "save you thousands in the Course of no long life."[33]

As Charley moved from a cloistered world presided over by priests into increasingly varied and complex social environments, the accounts he kept in response to Papa's instructions charted his transformation from a young provincial into a cosmopolitan gentleman. Participating in society while he studied at Bourges in 1758–1759 required that he attend balls and engage in apparently endless games of piquet, so he hired a dancing master and learned to play cards

32. CCA to CC, Sept. 30, 1754, Carroll-McTavish Papers; CCA to CC, Jan. [13], 1758, Carroll-Harper Papers, MdHi.

33. CCA to CC, Aug. 30, 1758, Carroll-McTavish Papers.

adequately, though not well, judging from the frequent losses he dutifully recorded. So consistently did these debits appear in Charley's accounts over the years that in July 1761, Papa, who scrutinized all his son's expenditures, finally asked in exasperation, "Now as I find you charge all the Money you lose at Cards you ought to Cr: wt: you win, for I cannot [suppo]se you so unfortunate as not to win sometimes." The purchase of a shuttlecock and two racquets allowed Charley to play badminton at Bourges, to which diversion he added tennis and riding parties when he returned to Paris. In both venues he kept a servant. Having acquired worked ruffles in Bourges, he then augmented his Paris wardrobe with a nightgown for which he spent £2.10.0 and a velvet coat that cost him £7.8.0, and he seemed continually to be purchasing silk stockings and paying to have them laundered. In at least one area, however, he clearly ignored Papa's insistence on moderation — and regretted it. Immediately following one of many entries for "Bavarian cremes," a confection Charley frequently consumed, there is noted the cost of "two bouillons during my illness."[34]

In London, Charley's social life, conducted for the first time away from the constant gaze of his Jesuit mentors, expanded considerably, as did his allowance, which Papa raised to three hundred pounds sterling a year. Giving treats and suppers at his chambers required him to buy "several little conveniences," including a tea service; and attending plays, concerts, and operas, visiting the pleasure gardens at Ranelagh and Vauxhall, taking trips into the surrounding countryside, and joining the Robin Hood Society, a tavern debating club, all cost money. The most distinctive item he added to his wardrobe was a silver-hilted sword, and he regularly spent money attending to the barbering, curling, and powdering of his hair. As he had in France, he kept a servant; and, despite the fact that his father did not entirely approve, he maintained a horse of his own at a London stable. Along with these expenses he continually added books to his library, some at Papa's direction and others of his own choosing. The younger Carroll's style of life did not go unnoticed. In 1760 his kinsman and St. Omers schoolmate Jacky Carroll, by then well on his way to becoming a priest, wrote, a trifle dourly perhaps, to his brother Daniel in Maryland about the "Great improvement" Charley had made in France and his "Elegant way of living in London."[35]

34. Ibid., July 10, 1761; CC, Account of Expenses, November 1758–September 1759, Carroll-Maccubbin Papers, MdHi.

35. CC to CCA, Feb. 30, 1760, Carroll Papers, MS 206; John Carroll to Daniel Carroll, Mar. 15, 1760, quoted in CCA to CC, July 14, 1760, Carroll-McTavish Papers.

"Sound & Strong"

By entrusting the first eleven years of Charley's education to the Society of Jesus, Papa reaffirmed his family's traditional allegiance to the Jesuit order and brought to bear upon his son what he conceived to be the finest combination of intellectual rigor and moral rectitude on earth. Daunted at first by the St. Omers curriculum, Charley persevered; and, once he mastered the problems that necessitated his remaining in "little figures"— elementary Latin — for an extra year, he did well.[36] By 1751 his Irish cousin and tutor, Father Anthony Carroll (Anthony Carroll of Lisheenboy's grandson) reported to Papa that, while not yet a "leader," Charley usually managed to place among the top five scholars, even though he was one of the youngest students in a "strong school." Two years later, he ranked third, an achievement that Papa noted with "great Pleasure" as a predictor of even greater future accomplishments: "As your Judgment unfolds it self and ripens I expect to hear of your still Rising."[37]

The most ringing endorsement came from Charley's master, Father John Jenison, late in 1753, just as the sixteen-year-old boy was leaving St. Omers to continue his studies at the Jesuit college in Rheims. Although "not in a disposition of Writing Letters," Jenison informed Papa that he had "lost this morning

36. The *Ratio Studiorum*, the basic curriculum at the English Jesuit College at St. Omer, was a course of study originally conceived by St. Ignatius of Loyola (1491–1556), founder of the Society of Jesus, and developed into its final form by Father Claudius Acquaviva (1543–1615), fifth general superior of the Society, between 1581 and 1599. Of the three main divisions within the course of study — literature or humanity, arts, and theology — it was the first, a five-part program beginning with Lower Grammar and progressing through Middle and Upper Grammar to Poetry and Rhetoric, that occupied Charley at St. Omers. "Figures," one of the two divisions of Lower Grammar (the other was Rudiments), introduced the student to the first elements (nouns, substantive verbs, simple verbs) of Greek and Latin. The initial year was devoted to "little" or "lower" figures, and a second year to "great" or "higher" figures. Muir, *Stonyhurst College, 1593– 1992*, 157; A. C. F. Beales, *Education under Penalty: English Catholic Education from the Reformation to the Fall of James II, 1547–1689* (London, 1963), 132, 146–148; Hughes, *Loyola and the Educational System of the Jesuits;* R. R. Harris, ed., *Douai College Documents, 1693–1794*, Catholic Record Society, LXIII (London, 1972), esp. 133–157. The author thanks Professor Philip Gleason of the University of Nortre Dame and Father Geoffrey Holt, London, for clarifying this educational method.

37. Anthony Carroll to CCA, Feb. 26, 1751, Carroll Papers, MS 206; CCA to CC, Oct. 10, 1753, Carroll-Harper Papers. The scholastic environment at St. Omers was highly competitive, with prizes awarded for academic distinction. The rigorous schedule of formal instruction, study periods, recreation, and prayers kept the boys busy from 5:00 A.M. until 9:00 P.M., with two free afternoons a week. Muir, *Stonyhurst College, 1593– 1992*, 28, 158.

the finest young man, in every respect, that ever enter'd the House." Not only had Charley "never deserv'd, on any account, a single harsh word" while under Jenison's care, but his "sweet temper" had also "rendered him equally agreeable both to equals and superiors, without ever making him degenerate into the mean character of a favorite which he always justly despis'd." Even when Charley learned that he would not be allowed to return to Maryland upon completing his course (his cousin Watty Hoxton was already home), his "application to his Book and Devotions" remained steady. "This short character," Father Jenison concluded, "I owe to his deserts; prejudice I am convinc'd has no share in it, as I find the public voice confirms my private sentiments."[38] By contrast, Charley's retrospective view of the institution to which he had been sent not only to be "a learned man, but also advanced in piety & devotion," was revealing and critical. Writing to Papa in 1761 about the shortcomings he perceived in the son of a mutual acquaintance, Charley attributed the lad's ignorance and inexperience to his being schooled too long at St. Omers: "That education is only fit for Priests."[39]

Though he did not intend that Charley should take holy orders, Papa deliberately sought to increase his piety and to protect his "Health," "Virtue," and "Innocence" by having him spend his adolescence under the care and supervision of men of the cloth. Beyond the concerns of personal piety and a sincere attachment to his faith, the elder Carroll viewed religious observance as a critical tool for enjoining discipline and imposing order on one's life, and he believed

38. Although most Catholic schools placed a master, aided by several assistants, in charge of as many as half a dozen classes at once, St. Omers employed a different system, giving one master charge of a single class from the time of its matriculation until its members completed their course of study (Muir, *Stonyhurst College, 1593–1992*, 28). The relationship between English Jesuit John Jenison (1729–1792) and CC continued for nearly a decade after the boy left St. Omers. Brantz Mayer includes Jenison's letter in his "Autobiographic Sketch of Charles Carroll of Carrollton," in Mayer, ed., *Journal of Charles Carroll of Carrollton during His Visit to Canada in 1776, as One of the Commissioners from Congress, with a Memoir and Notes* (Baltimore, 1876), 107–108. According to Mayer, both the document and its envelope were part of his "collection" of autobiographical "scraps," and the envelope bore an endorsement in CCA's hand that read "A Character of my Son: By Mr. Jenison his Master." Beneath those lines, CCC had written the following: "I fear this letter was dictated by Mr. Jenison's partiality to me. I never found till this day (27th July, 1782) that he ever wrote to my Father about me." Rowland later included this material in her *Life of Charles Carroll of Carrollton*, I, 62–63. No manuscript copy of Jenison's letter has been found; it is not at the Maryland Historical Society as indicated by Rowland's citation.

39. CC to CCA, Mar. [1751], Dec. 19. 1761, Carroll Papers, MS 206.

the regimentation of a Jesuit education would instill these values at a tender age. "Business Company late hours &c," he warned Charley in 1758, "gradually seem excuses for first Postponing & then neglecting our Prayers & this Rampart being once overthrown it's impossible to Enumerate the sad Train of Evils wch inevitably enter at the Breach." Regarding the Jesuits' critical role in transmitting such values, "I have I thank God been bred among them," he wrote Charley emphatically in the spring of 1762, "& if you do wt: they have taught you & nothing contrary to it, you will be happy here & hereafter." [40]

When Charley became a student in London, his father continued to remind him of the efficacy of habitually attending to religious obligations. Spiritual diligence alone would not suffice, however. Papa also emphasized in a typically eighteenth-century Enlightenment fashion the role of reason as a means by which an individual could control himself and the forces that shaped his destiny. "Sight with our other Senses is bestow'd on us by Providence for Our Benefit and happiness, but it mus[t] be kept under the Dominion of Reason," he counseled seventeen-year-old Charley in September 1754. This juxtaposition of faith and reason can also be seen in the kinds of books Papa called to Charley's attention: the *Retraite spirituelle* of Father Louis Bourdaloue, Isaac Berruyer's *Histoire du peuple de Dieu* (parts of which were consigned to the Index Expurgatorius in 1732, 1754, and 1758), the Jesuit missionary epistles entitled *Lettres édificantes et curieuses*, Robert Manning's treatises on controversy, and the works of the eighteenth century's celebrated satirist and ardent critic of the Roman Catholic church, Voltaire.[41] A tough-minded, independent man who saw no contradiction between his Catholicism and the exercise of critical thinking, the elder Carroll placed his ultimate reliance on the test of reason and rejected out of hand blind faith and mechanical genuflection to any authority, religious or civil. As he wrote to Charley in April 1762, "Wt: ever a man may grant, wt: ever Rules he may lay down, wt: ever Doctrines he may profess, if they be inconsistent with reason

40. CCA to CC, Aug. 30, 1758, Apr. 8, 1762, Carroll-McTavish Papers.
41. CCA to CC, Sept. 30, 1754, ibid. This is by no means an exhaustive list of the Carrolls' reading matter, but merely a sample of some of their interests. For a comprehensive bibliography of the Carroll library, see Michael T. Parker, "'The Fittest Season for Reading': The Library of Charles Carroll of Carrollton" (master's thesis, University of Maryland, 1990); Ronald Hoffman, Sally D. Mason, and Eleanor S. Darcy, eds., *Dear Papa, Dear Charley: The Peregrinations of a Revolutionary Aristocrat, as Told by Charles Carroll of Carrollton and His Father, Charles Carroll of Annapolis, with Sundry Observations on Bastardy, Child-Rearing, Romance, Matrimony, Commerce, Tobacco, Slavery, and the Politics of Revolutionary America* (forthcoming), appendix 2.

& Contrary to Morality Justice & Religion they are in themselves void & can have no ill Effect."[42]

Charley more than met his father's expectations in this regard: his study of the works of Locke, Newton, and Montesquieu made him a thoroughly "enlightened" man. Writing to Papa in October 1761 concerning the difficulties the Jesuits were experiencing in France, he even chastised the order for its uncritical dependence on authority and judged "dangerous to the state a body of men who implicitly believe the dictates of one Superior, & are *carried on to the execution of his orders with a blind impetuosity of will & eagerness to obey without the least enquiry or examination.*" In this case, however, Papa found Charley's "reasoning" defective. "The implicit Obedience professed by the Jesuits cannot be meant by Common Sense & Justice to extend beyond things innocent, indifferent & Just," he retorted in his reply on April 8, 1762. "Have they murdered, burnt or destroy'd in virtue of their Obedience?" In Papa's view, the Jesuits were suffering because "their Eminen[t] Merit & Virtue" had made them objects of envy and "provoked this persecution."[43]

Charley left the cocoon of direct Jesuit supervision in September 1759 when he departed France for England, where Papa had directed he spend five years studying the common law. Believing London to be a sophisticated and corrupt metropolis, far different from the insular world Charley had known, the older man found it necessary to impress upon his twenty-two-year-old son the grave dangers of the situation he was entering. The first letter he wrote after Charley crossed the Channel emphasized that Britain's capital was "an open & wide Ocean of danger" wherein "the greatest Resolution will be necessary to withstand the many Temptations you will be exposed to." Indeed, Papa warned, "so abandoned will you find most men as to be asham'd of even appearing Virtuous." To finish his education creditably and maintain his virtue in such an environment would require that Charley apply himself with unstinting vigor, "for nothing is more certain than that Idliness is the Root of all Evil."[44]

The younger Carroll's wide-eyed reaction to London vividly underscored the validity of his father's concerns. Acknowledging, almost breathlessly, that his "present situation is the most dangerous of any I have hitherto been in," he guilelessly revealed his awareness of the exciting possibilities that the great city's

42. CCA to CC, Apr. 8, 1762, Carroll-McTavish Papers.
43. CC to CCA, Oct. 22, 1761, Carroll Papers, MS 206; CCA to CC, Apr. 8, 1762, Carroll-McTavish Papers.
44. CCA to CC, Oct. 6, 1759, Carroll-McTavish Papers.

"Sound & Strong"

opportunities presented: "A Young person's passions are strong of themselves & need no outward encouragement," he told Papa, "but when roused by occasions, strengthened by example, fired with wine & Jovial company become almost irresistible." Would the values inculcated by his eleven years of Jesuit mentoring hold fast against such allurements? Highly impressionable and demonstrably inexperienced, Charley could not be sure. Although he knew full well that "the greatest resolution, prudence, & virtue are requisite to protect me from such contagion," he nevertheless wondered, with an ambivalent candor that must have given Papa pause, "Who can not promise not others but even himself, of remaining always virtuous?" [45]

Chief among Papa's concerns as Charley approached young manhood were his contacts with the opposite sex. From the older man's perspective, women posed a particular threat both to the Carroll resources and to the realization of his plans for Charley, but he also knew that association with them would contribute to his son's genteel socialization. A proper balance must therefore be achieved. Paternal instruction to this end commenced in the late summer of 1758, with a terse order that the young man must "avoid any intimacy or familiarity with the Fair Sex especially Visits or Conversations without witnesses." Moving immediately to the other side of the equation, the elder Carroll then emphasized that properly chaperoned socializing was both acceptable and desirable because women's ability "to soften & polish yr: Manners" would produce "a chearfull lively easy & polite Behaviour . . . in no way inconsistent with Religion or your Duty to God." [46]

45. CC to CCA, Jan. 29, 1760, Carroll Papers, MS 206. CCA edited this sentence to read "and who can promise to others, even to himself, to remain always virtuous."

46. CCA to CC, Aug. 30, 1758, Carroll-McTavish Papers. Papa's decision to address the subject was undoubtedly triggered by Charley's enthusiastic report from Bourges the previous February that he had been the escort and dancing partner of "one of the most butifull young ladies I ever saw" at a Shrovetide masked ball. CC to CCA, Feb. 11, 1758, Carroll Papers, MS 206.

Chaperoned socializing: CCA to CC, Aug. 30, 1758, Carroll-McTavish Papers. Papa's caution proved timelier than he knew: letters he had not yet received from Charley, written on June 14 and August 10, 1758, contained Charley's accounts of a brief (and probably innocent) encounter with one Miss Alcock, the "young, pretty, witty daughter" of an English button manufacturer at La Charité, a small town about thirty-six miles from Bourges. Charley met Miss Alcock, whom he described as possessing "no wealth other than her wit and beauty," during a summer holiday jaunt through central and southern France. What most unnerved Papa was Charley's report that the lady had so captivated one of his St. Omers school chums, Willoughby, a young man of "considerable" wealth, that the fellow was ready to marry her, "if she had wished, even without the consent of

Charley's move to London a year later required more specific directions from his father, this time regarding "the Women of the Town," who must be avoided "as you wou'd a Rattle Snake." In graphic terms, Papa made clear that failure to heed this warning risked the direst consequences: "By several Examples within my own knowledge they have proved as fatally, nay almost as suddenly venomous." Continuing in the same ominous vein, the elder Carroll proceeded to chapter and verse: "I have known some young men after as much time & Money spent on their Education as has been on yrs snatched from their Expecting Parents by the poison reced from Prostitutes, Others I have known long to linger in a State of Rottenness & at last to die objects of horror, therefore," he concluded, "if the more noble & pure Sentiments of Virtue & Duty should fail to keep you innocent, let a regard to yr: health deter you from a Crime wch may in this world make you most miserable."[47]

Charley's playful responses to Papa's advice about women seem less serious than the older man perhaps desired and, like his reaction to the "dangers" of London, reveal his unmistakable delight in the chance for female acquaintances. Exclaiming that he had found nothing as "decieving" or "engaging as women," he "wondered why Providence has bestowed such art, such sagacity on that sex, and at the same time so much beauty" and readily admitted, "The most beautiful are always the most powerful, at least with me." Even knowing that "the Strongest, wisest, best of men have been ensneared by women, & brought to utter destruction" did not curb his enchantment with "the charms of that pleasing deceitfull sex . . . surpassed by nothing but their art in setting them off to the best advantage & in rendering them more fatel." Nor did Charley's assurances to Papa that he would never "think of marriage without your previous consent & knowledge" preclude his behaving in a flirtatious manner toward the opposite sex. His cavalier attitude earned him a gentle rebuke from his mother, who chided him for the way he wrote of "the Ladys" and warned that he might someday meet one "that may make you pay for all the slights shewn to her Sex, by keeping you in her Chains & haveing no Mercy on you."[48]

his Father." Replying to Charley in February 1759, Papa stated that he was "well pleas'd to find that tho you give Miss Alcock the Merit of her wit & beauty[,] you think your Friend Willoughby would have acted foolishly in marrying her[.] You judge right, such a step is not to be made so early in life & hardly ever without the Consent of Parents." CC to CCA and EBC, June 14, Aug. 10, 1758, Carroll Papers, MS 206; CCA to CC, Feb. 9, 1759, Carroll-McTavish Papers.

47. CCA to CC, Oct. 6, 1759, Carroll-McTavish Papers.

48. CC to CCA, Jan. 29, 1760, Carroll Papers, MS 206 (nos. 47, 47a); EBC to CC, Sept. 10, 1760, Harper-Pennington Papers.

Although Charley lightheartedly declared himself to be so "frighted at the clincking of matrimonial chains" that he could resist even the most winsome charmer, Papa had no intention of leaving the matter to chance.[49] Like other ambitious colonial men, most notably his own father, Charles Carroll of Annapolis certainly understood that wedlock offered the possibility of achieving desirable goals — the forging of alliances between families, the enhancement of fortunes, the solidification and even the improvement of social status. But, as the calculated manner in which he dealt with Elizabeth Brooke demonstrates, he saw with equal clarity the real personal and material risks in using matrimonial strategies to pursue these ends. In Papa's view, the stakes could not be higher, and he transmitted the weight of his experience to Charley in the fall of 1762.

Acknowledging that his son had reached an age when "it is Naturall to think of Establishing yr self in the World by Mariage," Papa began by listing the values Charley must look for in a mate in order to assure his "Future Happyness." First, she must be "Virtuous, Sensible, good natured, Complaisant, Complying & of a Chearfull Disposition." Second, she must come from a good family, one worthy of the Carrolls' princely Irish lineage. Third, her fortune must be evaluated in proportion to the sixty thousand pounds sterling Charley could expect to inherit. And last, but by no means least, her religion must be taken into account, for Papa strongly recommended that Charley not under any circumstances "Marry a Protestant, for beside the risque yr Offspring will Run, it is Certain there Cannot be any Solid Happyness without an union of Sentiments in all Matters, Especially in Religion."[50]

Having enumerated the qualities to be sought in a wife "by a Man of Sense," Papa then set down the method Charley should use in searching for her. Aware of his son's admitted susceptibility to pretty faces, the elder Carroll immediately put this attribute in a proper perspective. While not to be "under valued," beauty was "too transient & Lyable to too many Accidents to be a Substantiall motive to Mariage." The chief danger lay in beauty's ability to affect "Our Propensity to Lust so strongly, that it makes most Matches, & most of those Matches Miserable unless when Beauty is gone, Virtue, good sense good Nature, Complaisance & Chearfullness Compensate the loss." Similarly, a man in search of a wife must not allow his heart to rule his head, lest "Passion Blind our Understanding." Moreover, the wise suitor would conceal his intentions in order to

---

49. CC to EBC, Mar. 31, 1761, Carroll-McTavish Papers.

50. CCA to CC, Sept. 1, 1762, Carroll Papers, MS 206. The version quoted is that signed by CCA. A second, unsigned copy, endorsed by CCA as a copy, is filed in the same collection.

discover the true character of the women under consideration: "The Sex are the most Artfull Dissemblers, But Nature will shew it self." The most serious scrutiny must be given to the character and "Regularity of the Family," in order to determine whether daughters had been "confined Early to their Book Needle & Works Sutable to their Station & Properly instructed in the Principles of Religion" or had been "Humoured when young & Bred in Dissipation & inattention to things necessary & Laudable." The former sort, Papa assured Charley, would make "good Wives"; with the latter, "the Contrary is much to be dreaded." Physical and mental health deserved attention as well: "It is of Importance to the Offspring that a Man & Woman should be of a good Size well Proportioned" and that they possess none of a host of "naturall defects," among them such undesirable traits as "Lameness Deafness Squinting stammering stuttering" and "Hereditary disorders Such as the Gout Gravell Consumption" and "Madness." With unveiled contempt, Papa dismissed any nobleman who "would not suffer an undersized Pyebaled Walleyed Spavined Mare in his Stud" but would "Urge his Son to Marry a Humpbacked Puny Woman with a great fortune." Does not such a man, the elder Carroll asked derisively, have "a greater Afection for his Beasts than his Family?"[51]

Papa devoted the final section of his letter to money. "Not that a fortune in Prudence ought to be overlooked," he explained, "but it ought not to be Prefered or even put in Competition wth the other good Qualities I have taken Notice of & wh I wish you may find in a Wife." To underscore his sincerity, the older man stated explicitly that, although the Carroll wealth made his son an extremely viable contender for the hands of rich daughters on both sides of the Atlantic, he would not object if Charley "Should Condescend to take a Woman unequall to you in Point of fortune," provided that the "inequality will be Compensated in Point of Family, by her Virtue & the other good Qualities of her mind & Person." Nor would he ever try to "perswade or influence you to Marry against yr inclinations," although he expected Charley not to "marry against myne" if he married in Maryland. If his son decided to wed an English bride, Papa pledged to "settle on yr Wife as a Dower Si[x] Pounds a year during her life if She Survive you, for every Hundred Pounds she shall bring you as a fortune," provided that Charley protect the Carroll fortune by making a formal prenuptial agreement.[52]

Although similar in some respects to other eighteenth-century parental injunctions prescribing the qualities essential for a happy union, Charles Carroll

51. Ibid.
52. Ibid.

of Annapolis's directions to his son on how to pick a wife are in other ways a unique product of his own character and experience. His forceful recommendation that his son not marry a Protestant signaled the uncompromising nature of his Catholic identity and confirmed the distance between the Carrolls and Protestant society. Eliminating Protestants also gave Charley a much smaller pool from which to choose, for there were, as Papa readily and proudly asserted, few "Roman Catholick Families in the Kings Dominions wh Could give their Daughters fortunes Proportioned to yours."[53] Similarly, the elder Carroll's insistence that financial arrangements be set down in a marriage settlement before Charley entered wedlock reaffirms his determination to prevent Carroll wealth from being siphoned away by a widow's remarriage.

However undeniable, Papa's hard-nosed practicality is not the whole story. His instructions also evince an equally genuine desire that Charley choose wisely in order to find "a Marryed state a Happy one." The knowledge that conjugal unions could produce personal happiness grew out of Charles Carroll of Annapolis's oddly configured relationship with his son's mother, whom he eulogized upon her death in 1761 as "the best of wives being a Charming Woman in every sense, remarkable for her good Sense evenness & Sweetness of her temper." Elizabeth Brooke Carroll had similarly endorsed the felicity of their marriage in a letter written to Charley in September 1760. Assuring her son that he would have no trouble finding a wife, she asserted, "The only difficulty will be to get a good one, one of good [mi]n[d] & temper & every other way agreable to make you intirely happy." Should he marry, preferably "about 3 or 4 years hence," she would only "wish you as happy in that State as yr [P]apa & I am."[54]

Charley reacted to his father's matrimonial advice more seriously than he had

53. Ibid. Quantifying the characteristics deemed desirable in female mates from some sixty marriage notices in the *Maryland Gazette* (Annapolis), Allan Kulikoff found that being well accomplished and agreeable led the list, followed closely by being virtuous and estimable. *Tobacco and Slaves: The Development of Southern Cultures in the Chesapeake, 1680–1800* (Chapel Hill, N.C., 1986), 176.

For discussions of eighteenth-century gentry views of marriage that do not take into account religious affiliations, see Jan Lewis, *The Pursuit of Happiness: Family and Values in Jefferson's Virginia* (New York, 1983), chap. 5; Daniel Blake Smith, *Inside the Great House: Planter Family Life in Eighteenth-Century Chesapeake Society* (Ithaca, N.Y., 1980), chap. 4; Kathleen M. Brown, *Good Wives, Nasty Wenches, and Anxious Patriarchs: Gender, Race, and Power in Colonial Virginia* (Chapel Hill, N.C., 1996), chaps. 8–10; Jay Fliegelman, *Prodigals and Pilgrims: The American Revolution against Patriarchal Authority, 1750–1812* (New York, 1982), 123–131.

54. CCA to CC, Mar. 22, 1761, Sept. 1, 1762, Carroll Papers, MS 206; EBC to CC, Sept. 10, 1760, Harper-Pennington Papers.

to the older man's earlier cautionary instructions concerning women. In the winter of 1763, he expressed his appreciation for "the liberty of choice" allowed him and averred, "To force a child's inclination in a concern of such importance is the highest cruelty a father can be guilty of." He even declared boldly that he would "rather be disinherited than obliged to marry against my inclination." Far more subdued than he had been during his first two years in London, the younger Carroll now perceived a great scarcity of the kind of women Papa recommended. In Charley's jaded view, "A chearful sensible virtuous, good natured woman is rara avis in terris [a rare bird on earth], a Prodigy, a miracle, a deviation from the general & fixed laws: not one in 10000 is endowed with all those good qualities." Moreover, even if he found a suitable "lady of family," he doubted that he would ever be able to prevail upon her "to leave her Home, her friends & relations & follow me to a barbarous uncivilised country." Wealthy ladies, whose "love of pleasure is stronger than their love of riches," would prove the most resistant. Professing a lack of interest in the opposite sex that contrasts sharply with his initial delight, Charley told his father firmly that he knew of "no R: Cath: lady that will suit me," that he had "never as yet seen the woman I shou'd chuse to marry" — "I have never been in love & hope I never shall be." [55]

Pleased as he was by Charley's promise of obedience in this all-important area, Papa nevertheless found his avowals excessive. "[I] am Convinced You Entertain an Opinion by far too disadvantageous of Women," he replied in a short letter written the following June. "What not one Chearfull Sensible Virtuous Good Natured Woman in 10,000; Pray How many Chearfull Sensible Virtuous Good natured Men do you Reckon in a like Number," he inquired dryly. "To do the Sex Justice they would outnumber us in good Qualities." Nor did the older man accept the younger's pessimistic conclusion that no suitable mate willing to brave the colonial wilderness could be found. Did not Charley's personal qualifications and potential wealth constitute an irresistible combination? Dismissing his son's pointed reminder that metropolitan elites regarded the colonies as "barbarous" and "uncivilised," Papa declared,"I should be sorry if You should ever happen to like a Woman so Silly as to make Such an Objection," it being just as possible to enjoy "Domestick Happyness . . . in Maryland as in London." Quoting, with evident amusement, the younger man's adamant declaration that he had *never been in Love & hope I never shall be,*" Papa agreed not to insist that Charley marry, but, he pointed out, "Many Men talk as you do untill they are far

55. CC to CCA, Feb. 19, 1763, Harper-Pennington Papers.

Advanced in years, Some untill they are past their Grand Climacterick & then become fond Doting Husbands."[56]

Full of new and exciting social opportunities, especially encounters with women, the London scene encouraged Charley to try his wings in ways that were bound to affect his relationship with Papa. The deference and obedience with which he had unquestioningly acceded to paternal direction in France affirmed the success of the elder Carroll's campaign to mold a worthy heir; and, until the fall of 1759, the father found the clay of the son's character entirely malleable. Canny realist that he was, Charles Carroll of Annapolis anticipated that exposure to women and cosmopolitan society might well induce a maturing young man to challenge a parent's authority, and thus he addressed those issues directly. What he did not expect, however, was that the study of the common law, the undertaking he regarded as the crowning accomplishment of his son's efforts, would itself become the nettlesome core of Charley's resistance.

Within six weeks of his arrival in the British metropolis, Charley began to question his father's plans. Having acquired an evidently sufficient command of civil law at Bourges and Paris, he now confronted the necessity of mastering an equally tedious subject that his religion prevented him from ever putting to practical use.[57] Aware that merely expressing a dislike of the law would not suffice, the younger Carroll mounted an argument with practical appeal — the expense involved in pursuing a legal education by gaining entry to the Inns of Court's Inner Temple, where his grandfather, Charles Carroll the Settler, had matriculated. "I shou'd be glad to know wether you wou'd have me entered of the temple," he asked his father in November 1759, "as the Roman Catholick religion is an obstacle to my being call'd to the Bar, I don't see the necessity or need of it, especially as I cannot be entered as a member under 20 pounds."[58]

This letter crossed one from Papa that answered the question by fully illumi-

---

56. CCA to CC, June 22, 1763, ibid. A "climacterick," a period in a person's life during which he is supposedly especially vulnerable to crises of health or fortune, was calculated by using multiples of 7 and 9. The "Grand Climacterick," a particularly critical time, came at the age of 63 (the product of 7 times 9). Born in 1702, Papa was 55, 8 years shy of his grand climacteric, when he married Charley's mother.

57. The previous fall, Charley had candidly acknowledged that he would need some powerful assistance — "the help of Domat, and the aid of God" — to gain any "understanding" of the civil law. (The reference is to Jean Domat, *Les lois civiles, dans leur ordre naturel* [1689].) CC to CCA, Nov. 7, 1758, Carroll-McTavish Papers.

58. CC to CCA and EBC, Nov. 13, 1759, Carroll Papers, MS 206.

nating the centrality of a legal education in his grand design for Charley. Besides its utility in preventing a gentleman from a distasteful dependence "on ev'ry dirty Petty fogger," proficiency in the law gave a wealthy man the ability "to advise & assist his friends, Relations & Neighbours of all sorts," thereby greatly increasing his "weight . . . on the Circle of his Acquaintance." Moreover, in England, a legal career often led not only to wealth but also to the "highest honours," like the peerage. Admitting that "as things now stand you are shut out from the Bar," Papa countered by pointing out that religious proscription did not extend to the less prestigious but still quite lucrative legal career of "acting as a Counsellor." But even more important than status and material gain, a competence in the law was "absolutely necessary to ev'ry private Gent: of fortune who has the least Idea of being Independant." Charley must therefore not spare himself in reaching this goal, an expectation his father conveyed to him in the clearest possible manner. "I do not send you to the Temple to spend (as many do) 4 or 5 Years to no purpose, I send you to Study & Labour, it is wt I expect from you do not disappoint my hopes." Everything Charley had previously accomplished was "but a preparation to do this well." Now he must "Finish worthyly, & apply as if yr: whole & sole Dependance was to be on the knowledge of the Law." [59]

Temporarily thwarted, Charley decided to employ more subtle tactics. In praising the creation of a chair of common law at Oxford as a much-needed corrective for the legal discipline's "want of a certain method & order," he noted, almost offhandedly, that Roman Catholics were not allowed to attend the lectures given by the chair's occupant, William Blackstone. He dutifully bought law books, though they were "extremely dear," but he doubted self-deprecatingly that he possessed the "bright capacity" requisite to gaining from them a thorough understanding of the law. Fifteen months after his arrival in London, he candidly confessed that despite "a pretty serious application during this time to the Law, I have made little or no advance in it . . . owing to my incapacity, to the difficulty of the study and to want of instruction." More than once he asked with a studied casualness how long he must stay in London. Having agreed to occupy his chambers for three years in order to get them painted, he wondered whether that would not be quite enough time for acquiring the "tincture" of legal knowledge that he would need to continue his studies in Maryland. Only occasionally did he risk expressing his real antipathy to complain of the law's dryness and intricacy, decrying its "barbarous language" and "unintelligible Jargon" and describing its practice as nothing more than "the mean but gainful application to

59. CCA to CC, Oct. 6, 1759, Carroll-McTavish Papers.

all the little arts of chicane." Through it all, Papa remained unmoved: Charley must enter the Inner Temple and spend four full years acquiring "a perfect knowledge of the law without wch I may say a Gent: is unfinished."[60]

In the midst of these periodically testy exchanges an event occurred that left an indelible mark on Charley's personality and perceptibly altered the balance of power between him and his father. Early in June of 1761 he received Papa's letter of the previous March conveying to him the "afflicting news" of his mother's death. The young man was devastated. For more than a year, information conveyed by Maryland visitors to London had made him uneasy about the state of her health. Dismissing as highly improbable suggestions that the mysterious swelling with which she was afflicted indicated a pregnancy, he worried instead that her condition signified dropsy. The illnesses and deaths of his Aunt Jenny and his grandmother within a year of each other increased his anxiety, and, fearful that Mama's sorrow at the loss of her closest female relatives would bring her further harm, he had urged Papa to "try every expedient that may allay her grief." A proper understanding of death as "the end of misery, the commencement of never ending happiness," combined with "company . . . the best preservative against melancholy," would certainly, the son advised, produce salutary effects.[61] Encouraged by the generally positive reports from Papa during the summer and fall of 1760, Charley began to believe that the crisis had passed, and by the spring of 1761 he could acknowledge that the distance separating him from his mother had perhaps unduly accentuated his apprehension. This more hopeful outlook, so recently acquired, made him particularly unprepared to learn that the event he most dreaded had indeed occurred.

The last phase of Mama's illness had begun in mid-December; and, despite the best efforts of four doctors, the end came on March 12, 1761. Acknowledging the searing depth of their loss — "To you she was a most tender Mother, to me the best of wives" — Papa reminded his son that they would find true solace only in religion. The dutiful Christian willing to submit himself to God's will would receive in return for his faith "that ease wch nothing else can give him." One additional comfort remained for Papa: "You are left," he told Charley, "the Pledge of our love & friendship."[62]

60. CC to CCA, Jan. 29, Feb. 30 (*sic*), Apr. 10, Sept. 16, 1760, Jan. 1, May 15, 1761, Carroll Papers, MS 206; CCA to CC, July 14, 1760, Carroll-McTavish Papers.

61. CC to CCA, Feb. 13, Mar. 28, 1761, Carroll Papers, MS 206. Charley had not learned of his mother's death when he wrote Papa on March 28.

62. CCA to CC, Mar. 22, 1761, ibid.; CCA to CC, May 21, 1761, Carroll-McTavish Papers.

Charley's anguish pierced to the core of his being. There was no sufficient comfort for the loss of his mother. Deprived of the "fond delusive hopes" of their eventual reunion that had for so many years sustained him, he bitterly pronounced himself "too credulous . . . all my imaginary Joys are vanished in an instant." The pious platitudes he had so recently penned to Papa concerning the attitude Mama must adopt toward the deaths of Aunt Jenny and his grandmother must have echoed mockingly in his heart. Never again to see his mother, he now was forced to acknowledge that his father might also be "snatched" from him, leaving him adrift in the world, friendless and without emotional support. Surely now he would be permitted to come home; could he not leave in the next fleet? "I am only doing here what I cou'd do as well at home. . . . I can apply as closely to the Law in yr. House as in the temple: what more distractions shall I meet with in Annapolis than in London?"[63]

Charley's cry of pain failed to move his father. The answer was no: he must stay and finish his course. Always aware that his plans for Charley carried the risk that one parent or the other might never see their son again, Papa never flinched. Having consistently privileged the achievement of competency over sentiment in his dealings with his son, the elder Carroll saw no reason to behave any differently in the current crisis. Educational and social skills and a reasoned, calculating intelligence must always take precedence over human feelings. Although Papa denied neither their existence nor their sincerity, such emotions were to be contained and borne and on no account allowed to interfere with the critical steps one must take to confront life's practical challenges successfully. His own experience offered a precedent: being called home from school abroad upon the Settler's death in 1720 forced Charles Carroll of Annapolis to give up the study of law that his father had intended for him. Regretting that loss for the rest of his life, he would not, under any circumstances, allow a similar fate to impede his son. Despite the severity of their loss and the weight of personal loneliness he and his son must bear, Papa expected Charley to maintain a reasoned perspective: grief, however deeply felt, must not interrupt his diligent acquisition of legal knowledge. For Papa, the inevitability of parental mortality simply affirmed the fundamental wisdom of his plan: the size of the Carroll estate made it "lyable to Many Disputes, Especially as A Roman Catholick stands but a Poor Chance for Justice with Our Juries in Particular."[64] In the same way that they had shaped Charley's earlier educational life, those realities now dictated that he remain in London and acquire a thorough grasp of the law.

63. CC to CCA, June 10, 1761, Carroll Papers, MS 206.
64. CCA to CC, Sept. 9, 1761, Carroll-McTavish Papers.

But Mama's death took a greater toll on Charley than the elder Carroll had anticipated, and, despite paternal testimonials to the efficacy of prayer and "the comfortable & Animating hope of enjoying her in a happy Endless Eternity," the young man could not shake off his melancholy. Nothing seemed to help. Though "pleasant, instructive, & agreeable," a journey into the English countryside several months later did not prove restorative, because Charley's constant awareness of his mother's death so frequently "threw a damp upon my spirits even in the midst of company." In late October 1761, a letter from his cousin Rachel Darnall, who had cared for Mama during her final illness, brought him to tears. Unable to muster sufficient self-discipline or "Christian resignation" to assuage his sorrow, he could only hope that the passage of time would eventually dull the pain and bring him relief. Nor did his anxiety that his father might also die diminish in the months after his mother's death. Such a loss, Charley reiterated in the spring of 1762, "wou'd be the greatest misfortune that can befall me."[65]

Distraught with grief and the anticipation of the even more devastating loss of his father, Charley found it impossible to concentrate on anything. His detestation of the law increased, and he no longer minded confessing that he made no progress in it. The litany of his dissatisfactions expanded: the tedium of the legal curriculum taxed his health, there were no proper instructors, the Inns of Court exposed him to bad company, the London air made him ill. And suppose Papa should die. "To what difficulties woud you leave me exposed?" he asked plaintively on more than one occasion.[66] Pleading for an early return to Maryland, he argued that his father could then profitably instruct him in the intricacies of Carroll business affairs, thereby providing him with knowledge far more essential to his competence as heir than anything he could possibly gain by prolonging his stay in London.

Papa forbore Charley's state of mind patiently for about six months before calling a firm halt to overt mourning. Although they would always think of Mama and pray for her, he and his son must in the future refrain from discussing her: the time had come to concentrate exclusively on the unfinished business that must be addressed during the rest of Charley's tenure in England. In addition to mastering the law, the young man must undertake the Italian method of bookkeeping, arithmetic, and surveying. He should apply the final gloss to a truly cosmopolitan character by observing and internalizing his im-

65. Ibid., May 21, 1761; CC to CCA, Oct. 13, Dec. 16, 1761, Mar. 17, 1762, Carroll Papers, MS 206.

66. CC to CCA, Mar. 17, 1762, Carroll Papers, MS 206.

pressions of the most prominent Englishmen of the day, lest he appear ignorant and ill informed upon his return home. "We live in the world & ought to know it," his father told him sagely in the summer of 1762, emphasizing that, because such "knowledge gives us weight in it, & makes us agreeable in Company & Conversation, some time & some money ought to be sacrificed to that end." Deeming Charley's persistent desire to scuttle his legal studies and leave London early as shortsighted and "unbecoming yr: good Sense," Papa reiterated the benefits of gaining proficiency in the law — the ability "to transact yr: affairs with ease & Security . . . to state yr: own Cases, to instruct those you employ," and to judge the service such persons rendered. The younger man's emotional state had similarly distorted his perception of the disadvantages he would suffer should his father perish before he returned to Maryland. Charley's own aptitude and instruction by their kinsman and confidant Richard Croxall would, Papa assured him, quickly yield "a thorô knowledge of my Affairs & yr: Interest." The critical importance of a legal education to his son's future "Wellfare, Interest & happiness" had steeled Papa to set aside his "natural fondness & propensity to see you & have you with me," and he would not "alter my Resolution in this Respect."[67] Moreover, he expected Charley to behave with comparable self-discipline, rationality, and fortitude.

When his efforts to reason and persuade did not produce the desired results, the elder Carroll turned in exasperation to sterner measures. Writing to Charley in midsummer 1762 — "in my owne hand because I do not Care my Clerk should know that you still persist after what I have Said to You to desier to Come in next Spring" — the angry father gave no quarter. Allowing Charley to come home without finishing his four-year course of legal study would, in addition to making them both objects of ridicule to their contemporaries, abrogate all the years the younger Carroll had spent preparing himself for that crowning achievement. "Is a year to be Higgled for by a Man of yr Sense & Age?" Papa asked sarcastically. Expressing his "great uneasiness . . . that what you seem to do so unwillingly you will not do well," the father concluded with a threat: "I have done my duty, you will too late Repent yr not Corresponding with my Will & Intention."[68]

What lay behind the threat? If his heir proved unworthy, would Papa redraw the will? Were Charley's melancholia and desultory behavior in danger of costing him everything? Suffice it to say that the young man straightened himself

67. CCA to CC, Nov. 10, 1761, ibid.; CCA to CC, June 29, 1762, Carroll-McTavish Papers.

68. CCA to CC, July 24, 1762, Carroll Papers, MS 206.

"Sound & Strong"

out. Six months later he reported that he now understood "the theory of Italian bookkeeping" and could "follow that method if need be, in the transacting of my own business." He had engaged a professor of mathematics to teach him surveying and decided to supplement his understanding by also learning geometry and trigonometry. He had not entirely capitulated, however. Upon the most important point of contention — the law — he conducted a clever campaign of passive resistance. Because he was now spending "not less than 2 hours a day" on other worthy pursuits, he knew his father could certainly see why "my reading the Law will be somewhat interrupted at least for some while." The most serviceable defense of all was one to which he knew Papa to be especially vulnerable, and he did not hesitate to employ it: "My health will not permit me to apply as closely and as long as I could wish," he informed his father early in 1763, adding that he was sure the elder Carroll "would not have me upon any account endanger my Constitution which tho' pretty good is none of the stoutest and will not bear too much fatigue; study may certainly be stiled such. There is no fatigue greater than that of the mind." [69]

Charley's attack of smallpox, and recovery, in the spring of 1763 would have strengthened such an argument to his visibly shaken, vastly relieved father. But, by then, the die had already been cast. In December 1762, several months before his son's life-threatening illness, Papa wearily penned his concession: "I acquiesce to your Resolution of not entering yourself of the Temple." A variety of stresses had worn the elder Carroll down. His misery between January and March 1761 because of his wife's illness and death had been added to by his dispute with his nephew Charles Carroll of Duddington. Dissatisfied with the accounts Charles Carroll of Annapolis had prepared and submitted to them for arbitration, Messrs. Hill and Waring had begun to press for additional information and detailed explanations just at the time Elizabeth lay dying. It was behavior, Carroll of Annapolis later recalled acidly, that would have "disgraced a Hottentot." [70] Compounding those troubles, a routine examination of loan office accounts by a committee of the Maryland general assembly in the spring of 1761 had discovered that Henry Darnall III, naval officer of Patuxent, had absconded with some sixteen hundred pounds sterling of the funds he had collected. Because Charles Carroll of Annapolis, together with the miscreant's brother John, had posted the one-thousand-pound-sterling security bond pre-

69. CC to CCA, Jan. 7, 1763, Dreer Collection, HSP; CC to CCA, Jan. 31, 1763, Carroll Papers, MS 206.

70. CCA to CC, Dec. 26, 1762, Carroll Papers, MS 206; CCA to Clement Hill, Dec. 24, 1761, Charles Carroll of Annapolis, letterbook 1757–1761, fol. 95, MdHi.

requisite for their kinsman's assumption of the post, the malfeasance meant a potentially heavy loss for the Carrolls. Although Carroll managed to protect himself by forcing Henry and his eldest son, Henry, Jr., to sign over all their property to him, he had to take that action just when his grief at Mama's demise was freshest.[71] In the midst of such troubles, the older man found himself less and less interested in continuing the tiresome contest with his son.

Papa's decision to relent on the matter of Charley's entering the Inner Temple diffused the tension between them and gave the younger man room to make a final recovery from his depression. The reprieve from formally pursuing the law did not, however, mean that Charley could leave England early, nor did it excuse him from completing the rest of his father's regimen for making him both competent and genteel. In addition to mastering arithmetic, surveying, and the double-entry method of keeping books, he must reaffirm his lineage by engaging a genealogist who could bring the Carroll line forward from at least 1500. This done, he would then assert his identity by having a bookplate made bearing "a fresh plate of our Arms stiling yourself the only Son of Cha: Carroll Esqr: of the City of Annapolis in the Province of Maryland & great Grand son of Danl: Carroll of Litterlorma Esqr: in the Kings County in the Kingdom of Ireland." As a precursor of his return, he would find time to have his "Picture drawn by the best hand in London," placed "in a Genteel gilt frame," and sent to Maryland, and he would give sufficient attention to his wardrobe to assure that the first impression he made upon reentering the province would be favorable. Thus, the younger Carroll sat for Sir Joshua Reynolds, who completed the portrait in time to be shipped in the fleet during the fall of 1763.[72] He had less success with the family pedigree and the bookplate. The precise lineage of his ancestors eluded the assiduous efforts of the researcher, and the size of his bookplate proved too small to encompass the text Papa desired.

Reflecting the subtle shift in the distribution of power within the father-son relationship, the tone of the elder Carroll's directions changed markedly after 1762. Instead of didactic instructions and imperious commands, the older man now sent requests that, while numerous and clearly meant to be attended to, were aimed as much at acquiring various material accoutrements of metropoli-

71. William Hand Browne et al., eds., *Archives of Maryland* (Baltimore, 1883–), LVI, lv–lviii; CCA to CC, May 5, 1761, Carroll-McTavish Papers.

72. CCA to CC, Sept. 20, 1763, Outerbridge Horsey Collection of Lee, Horsey, and Carroll Family Papers, MdHi; CCA to CC, Sept. 2, 1762, Carroll-McTavish Papers; CC to CCA, Nov. 12, 1763, Carroll Papers, MS 206. This portrait, Plate 16, is the only extant likeness of CCC as a young man.

PLATE 16. Charles Carroll of Carrollton. By Joshua Reynolds. 1763.
Courtesy The Yale Center for British Art, Paul Mellon Collection

tan culture as at shaping Charley's character and accomplishments. Having long wished to improve the quality and number of his horses, Papa wanted Charley to seek out and purchase pedigreed mares suitable for breeding stock and arrange to have them transported to Maryland. Charley must find a groom to care for the animals on board ship, and while he was at it, he should also find a workman skilled at applying stucco and persuade him to cross the ocean to ply his trade on the addition being built to the house at Doohoragen. And not just any "stuko man," either! Only one who could procure "a Certificate from some Master builder or undertaker" proving that "he is a good workman" would be acceptable. A gamekeeper would be another nice addition — several neighboring plantations had them — perhaps his son could secure one of those, too.[73] And, when Charley did come home to Maryland, he must travel as befitted one of his station by arranging to bring aboard with him "an Anchor of Brandy" (about ten gallons) so that he might, with the captain's permission, "now and then bestow a Bottle on the Sailors," a practice common among "Gent: Passengers." To finance the many commissions he had laid upon his son, Papa announced he would place £2,000 –£2,500 sterling in Mr. Perkins's hands "to Answer My owne & your Calls."[74]

Coincident with the change in the tone and thrust of the elder Carroll's concerns, an important expansion of his son's social life clearly signaled the abatement of his period of melancholy. During Charley's initial years in London his circle of personal acquaintances remained relatively modest, composed of such individuals as his father's principal mercantile agent, William Perkins, a couple of Roman Catholic conveyancers named Messrs. Hutton and Maire, several priests attached to the office of the London procurator, and the family, also Catholic, of a young man named Christopher Bird, the son of a marble merchant. In part, at least, this relatively narrow range can be attributed to Papa's similar preference for limited social contacts. His London associations were, he informed his son in the spring of 1760, confined mainly to tobacco merchants, against whose "Interested Civilities" he advised Charley always to be on guard. Beyond this group, the elder Carroll believed himself known only to "a few of our Roman Cath: Gentry" and "to a few more by report," but to none so well as to require that Charley invest either himself or his money in socializing with them.[75] The older man urged that his son adopt a similar reserve in dealing with any Marylanders he might meet in London. Toward those individuals, with the exception of their kinsman, ship captain Henry Carroll, whom they knew to be indisputably trustworthy, Charley should behave politely, respectfully, and reticently.

73. CCA to CC, Oct. 3, 1763, Horsey Coll.; CC to CCA, Jan. 27, 1764, Carroll Papers, MS 206; CC to CCA, Jan. 7, 1763, Dreer Coll.

74. CCA to CC, Oct. 3, 1763, Horsey Coll.; CCA to CC, Nov. 7, 1763, Carroll-McTavish Papers.

75. CCA to CC, May 1, 1760, ibid.

At the same time Papa also hankered to have his son rub elbows with the well-connected. Although he had instructed Charley to neither "decline or Sollicit an Acquaintance with Ld: Baltimore or his Uncle Mr: Cæcilius Calvert," Maryland's principal secretary, the elder Carroll was demonstrably pleased when a chance meeting at Mr. Perkins's house brought Charley to dine with those august personages and William Sharpe, the current provincial governor's brother.[76] Simply being in such company was not enough for Papa, however. He explicitly expected Charley to use such occasions either to rehearse in detail how perfidiously the proprietary family had treated Catholics in general and the Carrolls in particular or to solicit provincial appointments for persons sympathetic to their family and religion. Thus, when similar invitations followed the first — at least one from the proprietor and several from Calvert — Charley found himself in the unenviable position of trying to please his father without offending his hosts. A similar agenda informed Papa's insistence that he reestablish contact with some of his English classmates from St. Omers: in one instance, the elder Carroll directed the younger to entreat a schoolfellow's father to restore an annual pension to a formerly dissolute relative who had reformed himself and was now employed on Doohoragen Manor!

The most memorable of such encounters involved Papa's sending Charley to call on Daniel Dulany, the man who was, the elder Carroll readily acknowledged, "the best Lawer on this Continent." Recently appointed deputy secretary in Maryland and a member of the provincial council, the ambitious Dulany came to England in 1761 with the dual aim of improving his health and solidifying his relationship with principal secretary Calvert and the proprietary family. As orchestrated by Papa, the purpose of Charley's visit was to make himself known to Dulany and to solicit that gentleman's advice on a lawsuit in which he and the elder Carroll were mutually interested. Received coolly after some weeks of missed connections, Charley was additionally taken aback to find Dulany unsympathetic, even critical, of Papa's position in the case. Dulany did not return his call, and in April 1762, several months after their initial meeting, the deputy secretary returned the papers left with him concerning the suit in a manner that Charley considered indelicate and rude.[77] Almost a year later, Dulany insulted Charley again: after requesting and receiving two dozen bottles of wine from the younger Carroll, the great man did not acknowledge their receipt or express his appreciation for more than three months. The visit Dulany finally

76. CCA to CC, Oct. 6, 1759, ibid.
77. CCA to CC, Apr. 17, 1761, CC to CCA, Apr. 26, 1762, Carroll Papers, MS 206.

got around to paying Charley in the spring of 1763 did not erase the younger man's memory of the arrogance and bad manners that had characterized the deputy secretary's previous behavior. Neither man had any way of knowing it, but the unpleasantness of their first contacts unerringly predicted the pattern of their future association.

Until the winter of 1763, therefore, Charley socialized primarily with a modest set of daily acquaintances. Once in a while he visited the country homes of a couple of his St. Omers classmates or found himself included in the company of Lord Baltimore and his minions, although the behavior his father's agenda required of him on such occasions undoubtedly made him distinctly uncomfortable. The most distinguished American name Charley could drop was Philip Ludwell III, "a Virginia gentleman & one of the council in that Province." Within a year of meeting Ludwell, Charley had also begun an enduring friendship with lawyer Edmund Jenings (1731–1819), who had received his legal training at Lincoln's Inn. A Marylander by birth and the son of a proprietary official, Jenings had returned to England as a child and lived there for the rest of his life.[78]

Those tentative beginnings aside, Charley did not become part of a group of men whose interests and education meaningfully paralleled his own until he entered a friendship with William Graves. Several years Charley's senior and a graduate of Balliol College and the Middle Temple, William Graves (1724–1801) had recently become a master in chancery when he and the younger Carroll met.[79] The rapport they enjoyed appears to have been instantaneous, and Graves soon introduced Charley to his "set," which included Richard Hussey (c. 1715–1770), attorney general to Queen Charlotte, the wife of George III; Daines Barrington (1727–1800), whose older brother, as Charley took care to let Papa know, was a viscount; Robert Pratt (c. 1728–1775), a member of Parliament for Horsham, 1763–1774; Anthony Champion (1725–1801), also a current member

78. Describing Ludwell as a man whose "esteem wou'd redound to my praise," Charley avowed, "T'is glorious to be esteemed by men of worth," among whom the Virginian deserved to be placed for possessing "true politeness, solid sense, a virtuous mind & a good heart." CC to CCA, July 15, 1761, ibid.; Elizabeth B. Gibson, *Biographical Sketches of the Bordley Family, of Maryland, for Their Descendants* . . . (Philadelphia, 1865), 25–26; Owings, *His Lordship's Patronage,* 128–129; J. Thomas Scharf, *History of Maryland from the Earliest Period to the Present Day* (Baltimore, 1879), II, 18, 49, 504; CC to CCA, Aug. 6, 1762, Horsey Coll.

79. *DNB,* s.v. "Graves, Thomas, Baron Graves"; Lewis Namier and John Brooke, *The House of Commons, 1754–1790* (New York, 1964), II, 534; *Debrett's Peerage of the United Kingdom of Great Britain and Ireland,* 18th ed. (London, 1829), 347.

"Sound & Strong"

of Parliament; and Thomas Bradshaw (1733–1774), from Hampton Court in Middlesex, known for his conviviality and extravagance, who served as chief clerk at the Treasury, 1761–1763. The pleasure Charley took in his status among his new acquaintances is suggested by the request he forwarded his father in January 1764, asking that a buck be sent from Maryland, "cut up in several joints, each joint covered with bay salt and closely packed in a separate box," as a gift for "the company."[80]

One final adventure still remained to Charley before he took his leave for Maryland. Having assiduously applied himself to surveying so as to finish everything in Papa's curriculum (except, of course, the legal studies), Charley rewarded himself with a trip to the Continent. William Graves would accompany him, and together they planned an itinerary that included Belgium, Germany, France, and Holland. They soon discarded Germany, however, as not only too far given the time they had but also because "Germany at all times a bad country to travel in must certainly at present be worse than ever when over & above the bad accommodations the roads are infested with robbers and Banditti." Settling in the end for Dunkirk and then Bruges, where Charley "found my old Preceptors removed from St. Omers" because of France's suppression of the Jesuits, they went next to Ghent for a visit with cousin Jack Carroll before going on to Holland and ending in Paris.[81] Little did Charley know, when he and Graves set off from London on July 17, 1763, that he would return from his journey changed in the most profound and unexpected ways. The young man who had boasted so blithely to his father of never being in love was about to come a cropper.

Seventeen-year-old Louisa Baker, the young woman who captivated Charley, was "introduced" to him in Paris by the Carrolls' old friend, Father Alexander Crookshanks, procurator of the Jesuit mission in England and Scotland. Whether by "introduced" Charley meant that he actually met Louisa in person, saw her in a group or from afar, simply received a glowing description of her from Father Crookshanks, or some combination of these possibilities is not altogether clear. Whatever happened, the impression Louisa made upon him was immediately favorable. Pronouncing her "an agreeable person and good natured," he assured Papa that Crookshanks could not only vouch for her father's wealth but could also confirm that the "temper & amiable qualities" of the lady, currently a student at the Ursuline convent, left nothing to be desired. With this

80. CC to CCA, Jan. 27, 1764, Carroll Papers, MS 206.
81. CC to CCA, June 14, Aug. 8, 1763, ibid.

sketchy portrait, the younger Carroll then announced, presumably to his father's astonishment, that he intended to marry Louisa. "Provided I can obtain the Father's & the daughter's consent I flatter myself you can have no objection to the match." He intended to visit Mr. Baker early in November to secure permission to court Louisa, and he felt smugly certain that the conquest of her heart would prove no difficulty: "Her inexperience will favour my design."[82]

Lest Papa think him romantically distracted, Charley moved quickly to a discussion of the financial implications attached to his matrimonial plans. By his estimate, the jointure (the annual sum to be provided by the Carrolls for Louisa's maintenance should Charley predecease her) might run as high as eighteen hundred pounds sterling, with the amount of money Louisa brought with her determining the final figure and the rate of interest to be applied to it. All such arrangements would, of course, be firmly established by the marriage settlement that preceded the union. But, Charley wondered, could they afford such a sum — "Will our estate be equal to so heavy an incumbrance?" Considerations of health dictated that he proceed with extreme caution, for, smitten as he was, Charley had not forgotten what Papa had taught him: "If I die young, which is not improbable as I am of a weak constitution, my widow may marry a second Husband & carry the greatest part of the estate into a nother family."[83]

Charley had scarcely posted the letter informing Papa of these amazing developments when he learned that Louisa's father was not as rich as Mr. Crookshanks had thought; rather than being a sole heiress, she had four brothers. Although disappointing, the news was not entirely bad. From his holdings in the West Indian island of St. Croix John Baker realized an annual income of £3,500 sterling. The estimate of his net worth presented to the Carrolls was £50,000 sterling, an impressive figure but substantially less than the Carrolls' net worth, nearly £90,000 sterling.[84]

82. CC to CCA, Oct. 3, 1763, ibid.

83. Ibid.

84. Father Crookshanks had evidently formed his judgment of John Baker's "Circumstances" from observing "the Unlimited Credit he allows his Daughter." CCA to CC, Jan. 10, 1764, Carroll Papers, MS 206.

Baker's wealth: Nicholas Tuite, Dec. 22, 1763, "A list or valuation of the Estates of Jno Baker Esqr. in the island of St Croix in america," enclosed in CC to CCA, Jan. 27, 1764, CCA to CC, Jan. 9, 1764, Carroll Papers, MS 206. Nicholas Tuite (1705–1772), who provided the financial report on John Baker to the Carrolls, was an Irishman whose County Westmeath family lost its property for fighting against the crown. Emigrating to the Leeward Islands, he played a prominent role in the development of St. Croix. Tuite kept residences in London and at Bath as well as on St. Croix. Philip C. Yorke, ed., *The Diary of*

Baker lived as befitted a wealthy West Indian planter, dividing the time he spent in England between his home in Twickenham, on the outskirts of London, and his country residence, Grove Place, near Southampton. His diary reveals an active social life, filled with such activities as drinking tea, dining, dancing quadrilles, playing whist, piquet, and draughts, hunting, and going to church. Not entirely a man of vain pursuits, he read widely and enjoyed conversing in Latin. Satisfied with his station in life and firmly committed to his Roman Catholic faith, Baker moved within the small circle of affluent English Catholics whose limited presence no longer troubled the vast Protestant majority. Part of a network that reached far beyond the shores of Great Britain, these Catholic gentlemen knew about their counterparts in other regions of the Atlantic world. As Baker told Charley, he had certainly heard of the Carrolls: "Tis true Sr: I have not the pleasure of personally knowing you tho' I am [far] from being altogether a stranger to the name of your family." [85]

But did this comfortably situated absentee planter want the scion of a North American colonial family, however wealthy, for a son-in-law? Obtaining an answer to that question took many months of carefully choreographed negotiation. Evidently too impatient to wait for his priestly Cupid, Mr. Crookshanks, to procure him an introduction, Charley wrote to Baker himself in early December 1763 and received a timely, though cagey, reply. His only daughter, "who from her infancy has been so exceeding dear to me," was still too young "to engage in the married state." At the same time, Baker clearly respected the Carroll fortune. Noting candidly that the Carrolls' wealth far exceeded anything "my daughter might be (what the world calls,) intitled to," Baker wondered whether Charley's father could actually be persuaded to overlook the discrepancy. Notwithstanding his questions on that score, the Englishman seemed well enough disposed toward his daughter's prospective suitor to continue their exploratory discussions. Indeed, Baker expected that a closer look into Charley's "situation & character" would probably remove any obstacles to his visiting Louisa: "All I can assure you is that I should not affect to raise any: and will even ingenuously own to you that I seem to observe in yr: manner of writing certain marks of candour & worth that rather incline me to wish I might not find any." [86]

John Baker, Barrister of the Middle Temple, Solicitor-General of the Leeward Islands, Being Extracts Therefrom (London, 1931), 10–11, 62–63n, 182.

85. For Baker's activities, see "Diary of John Baker of Horsham," Accession 8241, West Sussex Records Office, Chichester, England. The quote is from John Baker to CC, Dec. 15, 1763, Carroll Papers, MS 206.

86. John Baker to CC, Dec. 15, 1763, Carroll Papers, MS 206.

Charley's dialogue with John Baker was well under way by the time the startling news of his matrimonial quest reached Papa. The older man reacted predictably. After a cursory review of the qualities — character, disposition, and family — that he insisted counted far more than wealth in choosing a wife, the elder Carroll focused his attention exclusively on money. Since the lady's family appeared to possess substantial resources, he urged Charley to drive a hard bargain. If Louisa's dowry were to be exclusively in cash, Charley should offer a marriage settlement bearing interest of 6 percent on the cash contribution alone, rather than on the estimated value of the estate she might ultimately inherit. Charley should also negotiate an arrangement that would preserve whatever "Lands & Negroes" bequeathed to her by her father for the male issue of their union. Other considerations also occurred to Papa, but none obscured the fundamental concern he expressed with unmistakable clarity: "Get his Estate settled on the Lady." [87]

Having dispatched several letters in this vein to Charley by mid-January, Papa grew increasingly anxious for further news. When letters from his son finally arrived near the end of February, the elder Carroll found them wanting in every respect. Having learned very little about John Baker's fortune, except that it was to be divided among his five children, making Louisa's portion much less generous than originally anticipated, Charley seemed primarily concerned about whether the Bakers would "object" to their daughter's living in the wilds of North America. Exasperated by his son's fixation on this point — of little consequence compared to the strategic potential of marital alliances for extending, enhancing, and securing family fortunes — Papa more or less exploded. "You leave me in the Greatest State of Uncertainty," he told his son irritably. "Could you not learn what Mr. Baker is supposed to be Worth Where his Estate lays of what it Consists, what Sum You Suppose he may, or may be able to give his Daughter. I suppose you had some Information as to those Particulars & to Many more before you wrote to him." The older man left no doubt about the source of his frustration: "I Cannot write to you as fully as I would do were you more Explicit." [88]

Fully informed or not, the elder Carroll continued to bombard the younger with astute financial advice. Reiterating that the Carrolls must agree to pay interest only on the dowry and not on any potential inheritance — to do otherwise would be to "give a certainty for an uncertainty" — Papa was nevertheless

87. CCA to CC, Jan. 10, 1764, ibid.

88. CC to CCA, Nov. 12, 1763, ibid.; CCA to CC, Feb. 28, 1764, Carroll-McTavish Papers.

"Sound & Strong"

willing by early April to raise that interest from 6 to 8 percent. As security for the marriage settlement, the elder Carroll initially authorized the younger to pledge only the properties that would be bestowed upon him when he returned to Maryland: the 12,700-acre Carrollton Manor, from whose tenants £250 sterling was annually realized, and a one-fifth share in the Baltimore Company iron-works that currently brought in £400 each year. By spring Papa was prepared to go even farther and offered to make his "whole Fortune Lyable to the Settlemt & Jointure" if "the Lady's Fortune could demand it." His terms were quite point-edly gender-specific, however: his "Mannor of Doohoragen 10000 A[cres] & 1425 A[cres] called Chance adjacent thereto on wch: Seats the Bulk of Negroes are settled" were to be used to secure the male Carroll line. Daughters were to be provided for "out of your personal Estate" in amounts "proportioned to their Mothers fortune." Satisfied that he had made a generous commitment, Papa stressed that Charley was at liberty to show Baker or his agents any documents or letters that would help close the negotiations and to do whatever else he deemed "reasonable" in pursuit of the end desired.[89]

Although Papa's professed reason for the increasingly generous settlements he offered between January and April 1764 was his son's happiness, it seems more likely that his growing liberality revealed the intensity of his desire for a successful outcome. Charley's behavior over those same months indicated a similarly strong ambition. He ingratiated himself sufficiently with John Baker to secure an invitation to Grove Place, where he spent a couple of weeks in January 1764 hunting, gaming, dining, and conversing in a supreme effort to make a favorable impression on Louisa's parents.[90] The results, to his disappointment, were decidedly mixed. He believed that he and Mr. Baker had established a certain rapport. Indeed, the gentleman told Charley quite candidly that he presently found himself "somewhat embarrassed" by a debt of ten thousand pounds sterling he had borrowed "to clear, settle, and plant his sugar lands," which suggested no "ready money" was apt to come with the bride.[91]

Louisa's mother was another matter entirely. A daughter of Thomas Ryan, an Irish Catholic expatriate turned West Indian planter, Mary Ryan Baker (d. 1774)

89. CCA to CC, Apr. 10, 1764, Carroll Papers, MS 206.

90. Ibid. Charley's presence at Grove Place is noted in several entries in Baker's diary, Jan. 9–24, 1764, although Baker does not mention that marriage negotiations were tak-ing place. Both Baker's diary and Charley's correspondence also confirm that the two men first met in Bath on Dec. 20–22, 1763. CC to CCA, Jan. 27, 1764, Carroll Papers, MS 206.

91. Ibid.

was Baker's second wife, and Louisa the only child of their union.[92] From the outset, this apparently formidable woman made it clear to Charley that she did not wish her daughter to live in North America, and neither the younger Carroll's accomplishments nor his wealth could change her mind. In mid-March, some two months after being a guest at Grove Place, Charley wrote forebodingly to Papa that he had begun to think "I shall not succeed with miss Baker." For young ladies, "the going to America is a prodigious objection," he informed his father. Moreover, even if the daughter's "good sense & inclinations" allowed her to transcend the difficulty, Mrs. Baker's attitude had convinced him that maternal consent would not be forthcoming. "Had I known the mother before I opened the affair to Mr. Baker I should have entirely dropt the thoughts of that marriage." Mr. Baker's suggestion that Charley solve the problem by remaining in England elicited a highly indignant response from the younger Carroll: to spend the rest of his life "absent from a father, whom I most tenderly love, to whose company & conversation I would willingly sacrifice every other enjoyt.," was unthinkable. Fully prepared to wrench Louisa away from her parents with no expectation of a future reunion, Charley pronounced Baker's suggestion that he follow a similar course "unnatural"; complying with it would evince the "utmost ingratitude & cruelty." He would rather, he told his father virtuously, "forego my own happiness than make a Parent miserable."[93]

By early May the outcome Charley morosely suspected in March had become reality. The previous month he presented Papa's initial offer carrying an interest rate of 6 percent to Baker by letter, along with the assurance that he had obtained his father's permission to "pay my addresses" to the young lady.[94] He also told Baker that he intended to return to America as soon after the wedding as possible, a plan that he realized might not be acceptable to Louisa's mother. Should Mrs. Baker find it impossible to give up her daughter, Charley averred he would not contest her. Meeting Baker to discuss these matters shortly thereafter, Charley found the gentleman far less receptive than he had earlier seemed. Despite the detailed proposal transmitted to him, Baker never broached the subject of the marriage settlement and instead confined himself to vague suggestions about postponing the courtship. Perhaps the two young people might meet

92. Thomas Ryan owned property on the Leeward Islands of Montserrat and St. Croix; John Baker's holdings lay on St. Croix. Yorke, ed., *The Diary of John Baker*, 10–11; Tuite, "A list or valuation of the Estates of Jno Baker Esqr.," enclosed in CC to CCA, Jan. 27, 1764, Carroll Papers, MS 206.

93. CC to CCA, Mar. 21, 1764, Carroll Papers, MS 206.

94. Ibid., Apr. 19, 1764.

when his daughter next came to London; if they liked each other, Charley could go home to Maryland. Later, when Louisa had attained an age more suitable for marriage, he could return to England and resume his suit.

Charley found the idea preposterous: how likely was it, he asked his father sarcastically, that "a young lady will retain her affection 4 years for a gentleman with whom she can be but slightly acquainted & from whom she will be separated by the Atlantick?" And suppose in the meantime he met someone he liked in Maryland? He could only conclude that the combination of Mrs. Baker's antipathy and the insufficiency of the settlement Papa offered — 8 or even 10 percent were the common figures in England, Charley now knew — had scuttled the match. Although he subsequently received "a very fair opening" to renew his quest, he declined to. Despite Papa's willingness to increase the interest to 8 percent, which he appreciated, Charley declared firmly that the affair was over.[95]

What is to be made of this courtship and of the young woman around whom three wealthy, ambitious men danced an elaborate minuet for some six months as they contended for her future? Trying to discover Louisa through her father's diary yields meager results. Not only does John Baker inexplicably refer to her as "Patty" but, beyond commenting approvingly on her musical talents and the "pretty" and "lively" girls that composed her circle of friends, he provides no enlightenment about her personality, appearance, or the qualities that so endeared her to him.[96]

Although Louisa clearly made a stunning impression on Charley, his correspondence reveals very little more than that she was agreeable and "good natured" or "good tempered." Only several years later does he intimate that she was also quite beautiful. Moreover, the amount of time he actually spent in her presence eludes us. Having been "introduced" to her by Father Crookshanks in Paris in the fall of 1763, he subsequently sought her father's permission to "visit" her, a request to which Mr. Baker indicated that he was favorably disposed. But whether, when, and where such encounters ever took place remain a mystery. In March 1764, three months after he initially approached Baker, Charley had still not managed to bring about the "better acquaintance" with Louisa essential to finding out whether "she answers the character all her friends give her." When all hopes of the match had flickered and died, Charley professed himself not un-

95. Ibid., May 1, July 26, 1764.

96. "Diary of John Baker," entries for May 12, 13, 1763. Yorke's introduction to his edited version of Baker's diary gives the daughter known to Charley as Louisa the name Martha, for which Patty is a diminutive.

duly disappointed: "I might perh[aps] have liked the young lady in time & upon a farther [acquaintance] but I knew too little of her to be in love." By midsummer 1764, he spoke of her quite caustically: "The young lady has been bread up with very high notions not at all answerable to her fortune; a domestick wife not so fond of show and parade, who is not above the business of her family will best suit me." Having concluded that "the mother is a vain empty woman," Charley chose not to risk the chance that "the daughter may take after her."[97]

Strong words, indeed, but they were not strong enough to banish Louisa's memory. Nearly four years after last seeing her, he could think of no higher compliment to pay his betrothed than to assure a friend that he preferred the woman he planned to marry "to all the women I have ever seen, even to Louisa."[98] Equally telling is the persistence of Louisa's name. Before Charley's ill-fated quest, that name had never appeared in the Carroll family, but he would give it to his third daughter and see it bestowed upon one of his granddaughters as well. All his protestations to the contrary, Charley never completely erased the image that the unattainable Louisa had engraved on his heart.

Why did the memory of this elusive young woman remain so deeply embedded in Charley's consciousness? Most obviously, his inability to win her denied him a sweet moment of triumph. Had he brought home to the colonial periphery an English wife of genteel birth and some fortune, his achievement would have made a significant impression upon the Chesapeake gentry, Protestants as well as Catholics, and earned the colonial Carrolls similar respect and recognition in the mother country as well. Indeed, the elder Carroll found this prospect sufficiently alluring to raise the interest he was willing to pay on the jointure from 6 to 8 percent and to pledge his entire fortune to secure the settlement. Although peripheral to the material enhancement and status the match with Louisa offered, Charley might also have had at least a fleeting thought that securing a metropolitan bride would more than adequately compensate any lingering disappointment his father might feel concerning his lackluster performance in studying law. And, perhaps, at a deeper level, Louisa became a symbol of unrequited love — a living loss that paralleled the incompleteness left by his mother's death. This much can certainly be said: the wound to Charley's pride inflicted by the Bakers' rejection further accentuated his tendency to draw inward and mask his feelings with a studied posture of distance and reserve. Rooted in his isolation from the intimacy of family in his formative years, cru-

97. CC to CCA, Oct. 3, 11, 1763, Mar. 21, May 30, July 26, 1764, Carroll Papers, MS 206.
98. CCC to William Graves, Jan. 16, 1768, Charles Carroll of Carrollton, letterbook 1765–1768, MdHi.

elly reinforced by the loss of his mother, and painfully aggravated by the experience of being unacceptable to John Baker's family, the emotional reserve that characterized Charley's conduct for the rest of his life was a well-developed facet of his personality by the time he ended his long sojourn in Europe and returned to Maryland.

With his courtship in ruins, the time for Charley's homecoming had at last arrived. Charley had fulfilled all of Papa's requirements except the one to which all the others were preliminary — the mastery of the law. Still, his father longed to see him; it was time to bring the sixteen years of separation to an end. Having planned everything else regarding his son's foreign education, Papa had firm advice to bring him safely home: "Do not come in a Ship with Fellons or Servants, & it will be agreeable to you not to be crowded with Cabin Passengers 2 or 3 you will find to be Company enough, try to get a neat Capt: & one who loves to live well. Be very inquisitive as to the Age of the Ship & whether she be sound & strong, & well found." [99] "Sound & strong" — Papa could just as well have been talking about the character he believed he had forged in Charley, his only son, his worthy heir.

99. CCA to CC, [Apr. 28], 1763, Carroll-Harper Papers.

CHAPTER 5

Affairs of the Heart: 1765–1773

The provincial world to which Charley returned was vastly different from the sophisticated continental and British environments of his formative years. Planning for that reentry a good two years before it took place, Papa issued instructions in the fall of 1762 that not only emphasized the importance he attached to the occasion but that also unwittingly underscored the contrast between the style of life routinely available to Old World gentry and that accessible to their New World counterparts. Although pleased by Charley's decision to "dress plainly" in London and quite willing for him to be again "as plain as you please" after his "1st Appearance" in Maryland, Papa nevertheless intended for Charley's arrival to make an important statement about his family's position in general and the young man's identity in particular. Relishing the chance to display his polished, European-educated, consummately genteel son, the elder Carroll took care that the younger would look the part.[1]

"As dress introduces a stranger into most Companies perhaps with stronger Impressions than the best Recommendations," he wrote Charley in 1762, "I think you shd: have Cloths suitable to such occasions & upon yr: first appearance among us some shew may not be improper." With this end in mind, Papa directed Charley to "contrive to be supply'd with 2 or 3 Waste coats, silk for two genteel Summer Suits, Velvets &c from France at the best hand & in the newest Taste." In addition, Charley was also to bring with him "a Genteel set of Horse furniture." It would not be necessary, however, for him to "by Pistols," since Papa already possessed "a very neat pair mounted with Silver wch: are at your Service."[2]

Outfitting himself for the part he was to play proved less of a challenge to

1. CCA to CC, Sept. 2, 1762, Carroll-McTavish Papers, MdHI.
2. Ibid.

Charley than getting himself to the stage upon which he was to perform. Equipped according to, if not in excess of, Papa's desires (included in what he called his "pretty considerable" baggage was an English desk) Charley embarked from Gravesend on September 19, 1764, his twenty-seventh birthday. By the end of October, his ship had reached Bermuda, but, buffeted by strong northwest winds, the vessel "scarce made 100 leagues" during the entire month of November. When he finally landed at Hampton, Virginia, on December 8, Charley had been at sea for eleven weeks. Mindful of the tragic demise of his older brother Henry off the capes of Virginia nearly half a century before, Papa must have received Charley's letter announcing his safe arrival with enormous relief and greeted with corresponding impatience his son's intention of not getting home to Annapolis until soon after the first of the year.[3]

Uncooperative weather delayed the much-anticipated homecoming even longer, however. For six weeks beginning early in January, an ice-locked bay prevented Charley from crossing from Maryland's Eastern Shore to Annapolis.[4] As a result, the younger Carroll's "first appearances among us" took place, not in the provincial capital as planned, but instead among the wealthiest stratum of the Eastern Shore gentry, several of whom were distantly related to him. Moreover, his splendid wardrobe remained just out of his reach on the boat, resting at anchor between the Carrolls' Poplar Island and Kent Island until more favorable conditions prevailed. Whatever his chagrin at this turn of events, Papa must have been somewhat mollified by Charley's reports of the warm reception extended to him by such substantial persons as Colonel Richard Tilghman III of the Hermitage on the Chester River; Colonel Edward Lloyd III (Lord Baltimore's current agent and receiver general) and his son Edward Lloyd IV, a family whose resources equaled the Carrolls'; Edward Tilghman of Wye, whose wife, Julianna Carroll Tilghman, was Charley's cousin; Richard Tilghman IV; William Cooke, another cousin; Francis Hall of Bolingly and his wife, Martha Neale Hall, both of old Roman Catholic families; and cousin Sarah Darnall Blake of Sportsman's Hall on Wye River. Neither was the cordiality of merchant

3. CC to CCA, Dec. 8, 1764, Carroll Papers, MS 206, MdHI.
4. As he reported to Papa in a letter written Jan. 10, 1765, Charley left Old Point Comfort in Virginia on December 26 but was delayed when the boat ran aground off Maryland's Tangier Island. By January 5 "the frost" had impeded all further progress, forcing the vessel to anchor at Kent Island. Although he considered traveling to Annapolis by land from the Eastern Shore, following the course around Head of Elk taken by the bearer of his letter, Charley was dissuaded by his new acquaintances, who told him such a "scheme" was "attended with a good deal of danger" and that he would reach the capital more quickly by waiting for "a thaw." Ibid., Jan. 10, 1765.

William Carmichael, Sr., and his son-in-law John Brown unwelcome. At length the cold weather moderated, and on Tuesday, February 12, 1765, Charley crossed the threshold of Papa's house on Duke of Gloucester Street in Annapolis, home at last.[5]

With a population of just over one thousand, Annapolis must have looked minute to Charley after the vast metropolitan landscape of London, center of an empire. In size and appearance Maryland's capital had not changed much since the younger Carroll's departure in 1748. Its population had grown, but only by a couple hundred souls, and the governmental establishment continued to be its chief enterprise. A steady growth in the volume and value of business conducted for the proprietor and the public had increased the incomes and the influence of an emerging urban elite composed largely of proprietary appointees, office-holders, and lawyers. However, the commercial disruption of the Seven Years' War had prevented these men from immediately impressing their expanding wealth and power on the physical character of the town. Thus it is not surprising that a visitor in the summer of 1762 found Annapolis unimpressive: "The Houses are Old, Ill Built, but 2 New ones as I could See now Building & but Very Little Trade Stirring." With the cessation of hostilities in 1763, commerce not only resumed but also expanded rapidly as merchants responded to the gentry's demand for goods commensurate with its status. By the time Charley returned home in late winter 1765, Annapolis stood poised on the threshold of its "golden age" — a decade that saw the construction of elegant town houses and the blossoming of an upper class of sufficient means to initiate and support a theater, a jockey club, a gentlemen's social club, and fortnightly assemblies.[6]

5. Ibid., Jan. 10, 25, 1765; *Maryland Gazette* (Annapolis), Feb. 14, 1765. Edward Lloyd IV was the heir of Richard Bennett (1666–1749), the Settler's and Papa's old ally. Julianna Carroll Tilghman was the daughter of Charley's second cousin Dominick Carroll (d. 1736), son of Michael Carroll and grandson of Anthony Carroll of Lisheenboy (see Appendix 6, chart B: "Descendants of Anthony Carroll of Lisheenboy," below). William Cooke's maternal grandfather, Major Nicholas Sewall (1655–1737), was Charley's maternal great-grandfather. Sarah Darnall Blake was Colonel Henry Darnall I's granddaughter; Charley was his great-grandson.

6. Victor Hugo Paltsits, ed., *Journal of Benjamin Mifflin: The Record of a Tour from Philadelphia to Delaware and Maryland, July 26 to August 14, 1762* (New York, 1935), 12; Edward C. Papenfuse, *In Pursuit of Profit: The Annapolis Merchants in the Era of the American Revolution, 1763–1805* (Baltimore, 1975), 10–34; William Eddis, *Letters from America, Historical and Descriptive, Comprising Occurrences from 1769 to 1777 Inclusive*, in Aubrey C. Land, ed., *Letters from America* (Cambridge, Mass., 1969), 20–21, 54; Gregory

Affairs of the Heart

Whatever his initial impressions of his surroundings, Charley must have been preoccupied with past realities rather than with future possibilities as he stepped into Papa's plain but imposing mansion, where his beloved Mama had died. Surely the stark realization of her absence struck Charley anew, tempering the joy of his long-anticipated homecoming with painful recollections of that searing loss. Perhaps the presence of his cousin Rachel Darnall, who had cared so devotedly for Mama during her final illness and now served as Papa's housekeeper, mitigated the somber memories, and the youthful spirits of Rachel's fifteen-year-old daughter, Molly, a member of the household since 1761, undoubtedly enlivened the atmosphere in the big brick house. Beyond his immediate family, Charley appears to have quickly renewed his friendship with his cousin Daniel Carroll II of Rock Creek, left a widower with two young children by the death of his wife, Eleanor, in 1763. Durable and mutually satisfying, his relationship with Daniel offered Charley an important source of support amid the unpleasantness of the continuing litigation between Papa and his nephew, Charles Carroll of Duddington. Indeed, Daniel's unwavering commitment to Charles Carroll of Annapolis's position in the "cause" and his steadfast refusal to give any credence to the claims advanced by his brothers-in-law, Charles Carroll of Duddington and Ignatius Digges, in suits that he also could have joined exemplified the loyalty that made him a confidant of both father and son. It must have been with real regret that Charley saw cousin Daniel embark in midsummer 1765 for a yearlong trip to England and Ireland.

In the end, however, nothing eased the discomforts and difficulties of Charley's readjustment to Maryland as effectively as the sheer happiness of being reunited with Papa. A few lines from a letter he wrote to his English friend William Graves in September 1765 capture his mood: "The gentleman who informed you of my Fathers having presented me with £40000 Cy. on my arrival was misinformed, or was willing to impose on you a piece of news of his own coining — not only 40000 pounds but the whole of my Father's estate is at my disposal we are and we like to continue, on the best terms, never a Father & Son were on better." Underscoring his recommitment to home and family after his long exile, Charley signed his letter to Graves with the appellation he had recently chosen, primarily to distinguish himself from similarly named relatives

---

A. Stiverson and Phebe R. Jacobsen, *William Paca: A Biography* (Baltimore, 1976), 55–56. For estimates of Annapolis's population in the 1760s, see Papenfuse, *In Pursuit of Profit*, 14, table 1-1.

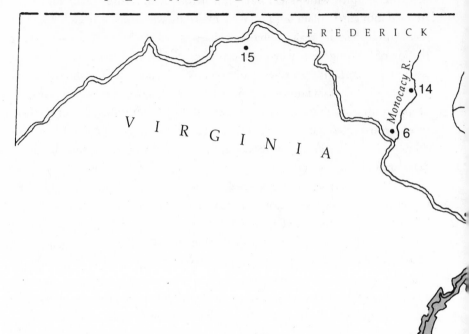

PENNSYLVANIA

FREDERICK

VIRGINIA

Monocacy R.

- 15
- 14
- 6

1. Elk Ridge Landing
2. Doohoragen
3. Annapolis
4. Annapolis Quarter
5. White Hall
6. Carrollton Manor
7. Bashford Manor
8. St. Clement's Manor
9. Baltimore Town
10. Baltimore Co. Ironworks
11. St. Mary's City
12. Mellwood
13. Rock Creek
14. Frederick Town
15. Berkeley Springs
16. Poplar Island
17. Duddington Manor
18. Head of Elk

MAP 6. The Carrolls' Maryland World, 1765–1782. *After Joshua Fry and Peter Jefferson,* A Map of the Most Inhabited Part of Virginia, Containing the Whole Province of Maryland . . . *(London, 1775); and Lester J. Cappon et al., eds.,* Atlas of Early American History: The Revolutionary Era, 1760–1790 *(Princeton, N.J., 1976). Drawn by Richard Stinely*

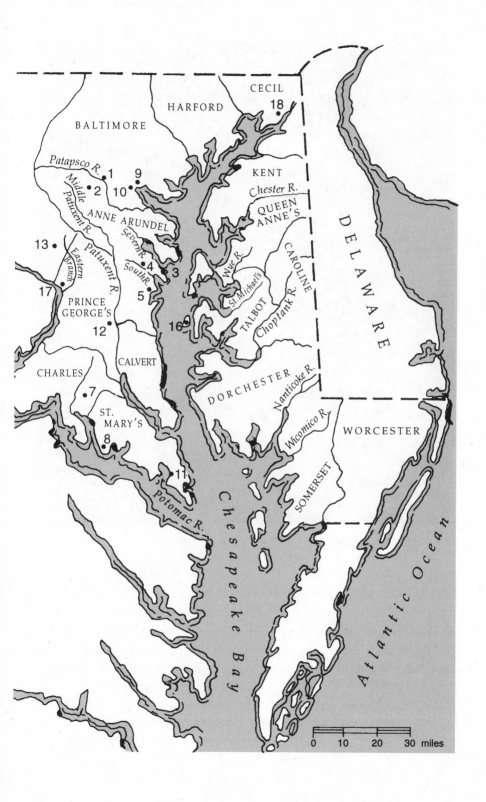

PLATE 17. Daniel Carroll II of Rock Creek. By John Wollaston. 1753–1754.
Permission Maryland Historical Society

but also to identify firmly with Maryland: Charles Carroll of Carrollton. He would use it unvaryingly, both in public and in private, for the rest of his life.[7]

Though sweet, the joys of reunion could not alter the fact that new challenges and expectations confronted Charley now that he was home. Most obviously, provided he could "escape the fever & agues this season," thereby acclimating

7. CCC to William Graves, Sept. 15, 1[76]5, CCC, letterbook 1765–1768, fol. 22, MdHi. In a letter to his cousin Daniel Carroll ten days before, Charley had signed his name simply "Charles Carroll." The letter to Graves follows immediately in the letterbook. CC to Daniel Carroll, Sept. 5, 1765, ibid., fol. 20.

Affairs of the Heart

himself to Maryland, he must learn to manage Papa's various enterprises.[8] Equally important, he must find himself a wife. Notwithstanding his professed commitment to bachelorhood after Louisa Baker's rejection, Charley knew he had responsibilities in this area and was not getting any younger. Moreover, success in business and matrimony would, besides pleasing his father, greatly assist Charley in establishing an identity of his own in Maryland. Far too subtle and complex to be accomplished simply by adding "of Carrollton" to his name, this process posed public and private dilemmas that required the younger Carroll to conduct himself with remarkable patience and restraint for a decade. His major opportunity for self-assertion would not come until the American Revolution.

Between 1765 and 1775, the circumstances of Charley's life frequently pitted his carefully honed personal attributes against seemingly intractable social realities. His fine European education, the knowledge of the world acquired on his travels, and the wit and sophistication that had earned him a place within a well-connected, upwardly mobile set of young English gentlemen were surely enough to recommend him to their provincial counterparts in the Forensic Club. Formed by William Paca and other Annapolitans in 1759 for serious discussion, speechmaking, and conviviality, the Forensic Club continued its activities until at least the spring of 1767, two years after Charley's return. Yet, he was never invited to join, an indication that anti-Catholic discrimination still defined Maryland's social as well as its legal and political life.[9]

Similarly, the very wealth that qualified Charley for gentry status carried with it the indelible imprimatur of his father, whose tough-mindedness in expanding the Carroll fortune had earned him widespread enmity, if not notoriety. And nowhere did the shadow cast by this obstreperous, socially cantankerous father envelop Charley more pervasively than in family relationships, for the arrangement that had characterized the Carroll household until his twentieth year was still a matter of comment in 1765, eight years after his parents had finally married and four years after his mother's death. A diary kept by an anonymous Frenchman traveling in the colonies in the mid-1760s provides a dispassionate synopsis of the attitudes toward the Carrolls during the first summer of Charley's return. On July 3, 1765, this gentleman recorded that he had "Dined with old Squ'r Carrol of anopolis," noting, "He is looked on to be the most moneyed man in maryland but at the same time the most avaritious. he is a stanche

8. CCC to Daniel Carroll, Sept. 5, 1765, ibid., fol. 20. The "fever & agues" was probably malaria.

9. Stiverson and Jacobsen, *William Paca*, 36–39; "Rules and Minutes of the Forensic Club," typescript, n.d., MdAA.

Roman Catholique keeps but very litle Company owing perhaps to his Distaste to the protestants." As if to counter any lack of hospitality he implied, the writer went on to assert, "I was never genteeler received by any perssonne than I was by him." Then the Frenchman concluded the day's entry with a final observation: "He has no family, only a b. son who he Intends to make his sole heir. he had part of his education in France." Since a man of Charles Carroll of Annapolis's character would have hardly discussed his personal business with a stranger during dinner, the French traveler most likely recorded the standard assessment of the Carrolls as conveyed to him by the assortment of merchants, lawyers, and public officials he had already met during his stay in Maryland.[10]

Given his problematic social situation, Charley was fortunate in having a coterie of English friends with whom he could continue, through correspondence, the invigorating political discussions he had enjoyed at the Crown and Anchor and other London coffeehouses and share his impressions of Maryland and the details of the life he intended to fashion there. Regularly sending mail to England, he wrote at least sixteen letters to his four closest companions, William Graves, Thomas Bradshaw, Edmund Jenings, and Christopher Bird, between July 1765 and the end of October 1766.[11] Although increasingly dominated by the issues associated with the Stamp Act crisis, those letters address a variety of other

10. "Journal of a French Traveller in the Colonies, 1765," part 2, *American Historical Review*, XXVII (1921–1922), 74. Among the Marylanders the Frenchman had met before dining with Charles Carroll of Annapolis were merchants Daniel of St. Thomas Jenifer, Samuel Galloway, and James Christie; Attorney General Edmund Key; John Brice II, commissioner of the paper currency office; Dr. George Steuart, cojudge of the land office; Governor Horatio Sharpe; and Papa's adversary Ignatius Digges (ibid., 70–74). There is no evidence in the Carrolls' papers to suggest whether Charley dined with his father and the Frenchman on this occasion.

11. Twelve of these letters have survived in draft form in CCC's letterbook, 1765–1768. Two others, to Thomas Bradshaw on Dec. 8, 1765, and to Christopher Bird on Dec. [30], 1765, were cut out of and stolen from this letterbook in the late 1960s and subsequently sold by the Mercury Stamp Company in New York in June 1970. Efforts to enlist the Mercury Stamp Company in finding the present owner yielded no results. The letters are known, however, through their appearance in Thomas Meagher Field's unreliably edited collection, *Unpublished Letters of Charles Carroll of Carrollton, and His Father, Charles Carroll of Doughoregan* (New York, 1902), 101–102, 107–108. The existence of another letter from Charley to Edmund Jenings, dated Sept. 30, 1765, is evident from its publication in J. C. Carpenter, "Doughoregan Manor, and Charles Carroll of Carrollton," *Appletons' Journal*, XII (Sept. 12, 1874), 323; no manuscript copy has been found. Finally, a letter written to Christopher Bird in July 1765 is known only by Carroll's reference to it in his correspondence of Sept. 28, 1765, CCC, letterbook 1765–1768, fol. 27.

topics, among them transatlantic gossip about mutual friends, exchanges of flora and fauna (wild turkeys and a flying squirrel from Maryland for a Parmesan cheese and grafts of morello cherry trees from England), and the weather. Having survived his reintroduction to Maryland's warmest months, Charley acknowledged to Edmund Jenings in November 1765, "The heats of the summer are indeed dangerous & disagreeable to persons who are obliged to expose themselves to the sun," but reassured him that, with the exception of only a few days, the climate was generally "very supportable to one in my situation who can confine himself to his house." [12]

Intent upon building a library worthy of any "english gentleman," Charley relied upon William Graves to fulfill his requests for books as well as to keep him supplied with "the most interesting Pamphlets." Although he did ask for and receive several volumes from Graves, the largest addition to his library during the late 1760s came by means of an unexpected bequest from the prominent Virginian Philip Ludwell III, whom he had known and admired in London.[13] To Charley's evident surprise, Ludwell, who died in England on March 25, 1767, specified in his will that "my friend Charles Carrol Junr Esq. of Maryland" should have "such of my books in my study in Virginia as he shall choose." Clearly flattered by the remembrance, Charley wrote Ludwell's executors that he accepted the legacy as a proof of the "very sincere friendship" he and Ludwell had enjoyed, rather than "from any real want of the books I have selected from his collection for my own use." With only one exception — Sir Philip Sidney's popular sixteenth-century romance *The Countess of Pembroke's Arcadia* — Charley chose about sixty weighty tomes, some in Latin and Greek, on subjects ranging from ancient and modern history, biography, religion, philosophy, and law to husbandry.[14]

12. CCC to [Edmund] Jenings, Nov. 23, 1765, CCC, letterbook 1765–1768, fol. 37.

13. CCC to [William] Graves, Sept. 15, 1765, Nov. 7, 1767, ibid., fols. 22, 112.

14. Will of Philip Ludwell III, printed in Lothrop Withington, *Virginia Gleanings in England: Abstracts of Seventeenth and Eighteenth-Century English Wills and Administrations Relating to Virginia and Virginians* (Baltimore, 1980), 309–310 (from *VMHB*, XIX [1911], 285–289); CCC to Richard Corbin and Robert Carter Nicholas, Nov. 8, 1767, Paine Family Papers, Signers of the Declaration of Independence, II, American Antiquarian Society, Worcester, Mass. Annotated lists of CCC's copy of his selections may be found in Ronald Hoffman, Sally D. Mason, and Eleanor S. Darcy, eds., *Dear Papa, Dear Charley: The Peregrinations of a Revolutionary Aristocrat, as Told by Charles Carroll of Carrollton and His Father, Charles Carroll of Annapolis, with Sundry Observations on Bastardy, Child-Rearing, Romance, Matrimony, Commerce, Tobacco, Slavery, and the Politics*

Of all the topics Charley discussed with his English friends during the first two years of his return, none, not even politics, intrigued him more than the mysteries and possibilities of matrimony. Although he wrote to William Graves, "Matrimony is at present but little the subject of my thoughts," his letters to Thomas Bradshaw and Christopher Bird suggest the contrary. Trying to portray himself as a cool and indifferent bachelor — "a man of common sense at 28," whose reason had long since triumphed over "youthful heat"— Charley instead revealed his avid interest in all aspects of the conjugal relationship, an interest tempered, not by his intellect, but by his lingering disappointment at failing to persuade Louisa Baker to embark upon the matrimonial adventure with him. Nowhere is this more evident than in his September 1765 letter to the recently wed Christopher Bird. Unable to resist the opportunity Bird's marriage provided for getting accurate information, Charley questioned the bridegroom closely about what being married was like "now the honey moon is over." After cautioning Bird not to "read this to yr. wife," Charley pressed him for his "real sentiments of that sweet slavery: is the way strewed over with flowers? Are there not some thorns & sharpe ones too?" Despite his tolerable health and substantial fortune, Charley found something still "wanting" in his life, a yearning he attributed, in a veiled reference to Louisa, to "too good a memory or too much sensibility." [15]

Writing to Thomas Bradshaw two months later, he affected a more pragmatic, emotionally distant stance, observing that men of his age recognized "the emptiness of that passion wh exists nowhere no where but in romance" and therefore would not choose "a meer mistress" for a wife, but "an agreeable, sweet tempered sensible companion." Should a mature man marry, he opined coolly, he would do so "from affection, from esteem, & from a sense of merit in his wife whom he will look upon in a better light than a meer bed fellow." This being so, he regretted that most women spent more time on improving their appearance than their minds, for physical charms lasted "in the eyes of a husband but as few months." A woman who wished "to secure the affection of a husband & to perpetuate that empire, wh beauty first established," must rely instead upon the enduring virtues of "good nature, & Good sense, improved by reflection, by

---

of Revolutionary America (forthcoming), appendix 3; and in Michael J. Parker, "The Fittest Season for Reading: The Library of Charles Carroll of Carrollton" (master's thesis, University of Maryland, 1990), 99–118.

15. CCC to [William] Graves, Sept. 15, 1765, CCC, letterbook 1765–1768, fol. 22; CCC to [Thomas] Bradshaw, Nov. 21, 1765, fol. 33; CCC to Christopher [Bird], Sept. 28, 1765, fol. 27.

Affairs of the Heart

reading & by the conversation of men of sense." Charley could imagine nothing "more dreadfull" or "more irksome" than being "linked for life to a dull, insipid companion, whose whole conversation is confined to the colours & fashions of her dress, the empty chit chat of tea table, or to the salting of hogs."[16]

Six months later, in May 1766, Charley rather offhandedly penned his friend Edmund Jenings the surprising news that he would shortly enter what he now called "the holy state of matrimony," having "made choice of a lady about 23 years of age, handsom enough, genteel, sensible & good natured." Her name, which he never mentioned to Jenings or to any of the English friends to whom he subsequently extolled her virtues, was Rachel Cooke, and she was the sister of the William Cooke he had met during his sojourn on the Eastern Shore in the winter of 1764–1765. Catholic, she was certainly, as Charley told Graves, "well bred," since her mother, Sophia Sewall Cooke, and Charley's maternal grand-mother, Jane Sewall Brooke, had been sisters, making the prospective bride and groom first cousins once-removed.[17] Her father, John Cooke, was a Prince George's County planter, whose seat, Graiden, where Rachel lived, lay some twenty-two miles from Annapolis. How long Charley had been courting her is unknown, but the nuptials were set for July 8, 1766. Then in June Charley fell ill with a fever that did not finally abate until late July, forcing postponement of the wedding until the fall.[18]

Though he accepted the need for this period of "recruiting" from the "great shock" illness had given "to a frame naturally weak," Charley was disappointed at the delay. As he waited out the intervening months, he commented upon the union with a lighthearted frequency that bespoke his growing anticipation. Hav-ing received a report of marital happiness from Christopher Bird, Charley re-plied in late July that he agreed with Bird's assessment "that every State has i'ts thorns, & that the matrimonial one if entered into with prudence, hath the fewest." In August he confided to Bradshaw that there were indeed many "ratio-nal enducements to marriage" and that he could not agree "with Swift that no wise man ever married from good sense." Then in September he penned Bird the ultimate endorsement of his intended: "A greater commendation I can-not make of the young lady than by pronouncing her in no ways inferiour to

16. CCC to [Thomas] Bradshaw, Nov. 21, 1765, ibid., fol. 33.

17. CCC to [Edmund] Jenings, May 27, 1766, CCC to [William] Graves, July 16, 1766, CCC, letterbook 1765–1768, fols. 39, 45.

18. E. Alfred Jones, *American Members of the Inns of Court* (London, 1924), 51; CCC to Christopher [Bird], July 22, 1766, CCC to [William] Graves, July 16, 1766, CCC, letter-book 1765–1768, fols. 45, 85.

Louisa." Indeed, the prospective bridegroom staunchly insisted that Rachel's disposition and amiability had "contributed to efface an impression which similar qualities had made on a heart too susceptible perhaps of tender feelings & on a mind not sufficiently strengthened by Philosophy to resist those & the united power of good sense & of beauty."[19]

Having settled upon the first week in November as the time he would be "initiated in the misterious rites, as Milton calls them of Hymen," Charley turned his attention to the practical matter of ordering finery from London to enhance Rachel's wardrobe. Writing at length to Christopher Bird's aunt Esther, whose "obliging temper, & pleasing fancy" he admired, Charley requested her assistance in choosing the "silks and other articles" he desired. Maintaining that "magnificence & finery in Cloaths is neither mine nor the lady's taste" and that Rachel would "chuse them decent, handsom & genteel," he nevertheless made it clear that, "if handsom necklace or suit of lace could be bought at twenty guineas for instance, I should not begrudge 10 or 12 guineas more to purchase them handsomer & of a better design & more highly finished." Beyond this stipulation and a few "general directions" regarding the silks, Charley professed to be content to rely upon Esther's "prudence, œconomy & taste" and moved on, ostensibly to present the merits of his bride-to-be. It was a discussion that eventually brought him, by a disingenuously circuitous route, to Louisa.[20]

Beginning with the supposition that his correspondent, who had been privy to his previous courtship, might have "some curiousity to know what sort of choice I have made," Charley gallantly declared Rachel's "chiefest commendation" to be her similarity to Esther. "She has your good sense, a temper equally as sweet as yours, and a modesty that would charm a Rake." Abruptly leaving Rachel behind, he then veered off gaily into an exploration of why "Rakes . . . are as fond of modesty in a wife, as any other set of men" and why "the ladies" are "fonder of Rakes than of other men," but he closed these musings short of definitive conclusions lest Esther interpret his comments as "a satyr upon your sex," the very sort of "little inadvertencies" that had, at a critical moment in the past, produced an unfavorable opinion of him from someone for whose approval he "would have given the world." Having gotten to it at last, he broached the matter with studied casualness:

19. CCC to [Thomas] Bradshaw, Aug. 26, 1766, CCC to Christopher [Bird], July 22, 1766, Sept. 17, [1766], CCC, letterbook 1765–1768, fols. 49, 59, 63.

20. CCC to Christopher [Bird], Sept. 17, [1766], CCC to [Esther Bird], Oct. 6, 1766, ibid., fols. 63, 65.

Affairs of the Heart

Well then since the subject has some how unaccountably led me to the lady: I may mention her name. How is Louisa: There [was] once more musick in that name than in the sweetest lines of Pope: but now I can pronounce it as indifferently as Nancy, Betsy or any other common name — if I ask a few questions, I hope you will not think that I am not quite as indifferent as I pretend to be — but I protest it is mere curiousity or mere good will that prompts me to enquire after her — is she still single? Does she intend to alter her state, or to remain single — if she thinks of matrimony, my only wish is that she may meet with a man deserving of her.[21]

Absorbed in demonstrating his indifference to Louisa and all that failed courtship represented, Charley belatedly remembered several vital points of information concerning the order. "I had almost forgot to mention that I would chuse to have the silks made up in London: I have accordingly sent the measure of the ladys stays, & of the skirts of her Robes," he added in a hasty postscript that perhaps provides the truest measure of his indifference.[22]

A week after his blithe letter to Esther Bird, Charley and Rachel received, from the Jesuit superior in Maryland, the waiver of consanguinity required for a valid union between closely related cousins. The wedding date was set for November 5, the anniversary of the Gunpowder Plot! It was "no wonder," the bridegroom commented to his English friend Edmund Jenings, "that a blooded minded Papist would chuse for feasting & merriment a day wh had like (if you believe the story) to have proved so fatal to a Protestant King & Parliament."[23] He commissioned Maryland merchant Charles Digges to buy a fashionable two-seated, two-wheeled chaise called a curricle for him when Digges next went to London, and instructed his agents in that city to have money ready for the purchase. Then, on November 1, when all was in readiness for the wedding, Rachel

21. CCC to [Esther Bird], Oct. 6, 1766, ibid., fol. 65. Although she was still single at the time Charley wrote this letter, Louisa [Martha] Baker married Henry Swinburne (1743–1803) on Mar. 27, 1767. Philip C. Yorke, ed., *The Diary of John Baker, Barrister of the Middle Temple, Solicitor-General of the Leeward Islands, Being Extracts Therefrom* (London, 1931), 26.

22. CCC to [Esther Bird], Oct. 6, 1766, CCC, letterbook 1765–1768, fol. 65.

23. CCC and Rachel Cooke, dispensation to marry, Oct. 14, 1766, Carroll-McTavish Papers; CCC to [Edmund] Jenings, Oct. 14, 1766, CCC, letterbook 1765–1768, fol. 72. Charley's reference is to the failed plot by a small band of English Catholic conspirators to blow up the English Parliament and James I on Nov. 5, 1605, commemorated as Guy Fawkes Day. Distressed by the increasing harshness of the penal laws, the collaborators hoped to precipitate an uprising of English Catholics.

fell ill. At first, the doctors did not consider her malady serious, but she continued to weaken. Visiting her regularly during her illness, Charley was present when she died on November 25, 1766. His shock, deepened by not being warned that Rachel was in mortal danger, led him to express his feelings for her more openly and with much greater warmth after her death than he had ever done while she was alive. "The young lady to whom I was to have been married died the 25th. Instant," he wrote Graves two days later. "She was acknowledged by all her acquaintance, to be a most sweet tempered, amiable & virtuous girl: I loved her most sincerely & had all reason to believe I was as sincerely loved — Judge of my loss & by it of what I now feel — but I must drop this melancholy subject; my heart is too full & my mind is at present too discomposed, to permit me to be as full & circumstantial as usual." Writing to Christopher Bird three months later, Charley described Rachel's final hours in more detail: "She retained her senses almost to the last: perfectly resigned to her fate she seemed to feel much more for me than for herself." Although he had no doubt that her virtue would gain her "perfect happiness" in any "future state" that might exist, that confidence had clearly not assuaged the feelings he had experienced at her deathbed, a "distresful scene of wh I was not only an eye witness but the Principal Sharer." He was certain that Bird's "heart is too tender not to partake even at this distance of yr. friend's grief & to sympathise with him." [24]

With nothing remaining of his second unhappy courtship but "a pleasing melancholy reflection of having loved & being loved by a most deserving woman," for several months Charley felt "quite indifferent to every thing in this world even to life itself." [25] Although still disconsolate in the spring of 1767, his spirits had undergone a remarkable transformation by that summer's end. Comfort and reinvigoration had come through his eighteen-year-old cousin, Molly Darnall, who had lived with her mother Rachel in Papa's household since 1761.

The niece of Charley's beloved Mama, Rachel Brooke Darnall had originally joined the Carroll ménage as her aunt's companion in 1759, at the age of twenty-eight, but her ten-year-old daughter Molly, for reasons unknown, lived elsewhere. In Mama's view "a very worthy agreable y[ou]ng Woma[n]," Rachel had unfortunately chosen a spendthrift for a husband. Although the gentleman in question, Henry Darnall, Jr., was a great-grandson of Colonel Henry Darnall,

24. CCC to [Perkins, Buchanan, and Brown], Oct. 15, 1766, CCC to [William] Graves, Nov. 27, 1766, CCC to Christopher [Bird], Mar. 8, 1767, CCC, letterbook 1765–1768, fols. 77. 78, 85.
25. CCC to Christopher [Bird], Mar. 8, 1767, ibid., fol. 85.

Affairs of the Heart

the Settler's mentor and father-in-law, his distinguished antecedents did not compensate for his disreputable behavior. When Rachel came to live with the Carrolls, she and her husband had been separated for seven years. Relegated by that separation to having neither the protection the law accorded a married woman nor the rights it generally guaranteed a single one and left with few material resources, Rachel welcomed the sanctuary that the Carrolls provided. The two women, each forced to live apart from a well-loved, only child, quickly formed a special bond, and in May 1760 Mama reported to Charley that her niece was an "agreable Companion" and seemed "quite contented & happy with us." Rachel's tender care of Elizabeth Carroll during her final illness earned Charles Carroll of Annapolis's enduring gratitude. In the painful aftermath of his wife's death, the elder Carroll invited the younger woman to continue to live with him and to keep his house and welcomed her daughter Molly, now twelve, to reside under his roof as well.[26]

When Charley arrived home in February 1765, Molly had been a member of his father's household for nearly four years. A month shy of her sixteenth birthday, she then received only the courteous, formal attention that an older, erudite, well-traveled gentleman would properly extend to a young female relative. Although Papa's affection for Molly was undoubtedly apparent to Charley, the qualities that endeared her to the father — "great . . . good sense, a solid Judgement," strict virtue, and good nature, as the older man later enumerated them — initially made no impression upon the son. Emotionally absorbed by his reunion with Papa and then by his courtship of Rachel Cooke, Charley had no reason to take more than cursory notice of this girl a dozen years his junior who just happened to reside in his father's house. Indeed, if he thought of Molly at all, it was only as part of the Carrolls' domestic scene, as his sole reference to her in the letters he wrote to England between February 1765 and August 1767 indicates. In October 1766, asking Esther Bird to purchase a number of items for his fiancée's trousseau, the prospective bridegroom also ordered some silk for Molly, or, as he identified her to Miss Bird, "a young lady who lives with us."[27]

Molly's initial reaction upon her introduction to Charley, presumably resplendent in the fine continental attire purchased for the occasion of his return, can only be imagined. Her previous knowledge of his appearance would have been conditioned by the two likenesses of him that adorned the Carroll home —

26. EBC to CC, Mar. 4, 1759, May 5, 1760, CCA to CC, Apr. 16, 1761, Carroll-McTavish Papers.

27. CCA to [William] Graves, Dec. 23, 1768, Carroll Papers, MS 206; CCC to [Esther Bird], Oct. 6, 1766, CCC, letterbook 1765–1768, fol. 65.

one, now lost, but known to have been drawn of him for his mother in 1756, when he was nineteen, and the other, the portrait painted by Sir Joshua Reynolds in 1763.[28] Any suppositions she might have entertained about his personality reached her from two very different sources. Her mother Rachel undoubtedly related to her many of the fond remembrances of a long-absent son that Elizabeth Carroll had shared with her. By contrast, the impressions of Charley conveyed to Molly by Papa, with whom she enjoyed a warm paternal relationship, would have suggested a far more formidable character — a man of considerable intellectual accomplishment and social grace who had lived in both Paris and London. For a girl like Molly, whose experience of the world had been confined to Annapolis and Doohoragen, Charley and his adventures must have seemed almost larger than life, a notion that the impatience and pride animating Papa on the eve of his son's return accentuated. Perhaps Molly was therefore somewhat relieved to see, on that cold February morning, that, for all his learning and fine clothes, Cousin Charley, slightly built and not more than five feet, five inches tall, at least did not look so imposing.[29]

Between the winter of 1765 and the spring of 1767, the two had ample time to get used to each other's presence, but only after the death of Charley's fiancée did the possibility of a romantic relationship between him and Molly emerge. Newly turned eighteen that March and in the fresh blush of young womanhood, Molly had probably lost any shyness or self-consciousness she had felt when Charley first came home, and the poignancy of his loss undoubtedly softened his polished veneer, opening him, perhaps unawares, to her genuinely sympathetic concern. Precisely when romance blossomed is unknown, but matters progressed so rapidly that, when Charley wrote to Edmund Jenings in early August 1767, he mentioned rather offhandedly that he might well be married before his friend even received his letter. "I have," he told Jenings casually, "been so successful as to gain the affections of a young lady endowed with every quality to make me happy in the married state; virtue: good sense & good temper," at-

28. In his letter to Charley of Oct. 10, 1753, Papa directed that he have a portrait of himself made "in the Compass of 15 Inches by 12" (Carroll-Harper Papers, MdHi). Presumably, this was the picture his mother received in September 1756. EB to CC, Sept. 8, 1756, CC to CCA, Apr. 29, 1763, Carroll Papers, MS 206.

29. In May 1760, Papa noted that Charley had measured five feet, five inches when he had "last" seen him, which would have been in France in 1757. Since Charley was already twenty-one at that time, it is unlikely that he grew any taller thereafter. CCA to CC, May 1, 1760, Carroll-McTavish Papers.

tributes that "receive no small lustre from her person, which the partiality of a lover does not represent to me more agreeable, than what it really is." Having suggested, in an urbane and convoluted way, that his intended bride was pretty, Charley then confessed that this "sweet tempered, charming neat girl," whom he did not identify, was "a little to young for me . . . especially as I am of a weak & puny constitution." [30]

Relaying similar information to William Graves later the same month, Charley's lively candor attested to the return of his good spirits while allowing him to distance himself from any emotional investment in his third serious courtship. Graves, a confirmed bachelor, had obviously been urging Charley to put aside his disappointments and, for practical as well as personal reasons, to resume the search for a suitable wife. No longer as resistant to such counsel as during the wintry days of his melancholy, Charley now informed his adviser that he had adopted "all yr. arguments in favor of the matrimonial state" and that he intended to be married in the fall. This time, Charley even disclosed part of the prospective bride's name, along with her other vital statistics. "The lady's name is Darnall"; she was "of a good family, without any money," but "in every other respect . . . such as you would recommend to yr. friend: chearful, sweet-tempered, virtuous & sensible." To this routine recitation of desirable female virtues, Charley then added an unexpected twist: he wanted his old friend to know that Miss Darnall's "person is agreeable & cleanly." These were qualities that he had often found "wanting in the fair sex," though he recognized that Graves might "have had better luck than yr. hum: servant" in such matters. "If women who live by a certain profession are so deficient in an essential point of their calling, what are we not to apprehend from wives, who are above those little arts of pleasing?" he wondered, and ended his discussion of the hygienic habits of eighteenth-century females by observing: "Many married men have complained that prostitutes are neater than their wives. I presume they spoke from experience." [31]

Whatever else these remarks suggest, they most certainly belie Charley's efforts to present himself as a thoroughly rational, self-disciplined gentleman devoted to far more edifying matters than human physicality. Even if his statements reflect more youthful bravado than actual experience, it is nevertheless clear that, for all his declarations about virtuous living, the younger Carroll retained an intense interest in and curiosity about intimate relationships between men and women. Seen in this context, his mounting anxiety over the self-

30. CCC to Jenings, Aug. 13, 1767, CCC, letterbook 1765–1768, fol. 96.
31. CCC to Graves, Aug. 27, 1767, ibid., fol. 99.

imposed legal and financial difficulties that delayed his marriage to Molly for nearly ten months reveals a man frantically at war with himself.

Although he knew by early fall that his eagerly anticipated wedding would be delayed, Charley proceeded with his matrimonial plans. Perhaps to console himself and his intended bride for the unexpected interruption of the original schedule, he ordered nuptial finery from England. Instead of relying on his old friends the Birds, who had unaccountably failed to return the money advanced to cover the purchases for Rachel Cooke (an order Papa had countermanded the day after her death), Charley entrusted the new commission to William Brown, nephew and business partner of the Carrolls' longtime London correspondent William Perkins. Requesting that Brown's wife select the items Molly desired, Charley provided no hint of what his fiancée wanted and merely stipulated that "the things be bought at the best rate — but at the same time handsome and genteel," estimating that £150–£200 sterling would cover the bill. Concerning his own purchases for the "approaching solemnity," he was a good deal more specific, however, and instructed his London tailor to make him a "marriage suit" consisting of a frock coat, waistcoat, and breeches of "superfine white cloth," in a style that was "genteel without any lace about it either of gold or sylver."[32]

The necessity of postponing the wedding arose, not from the need to allow sufficient time for the nuptial wardrobe to traverse the Atlantic, but from the self-protective, practical considerations to which the Carrolls unfailingly adhered, even in their most intimate, personal arrangements. Like Charley's Mama before her, Molly must sign a prenuptial agreement relinquishing her dower right to a third of her husband's real and personal estate, should she outlive him, in exchange for an annual cash stipend — amounting in this case to three hundred pounds sterling. Although Molly and her family were perfectly willing to accept the settlement that accompanied the "Advantageous offer of Marriage" she had received, her not yet being of legal age raised questions concerning the validity of her consent. To guarantee the enforceability of the contract, Charley deemed it necessary to secure a private act from the Maryland legislature that would enable Molly to function as an adult. However, the assembly had been dissolved pending new elections, and the implementation of Charley's plan must wait until the new members convened in the spring.[33]

32. CCC to [William] Brown, Oct. 17, 1767, CCC to Mr. Harrison, Oct. 19, [1767], ibid., fols. 110, 111.

33. CCC to Graves, Nov. 7, 1767, ibid., fol. 112. Quote taken from "The Humble Petition of Henry Darnall Junior, of Rachel Darnall Wife to the said Henry Darnall Junior,

Affairs of the Heart

By January of the new year, the possibility that the assembly might not actually meet until the fall had reduced Charley to a state of agitated frustration. With his wedding date receding rapidly into the future, he began to search for another way to safeguard the Carroll wealth. Seeking expert legal advice, he received contradictory opinions, some advising that the sanction of a legislative act was not required to legalize a minor female's relinquishment of her right of dower, and others the opposite. Increasingly alarmed by the prospect that the only sure solution might be to wait until Molly turned twenty-one two years hence, Charley turned to William Graves, who had assisted him in framing his proposal to John Baker five years earlier. Imploring Graves to obtain the best legal counsel available in London, Charley emphasized that his chief concern lay in protecting his personal estate — thirty thousand pounds sterling lent at interest and slaves valued at nine thousand pounds sterling — from being "carried into another family, to the prejudice of my own children, or of the heir at Law," should his wife outlive him. Enclosing a blank draft drawn against his London agent William Perkins, Charley urged Graves to spare no expense in finding a secure way of resolving his dilemma. And then, lest Graves should think all this meticulous attention to preserving his fortune implied "an objection" to his impecunious fiancée, Charley stoutly assured his old friend, "I prefer her thus unprovided to all the women I have ever seen, even to Louisa."[34]

By the spring of 1768 the certainty that the Maryland legislature would shortly convene had relieved the prospective bridegroom's anxiety about his "critical & very uneasy situation." On May 30, 1768, six days after the assembly finally went into session, Molly Darnall, her father (the ne'er-do-well Henry Darnall, Jr.), her mother, and her uncle (Robert Darnall, Charley's old St. Omers schoolmate) petitioned the upper house. They asked that a bill be enacted "to impower the said Mary Darnall, by and with the Advice of your Petitioners," to assent to the proposed settlement securing her jointure and barring her "Right of Dower and the Share She might Claim of the personal Estate, by the Law or Usage of this Province," and that the settlement be made as legally binding upon her "as if she were of full Age." Aware that the legal imbroglio over "the apprehended invalidity of the settlement" had caused the marriage to be "deferred," the members of the upper house quickly assented to the request and ordered it submitted for consideration by the lower house. Before it left the council chamber, however,

---

of Mary Darnall aged Nineteen Years, Daughter of the aforesaid Henry Darnall Junior and Rachel Darnall, and of Robert Darnall, Uncle to the aforesaid Mary Darnall," in William Hand Browne et al., eds., *Archives of Maryland* (Baltimore, 1883–), LXI, 291–292.

34. CCC to William Graves, Jan. 16, 1768, CCC, letterbook 1765–1768, fol. 115.

the document upon which Charley had hung his matrimonial hopes received a dissenting analysis from the Carrolls' occasional nemesis, Daniel Dulany. According to the official record of the day's proceedings, "Daniel Dulany Esqr. declared, that tho' he thought the Provision proposed, in respect of the Annual Sum to be Settled was unexceptionable and even liberal, He was against the Question, because it is a Standing Rule of this House not to pass Acts in Consequence of private Petitions, where the remedy or purpose sought is sufficiently provided for by the general existing Laws."[35]

Whatever his opinion, Dulany did not sway his fellow councillors, and they sent the petition on to the lower house, where the delegates approved it and wrote and passed the required legislation in a single day. When Maryland's governor Horatio Sharpe signed the bill into law on June 4, Charley's long journey to the altar had almost reached its destination. With a waiver of consanguinity permitting cousins to marry already in hand, the only unfinished prenuptial business was the execution of the marriage settlement, the "Indenture Quinquipartite," to which the five signatories — Charley, Molly, her parents, and her uncle — affixed their names as soon as the governor's signature on the "enabling act" was dry. The wedding took place the following day, June 5, 1768, and received a short notice in the Annapolis paper: "On Sunday Evening, was married at his Father's House, in this City, Charles Carroll, Jun. Esq; to Miss Mary Darnall, an agreeable young Lady, endowed with every Accomplishment necessary to make the connubial State happy."[36]

35. CCC to Edmund Jenings, Apr. 14, 1768, ibid., fol. 128.; "The Humble Petition of Henry Darnall Junior," in Browne et al., eds., *Archives of Maryland*, LXI, 292–293.

36. An Act to Enable Mary Darnall an Infant to Enter into and Accept of a Marriage Settlement and Agreement, in Browne et al., eds., *Archives of Maryland*, LXI, 422–423; Thomas Digges to CCC, June 3, 1768, Carroll Papers, MS 216, MdHi; CCC with Mary Darnall, Rachel Darnall, Henry Darnall, Jr., and Robert Darnall, marriage settlement, June 4, 1768, Carroll-McTavish Papers, oversize; *Md. Gaz.*, June 9, 1768. After signing his daughter's marriage settlement, Henry Darnall, Jr., disappears entirely from the voluminous records pertaining to the Carroll family except for one intriguing reference in 1772. In the letter to Charley on September 6 of that year, Papa confesses, "Without reflection I gave yr letter to Molly, I am sorry for it as the Acct of Her Fathers being Executed made Her low Spirited & Yr being unwell" (Carroll Papers, MS 206). The letter containing this news, written by Charley on either Aug. 31 or Sept. 4, 1772 — Papa notes he has received correspondence so dated from his son — has not been found, nor is the matter ever mentioned subsequently in any of the family's papers or in Maryland newspapers or court records. Therefore, it has proved impossible to learn whether "being Executed" means that Molly's wastrel father was actually put to death, or that he simply lost whatever property he still possessed through some sort of legal judgment "executed" against him.

The *Maryland Gazette*'s assessment was one with which Papa completely agreed, and his enthusiasm for the union had not diminished six months later when, on December 23, he wrote a long letter to Charley's friend William Graves. Papa had never met Graves, but "the Friendship you bear my Son," as demonstrated by their extensive correspondence, left the old man "no rome to doubt a letter from me may be acceptable to you, Especially as it will informe you that His Mariage was entierly to my Satisfaction, & that I think He has a well grounded prospect for as much Happyness as Can be Hoped for in a Conubiall state." Pronouncing himself completely delighted with his "very agreable" daughter-in-law, Papa assured Graves that his "Character of Her" was no fond, idle wish, but rather was "founded on a long & intimate Acquaintance: She has lived with me since she was 12 years old & in the Course of more than Seven years I have not had Reason to Chide Her." Notwithstanding his ringing approval of and paternal fondness for the bride, Papa emphatically wanted Graves to know that Charley had chosen her on his own: "He had not the most distant Hint from me," insisted the masterful old manipulator, "that Miss Darnall would make a good Wife." [37]

Following the wedding, Papa and Rachel Darnall, Molly's mother, retired to Doohoragen Manor, and the younger Carrolls set up housekeeping in town. Ensconced in the brick house and adjoining frame structure that constituted the Carrolls' Annapolis residence, with an annual income of at least one thousand pounds sterling, Charley and Molly entered the "Conubiall state" with an enviable degree of material security.[38] For Charley, long accustomed to the benefits of an "independent fortune," nothing very much had changed, for there was no appreciable difference between the style of life he had enjoyed as a bachelor and the way he expected to live as a married man. For Molly, cast adrift by her wellborn, wastrel father and forced, by his folly and the malfeasance of his father before him, to depend upon Papa's largesse for her livelihood, the panorama of possibilities that spread before her on her wedding day was truly breathtaking. As the wife of her benefactor's son, Molly became the mistress of one of colonial Maryland's most affluent, economically powerful, and educationally distinguished households, and her place at the center of this domestic sphere gained her four enormously important advantages: the protection of wealth, a position of social respectability, a well-defined and meaningful familial role, and as much control over her own life as any female of her day could reasonably expect. The

37. CCA to [William] Graves, Dec. 23, 1768, Carroll Papers, MS 206.
38. Ibid.

roof over Mrs. Charles Carroll of Carrollton's head might have been the same one that sheltered Molly Darnall, but everything else had been subtly and profoundly transformed. And it is the contrast embodied in this transformation — the juxtaposition of Molly's painful past with her well-founded hopes for a glowing future — that forms the backdrop for the poignant personal drama of the Carrolls' marriage.

Within ten months of her wedding, Molly Carroll performed one of the principal duties of a "good Wife" by giving birth to a child. Although the little girl delivered on April 3, 1769, was not the son and heir undoubtedly hoped for, the baby's arrival still confirmed Molly's reproductive capacity, and the fact that the infant received the name Elizabeth, in honor of Mama, attests that both her father and grandfather welcomed her warmly. Neither their happiness nor Molly's was destined to endure, however. In August, scarcely five months after he had recorded Elizabeth's birth in the pages of the old Gaelic genealogy, Charley added the grim notation of his little daughter's death. The loss must have been especially difficult for the twenty-year-old mother to bear. Already pregnant again, Molly miscarried later in the fall, probably owing in part to her distress over Elizabeth's death and the intense anxiety generated by a brief but extremely unpleasant public dispute between Charley and Lloyd Dulany, Daniel's younger half brother.[39] Molly's third pregnancy, begun before the turn of the year, proceeded uneventfully, and Papa, barely able to contain his delight at the prospect of another grandchild, scolded his daughter-in-law if she failed to give him up-to-the-minute reports of every development. "Molly Writes to Her Mama that she felt the little one 4 Weeks past," he told Charley in a letter written in early May. "Tell Her I think Her a perverse Girl for not letting me know it sooner." Mindful of the misfortunes of the previous year, Papa monitored Molly closely; although he did not object to her accompanying Charley on a pleasure voyage to the Eastern Shore in the spring, he reacted negatively to the news that his son had permitted her to attend a play in late August, when the baby's birth was imminent. "I wish the Heat of the Theatre may not Have been too great for Molly," he wrote Charley on August 28, adding tersely, "Had I been with Her I Believe I should not Have Consented to Her going to the Play."[40]

39. "Genealogy of O Carroll," MS, Carroll-O'Carroll Genealogies, MdHi. For the miscarriage, as for my interpretation of the Carrolls' conjugal relationship, I have relied upon Sally D. Mason's essay "Mama, Rachel, and Molly: Three Generations of Carroll Women," in Ronald Hoffman and Peter J. Albert, eds., *Women in the Age of the American Revolution* (Charlottesville, Va., 1989), 244–289, esp., in this case, 281.

40. CCA to CCC, May 4, Aug. 28, 1770, Carroll Papers, MS 206.

Affairs of the Heart

Notwithstanding her father-in-law's concern, Molly suffered no ill effects from her outing, and on September 2, 1770, with her mother in attendance, she bore another daughter, to whom she gave her own name, Mary. Whatever disappointment Papa might initially have felt that it was once again not a boy that "it has Pleased God to send us" soon dissipated. The more he came to know little Molly — or little "Pol" or "Polly," as the family occasionally called her — the more he adored her. Precociously displaying the charm for which she would be renowned as a woman, this tiny female would quickly make a conquest of Papa's heart; and, by the time she reached her first birthday, little Pol had transformed the man known to his adult contemporaries as an outspoken and abrasive curmudgeon into a doting grandfather. After a short visit to Annapolis in late September to attend the races and be introduced to the new arrival, Papa dutifully returned to Doohoragen; but, by the end of November, he was writing wistfully to Charley, "I long to see Our little Girl." It was even harder for him to tear himself away following his annual two-to-three-month winter stay with Charley and Molly in Annapolis, and in early April, his affection for the child led him to make an uncharacteristically effusive suggestion. "I shall hardly Mention the little Girl in my future letters, but I allways Mean that Molly should kiss her for me on the Receit of Every letter & oftener & when she brings us another I believe I shall take my little Darling to my self if Molly Can bear it." [41]

Needless to say, Molly had no intention of even considering such an arrangement, and, when her sentiments, conveyed in a letter to her mother, were brought to Papa's attention, he protested that he "never designed to Have my little Darling with me unless it was agreable to Her Mama." Defensive in his disappointment, the old gentleman insisted, "It is far from me to gratify my self by anything wh would give Her Pain," adding, "I saw what she wrote to Her Mother." Papa's pique was short-lived, however, and in June Molly brought the baby on her first visit to Doohoragen. Papa welcomed them with unabashed delight. "My little Girl was Coy at first," he reported to Charley, who had stayed behind in Annapolis. Nevertheless, he continued confidently, "We begin to be [Acq]uainted." [42]

Molly gave birth to her third child, a girl, in April 1772, but the new arrival did not diminish Papa's attachment to little Pol. She remained his "little Darling"

41. CCA to CCC, Sept. 4, 1770 (quoted in Mason, "Mama, Rachel, and Molly," in Hoffman and Albert, eds., *Women in the Age of the American Revolution,* 281), Nov. 30, 1770, CCA to CCC, Apr. 2, 1771, Carroll Papers, MS 206.

42. CCA to CCC, Apr. 12, June 3, 1771, Carroll Papers, MS 206.

and the recipient of the countless kisses his letters instructed her mother to bestow upon her, always with the message that her "Grand Papa" had sent them. The existence of her younger sister he acknowledged more generally in his affectionate good wishes for the well-being of "the little Ones" or "my Dear little Grand Children." The baby did have a name of her own, however, and a curiously interesting one at that — Louisa Rachel. While it is probable that her second name was given in honor of Molly's mother, Rachel Darnall, and not as a tactless reminder of Charley's ill-fated fiancée, Rachel Cooke, there is only one plausible source for Louisa. In his seventieth year and content with the present circumstances of his life, Papa might well have forgotten some of the details of his son's bittersweet first romance, and Molly, who was only fourteen or fifteen at the time of the negotiations with John Baker, might never have known the name of the young woman involved. But there can be no such suppositions about Charley who — probably without his wife's awareness — simply enshrined his memory of the unattainable Louisa in the bosom of his family by giving her name to his daughter. But Louisa Carroll's life ended abruptly when she succumbed to an unexplained illness in November 1772; yet, her brief presence and the echoes of the past it evoked for Charley were not forgotten. In 1791, little Pol, grown up and married, would christen a daughter of her own Louisa.

Two weeks after little Louisa's death, Papa readily admitted to Charley that the sad event and his concern for Molly had made him "more Grave & thoughtfull . . . than usual," but Charley's reaction to the loss of a second child is unknown. Indeed, his relationship with his children never exhibited the spontaneous warmth that characterized Papa's behavior toward them, and occasionally the old man saw fit to admonish his son for his reserved demeanor. "Tell Molly to give littell Molly a Kiss for me I know you will not do it," he told Charley in March 1771, and in August he echoed the same refrain: "Kiss my little Darling for me, if you will not Molly will." Papa even reminded Charley on September 2, 1772, "This is my Dear Little Polly's birth day," adding pointedly, "I shall drink Her Health, it is odds You will not do so." The same emotional detachment suggested by Papa's remarks is also evident in the descriptions of family life that Charley penned to his English friends during the early 1770s. Bringing William Graves up to date in March 1772, six or seven weeks before Louisa's birth, Charley reported, "I have one daughter alive, & Mrs. Carroll will soon make an addition to her family." He then went on to express his agreement with an "observation" Graves had apparently written to him concerning the desire of wealthy men for legitimate heirs. "I may venture to say there never was a rich man, but who sincerely wished for descendents of his own body — tho' the reflection that they might possibly not be of his *own body* has deterred many a one from using the means." In the same vein, Charley informed Graves that the anticipated expansion of his family had occurred by remarking, "I am now the father not of many children but of two girls, at least Mrs. Carroll tells me so, and Pater est quem nuptiae demonstrant [The father is he to whom the marriage points]." Concerning Louisa's death, Charley wrote only a single, brief sentence, which effectively distanced him from the event: "Mrs. Carroll & her little girl (she has only one alive) are both well." [43]

Describing his state of mind and style of life to William Graves in August 1772, Charley reported languidly, "Notwithstanding matrimony & the heat of the climate, my poor little thin carcass keeps its own, and my spirits are kept up, as you have guessed, by a variety of employments, business, exercise, & study: in short I never allow myself time to be idle, or the spleen to pray upon me and to this perpetual occupation I ascribe a nearly equal flow of spirits, which I cannot say is constitutional, being naturally rather of a melancholy & contemplative cast." In part, Charley's lassitude reflected his general uninterest in parenthood and the strictures it had imposed upon the erotic vision that had led him to pursue wedlock so vigorously. Not fathering a son provided an additional incentive for cultivating a posture of limited domestic involvement, which he maintained when Molly became pregnant again in late summer 1774. Conveniently distancing himself from such hopes by displacing them onto Papa, he described Molly to Graves as "big with a son and heir — at least So the old gentleman wishes — I believe he will lose all patience should it turn to a girl." [44]

Molly saved her father-in-law's equanimity by giving birth to a healthy boy on March 2, 1775, at the Carroll house on Duke of Gloucester Street. Not yet having ended his winter sojourn in the capital, Papa was on hand for the momentous occasion, and who can tell what memories of the Carroll past surged through his mind as he gazed at the grandson in whom so many future hopes would now be vested? Believing that "a Child's temper & disposition" would be "influenced more or less by its nurse," the elder Carroll regretted that Molly was unable to breast-feed her son; but, to his relief, little Charles prospered anyway. With proprietary pride, Papa reported the good news to William Graves in late May: "I will end with what will please You," he wrote. "I had a Grandson the 2d

43. CCA to CCC, Mar. 28, Aug. 8, 1771, Sept. 2, Nov. 19, 1772, ibid.; CCC to [William] Graves, Mar. 7, Aug. 14, 1772, Sept. 7, 1773, CCC, letterbook 1770–1774, fols. 21, 24, 29, MdHi.

44. CCC to [William] Graves, Aug. 14, 1772, Aug. 15, 1774, CCC, letterbook 1770–1774, fols. 24, 30.

of last March who is now a fine stout Hearty thriving Child." But even though he was always especially concerned to hear that "the little Boy" was doing well, Papa insisted that his attentiveness did not mean "that I love Him better or so well as my Dr little Molly." It was only, the proud grandfather declared firmly to his son, that the infant's "tender state makes me More Sollicitous for Him."[45]

True to his word, Papa remained as absorbed in his granddaughter after the birth of her brother as before. Little Charles might indeed be "the finest Boy in the World as Molly says to Her Mama," but, even so, no one could take little Pol's place in her grandfather's heart. He looked forward to her visits to Doohoragen, especially when she came to stay with him and Rachel without her parents, and he treasured the notes she began to send him from Annapolis. "Thank little Molly for Her letter," he told Charley in July 1775; "it did not contain a Sylable of Nonsense." And what about Charley — did the arrival of a son and heir soften his reserve and kindle some dormant spark of demonstrative fatherly fondness? Judging from Papa's refrain, Charley seems to have made some progress with his daughter — "Kiss little Molly," the old gentleman instructed him straightforwardly in August 1775 — but not with his son. Concluded Papa, "& tel Molly to Kiss the Boy for me."[46]

Charley did occasionally refer approvingly to his children — "Molly growes a fine girl full of life & prattle," he wrote Papa in May 1772, and two years later he characterized her to Graves as "a fine child . . . & of a sweet & lively temper." An early Carroll biographer archly attributed Charley's remoteness to a distaste for all "soggy, squalling infants," overlooking the possibility that a more profound dynamic was at work. Although sparse, the evidence from Charley's earliest years — before being sent away to school in France — portrays him as an openly affectionate child, "lolling & fondling" about his mother, who responded warmly to his declarations of love.[47] Nothing is known about his interaction with Papa during this period, but the strict subordination of fatherly sentiment that the elder Carroll deemed essential to his plan for creating a worthy heir is fully documented thereafter. Thus Charley's conduct toward his young children is both a reprise of the strict emotional discipline of his own father and a prod-

45. CCA to CCC, Apr. 2, 10, 1775, CCA to William Graves, May 2[9], 1775, Carroll Papers, MS 206.

46. CCA to CCC, May 17, July 6, Aug. 14, 1775, ibid.

47. CCC to CCA, May 27, 1772, ibid.; CCC to William Graves, Aug. 15, 1774, CCC, letterbook 1770–1774, fol. 30; Ellen Hart Smith, *Charles Carroll of Carrollton* (Cambridge, Mass., 1942), 90; EBC to CC, Sept. 8, 1756, Carroll Papers, MS 206, and Sept. 10, 1760, Harper-Pennington Papers, MdHi.

Affairs of the Heart

uct of the reserved personality thereby produced. Moreover, his restraint shielded him against the potentially devastating pain that giving his offspring up, whether to death or to life's demands, might bring. By contrast, as a patriarch long accustomed to controlling the circumstances and setting the contours of other lives — such as those of his wife, her niece, his son and daughter-in-law, his slaves — Papa dealt differently with the risks of human existence. Squarely confronting the inevitability of personal loss, he allowed himself to suffer even as he steeled himself against permitting his feelings to interfere with rational decisions.

Although Charley was consistently aloof toward both his male and female children, gender might have configured Papa's attitude toward the youngest members of the family. Of the seven children eventually born to Molly and Charley, six were girls, two of whom, Pol and Kitty, survived to adulthood. As revealed in his discussion of the attributes to be looked for in choosing wives, the senior Carroll held firm convictions regarding the deportment and character of genteel women and about the rearing most likely to produce them, such as religious instruction and early confinement to "Book needle & Works Sutable to their station." [48] At the same time, Papa clearly relished the opportunity to indulge and enjoy his granddaughters, thereby introducing them to the art and rewards of simply being charming. It is also true that the elder Carroll displayed a similar warmth for his grandson. The birth of what all hoped would be another worthy heir accounted for no small portion of the joy with which Papa greeted Charley's only son in March 1775. However, training in the weighty responsibilities of Carroll heirs did not commence during little Charles's earliest years. Thus while Papa might have later expected the same high performance from his grandson that he had demanded of Charley, that imperative lay ahead. Until the new generation of Carrolls was old enough to be groomed for future roles, Papa's sterner side could wait, and he could be the doting grandfather.

If Charley found marriage less fulfilling than he had anticipated and the parenting of young children a somewhat disagreeable, if endurable, necessity, one area of domestic activity interested him enough to keep up his spirits and ward off attacks of "the spleen." As befitted an English gentleman, and several of his provincial contemporaries as well, Charley began in 1770 an extensive renovation and improvement of the Carroll grounds and dwellings on Duke of Gloucester Street. His plans, implemented over the course of several years, make it clear that, despite his protestations to Graves concerning his "naturally . . . melan-

48. CCA to CC, Sept. 1, 1762, Carroll-McTavish Papers.

choly & contemplative cast," Charley intended to establish a far more visible social presence in Annapolis than his eccentric, unconventional father had ever cared to. Maryland law still barred Catholics from politics, but the overtly hostile feelings unleashed against them during the Seven Years' War had receded by the end of the 1760s. Even a staunch papist with a confrontational family background like Charley's might, in this more benign climate, enjoy some of the pleasurable pastimes — card games, horse races, dinner parties, balls, theatergoing, and other such entertainments — that occupied the leisure hours of the genteel Protestant elite. Some areas continued to be off-limits: Charley was not invited to join the Homony Club, a convivial group organized in 1770 and similar to its predecessors, the Tuesday and Forensic Clubs, although William Deards, the Englishman he had employed as his clerk in 1769, appears to have been a member. So were the new provincial governor, Sir Robert Eden, and his secretary, William Eddis, the Reverend Jonathan Boucher, rector of St. Anne's, Annapolis's Anglican church, merchant Charles Wallace, Lloyd Dulany, and many former Forensic Club participants.[49]

His exclusion from the Homony Club's gatherings at the Coffee House on Church Street did not deter Charley from frequenting that establishment on other occasions or from partaking of Annapolis's other social opportunities — activities that brought him and Molly on occasion into Protestant gentry circles. Thus, in refurbishing his house and redesigning his garden, he provided himself with surroundings that not only reflected his ambitions but also emphasized his attractive credentials: wealth, erudition, exceedingly good manners, and a pretty young wife who manifestly enjoyed giving and going to parties. Sometimes Molly's delight in festive diversions annoyed Charley to the point that he criticized her "levities" to his father, only to receive the older man's assurance that "a little time & Experience" would soon mitigate this girlish enthusiasm. Molly's youthful gaiety undoubtedly won a more sympathetic response from her best friend, Mary Ogle Ridout, who lived in a fine Georgian house a short distance from the Carrolls on the opposite side of Duke of Gloucester Street. Three years Molly's senior, Mary Ridout shared with her the experience of being married to an older man — in 1764, at the age of eighteen, she had wed thirty-one-year-old John Ridout, secretary to Horatio Sharpe, then governor of Maryland.[50] The

49. Joseph Towne Wheeler, "Reading and Other Recreations of Marylanders, 1700–1776," *Maryland Historical Magazine*, XXXVIII (1943), 171–180; Stiverson and Jacobsen, *William Paca,* 55–57.

50. CCA to CCC, May 4, 1770, Carroll Papers, MS 206. Mary Ogle Ridout (1746–1808) was the youngest child of former Maryland governor Samuel Ogle (c. 1694–1752) and his

friendship between the Carrolls and the Ridouts must have been firm; in the fall of 1771, the two couples took a trip of several weeks together, visiting Philadelphia and New York. Charley later described the journey as "very agreeable," owing to "the company the fine weather & the civilities we received" in both cities, but Papa distinctly disapproved of what he regarded as a frivolous undertaking. Aware that he would be forced to stay in Annapolis while the younger Carrolls were away, Papa let Charley know in mid-September, before the departure, exactly what he thought: "I never liked Yr: Northern Jaunt but I did not Chuse to thwart Mollys inclination tho I think she will when it is over be of Opinion that the Pleasure will not Answer the Expence fatigue & other Inconveniences attending it. You Cannot be well spared from Annapolis & it will be very Hurtfull to our interest Here for me to be so long absent at this Season."[51]

Notwithstanding their differences in age and temperament, Charley and Molly agreed about the need to improve and embellish their Annapolis domicile. Although imposing, especially when viewed from the shoreline of the creek that bordered the Carroll property on the south, Papa's brick house was essentially a simple, gambrel-roofed structure consisting of four bays bounded on the east and west ends by enormous chimneys. A story and a half on the land side and two and a half on the side facing the creek where the terrain fell naturally away to the water, this building was undeniably substantial, but its visual effect, which included the Settler's eleven-room frame dwelling at its eastern wall, lacked the elegance of the Georgian residences built in Annapolis in the late 1760s and early 1770s by Matthias Hammond, James Brice, Lloyd Dulany, the Carrolls' near neighbors Dr. and Mrs. Upton Scott (immediately west on Shipwright Street), and the Ridouts. Nor could the landscape surrounding the Carroll dwellings, dotted with various outbuildings and dependencies, compare with the gardens of other Annapolitans, the most notable being the harmonious arrangement of terraces, walkways, and plantings that graced William Paca's grounds.

For Charley to raise the plain and practical Carroll establishment to a par with the newer urban demesnes of his contemporaries would require a considerable outlay of time and money, and it was bound to bring him into conflict with his father. Conditioned to frugality by the adversarial and always uncer-

---

wife, Anne Tasker Ogle (1723–1817). John Ridout (1732–1797) came to Maryland with Horatio Sharpe in 1753. Edward C. Papenfuse et al., eds., *A Biographical Dictionary of the Maryland Legislature, 1635–1789* (Baltimore, 1979–1985), II, 691–692.

51. CCC to Charles Carroll, Barrister, Dec. 3, 1771, CCC, letterbook 1770–1774, fol. 19; CCA to CCC, Sept. 15, 1771, Carroll Papers, MS 206.

tain circumstances of his life and possessed as well of a distaste for ostentation, Papa considered it unconscionable to allow present expenditures to undermine careful planning for the future, and he strongly reiterated this view to his son and daughter-in-law shortly after little Pol's birth in 1770: "Can fine furniture Cloaths &c be put in Competition with a provision for Children?" he queried sternly. "Pride & Vanity are not to be indulged at their Expence, nor are You to be fools because many are So, what is decent & Convenient, You ought to Have, there is no end to a desier for finery of any sort, the Sumptuousity of Princes leaves roome for desier, I wish Yrs & Mollys to be governed by Reason be content with what is Neat Clean & Necessary."[52]

As long as the improvements appeared to have a solid, practical purpose, Charley could count on his father's approval. Papa regarded the seawall Charley began to plan in the spring of 1770 as a necessary expense dictated by the erosive action of the creek, although he might not have fully realized that his son deemed the barrier equally essential to the elaborate formal garden he intended to lay out. At any rate, Papa advised Charley fully about the materials and methods of construction to be used for his "Wall in the Water," urging him to forgo the cheaper, more accessible, but less durable Susquehanna stone for a harder variety that could be squared and laid in tightly fitted courses capable of retaining the soil. Unfazed by the knowledge that his way would take longer and make the work a good deal more arduous, Papa asserted, "I had if necessary rather be 10 years a doing it than not do it well." Following his advice, Charley used a ferruginous sandstone plentiful in Anne Arundel County and completed the work five years later, in 1775. Similarly, Papa recognized the wisdom of replacing the rail fencing along Duke of Gloucester Street with a brick wall that would protect the fruit trees and other foliage from vandalism by "idle disorderly Persons" who periodically scaled or broke down the wooden poles and trespassed on the grounds. Nor did the elder Carroll object to his son's attentions to the outbuildings, contenting himself with counseling Charley to act frugally by making "the Roof Seats &c of the Necessary Serve again" and reusing as much of the "Bricks stone &c" of the old privy as possible. The addition to the coach house undertaken in 1771 might well have raised Papa's ire, since it was needed to provide space for the fancy, four-horse carriage Charley had ordered from England, but instead the ever-pragmatic old gentleman simply directed that a shed large enough to house a couple of horses and several cows be attached to one side of

52. CCA to CCC, Nov. 30, 1770, Carroll Papers, MS 206.

Affairs of the Heart

the new structure, so that the former cowhouse could be used for storing the family's smaller equipages.[53]

The expenditures that triggered negative reactions, from grudging acquiescence to stinging reproof, involved conspicuous consumption. Papa's self-definition as a Catholic outsider both sanctified his economic aggression and conditioned him against the behaviors and costly material outlays calculated to buy broad social favor. "Shew," as Papa defined it, was a tool to be employed only on specific occasions, such as Charley's return to Annapolis from his studies abroad, and then in limited amounts. Under no circumstances was display to become a way of life. Papa was thus able to understand that a young couple who wanted to participate in Annapolis society might require a fancier parlor than the one he found adequate, and he did not object when Charley refurbished his public rooms. At the same time, Papa did not want Charley to misread his sentiments as permission for an unlimited expansion of such endeavors. To make sure his approval would not be misconstrued, he referred pointedly to two other Annapolis gentlemen, Samuel Chase and Edward Lloyd. Financially strapped and unable to complete the ambitious dwelling he had begun on Northeast Street in 1769, Chase sold the partially built structure in 1771 to Lloyd, whose inherited fortune equaled the Carrolls', for £504.8.2 sterling and £2,491.17.7 current money. To finish and furnish the house would, according to estimates Charley had relayed to his father, require Lloyd to spend an additional £6,000 current money. Briefly and bluntly, Papa let Charley know his opinion of these transactions: "Were Loyd my Son I should not like His Sinking £10,000 in a House, ease & Convenience is the most the Best fortunes in Maryland will at present Bear, shew among us in any shape is folly."[54]

Charley never intended to keep up with the Lloyds, but he did mean to live more stylishly than Papa. To this end, he ordered a complete set of furnishings from England for his renovated rooms, including such items as "two handsome gilt carvd girandoles," each having two lights; four "crimson silk & stuff damask

53. CCA to CCC, Aug. 12, 1770, May 30, Aug. 30, 1771, ibid.; William Voss Elder III, "The Carroll House in Annapolis and Doughoregan Manor," in Ann C. Van Devanter, ed., "Anywhere so long as There Be Freedom": Charles Carroll of Carrollton, His Family, and His Maryland (Baltimore, 1975), 68; Md. Gaz., June 14, 21, 1770.

54. James Haw et al., Stormy Patriot: The Life of Samuel Chase (Baltimore, 1980), 29–30. Charley's letter to [Charles] Carroll [Barrister], of Aug. 9, 1771 (CCC, letterbook 1770–1774, fol. 9), contains his estimates of the cost of completing Chase's house. He undoubtedly had given Papa the same information in a letter written August 10, which has not been found. CCA to CCC, Aug. 16, 1771, Carroll Papers, MS 206.

window Curtains . . . to be made up in the newest taste with Fringe"; a matched set consisting of "one fashionable Sopha" and twelve chairs "in the newest taste neat & strong wth cheque covers"; two framed pier glasses, carved and gilded to match the girandoles and sturdy enough to withstand Maryland's "extreams of Heat & cold" and "the rough treatment of negro servants"; and a couple of "fashionable Card Tables, no superflous Carving about them." In the event that the "Turky carpet" wanted for the floor could not be acquired, a carpet from "Axminster, Wilton — or any other English manufactory" could be substituted; and, to improve the appearance of the fireplace, Charley specified a mantle and jambs of white marble and a pair of "very neat Andirons — Brass topped, with a Shovell — a pair of Tongs and a neat brass pierced Fender." In two letters to West and Hobson, the firm handling this order, Papa insisted that the furniture be chosen carefully by "a Person of whose Judgement & Taste" his son had "a good Opinion," and on no account were goods of poor quality to be sent. To cover the cost of the order, £450 was left in the merchants' hands, and Papa directed them to "answer" any "Bills or orders." [55] Invoices for further refinements that arrived the following year elicited something close to a diatribe from Papa, however. "I return You Mr. Deards Shop note of Plate with some Remarks which Will Shew How Ridiculous & foolish it is to lay out Money that way for anything but spoons, for they Seem to me the only Necessary Plate Article," he began irritably. Warming to the subject, he then delivered a sharp reiteration of his values as a critique of Charley's:

> A rich side board Elegant & Costly furniture May gratify our Pride & Vanity, they may Excite the Praise & admiration of Spectators, more commonly their Envy But it Certainly must give a Rationall Parent infinitely more Satisfaction to Save the Money so dissipated as a Provision for younger Children, & an Ample Provision it would prove to be, in a Saving of 30 or 40 Years for Severall. Enjoy yr Fortune, keep an Hospitable table, But lay out as little money as Possible in dress furniture & shew of any Sort, decency is the only Point to be aimed at. [56]

Undeterred by his father's dislike of "shew" and dedication to the dictates of "decency," Charley continued to use a portion of his wealth to call attention to

55. CCA to West and Hobson, Oct. 26, 31, 1771, Charles Carroll Letter-book, 1771–1833, fols. 4–6, Arents Collections, New York Public Library, Astor, Lenox, and Tilden Foundations.

56. CCA to CCC, June 1, 1772, Carroll Papers, MS 206. John Deards, brother of CCC's clerk William Deards, was a London silversmith.

Affairs of the Heart

his presence in Annapolis. By September of 1772 he had joined the Maryland Jockey Club; and, during the race-week festivities that began in early October, his dinner guests included a Virginia planter named George Washington, whom he had probably met at the Ridouts the previous year.[57] Participating even more actively in 1773, Charley entered his stallion Marius in the fall races and watched with pleasure as the chestnut horse finished second in each of the three two-mile heats. The cancellation of the Annapolis races in 1774, in deference to the worsening imperial crisis and the resolves of the First Continental Congress, abruptly closed that particular avenue of social display, but the style of life Charley and Molly enjoyed at their Duke of Gloucester Street home on the eve of the American Revolution continued to reflect a taste for refinement and gentility that differed dramatically from the frugal simplicity Papa had imposed. The young Carrolls did indeed keep a "hospitable" table set with a service of imported blue-and-white china and blue water glasses and laden with a well-seasoned variety of foods, claret from Madeira, and such delicacies as raisins, chocolate, nuts, and truffles. Presided over by a pretty and charming hostess and an urbane host who regularly read not only the Maryland and Pennsylvania papers but also the *London Evening Post* and the *London Magazine* and served by a household staff of eight adult slaves, the three men among them outfitted in green serge liveries, the Carroll ménage could hold its own with any upper-class household in Annapolis.

57. CCA to CCC, Sept. 22, 1772, ibid. According to his diary entries, Washington dined at the Ridouts on Sept. 26, 1771, at "Mr. Carrolls" before going to "the Ball" on Sept. 27, 1771, and again at "Mr. Carroll of Carrollton" on Oct. 10, 1772. Donald Jackson and Dorothy Twohig, eds., *The Diaries of George Washington*, III (Charlottesville, Va., 1978), 56, 137.

CHAPTER 6

"A Prudent Management"

From the moment of Charley's return from Europe, Papa had begun to instruct him in handling the range of business affairs upon which the family's wealth depended. Among the first responsibilities the elder Carroll assigned his son was the still-pending lawsuit over the settlement of the Settler's estate, which pitted Papa against his nephew, Charles Carroll of Duddington, and his niece's husband, Ignatius Digges. Thrust into a legal thicket as thorny as any encompassed by the law curriculum he had so detested in London, Charley found the task as onerous as it was inescapable. "I have been pooring these two or three days past over old Accts of near thirty years standing that are now become the subject of a chancery suit[.] My spirits are quite sunk with the fatigue," he complained to Christopher Bird in September 1766. However, he intended to press on, trusting that his "perseverance and application will . . . enable me to expose the folly & malevolence of my advisaries." [1]

Had Charley known that it would take him another nine years to resolve these old conflicts, he might well have found his weariness insurmountable. Delayed by persistent family skirmishing and only occasional legal action, the case did not come to court until April 1771. By then, Charley had engaged Thomas Johnson, Jr., a politically ambitious young attorney, and his partner, William Cooke, brother of the ill-fated Rachel, to represent the Carrolls. The stir created in Annapolis by the courtroom airing of the long-standing family feud can be readily inferred from the description that Charley sent to Papa, who had chosen not to be present. After reporting that Digges's lawyers had spent an entire day accusing the elder Carroll of misconduct by misrepresenting and even ridiculing his administrative accounts, Charley turned to the defense mounted by

1. CCC to Christopher [Bird], Sept. 17, [1766], CCC, letterbook 1765–1768, MdHi, fol. 63.

Thomas Johnson: "He spoke four hours — I never heared a man speak more forcibly, more pertinently, more eloquently — He really was affected & touched with the ingratitude of this whole proceeding: he affected others — many in court could not refrain from tears; two or three left the court unable to conceal their sorrow." In the end, "Mr. Johnson who softened all the hearers, could not resist the tender feelings of his own heart, a sudden flow of grief put an abrupt stop to the most rational, eloquent, & pathetic discourse I ever heared."[2]

For Annapolitans, it must have been quite a show. For Charley, it became an acute embarrassment. The amount of speculation and gossip generated by the examination of his father's conduct in a courtroom that was, by his own account, "exceedingly crowded," can readily be imagined. For weeks, intermediaries from Governor Robert Eden, the presiding officer in chancery, conveyed messages urging that the suit be settled privately and implying that, if it were not, the court's decision would have "the *old gentleman* . . . upon *the high ropes.*" On one social occasion, the governor made oblique and unfavorable references about the case to Molly, and, during a similar gathering at the Ridouts' estate White Hall, both Eden and his assistant spoke directly to Charley about the desirability of compromise. Pressed equally hard in private by a father determined on public vindication as "a faithfull trustee & an Affectionate Uncle," Charley eventually managed — in 1774 — to resolve the matter in a way that satisfied his adversaries' pocketbooks and Papa's insistent self-righteousness.[3] By then, popular interest in the matter had long since waned. But, for Charley in the spring of 1771, engaged as he was in establishing his presence in Annapolis, the public examination of the legality and morality of his father's behavior must have been unsettling, a sharp reminder of how his family's defiant patterns of behavior reinforced its inherent vulnerability.

In the fall of 1766, Papa had delegated to Charley a second responsibility, which would not bring him any serious public embarrassment: the management of the tenanted portion of the Carrolls' landed estate. By the terms of the March 1757 agreement that settled the landed portion of the Settler's estate, Papa had transferred to his nephew, Charles Carroll of Duddington, five of the tenanted tracts he had developed: Clinmalira, Ely O'Carroll, and Litterluna in Baltimore County, and Clouen Couse and the Girles Portion in Prince George's County. The remainder of the lands he had begun to lease in the 1730s he kept for himself: Western Branch, composed of Concord and Outlet in Prince

2. CCC to CCA, [Apr. 14, 1771], Carroll Papers, MS 206, MdHi.
3. CCC to CCA, [Apr. 14], May 4, 7, 1771, ibid. The resolution of the dispute is discussed in Chapter 3, above.

George's County (1,325 acres), Carrollton Manor and the Addition to Carrollton in Frederick County (12,700 acres), and that part of Doohoragen Manor formerly possessed by his nephew (5,000 acres). He also retained control of the Settler's two St. Mary's County parcels, St. Clement's and Bashford (Basford) Manors, containing 11,400 and 1,500 acres, respectively. By placing the Prince George's, Frederick, and St. Mary's lands under Charley's supervision in the mid-1760s, Papa substantially reduced the scope of his own duties, and, although he continued to keep the books and settle the accounts for Carrollton for another fifteen years, he confined his direct oversight to the ten tenements he leased on Doohoragen Manor.

Any notions Charley might have brought with him to the job of land management and landlord-tenant relations were the product of observations accumulated during his long sojourn abroad, particularly the five years he spent in England. He rather quickly discovered that those impressions were of little use in mastering the tasks Maryland presented. As he informed William Graves in September 1765, he had found that "Our estates differ much from yours" in two important ways. To begin with, he explained, unlike the English gentry, who lived exclusively off their rents, Maryland planters relied upon a far less certain source of income inextricably tied to "the casual rise or fall in the price of Tobo." Even the few planters who had tenanted their lands received their rents in tobacco. In the light of these "disadvantages," it would be difficult for Charley to replicate in Maryland the life of the English landed gentry as he evidently aspired — and as Graves had apparently urged him — to do. Nevertheless, he had resolved "to confine myself to the improvement . . . of my parental acres" and "to live as becomes a gentleman" by avoiding "every appearance of meaness, of prodigality & ostentation." While he would not commit himself, as Graves had advised, to reinvesting all his annual income in improving his property for his own and his neighbors' benefit, neither would he hoard his money or spend it extravagantly on "gaudy equippages, empty pomp & show and in company more empty than these."[4]

Whatever his regrets at finding Maryland unsuited for English country life, Charley addressed himself with serious determination to successful land management's most basic task — the updating and reordering of the Carroll rent rolls, several of which had fallen into considerable disarray. He began sometime before September 1766 by interviewing the Carrollton Manor steward Joseph Johnson, from whom he learned of a number of situations detrimental to the

4. CCC to [William] Graves, Sept. 15, 1765, CCC, letterbook 1765–1768, fol. 22.

family's interests. One involved tenants who had ignored the restrictions on cutting timber specified in their leases and were now complaining about not being allowed to clear and farm the new ground. Charley also discovered from Johnson that unauthorized movement was taking place, with people swapping tenements or improperly transferring them to new residents without paying the required alienation fee to the Carrolls. Finally, an undetermined number of leaseholders had apparently abandoned their tenements and disappeared from the manor without settling their accounts.[5]

Organizing Johnson's information into a series of statements and questions, Charley then sought clarification from his father; by carefully recording Papa's replies, he not only found ways of resolving the present difficulties but also created a compact guide for subsequent dealings with other Carroll tenants. The plight of newcomers who had purchased tenements from their occupants without following established procedures did not elicit the elder Carroll's sympathy. Such people "ought to have known my terms before they purchased & not given Slater & Foster [the former tenants] what was due to me." Tenants who had destroyed timber received an equally stern response: he had no intention of allowing them to remain on his property if they committed similar violations in the future. Nor did Papa look kindly on tenant Basil Pearle, who, according to Charley's notes, had forsaken his tenement and "gone to his father's Rob: Pearl's place." Papa's reaction was curt: "Basil Pearle has no better right to his father's place than he has to the 50a[cres] he took of me; if therefore he does not chuse to hold the 50a[cres] I do not chuse he shall hold his father's place."[6]

As subsequent records confirm, Basil Pearle accepted Papa's dictum and continued to farm 150 acres on Carrollton until 1775. Most of the other difficulties uncovered by Charley's investigation were also satisfactorily resolved, as an analysis of the tenant population in 1771 reveals a remarkable stability, with more than 85 percent (fifty-four) of the sixty-two renters having taken up their tenements before 1760.[7] Rent collections for 1771 suggest that this stability trans-

5. [CCC], Queries and answers about Carrollton tenants, [c. September 1766], Carroll Papers, MS 216. The date is based on the document's internal evidence combined with information about CCC's activities gleaned from other manuscripts. Joseph Johnson (d. 1781), an Englishman by birth, assumed the post of steward on Carrollton about 1764.

6. Ibid.

7. Basil Pearle's father, Robert Pearle [Pearl, Perle], leased two hundred acres on Carrollton in March 1745 for a term of seventeen and a half years (Prince George's County Land Records, liber B.B. no. 1, fols. 264–265, MdAA. Basil's decision to move was prob-

lated into productivity: according to the balances recorded on September 29, the Carrolls received tobacco rents amounting to 57,260 pounds, just over 1,100 pounds more than the 56,076 pounds annually due. Although impressive, these figures do not tell the whole story: the tobacco paid by their leaseholders still fell nearly 26,000 pounds short of the cumulative total the Carrolls noted was actually owed them. The arrearage probably represented both the lingering effects of the problems Charley addressed in the 1760s and a more general pattern. As Papa had observed a decade earlier, no one could realistically expect to collect all that was due him every year. Despite such deficits, Carrollton's contribution to the family coffers continued to please both father and son: upon settling accounts with steward Joseph Johnson in September 1772, Papa happily informed Charley, "Yr Estate at Monnoccasi has Produced this Year upwards of £680 ster."[8]

---

ably occasioned by Robert's death in 1765. In addition to Basil, Robert Pearle left at least one other son, Daniel (d. 1774), who farmed one hundred acres on Carrollton from the 1740s or 1750s until his death. Two other tenants with similar tenures — James Pearle (d. 1774) and Thomas Pearle, who was still on the manor in 1779 — were also sons of Robert Pearle. (CCA, Account Book and Index, 1754–1784, fols. 33, 41, 42, 45, MdHi; [CCA], account with Danll. Pearle, 1752–1759, Carroll Papers, MS 216; rent roll and list of balances due on Carrollton, Sept. 29, 1771, and rent roll for Carrollton, Sept. 29, 1777, Carroll-Maccubbin Papers. Probate records exist for James Pearle: Frederick County Inventories, box 8, folder 44; and for Daniel Pearle: Frederick County Wills, box 5, folder 77, MdAA.) James Pearle's will names his wife, Elizabeth, executrix, lists no children, and designates Basil and Thomas Pearle as "next of kin." For a fascinating account of the Pearles, a mulatto family, see Mary C. Jeske, "Autonomy and Opportunity: Carrollton Manor Tenants, 1734–1790" (Ph.D. diss., University of Maryland, 1999), chap. 1.

The persistence of tenures on Carrollton has been calculated using Charles Carroll of Annapolis's Account Book and Index, 1754–1784 (a ledger titled MT) in conjunction with the 1768, 1771, and 1777 Carrollton rent rolls, the only documents of this kind that have been found. Ledger MT was begun by Charles Carroll of Annapolis in the mid-1750s, when an earlier book, liber T., had been completely filled. Although liber T., presumably standing for Tenants' Book and containing records of all Carroll leaseholders, has not survived, the accounts of Carrollton tenants carried from that ledger into the new one (MT, for Monocacy Tenants) are designated as coming from liber T. Although the bulk of the transfers (forty) were made in 1767, one account, that of Thomas Brashears (fol. 64) was entered in 1754. Entries in ledger MT to 1782 are in CCA's hand.

8. Carrollton rent roll, Sept. 29, 1771, Carroll-Maccubbin Papers; CCA to Clement Hill and Basil Waring, Nov. 21, 1760, CCA, letterbook 1757–1761, fol. 19, MdHi; CCA to CCC, Sept. 10, 1772, Carroll Papers, MS 206. Comparing rent roll summaries with specific entries in ledger MT, Jeske concludes that arrearages fluctuated, with tenants making up

"A Prudent Management"

Having cut his teeth, so to speak, on Carrollton, Charley next turned his attention to the even thornier situation on St. Clement's and Bashford Manors in St. Mary's County. Assembling the records of his father's and grandfather's tenures as lords of these manors, Charley quickly learned that the problems presented by the occupants of the St. Mary's County lands differed greatly from those of his Frederick tenants and that the present trouble was essentially a replay of long-standing difficulties. Unlike the tenants on Carrollton whom Papa had purposefully recruited to settle and develop the land, the vast majority of the people living on St. Clement's and the adjoining Bashford Manor were descendants, either by blood or marriage, of the individuals who had been granted tracts between 1652 and 1694, under very different agreements from those by which the Monocacy tenements were let.

The history of a five-hundred-acre tract called Bedlam Neck provides a typical example. On August 29, 1652, Thomas Gerard, the original owner of St. Clement's Manor, granted Bartholomew Philips this parcel with "full liberty of Hawking fowling fishing and Hunting after any Game Wild hoggs only Excepted" on the rest of the manor and permission to cut timber for his own use. In return, Philips agreed to reserve for the lord of the manor a fixed rent of "one Barrell of Good corn" a year and a hogshead of "Good Sound Tobacco, or the value thereof," at the end of every seven years.[9] Although the quainter provisions of such arrangements might not have survived Gerard's death in 1673, the lord of the manor's right to collect the rents and to grant vacant or escheated tracts remained in effect and was evidently judged to be of considerable value, since Charles Carroll the Settler paid six hundred pounds sterling in 1711 to acquire it from Gerard's daughter-in-law Sarah and her second husband, Michael Curtis.

Realizing a return on the investment proved harder than the Settler had anticipated, largely because Curtis had not demanded the rents with any regularity for many years. To remedy this neglect, the Settler appointed an agent to prepare a roll of the possessors on St. Clement's and Bashford Manors, noting the acreage they held, the right by which they held it, and the amount of the rent to be rendered to the manor lord. Known to us only by the meticulous reports he prepared, the agent canvassed the manors thoroughly and found things amiss

---

deficits in some years and incurring them in others ("Autonomy and Opportunity," chap. 7).

9. Thomas Gerrard to Bartholomew Philips, Aug. 29, 1652, Deed to Bedlam Neck, Carroll-Maccubbin Papers.

on both of them. Bashford, the smaller of the two, had only ten occupants on twelve tracts and seemed to be in general disarray: "The Bounds of this manor are Doubtful," wrote the agent, cautioning that they might well "in process of time . . . be utterly forgotten" were they not "timely Looked into." Slightly different circumstances obtained on St. Clement's Manor. There, none of the forty-odd tracts was unoccupied, but "Several of the plantasons" were found to "Containe more land than is specified in their grant, for wch.," the agent noted, "the lord of manor payeth rent to the proprietary wch. seems Injust, the reserved rent not amounting to the quit rent." [10]

Most troubling, and prescient, many of the residents resented being questioned and insisted that no rents had ever been reserved on their tracts, or that such fees had been abrogated through special arrangements with Curtis. The occupants who explicitly resisted the Settler's demands were closely related to the three most prominent Associator families who had spearheaded the 1689 Protestant rebellion — the Coodes, the Blakistons, and the Cheseldynes. Those antagonisms, combined with the political climate in Maryland of 1715–1720, must have given a particular edge to the Settler's attempts to collect his rents in St. Mary's County. Notwithstanding this resistance, the agent concluded that the Settler could by right expect some 53 barrels of corn, 840 pounds of tobacco, and £7 in cash from his St. Mary's lands per year. [11]

Unfortunately, no records listing payments actually received from St. Clement's and Bashford Manors during the Settler's lifetime have survived, so the practical value of all this reportage remains unknown. Early in February 1729, however, the Settler's son, Charles Carroll of Annapolis, received the report of Joshua Doyne, the man he had hired to update the work of the anonymous

10. "A List or Roll of all the Plantations or tracts of land in St. Clements and Bashford manors which lie Contiguous and Belong to the honble. Charles Carroll Esqr: with an account of the quanty of acres grantee, grantor and possor & rents of each tract," n.d., but between 1711 and 1716, Carroll-Maccubbin Papers. The second date is based on the fact that two of the persons shown to be active by the list (one being Michael Curtis) died in 1716. The anonymous agent might have been John Baptist Carberry, who died c. 1729, the year that Joshua Doyne assumed identical responsibilities for the Carrolls. Carberry's death date courtesy of Dr. Lois Green Carr, St. Mary's City Commission.

11. "List or Roll of all the Plantations," Carroll-Maccubbin Papers. Twelve renters had a choice of paying in tobacco, corn, or cash. Had all chosen to pay tobacco, the tobacco intake would have risen by 1,900 lbs., with a corresponding reduction of 19 barrels of corn. In general, the rent schedule specified a barrel of corn or 100 lbs. of tobacco or 10 s. sterling per 100 acres, plus two capons. Ibid.

"A Prudent Management"

agent. Both Doyne's experience and his conclusions replicated those of his predecessor: the thirty-eight St. Clement's residents and the sixteen on Bashford Manor were markedly uninterested in rendering rents to Carroll. Moreover, they questioned the authority by which he demanded such payments, on the grounds that his claim to the manor lordship was suspect because of improprieties surrounding its sale by the Curtises to his father. This charge eventually forced Charles Carroll of Annapolis to petition the legislature to clear his title, a process he first initiated in 1735 and did not successfully conclude until 1747. Whether this challenge materially affected Doyne's collections cannot be determined, since the only record of rents received during his tenure (1729–1743) consists of an undated summary showing amounts similar to those estimated to be due by the Settler's agent: 268 bushels of corn (54 barrels), 4,200 pounds of tobacco, and about £7 sterling.[12]

Once the general assembly had confirmed his position as manor lord in June 1747, Charles Carroll of Annapolis mounted a more aggressive campaign to collect arrears as well as amounts currently due. These demands, pressed by John Bond, Doyne's successor, met with generally uncooperative responses. Only four individuals refused outright to pay, but another twenty-four hedged by making their compliance contingent upon Carroll's resuming payment of the quitrents or by agreeing to pay only for the time they had actually possessed their tracts. Eight declared themselves willing to pay but pleaded that poverty prevented them and requested abatements. The prevailing attitude was perhaps best summed up by Mr. John Blakiston, who, Bond recorded, "grumbles Curses and Swears, he does not Say he will pay, nor denys paying, but Says if every body pays he will pay." And some did pay. Bond's sole surviving account, dated October 9, 1749, shows that he received 141 bushels (about 28 barrels) of corn and 2,500 pounds of tobacco for five years of arrearage from six tenants, plus 243

12. Joshua Doyne to CCA, Feb. 7, 1729; the Annuall Rent of St. Clements Manor and Bashford Manor, n.d., but between 1729 and Doyne's death in 1743, with notes in CCA's hand, ibid.

The slow progress of CCA's legislative petitions is related in William Hand Browne et al., eds., *Archives of Maryland* (Baltimore, 1883–), XXXIX, XLIV. In 1738, two years after his initial request failed to pass, CCA was again thwarted when the chancery court declined to uphold his title, and his testy relationship with Governor Samuel Ogle and the upper house in 1739 might have resulted from his anger over the defeat (XXVIII, 162–164). However, when he renewed his quest in the late summer of 1745, Samuel Ogle was still governor, and the bill passed in about two years (XXXIX, 373, 380–387, 413, 415, 421, XLIV, 81, 86, 460, 469, 501, 667–668).

bushels of corn (about 48 barrels) and 7,079 pounds of tobacco in annual rent from another thirteen.[13]

At this point in his review of his family's generally futile attempts to collect the St. Clement's and Bashford rents, it must have occurred to Charley that many years of effort had yielded very meager results. Whatever the case, he certainly saw that the source of the present problems on the manors lay in the decade of neglect that followed Bond's reasonably successful tenure as agent in the 1740s and 1750s. Preoccupied by more pressing problems in other areas, Papa had failed to appoint a receiver during that period, and, not surprisingly, payments once again stopped completely.[14] To reinstate them, Charley engaged Raphael Neale, a St. Mary's County native, as his steward and dispatched him to St. Clement's Manor in March 1767 armed with the rent rolls compiled by Doyne and Bond and a set of stern instructions that showed how well his experiences with Carrollton had taught him. Besides determining how many leases for lives were still in effect on the different tracts within the manor's bounds, Neale was authorized to "Turn off all such who have trespassed on the Swamp; such I mean who have settled on it without any colour of right," and to warn anyone cutting timber without permission that the Carrolls would prosecute. With regard to squatters, Charley directed Neale to inform him about any persons "settled on the Manor, who have no other right but mere possession . . . for if the original grantees have left no heirs or died intestate without as signing over to others their tenements by deed in their life time, such lands or tenements by right are escheated to the lord of the Manor." Neale was also to compile "an exact list of all the tenants" on Bashford Manor, including "the names of the lands they hold, and the annual rents." These tenants could, Charley noted as he completed his orders, "expect to be treated with the same indulgence as my tenants on St. Clement's Manor have met with."[15]

If Charley expected his "indulgence" to produce cooperation and gratitude, he was sorely disappointed. By the end of the summer, Neale had "bin Round to all your tenants" and found them generally displeased and defensive. "Most of Your Tenants," he reported to Charley on September 12, "Tells me they have

13. The ansrs. of the Tents. refer'd to the book 1747, and John Bonds acct. of Rents Rec'd in St. Clements & Bashford Manor's, Oct. 9, 1749, Carroll-Maccubbin Papers.

14. The resurgence of overt anti-Catholic feeling that swept Maryland during the 1750s brought about new laws that threatened the Carrolls' economic interests. In such a climate, it is not surprising that Papa ignored his St. Mary's lands.

15. CCC, "1767 — Instructions left with Mr. Raphael Neale," [c. Mar. 17, 1767], Carroll-Maccubbin Papers.

paid a grate dele more Corn &c. to, John Bond then thay Have Recpts. to show for, Sume declear To me thay have paid him and never took aney Recpts," while there were "a Few others that Refuses Leting me see theare Recpts or giving me A Copy of them." Indeed, Neale concluded, "The gratest part of your Tenants Seams to Expres a Very grate desire, of Seeing you, in St Mareys, County, that Thay may be able to Lay down thare agrevinces them Selves to You." [16]

These "agrevinces," as Neale initially recorded them in his notebook, were a good deal more rancorous than his letter to Charley indicates and suggest that the Carrolls' efforts to reimpose their authority on the residents of St. Clement's Manor threatened to raise individual recalcitrance to the level of crudely organized resistance. According to Neale's notes, none of the tenants was willing to assume responsibility for arrearages; although the majority (twenty-six of thirty-nine) said they would "pay you for Time to Cume," their acquiescence carried with it the condition that all their "nabors" do the same. A few were openly defiant: George Slye, holder of one thousand acres called Bushwood, "Says he bleves he Shant pay you aney," Neale noted, while Thomas Redor "Says he dont owe you a farthing." Before taking a stand either way, William Mills "Says he wants to see you him Self." James Jordan not only refused to "pay you aney thing," but he had also hired John Hall, a prominent Maryland attorney, "in order to Stand you Trial," though Jordan later modified his position and agreed to make payments in the future, provided the Carrolls would "pay the Quit rents and Indemnify him" for covering that expense himself in the past. Most worrisome of all, John Gibson insisted that "he Dose not Pretend to Dispute Lorships with you," but he had nevertheless informed Neale that "he has bin asked By mr Saml Jordan to Subscribe to a paper in order to Stand you Trial, wch. he has Refused, althou Sume others, has Done it." [17]

The St. Clement's folk do not seem to have made good on their threat to take Charley to court — neither existing legal records nor the family's papers mention such a confrontation. The outcome of their contention suggests that they did not need to go that far. Based on an account of rents owed in 1767 and paid by May 1768, the tenants held their own and in some cases prevailed. According to this compilation, jointly prepared by Charley and Raphael Neale, the occupants of St. Clement's Manor won the day with respect to arrearages, as the amounts stated as due reflect the old schedule of a barrel of corn per one hun-

16. Raphael Neale to CCC, Sept. 12, 1767, ibid.

17. Answers of the Tenants of St. Clements Manor to the demands made for rent due & returned by Mr. Rap: Neale, ibid.

dred acres. Tenant Kenelm Cheseldyne, who had stubbornly resisted the Carrolls' demands for at least twenty years on the grounds that "his father bought the rents of old Mr Curtis that was due or Should become due" on his four St. Clement's tracts, finally reaped the rewards of his persistence: following Cheseldyne's name, Neale penned the terse notation "Curtisus Recpt Clears." Although Charley's notes indicate that the equally defiant George Slye had not yet achieved like success, neither had he given an inch in the dispute. "He refuses to pay," Charley wrote, "because my Father promised to refund what corn he had *red* from Slye, unless he made all the tenants pay & because I promised to refer the matter to arbitration."[18]

From the Carrolls' standpoint, the most discouraging aspect of the 1767–1768 returns must have been their confirmation that passive resistance was alive and well on St. Clement's Manor: although most of the forty-one tenants promised to pay, more than half (twenty-two) avoided doing so, and another four made only partial payments. Of the 197 bushels of corn (39 barrels), 1,500 pounds of tobacco, and 41s Charley calculated was owed him, he actually received no tobacco, no cash, and only 85 bushels (17 barrels) of corn.[19]

Such a paltry yield after a year's endeavor indicated to Charley that St. Clement's Manor was a good deal more trouble to his family than it had ever been or was ever likely to be worth, an assessment that subsequent years invariably confirmed. Not only did collections fail to improve, but difficulties also arose in other quarters when claimants descended from the Gerards began once again to challenge the Carrolls' title. In the fall of 1774, Charley wearied of continuing the contest and accepted from John Lewellin, the most persistent Gerard descendant, an offer to buy the manor lordship for five hundred pounds sterling, one hundred pounds less than the Settler had paid for it. The younger Carroll urged his father to approve the deal rather than confront the many difficulties surrounding the title. Dogged persistence had allowed Charley to retrieve some of the back rents, but he deemed the prospects of making future collections extremely doubtful. "All circumstances considered," he concluded, "I have got more, than I ever expected to receive from that Manor; I hope you will be of the same opinion, & confirm the agreement." Reluctantly, perhaps, Papa did.[20]

By contrast, Charley brought matters at Concord and Outlet, the two tenanted Prince George's County tracts also known as Western Branch, to a rapid

18. The ansrs. of the Tents. refer'd to the book 1747, and St. Clement's Maner Rent: all for the Year 1767, ibid.

19. St. Clement's Maner Rent: all for the Year 1767, ibid.

20. CCC to CCA, Oct. 26, 1774, Carroll Papers, MS 206.

conclusion. His investigations in late 1767 confirmed the existence of the abuses his father had suspected: the tenants routinely employed more labor than the single taxable allowed by their leases, thereby working the land too hard, and several had paid, or tried to pay, their rents with substandard tobacco. Punitive action followed swiftly, with at least two of the offenders being turned off. Then, in February 1768, the Carrolls sold Concord and Outlet to Prince George's County planter Jeremiah Berry for £2,602.10.0 sterling. As a result of this transaction, it fell to Charley to settle accounts with the Carrolls' former tenants, a job he soon found could not be completed without legal action. The accounts of the Western Branch tenants needed to be copied and the balances certified, he told Papa firmly in October 1769, adding, "Without bringing suit you need not flatter yourself with being paid." [21]

In June 1767, as Charley's skill in clarifying the Carrolls' tenant relations became evident, Papa assigned his son a final major responsibility by transferring to him his one-fifth share in the Baltimore Company. Immediately becoming active in ironworks affairs, Charley found that the enterprise now consisted of three forges — Mount Royal, Hockley, and the "old," or Baltimore, forge — as well as the original furnace. The partnership roster had also changed by 1767. At twenty-nine, Charley was the youngest of the partners. His cousin Charles Carroll of Duddington was thirty-eight; Daniel and Walter Dulany (who split between them the share they had inherited from their father) and Charles Carroll, Barrister (who had inherited a share from his father, Dr. Charles Carroll), were all in their mid-forties; Benjamin Tasker (the only original stockholder still involved in the company's operation) was seventy-seven.

Neither his youth, inexperience, nor the anomalies of his social position deterred Charley from asserting himself; with an acumen that must have pleased his father, he began almost at once to press his partners to adopt his proposals for reducing costs and increasing profits. That these older men were generally amenable to his suggestions, with relatively minor adjustments, attests in some cases to a recognition of his business ability and in others reveals something about the relationships of the partners to each other and to the company. Charles Carroll of Duddington seems to have taken little interest in the operation of the ironworks beyond the marketing of his share of the pigs and bars produced. The aged Tasker, who had been fond of Charley as a boy, continued to

21. CCC and CCA, memoranda, November 1767, memorandum of acreage sold to Jeremiah Berry, Feb. 7, 1768, Carroll-Maccubbin Papers; CCC to CCA, Oct. 30, 1769, Carroll Papers, MS 206.

regard him benignly and probably appreciated his energy and desire for improvements. The acrimony that existed between Papa and Dr. Charles Carroll did not descend to their sons, who got along quite amicably, and Charley and Walter Dulany appear to have been on acceptable terms. Such was not the case with Walter's older brother Daniel Dulany, the powerful and, in Charley's view, imperious provincial secretary and councillor to the governor. Quick to take offense and to suspect Daniel Dulany of intending to give it, Charley resented that gentleman's high-handed manner.

Aside from occasional clashes of egos, perennially the most divisive issue among the Baltimore Company partners involved the annual settlement of the shareholders' accounts with the company, upon which Charley insisted as essential to good business. To his annoyance, it always seemed to take much longer to close the books at year's end than it should have taken. Other serious difficulties proved equally intractable. Among these, none was more crucial than securing an adequate labor supply. In 1767, during his first summer as a partner, Charley realized that the most economical means of resolving the company's chronic need for hands was to replace expensive "hirelings" with slaves. Having learned that slaves could be bought in Virginia for "£25 or 30 pounds Sterling a head," a price he considered cheap, he urged his partners to authorize the company's clerks to travel south and "purchase such negroes, as they Judge will be most serviceable." Although the partners accepted his recommendation, neither that sale nor others similarly advertised offered laborers suitable for the grueling work the furnace and forges required. The situation did not improve, and by 1773 Charley calculated that the company's annual labor cost for the past five years ranged between £2,550 and £3,000 current money. In his view, the remedy remained the same: the company must replace its hired labor with a slave force of thirty-five to forty "young, healthy and stout country born negros." The capital outlay required for such an investment was, as Charley well knew, considerable: a total of £2,000 sterling, or £400 per partner. But because the company would realize immediate savings in "annual disbursements in hireling wages [of] 901.5.0 Sterlg.— a prodigious saving," the younger Carroll deemed the expenditure reasonable and entirely justified.[22]

The other stockholders did not agree. Two of them stated that the proposal required further consideration, and another said he knew too little about company business to make a judgment. This lack of enthusiasm was primarily at-

22. CCC to Walter Dulany, Aug. 29, 1767, CCC to [the Baltimore Company], Sept. 22, 1767, Richard Croxall to Charles Carroll & Co., Mar. 12, 1768, CCC to the Baltimore Co., Dec. 8, 1773, Carroll-Maccubbin Papers.

"A Prudent Management"

tributable to the worsening economy that plagued Maryland in the early 1770s, but it also reflected the changes in the partnership itself since the acceptance of Charley's original proposal to replace hired labor with slaves. Three of the men who had been partners in 1767 had died, Tasker in 1768, Charles Carroll of Duddington in late 1771, and Walter Dulany in September 1773; Daniel Dulany had given his one-tenth share to his twenty-three-year-old son, Daniel III, in 1772.[23] Tasker's stock, sold at public auction as provided by his will, was acquired by his son-in-law Robert Carter of Nomini Hall, in Westmoreland County, Virginia, for £6,150 sterling. The company's chief clerk, Charley's kinsman Clement Brooke, kept Carter well informed about the company's business, but the Virginian's distance from the works usually meant that he was consulted after rather than before decisions were made. Walter Dulany had devised his one-tenth share to his son Daniel, age twenty-seven, and Charles Carroll of Duddington left his stock to his widow, Mary Hill Carroll, in trust for their three minor sons.[24]

Although Charley routinely conducted the "Widow Carroll's" ironworks business for her, his control of two shares of stock did not permit him to prevail. The two young Dulanys probably did not see the wisdom of committing so much sterling to buying slaves, nor did the Barrister wish to make such a large investment. Early in 1774, the partners reached a compromise by agreeing to buy five slaves and five white servants for the company in that year and a like number in 1775. A dissatisfied Clement Brooke lost no time in informing his employers that their course of action would not solve the problem: in the first place, the manager had already bought five convicts and did not want more than ten such servants in his workforce at a time. Beyond that, twenty workers of any sort would still not provide sufficient labor. The company needed a minimum of thirty slaves, and, to acquire them, Brooke advised the partners to buy five a year "'till that number is got, so that by degrees you will get rid of hirelings and carry on the Works with your own hands greatly to your Advantage." He added hopefully that, by buying ten slaves a year instead of five, they "wou'd furnish the stock necessary" in three years instead of six.[25]

---

23. CCC to the Baltimore Co., Dec. 8, 1773, partners' replies appended, ibid.; CCC to the [Baltimore] Co., Sept. 15, 1772, Gratz Collection, HSP. The note of Daniel Dulany, Jr., appended confirms the transfer of his tenth-share to Daniel Dulany III.

24. Aubrey C. Land, *The Dulanys of Maryland: A Biographical Study of Daniel Dulany, the Elder (1685–1753), and Daniel Dulany, the Younger (1722–1797)* (Baltimore, 1955), 346n. For Brooke's reports to Carter, 1769–1783, see the Carter Papers, MdHi.

25. Clement Brooke to the Baltimore Co., Feb. 4, 1774, Carroll-Maccubbin Papers.

Meeting in March, the partners accepted Brooke's limitation on white labor, authorizing the purchase of just five more convicts, and by July they had decided that ten slaves must immediately be bought for the works. Implementing the latter decision was delayed for many months, however, evidently because no suitable slaves could be purchased for the price the partners were willing to pay. With the problem still unresolved in April 1775, a weary Brooke tried once again to impart his sense of urgency to his superiors: "Your interest is daily suffering here from the want of hands of your own; and unless the Negros agreed to be bought last June, are soon bought & sent to the Works, & without a regular supply of the Quotas of corn, it will be impossible for me to carry on the business." [26]

As Brooke's lament indicates, keeping the ironworks supplied with corn and other necessities presented a problem as persistent as trying to procure an adequate workforce. For many years, provisioning the works was accomplished by assigning each partner a fifth of what the manager estimated would be needed, to be paid either in kind (bushels of corn or barrels of pork) or in cash. The amount required was considerable: between 1771 and 1775, for example, each partner's corn quota ranged from a low of sixteen hundred bushels to a high of two thousand, for a total average use by the works of nine thousand bushels a year.[27] Every shareholder kept his own record of his disbursements to the company, with adjustments being made when the accounts were settled with the clerk at the close of the business year.

The system had some obvious defects. In addition to tardiness in submitting their accounts, the partners, with the exception of Papa, and then Charley, tended to be chronically late, or short, in delivering their share of provisions or

26. Baltimore Co. resolves, Mar. 18, July 11, 1774, Carter Papers; Clement Brooke to the Baltimore Co., Apr. 10, 1775, Carroll-Maccubbin Papers. Carter was not present at either meeting.

Among the Baltimore Co. partners, apparently only Robert Carter had slaves to sell, and on July 15, 1774, Brooke wrote to ask his price, as the other shareholders were interested in buying. The following January, however, Brooke informed the Virginian, "The Gentn. of the Company who want to buy negroes for the works thought your price too high" (Clement Brooke to Robert Carter, July 15, 1774, Jan. 10, 1775, Carter Papers). By April 1775, at least one of the partners—Daniel Dulany, son of Walter—had met Carter's price and bought a slave from him for sixty-five pounds. Whether or not he dealt with Carter, Charley also paid sixty-five pounds apiece for slaves to fill his and the Widow Carroll's obligation to the works. Clement Brooke to the Baltimore Co., Apr. 10, 1775.

27. CCC, accounts with the Baltimore Co., 1771, 1773, 1774, 1775, Carroll-Maccubbin Papers; Clement Brooke to Robert Carter, Oct. 2, 1771, Carter Papers.

"A Prudent Management"

in putting up the cash equivalent. Without ready money in hand, the clerk had no way of handling the deficiencies except to keep reminding the delinquent parties of the hardships their delays were causing. In November 1766, several months before Charley became active in the company, the partners adopted a new procedure whereby anyone unable to meet his quota in kind must pay in cash on thirty days' notice from the clerk. If no payment were made before the deadline passed, the clerk was authorized to sell enough of that partner's iron to cover his deficit. The merits of the change were readily apparent to Charley, and in September 1767 he strongly endorsed the new policy, pointing out that, with money in hand, the clerk might well be able to realize savings in the purchase of corn and other items. Moreover, the Carrolls, unlike some of the other partners, raised corn, and Charley anticipated selling the surplus to the works "at the market price." [28]

The younger Carroll had no sooner made such a proposal to the company in October 1767 than Daniel Dulany reacted negatively. Certain that he had detected a conflict of interest, Dulany declared that Charley's proposition ran counter to company policy, which charged the clerk with the responsibility of buying corn as cheaply as possible. In return, Charley maintained that his offer "plainly implies" that the clerk should buy his corn "at as cheap a rate as he can purchase it of another person or in other words not to allow me more for my corn, than what other Partners give for theirs." Supported by Tasker and Walter Dulany, Charley prevailed in this instance, but not long afterward the partners rescinded their 1766 procedure and returned to the old way of doing business. Four months later, Charley reminded his colleagues that, as a consequence of their decision, they would be returning to the protracted procedure of settling their annual accounts: "As the resolution empowering the clerk to stop Iron & sell it to raise money, is now departed from, an annual settlement of our accounts is again become necessary." He therefore hoped that "the gentlemen have furnished the Clerk with their respective accounts agt. the Company, that he may settle & adjust them in order to be signed by the gentlemen as soon as possible." [29]

In affairs of business, as well as those of the heart, Charley proved equal to the

28. CCC to [the Baltimore Company], Sept. 22, 1767, Carroll-Maccubbin Papers; CCC to [the Baltimore Company], Oct. 28, 1767, Charles Carroll of Carrollton Collection, MdHi.

29. CCC to [the Baltimore Company], Oct. 28, 1767, Charles Carroll of Carrollton Collection; CCC's remarks appended to Daniel Dulany to Charles Carroll Esqr of Carrollton & Company, Feb. 5, 1768, Carroll-Maccubbin Papers.

tasks placed before him. With patience and increasing self-assurance, he consolidated the tenant accounts, sold off properties that no longer produced adequate income, and achieved some improvement in the conduct of the ironworks' business. Charley's accomplishments pleased Papa greatly because they both demonstrated the competence of his worthy heir and sharpened and strengthened the management of Carroll interests. Equally important, Charley's acumen freed Papa to devote the major portion of his attention to directing and developing the sector of the family's holdings that he most cherished — the agricultural enterprise known as Doohoragen Manor.

"A Prudent Management"

"The Occupation of Agriculture"

Lying in the fertile, gently rolling piedmont of western Anne Arundel County, in the broad stretch of land between the Patapsco and Middle Patuxent Rivers, Doohoragen Manor had been designated by Charles Carroll the Settler as his family's principal New World seat. Named by him for an ancestral territory in his native Irish midlands, Doohoragen's original 7,000 acres had expanded to 12,500 (counting the addition of the adjacent tract called Chance) by the early 1770s. For the Settler, the manor, which did not become a mature plantation during his lifetime, symbolized the dreams of power and dynastic resurgence that had brought him to Maryland. As the inheritor of his father's vision, Charles Carroll of Annapolis applied himself diligently to consolidating the tract that constituted the core of the Settler's landed estate and then to its development and expansion. The Settler's sole surviving son found therein his true vocation.

Transcending cultural lineage and economic aggrandizement, Doohoragen had, by the time Charley married, become for Papa more than a statement of prowess. Despite the endless challenges in making and keeping it productive, the manor offered Papa a depth of satisfaction that far exceeded any he received from other Carroll ventures. So, with happy anticipation, he turned over the daily management of the rest of the family's enterprises to Charley and settled himself at Elk Ridge to indulge his appetite for a planter's life. Writing to William Graves in December 1768, he sketched an idyllic description of his situation. "My Son," he told Graves, "lives in my House at Annapolis, I am Retierd to a very Pleasant Healthy Seat in the Country where I employ my Self in Farming, Planting Meadow Making &c Amusements very agreable to me, & when I want Money I Call on my Son to supply me."[1] His immense enjoyment of his

---

1. CCA to [William] Graves, Dec. 23, 1768, Carroll Papers, MS 206, MdHi.

PLATE 18. Doohoragen Manor. Nineteenth century.
Courtesy the present owner

new life did not, however, cause Papa to forswear his didacticism, and, as he concentrated on his planting activities, he often called attention to his own behavior as a model for Charley to emulate in the handling of their mutual affairs. Sometimes he criticized his son for a tendency toward indolence — for not wishing to "stir from home" — but in his occasional dissatisfaction he never threatened to reassume the duties that he had delegated.

Of all of Charles Carroll of Annapolis's rules for living, none was more sacred than being independent. Although the goal of self-sufficiency was not unique to Carroll, his relentlessness in improving his estates, his tenacious monitoring of commercial accounts, and his disciplined habits of consumption reinforced the distinction imposed by his Catholicism in setting him apart from other members of the Chesapeake gentry. Despising debt as the insidious enemy of independence, he labored more than four decades to build a self-sustaining, interlocking series of enterprises intended to guard his family's economic security. Doohoragen Manor served as the core of the Carrolls' agricultural operations, which also included two other plantations — the one-thousand-acre Poplar Island near the Eastern Shore of Chesapeake Bay, opposite Annapolis, and An-

"The Occupation of Agriculture"

napolis quarter on South River, some three miles outside the capital. Geared to the production of specific commodities — wheat, tobacco, salt, and corn on Poplar Island, and at Annapolis quarter corn, some wheat, and a portion of the vegetables, fruits, and livestock that fed the household on Duke of Gloucester Street — these smaller units also exchanged goods and services with the manor at Elk Ridge. The senior Carroll designed his system of plantation management to withstand the vagaries that threatened planters: fluctuations in commodity prices, swings in the weather, dissatisfied merchant creditors, and, in the 1770s, the deterioration of trade between England and her mainland North American colonies. His efforts achieved considerable success. In 1770, he could assure his son that, despite a bout of inordinately severe and damaging weather, the family was "well able to bear any loss we Have or may Sustain."[2]

Papa's organization of Doohoragen Manor reflected the importance he attached to the details of proper management, and his letters to Charley demonstrate his exacting involvement in all aspects of production and life on his lands. By the 1770s Doohoragen was divided into ten operating quarters, four of which were run by white overseers. James Riggs administered the manor's largest quarter (the home quarter), where 130 slaves lived, and he "overlooked" the six quarters headed by slaves — Sukey's, Moses', Jacob's, Mayara James's, Sam's, and Glen and Organer's, each with approximately twenty slaves. After Papa, James Riggs exercised the greatest control on Doohoragen, and his handsome annual salary of forty-five pounds sterling attested his employer's regard for his competence. The elder Carroll found Riggs "a thinking active Man" and particularly applauded his hard-driving style: "He proposes the saw mil shall work by Day & the Grist Mil by Night, by wh Method they may both work Constantly & Have a Sufficient Supply of Water." Charley once pointed out that the overseer could "scarce read & write, & must consequently want method," but his father prized Riggs for his loyalty and thoroughness. Nonetheless, even Papa occasionally found Riggs's dedication to his job excessive: "Riggs was Marryed last thursday," he reported to Charley one Monday in March 1774. "I did not know it untill Saturday, He stayed that night wth His wife, unless He is gone to Her this Day I do not know that He has seen Her Since Friday Morning, He is a strange Cur."[3]

Despite Riggs's idiosyncrasies, Papa remained pleased with his performance until he left the Carroll employ in the fall of 1778, perhaps to devote more time to his own agricultural enterprises, or perhaps, given his death two years later,

2. CCA to CCC, Apr. 20, 1770, ibid.
3. CCA to CCC, June 9, 1772, Mar. 21, 1774, CCC to CCA, Aug. 27, 1777, ibid.

for reasons of health. Although Riggs's marriage into the relatively affluent Howard family undoubtedly increased his wealth, the amount of property he willed to his heirs suggests that he and Papa had done well by each other. Probate records valued James Riggs's estate at £631 sterling, with an inventory, including twenty slaves, worth £1,164.[4]

James Frost came to Doohoragen in the fall of 1770 and remained for ten years, managing a quarter with a slave population of thirty-seven. Papa considered him "a Sober Diligent Industrious & Managing Man & not at all given to Rambling," and he also approved of Mrs. Frost, a "neat Housewifely Woman," whom he placed in charge of the dairying activity and poultry work on the quarter under her husband's care. For most of the decade Frost, a skilled farmer, satisfied Papa that he was worth his annual salary of twenty-seven pounds sterling. But he acquired a reputation for being hard on his slaves, and in 1780 Papa dismissed him for treating the hands abusively and taking better care of his own livestock than he did of the Carrolls'. The first signs of trouble surfaced in April of that year when Papa reported to Charley the disturbing tales he had heard about Frost: "He has winterd His owne Stock of Cattle & sheep on me, He has made a way with my Corn & meat, but as this is Negroe information I have not yet spoke to him." Upon confronting Frost and confirming the rumors, the elder Carroll decided that the overseer must go, even though the time of the year, May, was critical to the planting cycle. He would, he explained to Charley, have to rely on his enslaved drivers to fill the breach: "I must in a great measure trust to the gang Leaders who have promised to do their duty well. I could not continue Frost, He would have abused the People & made no Crop."[5]

The third of the white overseers ran the quarter called the Folly, where the most intensive cultivation of wheat took place. During the 1760s and 1770s three different men oversaw it. The first, John Heeson, was sent to Papa from England in 1763 as a gardener. Annoyed that Heeson had brought along a wife, Papa nonetheless retained him to manage the Folly, but at an annual wage of only twelve pounds sterling, plus a share of the crop, arrangements that might have precipitated his sudden departure in 1771. Whatever the cause, the abrupt exit clearly provoked Papa: "Jo: Heeson left the Folly the 17th & I have not seen Him

4. CCA to CCC, Mar. 21, 1774, ibid.; Anne Arundel County Wills, liber T.G. no. 1, fol. 10; Anne Arundel County Inventories, box 4, folder 61, liber T.G. no. 1, fol. 83; Anne Arundel County Administration Accounts, box 4A, folders 3, 11, liber G.N., fol. 15, liber T.G. no. 1, fols. 24, 41, 35, 101; Anne Arundel County Testamentary Papers, box 2, folder 7, all at MdAA.

5. CCA to CCC, Nov. 30, Dec. 5, 1770, Apr. 11, May 12, 1780, Carroll Papers, MS 206.

Since," he wrote Charley angrily. "I think to put His Acct in Suit He deserves to Rot in a Prison." The elder Carroll quickly hired Edward Clarke, "a Valuable & profitable Servt:," at twenty-four pounds sterling per year. Unfortunately, Clarke could not handle the job, and early in 1774 Papa transferred him to the weaving house, where he was apparently more successful. To replace Clarke at the Folly, Papa chose an Irishman, John Flattery, whom cousin Daniel Carroll II of Rock Creek brought to his attention. Although initially unhappy about the size of Flattery's family, Papa gave the man a chance, and within a few months the new overseer had begun to prove his worth. "I think Flattery will doe very well at the Folly," the senior Carroll wrote his son. "He is understanding & Diligent & allways with his People." Flattery continued to please and to build character with his employer. On one occasion Papa lent him two hundred pounds to purchase 150 acres, and in 1778, on Flattery's recommendation, the Carrolls hired another young Irishman, John Meara, as a clerk. Papa's only recorded displeasure occurred in 1780, when Flattery, who had moved from the Folly to the home quarter to assume Riggs's responsibilities, privileged some of his own livestock and manufacturing interests over the Carrolls'. Having "Spoke freely to Him," Papa was sufficiently satisfied with Flattery's explanation to continue him as Doohoragen's chief overseer.[6]

In addition to the overseers, a number of other white employees lived at Doohoragen. Riggs's predecessor, Captain John Ireland, for whom the Carrolls had genuine affection, had by 1773 retired to Doohoragen's smallest quarter, with only eight slaves. Born to a well-bred Yorkshire family whose estate had afforded him four to five hundred pounds a year, Ireland had misspent his youth. Marrying before his eighteenth year, he ran through his money; although some of his titled English relatives occasionally made minimal provision for him, he was reduced to soldiering for his livelihood in the French and Austrian armies. How Papa came to know him is unclear, but sometime during the early 1760s Ireland wound up in Maryland and went to work at Doohoragen, where his tireless labors won Papa's approbation. In the early 1770s, when Ireland's health rendered him no longer equal to the job, Papa rewarded his loyal service by allowing him to continue living on the small quarter, taking care to relieve him of his responsibilities in a way that did not offend the old man: "I had a good opportunity," he told Charley, "& I embraced it to Propose to Mr Ireland to move to His owne Plantation, I did it in such a manner, that He was Pleased with it, I in-

6. CCA to CCC, Aug. 23, 1771, May 11, 1774, Apr. 11, 1780, Carroll Papers, MS 206; CCA, Account Book and Index, 1754–1784, fols. 26, A, MdHi

tend to add to His House there a Snug & Warme roome for Him."[7] Much less well loved were the two chaplains the Carrolls retained. A cousin, John Ashton, whom Papa had brought over from Ireland in 1767, made such a nuisance of himself that Papa was delighted to see him leave. His replacement, Father Bernard Dederick, proved innocuous and unobtrusive.

Papa concentrated all of his artisans, white as well as black, on the home quarter that James Riggs managed from 1771 to 1778. The whites included at least half a dozen indentured servants and nine or ten skilled or semiskilled wage employees. Some were paid by the month and others yearly. Two carpenters, Thomas Gordon and William Sibthorp, each received £3.10.0 per month current money, and wheelwright William Ward earned £12 current money annually. Ward's salary was the lowest among the men, but two white women, Magdalen Belisle and Ann Le Blanc, received even smaller compensation, £6 current money each per year, for their work in the cloth manufactory (known variously as the weaving house or workhouse) that Papa built in 1770. Other wage-workers did measurably better. Gardeners Joseph Burgess and John Turnbull earned £12 sterling and £18 sterling a year, respectively; Timothy Laws, a cobbler, got £12 sterling; and Papa's two vignerons, John and James George, were paid £12.12.0 sterling apiece. With his tanner and his fuller, both of whom he had helped set up in business, Papa negotiated individual contracts. James Donnington, the tanner, paid £5.12.0 rent for the tanyard and £2.10.0 for ten acres and received a salary of £30 current money. A different arrangement covered the fuller, Alexander Malvell. Having spent £236.8.8 on the supplies needed to put the fulling mill in operation, the elder Carroll calculated Malvell's annual rent at 12 percent of that sum (£28.7.5) as a means of ensuring repayment of the debt. He did not, however, pay Malvell a salary, enjoyed preferred access to his business, and debited his account for any cloth he spoiled. Papa bragged to Charley about his sharp dealings with Donnington and Malvell: "Thus You see in these two Articles," he told his son pointedly in the spring of 1770, "a pretty little Annuall Estate Raised, & that Every shilling I lay out, is layed out to profit."[8]

In sustaining his plantations, Papa planned carefully for the supply of food required by the 386 Carroll slaves, the labor force at the ironworks, the twenty or more whites on Doohoragen, and the livestock on the various quarters. Corn (maize) and wheat were raised at Doohoragen, the Annapolis quarter, and Pop-

7. CCA to CCC, Sept. 17, 1761, Carroll-McTavish Papers, MdHi; CCA to CCC, May 7, 1771, Carroll Papers, MS 206.

8. CCA to CCC, Apr. 27, 1770, Carroll Papers, MS 206; CCA, Account Book and Index, fols. 5–14, 16, 17, 22, 25–29, 71, 88.

"The Occupation of Agriculture"

lar Island. For several years when the demand for corn outstripped the supply, Papa had to purchase it on the open market, an option he generally preferred to feeding his laborers wheat, although sometimes during the winter months his slaves helped themselves generously to his store of that commodity. To meet the ever-increasing demand for food, Papa contrived to clear land, especially for corn: "There is so much New ground Cleared Here & at Sucky's," he wrote Charley in March 1772, "that I shall plant the Greatest part of the Pasture old field in Corne (for Corne ground is most Wanted) the rest I shall lay downe in Oates & Clover."[9]

All of the plantations maintained large kitchen gardens, where a remarkable variety of vegetables were grown; orders to London in 1773 asked that seeds be sent for a wide assortment of cabbages, broccolis, endives, lettuces, greens, onions, and beans. The Carroll orchards produced an equally varied array of apples, pears, peaches, and cherries; currants, gooseberries, and strawberries were also grown. Between 22,000 and 23,000 gallons of cider and as much as 180 gallons of "Country Wine" were produced annually.[10] To support these activities, Papa maintained a nursery at the Annapolis quarter. The slaves supplemented their food supplies with private garden plots and also earned some money through local sales and exchange, though the Carrolls were not among their customers. In the fall Papa slaughtered hogs at Doohoragen; the quarters at Annapolis and Poplar Island supplied additional meat. Sometimes sheep were killed, but, as the Carrolls' weaving operations expanded, Papa increasingly used sheep only for their wool.

The various quarters and plantations continually exchanged labor and foodstuffs. A steady stream of people and items flowed back and forth between Doohoragen and Annapolis, a distance of thirty-two and a quarter miles, easily covered in a day. When the fences at the Annapolis quarter required repair, Papa sent several hands from Doohoragen, and, when a corn house was needed on Poplar Island, he dispatched carpenters from the manor to frame it. From Annapolis, where Charley's clerk, William Deards, superintended a large storehouse filled with imported supplies, came all kinds of articles: window glass, "Best Bed Blankets," gunpowder, milk pans, wines of all varieties (with Côte Rôti and Hermitage from the Rhone Valley being the most preferred), leather, clayed and brown sugar, molasses, nails, "Lamp Oyle," and much more. In re-

9. CCA to CCC, May 22, 1770, Mar. 11, 1772, Carroll Papers, MS 206.

10. CCA to Shiells & Cowrie, Sept. 20, 1773, Charles Carroll Letter-book, 1771–1833, fols. 26v–27v, Arents Collections, New York Public Library, Astor, Lenox, and Tilden Foundations, New York; CCA to CCC, Oct. 22, 1775, Carroll Papers, MS 206.

turn, Doohoragen provided the family in town with barrels of flour, pots of butter, fruits, vegetables, and cattle for meat and sent homemade implements for household and farm use to the Annapolis quarter and Poplar Island. Charley theoretically oversaw the continual movement of these items, since he was in charge of purchasing, but most of the actual responsibility rested on William Deards. Naturally, Papa did not hesitate to tell his son how the clerk should do his job: Deards should make a thorough inventory so as to anticipate the family's future needs. "If He reflects, He must after the Experience He Has Had, know every common Article that will be wanted." [11]

Whenever possible, Papa supplied his own wants. At Doohoragen, he maintained tobacco barns, a prize house (for packing tobacco), flour and gristmills, a workhouse used for weaving, a cobbler shop, a blacksmith shop, a fulling mill (for cleansing and thickening cloth), a tanyard, a ciderhouse, a brickyard, a repair yard, and, nearby, a quarry. With the white and slave artisans concentrated on the home quarter near his house, Papa could supervise a range of building, manufacturing, and repair projects: "Pray go with Timothy to Mr Ridouts study," he typically directed Charley, "& desier the favour of Mr Ridout to shew Him How His Stove is Constructed to try to Make Timothy understand it, so that He may build Such in my new Work House & Else where." By contrast, the goods he ordered from England often defied his efforts at quality control. The steel he bought in 1770 was not "fit for Axes or any Tools," and the shoemaker's thread sent at the same time by one of their English suppliers was so "Scandalously Bad that I would not Pick such from a Dunghill." So, too, the clothes made for his slaves out of the Welsh cottons imported for that purpose shrank so much the first time rain fell on them that they could not be worn again. [12]

Even more intense than the pride Papa took in organizing and managing his plantations was the sheer joy he received from his physical experience of the land. Nothing so filled his spirits as riding through his fields or taking quiet evening walks on Doohoragen. As he wrote Charley poetically in June 1772: "I took a tour this Morning to Jacobs, the Folly & by the Pool meadow, all my Fields smiled on me." That slaves performed for him the grueling work of making those fields smile did not detract from his enjoyment. He spent the winter months with Charley and Molly in Annapolis, usually arriving with Mrs. Darnall in early December and returning to Doohoragen in mid-March. Within several days of getting back to the manor, he would make an inspection of the

11. CCA to CCC, Mar. 26, 1772, Carroll Papers, MS 206.

12. CCA to CCC, Aug. 9, Oct. 18, 1770, ibid.; CCA to West & Hobson, Oct. 31, 1771, Charles Carroll Letter-book, 1771–1833, fol. 6, Arents Collections.

"The Occupation of Agriculture"

quarters, and his descriptions reflected both the pleasure he took in his plantation and his satisfaction in the scope of its activities. "We were 7 hours & ¼ getting here, the latter part of the road being Chiefly Clayey made travelling Heavy," he reported to Charley upon his return to the country in March 1772, acknowledging that "the day was as good as we Could Expect at this Season." He commenced his reconnaissance of the plantation at the beginning of the next week. "On monday in the Afternoon I rode about this & Succys Plantation Yesterday I went by Reads to the Folly, Frosts, the Pool meadow & the Saw mill, I every where found more Work done than I Expected." He was equally pleased in 1775: "I went to Moses's this Morning where there is the Frame of a good Barne raised, a large Piece of Ground Cleared including the Glades & all Ploughed or broken up. I returned by the low grounds Cleared between Sucky's & Jacobs, they are all most all Ploughed or Broke up, well disposed into Severall fields & Substantially fenced. A good Piece is added to the Turnip patch." [13]

The rhythm of the agricultural year followed a set pattern. Having returned to Doohoragen and surveyed with Riggs and the other overseers the work completed in his absence, Papa first concerned himself with evaluating the progress of the winter wheat. As the seeds sown in the fall began to shoot in late March, Papa watched the weather anxiously and worried about its effects on the grain. With a practiced eye, he reported to Charley in 1772, "It will not be mild & Settled Weather untill the Wind goes Regularly Round from N to E, S & West." When April calmed March's fierce bluster, the prospects for the first months of planting became easier to gauge: "Our Wheat & Rye looks charmingly & our Pastures begin to look green & we shall soon have Plenty of Grass if we have not Pinching Cold Winds to Check its Growth." Early April was also the time for sowing oats and sometimes a small amount of spring wheat. Once the oats were in the ground, the heavy work that readied the ground for putting in the corn began. Papa planted two varieties of this crop, "Indian Corn" and Virginia gourd seed corn, because of their staggered growth cycles. [14]

May's demands exceeded those of April. Like most colonial planters, Papa turned his livestock out to feed, but beginning in May 1770 he took the unusual step of ordering the planting of extensive crops of potatoes to be used for fattening up his cattle and swine in the late fall and winter. Checking his corn, he directed that those areas that did not suit him be replanted, but tobacco consti-

13. CCA to CCC, Mar. 11, June 23, 1772, Mar. 30, 1775, Carroll Papers, MS 206.

14. CCA to CCC, Apr. 10, 1770, Mar. 20, Apr. 10, 1772, Apr. 1, 1773, ibid. See also David O. Percy, *Corn: The Production of a Subsistence Crop on the Colonial Potomac,* National Colonial Farm Research Report no. 2 (Accokeek, Md., 1977), 2–3.

tuted the most important early summer activity. From late April until early June, the slaves carried the young tobacco plants from their seedbeds to the fields, placing them in individual "hills," mounds of dirt standing about knee-high, generally setting out four to five thousand plants per acre. Because the staple required moisture, special care had to be taken to guard against the ground worms that also thrived in damp soil and could level the seedlings.[15] Hornworms constituted an even greater threat. A constant menace, they could devour an entire crop in a matter of days, especially during hot, humid weather, when they had to be removed daily.

With tobacco planting completed by mid-June, the plantation hands turned to cleaning the cornfields, mowing early clover, and shearing sheep. By 1775, Papa had 182 sheep and 99 lambs on Doohoragen, and he produced 348 pounds of worked wool that year, all of which went to his weavers. In late June, the pace of the work quickened rapidly as the harvest of the large winter wheat crop, normally two thousand bushels, loomed. "We began yesterday to Cut some Rye," Papa informed Charley in June 1773. "I think our Wheat Harvest will Come in sometime next week."[16]

Each July Papa mobilized his entire workforce for reaping. The artisans of Riggs's home quarter, the house servants at both Doohoragen and Annapolis, the white indentured and convict servants, the wageworkers, and, when necessary, hired day laborers joined the field hands. First they cut the winter grains and later in the month the spring oats. The meadows were also mowed in late July, and, while some hands stacked the hay, others continued to tend the tobacco and corn. If the rain had been good, the corn would have begun to shoot by the end of the month.

As the searing heat of August baked the Chesapeake, the field hands' work became backbreaking. Some slaves were kept checking the tobacco leaves for spot, a discoloration that could seriously diminish the value of the crop; others finished the job of topping the tobacco, the cutting off of the top leaves and seed-forming buds to increase the size of the maturing leaves. The topping done and the danger of worms contained, there remained the task of suckering — the weekly removing of shoots that drew nourishment from the plants and reduced the size of the leaves. Workers not engaged in the tedious job of tobacco tending stacked the hay, oats, rye, and wheat that had been cut, and began sowing the

15. CCA to CCC, May 22, 1770, Carroll Papers, Ms 206; David O. Percy, *The Production of Tobacco along the Colonial Potomac*, National Colonial Farm Research Report no. 1 (Accokeek, Md., 1979), 14–15, 20–21.

16. CCA to CCC, June 24, 1773, June 20, 1775, Carroll Papers, MS 206.

"The Occupation of Agriculture"

next year's grain: "They are sowing my Rye & I hope to have all my wheat at this Plantation in the Ground in less than a fortnight," related Papa in early August 1771. During the latter part of the month the initial stages of cutting and housing tobacco began. "We have great Crops of tobo & the tobo of an Extra ordinary size: We began to House it yesterday," Papa told Charley in late August 1773. Indeed, the crop was so great, he continued, that "we shall not be able to find House roome for it." Papa's optimism was not misplaced; tobacco production on Doohoragen climbed in the mid-1770s to between ninety and one hundred hogsheads per season.[17]

As the cooler temperatures of September eased the summer heat, the pace of housing tobacco increased. After cutting the plants and allowing them to wilt in the fields for several days, the field hands brought the leaves to the tobacco house for curing, which required four to six weeks. To prevent damage from dampness during this period, the senior Carroll, like all major planters, kindled small fires on the floors of his tobacco house, which had to be patiently monitored so as not to burn the crop. Normally, about half of the tobacco had been housed by the end of September, with the operation continuing into the fall. As Papa wrote Charley in late October 1772: "For 3 Weeks past there has been thick Close foggy & Warme weather it is not only unusuall at this Season but unwholesome & very prejudiciall to the tobo Housed, We are obliged to keep fiers in all the Houses at no small risque (the tobo being mostly Cured) to Prevent House burning & Mold, if this is not Generally done Much tobo will be spoiled in the Province."[18]

Although the curing of tobacco and the corn harvest occupied the field slaves for most of September and October, the planting of winter grains also continued until by mid-October all of the next year's wheat, rye, barley, and spelts (a southern European relative of wheat usually fed to livestock) were in the ground. At about the same time, Papa oversaw the harvesting of his potatoes, which yielded more than seven thousand bushels by the early 1770s. In addition, his slave carters transported the previous year's tobacco crop to Elk Ridge Landing on the Patapsco River for inspection and, depending on his assessment of the market, shipment or storage.

The intense activity at Doohoragen did not slacken with the beginning of the deep fall in November. Despite the kindling of fires in the barns, mold invariably formed on some of the tobacco leaves, making rehanging necessary. "House burnt," or mold-damaged, tobacco was not ruined and could be restored by

17. Percy, *Production of Tobacco*, 24–25; CCA to CCC, Aug. 8, 1771, Aug. 26, Sept. 17, 1773, June 26, 1774, Carroll Papers, MS 206.

18. CCA to CCC, Oct. 19, 1772, ibid.

proper curing. The hard labor of bringing in the manor's nearly three hundred acres of corn, some two thousand barrels, began in September, and proceeded well into November and even December.[19] The ripened corn had to be thoroughly dried in order to be stored safely. To hasten this process, sections of corn were left standing in the fields until a good frost dried the ears enough to prevent spoilage.

With all of the corn in, the best ears were hung to dry through the winter, the seeds saved to be used for the next year's crop. The best tobacco seeds were similarly stored for raising tobacco seedlings early the next spring. The livestock that had been allowed to roam free since March were penned; and, with cold weather a guarantee against spoilage, many of the hogs were slaughtered for meat. The growing part of the year's work done, Papa, before departing for his winter stay in Annapolis, would lay out for Riggs and the other overseers the projects, such as the ditching and draining of fields and meadows, that he expected to be accomplished in his absence. Just before leaving Doohoragen in November 1773, he wrote typically to Charley, "I have marked all the Places in the last Years Wheat field where stops are to be made to fill up the Gullies in that field, wh are very Numerous & Many of them deep, without this Precaution & trouble the field would be ruined." Papa clearly expected "all the Works of the Season" to be carried on while he was away.[20]

Not only did Papa manage the manor with a firm hand, but he also rarely passed up an opportunity to offer gratuitous advice on Charley's administration of the quarters at Annapolis and Poplar Island. Although both operations were small in comparison to Doohoragen — the Annapolis quarter had seventeen slaves and the Island twenty-six — Papa nevertheless kept smartly abreast of their progress and periodically preached to Charley one of his favorite litanies: "A man to have His business well done must do it Himself." By this measure he often found Charley's running of his quarters wanting. His son's handling of Mr. Young, the Annapolis quarter overseer, for example, seemed unnecessarily indecisive: "I suppose You Have upbraided Young with His Knavery & Lazyness, let Him know before Evidence that You will Charge Him 20/ a day for every day you Can prove Him to be absent from the Plantation without yr leave, This may Have a good Effect, Especially if you Season it with Hopes of Continuing with you." Papa's patience with Charley grew even thinner when he learned that Young had failed to take care of simple repairs: "I send two Carpenters if you have nothing for them to doe but hang yr Gates, it is what Young ought to doe,

19. CCA to CCC, Nov. 18, 1773, ibid.
20. CCA to CCC, Oct. 28, 1772, Nov. 26, 1773, ibid.

"The Occupation of Agriculture"

for He is a poor Overseer that Cannot do that, let Young know what I write & Send back the Carpenters as soon as possible for they are much Wanted Here."[21]

In addition, Papa sometimes found his son deficient in method. When Charley decided to build a new stable in Annapolis, Papa agreed to it but then added: "I advise you not to Build yr New Stable before Next Spring, do not do it then unless you Have every Article in Place." Several months later he observed that Charley had too many projects going simultaneously. "It is imprudent," he sniffed, "to Have Many Irons in the fier at Once, Some must Burn." Such practices, Papa felt sure, contributed to Charley's mishandling of some of the simplest duties that took place on his quarters. "I will look out for two Cowes for You," he told his son in April 1771. "But it is my Opinion that they in a short time will be of as little Service as those You have, Care in Milking & feeding is what is wanted." Occasionally, Charley's mistakes left Papa incredulous: "How Came You to feed with the seed Oates formerly Sent You, be more Carefull, I could illy Spare the Oates Seers Carryed wth Him, I must sow Common Oates."[22]

In part Papa's exasperation sprang from the continual delight he derived from managing his agricultural operations well — a passion his son did not share. Continually experimenting with new crops and techniques and trying dozens of ways to improve his lands, the old gentleman planted potatoes in the early 1770s for stock feed when virtually no other Chesapeake planter did so, and he continually tested different varieties and methods to improve the quality and quantity of his output. Proudly he told Charley of confounding the cultivation reports of others and producing more than their predicted five bushels per acre, "A Result Contrary to what I was told would happen."[23] Papa conducted similar trials with different grasses — timothy, sainfoin, and especially alfalfa — "the Planting of my Lucern is a Tedious & troublesome Job But I do it well & doubt not it will fully Repay the trouble & Cost," meaning, presumably, that he meticulously oversaw the work to ensure that his slaves or white laborers performed it to his satisfaction. He spent hours grafting plants and fruits and raising cucumbers and other vegetables in a greenhouse. Always eager to learn more, he closely perused the writings of agriculturists like Arthur Young and was fascinated by new farm machinery. In 1770 he told Charley that he very much wanted to own a "Clayton Machine," a device powered by one man and one horse that

21. CCA to CCC, Apr. 25, 1770, Apr. 2, 1771, Nov. 18, 1773, ibid.
22. CCA to CCC, May 22, Aug. 17, 1770, Apr. 2, 1771, Mar. 25, 1773, ibid.
23. CCA to CCC, Nov. 2, 1770, ibid. David O. Percy, who generously shared with me his extensive knowledge of colonial agricultural practices, brought to my attention that CCA was unique among Chesapeake planters in cultivating potatoes for feeding livestock.

supposedly thrashed fifty bushels of wheat per day. Although he apparently never acquired the thresher (the inventor, a local man, might not have been able to build what he had promised), he often procured smaller items and gadgets. "Pray Write," he directed Charley, "to Mr Thos: Philpot for a Turnep Slicer According to the Plate in the 3d Volume of Youngs Six Months Tour Page 440 Invented by Cuthbert Clarke[.] The whole Machine Can be Afforded Compleat for Two Guineas." [24]

Papa knew that not everyone shared his zest for new projects, and he sometimes expressed a certain amount of wry sympathy for James Riggs, the chief recipient of his boundless ideas. "Business in generall goes on well, the Weather Has put us much Back, but Rigges says He Hopes to bring all into order in good time," he told Charley in April 1772, adding that the overseer "says Frost is much forwarder in His Business than Himself, No Wonder for a Home Plantation with a Master who has many Jobs on Hand is a Great Hindrance." Most of the time Riggs seems to have gone along with what his employer wanted: he accepted the need for regular ditching of the bottomland fields on the east side of the middle branch of the Patuxent, and he seconded Papa's desire to take advantage of the manor's liberal water supply to increase capacity of its mills. In the autumn of 1774, Papa decided to dam the river and directed the construction of a four-and-a-half-foot waterfall, an admittedly formidable undertaking, it being "no easy matter to bring up the Bed of a Stoney gravelly River 4 feet deep & at least 12 feet wide, they are now at Work at the Dam above the Watergate & from thence to the Mill the distance is as Clarke tells me 600 yards." Undaunted by such difficulties, Papa pursued the project whenever the crop cycle permitted through the rest of 1774 and all of 1775. Despite heavy rains and rock that had to be blasted, he pushed Riggs and the hands working with him not to let up, and, as 1775 drew to a close, he told Charley that the end was in sight. [25]

Papa's most enduring obsession was his vineyard. For more than ten years, he doggedly pursued his dream of producing a fine domestic wine, but his efforts proved largely unsuccessful. A combination of factors, including unpredictable climatic conditions, the vulnerability of imported cuttings to disease, and the unrefined quality of wild American grapes, frustrated him as they did most colonial planters who attempted viticulture. Nonetheless, he derived enormous satisfaction from the work and the beauty of his vineyard. Charley captured the

---

24. CCA to CCC, Oct. 18, Nov. 11, 1770, May 7, 1771, Apr. 1, 1773, ibid.; William Hand Browne et al., eds., *Archives of Maryland* (Baltimore, 1883–), LXII, 315–316.

25. CCA to CCC, Apr. 14, 1772, Oct. 6, 1774, Dec. 7, 1775, ibid.

spirit of the enterprise in a letter to his London friend William Graves in 1772. His father, he told Graves, "has spared no pains or cost to deserve success. . . . The vineyard is planted with several sorts of grapes, that we may learn by trial & experience, which sorts are best suited to our climate."[26]

Papa's first efforts at raising grapes began in April 1770 when he set out four beds of vines. Later that fall he directed that "two Ranges of Terraces" be added, which, he told Charley, "look prettily." Experimenting with different varieties of grapes by 1772, he had also initiated an intensive search for one or two vignerons from France. A family friend at Liège, the Reverend John Williams, had agreed to help. Convinced that Williams would succeed, Papa directed his mercantile correspondent in London to pay the priest forty-five pounds for his trouble and to arrange for transporting the vignerons to Maryland. A year later, with his French vignerons, John and James George, in place, Papa proclaimed his vineyard a success, although the defensive tone in which he announced his triumph to Charley suggests that he still harbored doubts. "The Wine I made is allmost fine & has a good Colour & is much improved Since December & has a good Body, I think it sound, but I believe You will not, thô it is not nigh so tart as Renish 3 year old."[27]

If the quality of the vineyard never quite satisfied, its output increased, and Papa never tired of lavishing attention on its beautification. Enlarging the hilltop site until it covered more than four acres, he added walkways, sloped its sides, turfed it, and considered blasting to clear the summit. A visitor to Doohoragen in the late 1770s, struck by the loveliness of the spot, recorded her impressions. "The next day they drove us out to show us their vineyard, which was very elegant and surpassed our expectations. At first we drove through a large orchard. Then we climbed up a winding path to the vineyard. The grapevines were planted alternately with hollyhocks and amaranths. The view from both sides of the hill and looking down from the top was the most beautiful sight I had ever beheld in the whole part of America I had visited."[28]

Papa's commitment to his vineyard did not prevent him from devoting considerable time to improving his house and garden as well. His white mason,

26. CCC to [William] Graves, Mar. 7, 1772, CCC, letterbook 1770–1774, fol. 21, MdHi.

27. CCA to CCC, Apr. 20, Oct. 11, 1770, Apr. 1, 1773, Carroll Papers, MS 206; CCA to John Buchanan, July 1, 1772, Charles Carroll Letter-book, 1771–1833, fol. 11v, Arents Collections.

28. Marvin L. Brown, Jr., trans. and ed., *Baroness von Riedesel and the American Revolution: Journal and Correspondence of a Tour of Duty, 1776–1783* (Chapel Hill, N.C., 1965), 88–90.

Timothy, and two slave masons seemed forever engaged in expanding his porch, laying new pathways, improving the garden walk, and enhancing the outward appearance of his story-and-a-half brick dwelling and its adjacent dependencies, a kitchen and a chapel. In 1774 he consulted the Annapolis architect Joseph Horatio Anderson about an elaborate alteration to his house. He expanded his garden, seemingly each year. His efforts did not go unremarked. The woman who so admired Papa's vineyard also took note of his home and garden: "We came through a large court to a very handsome house," she recorded. "The Garden was magnificent." [29]

Most of the men and women whose labor made Doohoragen a place of beauty and productivity were slaves; the twenty or so white workers included indentured servants, redemptioners, and tenants. Papa built his slave force slowly. Initially inheriting 56 slaves from his father, he acquired another 96 upon his brother's death in 1734 and between 20 and 30 more when his mother died in 1742. In the mid-1740s he held between 170 and 180 slaves, and by 1764 that number had increased to 285. The most detailed surviving count is the census he took in 1773, when he recorded by name, age, and family the 386 enslaved African Americans belonging to the Carrolls. The age profile of the 1773 population indicates that he possessed a workforce capable of sustaining both a wide range of agricultural operations and a high rate of reproduction (see Figure 1.)

Papa organized his slaves along two roughly parallel lines, by quarters and by families. In work and residence, he distributed his "People" on the ten quarters at Doohoragen, at the Annapolis quarter, Charley's house in Annapolis, and the quarter at Poplar Island (see Table 3). One or two families formed the nucleus on most of the quarters, with more than two-thirds of the children living with their parents. In some instances, families were distributed on different quarters, but even those children who did not reside with a parent usually stayed with a sibling or grandparent, so that virtually none of the young slaves lived without kin.[30]

29. CCA to CCC, Sept. 29, 1774, Carroll Papers, MS 206; Brown, trans. and ed., *Baroness von Riedesel*, 88–90. For a perceptive analysis of the house at Doohoragen Manor, see William Voss Elder III, "The Carroll House in Annapolis and Doughoregan Manor," in Ann C. Van Devanter, ed., *"Anywhere so long as There Be Freedom": Charles Carroll of Carrollton, His Family, and His Maryland* (Baltimore, 1975), 59–81.

30. Mary Beth Norton, Herbert G. Gutman, and Ira Berlin, "The Afro-American Family in the Age of Revolution," in Ira Berlin and Ronald Hoffman, eds., *Slavery and Freedom in the Age of the American Revolution* (Charlottesville, Va., 1983), 178–179.

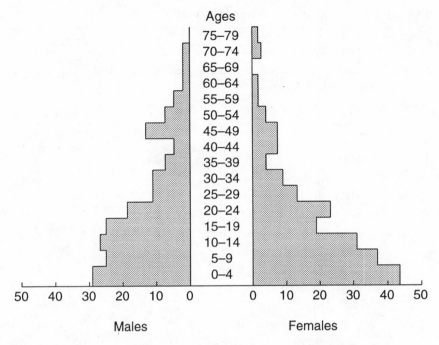

FIGURE 1. Population Pyramid of Carroll Slaves, 1773. *From slave lists in ledger X, Carroll-McTavish Papers, MdHi. Prepared by Daniel B. Deans. Drawn by Richard Stinely*

Although the records are regrettably silent on the important question whether the elder Carroll recognized and encouraged slave marriages, the organizational and genealogical structure revealed by the census he prepared in 1773 demonstrates the importance he ascribed to enslaved families. The centrality of those families within Papa's administrative scheme similarly affirms the enslaved population's insistence that the Carrolls acknowledge and respect their kinship attachments. With few exceptions, every slave identified by Papa is linked to one of twelve matriarchal lines: those of Old Grace, Old Fanny, Rachel, Goslin Kate, Battle Creek Nanny, Banks Nanny, Old Moll, Suckey, Nan Cook, Old Peg, Old Nell, and Sam's Sue. Moreover, of the 386 blacks that appear on Papa's 1773 list, 51, or roughly 13 percent, were recorded as skilled, with certain trades concentrated in specific families. Typical was Carpenter Harry, two of whose sons, Abraham and Harry, were also carpenters, and two others, Elisha and Dennis, were wheelwrights. Similarly, three generations of another family were involved in coopering — Cooper Joe, his son Cooper Jack, and his grand-

TABLE 3. Distribution of Carroll Slaves, 1773–1774

Site	No. of Slaves	Total No. of Slaves
Doohoragen Manor		330
Rigg's (home quarter)	130	
Sukey's	22	
Moses'	19	
Jacob's	21	
Mayara James's	28	
The Folly	20	
Sam's	22	
Mr. Frost's	37	
Glen's and Organers	23	
Captain Ireland's	8	
Annapolis quarter		17
Poplar Island		26
Annapolis (house servants)		13
Grand total		386

Source: Ledger X, following fol. 62, Carroll-McTavish Papers, MdHi.
Note: Writing to Charley on Dec. 3, 1773, shortly after completing an inventory of slaves on Doohoragen, Papa noted that he had compared the new total of 330 with a similar census taken in 1767 and discovered that the increase over the six years amounted to 57. The 1767 document has not been found. CCA to CCC, Dec. 3, 1773, Carroll Papers, MS 206, MdHi.

son James. Papa and his slave artisans had a mutual interest in the continuance and stability of these skilled enslaved families.[31]

For their part, the slaves who toiled on the Carroll lands expressed their commitment to family through naming patterns. As a whole, the population divided into fourteen principal families, within which names from previous generations were perpetuated from the early eighteenth century to the Civil War. By giving children the names of their parents, grandparents, or other close relatives, the slaves created and reinforced a sense of community that Papa understood and employed in organizing his bondsmen and bondswomen into a productive workforce.[32]

31. Daniel B. Deans, "The Carroll Family Slaves, 1721–1833: Genealogies," MS, University of Maryland, 1990.
32. Ibid.

"The Occupation of Agriculture"

There is no evidence that Charles Carroll of Annapolis ever questioned the morality of slaveholding or that he felt any guilt about its practice. Presumably, he judged his behavior toward his enslaved population by the same standards he applied to other areas, where he regarded himself as a rational man given to neither conspicuous cruelty nor special kindness. Nor do the surviving records suggest that the elder Carroll sought from his slaves the validation of his patriarchal role — or that it ever occurred to him to care what they thought of him. A practical man who prided himself on never letting his passions overrule his reason, he considered his slaves a major investment, and he wanted them treated in a way that allowed them to labor most efficiently and productively. Therefore, his people must have enough to eat, serviceable clothing, and adequate places to live. Compared with other Maryland slaveholders, Papa believed he met these requirements satisfactorily. He expressed his attitude clearly to Charley in 1771: "You will have it that my People are not well fed, it is true they do not live so well as our House Negroes, But full as well as any Plantation Negroes & think I Can safely say no Man in Maryland Can shew in proportion to Our Number, Such likely well looking Slaves." Similarly, when his son complained that the condition of the stallions he had left at Doohoragen had been allowed to deteriorate to the point that they were currently "unfit to go to Mares," Papa caustically rebuked Charley's shortsightedness and impracticality. Corn, he reminded Charley, had been in short supply, and "in Such a Want it would not be Reasonable to Pamper my Horses & Pinch my slaves, Under these Circumstances you need not Wonder I was fretted to Hear you complain of the Condition of the stallions, you sometimes Speak without deliberation." [33]

Notwithstanding those considerations, Papa never hesitated to administer punishment. Although his slaves might have regarded their behavior as legitimate resistance, conduct the elder Carroll judged as wrongdoing earned the offender a collar or a whipping. He meant not to have any trouble from his slaves or servants, and generally he did not: "I lost a pair of thread Stockings When last with you," he told Charley in the fall of 1772. "Pray enquier for them, Nanny is not the only thief in Yr: House, I think to Give Molly & Henny a Severe whipping When I go downe if my stockings are not found." When the problem of light-fingered house servants persisted, Papa took further action:

33. CCA to CCC, Sept. 15, 1771, June 1, 1772, CCC to CCA, May 27, 1772, Carroll Papers, MS 206.

"Little Nan has been whipt about Mrs Moretons shifts, She Confessed she stole them & said she gave them to Moll, Search Molls Box &c privately, But it is probable she Has sold them. I am determined to see Moll & Henny well Whipped when I go downe." Misbehavior, he directed Charley, must be corrected immediately: "I do not Hear that Giles is Come Home, He Certainly got Drunk lost or sold the shoes, He shall be Whipped." Clem learned the same lesson. "I did not write by Johny Expecting a letter from You by Clem who Came Home this day about three a Clock, He says you gave Him leave to goe to the Marsh to see His Aunt, I have orderd Him a good Whipping." Charley absorbed his father's methods without question. Finding his slaves at the Annapolis quarter sullen and uncooperative upon the arrival of a new overseer, he did not hesitate to order a round of lashings for three of the approximately twelve adults: "The negroes at the quarter were at first very refractory: two of them have been well whipped, & Will shall have a severe whipping tomorrow — they are now quite quelled." [34]

Papa recorded few instances of major slave sabotage, although such suspicious incidents like that involving Charity occasionally took place. This young woman resided at Riggs's with her three young children, Nancy, Betsy, and Johnny, while her husband, Johnny, lived at Charley's house in Annapolis, and the bad temper for which she was known might well have been related to those arrangements. Whatever the reason, Papa distrusted her and on one occasion suspected her of killing a horse: "If the Mare was killed by a Stab I suspect Johnys Wife, She was whiped before I went to Annapolis, She is of a Sulky Malicious temper & May have done it, it is only Suspicion & therefore doe not Mention it." [35]

Punishments, Papa reasoned, were to be inflicted for the purpose of maintaining a well-ordered plantation, but punitive measures dealt out gratuitously disrupted the smooth operation of Doohoragen and the other quarters and offended his sense of fairness as well. In most instances, he rarely interfered in the overseers' domains, preferring that they discipline their hands. Two overseers, Frost at Doohoragen and William Sears at Poplar Island, tended to be overly harsh, and the senior Carroll intervened. "Fanny's Sam One of the wood Cutters is Returned," he informed Charley in November 1775. "He says Sears threatned to Whip Him very Severely for a fault He Committed four Years past & for which He was Corrected by Mr Frost, if He tells the truth Sears deserves to loose His

34. CCC to CCA, Oct. 30, 1769, CCA to CCC, Oct. 19, 28, Nov. 23, 1772, Apr. 13, 1773, ibid.

35. CCA to CCC, Oct. 11, 1775, ibid.

labour for His unforgiving temper & ill timed Severity." Frost, as previously noted, became so abusive to the "People" that Papa finally fired him because the slaves refused to make a crop under his authority.[36] In the slaves' eyes, Frost had broken the tacit understanding that their labor constituted a repayment for treatment they defined as acceptable.

Both Papa and Charley refrained from inserting themselves into the personal lives of their enslaved population except when it served their specific purposes, as in the case of the work regime. A visitor to Doohoragen in 1779 grasped a sense of the separate spheres of the place. The long lane that passed through Riggs's quarter on the way to the manor house led, she recounted, "through a very pretty village, inhabited entirely by Negroes, each of whom had his own garden and had learned a trade." Virtually all of the families on Doohoragen's quarters had private gardens. The produce supplemented their own diets, thus benefiting Papa as well as themselves, but what was not consumed could be sold. Papa and Charley had no objection to this active private economy and when necessary served as intermediaries and made their clerks, William Skerrett and John Meara, available to handle financial transactions. "Skerret," wrote Papa to Charley on one occasion, "sent a parcel of the Negroes money to Meara to be changed for very smal Bills, desire Him to return the change."[37]

Papa and Charley also kept their distance with regard to the spiritual content of their slaves' lives: there is no evidence that they ever sought to encourage Catholic conversion or Christian morality in any form. Their chaplain and kinsman from Ireland, Father John Ashton, took a very different view and complained insistently to Charley that William Sears, the Poplar Island overseer, had become intimately involved with Henny, a female slave who lived with her husband and children under Sears's supervision. Charley found Ashton's interference unwarranted and exceedingly inconvenient. Removing Henny from the island quarter meant going to the trouble of finding another "good house wench" to replace her; although he acknowledged that "the crime of adultery is certainly great," Charley doubted that altering Henny's current situation would prevent it. "Deorum injuriæ diis curæ [injuries to the gods are their concern]," he concluded irritably. "We do want Henny in our family." Papa agreed wholeheartedly. Ashton, he later acknowledged, was "a silly Peevish disagreable Man." Nevertheless, as a result of the priest's complaints, Charley did remove Henny from

36. CCA to CCC, Nov. 21, 1775, May 12, 1780, ibid.
37. Brown, trans. and ed., *Baroness von Riedesel*, 88–89; CCA to CCC, Apr. 10, 1781, Carroll Papers, MS 206.

Poplar Island to his house in Annapolis. Her husband and sons remained on the island, and a daughter resided with her.[38]

Though disinclined to become involved in most aspects of their slaves' private lives, Papa and Charley did take an active interest in their health, especially of the adult males. "Pray keep Shoemaker Jim with You untill He is killed or Cured," wrote Papa in 1770. "He is a Valuable Man & should not be Neglected." The children's well-being was also a source of obvious concern, particularly when the danger of smallpox was present. Not only did Papa inoculate against the pox, but, in an effort to control the spread of the disease, he also ordered that mothers and children be separated. Much to his frustration, his instructions were not followed. "Negroes & their Nurses are so Stupid that they Cannot be kept in order, nor Can they be prevailed on to follow directions; I did not innoculate the Sucking children & orderd their Mothers not to Visit their Innoculated Children, they did not observe those orders & I am apprehensive Some of the Sucking Children Have taken the Pock from their Mothers."[39]

When death came to their slaves, both father and son generally reacted with detachment, especially if the deceased was young or a hand with whom they had limited contact. "The Boy Antony who was So ill when You was Here dyed this Morning," Papa informed Charley dispassionately in September 1772. "Howard Opened Him & told me He was filled with Worms, it is od the Faculty Cannot Stumble on an Effectual Vermifuge, most Negroes are killed by them."[40] A similarly distant, almost dehumanized, attitude characterized Charley's remarks when, in telling Papa of the death of a young slave, he spent more time describing the illness, probably tetanus, than lamenting the human aspects of the event:

> Little Mulatto Bob a fine boy about 10 years old died last night at the quarter of a very singular disease, to wh the Doctors give the hard name of Opisthotonos — he was seized yesterday forenoon with a ridgidness or stiffness in all his joints, so that he could not move himself: he continued in that situation till his death, without taking the least nourishment of any kind and retained his senses to the last. . . .
>
> As you may be desirous to know the signification of Opisthotonos I give you Chamber's definition or rather his explanation of the word: but more on Mrs. Darnall's acct than yours: "a kind of convulsion, wherein the body is

38. CCC to CCA, Oct. 30, 1769, CCA to CCC, Nov. 12, 1773, Carroll Papers, MS 206; "List of Negroes — House Servants at Annapolis — taken the 4 July 1774," ledger X, Carroll-McTavish Papers.

39. CCA to CCC, May 4, 22, 1770, Carroll Papers, MS 206.

40. CCA to CCC, Sept. 17, 1772, ibid.

bent backwards, so as to form a kind of bow." NB the word is compounded of the greek, οπισθεν, backward, behind; and τεινειν, tendere, to Stretch, or bend.[41]

But when an old hand or one of the matriarchs, like Old Grace, who had been with the family since the time of the Settler, died, a subdued sense of loss crept into the Carrolls' writing. "Poor old Grace died Suddenly last friday morning between the hours of 10 & 11," related Charley to Papa in the spring of 1773. "'Her death was instant and without a groan.' She had long been sick but that morning she eat a hearty breakfast, & told her mistress she hoped now the warm weather was coming on, she should get well. I saw her about 8 o'clock in the old Kitching that morning — poor old Creature. I hope she is happy."[42]

In sum, Papa believed that he had done right by his "people." He fed them well, gave them habitable places to live, cared for them in sickness, and allowed them to lead partially private, if obviously restricted, lives. He believed that he behaved equitably and acted with essential decency in managing his enslaved labor force, and he assumed that for the most part he could rely upon their loyalty. Just as the Carrolls made the whip or the collar the consequences of "bad" conduct, they devised a system of graduated privileges and rewards to recognize and motivate the kind of behavior they defined as "good." Felt hats ordered from London constituted one such incentive. These were distributed, as Charley explained it, to "some of my best negros in order to encourage them to do well."[43] By virtue of their positions and responsibilities, gang drivers and house servants enjoyed more freedom of movement, and some of them were entrusted with carrying large sums of money, even gold, without supervision, between Doohoragen and Annapolis and other locales. Others were allowed to spend extended periods of time away from their quarters, and none of them was ever recorded as permanently running away.

Late in the Revolutionary war, when the Maryland general assembly considered raising a 750-man "negro regiment," neither Charley nor Papa had any serious objection other than that the large slaveowners would probably have to bear a disproportionate cost of the draft. Charley hoped that "none of our negroes will inlist," because the price to be paid even if "in ready & solid coin is not equal to the value of healthy, strong, & young negro men." Neither Carroll speculated about what slaves who did enlist would likely do after completing their

41. CCC to CCA, Nov. 14, 1774, ibid.
42. CCC to CCA, Apr. 3, 1773, ibid.
43. CCC to West & Hobson, Sept. 21, 1772, Charles Carroll Letter-book, 1771–1833, fol. 14v, Arents Collections.

military service, evidently because both father and son assumed their property would return or be returned to them. Similar assumptions underlay the Carrolls' response to their slaves' behavior when the British raided Poplar Island in the spring of 1781. The island blacks did not seize the opportunity to leave, a decision the Carrolls interpreted as "a proof of their attachment." It did not occur to either Charley or Papa that the slaves "attachment" might be to their own kin rather than to their owners. Rewarding what they perceived as loyalty, the Carrolls transferred the Poplar Island blacks en masse to Doohoragen, thereby honoring the group's express wish that they not "be parted." [44]

If anything, the Carrolls treated their white servants as harshly in terms of punishment as they did their black slaves. This was particularly true for the convict servants, several of whom Papa and Charley subjected to severe discipline. The Carrolls generally recruited skilled workers, either redemptioners or indentured servants, by making them attractive offers and treating them well. But a number of men in their service behaved in ways that suggest that they had been forced to come to the colonies. Papa's method of managing such individuals relied upon swift and sure retribution. The case of Harry (Henry White), one of the Carrolls' white gardeners, whom Charley had been unable to control, is representative. "The best Servants," wrote Papa, "must be minded, indifferent & Lazy Ones Corrected: Harry shall have a good flogging & a Collar this Evening." The next day Papa, in his inimitably didactic manner, told Charley why it was important to act decisively: "Harry has had His flogging & is Colard, it is imprudent to threatten to whip Servants or to keep them in dread of it, when they really deserve it, give it to them as soon as possible." Charley agreed but attributed Harry's misconduct, not to inadequately administered discipline — "Since he has been with me, I think he has had 6 or 7 floggings" — but to the distracting effect the diversions of Annapolis had upon his servant. The more isolated setting at Doohoragen, he reasoned, should improve the man's tractability. But when Harry proved just as recalcitrant at the manor, Charley endorsed further punishment: "I am very glad you have ordered Harry a good whipping: he richly deserves it: he has been exceedingly idle: never was a garden in a worse condition than mine." [45]

Harry's coworker in the garden, John Turnbull, could be just as difficult, especially when he was drunk. And he was often drunk. "Turnbull was flogged yesterday," Papa reported disgustedly to Charley in April 1774. "He got Drun[k]

44. CCC to CCA, Apr. 11, 12, June 4, 1781, Carroll Papers, MS 206. The British did take two children with them, a boy of eight and a girl of twelve.
45. CCA to CCC, Sept. 28, 29, 1774, CCC to CCA, Sept. 29, 1774, ibid.

"The Occupation of Agriculture"

last Week & most grossly abused Mrs. Darnall, I ordered Him to be Corrected but she foolishly begged Him of[f]: On Wendesday He Carry[ed] Kenneday out & they both Came Home drunk at Night, no One more dreads a Whipping & no One is less Carefull not to deserve it." If Turnbull, whom the elder Carroll judged "a perfect Blackguard & Brute when He is Drunk," wanted to continue at Doohoragen after his time was up, he would have to agree "to be Whipped When He deserves it, upon no other terms will I accept His Service, the fear of the lash Can only keep Him within any tollerable Bounds." The elder Carroll, who was prepared to offer Turnbull a good wage, predicted that Turnbull would stay. "He talks of leaving me, but I do not think He will." That prediction proved wrong — Turnbull had tasted enough of the lash.[46]

Another servant, Daniel Squiers, a stonemason, ran away, possibly because of the discipline at the manor. Once Squiers had been apprehended and returned, Papa pronounced the expected sentence: "He is this Evening to Have 15 lashes well laid on & a Collar: Witho[ut Pu]nishment there is no keeping Servants [of a]ny Sort, His Chastiment may deter my other [Se]rvants from following His Example." But this time the senior Carroll relented — no whipping, possibly because of Squiers's pledge of future good behavior. "Squiers was not whipt, He Wears a Collar in terrorem to others & as a Punishment wh He justly deserves, but I think to take it of[f] soon." Papa also showed leniency to Timothy, a mason at Doohoragen. "Timothy was very Penitent, He Came to me knelt downe begged my Pardon, promised never to behave so again[.] I forgave him & told Him I should forget his fault provided He Behaved well for the future, wh He promised, He was much Scared & I believe will keep His promise."[47]

The elder Carroll sought to maintain an orderly work environment at Doohoragen. For bound white laborers he preferred German redemptioners, known as "Palatines." Unlike indentured servants, whom one acquired sight unseen, a buyer could examine redemptioners in the flesh before contracting for their labor in exchange for paying (redeeming) the ship's captain for their Atlantic passage. Skilled white labor was generally dear and hard to come by, and the Carrolls sometimes had to take what they could get. In need of spadesmen for ditching meadows in the spring of 1770, Papa hired for three pounds per month a gardener whose appearance made him wary. "I do not like His looks as they are very Sottish," he informed Charley forebodingly. "He may buy Rum & get Rum, I will not allow him any, I Cannot doe it, without allowing it to all my other Servants which would be Endless, they all Mess togeather & are

46. CCA to CCC, Apr. 8, May 5, 1774, ibid.
47. CCA to CCC, May 4, Aug. 28, 31, 1770, ibid.

allowed 3 Quarts of Cyder each pr Day wh I think full Allowance for any Man." Nor could white laborers who ran afoul of the law expect any sympathetic intercession: a "heirling" named Dennis Flanigan went to jail in October 1770 for stealing "a Napkin two Towels & a Tea Cloath." By making the standards clear and by shaping the workers' environment, Papa believed that a climate of discipline, purpose, and steadiness could be established. His advice to Charley concerning Henry White (the Harry described earlier) succinctly makes the point. White would, the older man told his son in 1772, "make a good kitchen Gardener & an orderly Servt if you keep him Constantly employed & do not spoil Him by too much indulgence & suffering him to goe into Towne & keeping Idle Company." It was Charley's inability to enforce such a regimen that led to Harry's transfer to Doohoragen two years later.[48]

Papa also considered himself a masterful teacher in the handling of another class of men — merchants — and he spared no pains in impressing his views on Charley. Prudence dictated, he explained, that merchants be viewed somewhat like adversaries. Hence, he advised his son, "it is a Generall Rule Never to let a Man know more than is absolutely Necessary for yr owne Purpose." Charley could never be too cautious or thorough in commercial transactions. "I must desier you to Read over all yr letters to others, if they any ways Relate to Business, for fear you should say to them what You do not intend to say. Never do any thing in a Hurry, thought & Reflection ought to Accompany the most trifling transactions." Not surprisingly, Papa had a reputation for driving a hard bargain. With a large supply of high-quality tobacco to sell (as much as 300 hogsheads in some years), the elder Carroll negotiated tirelessly for the highest possible price. He succeeded admirably. In 1772, despite a depressed market, West and Hobson paid £1,270.11.9 sterling for 130 hogsheads, or nearly £9.15.0 per hogshead. In his view, the trade to the Chesapeake operated according to a simple equation: "Tobo," he told Charley, "gives the Merchants so large a Credit & they in Generall stand so much in need of Credit, that they must import tobo to obtain it." For that reason and because of the quantity that Papa had to offer, he did not approach the merchants. Instead, the reverse occurred: "Our Case is quite different, we are knowne to Have a large Quantity for Sale & I Have allways been applyed to."[49]

The major decision to be made each year was whether to sell the tobacco "in the country" or to consign it for sale on the London market. Assets and liabilities figured in each calculation. Selling in the country eliminated the problems

48. CCA to CCC, Aug. 27, Oct. 11, 1770, Aug. 14, 1772, ibid.
49. CCA to CCC, Nov. 13, 1769, Apr. 10, May 22, 1770, Aug. 31, 1770, ibid.

"The Occupation of Agriculture"

of insurance, weight loss, and pilferage that invariably accompanied transatlantic shipment. However, the price in the country was almost always lower than in London. Ideally, the elder Carroll preferred to sell from one-third to one-half or more in the country. The important thing, he repeated to Charley, was never to give a hint about which way one was leaning. "A Man who wishes to Sell, should not let it be knowne that He is willing to ship, He may Cast about so as to look out for & be Certain of Securing a Freight, without letting His Intention be knowne." In making his decision, Papa demanded the maximum intelligence, so he haunted the Patapsco landing at Elk Ridge and urged his son to do the same at Head of Severn near Annapolis, but Charley sometimes displayed a lack of energy that annoyed and displeased him. "If You are not offerd more than 21/ pr ct [shillings per hundredweight] & 4 pr Ct [percent], take it, if that be not offerd I intend to ship it. I do not Believe you ever Enquier what tobo sels at, if You do, You do not advise me which Comes to the Same thing."[50]

In the late 1760s and early 1770s, Papa and Charley dealt with seven London merchants, playing one off against the other and relentlessly pushing for the most lucrative arrangement. During this short period, two of these mercantile houses, John Buchanan, and West and Hobson, failed, and the Carrolls quit a third, Thomas Philpot, after nearly twenty years. Increasingly dissatisfied with the others, they finally secured such an advantageous deal with the new firm of Wallace, Davidson, and Johnson in 1773 that its principals begged them to keep the terms secret for fear that their other suppliers might demand the same treatment. Papa negotiated ferociously, demanding to know the minute details of all transactions and the precise status of his account. He also insisted on securing the maximum for the cask as well, usually holding out for five shillings.[51]

The senior Carroll's most consistent complaints about tobacco merchants centered on the issues of weight loss, crop damage, and what he defined as the "iniquitous Custom" of merchants who reserved for themselves all the profits from duty-free tobacco. The loss of weight between the time of shipment from Maryland and arrival in England constituted a perennial problem, with the merchants contending that the losses resulted from the tobacco "laying long in the cuntry" and Papa maintaining that the true reason came from "unfair play," specifically the "pillage" of the hogsheads while on board ship. The Carrolls became so annoyed by the excuses offered by their merchants that they even threatened to sue. Papa took the same stand on the deductions made by merchants for "damage." When John Buchanan deducted £23.15.2 for "damaged

50. CCA to CCC, Aug. 27, Sept. 4, 1770, ibid.
51. CCA to CCC, Aug. 31, 1770, Oct. 21, 1774, CCC to CCA, Oct. 26, 1774, ibid.

Tobo" in 1772, Papa refused to accept the charge, arguing that he had taken out insurance against shipboard destruction. He further dismissed as patently false Buchanan's claim that nearly five thousand pounds had been damaged before being loaded. "I have heard," wrote Papa, "that a pretence hath been sometimes made, and a distinction set up between Country & Ship Damage — that cannot take place here, as the bill of lading is explicit, that the Tobacco is shipped in good order & condition." [52]

Papa fought the issue of duty-free tobacco with equal vigor and ultimately prevailed. From each hogshead of tobacco imported into England, a proportion, normally 10 percent, sold duty-free. This waiver gave the duty-free tobacco a higher profit margin, which the merchants customarily retained. Refusing to accept this arrangement, Papa argued that the additional profit belonged to him: "An iniquitous Custom," he lectured John Buchanan, "cannot be supported by a practice of it." Buchanan did not relent, but his bankruptcy shortly made his position academic. The Carrolls then moved to Wallace, Davidson, and Johnson, a firm that wanted their business enough to make the concession. As that firm well knew, the Carrolls, for all their demanding tenacity, were excellent customers. They marketed large amounts of fine tobacco, consigned substantial shipments of iron, sold grain locally at the prevailing price, and each year ordered considerable amounts of high-quality goods from London, for which they always paid cash. A great deal of business and sizable commissions awaited merchants who possessed the mettle and stamina necessary for dealing with Papa. For his part, Papa had built his reputation carefully, and he knew quite well what he thought of merchants and how they regarded him. As he had explained to Charley during his student days in London, "It is true I am known to our Tobo Merchts they are but Merchts & they can Consider me in no other light than as a good man (according to their phrase) that is as a man able to answer his Engagements." [53]

52. CCA to John Buchanan, Feb. 11, 1772, CCC to Perkins, Buchanan, and Brown, Aug. 10, 1772, Charles Carroll Letter-book, 1771–1833, fols. 13v–14, Arents Collections.

53. CCA to John Buchanan, Feb. 11, 1772, ibid.; CCC to CCA, Oct. 26, 1774, Carroll Papers, MS 206; CCA to CC, May 1, 1760, Carroll-McTavish Papers. The extent and variety of the Carrolls' orders to London is indicated by the standard categories of goods they included: "Ironware, Hardware, Braziery, Cutlery &c"; "Linnens"; "Wollens"; "Haberdashery"; "Glover"; "Upholstery, Blanketting &c"; "Stationary"; "Medicines"; "Perfumery"; "Leather"; "Oils, Pickles &c"; "Cordage &c"; "Cheese"; "Garden Seeds"; "Hat maker"; "Porter"; "Candle Wick"; "Dyes"; "Lead"; "Tinware"; "Window Glass"; and "Pewterer."

TABLE 4. Carroll Loans Outstanding in 1776

Sum	Number	Amount	Proportion
Sterling			
£1–99	16	£921.03.04 ¾	2.4%
£100–249	20	£3,046.14.11	7.8%
£250–499	23	£7,498.08.08 ¾	19.3%
£500–999	13	£8,892.17.08 ½	22.9%
£1,000–2,499	4	£4,796.19.05 ¼	12.3%
£2,500–4,999	0		
£5,000+	2	£13,723.11.00 ¼	35.3%
Total	78	£38,879.15.02 ½	100.0%
Maryland and Pennsylvania Currency			
£1–99	7	£333.06.09 ¾	10.1%
£100–249	9	£1,443.13.03	43.6%
£250–499	3	£959.02.02 ½	29.2%
£500–999	1	£560.00.00	17.0%
Total	20	£3,296.02.03 ¼	99.9%

Source: Ledger X, Carroll-McTavish Papers, MdHi.
Note: Deviation from 100.0% is due to rounding.

The senior and junior Carrolls collaborated most closely in lending money. About eighteen months before Charley returned home, Papa calculated the total amount of money he had lent at interest at £24,000 sterling. By 1768 the sum had climbed to more than £30,000, and eight years later, on the eve of the Revolution, to slightly more than £41,000. In all, Papa and Charley held seventy-eight sterling accounts by 1776. Six of them comprised 47 percent of the total, with two debtors alone responsible for 35 percent (see Table 4). At the other end of the spectrum, thirty-six of the loans totaled slightly more than 10 percent of the capital the Carrolls had extended. Papa and Charley also made loans in Maryland and Pennsylvania currency, but only one of them exceeded £500.

The total amount of the money the Carrolls had placed at interest grew for two reasons. First, they were generally prepared to extend credit as long as the client possessed adequate resources, principally land and sometimes goods and chattels, to secure the loan. Second, Papa always added any unpaid interest to the principal of the note, consequently increasing the principal of many loans by as much as six percent a year. However, if too many years passed with nothing paid against the debt, the elder Carroll would foreclose without hesitation or else demand additional security. The experience of James Dilling of Baltimore County offers a telling vignette of what borrowing money from the Carrolls might be like. Sometime before 1771, Dilling had borrowed a modest sum, less than £50 Maryland currency. He had apparently intended to retire his debt in the fall of 1771, but, as Papa told Charley, bad luck intervened: "Poor Dilling had got the Money ready last fall to Pay me But Broke His leg by a fall from His Horse, He spent all the Money on Doctors who at last [C]ut of[f] His Leg, He proposes this fall to Mortgage His Land to me as a better Security."[54] Papa accepted the deal, lending Dilling £50.1.9 against his tract, Baker's Discovery. By the time of the Revolution, Dilling's loan had climbed to £59.4.7.

As for land speculation, the Carrolls made no sustained moves before the Revolution but continued buying and selling on a limited basis. Dealing primarily in small tracts, they foreclosed on unpaid mortgages and took some interest in renting and leasing town lots in Annapolis and Baltimore. Their most substantial sale involved the eleven hundred unimproved acres of the Frederick County tract, Carroll's Delight, which netted them close to two hundred pounds.[55] Rather than speculating or adding to their landed estate, the Carrolls concentrated their energies on determining the metes and bounds of the properties they already possessed, an endeavor that immersed them in seemingly endless lawsuits with friends, neighbors, and enemies. Charley shouldered the main burden of these prosecutions and generally managed to please Papa with his performance. As the 1760s gave way to a new decade, however, the son's most promising opportunities for earning his father's approval lay increasingly in the public arena, where shifts within the provincial power structure offered tantalizing possibilities for regaining the access that had been denied Roman Catholics since the Settler's day. Papa saw Charley as uniquely qualified by intellect, wealth, and training to extract meaningful gains for himself and his family from the newly fluid political situation, and in this his son would not disappoint him.

54. CCA to CCC, Oct. 14, 1772, Carroll Papers, MS 206.
55. Frederick County Land Records, liber O, fols. 361–362, 365–367, 385–386, 394–401, MdAA.

"There Is the 1st: Citizen": Political Beginnings

On November 1, 1765, eight and one-half months after the younger Carroll's long-desired homecoming, George Grenville's Stamp Act went into effect. In theory the measure constituted the centerpiece of a new British program aimed at reforming and more equitably distributing the costs of administering the enlarged empire gained from the Seven Years' War. In reality, however, the Stamp Act precipitated the first vigorous wave in a series of protests in the British North American mainland colonies that ultimately led to rebellion and revolution in 1776. No one — least of all Charley — could have predicted such an outcome in 1765. Nor could he have foreseen how those events would transform him from an outsider into a leading political figure in Maryland and make him one of the select group of men who signed the Declaration of Independence.

Charley's experience in the Revolution contrasts sharply with the marginalization to which he, Papa, and the Roman Catholic gentry of Maryland had been previously subjected. Until his return to the colony, much of Charley's awareness that his religion placed him outside the mainstream of Anglo-American society had come to him secondhand. He first encountered statutory discrimination when he arrived in England, after eleven years in Catholic France, but the British monarchy's benign attitude toward members of the Roman church muted the enforcement of those measures. Although the younger Carroll was well aware that "the most tyranical laws" remained on the books and that Parliament would activate them at a moment's notice "whenever it shall please the King," such a possibility seemed unlikely in the relatively tolerant atmosphere of eighteenth-century London. By contrast, the grim history Papa recounted of Catholic suffering in Ireland and Maryland dismayed him and made him wish, like Dido in Virgil's *Aeneid,* that "some avenger might spring up from our bones." Longing as he did for the day he would be allowed to return to Maryland, Charley found it particularly unjust that the "malicious prosecutions" of Catholics might cause his father to quit the province entirely before the happy day of his homecoming arrived. His response to the fate of Catholics in Ireland was to distance himself from those oppressions as a way, perhaps, of denying that he too was liable to similar misfortunes. After toying briefly in 1760 with the idea of visiting Ireland, he laid the thought aside, explaining to his father: "The present situation of that Isleland, will only renew the memory of past wrongs. . . . Fuit Ilion, et ingens gloria Dardanidum. . . . how unavailing to remember what we can not revenge! How melancholy to behold, ancient, noble, and once flourishing families now reduced to beggary!" [1]

Papa's long memory of the oppression that had defined his family's past — and the immediacy of his own experience of injustice and perfidy — convinced him that he as a Catholic might protect himself and his family in a Protestant society only by building a bastion of economic security. Fueled by the dynastic ambitions instilled in him by the Settler and his own aspirations and experience, he carried one tenet of eighteenth-century liberalism in the very core of his being: the possession of substantial property made a man independent and freed him from the patronage of the politically powerful and well-connected, all of whom at that time were Protestants. At the same time, the elder Carroll, like his coreligionists, knew full well that, along with the pretext of religious belief, economic self-interest constituted an equally potent incentive for anti-Catholic action. Catholics with the most to lose made the most tempting targets, and a defiantly Catholic man of wealth like the elder Carroll was particularly at risk. Undeterred, Charles Carroll of Annapolis continued to build his fortune, and he met all threats to his property, whether from provincial, proprietary, or imperial policies, with maximum resistance.

Although the Carroll past shaped his perceptions and molded his character in unique ways, the elder Carroll also shared the general assumptions and values of the colony's Catholic gentry. For all these men, the tenets of Whig republican ideology had selective meaning. Stripped of the right to vote and shut out from the possibility of holding office, the Catholic elite found little relevance in the ideal of civic representation as a means of protecting private property and

1. CC to CCA, Dec. 10, 1759 (quoting Virgil, *Aeneid* 4.625), May 22, Sept. 16, 1760, Carroll Papers, MS 206, MdHi. Translated, the whole Latin passage "Fuimus Troes, fuit Ilion . . ." (Virgil, *Aeneid* 2.325–326), one of Charley's favorite allusions, compares Ireland to Troy: "We were Trojans, Troy and the immense glory of the Trojans are no more." CC to CCA, Mar. 28, 1761, Carroll Papers, MS 206.

expressing the popular will. Beyond supporting the Catholic community, notions of civic virtue that called for subordinating private interests to the public good were largely bereft of meaning. Conversely, republican emphasis on the dangers of consolidated power and the corrupting influence of centralized wealth were a clarion to the Catholic gentry — especially when the governing authorities were Protestant.[2]

By the 1750s, Maryland's Roman Catholics accounted for approximately 16,000–17,000 souls in the province's total population of 160,000, and the amount of land they held was slightly less than their proportion of the population.[3] As in Charles Carroll the Settler's day, most were still small farmers, but the wealth and highly self-conscious mentalité that characterized the families at the top of this pyramid made the Catholic presence in Maryland seem larger than its numbers. Although half of the province's twenty largest fortunes belonged to Catholics, these elite families found that the possession of substantial assets in a context of political impotence underscored their vulnerability.[4] Their success in capitalizing upon the colony's opportunities for accumulating wealth certainly made their lives more comfortable and placed them above ordinary men, whether Protestant or Catholic, in the provincial social order. Less clear is the extent to which their command of resources also brought them any meaningful ability to influence either the government's formal exercise of power or the popular will. Except for practicing law and holding public office, the various profitable activities that composed the Maryland economy were open to Cath-

2. For a vigorous statement of Papa's philosophy, see CCA to William Graves, Dec. 23, 1768, Carroll Papers, MS 206.

3. Writing to the proprietor in 1758 about the results of a census he had recently taken, Governor Horatio Sharpe reported that Catholics "do not at present make a Thirteenth Part of the Inhabitants" of Maryland and "that they are not possessed of a Twelfth Part of the Land" (Sharpe to Lord Baltimore, Dec. 16, 1758, in William Hand Browne et al., eds., *Archives of Maryland* [Baltimore, 1883–] IX, 315). Beatriz Betancourt Hardy notes that Richard Challoner, vicar apostolic for the London District, set the Catholic population of Maryland at sixteen thousand in an August 1763 report to Pope Clement XIII ("Papists in a Protestant Age: The Catholic Gentry and Community in Colonial Maryland, 1689–1776" [Ph.D. diss., University of Maryland, 1993], 323n). My estimate of Maryland's population in the 1750s is based on John J. McCusker and Russell R. Menard, *The Economy of British America, 1607–1789* (Chapel Hill, N.C., 1985), 136.

4. The gentry families that remained Catholic in Maryland after 1720 included Bennett, Boreman, Brent, Brooke, Carroll of Annapolis, Carroll of Duddington, Carroll of Upper Marlboro and Rock Creek, Digges, Fenwick, Gardiner, Hall, Hill, Lancaster, Neale, Pye, Sewall, Waring, and Wharton.

olics; like upper-class Protestants, they engaged in planting, trade, business ventures such as ironworks, and moneylending with varying success. When religious animosity in the colony was quiescent, as it generally was between 1720 and the early 1740s, great Catholic planters or merchants might work closely with Protestants in behalf of common economic goals.[5] Planters of all religious persuasions certainly cooperated to improve tobacco prices in the late 1720s, and, of the five partners who incorporated the ironworks known as the Baltimore Company in 1731, three were Catholics and two Protestants.

The test invariably came when power struggles within the colonial government or international conflicts between Great Britain and a Catholic enemy like France or Spain shattered the veneer of provincial civility. In these times — such as the 1745 rebellion led by Charles Edward Stuart, the Young Pretender, or the Seven Years' War waged by the British against the French and their Indian allies — Maryland's Catholics were regarded with deep suspicion, accused of disloyal and even treasonous activities, and repeatedly threatened by new statutes aimed at penalizing them even further. For elite Catholics, the fragile dominion over land, slaves, and other forms of property that ostensibly gave them an informal influence in provincial life now cut the other way. Instead of protecting them, the law exposed them to and sanctioned the designs of envious and ambitious Protestants.

The inability of the Catholic elite to bring about the repeal or substantial mitigation of the statutes in force against them suggests the severe limits of whatever informal authority they possessed. Beyond educating their sons in Catholic schools abroad without incurring the prescribed legal penalty, they never, from 1720 until the American Revolution, succeeded in persuading Maryland's governing authorities to rescind any of the laws that deprived them of their civil liberties. In crises they became convenient scapegoats, their loyalty was viciously attacked in the press, and, despite concerted efforts, they could not get enough sympathetic legislators elected to make any difference, nor could they prevent additional anti-Catholic legislation from being proposed and enacted. The best they were able to do, after a three-year campaign (1756–1759) that involved sending a special emissary to the proprietor in London, was to secure an order to the governor from Cecilius Calvert, Lord Baltimore's principal secretary for the province, that no *future* penalties would be imposed upon Catholics "without Sufficient Cause of their Offence."[6]

5. Hardy, "Papists in a Protestant Age," 214–236.
6. Cecilius Calvert to Horatio Sharpe, Mar. 30, 1759, in Browne et al., eds., *Archives of Maryland,* LVI, 256, quoted in Hardy, "Papists in a Protestant Age," 299. For the anti-

Notwithstanding their material advantages, the Catholic gentry thus remained exposed to the same kind of legal sanctions that had in the not-so-distant past dispossessed a majority of their coreligionists in England and Ireland. Against this threat, the only sure defense was to change their religion and thereby gain both the security and the opportunities for advancement available to the Protestant establishment. Papa's kinsman, Dr. Charles Carroll, followed such a course. Immigrating to Maryland about 1715, from the same section of the Irish midlands as Charles Carroll the Settler, Dr. Carroll had prospered as a land speculator and businessman, but during the 1730s he joined the Anglican Communion and subsequently gained a seat in the general assembly's lower house. Catholics less willing to commit apostasy might select other protective strategies. Some families like the Bennetts retained their Catholicism but intermarried with powerful Protestants. Others, among them Henry Darnall III, grandson of the Settler's father-in-law, chose partial conversion, whereby the men entered the established church while their wives and children remained Catholic. A last group, including most notably the descendants of the Settler and of Daniel Carroll I of Upper Marlboro, refused to make any compromises at all, electing to survive by sheer force of will and tenacious business practices.

Embittered by the collective experiences of his forebears, Papa placed no confidence in the promises of Protestant governments. The apostatizing Calverts' treatment of his father, Charles Carroll the Settler, constituted the iron proof of that conviction, and he insisted that the abuse loyal Catholic families like the Carrolls had sustained be embedded in Charley's consciousness. "Remember the ill treatment yr: Grandfather met with after so long a Series of Services," he wrote his son in October 1759, "remember the cruel usage of the Rom: Catholicks by the late and present Ld: Baltimore, & let that so weigh with you as never to Sacrifice yr: own or yr: Country's Intt: to promote the Intt: or power of the Proprietary family." During Charley's student days in London, Papa urged him to confront Lord Baltimore and Secretary Calvert with all the instances of the proprietary family's perfidy toward the Carrolls. The elder Carroll also insisted that his son remind these powerful gentlemen that every single law de-

---

Catholic campaign mounted by the *Maryland Gazette* in 1746 and 1747, see "Papists in a Protestant Age," 244–250. Catholic efforts to influence lower house elections in 1751 and 1752 achieved modest success in 1751, with fifteen of the twenty-three anti-Catholic delegates winning reelection, versus eleven of the fifteen judged somewhat sympathetic to Catholics. In 1752, only eight of twenty delegates who "had voted in favor of Catholic positions at least half the time" were reelected. Hardy, "Papists in a Protestant Age," 268–270, 278–280.

priving Roman Catholics of their liberties as well as other discriminatory legislation intended to "vex them" remained in effect. Two such discussions eventually took place, one in the spring of 1760 and the other in February of the following year, but neither produced a satisfactory result. Calvert acknowledged that Governor Sharpe had confirmed that Catholics posed no threat to civil order, but he did not promise that the discriminatory statutes would be repealed. Papa's responses thereto reiterated his position: "The memory of the favours confer'd on yr: Grand Father will always incline you to promote the Intert: of the Proprietary family where you can do it with Honour & Justice." "But at the Same time I think You will act foolishly if from Principle You Espouse the Interests of a Family, who have Plainly shewed they have no Principle at all."[7]

During the late 1740s and early 1750s, while Charley studied abroad, political developments in Maryland heightened the dangers inherent in the Catholic gentry's situation. In 1744 the council directed that Catholics no longer be enrolled in the militia, that those already in service be discharged, and that they turn in any public arms in their possession. The Jacobite rising in Scotland and England in 1745 increased suspicion of the province's Catholics, especially the Irish variety, already considered the most dangerous of all "his Majesty's Roman Catholick Subjects."[8] As the threat of open warfare with France intensified in the early 1750s, the lower house of assembly asserted that Roman Catholics constituted an ever greater menace. Bitter disputes between the two houses of the legislature aggravated tensions within the colony; the forces of political turmoil, religious bigotry, and hatred of the French and their Indian allies coalesced into a potent brew that posed enormous dangers to Catholics, the one group against whom all Protestants could unite. Standing at the center of this storm, Charles Carroll of Annapolis recognized that, save for his intelligence and inflexible will, he was as defenseless as his father and the Irish Carrolls of decades past. Unprotected by English law, Catholics were instead its victims.

The first major confrontation occurred in 1751 when the lower house's Com-

7. CCA to CC, Oct. 6, 1759, Carroll-McTavish Papers, MdHi; CC to CCA, Apr. 10, 1760, Feb. 13, 1761, CCA to CC, Oct. 13, 1760, Carroll Papers, MS 206.

8. Browne et al., eds., *Archives of Maryland*, XXVIII, 315, 340; Hardy, "Papists in a Protestant Age," 245. The assembly's upper house had made this statement in the summer of 1740, in the course of protesting the lower house's appointment of Dr. Charles Carroll, one of several "late Converts from Popery," as receiver of levies raised to finance an expedition "against the Territories of the Catholick King in the West Indies." Browne et al., eds., *Archives of Maryland*, XLVII, 5, 19; Hardy, "Papists in a Protestant Age," 243–244.

mittee on Grievances and Courts of Justice warned of the dangerous growth of "Popery" in the province and urged that, to combat it, the English penal statutes be fully enforced in Maryland. The chief instigator of this document was Dr. Charles Carroll, with whom Charles Carroll of Annapolis was involved in a bitter dispute over the will of their cousin, James Carroll, for whose extensive estate they had been named coexecutors. Still a Catholic when James died in 1729, the doctor was a member of the vestry of St. Anne's, Annapolis's Anglican church, by 1740. Striving assiduously to overcome the persistent suspicion that being Irish attached to his renunciation of Catholicism, Dr. Carroll became in the 1750s the lower house's leading proponent of enforcing existing anti-Catholic statutes and its chief drafter of new ones.[9]

The motives underlying Dr. Carroll's conversion and his attacks on his former coreligionists reflected the same virulent ambition and self-interest that repeatedly sparked anti-Catholic activity. In this instance, the doctor had appropriated for his personal use a large portion of the handsome bequests that James Carroll had devised to several Irish nephews. When Charles Carroll of Annapolis demanded the release of these legacies in full, including both principal and interest, Dr. Carroll replied that he was "incapable of refunding the whole sum without distressing his family" and offered instead to make a partial settlement equal to approximately half of what was due. Rejecting his coexecutor's vigorous insistence that the entire amount be returned, Dr. Carroll justified his action on the grounds that English penal law denied James's legatees the privilege of inheritance because they had become Roman Catholic priests.[10]

Thoroughly incensed, Papa nailed a petition protesting his kinsman's conduct to the door of the State House while the general assembly was meeting. Accepting Dr. Carroll's interpretation of this action as an affront to the dignity and prestige of their chamber, the members of the lower house ordered its perpetrator confined to his residence until the end of the session and then debated whether to discipline him further by incarcerating him in the Annapolis jail.

9. Browne et al., eds., *Archives of Maryland,* XLVI, 549–550; Edward C. Papenfuse et al., eds., *A Biographical Dictionary of the Maryland Legislature, 1635–1789,* 2 vols. (Baltimore, 1979–1985), I, 194–195.

10. [George Hunter], "A short Account of the proceedings of the Assembly of Maryland in regard to the Rom. Catholicks settled there, together with a justification of their conduct & behaviour, the whole proved from authentick copy's of the Provincial Record & other undoubted testimonys," Special Collections Division, Georgetown University Library, Washington, D.C.; Daniel Dulany to Cecilius Calvert, Dec. 26, 1752, Dulany Papers, MdHi.

Charles Carroll of Annapolis escaped this fate by six votes, a margin that a contemporary Protestant observer named Henry Hollyday described to a correspondent in England as "a small majority."[11]

For Hollyday and, undoubtedly, other upper-class Annapolitans, those events constituted "laying a great Man by the Heels." As Hollyday explained it, Charles Carroll of Annapolis was "very rich and consequently a Man of power, and whether a Check of this Kind may not be sometimes necessary you are as well able as I am to determine." This description points up the paradoxical nature of whatever power Maryland's Catholic gentry could command. Possessed of considerable wealth, they could not translate their economic strength into political influence, because the normal channels for such transactions were closed to them. Charles Carroll of Annapolis therefore chose another means to challenge the injustices visited upon him and James Carroll's heirs by a member of the Protestant power structure. Yet his protest, by focusing public attention and private envy on the unpalatable combination of his great fortune and his unacceptable religion, served only to make him even more obnoxious and vulnerable to the forces arrayed against him.[12]

The issues in this confrontation exceeded the dimensions of a personal feud. Dr. Carroll's assertion that the English penal laws dealing with the rights of inheritance should also be considered in effect in Maryland raised the possibility that the measures that broke the great Catholic fortunes in England and Ireland would be used to break them in the colony. The times within which the doctor mounted his aggressive campaign reinforced his chances for success. The specter of a Catholic menace revived by the Young Pretender's rebellion and Great Britain's fight against a Franco-Spanish alliance in King George's War was further enlivened by the reports of hostile exchanges between the mother country and France in the Ohio Valley. More immediately, Maryland's lower house,

11. Daniel Dulany to Cecilius Calvert, Dec. 26, 1752, Dulany Papers; CCA, "A List of Papers sent to England in defence of the Roman Catholics of Maryland," Spec. Coll. Div., Georgetown Univ. Lib.; Browne et al., eds., *Archives of Maryland*, XLIV, 573, 576, 582–583; Henry Hollyday to Philemon Hemsley, June 12, 1751, Maryland Diocesan Archives, Cathedral Church of the Incarnation, Baltimore. The vote was twenty-two for incarceration to twenty-eight against, with Dr. Carroll voting in the affirmative (Browne et al., eds., *Archives of Maryland*, XLIV, 582–583).

12. Hollyday to Hemsley, June 12, 1751, Maryland Diocesan Archives. No documents explicating the final outcome of CCA'S dispute with Dr. Carroll have been found. The doctor died in 1755, before "the Case was ripe for a Trial," but whether his son was eventually "oblig'd . . . to pay what his Father justly owed," as Papa hoped, is unknown. CCA to CC, July 26, 1756, Carroll-McTavish Papers.

rankled by losing a protracted struggle with Lord Baltimore and the upper house over legislative prerogatives and the control and collection of revenues, found Dr. Carroll's anti-Catholic measures a potent means of making trouble for its adversaries: it suggested that any hesitation in endorsing proposals to "prevent the Growth of Popery" brought the proprietor's loyalty into question. Indicative of the lengths to which the delegates were willing to go is the trip to England in 1752 by Dr. Richard Brooke, a Protestant who, like Dr. Carroll, had a keen interest in recovering for himself family property devised to relatives who were Jesuits. Acting as "an unofficial agent for the Lower House," Dr. Brooke presented to the earl of Halifax, head of the Board of Trade and Plantations, a memorial alleging that the proprietary government was demonstrably sympathetic to Catholics, allowing them great leeway in the public practice of their religion and in attempting to influence elections despite their overtly Jacobite behavior during the 1745 rebellion. That Halifax, who advocated closer crown control of the colonies, took Brooke's accusations seriously persuaded Lord Baltimore and the Maryland officials dependent upon his patronage to distance themselves from any appearance of countenancing papists.[13]

Thus, during the years 1748 to 1764 when Charley was studying in Europe, Maryland's Roman Catholic gentry feared for their safety and their property. If the holdings of their priests, repeatedly described in hostile legislation and petitions as "extensive," could legally be taken, the large estates of wealthy lay Catholics were equally at risk, and this oppressive uncertainty menaced them throughout the 1750s.[14] Most of the bills that sought to penalize them originated in the lower house only to be struck down by the upper, not because that chamber was pro-Catholic, but to assert superiority in the power struggle between the proprietor and his upper-house supporters and the elected delegates of the lower house. However, in April 1756, some eight months after Dr. Carroll, the lower house's chief instigator, died, the upper house passed a bill containing the most stringent disabilities of any legislation theretofore crafted. In addition to reiterating strictures against educating children in "popish seminaries" abroad, the upper house's Act to Prevent the Growth of Popery within This

13. Hardy, "Papists in a Protestant Age," 270–271, 274.

14. The petition of "The Freeholders and Inhabitants of Calvert County," May 22, 1756, supported the enforcement of English penal statutes against Maryland's Roman Catholics and emphasized "how much His Majesty's Protestant Subjects are disheartened to see Priests & Jesuits accumulating great wealth & enjoying some of the best Estates in the Province, contrary to Law & good Government." Browne et al., eds., *Archives of Maryland*, LII, 668–669.

Province denied all rights of inheritance to priests, prohibited anyone who had not sworn the prescribed oaths from instructing children even as a private tutor, and made the "conversion of a Protestant to Catholicism . . . punishable as high treason." When the lower house received the bill, the delegates promptly amended it to make it even more severe; they also changed its disposition of the fines and forfeitures. Both houses agreed that half of such revenues should be bestowed upon the informers who brought offenders to justice. But the lower house insisted that the remaining portion go to support free schools in the province, instead of to the proprietor "for the support of government" (meaning to proprietary appointees) as the upper house proposed. Thwarted in its attempt to secure any emoluments for its members, the upper house balked and refused its consent.[15]

Spared another set of disabling strictures thanks to legislative wrangling, Catholics would not be so fortunate again. French and Indian pressure on the frontier finally forced the two houses of assembly to lay aside their differences and work together to raise adequate funds for the colony's defense. The resulting Act for Granting a Supply of £40,000 for His Majesty's Service, passed by the assembly and assented to by the governor on May 15, 1756, mandated that the new land tax of two shillings current money per one hundred acres to be levied upon provincial landowners be doubled for Roman Catholics. For the Catholic gentry, the danger in the double tax arose not from financial hardship — Charles Carroll of Annapolis, owner of some forty thousand acres of land, would pay an annual toll of about forty pounds. The real threat was that, in breaching their economic bastion, the double tax had initiated a process that would lead to their dispossession.

Closing ranks, Charles Carroll of Annapolis and three other prominent and wealthy Catholics — Ignatius Digges, husband of his niece Mary, Basil Waring, and Clement Hill — led a desperate effort to block the bill.[16] Their failure attests the limits of whatever influence their wealth presumably accorded them and the

15. Ibid., xxxv, 430, 449.
16. All of Carroll's colleagues resided in Prince George's County: Digges (1701–1785) at Mellwood, Waring (1711–1793) at Heart's Delight, and Hill (1707–1782) at Compton-Bassett (Effie Gwynn Bowie, *Across the Years in Prince George's County: A Genealogical and Biographical History of Some Prince George's County, Maryland, and Allied Families* [Richmond, Va., 1947], 274–276, 433, 601; Christopher Johnston, "Hill Family," Dr. Christopher Johnston Collection, filing case A, MdHi). By the end of the decade, however, the dispute between Papa and his nephew Charles Carroll of Duddington, in which Digges, Hill, and Waring had major roles, had splintered the bonds of cooperation and kinship that held the leadership of the colony's Roman Catholics together under siege.

"There Is the 1st: Citizen"

jeopardy in which their inability to exert meaningful pressure placed them. Petitioning Governor Sharpe, who had previously defended Catholics against charges made by the lower house, had no effect. Badly in need of funds for defending the frontier and fearful of giving "Clamorous & Factious people an Occasion of representing the Governor & Council as Favourers of Popery," the governor now abandoned the Catholics with alacrity, signing the legislation as soon as it was presented to him. Unable to make any headway in Maryland, the Catholic leaders decided to appeal directly to the proprietor, entrusting this mission to Father George Hunter, the Jesuit superior in Maryland. Armed with a set of documents detailing the treatment of Catholics from the time of the colony's founding, the priest left for England in September 1756.[17]

Those circumstances provoked Charles Carroll of Annapolis's decision, as he wrote to Charley abroad, to quit Maryland entirely for the Catholic colony of Louisiana. Having learned to survive and prosper despite political and religious disabilities, only to find himself under siege in his sole stronghold of economic security, he would not rely upon the uncertain hopes contained in appeals to the Protestants who governed Maryland. Angered by the perfidy of the double tax and fearful of its implications, he began to settle his affairs in Maryland, the first step in converting his fixed assets to portable ones. The initial hint of his plans appeared in the *Maryland Gazette* on May 27, 1756, thirteen days after the governor had assented to the supply bill. Announcing his intention "to wind up his Affairs as soon as possible," he called in debts due to him and offered for sale "several valuable Seats of Land" and his "Houses and Lots in *Annapolis*."[18] An even more striking indication that he had reached a fundamental decision about his family's future is the prenuptial agreement he concluded with Elizabeth Brooke on November 7, 1756, and their subsequent marriage in February 1757. In March, a month after he wed Charley's mother, he initiated the final settlement of his father's estate with his nephew Charles Carroll of Duddington.

Having made his Maryland property and its future disposition as secure as he could, Papa sailed for Europe on June 2, 1757. His destination, by way of London, was Paris, where he intended to negotiate the exchange of his Maryland holdings for a comparable estate in French (and Catholic) Louisiana. A deliberate mystery surrounds this journey, and the details of Papa's plans remain tantalizingly obscure, because the Carrolls and their friends took pains to conceal

17. Sharpe to Calvert, May 27, 1756, in Browne et al., eds., *Archives of Maryland*, VI, 419. The papers relating to Father Hunter's journey may be found in the Spec. Coll. Div., Georgetown Univ. Lib.

18. *Maryland Gazette* (Annapolis), May 27, 1756.

them. Neither is it known whether the venture was Papa's private "scheme" or whether a larger group of wealthy, disgruntled Maryland Catholics was involved. Governor Sharpe, writing to his brother William in London on July 6, 1757, speculated on rumors that Carroll had "Thoughts of leaving Maryland & carrying his Fortune to Europe" and predicted that he would probably settle in "some part of France as he seems by sending his Son to that Kingdom while he was very Young & by supporting him there since he has finished his Studies to prefer that Country."[19]

Such theories entirely missed the mark. Landing first in England, at Portsmouth on July 17, Papa reached Paris early in August, missing by some three weeks Charley's presentation of his thesis at the Collège Louis-le-Grand. Reunited after nine years, father and son spent the fall together, parting in December, when Charley left to continue his studies at Bourges. The reunion with his son, however happy, was not the principal reason for the elder Carroll's journey to the French capital, and during the four months he spent there he engaged in extensive discussions with several notable figures, among them Pierre de La Rue, known as l'Abbé l'Isle Dieu, who had been vicar of Louisiana since 1734, and Sébastien-François-Ange Le Normant de Mézy, the intendant in that colony, 1743–1748.[20]

The Carrolls subsequently destroyed all correspondence directly relating to those meetings. However, surviving references suggest that Papa's attempts to assist some of the French Catholic refugees deported by the English from Nova Scotia to Maryland in December 1755 opened doors for him in Paris two years later, even though the provincial government had prevented him from carrying

---

19. Horatio Sharpe to William Sharpe, July 6, 1757, in Browne et al., eds., *Archives of Maryland,* IX, 46. The possibility of a larger group's emigration is suggested by Eleanor Carroll's letter to her uncle Charles Carroll of Annapolis, dated Apr. 8, 1757. Fearful that she had been guilty of a breach of secrecy, Eleanor confessed that she might have replied too explicitly to a query from her mother about "what scheme the Roman Catholics were upon and particularly yourself." Regrettably, she gives no details. Eleanor Carroll to CCA, Apr. 8, 1757, Carroll-Maccubbin Papers, MdHi.

20. La Rue, born in 1688, served as vicar of Louisiana until 1776, when he retired. Le Normant de Mézy, whose position at the time of CCA's visit to Paris is unknown, subsequently held an administrative post in the ministry of marine for a brief period, June–November 1758. Ernest Lavisse, *Histoire de France depuis les origines jusqu'à la Revolution* (1900–1911; rpt. New York), VII, part 2, 272; Lee Kennett, *The French Armies in the Seven Years' War: A Study in Military Organization and Administration* (Durham, N.C., 1967), 6n.

"There Is the 1st: Citizen"

out the charitable actions he proposed. It is also clear that Charles Carroll of Annapolis placed a considerable sum of money — 4,800 livres tournois, equal to £207 sterling — at the abbé's disposal. The deposit did not produce the desired result, and, after two years of persistent effort on the part of Father Crookshanks (the priest who would later play a role in the Louisa Baker affair), the money was returned to the Carrolls. In December 1759, having received the payment that he, unlike his father, had long ago given up as lost, Charley informed Papa that he had burned all the letters in his possession relating to the affair and also "the memorial you drew up to be presented to the M ———." [21]

Failing to arrange matters as he wished in Paris, the elder Carroll moved on to London, where he spent three months conducting unspecified business and continuing to write to the abbé and Crookshanks. He sailed for Maryland in March 1758 and was home by June. Discouraging reports on the progress of his "scheme" — Le Normant de Mézy informed Charley in August that there was little hope the project would succeed — did not dissuade him, and he refused to relinquish his plans to move, despite the anxiety that possibility produced in his wife and son. In February 1759, he told Charley firmly, "I still persist in the Resolution to sell my Estate here" and underscored his intention by noting that he had already sold lands "to the value of £2000 Ster:" Though what he had sold "has not been under Value," he hoped that "upon a peace . . . my lands will go of[f] better & faster." Regarding the situation of Catholics in Maryland, he found "the disposition of our Lower House of Assembly is as inveterate as ever." Although the delegates' anti-Catholic campaign seemed temporarily stymied, he wondered, "Who would live among men of such dispositions that could live elsewhere?" Not even Father Hunter's success in gaining orders from Secretary Calvert to Maryland's governing authorities "not to molest the Catholicks for the future" dissuaded Papa from his course. As Charley ruefully acknowledged in February 1760, "By yr. last you seem still resolved upon Leaving Maryland." [22]

Unlike his mother, whose reluctance about quitting Maryland he deemed nostalgic and sentimental, Charley entertained more troubling reservations.

21. Many of the nine hundred Acadians sent to Maryland "would have met with very humane Treatment from the Rom: Caths here," Papa informed Charley in the summer of 1756, "but a real or pretended Jealousy inclined this Governmt: not to suffer them to live with Rom Caths." CCA to CC, July 26, 1756, Carroll-McTavish Papers; CC to CCA, Dec. 10, 1759, Carroll Papers, MS 206.

22. CC to CCA and EBC, Aug. 10, 1758, CC to CCA, June 22, 1759, Feb. 30 [sic], 1760, Carroll Papers, MS 206; CCA to CC, Feb. 9, 1759, Carroll-McTavish Papers.

Having spent more than a decade of his life in a Catholic country, he questioned whether, in moving to Louisiana, the Carrolls might find that they had merely exchanged religious oppression for the far greater evil of civil tyranny. However onerous, he reasoned, religious oppression, unlike civil, at least offered the faithful the wherewithal to withstand their trials with appropriate resignation. Shielded by time and distance from the immediacy of his father's difficulties, lulled by the current abeyance of anti-Catholic sentiment in London, and emotionally bound to dreams of a Maryland homecoming, Charley wanted to ignore the connection that British law had forged between adherence to a proscribed religion and the devastating loss of civil liberties. He preferred, he asserted, "to live under an english goverment rather than under any other: Catholick I mean: for I know of no Catholick country where that greatest blessing, civil liberty is enjoyed." [23]

The elder Carroll's determination to leave Maryland began to abate in the spring of 1761. Writing to Charley in April, a month before the supply bill's double-tax provision was due to expire, he evinced a degree of tractability that greatly relieved and pleased his son: "As I have often given you reasons to shew Maryland to be no desirable Residence for a Rom: Cath:, & as you have as often shewn it to be as much so as most others, you are quite at liberty to fix where you please." It was, he allowed, even possible that Charley "may be happy here," provided a "country life . . . with yr: Books & the amusements wch Farming &c afford" would suit him. Moreover, the resumption of trade in 1763 after the war allowed Papa to concentrate again on expanding the Carroll fortune, further defusing his desire to pull up stakes and quit the province. [24]

But, just as Catholics had begun to rest easier in postwar Maryland, they learned of their church's plans for installing a bishop in British North America. Although Rome had contemplated such action as early as 1677, a decade before the Glorious Revolution, church officials never implemented the idea and instead placed Catholics in the British North American colonies under the supervision of London's vicar apostolic. In the summer of 1763, Richard Challoner, the current vicar apostolic in London, revived the issue by encouraging Rome to send a bishop to the colonies now that the war with France had ended. In Challoner's view, the addition of the Catholic populations of Canada and Florida to British North America had vastly increased the scope of the London vic-

23. CC to CCA, Feb. 30, 1760, Jan. 1, 1761, Carroll Papers, MS 206.
24. CCA to CC, Apr. 16, 1761, Carroll-McTavish Papers.

"There Is the 1st: Citizen"

ariate's responsibilities and made the installation of a bishop in Philadelphia a necessity.[25]

The plan horrified the elder Carroll and his coreligionists in Maryland. Having finally seen the demise of the double tax, they wanted to avoid raising any issue that might possibly reignite anti-Catholic sentiments, and they forwarded a petition to London underscoring their opposition. Dated July 16, 1765, and signed by 259 Roman Catholics, with Charles Carroll of Annapolis's name leading the list, the appeal expressed unequivocal disapproval: "We think it our duty to god, ourselves, & posterity to represent our objections against such a measure, as what would give our adversaries, bent on our ruin, a stronger handle than anything they have hitherto been able to lay hold on." Writing privately to Challoner, the elder Carroll recalled the furor that had accompanied a Church of England proposal to place a Protestant bishop in the colonies. A move to extend the Catholic hierarchy so visibly would wreck his desire "to continue in the enjoyment of my spiritual peace, & a quiet possession of my Temporal goods." Should an "Apostolical Vicar for America" be appointed, he warned, the act, "I am afraid, will create great troubles here, & give a handle to our enemies to endeavour at the total suppression of the exercise of our Religion, & otherways most grievously to molest us." Convinced, although disappointed, Challoner withdrew his suggestion, and the idea of a Catholic bishop for America remained quiescent until after the American Revolution.[26]

Papa's reaction to Challoner's effort to install a Catholic hierarchy suggests the dimensions of his identity as a Roman Catholic. His devotion rested on a foundation of implacable loyalties to lineage and faith. Nevertheless, discipline and reason, not sentiment and sensibility, marked his behavior and attachments. His pride in his Irish heritage did not include a romantic longing for the country of his fathers. When he traveled to France in 1757, the first European landmass he saw was Ireland. His journal entry on that occasion consisted of a dispassionate description of the coastline's "wild ragged Appearance" and contained no hint of encumbered memory or stirrings of a Gaelic past. He referred in a similarly laconic tone to a site poignant in Irish history — Kinsale, the place where Hugh O'Neill sustained the defeat that ensured the Elizabethan conquest

25. Hardy, "Papists in a Protestant Age," 361–362.

26. Peter Guilday, *The Life and Times of John Carroll, Archbishop of Baltimore (1735–1815)* (New York, 1922), 154. No manuscript copy of the petition has been found. See also Thomas Hughes, *History of the Society of Jesus in North America: Colonial and Federal* (London, 1907–1917), II, 591–592.

of Ireland. Well aware of the implications of that event, he could hardly have failed to make the connection, but his brief note revealed no sense of tragedy: "At 8 at Night we heard several great Guns; We took them to be a Man of Warr's Guns at Kingsale."[27]

The fierce pride the elder Carroll took in his Catholic identity found its clearest expression in the respect and loyalty he accorded the Jesuits. As a boy he had studied under them at St. Omers and Douai, and he kept Charley under their care until age twenty-two. Convinced that they were persecuted because their "Eminent Merit & Virtue" had made them objects of envy and resentment both within the church and without, he brooked no criticism of them, even from his son.[28] The Jesuits personified the qualities that Papa deemed essential — austerity, steadfastness, integrity, and discipline combined with the reasoned use of the mind. He honored them because, in his judgment, they refused to compromise their adherence to ecclesiastical doctrine and never wavered in their central mission: protecting the true church from heresy through faith and reason and restoring it to absolute dominance.

Charles Carroll of Annapolis's Catholicism reflected the influence of the Jesuits who had shaped him. He did not question the teachings of the church; he was, as Charley would become, a devout Roman Catholic, who believed that strict doctrinal adherence was essential for salvation. He evidently harbored no doubts about the status of his own soul — at least no hints of vulnerability on that score ever left his pen. Instead, self-assurance pervaded his correspondence and conduct, a certainty that he lived his life according to the requirements and rituals of the church. When his father died, he engaged priests to say Mass for him. He married Elizabeth Brooke in a ceremony that complied precisely with the format prescribed by the Council of Trent, and upon her death he had masses offered for her in Maryland and forwarded Charley money for similar services in England. He prayed regularly and maintained a "Priest's roome" at Doohoragen. He wanted a priest nearby to say Mass, to help him make his Easter duties, which included confession, to give him last rites, to absolve him from sin. He wanted this for himself, for Charley, and for Mama, about whose salvation he was also supremely confident. He made it clear to Charley that he was

27. CCA, June 2 to July 18, 1757, Journal kept on a voyage to England, Carroll Papers, MS 216, MdHi. It should be noted that many of Papa's journal entries contained extensive and enthusiastic descriptions. He wrote admiringly, for example, of the order and productivity of the English countryside and of the military might reflected in the nation's shipyards.

28. CCA to CC, Apr. 8, 1762, Carroll McTavish-Papers.

"There Is the 1st: Citizen"

never to marry a Protestant, because offspring of such a marriage risked damnation if they were not raised Catholic.[29]

At the same time, the elder Carroll was not overtly pious. He freely complained about disagreeable qualities in the priests who served his family; in his letters he never used the common ejaculations "IHS" ("In this Man I see the Savior," etc.) or "JMJ" ("Jesus, Mary, Joseph"). Quite to the contrary, he steered his own course in many areas. The books he kept in his escritoire symbolized his convictions. Next to those volumes that emphasized traditional Catholic teachings—Francis de Sales, *An Introduction to Devout Life*, Richard Challoner, *A Roman Catholick's Reasons Why He Cannot Conform to the Protestant Religion*—Papa placed his copy of Voltaire's *Le siecle de Louis XIV*. Sometimes the works he instructed Charley to buy (like Isaac Joseph Berruyer's *Histoire du peuple du Dieu*) appeared on the Index Librorum Prohibitorum (the list of books forbidden by the Roman Catholic Church). The elder Carroll saw no contradiction between religious belief and an examination of Enlightenment ideals. Hence, Voltaire could sit beside his missal. He prized his independence of mind and did not regard rational inquiry and religious faith as mutually contradictory.

Papa set an independent course in other areas as well. His lack of interest in instructing in Christian doctrine the people he enslaved set him apart from most of the colony's Catholic planters. At the same time, he refused to make any of the religious concessions that many of his coreligionists routinely embraced, such as marriages in which the husband secured political privilege by becoming a Protestant while the wife and children remained Catholic. Instead, the elder Carroll responded to the penal statutes and Protestant authority with measured defiance: he openly maintained chapels at his residences at Annapolis and Doohoragen, where a priest said Mass once a month. He did not proselytize, but he did read controversy—the literary corpus that provided Catholics with argumentation for the veracity of their faith as opposed to Protestantism—and he insisted that Charley master those texts as well so as to be fully prepared to defend his theological beliefs. In short, Charles Carroll of Annapolis honored the faith that was integral to his Irish heritage; in denying either, he would deny himself.[30]

Charley's Catholicism followed his father's in most particulars. As a young

29. CC to CCA, July 15, 1761, CCA to CC, Sept. 1, 1762, Sept. 13, 1774, Carroll Papers, MS 206; John Bossy, *The English Catholic Community, 1570–1850* (New York, 1976), 269–270.

30. Beatriz Betancourt Hardy, "Slavery and the Catholic Church in Colonial Maryland," MS (1994); CCA to CC, May 1, 1760, Carroll-McTavish Papers.

boy his teachers wrote approvingly of his "application to his Book and Devotions," and as an adult he conformed strictly to the church's beliefs and practices. During his years in London, a more secular view of Christianity, which played down doctrinal differences and stressed instead the commonality of Christian ideals, had begun to make inroads into the Catholic Church in England.[31] How much these intellectual currents and those of the Enlightenment influenced Charley cannot be measured, but he certainly considered himself a warm friend of toleration: "I execrate," he wrote William Graves after his return to Maryland, "the intollerating spirit of the Church of Rome, and of other churches." He sometimes shared his father's annoyance with family chaplains: priests could indeed be "troublesome animals in a family — & occasion many chops & changes." But these sentiments were essentially background noise. Charley, like Papa, remained a devout Roman Catholic firmly committed to intellectual independence.[32]

By the time Charley returned to Annapolis in early 1765, the furor surrounding the "Catholic threat" during the war years had subsided, but for Papa and his fellow Catholics the reality of being outsiders remained. For twenty-seven-year-old Charley, whose emotional and personal development had taken place far from the Chesapeake, the social distance in being a member of a Catholic family that had suffered under Protestants reinforced his sense of being a stranger. The heightened sensibilities of class that he had acquired through his European experience and education further enhanced his sense of detachment from Maryland society. He returned to the colony a continental gentleman in breeding and outlook. His prejudices and tastes were those of French and English high society, and the more egalitarian overtones of his new environment were offensive and somewhat threatening. "As to the people," he wrote his friend Edmund Jenings in November 1765, "there is a mean low dirty envy which creeps thro' all ranks & can not suffer a superiority of fortune, of merit or of understanding in fellow citizen: either of these are sure to entail a general ill will & dislike upon the owner: my fortune will certainly make me an object of envy."[33]

31. John Jenison to CCA, c. November 1753, quoted in "Autobiographic Sketch of Charles Carroll of Carrollton," in Brantz Meyer, ed., *Journal of Charles Carroll of Carrollton during His Visit to Canada in 1776, as One of the Commissioners from Congress, with a Memoir and Notes* (Baltimore, 1876), 107–108; Bossy, *The English Catholic Community,* 377.

32. CCC to William Graves, Aug. 15, 1774, CCC, letterbook 1770–1774, MdHi; CCC to CCA, Oct. 30, 1769, Carroll Papers, MS 206.

33. CCC to Edmund Jenings, Nov. 23, 1765, CCC, letterbook 1765–1768, fol. 37, MdHi.

As the general crisis in America over the Stamp Act worsened, Charley's distaste both for the people of America and their politics intensified. He viewed the popular disturbances and agitation that swept through Maryland and the other colonies in the second half of 1765 and into 1766 as grossly unpleasant and ill advised, preferring instead a more orderly program of sustained economic boycotts. He was convinced that a trade embargo constituted a more reasoned approach, but, owing to his background, he was appalled and offended by democratic protest. As he sniffed in a letter written in March 1766 to his cousin Daniel Carroll, then visiting England, "The clamour of the people out of doors proceeds from their ignorance, prejudice and passion; it is very difficult to get the better of these by reasoning."[34]

Yet, Charley identified in principle with the colonial opposition to Great Britain. Indeed, he deemed all of Parliament's policies of the 1760s ignorant and wrong-headed because they threatened the enormous trade advantages that Britain derived from her colonies. And he argued the colonies' case against Parliament's new series of taxes and regulations effectively and cleverly, if somewhat dispassionately, in letters to his British friends. Erudite and perceptive, Charley deftly employed Whig republican rhetoric and allusions from the past to support his position. He loved the mental joust, for it attested the achievements of his Jesuit education and enabled him to display the keenness of his intellectual training. Moreover, he recognized rhetoric and ideology for what they really were — modes of reasoning and argumentation that literary combatants used to advance their own convictions and interests — but he never confused rhetoric with the actual motives of persons and institutions. Indeed, if anything truly aroused his passion, it was Britain's stupidity in not recognizing how destructive of the empire's true interests Parliament's policies were.

His rhetorical identification with the cause of the colonies notwithstanding, Charley continued to think, act, and behave with the feigned disdain of an outsider — a man set apart, possibly by preference and certainly by reality, from the society to which he had returned. Initially, he judged colonial politics so contemptible as to be almost beyond serious comment: "We have political parties

34. CCC to Daniel Carroll, Mar. 17, 1766, in Thomas Meagher Field, ed., *Unpublished Letters of Charles Carroll of Carrollton, and His Father, Charles Carroll of Doughoregan* (New York, 1902), 110. For the fate of the originals of the letters Charley wrote between Nov. 23, 1765, and May 27, 1766, see Chapter 5, note 10, above. Checking Field's transcriptions against manuscripts when available reveals numerous inaccuracies, including misidentification of recipients, silent excising of material, and occasional rewriting. I have thus used them carefully and sparingly.

amongst us," he wrote his English friend Edmund Jenings in November 1765, "but they are too trivial & of too little consequence for me to relate or you to hear: I shall only observe, they seem to me to spring from the same source yr. factions have theirs: the want of a sufficient number of lucrative offices to gratify the avarice or the ambition of the Outs." As the violence surrounding the Stamp Act mounted, however, Charley's dismissive attitude turned to a studied contempt shared by other wealthy men. Like them, the younger Carroll deplored the democratic character of the protest and the politicians — the "Patriots," he called them — whom he suspected of abetting disorder as a means of advancing their own interests. The ambitious, deceitful, inconsequential men who composed the Sons of Liberty sought, not the public good, but private advantage. The protesters Charley admired were those who attacked the Stamp Act nonviolently through pamphlets and petitions, even though the most prominent among such men in Maryland was the arrogant Daniel Dulany.[35]

Prevented by his religion from being an actor even if he wanted to be, Charley rationalized his exclusion by insisting that he preferred retirement because it allowed him to nurture his virtue and preserve his independence. Expressing his distaste for the unpleasant, aggressive character of public life in Maryland, he informed his English friends that he had "resolved never to give myself the least concern about politicks but to follow the sensible advice given by Candid[e] to

35. CCC to Edmund Jenings, Nov. 23, 1765, CCC, letterbook 1765–1768, fol. 37, MdHi; CCC to Daniel Carroll, Mar. 17, 1766, in Field, ed., *Unpublished Letters*, 112. Daniel Dulany's pamphlet, *Considerations on the Propriety of Imposing Taxes in the British Colonies, for the Purpose of Raising a Revenue, by Act of Parliament,* was published anonymously, but to great acclaim, in October 1765, in Annapolis. Focusing on the "essential principle of the *English* constitution" that linked taxation and representation, Dulany dismantled the British rationale that Americans could be taxed because they were "virtually" represented in Parliament. At the same time, Dulany carefully tried to distinguish between the impropriety of parliamentary taxation, which he decried, and Parliament's supreme power over the colonies, which he affirmed. Asserting that "prudence, as well as duty, requires submission" until redress could be obtained, he urged the colonists to mount spirited, vigorous, but orderly protests and to exercise economic pressure, particularly through "a vigorous application to manufactures." Aubrey C. Land, *The Dulanys of Maryland: A Biographical Study of Daniel Dulany, the Elder (1658–1753), and Daniel Dulany, the Younger (1722–1797)* (Baltimore, 1955), 263–265.

A month after it appeared in print, Charley described the pamphlet approvingly as written "with that strength & solidity of argument as must convince the understanding of the unprejudiced; & with that elegance & beauty of style as can not fail pleasing good judges & men of taste." CCC to Thomas Bradshaw, Nov. 21, 1765, CCC, letterbook 1765– 1768, MdHi.

"There Is the 1st: Citizen"

improve my own little spot to the utmost," thereby becoming both "independent & I hope virtuous, for virtue & independency are seldom separate."[36]

Papa's attitude contrasted sharply with the distant, uninterested posture Charley projected. Reacting to British policy in the 1760s with the same fervor he had manifested against the economic restrictions laid on Catholics during the previous decade, the elder Carroll condemned the Stamp Act as idiotic, abusive, and insulting. Regarding Britain's need for tax revenue, he told Charley's friend William Graves, now a member of Parliament, that the sorry state of the mother country's finances was entirely attributable to pervasive corruption, a situation the colonies had not caused and for the correction of which they bore no responsibility. "Do you apply to us as Beggars, Shew that you are reall objects of Charity," he fulminated to Graves in late 1768. "Supposing a Drunken profligate able Bodied Sturdy Beggar should apply to you for an Alms would you bestow it? When we see Princely Estates Suddenly made by Contractors &c When we See numberless Sine Cure Offices of immense Annuall Value Held, When we See great & unmeritted Pensions with out number bestowed to the 3d: & 4th Generation Can you Expect that we Can be prevailed on to Gratify yr Cravings or Contribute to yr Profusion?"[37]

Their differences in temperament aside, father and son confronted the same reality: politically, they were outsiders. Despite his handsome fortune, the elder Carroll's efforts at translating his wealth into political influence capable of fully integrating Catholics into provincial life had succeeded only in maintaining the status quo. Openly resentful of the statutory injustice that circumscribed the lives of Catholics in Maryland, Papa never hesitated to express his contempt for the men who had crafted and acquiesced in the continuance of those laws. Thus, when an opportunity developed in the early 1770s for the Carrolls to advance their political interests, Papa moved cautiously and deliberately to seize the moment and maximize his advantages. In securing such gains, he chose his son as his principal vehicle; once prodded into action, Charley relinquished his posture of affected indifference and proved equal to the task.

The events that allowed the Carrolls to move from outsiders to insiders had their genesis in the 1740s. The issue involved the collection of "officers' fees." Since 1747 the prices proprietary officials could charge for performing public services had been linked to legislation that regulated the colony's tobacco inspection sys-

36. CCC to Edmund Jenings, Aug. 13, 1767, CCC, letterbook 1765–1768, fol. 96.
37. CCA to [William] Graves, Dec. 23, 1768, Carroll Papers, MS 206.

tem. In 1755 and 1763 the act had been routinely renewed, but, starting in 1769, the level of the fees became hotly contested between the upper and lower houses of the general assembly. The points of contention were several, but the delegates raised their main objection over the proprietary practice of selling public offices, which, in the lower house's opinion, led officeholders to charge excessive fees for their services in order to recoup their expenditures. As a remedy, the delegates pushed in both 1769 and 1770 for the elimination of such sales and the institution of a reduced fee schedule. The upper chamber naturally opposed the measure. Several of its members, including Daniel Dulany and his brother Walter, enjoyed handsome incomes from their proprietary positions.[38] Complicating matters further, the expiration of the tobacco inspection act to which the fee schedule was attached engaged the lower house in a heated dispute with the colony's governor, Robert Eden, who oversaw the operation of the proprietary system. Weary of the wrangling, Eden took a drastic step. In November 1770, after an angry confrontation with the lower house over the conduct of two land office judges who continued to collect fees despite the absence of any authorizing legislation, the governor issued a fee proclamation directing the continued payment of revenues in accordance with the schedule enacted in 1763.[39]

Known in Maryland history as the fee controversy, this internal proprietary dispute not only enabled Charley to move into the center of political power but also allowed him to become a rallying point for other political aspirants who either wanted "in" or who were not "in" enough and wanted to vanquish the proprietary's interests. Perennial Carroll irritant Daniel Dulany provided the opening. Seeking either to improve his standing with Eden, who regarded him as a rival, or perhaps to solidify his ties to a new proprietary regime, Dulany published a clever essay defending the fee proclamation in hopes that, if he persuaded voters to select more moderate delegates in the forthcoming election, his

38. At the commencement of the legislative session in the fall of 1770, the lower house initiated an investigation into the amount of revenue earned by proprietary officials through the conduct of their offices. The results revealed that Daniel Dulany, deputy secretary of the colony, made £1,000–£1,500 annually, that his brother Walter garnered only slightly less from his post as commissary general, and that a pattern of high earnings existed throughout the proprietary establishment. The lower house then proposed a schedule of reduced fees, which the upper chamber rejected. A discussion of the fee controversy can be found in Ronald Hoffman, *A Spirit of Dissension: Economics, Politics, and the Revolution in Maryland* (Baltimore, 1973), 103–125; and Charles A. Barker, *The Background of the Revolution in Maryland* (New Haven, Conn., 1940), 348–358.

39. The details of the confrontation between Eden and the lower house are recorded in Browne et al., eds., *Archives of Maryland*, LXII, xxvii–xxix, 304, 379–380, 431.

"There Is the 1st: Citizen"

interests would be adavanced. Printed in the January 7, 1773, issue of the *Maryland Gazette,* the piece took the form of a dialogue between two adversaries, "First Citizen" (an Eden opponent) and "Second Citizen" (an advocate of the governor). Eden's benefactor triumphed, and First Citizen acknowledged the error of his misguided views.[40]

It is unlikely Dulany had calculated on what happened next. On February 4, Charley published a remarkably facile rejoinder under the pseudonym "First Citizen," thereby commencing a battle that raged in the pages of the newspaper for five months. Three lengthy pieces by First Citizen and three by Dulany, who chose to call himself "Antilon," appeared in the course of the contest. Replete with a host of classical, literary, and historical allusions and spiced with stinging personal invective, the exchange debated the legal and constitutional validity of Governor Eden's unilateral imposition of the fee schedule in November 1770. Dulany carefully distinguished between fees and taxes and emphasized that Eden's proclamation was in reality a protective measure taken in behalf of the public. With the expiration of the old law, he argued, the officers were free to raise their prices to any level they desired. Therefore, the governor had by his proclamation established a ceiling and prevented the charging of excessive rates. Dulany justified Eden's right and obligation to take such action by marshaling an impressive array of English and provincial precedents. Taxes, he contended, could be levied only by Parliament, but fees had often been assessed by various branches of government — the courts, the executive, even separate houses of the assembly — acting on their own accord.

In opposition, Charley warned against the grave dangers of an unbalanced constitution and the threats posed by absolutism once a legislative body's privileges, especially its control over public finance, were no longer respected. In direct opposition to Dulany, he maintained that fees were indeed a tax and that their regulation came under the authority of the general assembly. The governor's proclamation constituted a new law, but the commission to legislate unilaterally did not repose within the juridical purview of the governor's office. Charley justified his case by recourse to English history, interpreted according to the Whig tradition. But, while deploring the growing power of patronage controlled exclusively by the proprietary circle that had rendered the government increasingly less responsive to the people, Charley, in deference to Papa's

40. *Md. Gaz.,* Jan. 7, 1773. With the death of the proprietor, Frederick Calvert, sixth Lord Baltimore, in September 1771, Maryland succeeded to his illegitimate son, Henry Harford. This change in administration necessitated a new election, but difficulties posed for the succession by Harford's illegitimacy delayed the voting until May 1773.

wishes and his own sensibilities, took pains to suggest that he did not blame Eden for the colony's difficulties. Instead, he faulted Eden's "Minister," Dulany. Whatever the governor's opinion of the fine line Charley had tried to walk, the voting public did not hesitate to make its preference known: the elections held in May 1773 returned a lower house firmly sympathetic to the views espoused by First Citizen.[41]

Among the family conflicts in colonial Maryland, the testy, sometimes openly hostile relationship between the Carrolls and the Dulanys ranks as a classic. Thus, while the fee controversy undeniably was the overt political trigger in the First Citizen–Antilon debate, other powerful forces, some conscious and others perceived only dimly, shaped and animated the contest. Underlying the rivalry, perhaps subconsciously, reverberated echoes of Ireland's bitter past. The Dulanys were a Protestant Irish family, and, although by 1773 Daniel was two and Charley three generations removed from the clashes of their ancestors, the defining power of that history still formed a vital subtext for the rhetorical battle between Maryland's consummate insider and the upstart outsider who challenged him. As a member of the lower house of assembly, Daniel had opposed Dr. Carroll's campaign against Catholics during the 1750s with such vigor as to make himself unpopular among his Frederick County constituents, an outcome that dissuaded him from standing for reelection. Yet, as Antilon, he disparaged First Citizen as "a papist by profession" and noted that the laws disabling Catholics had been enacted because their "religious principles are suspected to have so great influence, as to make it unsafe" to allow their "interference" in matters concerning the established church or the civil government. First Citizen, Antilon pointed out acidly, "is not a protestant." And, with similar rancor, Antilon resurrected the old connection between papists and Jacobites.[42]

41. The best edition of the "First Citizen" letters is Peter S. Onuf, ed., *Maryland and the Empire, 1773: The Antilon–First Citizen Letters* (Baltimore, 1974). Onuf's publication was preceded by Elihu S. Riley, ed., *Correspondence of "First Citizen"–Charles Carroll of Carrollton, and "Antilon"–Daniel Dulany, Jr., 1773, with a History of Governor Eden's Administration in Maryland, 1769–1776* (Baltimore, 1902). For an informed discussion of the political controversies within Maryland in the early 1770s, see James Haw, "Maryland Politics on the Eve of Revolution: The Provincial Controversy, 1770–1773," *Maryland Historical Magazine,* LXV (1970), 103–129.

42. Land, *The Dulanys of Maryland,* 224–226; Hardy, "Papists in a Protestant Age," 279; Onuf, ed., *Maryland and the Empire,* 121–122, 186–189. Land suggests that Dulany's views on Roman Catholics in the 1750s were moderated by his sister Rebecca's first marriage to Catholic James Paul Heath (d. 1746) of Cecil County, a union that produced sev-

Exclusion from civic participation certainly sharpened the edge of the Carrolls' resentment of the Dulanys' control of some of the colony's most lucrative political offices. But, despite their political clout, the Dulanys envied the Carrolls' wealth and delighted in insulting them. Relations between the two families took a particularly nasty turn in the spring of 1768 when Charley went to the assembly for the enabling act to facilitate Molly Darnall's prenuptial settlement. Dulany chose that moment to deliver a pointed personal insult to the Carrolls by opposing the request. In June 1773, an anonymous muse recounted Charley's chagrin on that occasion in a poem that held him up to public ridicule:

When your letter I read, my heart leap'd for joy,
That I an occasion so apt might employ
My rancour, and[k] *venom innate* to let fly
At a man I abhor — and, I'll whisper you why.
I could not be married — (you've heard of the fact)
Before I had got "an ENABLING act."
For, a man, you'll allow, wou'd cut a poor figure,
(Tho' big as myself, or, perhaps, somewhat bigger)
Who, to any fair virgin his honour shou'd plight,
Without being ENABLED to do — what is right.
In this he oppos'd me; for which, oh, befal him
The *catholick* curse of — what do you call him!

[k] *Here it must not be construed, that the doctrine of John Locke of Oxford about* innate ideas, *is impugned. But it is* LUCE CLARIUS, *that no more is meant, than that the anima medica, when in embryo, may receive certain qualities and impressions, by the* potent applications of ar[t]. Anon.[43]

Compounding those tensions, Charley and Lloyd Dulany, Daniel and Walter's hot-blooded young half brother, had come unnervingly close to a life-and-death confrontation in 1769. In mid-September of that year, Daniel Dulany sent an objectionable letter to Papa, and Lloyd seconded his brother's comments in

———
eral sons. Land, *The Dulanys of Maryland*, 166; Papenfuse et al., eds., *Biographical Dictionary*, I, 285.

43. "A New Edition of the Answer to the Letter of Thanks, Addres'd by the Representatives of the City of Annapolis to the *First Citizen*, with Notes," *Md. Gaz.*, June 24, 1773. The poem is not mentioned in family correspondence.

an abusive letter of his own. In view of what then ensued, it is especially unfortunate that neither of these missives has been found. Stung by Lloyd Dulany's insults, Charley believed his honor was at stake and challenged his antagonist to a duel, explaining succinctly to Papa, "I shall take no further notice of LLoyd: but shall go prepared to blow out his brains."[44]

Declining to accept the younger Carroll's challenge, Lloyd replied contemptuously, referring to his antagonist as a "silly little Puppy" and suggesting that the ears of both Carrolls should have long ago been placed "upon a Pillory." Nevertheless, Charley bravely rode out anyway but saw no sign of his adversary. Reflecting on the perilous incident several days later when all danger had passed, Charley professed himself incensed both by Lloyd's behavior and by its distressing social implications. "If such outrageous abuse should go unpunished, if the grossest insinuations are permitted to be thrown out agt. a gentleman's character by such scoundrels with impunity," he fumed to Papa, "there is an end of civil society. Every sturdy insolent fellow confiding in his strength might insult a worthy honest man who might be weaker." Beyond that: "In the late instance had I been killed what dear connections should I have left behind me! & who would have grieved at LLoyd's death? I do not believe a single tear would have been shed on the occasion."[45]

Given the rancor between the Carrolls and the Dulanys and Papa's preference for direct confrontation, Papa's restraint during the fee controversy and the studied caution he urged upon Charley are striking. Believing a major opportunity had suddenly developed, the elder Carroll schemed intensely to advance his family's interests, and on all occasions his son deferred to his instructions. When Charley prepared the initial First Citizen letter, he and his father were wintering together in Annapolis. Clearly pleased with the essay, Papa expressed unmitigated delight at the celebrity accorded his son upon its publication. "A Gentleman," he wrote Charley after returning to Doohoragen in March, "told me You appeared at the County Court on Friday, that the Whisper immediately Ran there is the 1st: Citizen & that Every Eye was fixed on You with evident marks

44. CCC to CCA, [Sept. 30, 1769], Carroll Papers, MS 206.

45. Lloyd Dulany to [CCC], Sept. 29, 1769, enclosed in CCC to CCA, [Sept. 30, 1769], CCC to CCA, Oct. 2, 1769, ibid. In 1782, Lloyd Dulany died in London from wounds suffered in a duel with the Reverend Bennett Allen, formerly a rector of St. Anne's Church in Annapolis. Both men were loyalists and had returned to England to live. Papenfuse et al., eds., *Biographical Dictionary*, I, 285.

of Pleasure & Aprobation, that many sayed they did not know which to admire most yr strength of reasoning or yr calm & Gentleman like Stile."[46]

Not everyone was favorably impressed, however, and through the spring and into the summer Antilon's supporters presented their sharply different views in the press. The use of anti-Catholic invective in these diatribes was sufficiently pronounced to suggest that the writers believed enough religious animosity remained in Maryland to make playing the popery card an effective strategy. Such authors accused First Citizen of trying to make "A PROTESTANT *people* to *me* bend the knee" or of being the minion of a diabolical plot fomented by the Jesuits to "make way for popery . . . a complication of all the absurdities, rogueries, and errors, that ever appeared among men, or that the craft, folly, and malice of men is capable of." How could a "patriotic nursling of St. Omer" presume to attack a man like Antilon, whose pamphlet supporting the colonies' position during the Stamp Act crisis had earned him the approval of so notable a figure as William Pitt? "A Protestant Whig" expressed sympathy for Dulany, a "Gentleman of distinguished abilities, who has retired from the Bar," because his great talents seemed unlikely to save him from "the holy inquisition of *Jesuits* and *Independent Whigs*." One writer resorted to sexual innuendos to deprecate Charley as too "small" a man for the role he sought, and another tried to diffuse the public's approbation by referring to an equally tender spot — the Carrolls' reputation for charging compound interest. In midsummer, "Leixiphanes" deftly summed up First Citizen as "one in whom contradictions are reconciled, a papist and yet a friend to civil liberty — a receiver of compound interest, and yet an enemy to illegal exactions; of a noble elevated mind, tho' ———— curtail'd of fair proportion."[47]

The pitfalls that marked this volatile political landscape demanded that the Carrolls step carefully; as unpopular as Eden had made himself, he was still the governor and thus wielded considerable power. Basking in but not lulled by the warm glow of parental pride, Papa directed Charley to handle Governor Eden gently, to do all he could not to offend him, and to keep the lines of communication open. Relieved at learning Eden still appeared friendly, Papa was "glad to Hear the Govr invited you to dine with Him so soon after the Publication of yr: Answer to Antilon, althô it be no proof that yr answer has not

46. CCA to CCC, Mar. 17, 1773, Carroll Papers, MS 206.

47. A Protestant Whig, *Md. Gaz.*, Mar. 4, 1773; Clericus Philogeralethobolus, Mar. 25, 1773; "A New Edition of a Late Letter of Thanks to the First Citizen, June 10, 1773; "A New Edition of the Answer to the Letter of Thanks," June 24, 1773; Lexiphanes, July 22, 1773.

offended Him; His Behaviour & Hints which He may have dropt Since, will be more Certain indications of His sentiments." Charley must constantly observe, listen, and evaluate the governor's actions and demeanor: "His Behaviour you have seen, if He has Spoke, you probably Have Heared Some of the things He has sayed, Upon all Circumstances let me know what you think He thinks." Openly entering the fee controversy exposed the Carrolls to great risks — after all, the governor and Dulany might well triumph. To insulate themselves against an unfavorable outcome, Papa insisted that Charley reiterate to Eden their belief that he was not personally responsible for the unpopular proclamation but was rather the victim of Daniel Dulany's bad advice. Charley must, his father cautioned him, "Manage the Govr: as much as You Consistently Can with the Force & œconomy [of] it."[48]

Besides giving Charley detailed advice on how to behave toward Eden, Papa used third parties as couriers to apprise the governor of the Carrolls' continued support. Having approached Major Daniel of St. Thomas Jenifer, the proprietor's agent and receiver general, for such a purpose, the elder Carroll told the younger that he had done so "with a view that He might shew my letter to the Govr: wh: I doubt not He has done, it Can doe us no Harme, it will let the Govr see Plainly our Sentiments." Moreover, Papa thought that the major's answer to his letter "may draw something from Him & in order to that I seasoned it with some Complaisance."[49]

Precisely what Charley thought about these incessant maneuverings is unclear; he insisted that he remained uninterested and above the fray. "I did not write for reputation," he noted to his father, "but to instruct my countrymen, & to apprise them of the pernicious designs of Government. I hope I have in some measure succeeded; and this success gives rise to the Governor's resentment."[50] However modest his stated ends, Charley soon discovered that his new reputation opened avenues to power previously closed to his family. The collection of supporters that began to identify openly with him both before and after the May 1773 election clearly indicated his meteoric rise to prominence and growing influence. Charley's assault on the proprietary establishment had made him a rallying point for other opportunists who hoped to advance their own interests by capitalizing on the unsettled situation. Two of these ambitious young men,

48. CCA to CCC, Mar. 25, Apr. 16, 1773, Carroll Papers, MS 206. For an early expression of the conviction that Eden was a victim of bad advice, see CCC to Charles Carroll, Barrister, Dec. 3, 1771, CCC, letterbook 1770–1774, fol. 19, MdHi.

49. CCA to CCC, Apr. 8, 1773, Carroll Papers, MS 206.

50. CCC to CCA, Apr. 3, 1773, ibid.

"There Is the 1st: Citizen"

Samuel Chase and William Paca, succeeded at the polls and used their advocacy of First Citizen to vault themselves into positions of power in the lower house. Others, most importantly Thomas Johnson and Matthew Tilghman, coalesced around Charley to form the nucleus of a popular party — a coalition of men intent on diminishing the proprietor's authority and enhancing their own.

Although tremendously excited by the heady possibilities swirling about First Citizen, Papa acted with truly remarkable tact and restraint. Unlike his past confrontations with governmental authority when he had moved boldly, heedless even of his own personal safety, his deliberate conduct in 1773 took into full account the consequences of a misstep. The explanation for his uncharacteristic behavior lies in the nature of the situation. This time, Papa was on the offensive. Instead of mounting a defense to protect Carroll property, he now sought through delicate maneuvers to advance other family interests. Moreover, he perceived that the discriminatory attitudes that had so long prevailed against Maryland's Catholics had begun to shift, subtly but unmistakably. Dr. Charles Carroll, one of the main abettors of prejudice, had been dead for nearly twenty years, and his son, Charles Carroll, Barrister, had no interest in continuing his father's activities. The anti-Catholic hysteria precipitated by the Seven Years' War had dissipated, and whatever remained after Culloden of the Jacobite cause that had once reached across the Atlantic to fuel anti-Catholic sentiment in Maryland had gone to the grave with the Old Pretender in 1766. When anti-Catholic attacks on First Citizen in the press failed to arouse the public, Papa sensed that a new day might be coming, and with consummate skill he positioned the son he had so painstakingly shaped to take full advantage of its opportunities.[51]

During the rest of 1773 and into early 1774, Charley's supporters (Chase, Paca, Johnson, and Tilghman) attempted to parlay the power they had gained in the lower house into a resolution of the fee controversy. Desiring primarily the traditional advantages of power — money, prestige, and influence — they hoped to reach a compromise with the governor that would consolidate their recently

---

51. Despite the fact that the Jacobite "threat" made trouble for Catholics well into midcentury, Papa believed that the return of the Stuarts to power had ceased to be a possibility upon the death of Louis XIV in 1715. As he wrote to Charley on July 24, 1762: "Lewis the 14th was sincerely disposed to restore the Exiled family. Since his death the Chevalier & his Son have been but Cats Paws in the hands of France who may now have good reason to repent their double dealing with that unfortunate family" (Carroll-McTavish Papers). The Old Pretender, James Edward Francis Stuart, was recognized as James III in France until 1713 and was known thereafter as the Chevalier St. George.

won gains. While these efforts were continuing, and while Charley's friends worked to neutralize an even more radical lower house faction that refused to make any concessions to the proprietary establishment, the imperial controversy burst upon them and changed the context so dramatically that the proprietary dispute became moot.[52]

The final sequence of events that led to the dissolution of the ties between Great Britain and her North American mainland colonies began innocently enough with Parliament's decision to aid the financially ailing East India Company by passing legislation that allowed the company to sell tea directly to its agents in America without paying British export taxes. Designed to make the East India Company's commodity competitive with what the colonists acquired illegally from the Dutch East India Company, the measure nevertheless left in force the import duty first levied on tea in America. This tax, part of the so-called Townshend Acts, had been imposed by Parliament in 1767. Designed by the chancellor of the Exchequer, Charles Townshend, the measures were intended to raise revenue under pretext of regulating trade. Although some Americans, notably in New York and Philadelphia, had subsequently refused to purchase taxed tea, so many more of them had continued to that the British ministry did not expect the Tea Act to be resisted.

The ministry could hardly have been more mistaken. The arrival of the first ships carrying East India Company tea at Boston on November 27, 1773, created an impasse between popular agitators and local British authorities, with the former refusing to allow the tea to be landed and the latter, led by Massachusetts governor Thomas Hutchinson, refusing to allow the ships to leave. The stalemate persisted until the night of December 16, when a party of men disguised as Mohawk Indians boarded the ships and, before a large cheering crowd, broke up 342 cases of tea and heaved the contents into the water.

Parliament, most of whose members were infuriated by this defiance, responded in May 1774 by enacting a series of punitive measures. Known in the mother country as the Coercive Acts and as the Intolerable Acts in America, this legislation consisted of four parts. The first, the Boston Port Act, closed the port until the people compensated the East India Company and paid the tax on the destroyed tea. The second, the Administration of Justice Act, provided that a royal official accused of a capital crime committed while carrying out government policy would be tried in another colony or in Britain rather than in the

---

52. Hoffman, *Spirit of Dissension,* 126–128, 135–138.

"There Is the 1st: Citizen"

court with jurisdiction over his locale. The third, the Massachusetts Government Act, effectively annulled that colony's charter, drastically curtailed town meetings, and severely reduced the representative character of the government. The last disciplinary measure extended the Quartering Act by allowing British commanders to requisition buildings or private dwellings to house troops. A fifth measure, the Quebec Act, aroused such animosity among the colonists that they insisted on regarding it as part of the punitive program even though its intention was to regularize the government of Canada rather than to penalize the fractious Americans. Most objectionable were the clauses that reserved the levying of all but a few local taxes to the crown, denied jury trial in civil cases, extended Canada's boundary to areas of the Ohio country already claimed by Connecticut, Massachusetts, and Virginia, and granted civil and religious toleration to Roman Catholics.

The violence and destruction of property of the Boston Tea Party initially produced feelings of aversion and alarm in most of the colonies. Many men of property believed that the port deserved to be punished and should pay for the tea. But more radical men, known as popular leaders, vigorously denounced the Intolerable Acts as proof of Parliament's determination to reduce the colonies to virtual slavery. On May 25, 1774, a letter from the Boston Committee of Correspondence denouncing the Boston Port Act and calling upon the colonies to adopt nonimportation and nonexportation pacts arrived in Annapolis. That afternoon, a group of some eighty men gathered to discuss the message and to contend over how the province should respond. Feelings ran high. Leaders like Samuel Chase, Thomas Johnson, Jr., and William Paca, who owed much of their public support to Charley's talented pen, found themselves challenged by an even more radical faction headed by Annapolis lawyer John Hall and Anne Arundel County planter Matthias Hammond, whose support of First Citizen had won him election to the lower house in May 1773.

The radical nature of the "resolves" that came out of the meeting reflected its heat and the combativeness of men vying for leadership. A seven-member Committee of Correspondence was to communicate the resolves to the rest of the province and the Virginia House of Burgesses. The resolutions called not only for the immediate stoppage of all trade with Great Britain but also for incorporating that policy into an agreement to be sworn under oath. Any colony that did not adopt a similar course of action was to be boycotted. The most controversial provision demanded that provincial lawyers not file any suits for debts owed to British creditors until the Boston Port Act was repealed. As also mandated by the resolves, a convention of delegates from Maryland's sixteen counties convened in Annapolis, June 22–24.[53] Similar activities in other colonies culminated in a consensus that, as a prelude to collective action, representatives should be sent to a general meeting. Fifty-six such individuals from all the colonies except Georgia met in Philadelphia on September 5, 1774, as the First Continental Congress.

From the outset, Charley reacted to the Coercive Acts with indignation. "I flatter myself the Colonies will consider the case of Boston as their own," he wrote his mercantile agent in London in early June. Keenly aware of the direction in which events were rapidly moving, he predicted that "a Congress of deputies from the different Colonies" would be called to formulate a plan "to defeat the pernicious design of the British Administration" and adopt "some general Scheme of Union" for governing the American provinces. Nor had he any doubt that, "should the Minister persevere in his measures," trade between Great Britain and the colonies would come to a complete halt.[54]

Yet, for all his passion, he remained an outsider. His presence at the impromptu gathering on May 25 cannot be verified; the Charles Carroll who gained a place on the Committee of Correspondence selected there was certainly his Protestant kinsman Charles Carroll, Barrister. Although Charley gave his father a "Pleasing acct of the Provinciall meeting" that took place on June 22–24, he was an observer of rather than a participant in the first convention, the extralegal body that boldly assumed the powers formerly exercised by the proprietary assembly. In September, he accompanied the Maryland delegation selected by the convention to Philadelphia for the First Continental Congress, but, again, he was not an official member as were the men whose access to power his pen had so eloquently enhanced — Chase, Johnson, Paca, and Tilghman.[55] Passionately convinced that ministerial avarice, ambition, and corruption had brought the British Empire "to the brink of ruin," Charley nevertheless remained philosophical about his continued exclusion from the halls of power. "If my coun-

53. Ibid., 128–130; David Ammerman, "Annapolis and the First Continental Congress: A Note on the Committee System in Revolutionary America," *Md. Hist. Mag.*, LXVI (1971), 169–180; Papenfuse et al., eds., *Biographical Dictionary*, I, 68.

54. CCC to Wallace and Company, June 5, 1774, Charles Carroll Letter-book, 1771–1833, fol. 37v, Arents Collections, New York Public Library, Astor, Lenox, and Tilden Foundations, New York.

55. CCA to CCC, June 26, 1774, Carroll Papers, MS 206. The fifth member of Maryland's delegation was Robert Goldsborough (1733–1788), of Dorchester County on the Eastern Shore. Tilghman at 56 was the eldest of the delegates, followed by Johnson, 42, and Goldsborough, 41. Chase at 33 was the youngest; Paca was 34. Charley would have celebrated his 37th birthday while in Philadelphia.

trymen judge me incapable of serving them in a public station for believing the moon to be made of green cheese," he wrote William Graves three weeks before he left for Philadelphia, "in this respect their conduct (if not wicked) is not less absurd than my bilief, and I will serve them in a private capacity notwithstanding." "Nay," he concluded wryly, "I have done it." [56]

Charley arrived in Philadelphia on September 6, "dejected" by "the gloomy prospect before us." With the mother country showing no sign of bending, civil war seemed inevitable, and, should it begin, he feared the colonies had as much to dread from victory as from defeat. Nevertheless, he would, he wrote Papa firmly on September 7, "either endeavor to defend the liberties of my country, or die with them: this I am convinced is the sentiment of every true and generous American." His inability to monitor the Congress's meetings firsthand because the delegates admitted "no strangers" to their deliberations forced Charley to rely on whatever intelligence the official deputies were willing to breach their vow of secrecy to share with him. Gleaning enough information to give him a measure of reassurance, Charley decided there was still hope that the "men of strong sense" in the Congress would avoid armed conflict by steering "a proper course between Independency & Subjection." And, once satisfied that the Maryland and New England deputies were among the most moderate of all, the younger Carroll allowed himself to enjoy the company of a coterie of prominent Philadelphians, who included him in a variety of social functions. Associating with men of influence from all of the colonies, he gravitated ever nearer to the centers of action. He was not yet an insider, but he had come close enough to feel the allure of power, and he no longer pretended to be detached or to prefer the role of an independent outsider.[57]

Whatever part he played in Philadelphia during the first two weeks of September 1774, Charley's role in Maryland politics was assured thereafter. In early November 1774 he became a member of the Committee of Correspondence for Anne Arundel County and Annapolis and gained election to the second of the provincial conventions that constituted the provisional government of Maryland. Subsequently returned to the succeeding seven conventions, Charley also served on the first Council of Safety appointed by the deputies in the summer of 1775. His inclusion on these increasingly important bodies maintained his steady momentum toward political prominence, confirmed his growing influence, and kept him at the center of developments in the burgeoning imperial crisis. Certainly his activities during the fall of 1774 and throughout 1775 bore little resem-

56. CCC to William Graves, Aug. 15, 1774, CCC, letterbook 1770–1774.
57. CCC to CCA, Sept. 7, 9, 12, 1774, Carroll Papers, MS 206.

blance to the contemplative pursuits of a retired existence that he had once extolled to his English friends.

However, the pleasure he took in his expanding public career did not mask the grave reality that the relationship between Great Britain and its North American mainland colonies might disintegrate. By early 1775, the darkening cloud of revolution began to cast an ominous shadow over the Carrolls' daily lives and to infuse formerly routine transactions with a sense of foreboding. On January 8, Charley sent a voluminous order for goods to Wallace and Company's London agent Joshua Johnson. The length and variety of the invoice, with the accompanying letter, attest to the unsettled times as well as to Charley's own uneasy ambivalence, hoping that all difficulties would be resolved without a major disruption of trade while acknowledging that a prudent man would nevertheless stock his warehouse. Mindful that the strictures against imports from England and Ireland imposed by the Continental Association had taken effect on December 1, Charley took care to instruct Johnson that none of the hundreds of items ordered were "to be bought unless *All the Acts* mentioned by the continental Congress as unjust and oppressive, (and of which the repeal is solicited) should be Repealed. A partial Repeal I am satisfied will not content America," he added soberly; "now is the time for a total redress of grievances, and unless they be totally redressed, harmony and good understanding will never be re-established between the mother Country and her Colonies." Measured against those somber tones, the litany of complaints about the quality of goods previously sent with which Charley habitually closed his letters to Johnson—"the country shoes . . . were extreamly bad" and "the whole Jarr of Raisans sent to my house at Elk Ridge were totally decayed"—seems quite trivial. Far greater trials than shabby shoes and rotten raisins lay ahead.[58]

Like many other incipient patriots, both in Maryland and elsewhere, Charley retained his steadily diminishing hopes for several more months. In late January 1775 and again on March 6, he sent supplemental orders to Wallace and Company, but he balanced that optimism by supporting, as a member of the provincial convention that convened in midsummer, a range of defensive measures aimed at raising a militia, formalizing and regularizing the provisional government, and ensuring loyalty to the American cause. Yet, he still believed that there was time for the mother country to come to its senses and avoid civil war. Nor did he allow his newfound patriotism to interfere with his interests. He moved quickly to get the Carrolls' 1774 tobacco crop—141 hogsheads—

58. CCC to Wallace and Company, Jan. 8, 1775, Charles Carroll Letter-book, 1771–1833, fols. 42–46, Arents Collections.

shipped out of Maryland before nonexportation took effect on September 10 and then alerted his London agent that the rapidly worsening imperial situation might well prove advantageous to sellers by "giving a start to the market."[59]

Despite his economic concerns, Charley remained principally preoccupied with politics, as the local committees and the provisional government absorbed increasing amounts of his time. In February 1776, his public duties expanded significantly when the Continental Congress asked him to participate in a diplomatic mission to Canada for the purpose of engaging support for the American cause. Ironically, the very attributes that had contributed toward making him an outsider now recommended him for the job. His political ally, Samuel Chase, who promoted him for the position, pointed out to John Adams that the younger Carroll's religion and French education, especially his fluency in the language, would be major assets in the delicate negotiations. Although the Canadian mission itself was a failure, Charley's performance redounded to his credit both nationally and locally, and, shortly after his return to Maryland in June 1776, the convention chose him as a delegate to the Second Continental Congress.[60]

What is perhaps most remarkable about the Carrolls' support for the Revolutionary movement is that their enthusiasm persuaded them to ignore the danger to the propertied classes inherent in it. Beginning in October 1774 with the burning of the *Peggy Stewart,* a ship carrying tea owned by the Annapolis mercantile firm of Dick and Stewart, the potential for attacks on property became increasingly evident. Papa, who had always been acutely sensitive about protecting the Carrolls' worldly goods, seemed willfully to ignore the precedent suggested by firing the ship. Instead, he wholeheartedly endorsed the action as a symbol of what those who opposed the patriot cause might expect: "The Example will I hope deter others from the like Offence." Unlike the Dulanys, whose power and influence were steadily eroding, the Carrolls felt themselves to be riding the wave of the future. Describing to Papa, in October 1774, a suddenly tentative Dulany, forced by his ties to the proprietor into an increasingly negative position regarding the imperial dispute, Charley wrote exuberantly, "The Union of all America has swallowed him up in the great vortex, he follows its

59. Ibid., June 4, 1775, fols. 48–48v.

60. Paul H. Smith et al., eds., *Letters of Delegates to Congress, 1774–1789* (Washington, D.C., 1976–) III, xv–xvi, 276n. Charley also appears to have played a role in composing Maryland's Declaration of Independence. A rough draft of the document in his hand is in the Carroll Papers, MS 206.

motion, not daring to be the first mover, nor possessing a temper sufficiently intrepid to guide its course: he is carried away with the Whirlwind, he does not ride on it, nor directs the storm."[61]

The increasingly aggressive stance assumed by Papa and Charley throughout 1775 and into 1776 represented the culmination of the radical posture they had taken in opposing British policy. Only once, in December 1775, did Papa seem to apprehend what others already feared: that the dislocation within the empire and the rising anger in the colonies could lead to demagogic opportunism and social chaos. Writing to Charley after dining with Samuel Chase, Papa warned, "Chace dined with me & is with me, much talk of Politicks with Him. . . . We must Establish a Government, the Convention must say what sort of a One, Rogues & Enemies must be punished, nothing Essentiall to Generall safety Can be done as things are now."[62]

His somber mood of September 1774 forgotten, Charley seemed little impressed by the hints of an impending storm. Excited by the growing confrontation with England and invigorated by the prospect of his diplomatic mission to Canada, he commented to Papa in mid-March 1776, "Some people are still in hopes of peace, I see no probability of it." Before embarking on his Canadian journey, he composed two public letters that appeared in the March 26 and April 2 editions of *Dunlap's Maryland Gazette; or, The Baltimore General Advertiser*. Signed "CX," the essays showed Charley to be on the leading edge of proindependence sentiment by urging the establishment of a new government with clearly demarcated legislative, executive, and judicial authority. The expedient of provisional conventions like those that had governed Maryland since June of 1774 was, he argued, no longer appropriate, given England's rigid stand against meaningful compromise. "Our present government seems to be approaching fast to its dissolution; necessity during the war will introduce material changes; INDEPENDENCE, the consequence of victory, will perpetuate them." Leaving no mistake where he stood, the younger Carroll outlined some of the reforms he envisioned for the new constitution: an upper house reduced in authority but composed of men who would hold their seats for life, a more equitable form of representation for the lower house, and a weakened executive annually elected and permitted only three successive years in office. Despite the sincerity of these proposals, Charley's fundamental purpose in publishing the letters was to present independence as inevitable. Writing to Papa on May 5, from Montreal, he professed himself "anxious to hear what our Convention has done and how the

61. CCA to CCC, Oct. 21, 1774, CCC to CCA, Oct. 26, 1774, Carroll Papers, MS 206.
62. CCA to CCC, Dec. 1, 1775, ibid.

two papers signed C X are relished in Maryd. The doctrine perhaps is not so unpalatable now as when they were written: a few weeks, nay a few days make a great alteration in the political Barometer in such critical times."[63]

The Carrolls' enthusiasm put them at odds with many of the more conservative Maryland leaders, who had grown increasingly fearful of the colony's rapidly deteriorating situation. By the fall of 1775 and into 1776, widespread reports in all parts of the province told of insurrectionist activities among blacks and whites, servants and slaves, some indigenous, others instigated by the British. Accompanying them were lengthy communiqués from frightened militia commanders emphasizing the extent of desertion and disobedience, which threatened their commands' effectiveness. To some of the most perceptive Revolutionary leaders, these developments confirmed suspicions that the rebellion would unleash convulsive social tensions previously restrained by the old system of authority. They recognized that the rhetoric about liberty and their attacks on royal privilege might well come to be used on themselves, just as they had used them against Great Britain. In sum, a large segment of the provisional convention realized by the late spring of 1776 that hardly anything Britain could do would prove as threatening to their class as the Revolution itself.

Acknowledging that fear, the convention voted unanimously against Independence on May 21. Five weeks later, on June 28, the delegates reversed their vote. Until then, Maryland remained the sole colony, with the possible exception of New York, opposed to separation from the empire. Charley, who had returned to Philadelphia on June 11 from Canada and was back in Maryland by June 15, campaigned openly for Independence. Capturing the excitement of the moment Charley's ally Samuel Chase wrote John Adams: "I have not been idle. I have appealed *in writing* to the people. County after County is instructing."[64]

Charley's euphoria proved short-lived. Selected by the convention on July 4 to represent Maryland in the Continental Congress, he missed the vote on the Declaration of Independence but was present for the signing on August 2. A scant two and a half weeks later, his enthusiasm had waned rather dramatically. Unless "honest men," he confided urgently to Papa on August 20, could establish order, authority, and stability in Maryland, "anarchy will follow as a certain consequence; injustice, rapine & corruption in the seats of justice will prevail, and this Province in a short time will be involved in all the horrors of an ungovernable and revengeful Democracy and will be died with the blood of its best

63. CCC to CCA, Mar. 12, May 5, 1776, ibid.; *Dunlap's Maryland Gazette; or, The Baltimore General Advertiser*, Apr. 2, 1776.

64. Hoffman, *Spirit of Dissension*, 152–154, 163–168.

citizens."[65] No longer an outsider, Charley had moved to the vital center of politics and thus had helped to create a new reality that posed extraordinary threats to his family's propertied wealth. The allure of power had become a deadly game — the Revolution had come to Maryland. Now the Carrolls would have to ride the whirlwind.

65. CCC to CCA, Aug. 20, 1776, Carroll Papers, MS 206.

CHAPTER 9

A Broader Allegiance: The American Revolution

When they found themselves at the threshold of political power in late 1774, neither Papa nor Charley had anticipated what lay ahead. Long denied any chance to share in the governance and civic life routinely open to Protestants, the Carrolls moved to grasp the opportunities that suddenly appeared before them. The breakdown of the proprietary and imperial systems that these openings manifested concerned them only intermittently at first, but before long the momentum toward Independence forced them to confront the threats to propertied men inherent in the crisis. The upheavals unleashed as the colonies reconfigured themselves as states within a nation taught Charley, often abruptly and painfully, what he must do if he wanted his family to retain its wealth and newfound power in that brave new world. For Papa, who had tenaciously defended the Carroll fortune against arbitrary governments, religious enmity, and envy for more than half a century, the American Revolution brought a message of irrelevance: the ancient truths that had ordered his existence — loyalty to clan and family, unyielding defiance in the protection of his interests — were no longer an effective strategy. If the Carrolls were to avoid being swallowed up by "the great vortex," the Revolution demanded that old ways of doing business be discarded. Both publicly and personally, Charley and Papa would find the struggle challenging and arduous.

Early on, the Revolution impressed upon Charley the necessity to act in concert with others rather than contend with adversity in his father's fiercely independent style. Of all the alliances the younger Carroll formed after his success as First Citizen, none proved more critical to him and to the cause of the Revolution in Maryland than the relationship he developed with Samuel Chase. Chase had begun his political career in 1763 by advocating local reform in Annapolis. He entered the general assembly's lower house in 1765, having combined popular support from artisans and mechanics with backing from the powerful Dulany family. His championship of radical resistance to the Stamp Act cost him the support of the Dulanys, but his outspoken opposition to both Parliament and Maryland's proprietary government increased his political influence. He won election to the lower house in 1768 and 1773, served on Maryland's Committee of Correspondence (1773–1775), represented Maryland in the Continental Congress from 1774 to 1778, and in 1776 accompanied Charley on the congressional mission seeking support for America's rebellion from the people of Canada.

During that sojourn, Charley and Chase spent at least seventy-five days in each other's company and shouldered the main responsibility for the negotiations, especially after May 11, when the other two commissioners, Benjamin Franklin and Charley's Cousin Jack (now Father John) Carroll left. The two men provide a study in contrasts. Most obviously, Chase, robust and ruddy, stood six feet tall, whereas slight and slender Charley barely measured five feet six. Moreover, their manners matched their appearances: Charley, a cultured, refined continental gentleman, must have seemed almost effete next to the boisterous, rowdy, convivial Chase, whose "impious language" and "irregular conduct" had led to his suspension and eventual expulsion from Annapolis's Forensic Club in the early 1760s.[1]

The two men differed markedly in background as well. Chase's father, the Reverend Thomas Chase (c. 1703–1779), served as rector of St. Paul's, Baltimore's Anglican parish, beginning in 1745, but his remuneration — perhaps one hundred pounds sterling a year — did not permit him to live at the level of gentility to which he aspired. That the Reverend Mr. Chase found it difficult to reconcile his dreams and his means is evident from his incarceration for financial problems on two occasions: in 1746–1747, he was in jail for debt, and he was jailed again in 1765, on charges of misappropriating funds from the estate of a relative. Neither experience caused him to moderate his expenditures, however, and his most enduring legacy to Samuel would be a burning desire for wealth and a secure place within the gentry. Finally, the virulent anti-Catholicism that animated Thomas Chase during the 1750s and 1760s would certainly have made him anathema to the Carrolls. Fanatically convinced that Maryland's Catholics posed a real and present danger during the Seven Years' War, the elder Chase "scrupled not," in the words of a contemporary observer, "to intimate from the Pulpit to

1. Quoted in James Haw et al., *Stormy Patriot: The Life of Samuel Chase* (Baltimore, 1980), 11. For my treatment of Chase's background, early career, and personality, I have drawn on the very fine analysis contained in this volume, 1–16.

A Broader Allegiance

his Congregation that the State or Situation of the Protestants in this Province was at that time very little different from that of the Protestants in Ireland at the Eve of the Irish Massacre."[2]

Beneath these tremendous differences, however, there existed certain intriguing similarities, although it is unlikely that either man recognized them. For one thing, each had suffered the early loss of his mother: Chase never knew his at all, since she perished at his birth, and, in a very real sense, Charley "lost" his when he was sent away from Maryland at the age of ten; although Mama did not die until he was twenty-four, he never saw her again. Deprived of a maternal presence, both youngsters were left under the care and direction of their respective fathers, and in both cases these paternal personalities left an indelible imprint upon their offspring.

Although the Reverend Mr. Thomas Chase and Charles Carroll of Annapolis harbored similar ambitions for themselves and their sons in education and status, they necessarily followed different paths in achieving these goals. Lacking the wherewithal to send Samuel abroad to study, or even to a colonial institution, the clergyman, an accomplished classical scholar and gifted teacher, educated his boy himself. While Charley studied Horace, Virgil, and Cicero under the watchful tutelage of Jesuit priests at St. Omers, Rheims, Bourges, and Paris, Samuel Chase learned his Latin and Greek at his father's knee in the Baltimore boardinghouse where the two of them lived until the mid-1750s. In 1759, eighteen-year-old Sam Chase, having completed that course, scraped together enough money — between thirty-five and seventy-five pounds sterling — to secure a clerk's position in the successful Annapolis law office of John Hall and his partner, John Hammond, and moved to the capital to make himself a lawyer. During the same period when Charley was striving to maintain himself genteelly in London on the three hundred pounds sterling a year his father allowed him, Samuel Chase, who received nothing from his father, found it so difficult to meet his living expenses that he was occasionally reduced to selling some of his personal belongings. The attitudes of these young men toward the law differed

2. Gov. Horatio Sharpe to Lord Baltimore, Dec. 16, 1758, in William Hand Browne et al., eds., *Archives of Maryland* (Baltimore, 1883–), IX, 315–318, quoted in Haw et al., *Stormy Patriot*, 6. The Irish rising of 1641 began with an attack on the Protestant settlers of Ulster in October of that year. No reliable figures for the number of dead exist, but one modern authority places the number at two thousand. As vile as the actual massacre was, contemporary accounts quickly elevated the number of Protestants killed by Catholic treachery to highly exaggerated levels. These estimates were sustained and embellished by subsequent writers and persist in partisan tracts into the present. R. F. Foster, *Modern Ireland, 1600–1972* (London, 1988), 85–86.

as markedly as their means of pursuing it. Residing in the Inner Temple with access to the finest legal training available to a man of his time, Charley disdained the profession as inherently villainous, far too passionate, and likely to embroil its practitioners in the countless distasteful dilemmas of the human condition, few of which would be amenable to rational resolution. Toiling away in a law office in Annapolis, riding the county court circuit with his mentor John Hall, litigating case after minor case that brought him only a pittance in fees, Samuel Chase saw a legal career as an avenue to wealth and influence.

Both Charley and Chase had been shaped by their experiences as outsiders who resented the proprietary government that marginalized them. Although set apart for different reasons — religion in Charley's case, a perennial lack of money in Chase's — the personality traits each man displayed in dealing with ostracism cemented their alliance and made it indispensable to the success of the Maryland leadership's Revolutionary strategy. Later, when the most severe crises had passed, the same attributes would make inevitable an irreparable rift between them. By temperament, training, and experience, Charley found direct confrontation distasteful and sought to avoid it. Once the Revolution invited him into the political arena, he consistently preferred to conduct the business of governance in the company of educated and reasonable men in an environment removed from the pressure and demands of the populace.

Not so Samuel Chase. Kept an outsider by the requirements of the code of gentility rather than by the penal code, Chase intended to use whatever means were necessary to acquire the wealth that would permit him to live and to wield power as a gentleman. These desires frequently moved him to make impulsive decisions that his finances were unable to support, such as the construction of an elegant three-story mansion in Annapolis that he could not finish and reckless speculation in land. Moreover, where the Carroll fortune allowed Charley to give naive rhetorical allegiance to the ideals of disinterestedness and independence as the true motives for public service, Samuel Chase — with no fortune at all, consummate ambition, and, by the end of 1776, four motherless children to support — never enjoyed the luxury of espousing such notions, nor did he ever deceive himself about the benefits to be gained through the acquisition of political influence.

At the same time, Chase had his own set of convenient delusions. Despite his determination to attain his rightful place among men of property, his impecunious youth, reinforced by the straitened circumstances of most of his clients in his early legal career, gave him a genuine sympathy for "the people." By casting himself as their "champion" in the tumultuous fray of the lower house, Chase managed, for a time at least, to conceal from his colleagues — and perhaps even from himself—the undeniable self-interest that drove him. Before the war ended, Charley and Chase would come to despise each other for the very characteristics that had once made them effective allies — Charley's posture of disinterestedness and virtue and Chase's avarice and his ability to manipulate popular prejudices and resentments. But that division lay several years in the future. In the heady atmosphere of 1776, the dangerous course upon which they had embarked and their intense pursuit of apparently common goals compelled unity.

When Charley and Chase got back to Maryland in the second week of June after making their report to Congress, they worked together assiduously to persuade the convention to change the instructions it had adopted in late May binding the congressional delegates to vote against Independence. Both had by then witnessed a good deal of chaos in upstate New York and Canada, precipitated by the American invasion begun in September 1775 to gain control of the latter. Hence, neither man became unduly alarmed by the social unrest that had developed in Maryland during their absence and given such pause to their colleagues. Urged in Philadelphia to secure the reversal of Maryland's instructions and aflame with the excitement of revolution, Charley and Chase descended on the convention like a whirlwind. During the next several weeks, they made the most of the enhanced reputations they had gained on the front lines of the confrontation with England and their consultation with General Washington in New York on the way home.[3] By June 27, as Charley told Papa in a letter written early the next morning, the pressures unleashed in the convention — struggling with the issues of Independence, organizing the militia, and needing to form a permanent government — had grown so intense that "it was necessary to adjourn the house to prevent too great heats." By then, however, he knew that he and Chase had won the day on the all-important matter of separation from Great Britain. They had the votes, and Charley confidently predicted the outcome: "The instructions to our Deputies in Congress will certainly be rescinded."[4]

Another item of business, the seriousness of which Charley overlooked in his June 28 euphoria, claimed the attention of the convention on the same day it settled the question of Independence. Unrest on Maryland's lower Eastern Shore had risen to such a pitch that the delegates found it necessary to order militia

3. Writing to Papa on June 11, 1776, from Philadelphia, Charley reported that he had "just had the pleasure of an hour's conversation with Gen. Washington at N. York." Carroll Papers, MS 206, MdHi.

4. CCC to CCA, June 28, 1776, ibid.

units to Somerset County "to secure obedience to the resolves of the convention and peace and good order in that county" by disarming "all persons disaffected," taking them into custody, and bringing them before the proper authorities.[5] Although the turmoil across the bay had not yet intruded into Charley's thoughts, its growth and persistence would eventually become a major concern. Two other subjects the convention addressed before it adjourned on July 6 affected Charley directly. On July 3, the delegates prescribed that elections should be held on August 1 to select members for a ninth convention, whose chief task would be to draft a new plan of government. The next day, July 4, the convention selected a new slate of representatives to the Second Continental Congress — Robert Alexander, Samuel Chase, Thomas Johnson, William Paca, Thomas Stone, Matthew Tilghman, and Charles Carroll of Carrollton.

Charley professed that he accepted his new assignment reluctantly, having so recently returned from Canada, but his subsequent enthusiasm belied the weary resignation he feigned upon being appointed "a Deputy to Congress." Sometime around July 12, he and Chase left for Philadelphia, arriving on July 17 and taking their seats in Congress the next day. Appointed to the Board of War, probably because of his experiences in Canada, where he had observed both the difficulties of command and the problems of supply, he was brought face-to-face with trying to organize and equip a military machine that could challenge the forces of the British Empire. Equally daunting, Congress had to draft a plan of confederation that balanced the competing interests of the thirteen states, particularly with regard to voting and apportioning financial responsibility for the war. As he reported soberly to Papa on August 1, "We are engaged in very important business: I am in hopes justice & true policy will at last prevail over distinct & separate interests — if it should not, I will predict, that a confederation formed on partial & interested views will not be lasting."[6]

The seminal moment in Charley's life took place in Congress on August 2, 1776, the day after he wrote that letter, although at the time he did not comment

5. *Proceedings of the Conventions of the Province of Maryland, Held at the City of Annapolis, in 1774, 1775, and 1776* (Baltimore, 1836), 175–176.

6. CCC to CCA, July 5, Aug. 1, 1776, Carroll Papers, MS 206. Charley apparently returned from Canada with the idea that he had become something of a military expert. While still in Philadelphia in June, he took, in his words, "the liberty" of writing to General Horatio Gates, whom he thought would "probably be appointed to the chief command in Canada," to offer a few "hints" based on his own recent experiences in that country. The letter may be found in Kate Mason Rowland, *The Life of Charles Carroll of Carrollton, 1737–1832, with His Correspondence and Public Papers* (New York, 1898), I, 174–176.

on it. But then neither did any of the other men who signed the Declaration of Independence, with the possible exception of John Adams. Writing to his brother-in-law, Richard Cranch, the day the document was signed, Adams exulted over the "astonishing" alteration in the "Prejudices, Passions, Sentiments, and Principles" it represented — a change that had made the people and the states "republican" and had broken them of "Idolatry to Monarchs and servility to Aristocratical Pride." Adams's jubilation aside, Congress did not order the distribution of authenticated copies bearing the names of all the delegates until January 18, 1777, for fear of exposing the signatories to British retribution.[7]

Half a century later, Charley would assert that, in placing his name upon the Declaration of Independence, he had, as the only Roman Catholic signer, struck a blow for "not only our independence of England but the toleration of all sects professing the Christian religion and communicating to them all equal rights." However, nothing in his papers suggests that he entertained such thoughts on August 2, 1776.[8] Nevertheless, in the context of his life and the whole sweep of the Carroll experience, Charley's signing of the Declaration of Independence becomes a powerful metaphor for a personal mental and emotional transition of which he was as yet only dimly aware. Up to that moment, the burden of Carroll history had been conveyed to him through the filter of his father's memories. That history stressed the long train of sieges that the Carrolls had been forced to withstand, relying exclusively on their own wits and tenacity. There were no larger institutions beyond the family upon which Charley's forebears could rely — not the English government or English law, not the proprietary family or the Maryland assembly, and ultimately not even their own wealth. Each succeeding generation had accepted as its fundamental obligation the defense and perpetuation of the family. The world in which the Carrolls lived from

7. John Adams to Richard Cranch, Aug. 2, 1776, in Paul H. Smith et al., eds., *Letters of Delegates to Congress, 1774–1789* (Washington, D.C., 1976–), IV, 604–605; Worthington Chauncey Ford et al., eds., *Journals of the Continental Congress, 1774–1789* (Washington, D.C., 1904–1937), VII, 48 (hereafter *JCC*); John Hancock to the States, Jan. 31, 1777, in Smith et al., eds., *Letters of Delegates,* VI, 171.

8. Quoted in Joseph Gurn, *Charles Carroll of Carrollton, 1737–1832* (New York, 1932), 261. Charley wrote the words in 1829 in response to an overture made to him by the District of Columbia chapter of The Friends of Civil and Religious Liberty of Ireland.

The last letter Charley wrote Papa from Philadelphia that has been found is dated Aug. 1, 1776 (Carroll Papers, MS 206). He appears to have remained in Congress until about August 10. On August 15, he was elected to represent the city of Annapolis in the ninth convention and took his seat on the August 17. *Proceedings of the Conventions,* 212, 220.

the days of the Kildares and the Ormonds through the fall of the Stuarts and up to the final quarter of the eighteenth century increasingly proscribed their means of advancement and survival. Nevertheless, the Settler and Charles Carroll of Annapolis single-mindedly aggrandized their position through the accumulation of property and the shrewd manipulation of economic opportunities. Ever mindful of the past, they planted a new Carroll dynasty in a colony that kept Catholics vulnerable and off balance by depriving them of the rights and protections their Protestant counterparts took for granted. Relegated to the provincial periphery, they distrusted the governments in which they could not participate and maintained a wary distance from the society that excluded them.

But in the sweltering heat of that Philadelphia August — according to Charley, the city was "insupportably hot" — more than Britain's North American empire melted away.[9] Although he did not yet realize it, the younger Carroll had begun to forge a broader allegiance that extended beyond family and linked him irrevocably, not to other defiant Irish Catholics as with his ancestors in 1641 and 1689, but to a diverse band of men determined to create a republic. In signing the Declaration of Independence, Charley cast his lot and tied his family's future to a new enterprise shorn of the atavistic and irredentist characteristics that had animated the Carroll past. Stepping beyond the shadows of ancient prejudices, Charley asserted a place for his lineage in the sun of the new nation. On August 2, 1776, this descendant of a long line of Irish rebels became a full-fledged member of America's Revolutionary elite. And within less than three weeks he had begun to understand how steep and terrifying a price he might have to pay for it.

Returning to Maryland about August 10, Charley found confusion and disorder. So many irregularities had attended the voting for members of the ninth convention that ballots were ordered recast in five counties. To Charley's surprise, and certainly to his dismay, the Anne Arundel County voters declined to elect him, although he did manage to win a seat in the convention as a delegate from Annapolis.[10]

9. CCC to CCA, Aug. 1, 1776, Carroll Papers, MS 206.
10. As part of its call for the election of a new convention, the eighth convention specified that Annapolis and Baltimore Town would, for the first time, be allowed to choose two representatives each. As a consequence, the voters in those places were prohibited from participating in the balloting for delegates from their respective counties, Anne Arundel and Baltimore (*Proceedings of the Conventions,* 183). The elections in Anne Arundel County commenced on Aug. 1, 1776, while Charley was still in Philadelphia. By the following day, the Council of Safety, alarmed by the clearly observable trend in the voting, wrote Maryland's delegates in Congress to advise them that the county's voters

Despite the worrisome rejection at the polls of some of Charley's important allies, particularly Thomas Johnson, the seventy-eight men who formally assembled as the ninth convention in mid-August remained solidly representative of Maryland's traditional political and economic elite. On August 17, these delegates appointed a committee to draft a declaration of rights and a new state constitution.[11] Chosen along with Charley for this task were four of his old fee controversy allies, Matthew Tilghman, William Paca, Charles Carroll, Barrister, and Samuel Chase, and two men of prominent planter families, Robert Goldsborough and George Plater. The committee had barely begun its work, when Charley experienced the first major shock of just how volatile Maryland's politics had become in their new Revolutionary setting. On August 22 the *Maryland Gazette* would print a series of instructions that had been sent to the delegates of Anne Arundel County. Signed by 885 freeman, these directives called for a more open and democratic form of government. Unable to ignore such a large number of freeholders, the county's delegates prepared responses on August 19 for publication in the same issue of the newspaper. One delegate, Papa's Elk Ridge neighbor Rezin Hammond, did not object to the freemen's proposals, but the other three, Samuel Chase, Brice T. B. Worthington, and Charles Carroll, Barrister, voiced their opposition to the demands because of the danger they posed to property and liberty. With the express hope that the people would reconsider and rescind the instructions, Chase, Worthington, and the Barrister called for a public meeting on August 26.[12]

It is a measure of Charley's growing anxiety that he tried to stage-manage this gathering to prevent the faction behind the instructions from turning the occasion to their own purposes. For the younger Carroll, countering the threat meant neutralizing the influence of the fourth Anne Arundel County delegate, Rezin Hammond. Entering Maryland politics in 1774 as a delegate to the first convention, Hammond, a substantial planter, quickly became known for his aggressiveness both in opposing England and in behalf of democratic reforms. Once characterized by Papa, with whom he had engaged in numerous bound-

would probably not elect either Thomas Johnson, William Paca, or Charles Carroll of Carrollton. Council of Safety to the Maryland Deputies, Aug. 2, 1776, in Browne et al., eds., *Archives of Maryland*, XII, 163, quoted in Ronald Hoffman, *A Spirit of Dissension: Economics, Politics, and the Revolution in Maryland* (Baltimore, 1973), 170.

11. Edward C. Papenfuse and Gregory A. Stiverson, eds., *The Decisive Blow Is Struck: A Facsimile Edition of the Proceedings of the First Constitutional Convention of 1776 and the First Maryland Constitution* (Annapolis, Md., 1977), n.p.

12. *Maryland Gazette* (Annapolis), Aug. 22, 1776.

ary disputes, as "a Noisy obstinate fool," Hammond subsequently behaved in ways that solidly confirmed the elder Carroll in that opinion.[13]

During the summer of 1776, Hammond endorsed a lengthy "sketch of a form of government" prepared and circulated by members of the Anne Arundel County militia. This document advocated such democratic innovations as the popular election of local officials and militia officers. Then he campaigned successfully for a seat in the ninth convention by urging militiamen "to lay down their arms if they were denied the privilege of voting for it was their right and they ought not to be deprived of it."[14] Well aware of Hammond's activities, Charley feared that, "unless gentlemen will take some trouble and exert themselves a Governt. will be formed most destructive to Liberty & Property." Indeed, it was the "duty" of such men "to their country . . . to exert their utmost endeavours to save it from the danger with which it is now threatened by the secret machinations of evil and designing men."[15]

On August 20, two days before the announcement in the press of the meeting called by Chase, Worthington, and the Barrister, Hammond busied himself "persuading the People" not to attend. Urging Papa to prevail upon his neighbors to be present in Annapolis on the appointed day, Charley underscored his belief that the stakes were high: "If two or 3 hundred of the substantial freeholders were to mee[t] a check might be given in time to the desperate designs of the Hammonds & such fellows who are endeavouring to involve the country in the utmost confusion in this time of danger & distress." On August 23, two days before the gathering, he warned his father again: "Unless the Howards and gentlemen of Character [&] property will bestir themselves, and counteract the malicious falsehoods that are propogated about this county, & other counties, it will be impossible to have a good governt." Charley had begun to comprehend the dangerous instability of the situation amid which he and other like-minded members of Maryland's Revolutionary leadership intended to devise and then impose a new system of governance. He now saw that other men — men he believed by birth and breeding ought to know better — might embrace a more democratic governing structure to secure popular support for their bid for power. They would surely enflame the people and threaten the fragile authority

13. CCA to CCC, Nov. 26, 1773, Carroll Papers, MS 206.

14. *Md. Gaz.*, July 18, 1776; Deposition of Thomas Henry Howard, Aug. 27, 1776 (*Calendar of Maryland State Papers*, no. 4, *The Red Books*, part 2 [Annapolis, 1953], 82). Samuel Godman gave similar testimony about Hammond on the same day. For more information on Hammond, see Hoffman, *Spirit of Dissension*, 170–177.

15. CCC to CCA, Aug. 20, 1776, Carroll Papers, MS 206.

that the governing authorities currently exercised. "Men of desperate fortunes, or of desperate & wicked designs are endeavouring under cloak of procuring great privileges for the People to introduce a levelling scheme, by wh they (these evil men) are sure to profit."[16]

Despite Charley's efforts, the three delegates lost their bid to rescind the instructions and resigned. New elections on September 4 returned Chase and Worthington but replaced Charles Carroll, Barrister, with John Hall, a supporter of Rezin Hammond and a member of the faction that had precipitated the entire episode. Apparently resigned to saving two of the three contested positions, Charley remarked to his father two days later: "Our internal affairs, I mean of this Province, seem to be but in an indifferent way — I am afraid there are some men in our Convention not so honest as they should be. It is certain we go on very slowly."[17]

Throughout the Anne Arundel election dispute, the committee constituted by the convention to draft a plan of government continued its deliberations. When Charles Carroll, Barrister, lost his seat, the convention added Thomas Johnson, Jr., and Robert T. Hooe to the committee. The presence of Johnson, who had been rejected by the Anne Arundel County voters on August 1 but was subsequently elected from Caroline County, might have compensated somewhat for the Barrister's absence. On August 24, the drafting committee submitted to the convention the forty-four articles of the Declaration and Charter of Rights and within a fortnight reported their "Constitution and Form of Government." Giving the documents only a cursory reading, the convention postponed consideration to a later date to allow Johnson, Chase, and Paca to attend Congress in Philadelphia. Uncertain about the reception the plan of government would receive, the younger Carroll worried to the elder that the proposal did not seem to enjoy widespread support within the convention. He was further dismayed when the plan's opponents passed a resolution that the documents be printed and distributed throughout the province for "the consideration of the people at large."[18]

The ideological preferences of the committee, unmistakable in the document it devised, were the basis for the most conservative of all state constitutions developed during the Revolutionary era. By a series of high property qualifications, the draft restricted officeholding exclusively to the wealthy, propertied elements

16. CCC to CCA, Aug. 20, 23, 1776, ibid.

17. CCC to CCA, Sept. 6, 1776, ibid.

18. CCC to CCA, [Sept.] 13, 1776, ibid.; Hoffman, *Spirit of Dissension*, 180; Papenfuse and Stiverson, eds., *Decisive Blow Is Struck*.

of the society. A £500 real or personal property requirement limited eligibility for the House of Delegates to fewer than 15 percent of the province's free white males. Similarly, seats in the Senate and on the governor's council required owning a minimum of £1,000, a prerequisite that only 7–8 percent of that population could meet. Moreover, senators were to be chosen by an elected electoral college made up of men possessing £500. Elections for the Senate were to be held every seven years and for the lower house every three. Finally, the governor, to be chosen annually by the legislature, had to possess property worth £5,000.[19]

By the time the convention finally got around to considering the form of government early in October, Charley had begun to fear that something truly horrible might happen. The Continental army was in disarray, the military situation was rapidly deteriorating, and social disorder approaching anarchy increasingly plagued Maryland and the other fledgling states. In the absence of a governing authority capable of imposing order upon the distracted times and fragmented people, threats against men of property mounted. Forecasting the impending storm, the younger Carroll undoubtedly shocked his father on October 4 with the depth of his anxiety and despair: "In my opinion (entre nous) our affairs are desperate & nothing but peace with GB on tolerably reasonable terms can save us from destruction." As much as he feared the disintegration of America's military forces, Charley perceived equally grave dangers to the country from within. Not only were the colonies at odds with each other, but each of them was also fractured internally with "such a spirit of disunion & discord" that even in the unlikely event of success against the mother country, he predicted, "We shall be rent to pieces by civil wars & factions." The impossibility of then establishing free governments was, he declared grimly, "self-evident." [20]

The younger Carroll had clearly underestimated the social upheaval a war for Independence would unleash. Part and parcel of his transformation from outsider to insider, his decision to support Independence was the product of his finely honed Enlightenment mind and his family's long-thwarted desire for political power. His ambitions, inflamed by his increasing acceptance as an actor rather than just an exceedingly well-informed observer, encouraged him to ig-

19. Papenfuse and Stiverson, eds., *Decisive Blow Is Struck*. The earliest surviving draft of the constitution is a copy sent by Samuel Chase to John Dickinson for comment and suggestions on Sept. 29, 1776. Papenfuse and Stiverson, eds., *Decisive Blow Is Struck;* Constitutional Records: from the Charter of 1632 and the Act of Toleration of 1649 through the Constitution of 1851, Microfilm Collection of Early State Records: Library of Congress and University of North Carolina, MSA SC M 3145, MdAA.

20. CCC to CCA, [Oct.] 4, 1776, Carroll Papers, MS 206.

nore some of the difficulties endemic to revolutions. Men who had been active in the bitter, yearlong congressional debate over separation from Great Britain greeted Independence more realistically. Recognizing the severity of the trials ahead, John Adams somberly acknowledged that "Calamities still more wasting and Distresses yet more dreadfull" awaited America, and freely admitted that giving "unbounded Power" to the people whom he knew to be "extreamly addicted to Corruption and Venality" made him apprehensive. Others, like Philadelphian Robert Morris, voted for Independence but continued to hope for reconciliation. Certainly, few members of the Congress were as sanguine as Samuel Adams, who asserted with cavalier exuberance in late July 1776, "Was there ever a Resolution brot about, especially so important as this, without great internal Tumults & violent Convulsions!"[21]

If Charley was not alone in having second thoughts, none of his fellow signers of the Declaration of Independence (so far as is known) expressed his doubts with such vehemence or identified so explicitly the root cause of the disorder. What seemed plain to the younger Carroll was that ambitious men, determined to advance themselves at all costs, were appealing directly to the people, encouraging them to reject a constitution that kept authority in the hands of the propertied elite in favor of a more democratic form of governance. In Charley's view, this behavior was nothing more than an expedient, self-interested ploy bound to produce disastrous consequences. Writing to his father on October 4, he vented his contempt for such men: "I execrate the detestable villany of designing men, who under the specious & sacred name of popularity are endeavouring to work themselves in to power & profit, and to accomplish this their end, want to establish a most ruinous system of Governt."[22]

Two weeks later, Charley's spirits had reached their nadir. Convinced that the

21. John Adams to Abigail Adams, July 3, 1776, Robert Morris to Joseph Reed, July 21, 1776, Samuel Adams to Benjamin Kent, July 27, 1776, in Smith et al., eds., *Letters of Delegates*, IV, 373–375, 510–513, 551–552, quoted in Merrill Jensen, *The Founding of a Nation: A History of the American Revolution, 1763–1776* (New York, 1968), 702–704.

22. CCC to CCA, Oct. 4, 1776, Carroll Papers, MS 206. Early in September, Caesar Rodney of Delaware assigned to the Almighty the task of returning to the patriot fold "The Bulk of the people . . . lead astray from a Virtuous persuit by the Art and Cunning of Wicked and designing men. . . . more industrious than the Honest and Virtuous." Assessing the state of affairs in October, South Carolinian Edward Rutledge advocated hanging Quakers if they refused to take the Continental currency and predicted that a defeat of Washington's troops would bring the country to "the Brink of a Revolt." Caesar Rodney to Thomas Rodney, Sept. 11, 1776, Edward Rutledge to Robert R. Livingston, Oct. 2, 1776, in Smith et al., eds., *Letters of Delegates*, V, 134, 295.

delegates were about to reject his committee's plan of government in favor of democratic experimentation, he could only hope that reconciliation with Great Britain "on safe terms" could be negotiated. "If the colonies will not accept of such terms, should they be offered, they will be ruined, not so much by the calamities of war, as by intestine divisions and the bad governts. wh I foresee will take place in most of the united States: they will be simple Democracies, of all governts. the worst, and will end as all other Democracies have, in despotism." His pessimistic outlook had not improved two days later, when he informed his father that the convention had made some marginal progress by agreeing to a two-house legislature. He found less pleasing the reduction of the Senate's term from seven to five years and that of the lower house from three years to one. "God knows," he told Papa morosely, "what sort of a govt. we shall get." [23]

What appears remarkable in retrospect is that the two alterations in the form of government Charley mentioned were the only important changes made in the committee's draft. After several more weeks of discussion the convention adopted the constitution on November 8. By consolidating power exclusively in the hands of the propertied elite, the document secured the upper class's retention of power. Without question, the gentry's control over the drafting of the constitution ensured its continued dominance of governance.[24] Although Charley found writing the constitution a harrowing experience, the highly conservative structure of government that ultimately emerged reassured and steadied him. One thing is certain — throughout the remainder of the Revolution, he never again exhibited such a distracted state of mind.

Even Papa found Charley's anxiety excessive: "I agree our [Af]fairs have a very bad appearance," he told his son, but added comfortingly, "I do not think them desperate." [25] Charley believed differently. In the fall of 1776, he had confronted the grisly specter of anarchy and a disruption so profound that it might revolutionize the social order in ways that he had not remotely anticipated during earlier, headier days. And from that terrifying moment of recognition, Charley learned that his interests now transcended clan and family to bond with the cause of men of great property. He now understood that, if such men did not close ranks to combat the internal and external threats of the Revolution, they faced the very real possibility of losing everything, including their lives.

Having established a constitution that preserved the traditional prerogatives and privileges of the propertied elite, Maryland's Revolutionary leaders per-

23. CCC to CCA, Oct. 18, 20, 1776, Carroll Papers, MS 206.
24. Hoffman, *Spirit of Dissension*, 179–183.
25. CCA to CCC, Oct. 9, 1776, Carroll Papers, MS 206.

A Broader Allegiance

ceived that they must secure the acquiescence of an unsettled populace, a sizable portion of which often appeared dangerously disaffected. Failure to gain popular support would place both themselves and the Revolution in jeopardy. To rally the people to the cause and to win their endorsement of the new constitutional order, the leadership recognized that it had to give a real stake in the outcome to those who would be asked to fight and die to achieve it.

Daniel of St. Thomas Jenifer, once a proprietary official and now, like Charley, chosen to serve as a senator in the state government of Maryland, succinctly captured the situation the Revolutionary leadership faced in a letter to the younger Carroll on February 2, 1777, just before the new government convened. In Jenifer's view, the government was weak and unpopular, and would be unable to act effectively because the constitution's officeholding requirements deprived it of too many of the men best able to deal with the crisis. Even more disturbing: "The Senate does not appear to me to be the child of the people at large and therefore will not be supported by them." Once the assembly levied the taxes necessary for supporting the war effort, Jenifer expected an uproar that might ultimately bring down the government. "Taxes must be laid and the money made a legal tender," he wrote, but because those measures inevitably "may not alike suit every man hence will arise diversity of sentiment, warmth will ensue and your government immediately be dissolved."[26]

With these somber thoughts in mind, Charley took his seat in the Senate on February 5, 1777. The only interlude of sweet satisfaction he might conceivably have experienced occurred on February 14, when the House of Delegates and Senate elected Papa to a seat on the governor's council. The elder Carroll demurred, citing his advanced age as an insuperable barrier to effective service.[27]

It was a decision he would soon regret. The Maryland government began moving almost immediately to accomplish the twin goals of cohering the people's support for the Revolution and new constitution and meeting the state's financial obligations for the war effort. The legislation enacted for these purposes during the first half of 1777 constituted a radical fiscal program that reapportioned the tax burden and substantially reduced the level of personal debt owed to creditors within the province. Both measures required sacrifices from the propertied class that would be widely known and readily recognizable.

26. Browne et al., eds., *Archives of Maryland*, XVI, 108–109.

27. *Votes and Proceedings of the House of Delegates of the State of Maryland*, February Session, 1777, 14 (hereafter *VPHD*); CCA to Daniel of St. Thomas Jenifer and Thomas Sprigg Wootton, Feb. 18, 1777, Shea Collection, Georgetown University Library, Washington, D.C.

Adopted in February, the new system of taxation shifted the burden of assessment from polls to land and slaves, or, in essence, from the majority of the people to the planter elite. The second, a legal tender bill enacted in March, formed the centerpiece of the state's Revolutionary fiscal policy. This law authorized the repayment of loans made in pounds sterling with depreciated Continental and Maryland paper currency at a fixed rate of exchange. Charley disliked the latter policy intensely, and, for that reason and out of deference to his father, he spoke against the legal tender bill and voted against it when it came before the Senate. He was the only senator to do so.[28] Then he made his peace with it, because he understood what was being done and why. The wealthy creditor class, of which his family was the richest member, would have to make major sacrifices: if they did not bend in this situation, Charley believed, the Revolution would break them. As he put it succinctly in a letter to Papa in the fall of 1777, "The law suits the multitude: individuals must submit to partial losses; no great revolutions can happen in a State without revolutions, or mutations of private property."[29]

Papa did not share his son's perception of Revolutionary realities. Having spent a lifetime building the Carroll fortune, much of it based on lending money, and having exercised unstinting vigilance in protecting his wealth from the machinations of would-be saboteurs, the elder Carroll saw in the legal tender act the most insidious attack on property imaginable. If the assembly could pass this bill, he raged, what was to prevent them from deciding that "no man shall hold above 500 a[cres] of Land? that He shall sell all above that Quantity at the rate of £100 Curt: pr: Ct:, Why should not the Land Holder be obliged to part

28. *Votes and Proceedings of the Senate of the State of Maryland,* February Session, 1777, 44 (hereafter *VPS*). Reporting on Charley's protest several months later, a more objective observer commented pointedly on the reaction that continued opposition to the tender law by the Carrolls was likely to bring:

> The bill passed for Payment of Sterling Debts with Congress and Convention Money will be attended with the most distressing Consequences to many Persons, especially to the friends of Government, who have large Sums upon loan. Several of the Senate, whether from *Principle* or *Interest,* I know not, expressed, without Doors, their highest Disapprobation of this Act, but only Carol of Carolton had resolution to oppose it in the proper Place. He animadverted on the Injustice thereof, & protested against the same being passed into a Law, but his Objections procured him no great Reputation as it was generally believed that he was not altogether actuated by Sentiment alone.

William Eddis to Robert Eden, July 23, 1777, Fisher Transcripts, MdHi.

29. CCC to CCA, Nov. 8, 1777, Carroll Papers, MS 206.

with His Land as well as the Sterling Money Holder be obliged to Part with His Sterling Money?" In Papa's view there was nothing but dangerous leveling in the measure; the policy was a pernicious attack on property, and the men who supported it were "pickpockets and thieves." Caring not a fig for what his son insisted were the necessities of the times, the old man would not, as he later vowed, "let the tender law sleep, nor the rogues who have taken the advantage of it, nor the men who ought to repeal it."[30]

Its obvious aim of exacting a high toll from large moneylenders made the legal tender act a lightning rod of Revolutionary attention and comment. James Tilghman drew a sardonically accurate assessment of the measure in a letter to his brother Matthew in February 1777. Both men were well positioned to understand the impact the financial legislation would have on creditors like the Carrolls. Although suspected of loyalist sympathies, James had served on the Pennsylvania council until 1776, and he still lived in Philadelphia, where he kept himself informed about the deliberations of the Continental Congress. An early supporter of First Citizen, Matthew had subsequently chaired all but one of Maryland's conventions, led various delegations to Congress, and taken his seat in the first Maryland Senate just before he received his brother's letter. Reflecting on the recent sharp rise in Philadelphia prices, James Tilghman observed that, while farmers, tradesmen, and laborers could counter such increases by charging more themselves, "the man who lives upon his Rents or his Interest must go to destruction." As James saw it:

> The moneyed men are in a manner ruined, Even those who have been so guarded as to take their Securities in sterling cannot escape For the Congress have recommended to the Assemblies to oblige the receipt of Continental currency in discharge of sterling at 66-2/3 as I hear And our assembly have gone farther. They have made sterling debts Dischargeable at 55 p[er]Cent So that two thirds at least of every sterling debt must be lost. I suppose something of the same kind will be done with you, which I mistake not the man, will [put] Charles Carrolls Patriotism to the Test. In[deed it] would try any man to have all his care and attention So disappointed. God send a change Soon and for the better is the wish and prayer of.[31]

James Tilghman had pegged both Charles Carrolls. While Charles Carroll of Annapolis found the tender law and his son's acceptance of it a trial of consider-

30. CCA to CCC, Mar. 18, 1777, CCA to Daniel of St. Thomas Jenifer, July 30, 1779, ibid.

31. James Tilghman to his brother, Feb. 18, 1777, Revolutionary War Collection, MdHi.

able magnitude, Charles Carroll of Carrollton regarded the measure as a crucial test of the Revolutionary leadership's capacity to navigate the surging waters of Revolutionary upheaval. Perhaps some members of the gentry and general assembly would, as his father predicted, take advantage of the statute by reducing their debts with depreciated currency, but he did not think such abuses would be substantial. More important, he considered the possibility irrelevant. For the younger Carroll, the critical issue was, not what some members of the elite might do for private gain, but rather what steps he and his colleagues in the Revolutionary leadership must take to ensure their survival and, if lucky enough to manage that, to retain their privileges. The future he had glimpsed with such sudden and alarming clarity during the writing of the Maryland constitution had convinced him that protecting the wealthy, propertied class from the social disruption unleashed by the Revolution demanded acquiescence in the enactment of extreme measures.

Not surprisingly, Charley's position and the arguments he used to justify it outraged Papa. That the son whom he had shaped so carefully and for whom he had planned so diligently, and for whom he had such great affection, should in this crisis decline to stand firm and should argue instead that in Revolutionary times a potentially roiling populace must be placated — struck him as truly incomprehensible. Likewise, Charley found equally maddening his father's obstinate refusal to accept his reasoning and to abide by his instructions to refrain, for safety's sake, from publicly protesting the law.

For the next several years the two men argued their points strenuously and with total candor. Writing to Papa, Charley spoke eloquently for the wealthiest element of the aristocracy, articulating its rationale and explaining the strategy its members must employ in order to secure their continuance as a ruling class. The letters rang with anger in one paragraph and affection in the next. The father regularly censured the son for pandering after popularity and courting the rabble, and challenged him to cast off his "meekness of temper." "I look upon Yr fears & Prudence as Idle & out of Season. . . . Are You not too fond of Popularity & has not that Fondness biassed Yr: Judgement?" Still, he would also implore Charley to "drudge not . . . nothing is dearer to me than Yr health." And while castigating the father's behavior as meddlesome and certainly "out of season," the son would simultaneously plead with the old man to take care of himself more diligently.[32]

32. CCA to CCC, Nov. 7, 14, 1777, Dec. 8, 1779, CCC to CCA, Nov. 13, 1777, Carroll Papers, MS 206.

A Broader Allegiance

The Carroll correspondence of 1777–1780 tells the dramatic story of their confrontation. The fireworks began in mid-February 1777 when Charley first warned his father that a legal tender act would be proposed. The elder Carroll exploded with a series of instructions. First, Charley should be absolutely inflexible and in no way temporize in his opposition to the law: "Principiis obsta [oppose the beginnings], ought to be the inflexible Rule of Every man of Honour & Honesty." Second, Charley should form alliances with all the parties that might be hurt, including some of the Carrolls' longtime enemies, even though many of them had dissociated themselves from the patriot cause: "Dulany for Himself & Family, Ridout for Mrs. Ogle & [C]oll Sharpe are Interested. You cannot concert an Opposition directly with Dulany, But You may doe it indi[r]ectly by Ridout. The influence of all who are likely to Suffer should be exerted."[33] Finally, if the legislation should pass, Papa expected Charley to resign his Senate seat. "A man of Honour" should "quit a Service which associates You with Pickpockets." Thereby, he later noted, "Yr withdrawing may prove yr detestation of Rogues." Once the legislation had passed the Senate, Papa made clear his unyielding stance: "Who were present in the Senate when the Bill past? Invite none of them Here for I shall turn them out of doors."[34]

The Carrolls' sharply divergent reactions to the tender bill underscore the abiding differences in their personalities and life experiences and suggest the dimensions of Charley's new, broader allegiance. Of all the Carrolls, Papa had led the most harrowing life. His father, Charles Carroll the Settler, had come to Maryland with the position of attorney general and despite its loss had retained

33. CCA to CCC, Mar. 18, 19, Apr. 16, 1777, ibid. None of the persons included on Papa's list could be considered a warm friend of the Revolution. Daniel Dulany was a nonjuror and maintained a "neutral" status during the Revolution. His Baltimore County estate, Hunting Ridge, was sold under the provisions of Maryland's 1781 confiscation act. (For the Dulany family's politics during the Revolution and the losses sustained as a result, see Aubrey C. Land, *The Dulanys of Maryland: A Biographical Study of Daniel Dulany, the Elder (1685–1753), and Daniel Dulany, the Younger (1722–1797)* [Baltimore, 1955], 320–331.) Although John Ridout (1732–1797) signed the oath of fidelity before July 1778, he was regarded as a loyalist (Edward C. Papenfuse et al., eds., *A Biographical Dictionary of the Maryland Legislature, 1635–1789* [Baltimore, 1979–1985], II, 691–692). Former governor Horatio Sharpe (1718–1790) traveled to England in 1773 accompanied by Ridout's mother-in-law, Anne Tasker Ogle (1723–1817). In their absence Ridout assumed management of their affairs. Sharpe never returned to Maryland; Mrs. Ogle came home in 1784. Matilda Edgar, *A Colonial Governor in Maryland: Horatio Sharpe and His Times, 1753–1773* (London, 1912), 250–280.

34. CCA to CCC, Mar. 18, Apr. 1, 13, 1777, Carroll Papers, MS 206.

a lucrative private proprietary post throughout most of his lifetime. Moreover, the province's most rigorously anti-Catholic legislation had not been enacted until the last few years of his life. Charley's existence had always been materially secure. From his eleventh until his twenty-seventh year he lived comfortably, first in a Catholic country, France, and later in England, where a liberal allowance allowed him to lead the life of a protected, even pampered young gentleman and to travel with a handsome and well-to-do crowd. He had never experienced or contemplated want, and he had no reason to expect that he would ever do so.

In contrast to both his father and his son, Charles Carroll of Annapolis had grown up in a sterner, more uncertain, and more menacing world. Sent at the age of ten to be educated in France, he had studied during the second decade of the eighteenth century with classmates from Ireland and England, some related to him, whose families were being dispossessed of their power, wealth, and land under the penal laws. Returning to Maryland, in late 1720, several months after the Settler's death, he immediately confronted discriminatory barriers that had recently been reinforced by the anti-Catholic legislation precipitated largely by the behavior of his own father. For the next forty years the climate of hostility and adversity occasioned by these measures persisted, reaching a frenzy during the Seven Years' War, when Papa pursued his plan to "withdraw"—by selling off his Chesapeake possessions and moving to Louisiana.

Never had the elder Carroll considered himself a protected member of the upper class. How could he, as long as the most important guarantee British law afforded to its aristocracy—the inviolate sanctity of private property—excluded Catholics, leaving them vulnerable to dispossession under the penal statutes? Class status meant little in that equation. Striving within an envious, vindictive society for the economic success that constituted his only hope for security and a measure of authority over his environment, Papa saw the Carrolls as continually beleaguered and their wealth as perennially at risk. Forever on the defensive, he personalized all threats to his property, including the legal tender act. From the time he turned twenty-one in 1723, he believed that he had protected and enhanced the Carroll fortune solely by the assertion of his obstinate will. Now, having valiantly withstood numerous attacks from above, he suddenly found himself in 1777 facing the threat of dispossession from below. His response was automatic, the reflex of a lifetime of conditioning: he and his son must be uncompromising and single-minded in their determination to prevent the erosion of the family estate.

In sum, 1776 had been a watershed for Charley, but his father could not reinterpret the world. All Papa's instincts told him to protect the family's interests in the only way he knew: maneuver between the equally hostile contending powers for advantage and form alliances today with the enemies of yesterday if that would secure the family's wealth. The fact that he would urge Charley to ally himself with Dulany and Ridout — men completely out of power, of loyalty so suspect in Revolutionary Maryland that their presence was tolerated only because they lived quietly and inconspicuously — dramatically illustrates how completely the times had passed him by.

To Papa's initial disbelief and abiding consternation, Charley acted from a different perspective: experience had taught him that the radical demands inherent in the Revolution must be met. When his father commanded that he quit the Senate because it was full of "highway men" and "pickpockets," Charley, with biting sarcasm, posed the essential question: "Where shall I withdraw?"[35] There was nowhere else to go: neither assertions of obstinate will nor schemes of flight to Louisiana could change the reality that the Carrolls' fortune and future were now firmly embedded in the fate of Revolutionary Maryland. For Charley the painful legal tender act constituted the adroit and necessary sacrifice required of wealthy men — the price they must pay for retaining power. By placating the populace, the leadership bought the chance to survive until calmer times, when forceful and calculating action could restore a conservative economic order.

Of all the barbs Papa flung Charley's way during their acrimonious contest, none could have rankled the younger Carroll more than his father's charge that he temporized instead of mounting a frontal attack on the tender law because he "pandered" after popularity and courted "the rabble." An aristocrat to the core, Charley harbored a distaste for the people that greatly exceeded Papa's. Intended or not, the educational regimen upon which the elder Carroll had insisted and its environment produced in his son an unshakably hierarchical view of how society should be structured. As early as 1760, Charley had developed what would be a lifelong preference for the governance exerted by Maryland's upper house as opposed to "the malicious persecutions, of an ignorant, base, contemptible rabble"— the lower house — whose actions seemed calculated to drive the Carrolls out of the colony. He told Papa approvingly that Horace had it right: "Odi profanum vulgus, et arceo" ("I hate the common herd and keep them afar"). Every motive for containing a social revolution had been instilled in Charley by the time he was twenty-three, and, when he returned to Maryland, the "mean low dirty envy" he perceived as the prevailing attitude of the meaner and poorer sort, and many of higher rank as well, reinforced all his elitist sensi-

35. CCC to CCA, Mar. 15, 1777, ibid.

bilities.[36] Perhaps his first direct confrontation with people who had no compunction about standing their ground and challenging their betters came on St. Clement's Manor in 1767, when his tenants baldly threatened to "stand you trial" and demanded that he appear before them to answer their complaints.

But, however much Charley disliked the people, he had learned not to underestimate what they might do in a revolutionary situation or what measures their discontent might force the leadership to take. Hence, he appreciated, as his father did not, that in the unpredictable and volatile climate of Revolutionary Maryland attention must be paid to the "common herd" and its allies and that individuals obnoxious to these forces invited extremely unpleasant consequences, including beatings, draconian attacks on property, jail, and even death. As he tried to explain to Papa in November 1777, in an effort to curtail the older man's injudicious public railing against the tender law: "There is a time when it is wisdom to yield to injustice; and to popular frensies & delusions: many wise and good men have acted so. When public bodies commit injustice, and are exposed to the public & can not vindicate themselves by reasoning, they commonly have recourse to violence & greater injustice towards all such as have the temerity to oppose them, particularly when their unjust proceedings are popular."[37]

Not only did Papa misapprehend what was at stake for the Carrolls in Revolutionary Maryland, but he also conducted himself in ways that Charley deemed counterproductive and dangerous. Rather than behaving with his characteristic belligerence, the elder Carroll should take the long view and act coolly and with circumspection. "I have long considered our personal estate, I mean the monied part of it, to be in jeopardy," Charley explained patiently, but to no avail, in April 1777. "If we can save a third of that, and all our lands & negroes I shall think our selves well off." Even couching his appeal in the most intimate personal language—"If you love me, you will pursue this conduct," he implored the following June—failed to persuade Papa to cease his pugnacious attacks on the law.[38] Still trying to reason with the old man in November, Charley pleaded

> There are not in this state more than 500 men, who disapprove of the law, altho' thousands would acknowledge the injustice of it. . . .

36. CC to CCA, Sept. 16, 1760, ibid.; CCC to [Edmund] Jenings, Nov. 23, 1765, CCC, letterbook 1765–1768, fol. 37, MdHi.
37. CCC to CCA, Nov. 13, 1777, Carroll Papers, MS 206.
38. CCC to CCA, Apr. 4, June 16, 1777, ibid.

I have weighed this matter cooly, and I think I have formed a right judgt. such as 999 men out of a thousand would approve: such as all your friends would approve: why then will you not gratify me in a most reasonable request? I beg you to consider well, and suffer not your passion or your interest to get the better of your understanding.[39]

Moved neither by his son's advice nor by his pleas, Papa insisted on pushing his anger at the tender bill beyond the bounds of their personal relationship into the public arena. In doing so, the older man created an acute source of strain for Charley in his relationship with the Revolutionary leadership coalition. Aware from the outset of the exigencies that compelled the passage of a tender bill, he had acceded to his father's wishes by protesting and voting against the measure when it first came before the Senate. Having taken that bold step, Charley believed he had done all that was necessary "to shew my detestation of a most infamous action." Despite its obvious injustice, the act would certainly pass, and he expected Papa to accept the distasteful outcome and to "make yourself easy on this score."[40]

Getting the parentally required statement of principled opposition past his colleagues cannot have been comfortable for Charles Carroll of Carrollton. Undoubtedly, their tolerance assumed that the elder Carroll's overt opposition would diminish. Charley certainly seems to have expected the old man to retire from the fray, leaving him free to get on with trying to govern Revolutionary Maryland in a way that protected the Carrolls' property and their position. As political developments in the general assembly began to move haltingly in this direction, the younger Carroll found to his dismay that one of the chief impediments to continued progress was the patriarch of his own household. In short, Papa had no intention of holding his tongue, and, if his son would not heed him, then he would appeal to and, if necessary, berate other members of the elite for countenancing the tender law.

Increasingly, the old man directed his most vicious attacks at Samuel Chase, whom he held personally responsible for the promotion and passage of the measure in the House of Delegates. Chase, Charley's oldest and most important ally, had become the most powerful member of the lower house; thus, from Charley's perspective, Papa could not have picked a more dangerous target upon whom to vent his spleen. The elder Carroll's obstreperous behavior forced Charley, a

39. CCC to CCA, Nov. 8, 1777, ibid.
40. CCC to CCA, Apr. 4, 1777, ibid.

man vain of his self-control, to rely on the indulgence of Chase (whose conduct Papa likened, in a letter to the gentleman, to that of a "Publick Strumpet") and the forbearance of Major Jenifer and others to avoid a messy scandal and an open breech in the leadership's ranks. Writing to his father on June 26, 1777, Charley remonstrated bluntly: "I really do think your correspondence with Chase was imprudent: what good did you propose to yourself by it? & why should you wish to be called before the assembly? To treat them as you have treated Chase you say: the consequence would be a commitment; perhaps, to Goal. Can You at your time of life bear such confinement?"[41]

Undaunted, Papa persisted throughout the summer and into the fall of 1777 until Charley became completely exasperated. Regarding Chase, he retorted in November, "I really think, to speak my mind freely, he has acted with more wisdom than you have done & I hope you will not trouble yourself any more with letters to him or anyone else on the subject — Believe me your letters will not answer any good purpose: as to a repeal of the law, you must not hope for it." A week later, his patience exhausted, Charley penned a sharp dismissal to his stubbornly defiant parent: "I still retain my opinion respecting the impropriety of yr. writing to Chase & publications: you still retain yours; in this case the only way to ascertain which opinion is right is to appeal to the judgt. of some sensible man uninterested in the matter & a friend of both of us. I shall never say a word more to you on the subject."[42]

For the next two years Charley essentially adhered to his vow of virtual silence on the tender law. Between November 1777 and the fall of 1779, he confined himself to perfunctory comments to his father on the subject. Undeterred, Papa also remained true to his promise not to "let the tender law sleep" and continued to flail at the Maryland leadership in a manner reminiscent of his conduct in 1751, when he had nailed his protest to the door of the assembly while the delegates were in session. On two occasions the elder Carroll even managed to present his position directly to the Maryland legislature. In the first instance, during the fall 1778 session, he appeared before the House of Delegates to argue in behalf of his petition to repeal the tender law. In rejecting his appeal, the house noted predictably that it found the petitioner's language "highly indecent and justly ex-

41. CCA to Samuel Chase, June 9, 1777, CCC to CCA, Jun. 26, 1777, ibid.
42. CCC to CCA, Nov. 13, 20, 1777, ibid. Having refused on several occasions to deliver Papa's intemperate missives to Chase, Charley at length found himself with no alternative except to accede to his father's wishes. To his undoubted relief and equal humiliation, Chase saved the day by refusing to accept the letter. He would not read it, Chase told Charley bluntly: "I wish to avoid an altercation with your father."

A Broader Allegiance

ceptionable," but because of his "advanced age" the delegates declined to take any punitive action.[43]

Highly indignant at such treatment, Charles Carroll of Annapolis composed a snide pamphlet that condemned both the legal tender measure and the behavior of the general assembly. Published in early 1779, the document emphasized to the "Gentle Reader" how the assembly, composed of "the most disinterested men in the state," had raised the salaries of its members to keep pace with inflation while freezing the rate at which creditors had to accept paper currency for sterling debts. Since the delegates had indeed quadrupled their pay from ten shillings per day in early 1777 (when they enacted the legal tender law) to two pounds per day by December 1778, they found the elder Carroll's remarks decidedly unpleasant. Indeed, his pamphlet so aroused the House of Delegates that, when he appeared before it with a second petition in March 1779, he was received even more harshly. The delegates censured him, took him into custody, brought him before the bar, and demanded that he apologize or be placed in jail. Papa ruefully agreed to beg the pardon of the house, but he refused to desist from his efforts to have the law repealed. During the July 1779 session, when Charley was absent, having taken his wife to the medicinal springs at Bath (Berkeley Springs), Virginia, for her health, Papa once more attempted — this time unsuccessfully — to persuade the speaker of the house, William Fitzhugh, and then John Hanson, a delegate from Frederick County, to enter a petition on his behalf. Their refusals clearly proved to the old man that the vast majority of the Revolutionary leadership, many of whom were creditors, continued to accept the law as a necessity of the times.[44]

By the fall of 1779, however, Papa could at least take some comfort from the fact that Charley had finally become concerned about the financial toll that the tender law was taking on the Carroll fortune. When the measure was enacted in 1777, the younger Carroll had not believed it would substantially endanger the family's extensive credit holdings, nor did he really expect that many persons would attempt to discharge the sterling debts they owed the Carrolls in paper currency. Two years later, this hope had crashed against the reality his father had predicted. The elder Carroll's calculations through the end of 1778 showed that the tender law, in combination with a soaring inflation his son had also failed to anticipate, had already taken nearly four thousand pounds sterling out of the

43. [CCA] to Maj. [Daniel of St. Thomas] Jenifer, July 30, 1779, ibid.; *VPHD*, October Session, 1778, 17.

44. *VPHD*, March Session, 1779, 457–460; CCA to the Hon. Col. William Fitzhugh, July 15, 1779, CCA to CCC, Aug. 10, 17, 1779, Carroll Papers, MS 206.

Carrolls' pockets. With meaningful action in behalf of such losses beyond his reach, Charley moved to counteract whenever possible the ravages of inflation. So suspicious had the younger Carroll become of both Congress and the state government with respect to financial matters that he distrusted even their efforts at gold and silver coinage. Opting to take bonds for the sale of tobacco in bills of exchange drawn on English sterling rather than in gold or silver, he justified his preference by explaining to his father that he feared the Congress might soon begin to adulterate the coinage.[45] Determined to find a way to secure payments for tobacco in a currency immune both to violent fluctuations and the provisions of the tender act, Charley, on the advice of Maryland's first governor, Thomas Johnson, concocted an elaborate scheme for dealing in livres tournois, a medium of exchange not covered by the law.

The combined effects of the tender law and spiraling inflation began to fret Charley in another area. He worried about the family's ability to meet its tax assessments. Less anxious than his son about this matter, Papa nevertheless agreed that the money hovered on the verge of increasing "beyond concep[t]ion" and well might reach a point where it would "hardly answer in any way the intention of Money." When Charley decided to sell off his fancy carriage on the grounds that "every little helps in these most extravagant times," the old gentleman did not object.[46] As Charley now realized, his father's rantings about being "Robbed of the Greatest part of my Property" contained a depressingly large element of truth, and the demands of trying to deal with it all could wear a man down. "Molly tells me You do not look well, that You have lost Yr appetite," Papa wrote him solicitously in early December 1779, "wh She ascribes to a too close application & vexation at being so Shamefully robbed." Charley confirmed the report: "Confinement & thought & uneasiness at the situation of our affairs have taken away in some degree my appetite, tho' I find myself well. It is certainly vexatious to see oneself robbed by a Set of Rascals with impunity, & without any public advantage." He reached an even gloomier conclusion: "If the war Should continue much longer we may be robbed of our lands, as well as money."[47]

45. CCA, Account of Paper Money paid for sterling, CCC to CCA, Oct. 25, 1779, Carroll Papers, MS 206.

46. CCA to CCC, Oct. 24, 1779, CCC to CCA, Oct. 26, 1779, ibid. By the middle of 1780, Papa was mildly concerned about meeting the family's taxes, especially if his son did not curb his "disbursements," but Charley was no longer quite as alarmed. CCA to CCC, June 23, 25, 1780, ibid.

47. CCA to Thomas Jennings, June 7, 1778, CCA to CCC, Dec. 3, 1779, CCC to CCA, Dec. 4, 1779, ibid.

A Broader Allegiance

With the weight of his family's business pressing ever more urgently upon his mind, Charley began in the fall of 1779 to express guarded support for the older man's position. Although convinced that the people's support for the Revolution remained fragile and that their sensibilities and those of the lower house must still be carefully considered, he nevertheless told his father that, under certain very specific conditions, he would sponsor legislation in the Senate to rescind the tender law. He remained convinced, however, that the House of Delegates would reject it. His sober assessment reflected the challenge he and his Senate colleagues currently faced as they fought the House of Delegates' attempt to extend the law's reach. On November 20, 1779, the delegates passed, by a margin of forty-two to five, a bill to allow debtors whose tender of paper money was refused by a creditor to satisfy the debt in full by paying the money to the state treasurer. Undeterred by the measure's popular appeal, the Senate considered and then rejected it.[48]

Despite the discouraging short-term prospects for repeal, forces were already at work moving Maryland and the other states toward a more conservative financial posture. On November 19, 1779, the day before Maryland's House of Delegates overwhelmingly approved the addition to the tender law, the Continental Congress resolved that the states should adjust their legal tender laws to provide equity for both debtors and creditors.[49] Moreover, the necessity for using the tender law to defuse threats against the propertied elite lessened appreciably when the Maryland courts, through more energetic prosecution of groups that opposed the state government or flouted whig authority, reasserted their control in the waning days of 1779. The establishment of a vigorous system of civil governance and the reopening of the courts, particularly on the Eastern Shore, signaled unmistakably that Charley's class — the men he believed ought to govern — had solidified its hold on politics and society. Those actions persuaded him that the most acute period of social instability had passed. As 1780 wore on, it became increasingly evident that the principal issue now animating the Maryland leadership involved, not placating the people, but solving the fiscal crisis afflicting both the states and the central government so that the war could continue. By the end of the summer, Charley not only readily acknowledged that heavier taxes would have to be levied, but he also clearly believed that they could be. The Congress, he noted in a letter to John Hanson, one of Maryland's delegates, had "tried the pulse of the People already," and he predicted

48. *VPHD*, November Session, 1779, 13, 19; *VPS*, November Session, 1779, 17.
49. *JCC*, XV, 1292.

that new tax measures "may now be carried into effect without much convulsion or danger."[50]

Although clearly evident by the spring of 1780, the Maryland leadership's success in containing popular unrest and forging support for both the government and the Revolutionary cause did not automatically translate into the repeal of the tender law. Deprived of the convenient justification of political necessity that had previously cloaked their operations, "interested" men who had sought to use the law for their own gain now stood exposed as they fought openly for its retention. Chief among those Charley deemed a corrupt group loomed his old ally and onetime friend Samuel Chase. "There are many gentlemen among the Delegates, who wis[h] to promote their country's good, perhaps a majority," the younger Carroll wrote his father in May, "but their leaders, or rather leader, is all for himself: all his measures have a tendency to promote his own interest wh is incompatible with that of the Public." Whereas Charley had once chastised Papa for likening Chase to a "Publick Strumpet," he now condemned his erstwhile friend as "the most prostituted scoundrel who ever existed."[51]

Charley's outrage devolved from two separate sources. Undoubtedly his republican sensibilities were genuinely insulted when Chase's avaricious and opportunistic conduct first surfaced in the spring of 1778 with accusations that Chase was the principal protagonist in a scandal to corner the flour market. The charge — that Chase, by virtue of his congressional seat, had learned of huge flour purchases intended by the French and had sought to monopolize the supply — resulted in his exclusion from Maryland's delegation that fall. Although Charley deemed such conduct deplorable, he continued his alliance with Chase out of the conviction that the preservation of a unified leadership and the continuance of its contribution to the stabilization of the social order took precedence over all other considerations.

By 1780, however, the achievement of civil order in Maryland exposed other kinds of insidious threats. Convinced that further sacrifices were no longer required from men of wealth and stature, Charley no longer saw any reason to mask his contempt for and alarm at Chase's self-interested schemes. With the tender law still exacting its toll, Chase and his allies mounted a new drive that linked the measure with a proposal to confiscate loyalist property in Maryland, a move that endangered Carroll holdings abroad. In Charley's view, the lower house's opposition to repeal of the tender law sprang principally from the desire of Chase and his supporters to use their rapidly depreciating currency for the

50. CCC to John Hanson, Aug. 15, 1780, Carroll Papers, MS 206.
51. CCC to CCA, May 11, 1780, ibid.

acquisition of loyalist property. It was well known that Chase had his eye on the dwelling that Maryland's last proprietary governor, Robert Eden, had abandoned upon his return to England in 1776. Set on six acres of land, the grand two-story brick structure was known as "the best House in Annapolis."[52]

The meshing of the repeal of the legal tender law with the conflict between the Senate and the House of Delegates concerning the confiscation of British property increased the vulnerability of the Carrolls' economic interests. The question of confiscation had been raised as early as 1777, but did not gain significant support for another three years. In August 1780, Charley explained to his friend William Carmichael, who was then serving as secretary with John Jay's diplomatic mission in Spain, the high-minded rationale for his and the Senate's opposition: the measure violated the standards of "civilized nations." But Charley had more personal reasons: specifically, the Carrolls would certainly suffer further financial losses should the British reciprocate. In November 1779 he had advised Joshua Johnson, the Carrolls' mercantile correspondent then based in Nantes, about the developments in Maryland and urged him to take precautionary measures to protect all the family's liquid assets and other property in England from retaliation. Reiterating his concerns in May 1780, Charley directed Johnson to secure "your correspondents property which may be in England in Such a manner that it may be out of the reach of the british Government in case it Should make use of reprisals."[53]

Throughout 1780, Charley and his colleagues in the Senate pressed for the discontinuance of the tender law while Chase and the House of Delegates held firm in demanding confiscation. At the June 1780 session of the general assembly, three separate measures regarding repeal of the tender law were introduced. The first and second failed; the third passed. It required that all gold and sterling debts contracted after July 5, 1776, be repaid in gold or silver. However, all obligations entered into before that date could still be remitted in legal tender. Because nearly all of the Carrolls' extensions of credit had occurred before 1776, the so-called repeal did little to improve their situation, and both father and son regarded it with contempt. The motivation for it, Charley wrote acidly to Carmichael that August, "must be sought for in the iniquity of those who have plundered this State, and individuals, to benefit themselves, and are determined

52. Testimony of Robert Smith, Dec. 1, 1788, and Thomas Eden, Feb. 22, 1787, Loyalist Transcripts from the New York Public Library, microfilm, MdHi, quoted in Haw et al., *Stormy Patriot*, 30.

53. CCC to William Carmichael, Aug. 9, 1780, CCC to Joshua Johnson, May 1, 1780, Carroll Papers, MS 206.

at the expence of their reputation, to preserve the gains they have made by such scandalous frauds."[54]

When the next session of the assembly convened in October 1780, the drive to repeal the tender law and enact a confiscation measure intensified. Because the British during the summer sequestered Maryland funds held in the Bank of England, the Senate withdrew its opposition to confiscation. With that obstacle removed, and with the Continental Congress pressuring all of the states to reform their currencies by making Continental and state moneys reasonably equal in value, the House of Delegates began actively discussing the abrogation of the tender law. Near the end of November, Charley again became pessimistic, fearing that a flurry of negative votes signaled the end of the repeal effort, but he was wrong. On November 30, the house revoked the legal tender legislation, the Senate followed suit the next day, and on December 14 Governor Thomas Sim Lee (a relative of the Carrolls by marriage) signed the bill.[55] Remarked Papa to Charley three days later: "I much doubt the Assemblys ever doing justice to the Publick & Crs, however it is a comfort that we are not now exposed to be robbed." As for those debtors who had taken advantage of the tender law to liquidate their obligations to the Carrolls, Papa continued to hound them. Some he vilified in the press while others he wrote to privately demanding that as a point of "honor & conscience" they should repay him amounts equivalent to their original sterling debt.[56]

In the summer of 1780, Charley's cousin Daniel Carroll II of Rock Creek, a member of the governor's council, asked his help in the state's anti-inflationary efforts. Urging Charley to persuade Maryland's merchant community to accept the new congressional currency emission at the rate of forty old bills for one of the new notes, Daniel pleaded eloquently: "For God sake second our endeavour all you can — Nothing would more effectively do it than by a Number of the Principal farmers &c engageing to the Merchts to take the money at that rate for their produce — Men of property & of a liberal way of thinking may do great

54. "An Act relating to loans in specie, tenders for debts and contracts in future and the establishment of a bank for public purposes," *VPHD,* June Session, 1780, 213, 217, 219–221, 226–227; *VPS,* June Session, 1780, 116–117; CCC to William Carmichael, Aug. 9, 1780, Carroll Papers, MS 206.

55. Hoffman, *Spirit of Dissension,* 262; *VPHD,* October Session, 1780, 11, 12, 39–40; *VPS,* October Session, 1780, 12, 18. Governor Lee's wife was the stepdaughter of Charles Carroll of Carrollton's first cousin Mary Carroll Digges (1730–1825).

56. CCA to CCC, Dec. 17, 1780, CCA to John Llewellin, Jan. 2, Feb. 11, 1782, Carroll Papers, MS 206; *Maryland Journal, and the Baltimore Advertiser,* Nov. 20, 1781.

things — I wish for the sake of justice the Evills of the Tender law cou'd be remedied — I have strong hopes they will in some degree — I wish for the sake of my Country the effects coud be forgot — this Sacrifice is due to our Country from a good Citizen."[57]

Not surprisingly, Daniel's words fell on deaf ears. If virtue and disinterest had once been part of First Citizen's lexicon when he entered the political arena, the exigencies of the times had at length caused him to temper radically those ideals with more personal calculations. Although Papa's dire warnings had been correct about the losses that the Carroll fortune would sustain, the credit for preserving the bulk of their assets remained Charley's. By aligning his family with the Maryland gentry and by submitting, however painfully, to the strategic concessions necessary for solidifying the propertied classes' hold over society, the younger Carroll had endured the Revolution with a growing determination that Carroll wealth would never again be placed in jeopardy. Until late 1779, he had seen the greatest danger to his family in the turbulent behavior of the disenchanted populace. Once the reimposition of civil order had curbed that threat, Charley confronted the risks to his holdings posed by the schemes of ambitious men like his old ally Samuel Chase who sought to manipulate Revolutionary exigencies for private gain. Having risked everything by standing with the new Republic, Charley had gained for himself and his family the security and inviolate protection of law that had been denied to Irish Catholics from centuries before his birth through the lifetime of his own father. Emerging weary but triumphant from his political and personal ordeal, he carried with him the defining reality of a broader allegiance forged in the midst of peril. One truth would henceforth order his existence: in the world made by the American Revolution, the interests of men of substantial property transcended their differences.

57. Daniel Carroll to CCC, Aug. 26, 1780, Carroll Papers, MS 206.

The Family Economy: 1777–1782

During the years of the War for Independence, friction over the management of the Carroll estates occasionally echoed the contest between Papa and Charley in their struggle over the legal tender act. A visit to Doohoragen in August 1777 prompted the son to take the father sharply to task for the unsatisfactory conditions into which several of the manor's most important activities had fallen, singling out for particular criticism the older man's handling of the workhouse: "You know Magdalen, althô a hard working woman & a good spinner, has very little management, & is besides addicted to liquor. Blackwell you know to be a drunkard, & have the greatest reason to suspect of being a rogue: now, under the direction of two such hopeful persons, how can a man of sense expect to cloath this numerous family?" Charley judged as similarly deficient the labor of the smiths, coopers, wheelwrights, shoemakers, and carpenters: "I assure you from my own observation they want an overlooker very much: they do but little, & that too carelessly."[1]

Papa's reaction is unknown, but, when he discovered a shortage of some seventy-five pounds in his cash account several months later, he insisted that Charley's miscounting was responsible. The son responded by pointing out the older man's arithmetical shortcomings: "If you go over your cash account and examine carefully whether the additions and subtractions are right, and then if these are right if you count over your money you will probably find out the error." Imputing the mistake to carelessness, the younger Carroll suggested that his father had perhaps "omitted to count some small parcels of money: did you count the little silver & gold you have?" When Papa continued to resist, Charley simply reassigned the task to someone he clearly regarded as more competent in

1. CCC to CCA, Aug. 27, 1777, Carroll Papers, MS 206, MdHi.

the matter than his father: "Mr. Deards will go up with Mrs. Carroll, do get him to count over your money; he is expeditious & accurate in counting money."[2]

In the years 1777–1781 the rapidly appreciating burden of wartime taxes sharpened the bickering between father and son, with each blaming the other for frustrations caused by the war. "If You do not lessen Yr disbursemts:," Papa carped on one occasion, "I know not how we shall pay Our taxes, I do not enquire whether You gratify Real or imaginary Wants." Countered Charley defensively, "It is true money runs away very fast: but I am careful of it as I can be — you know of how little value it is." Such squabbling reflected a real and growing concern about their ability to pay their assessment: by 1778 their taxes had increased to nearly four thousand pounds; a year later the figure approached seven thousand pounds.[3] To meet these obligations, Papa and Charley pursued several strategies, among them raising their tenants' rents, arranging for a huge sale of tobacco in 1779, and expanding substantially their production and marketing of beef and other foodstuffs. In addition, they traded in an array of financial instruments, especially interest-bearing Continental loan office certificates and receipts, which they used, along with depreciated paper money, wheat, tobacco, and beef, to pay what they owed the state.[4]

Father and son differed somewhat in their attitudes toward these "obligations to the public." Although he could not stomach the tender law or his son's arguments about placating the populace, Papa accepted with equanimity the straightforward necessity of paying taxes: "What are they to the Value of Our lives Liberty & Freedom?" he asked Charley in May 1780. "Supposing Our Estate assessed to £130,000 We must pay 36400 tt tobo & £23,000, what proportion doe these Paymts: bare to the real value of Our Estate? Will the Bulk of Our People be less able to Pay than We are?" By contrast, Charley, now nearly four years into the struggle for Independence, did not share those magnanimous sentiments. Despite his political astuteness concerning Revolutionary necessities and the wisdom of accommodating them, he regarded as especially onerous additional assessments imposed to achieve certain goals: "We could easily enough pay this year's taxes," he told his father dourly in June 1780, "if it were not for the addi-

2. CCA to CCC, Nov. 15, 1777, CCC to CCA, Nov. 15, 20, 1777, ibid.

3. CCA to CCC, June 23, 1780, CCC to CCA, Apr. 20, 1778, June 24, 1780, ibid. See also Sheriff's Accounts, 1779, The Papers of the Carroll Family, box 3, DLC; CCA to CCC, Dec. 3, 1779, Carroll Papers, MS 206.

4. CCC to CCA, Apr. 8, 1779, CCA to CCC, Apr. 28, 1779, Apr. 18, 1781, Carroll Papers, MS 206. See also Sheriff's Accounts, 1779–1780, Papers of the Carroll Family.

tional tax of recruits wh will be exceedingly heavy." Charley initially estimated this expense would cost the Carrolls "£36000 over & above our other taxes." To his relief, the final bill was less than half that amount.[5]

In dealing with the financial necessities occasioned by the Revolutionary conflict, the Carrolls continued their prewar patterns of plantation management. Tobacco remained their principal cash crop, and, unlike other planters, they did not curtail production. Nonetheless, the disruption in trade caused by the fighting made supplying normal markets difficult.[6] Tobacco prices in Europe increased nearly tenfold in the years 1776–1781, but very little of the staple actually reached its intended destination, although some Baltimore merchants reported a brisk trade with France in 1778. As George Woolsey, a principal in the mercantile firm of Woolsey and Salmon, reported to an Irish correspondent that year, "Our Captains seldom meet with any accidents" because they sailed at night and possessed a thorough knowledge of the coastal inlets.[7] Planters who found international trade too risky could participate in the internal market,

5. CCA to CCC, May 12, 1780, CCC to CCA, June 25, 1780, Carroll Papers, MS 206. During its June 1780 session, the Maryland legislature enacted a measure to raise 2,000 men for the Continental army. The means to this end required the division of all property in the state into 2,000 classes, with every £9,000 worth of property providing one recruit or a cash equivalent not exceeding 25 percent (£2,250) of the class's property. Seeing no likelihood of finding the 16 men that would be needed to avoid a huge cash payment, the younger Carroll was relieved to learn that he need provide only 8 or be assessed £14,250. *Laws of Maryland, Made and Passed at a Session of Assembly, Begun and Held at the City of Annapolis, on Monday [June 7, 1780]* (Annapolis, 1780), chap. 10; CCC to CCA, June 23, 27, 1780, Carroll Papers, MS 206.

6. For a description of how other Chesapeake planters adjusted to the war years, I have, in a number of instances, relied on Lorena S. Walsh, " 'To Labour for Profit': Plantation Management in the Chesapeake, 1620–1820," MS.

Surprisingly, no authoritative account of the tobacco trade for the Revolutionary war years, 1776–1783, has been written. The most suggestive information for the period can be found in Jacob M. Price, *France and the Chesapeake: A History of the French Tobacco Monopoly, 1674–1791, and of Its Relationship to the British and American Tobacco Trade*, 2 vols. (Ann Arbor, Mich., 1973); and Edward C. Papenfuse, *In Pursuit of Profit: The Annapolis Merchants in the Era of the American Revolution, 1763–1805* (Baltimore, 1975). See also Jacob M. Price, "Reflections on the Economy of Early America," in Ronald Hoffman et al., eds., *The Economy of Early America: The Revolutionary Period, 1763–1790* (Charlottesville, Va., 1988), 317–322.

7. George Woolsey to Waddell Cunningham, Apr. 15, 1778 [Balto. to Dublin], Woolsey and Salmon Letterbook, Manuscripts Division, DLC. It is interesting to note that George Woolsey suggests on a number of occasions that merchants and planters did well in the tobacco trade during the war.

where the demand for tobacco continued to be robust. State and Continental agents made large purchases that were exported from Baltimore and Philadelphia to St. Eustatia and other Dutch and French Caribbean islands to pay for arms and supplies. Similarly, tobacco served as an important medium for levying and paying taxes and settling private obligations and constituted an excellent hedge against inflation as well.

Papa and Charley chose to hold the bulk of their tobacco off the market until 1779. By then they had stored between 260 and 270 hogsheads of excellent quality. With French ships able to put into Baltimore and Philadelphia that spring, Samuel Chase offered them twenty-five shillings sterling per hundredweight, a price that exceeded £12 sterling per hogshead. Even though such a sale would have yielded £3,250 sterling, Papa refused, holding out instead for thirty-five shillings per hundredweight. The elder Carroll expected to sell to Pierre Penet, an aggressive wartime trader based in Nantes; but, when James Howard, a local merchant, met his price, he closed the deal and delivered crop notes to Howard for 251,579 lbs. of tobacco. The total sale amounted to £4,402.12.17 sterling, more than £17 sterling per hogshead.[8]

Months before this sale brought them its rich return, Charley and Papa had begun to ponder how to invest their capital for maximum safety and profit in a wartime economy. Charley wondered whether they might "not place it at interest in some of the funds of Europe." Or perhaps "the best way of laying out that money" would be to buy land cheaply by paying for it in sterling via bills of exchange. Putting some funds in the Continental loan office offered another option, although father and son agreed that large sterling sums should not be risked on such certificates. For the elder Carroll, however, ventures closer to home were evidently another matter, and in June of 1780 he earned his son's disapproval for purchasing state bonds with money meant for other expenses: "We ought," Charley chided primly, "to pay our debts before we lend to the State."[9]

If the Carrolls' manipulations of wartime financial markets and the considerable profits they earned from tobacco helped assuage their tax burden and the losses they sustained from the legal tender act, other disruptions caused by the Revolutionary conflict inflicted measurable damage upon their prewar operations. The most serious of these involved two British raids on Poplar Island. From the start of hostilities, Papa and Charley recognized the vulnerability of their island plantation to British maritime incursion, and in March 1776 they

8. CCC to CCA, May 8, 1779, CCA to CCC, July 21, Dec. 3, 8, 1779, Carroll Papers, MS 206. To secure the sale, CCA had Howard draw his bond in livres tournois.

9. CCC to CCA, May 8, 1779, June 10, 1780, ibid.

agreed to move their herds of sheep from there to Doohoragen. Eighteen months later, just as the British fleet carrying General Sir William Howe's invasion force moved into the Chesapeake for its journey to the head of the bay, Charley directed his island overseer, William Sears, to begin transporting the rest of the livestock across the bay as well. The decision proved timely. Although the occupants of the enemy ships that anchored off Poplar Island on their way north were more interested in consuming crabs than bothering the Carroll establishment, this was not the case when the fleet returned after depositing Howe and his troops at Head of Elk. On September 16, 1777, while Charley was attending Congress in York, Pennsylvania, whither the delegates had fled as Howe advanced on Philadelphia, a small British raiding party landed on Poplar Island, destroyed the saltmaking operation, and carried off a few slaves and the plantation boat.[10]

Following the British withdrawal from the Chesapeake in 1777, life on Poplar Island returned to normal, and for the next several years the plantation functioned without incident. Returning from a visit of inspection in November 1779, Charley reported that erosion — "the washing of the Island" — constituted the most serious threat to operations there. The peaceful scene changed abruptly in March 1781, when a British party attached to the command of Admiral Marriot Arbuthnot, in the bay to support General Benedict Arnold's forces, razed much of the Carrolls' establishment. Papa deplored the destruction but tried to view the situation philosophically: "Such cruel Wanton inhuman & bar[ba]rous Waste is in consequence of Malice & Rage excited by disappointment. Our loss is great, but we have been lucky in Saving Our Negroes, & if we reflect on the distresses & total ruin of Many Opulent Gentn: to the Southward, We should be wanting in Gratitude did we not return thanks to God that we & this State have Sufferd so little."[11]

10. CCC to CCA, Mar. 25, 1776, Aug. 27, Oct. 5, 9, 11, 1777, ibid. The Calvert County militia subsequently recaptured the Carrolls' boat and found it contained "a Mulatto Man 10 good Muskets, 10 broad swords & 10 Cartouch Boxes." The slave, a twenty-year-old man named Frank, told the militia officer that he "belongs to Mr. Carroll of Carrolton & also the Boat — that he with two others were taken going from Cooks Point to Poplar Island Tuesday Evening." William Hand Browne et al., eds., *Archives of Maryland* (Baltimore, 1883–), XVI, 384; "List of Negroes on Poplar Island taken 18th Feby. 1774," ledger X, Carroll-McTavish Papers, MdHi.

For a British account of their activities off Poplar Island, see G. D. Scull, ed., "The Montrésor Journal," New York Historical Society, *Collections,* XIV (New York, 1881), 440–441.

11. CCC to CCA, Nov. 5, 1779, CCA to CCC, Mar. 30, 1781, Carroll Papers, MS 206.

Equally grateful that the "Island negroes" had not left with the British, Charley relocated all but two of them to Doohoragen, noting that he had acquiesced in their strong desire to remain together. "As they did not chuse to be parted," he told Papa, the overseer "sent them all up." Sharper and his wife Sucky, who headed the island's principal slave family, were left behind to watch over the surviving structures, the crops of small grain, and the orchards and to protect the trees from cutting by neighbors and watermen. Although he approved of Charley's decision, Papa knew that for the immediate future it meant a loss of productivity, not only because the island had lost its labor force but also because a period of adjustment would be required to integrate the transferred slaves into the pattern of work at Doohoragen. "I have distributed the Island Negroes among the Quarters," he told Charley soon after the twenty-four blacks arrived at Elk Ridge, where he hoped they would "at least make as much Corn as will maintain them next year." [12]

The war precipitated other changes in the Carrolls' plantation practices that paralleled efforts throughout the newly independent states to achieve self-sufficiency through home manufactures. Among these were a heightened emphasis on raising sheep and cattle and an expansion of clothmaking. The latter occasioned concentrated efforts both to improve the cultivation of hemp and flax and to increase the production of material, endeavors absolutely essential in providing clothing for slaves. Beginning in 1776 and continuing through the war, the manufacture of cloth at Doohoragen increased steadily until the Carrolls could largely meet their needs. As Charley explained to his chief commercial correspondent in Europe in the spring of 1782, "I am informed the coarse linens Shipped for the Negroes wears well; but as I am in hopes of Manufacturing linen enough to Cloath my People I shall not import any." [13]

Achieving that hopeful prospect was not easy, however, and the Carrolls occasionally found themselves in straitened circumstances. In October 1777, their acute need for cloth induced Charley to approach Richard Peters, secretary to

12. CCC to CCA, Apr. 11, 1781, CCA to CCC, Apr. 18, 1781, ibid. An inventory made on Feb. 18, 1774, lists a total of 26 slaves — 15 adults (6 men and 9 women) and 11 children — living on Poplar Island. The number estimated to have been transferred to Doohoragen in 1781 is derived from that figure. "List of Negroes on Poplar Island," ledger X, Carroll-McTavish Papers.

13. James A. Henretta, "The War for Independence and American Economic Development," in Hoffman et al., eds., *The Economy of Early America*, 45–87; CCC to Wallace, Johnson, and Muir, Apr. 18, 1782, Charles Carroll Letter-book, 1771–1833, fol. 59, Arents Collections, New York Public Library, Astor, Lenox, and Tilden Foundations, New York.

Congress's Board of War and Ordnance, about procuring two weavers "used to weaving coarse linens & woollens" from among the British prisoners. "I would prefer british workmen on account of language & superior skill to Hessians," he told Peters, "but rather than not get weavers I must take Hessians, or else my poor slaves must go naked this winter." Underscoring the urgency, the younger Carroll pressed Peters to "exert yourself in rendering me this essential piece of service," noting that his father was willing to pay each weaver three pounds a month.[14] By mid-November Peters had found two men, one skilled in weaving both wool and linen, the other able to work only in linen, from among the British captives held at York, and at month's end Papa sent Folly quarter overseer John Flattery to bring them to Doohoragen. One, "used only to fine Work," did not suit the Carrolls' purposes and was placed with a neighbor, but the other toiled in the manor workhouse for the rest of the war.[15]

Although driven by profitability rather than necessity, the raising and marketing of cattle also became increasingly important at Doohoragen as the Revolutionary conflict wore on. By 1780, Charley had come to believe that beef sales offered the best profit margin of all his family's plantation operations. Indeed, so important had it become that the 1780 assessment listed "beef in the Hoof" as an acceptable means of satisfying tax obligations.[16]

The useful, if limited, income provided by livestock pales when compared to the flow of money generated by tenant rentals. From the onset of the imperial crisis in the mid-1770s through the war, a large number of leaseholders continued to live at Carrollton Manor, and another ten families held tenements on Doohoragen. Critical gaps in evidence make systematic analysis of persistence, productivity, and profitability difficult.[17] Even so, combining references from family correspondence with the records that do exist provides telling vignettes

14. CCC to Richard Peters, Oct. 22, 1777, Etting Collection, HSP. At the time he wrote to Peters, Charley was an active member of the Board of War, to which he had first been appointed on July 18, 1776. The care and maintenance of prisoners of war fell under the board's jurisdiction.

15. Richard Peters to CCC, Nov. 18, 1777, Carroll Papers, MS 206; CCA to CCC, Dec. 5, 1777, Outerbridge Horsey Collection of Lee, Horsey, and Carroll Family Papers, no. 1306, MdHi.

16. CCC to CCA, Apr. 29, May 6, 1780, Carroll Papers, MS 206.

17. Only the rent roll dated Sept. 29, 1777, remains from the Revolutionary period. Ledger MT, the tenants' account book begun in the mid-1760s, was practically full by 1779, and its successor has not been found.

of how the War for Independence affected the activities of both landlord and leaseholder. Between 1771 and 1777, a period bracketed by two surviving Carrollton rent rolls and buffeted at the end by Revolutionary turmoil, the persistence rate on the Carrolls' Frederick County manor held at 50 percent. Thirty-four of the sixty-eight tenants on the manor in 1777 had been living there in 1771, and twenty-nine had been residents before the beginning of Charley's managerial involvement in 1767. The largest group exodus occurred in the years 1772–1774, when nine of the thirteen English Moravian families residing on Carrollton departed for the Brethren's settlement at Wachovia, in North Carolina.[18]

According to the rent rolls, the productivity of the Carrollton tenants remained stable from 1771 to 1774, with payments to the Carrolls averaging about 58,500 pounds of tobacco each year. Although Papa and Charley postponed the sale of the 1772 and 1773 crops as they tried to ride out the effects of the mercantile failures in England and the resulting depression of prices during those years, their ability to wait ultimately brought them a good return. Despite the loss of weight in transit, the 120 hogsheads of Carrollton tobacco shipped from Rock Creek landing on the Potomac River in the fall of 1774 brought a price of £11.6.2 sterling per hogshead. Papa's shrewd head for business squeezed every possible advantage out of the transaction. At his direction, Charley informed Charles Wallace, the Annapolis representative of Wallace, Davidson, and Johnson, that in return for giving the firm their business the Carrolls expected to pocket the money realized from the 10 pounds of duty-free tobacco allowed per hogshead.[19] In 1775, the impending stoppage of trade and the fact that the current Maryland and Virginia crop was "a Short one" augured for an even better market, and Papa urged Charley to sell "in the Country," where planters were reportedly getting 40s–41s current money per hundredweight. Evaluating carefully, the younger Carroll ultimately decided to consign his tobacco to Joshua Johnson, Wallace and Company's London agent, cautioning the merchant not to "speculate too deep" but to accept with alacrity any offer commensurate with what planters dealing locally were receiving. The following spring, Johnson

18. Rent rolls for Carrollton Manor, 1771, 1777, Carroll-Maccubbin Papers, MdHi; George Ely Russell, *Moravian Families of Carroll's Manor, Frederick County, Maryland* (Middletown, Md., 1989), 111–141.

19. CCA to CCC, Oct. 6, 21, 1774, CCC to CCA, Oct. 26, 1774, Carroll Papers, MS 206; CCC to Wallace & Co., Oct. 19, 23, 1774, Sept. 10, 1775, Charles Carroll, Letter-book, 1771–1833, fols. 40v, 51, Arents Collections.

wrote his partners in Annapolis that even mediocre tobacco was bringing 4d per pound — about 33s per hundredweight.[20]

The most obvious change the Revolution brought to Carrollton was the Carrolls' decision to shift from tobacco rents of one thousand pounds of the staple per 100 acres to cash rents at the rate of £20 current money for the same amount of land. First instituted in 1775, the new levy is further confirmed by the record of balances for 1776 and 1777. In September 1776, the rent stated as annually due on the manor's 6,826 acres of tenanted land lists the sum of £1,289.11.3 current money, £17.13.8 ¾ sterling (for quitrents), and only fifty-nine hundred pounds of tobacco. The figures for 1777 present a similar picture, with the rent roll for that year recording the annual rent on the 6,843 ½ acres leased as £1,260.10.0 current money and sixty-seven hundred pounds of tobacco, plus £15.8.6 ½ sterling for quitrents. The balances further show that Carrollton's tenants found it no easier to come up with the cash than they had the tobacco. The sum actually owed in 1776 was £2,784.10.8 current money, indicating a carryover of more than £1,600, and in 1777 the annual rent accounted for less than half of the £2,683.8.9 ½ noted as due. No returns from Carrollton have survived for 1778, but by 1779 the combined strains of a rapidly depreciating currency and a mounting tax burden made good collections from the manor imperative. "We must," Papa wrote Charley in April of that year, "make Carrollton more than Pay Our Assessments."[21]

To achieve that goal, Papa, whose role in managing the property had ex-

20. CCA to CCC, Aug. 14, 1775, Carroll Papers, MS 206; CCC to Wallace & Co., Oct. 4, Nov. 14, 1775, Charles Carroll, Letter-book, 1771–1833, fols. 51, 52–52v, Arents Collections.

Although the information Joshua Johnson relayed to his partners in April 1776 was known to the Carrolls that August (CCC to CCA, Aug. 20, 1776, Carroll Papers, MS 206), his final account of sales did not arrive until early 1777. Because Charley communicated this intelligence to Papa in person, rather than by letter, no written record of the Carrolls' final prewar tobacco transaction survives. Clues, however, make it possible to approximate the general value of the sale. Assuming that Johnson secured at least 4d sterling per pound for the 141,000 lbs. of the staple consigned him, the Carrolls would have realized a minimum gross return of £2,350 sterling. However, Wallace and Company's records show that prices for the tobacco consigned to them in October and December 1775 ranged from a low of 3.5d to a high of 9d per pound, so the Carrolls probably made even more than this calculation suggests. Edward C. Papenfuse, *In Pursuit of Profit*, table 2-8a, 69.

21. CCA to CCC, Mar. 19, 1777, Apr. 28, 1779, Carroll Papers, MS 206; rent roll for Carrollton, Sept. 29, 1777, Carroll-Maccubbin Papers.

The Family Economy

panded because of the demands of Charley's political career, took two steps designed to enhance the returns from the manor. Having raised the rents in 1779 from £20 current money to £40, he increased them again in 1780 to £100 per one hundred acres. The rampant depreciation of paper money meant that this change improved the Carrolls' cash flow without burdening their tenants — in hard money values, the rents were lower than they had been before the American Revolution. Second, the elder Carroll elected instead to "advance" the payment schedule by having steward Joseph Johnson collect twice, rather than only once, a year. The first biannual collection yielded a total of £1,906.14.0 current money — approximately half in April 1779, and the rest in December — confirming Charley's observation that the tenants would probably find paying in two smaller increments easier to afford.[22]

The improved collections notwithstanding, the havoc wreaked by the war on the value of money convinced Charley that the Carrolls would do even better if they returned to their old system of crop rather than cash rents. "I think the rents on Monocasi should be reserved in kind in Tobacco, or wheat — a thousand weight of Tobo, or 5 bushels of wheat for every hundred acres," he told his father in early December 1779. "The money is in so fluctuating a state, that no one can with safety deal in it." In addition, Charley suggested that tenants who still owed tobacco rents be charged "interest in Tobo" and made to pay at once. "This Tobo together with our own, will, I hope enable us to pay next year's (1780) tax."[23]

With a 1778 congressional ban on exporting provisions still in effect, Papa considered implementing only the part of Charley's recommendation that pertained to tobacco. In the spring of 1780 he proposed setting rents on Carrollton for 1781 at one thousand pounds of the staple per one hundred acres for "Bottom Tenants" and slightly less, eight hundred pounds for the same acreage, from "Upland Tenants."[24] However, this change was never put into effect, because the repeal of the legal tender law in December 1780 gave the Carrolls another, evidently preferable, course of action, that of levying rents in specie (hard money) at £20 per one hundred acres. An examination of the thirty-one tenants' accounts that survive for 1781–1782 reveals that, after March 1781, rents were no

22. Mary C. Jeske, "Autonomy and Opportunity: Carrollton Manor Tenants, 1734–1790" (Ph.D. diss., University of Maryland, 1999), chap. 7; CCC to CCA, Apr. 29, 1779, Carroll Papers, MS 206.

23. CCC to CCA, Dec. 4, 1779, Carroll Papers, MS 206.

24. CCA to CCC, Apr. 11, 1780, ibid.

longer charged and received in current money, but in specie.[25] The elder Carroll did impose one new restriction on the manor — a limitation that indicates tenant perception of opportunities the war offered. "I have," Papa informed Charley in mid-April 1780, "prohibitted the Sale of Tenements to prevent Emigrations; that Spirit prevails greatly." He had heard that "the Virginia Land Office was shut up, if it was so, it is again opened." Several of his acquaintances had already "sent thither for Land Warrt:" and planned "to sett out in a fortnight for Canetuck," a course of action he emphatically meant to deny to his Monocacy tenants.[26]

The difficulty Joseph Johnson experienced in making his collections during the spring of 1780 offers a tantalizing hint of how the proscription against sales was received on the manor. Apprised by Johnson in early April that the process was not going well, Charley grumbled irritably that the steward "is either grown too old for business, or dishonest," apparently never considering that tardiness in paying rent might well signify his tenants' displeasure and resistance. Unmollified by Johnson's subsequent presentation of £713.7.6 on May 1, the elder Carroll insisted that Charley go to Carrollton to put matters in order. The results of Charley's tour in mid-May were reflected in Johnson's December collection, a return that Charley still considered highly unsatisfactory but that his father defended on the grounds that the tenants had not yet completed harvesting and selling their grain. Indeed, Papa was pleased enough to order the steward "to informe the Tenants that I will have patience with them until the 1st: of March, to give them an opportunity of Selling the Produce of their Farmes to the best advantage, but after that day," the old man asserted sternly, "Johnson must distrain."[27]

Little of whatever distraining became necessary on Carrollton in 1781 was undertaken by Joseph Johnson. His service to the Carrolls ended abruptly with his death that May. Professing to be "sorry" for Johnson's demise, Charley replied that he believed the steward to have been "an honest man, tho latterly too indolent & indulgent to the tenants, at our expence." Finding a replacement with sufficient industry and integrity proved something of a challenge, but within a month Papa had appointed Joseph Smith, a distant relative living near the manor and highly recommended by family and friends. The beginning of

25. The Carrolls' practice of entering specie payments in a different column from those in current money confirms this change. Jeske, "Autonomy and Opportunity," chap. 7.
26. CCA to CCC, Apr. 11, 1780, Carroll Papers, MS 206.
27. CCC to CCA, Apr. 8, 1780, CCA to CCC, May 4, Dec. 9, 1780, ibid.

The Family Economy

Smith's stewardship coincided with another change on Carrollton: the tenants' initial payments of their rents in wheat at the rate of five shillings current money per bushel. Five of the tenants whose accounts are credited with wheat during those years paid eighty or more bushels, enough at five shillings apiece to satisfy an annual cash rent of twenty pounds. Moreover, at 7s 6d, the price the Carrolls were getting for their wheat in 1781, Papa and Charley stood to make a gross profit of 50 percent on every bushel they received from Carrollton.[28] With the provisions embargo lifted by 1781 and the demand for wheat strong, father and son could take a measure of satisfaction in their ability to keep the manor economically viable during a disruptive conflict, but they were well aware that Carrollton's future productivity depended upon the war's being brought to a successful conclusion.

The coming of the American Revolution also compounded the Baltimore Company's chronic problems and added new strains and pressures of such magnitude that it is a wonder the ironworks managed to survive the tumultuous period 1775–1783. Among the most detrimental effects on the company's interests was the increasing monopoly by the crisis of Charley's energy and attention, especially in the years 1776–1778, when his duties as a member of the Continental Congress frequently kept him away from Maryland for months at a time. Largely deprived of the guidance of its best businessman, the Baltimore Company relied heavily on its on-site manager, Clement Brooke, to deal with the difficulties of operating an ironworks during a war. Brooke's task was formidable. The military's need for manpower made labor scarcer and more expensive, and the slaves the partners sent to the works were often unfit to perform the strenuous tasks required of them. Joney, a "wench" sent by Robert Carter in 1777, was so subject to fits that she could not even "earn the victuals she eats," and Will, who came from Carter the following year, was disabled by a defective hand. By April 1778, the company's situation had become critical: with no hands to cut timber and make charcoal, Hockley Forge was "standing still," work at the other forge was barely moving, and, although the furnace had been primed and

28. CCA to CCC, May 18, June 9, 1781, CCC to CCA, May 21, 1781, ibid.; Accounts of Adam Kile, David Prish, Jacob Tivecot, George Yose, and James Bosley, CCA, Account Book and Index, 1754–1784, fols. 78, 81, 85–87, MdHi. In his letter to Charley dated Apr. 10, 1781, Papa noted that he expected to realize £300.0.0 from the sale of 800 bushels of wheat, or 7s 6d per bushel (Carroll Papers, MS 206). For an analysis of tenant productivity, 1776–1780, based on ledger MT, see Jeske, "Autonomy and Opportunity," chaps. 6, 7.

ready for several weeks, Brooke could not put it "in blast" because he lacked "a sufficient number of hands to coal."[29] Four years later, the beleaguered manager was still reciting the same lament, his employers having saddled him with at least five slaves who were crippled, sick, or otherwise "very unfit for the business." A year later, in 1783, Brooke registered a new complaint — the works had become so "burthened" with female slaves that he insisted no more women be sent.[30]

Whatever the quality of his workers, Brooke still had to feed them, but the outbreak of hostilities impeded both the production and the delivery of corn, especially when the British navy was either present in the Chesapeake Bay or conducting coastal raids. Even having enough laborers sufficiently well fed to be able to produce iron did not mean the end of the woes of the ironworks. The partners still had to contend with the unpredictability of the wartime market and the effects of rampant inflation on company profits. The price of bar iron, consistently more in demand than the brittle pigs, soared from £28 current money in 1776 to £300 per ton in 1778, and at the end of 1780, with the ratio between gold and paper at 90:1, Papa calculated one sale at £3,240 current (£36 gold) per ton. Within a month, the figures had spiraled upward again, and in January 1781 bar was selling at £40 gold per ton, and the exchange had increased to 110:1.[31]

Like the majority of the thirteen ironworks operating in Maryland by the time of the American Revolution, the Baltimore Company declined to contract with either the provisional or the state government to produce armaments for the war effort. Rather than undertaking the intricate process of casting cannon, which required the skills of a specially trained founder, Charley and his partners decided they would do better selling their pigs and bars to ironmasters interested in manufacturing war materiel. Accordingly, the company, in the spring of 1776, offered to lease William Whetcroft the old forge on the Patapsco River for the construction of a slitting mill. Although Whetcroft refused in favor of another site farther upriver, his operation was still expected "to make a good market for Baltimore Company iron." On at least one occasion, the company

29. Clement Brooke to Robert Carter, Apr. 8, 1777, Apr. 14, 1778, Carter Papers, MdHi. In the letter of April 14, Brooke offered to buy five "young healthy fellows about 22 years of age or thereabouts" from Carter for the works on behalf of Daniel Dulany, Charles Carroll, Barrister, and Widow Carroll and stated he would pay "£300 this money," presumably currency, apiece but did not want any slaves that were "vicious."

30. Clement Brooke to the Baltimore Co., Aug. 7, 1783, ibid., oversize.

31. Clement Brooke to Robert Carter, Mar. 3, 1777, Dec. 4, 1778, ibid.; CCC to CCA, Oct. 10, 1776, CCA to CCC, Dec. 9, 1780, Jan. 13, 1781, Carroll Papers, MS 206.

sold a sizable amount of timber and iron to the Baltimore Committee of Observation for the construction of a frigate, a transaction that netted each shareholder £135.[32]

Most sales continued to be conducted individually, however, since the war did not alter the company's long-standing marketing system, whereby each partner disposed of his own share of the pigs and bars produced, and references gleaned from the Carrolls' wartime correspondence indicate that between 1776 and 1782 they generally dealt with local buyers. Dr. Ephraim Howard, one of their principal purchasers, operated a saltpeter manufactory and, with his wife's cousins Samuel and Edward "Ironhead Ned" Dorsey, was involved in producing artillery at Dorsey's Forge on the Patapsco, near the Baltimore Company's Hockley Forge. Reflecting the emergence of Baltimore Town as Maryland's major trading center during the Revolution, the Carrolls sold iron to at least two mercantile firms located there — that of the elderly Glasgow merchant, Robert Christie, and later the newer partnership of Donaldson and Roe.[33] Finally, Papa and Charley continued to do business with their prewar customer James Hunter, the proprietor of a large slitting mill at Falmouth, Virginia. But, whoever the buyer, the Carrolls' transactions were invariably carefully calculated to minimize the ability of constantly shifting varieties of paper money to devalue their returns.[34]

32. Michael D. Thompson, *The Iron Industry in Western Maryland* (n.p., 1976), 17–18, 41–48; Robert Carter to CCC, Mar. 16, 1776, printed in Kate Mason Rowland, *The Life of Charles Carroll of Carrollton, 1737–1832, with His Correspondence and Public Papers* (New York, 1898), I, 143–144; Clement Brooke to Robert Carter, May 23, Oct. 23, 1776, Carter Papers. The site Whetcroft leased was Dorsey's Forge, owned jointly by Samuel Dorsey (1741–1777) and his brother Edward (1758–1799). John W. McGrain, "Defense Efforts at Dorsey's Forge," *History Trails*, VIII (1974), 13–16.

33. McGrain, "Defense Efforts at Dorsey's Forge," *History Trails*, VIII (1974), 14–15; Harry Wright Newman, *Anne Arundel Gentry: A Genealogical History of Some Early Families of Anne Arundel County, Maryland*, 3 vols. (Annapolis, 1970–1979), II, 172–173, 189–193. For a good discussion of the rise of Baltimore during the American Revolution, see Tina Hirsch Sheller, "Artisans and the Evolution of Baltimore Town, 1765–1790" (Ph.D. diss., University of Maryland, 1990).

34. The Carrolls note sales of iron to Christie in 1776, to Dr. Howard in 1779 and 1780–1781, to Walter Roe of Donaldson and Roe in 1779, and to James Hunter in 1772 and 1779. CCA to CCC, Sept. 17, 1772, Nov. 9, 1779, Dec. 9, 1780, Jan. 13, 1781, CCC to CCA, Oct. 10, 1776, Mar. 31, Oct. 26, Dec. 4, 1779, Carroll Papers, MS 206. For Hunter's identity, see Robert A. Rutland, ed., *The Papers of George Mason, 1725–1792* (Chapel Hill, N.C., 1970), I, lxiii.

Given the confusion and depreciation of the currency and the dearth of both company and individual records, it is impossible to determine whether the ironworks actually made any money for the partners during the war. Clement Brooke's assessment of the state of the business in January 1782 makes anything more than very modest profits seem highly unlikely. According to the ever-beleaguered manager, "The high prices of Labour, clothing, & almost every thing requisite towards supporting the works, together with the heavy taxes, takes almost all the iron made, considering the very low prices of iron in Maryland for upwards of twelve months until very lately." Most of the bar in stock, Brooke reported, had been sold to raise enough money simply to "maintain the works," or else had to be held in reserve against the demands of the tax assessor.[35]

Notes in an unknown hand concerning profits and losses at the Baltimore furnace for 1780–1781 underscore the effects of monetary chaos on the company's wartime finances: "A Profit of £3983.8.9 ¼ appears, but the accounts are so confused & the entrys so blended with continental money that it is impossible to tell what was real Profit or Loss those years." A similar situation prevailed at Hockley Forge during the same period. Noting that "a Profit of £1891.1.7" appeared for the forge in 1781, the anonymous scribe pointed out that "the Specie value of this sum must have been a very trifle" and admitted, "I know not what it was worth." Some improvement seems to have occurred at both the furnace and the forge over the next two years. For 1782–1783, a £3,787.12.7 ½ profit is attributed to the furnace, £385.10.9 ½ of it from sales of bar. Hockley Forge did even better. Regarding the £571.8.9 profit earned in 1782 and the £465.6.4 in 1783, the examiner commented revealingly, "This was real money."[36]

The partnership itself did not emerge from the war unscathed. The Dulany cousins, Daniel III and Daniel (son of Walter), remained loyal to the mother country, and both returned there to live, Daniel III in July 1775 and Daniel that September. Both left their ironworks shares with Daniel Dulany, Jr. A proclaimed neutral, the elder Dulany managed to protect a portion of his property from the fate that befell loyalists, but the holdings of his son and nephew did not escape. Under the provisions of An Act to Seize, Confiscate, and Appropriate All British Property in This State passed by the general assembly in February 1781, the state of Maryland acquired the Dulany stock in the Baltimore Company and

35. Clement Brooke to Robert Carter, Jan. 13, 1782, Carter Papers.
36. Daniel Carroll of Duddington Papers, Manuscripts Division, DLC (microfilm, reel 5). At the Baltimore Furnace sales of bar iron accounted for £962.4.7 ½ of the ephemeral profit. For the effects of the Revolution on the iron industry, see Sheller, "Artisans and the Evolution of Baltimore Town," 211–215.

acted as a full-fledged partner, contributing its allotment of labor and supplies, until 1785, when it sold the share at auction.[37] A less dramatic change occurred in June 1780, when the widow of Charles Carroll of Duddington remarried and her new husband, Ignatius Fenwick, assumed responsibility for managing her affairs in behalf of her three minor sons. Finally, the death of Charles Carroll, Barrister, on March 23, 1783, placed his Baltimore Company stock in the hands of his nephews, James and Nicholas Maccubbin Carroll.[38]

On August 7, 1783, four months after the Barrister's death, Clement Brooke summed up the state of the Baltimore Company for the new slate of partners. His litany was familiar, touching on all the old problems of labor and supplies. In remarks appended to Brooke's letter, Charley reiterated his strong support for the manager and urged the partners to give Brooke the authority to "lay in provisions, pay hirelings, other incidental charges, & taxes." In addition, the younger Carroll emphasized that anyone guilty of sending substandard labor to the works should take such hands back and immediately replace them with others who met Brooke's criteria. Calling for a meeting of the partners to be held "at the Furnace" in Baltimore on September 27, Charley concluded with a succinct summary of what he saw as the Baltimore Company's postwar agenda: "The Works, if carried on with spirit, and managed to the greatest advantage, might certainly be made very profitable: at present they hardly clear themselves[.] How to improve so improveable an Estate, is the object of the proposed meeting."[39]

There is no doubt that the war years exacted a toll from the Carrolls, but, despite the losses arising from the legal tender act, wartime taxes, British raids, and the

37. CCC to CCA, June 22, 1781, Carroll Papers, MS 206; Aubrey C. Land, *The Dulanys of Maryland: A Biographical Study of Daniel Dulany, the Elder (1685–1753), and Daniel Dulany, the Younger (1722–1797)* (Baltimore, 1955), 317, 321, 326–327; *Maryland Journal, and the Baltimore Advertiser,* Mar. 18, 1785. Baltimore merchants Abraham and Isaac van Bibber and William Smith purchased the Dulany share. Land (*The Dulanys of Maryland,* 369n) gives the price paid for Daniel III's tenth as £12,600. For evidence of the state of Maryland's participation in the Baltimore Company, see Clement Brooke to the Baltimore Co., Aug. 7, 1783, Carter Papers, in which Brooke notes that the state owes the works five men and two women.

38. Effie Gwynn Bowie, *Across the Years in Prince George's County: A Genealogical and Biographical History of Some Prince George's County, Maryland, and Allied Families* (Richmond, Va., 1947), 315; Edward C. Papenfuse et al., eds., *A Biographical Dictionary of the Maryland Legislature, 1635–1789* (Baltimore, 1979–1985), I, 197.

39. CCC to the Baltimore Co., Aug. 11, 1783, appended to Clement Brooke to the Baltimore Co., Aug. 7, 1783, Carter Papers.

shutting down of Poplar Island, the Carroll fortune, as documented by the Maryland tax list for 1783, remained substantial. The Carrolls' astute management during the years of fighting yielded highly profitable sales of tobacco, wheat, provisions, and, presumably, iron, which helped offset the effects of depreciation on their income from rents and loans. At war's end, Doohoragen contained some 11,716 contiguous acres and a slave population numbering 408. With an age structure ideal for labor and production, this labor force was valued at £14,762. The plantation's herds of livestock had swelled to 90 horses, 609 black cattle, and 256 sheep. By contrast, the manor's holdings of plate seem relatively modest — 362 ounces valued at £150.17.0. Doohoragen still bore the elder Carroll's unmistakable signature: it was a place of work.[40]

By contrast, the establishment on Duke of Gloucester Street, graced by 1,290 ounces of plate worth £537.10.0 and attended by nineteen slaves, served as a setting for show. Continuing the work on his gardens during the war, Charley had adorned his formal view by constructing two lovely pavilions overlooking the water. The 1783 tax list shows him to be the capital's wealthiest resident and, as the owner of twenty-eight lots valued at £3,255, its largest landlord. None of his neighbors came near to equaling him. His closest competitor, merchant Nicholas McCubbin, Sr., with four lots, eleven slaves, and 292 ounces of plate, possessed assets worth £2,475. Other wealthy Annapolitans sported fine homes, gracious tables, and liveried attendants, but none outshone the Carrolls.[41]

Yet, neither the glittering style of life and material security attested by the 1783 tax list nor the political and economic ordeals Papa and Charley encountered and overcame during the war fully explicates the family's Revolutionary experience. The ultimately tragic subtext of the years 1776–1782 is found elsewhere, in the poignant story of Charley and Molly's relationship.

40. "A Return of Property in Elkridge Hundred as Valued by Brice Howard, Assessor for the Year 1783," 1783 Maryland Tax List, MdAA.

41. "A Return of Property in Annapolis Hundred as Valued by Francis Fairbrother for the year 1783," ibid.; appendix B, part 3, "The Distribution of Total Assessed Wealth in Annapolis from the 1783 Tax List," in Papenfuse, *In Pursuit of Profit*, 263–268. It is important to note that the Annapolis home and properties of Nicholas Maccubbin, Sr., constituted virtually his entire estate, whereas the Carroll dwelling on Duke of Gloucester Street, although an important expression of the family's status, represented only a portion of its total wealth.

CHAPTER 11

Scenes from a Marriage: Charley and Molly, 1776–1782

As with the struggle for custody of the family's future between Papa and Charley over the legal tender law, the Revolution undeniably played a role in what happened to the Carrolls' marriage and especially to Molly. Two factors account for much of the strain that developed between husband and wife. Most obviously, Charley's wartime responsibilities kept him away from home for extended periods, particularly until he ended his congressional service in June 1778. Even more tellingly, his constant preoccupation with the Revolution's problems and pressures stiffened the emotional reserve that the separations of his childhood had made an immutable component of his personality. However, neither the Carrolls' waning intimacy nor Molly's steady decline can be attributed solely to the exigencies of war or Charley's insufficiency of personal warmth. In the end, the strictures that defined the lives of all eighteenth-century women also contributed powerfully to Molly Carroll's unhappy fate.

For Charley, who had expressed a certain dissatisfaction with married life as early as 1772, the coming of the American Revolution provided, in addition to political opportunities and economic challenges, a spectrum of exciting social diversions. His trip to Philadelphia in September 1774 during the meeting of the First Continental Congress gave him a taste of the convivial pleasures ahead. Notwithstanding his exclusion from the Congress's secret proceedings, he found himself immediately included — somewhat to his surprise and certainly to his delight — in the swirl of activities that animated the city's resident and visiting elites outside the room in Carpenters Hall where the official deliberations were taking place. On September 7, the day after he and Maryland delegate Thomas Johnson, Jr., arrived in Philadelphia and settled into their lodgings at the City Tavern, Charley spent what he described to Papa as "an agreeable evening . . . in company with several gentlemen who constitute what is called the Governor's Club." For more than thirty years, this set of prominent men had met nightly in a local tavern to, in the words of one observer, "pass away a few Hours in the Pleasures of Conversation and a Cheerful Glass." In its variety, the political complexion of the group Charley talked and tippled with reflected the tenuous and indecisive atmosphere that prevailed while Congress struggled to find a middle ground between subjection and independence.[1]

Most of the younger Carroll's companions owed their careers and influence to their close ties to Pennsylvania's proprietary party and the crown, a web that would ultimately prove too strong to break. Lawyer and former Pennsylvania governor James Hamilton (c. 1710–1783) and his brother-in-law William Allen (1704–1780), the distinguished jurist who had resigned as the colony's chief justice the previous April, were already known to Papa. Indeed, Charley reported, Hamilton had "enquired kindly after you." At least some, if not all, of Allen's four sons were present, and Richard Tilghman (1746–1796), a nephew of Charley's political ally Matthew Tilghman, completed the gathering's conservative contingent.[2] Within the next couple of years, two of these men, old William Allen and young Richard Tilghman, would return to England while the rest assumed a variety of loyalist positions in America. By contrast, Dr. William Shippen (1736–1808) and Dr. Thomas Cadwalader (c. 1707–1779), who also shared the cup and conversation at the Governor's Club that evening, were committed whigs and would boldly follow those principles into the whirlwind of revolution. Shippen, brother-in-law of the Virginia Lees (Francis Lightfoot, William, Richard Henry, and Arthur), became chief of the Continental army's medical department in 1777; Cadwalader, deemed too old for active duty, nevertheless volunteered his skills when hostilities commenced.

To most of the distinguished colonial gentlemen who gathered in Philadelphia on the meeting of the First Continental Congress, however, such painful and irrevocable decisions and the new dangers they would impose belonged to

1. CCC to CCA, Sept. 9, 1774, Carroll Papers, MS 206, MdHi; William Black (a Virginia official), journal during a visit to Philadelphia in 1744, cited in J. Thomas Scharf and Thompson Westcott, *History of Philadelphia, 1609–1884* (Philadelphia, 1884), I, 235.

2. CCC to CCA, Sept. 9, 1774, Carroll Papers, MS 206; Edward F. De Lancy, "Chief Justice William Allen," *Pennsylvania Magazine of History and Biography*, I (1877), 202–211; Edward C. Papenfuse et al., eds., *A Biographical Dictionary of the Maryland Legislature, 1635–1789* (Baltimore, 1979–1985), II, 822. Responding to Hamilton's greeting, Papa, clearly pleased by the recognition, noted that Hamilton and "Mr. Allen the Elder" were "the only Gentn: in Philadelphia whome I can Call old acquaintance." CCA to CCC, Sept. 13, 1774, Carroll Papers, MS 206.

Scenes from a Marriage

a future as yet only dimly perceived. Moderation was still the order of the day. Charley informed Papa quite happily: "Would you believe it? The new England & Maryd. deputies are as moderate as any — nay the most So." Social intercourse continued in its traditional channels and, without noticeable strain, encompassed men who did not agree about the causes and handling of the imperial crisis. On September 8, the day after his evening at the Governor's Club, Charley called on John Dickinson, "chatted with him half an hour chiefly on litterature, & a little on Politicks," and accepted an invitation to join "a large company" at his house for dinner the following day. On the afternoon of his initial visit to Dickinson's, Charley dined "quite in the familiar way" with Philadelphia merchant David Beveridge and his wife, both of whom, he told Papa, "desire their complts to Molly, & Mr. Beveredge to you." Before attending Dickinson's fete on the ninth, Charley took time to write his father: "Invitations are become very frequent. I have 3 invitations to dine out — & probably shall have many more." On September 12, he verified his prediction: "Except this day I am engaged to dine out every day this week."[3]

Although some of the men upon whom Charley called or with whom he dined — merchants Henry Hill, Stephen Moylan, and David Beveridge, for example — were already known to his family through trade, others, notably Pennsylvania's current governor John Penn and his brother Richard, represented a significant widening of the Carrolls' acquaintance.[4] That circle expanded again on September 14 when Samuel Chase, who had lost no time making himself known both as a congressional delegate and socially, introduced Charley to John Adams. Adams's diary entry records what impressed him most about Carroll and, in its exaggeration of his family's wealth, illustrates Chase's penchant for hyperbole. "This Day Mr. Chase introduced to us, a Mr. Carrell of Anapolis, a very sensible Gentleman, a Roman catholic, and of the first Fortune in America.

3. CCC to CCA, Sept. 9, 12, 1774, Carroll Papers, MS 206.

4. CCC to CCA, Sept. 12, 1774, ibid. Moving from his native Maryland to Philadelphia as a child, Henry Hill (1731–1798) and his father, Richard Hill, became successful wine merchants. The renown of "Hill's Madeira" accounts for the Carrolls' transactions with the firm, madeira being one of the family's favored vintages. Charley called at Hill's country seat near Germantown. Stephen Moylan (1737–1811) emigrated to Philadelphia in 1768 from Cork, where his family was successful in trade. Wm. H. Egle, "The Constitutional Convention of 1776: Biographical Sketches of Its Members," *PMHB*, III (1879), 441; Hill, Lamar, and Hill to CCA, Mar. 29, 1755, Carroll Papers, MS 206; Harold Donaldson Eberlein and Horace Mather Lippincott, *The Colonial Homes of Philadelphia and Its Neighbourhood* (Philadelphia, 1912), 258; CCC to CCA, Sept. 12, 1774, Carroll Papers, MS 206.

His Income is Ten thousand Pounds sterling a Year, now, will be fourteen in two or 3 years, they say, besides his father has a vast Estate, which will be his, after his father."[5]

On September 16, two days after making Adams's acquaintance, Charley brought his Philadelphia visit to a glittering climax by attending the gala dinner that the "gentlemen of the City" gave in honor of the "Gentlemen of Congress." Intended by its sponsors to be "the greatest entertainment that was ever made in the City" and expected to cost one thousand pounds, the event took place in the Pennsylvania State House, where, according to Massachusetts delegate Robert Treat Paine, "abt. 500 dined at once." The printed list of toasts (thirty-two in all) that Charley brought home to Papa covered a wide spectrum of possibilities. Beginning with "The King," "The Queen," and other members of the royal family, the assemblage moved on to endorse "Perpetual Union to the Colonies," to hope that "the Cloud which hang over Great-britain and the Colonies, burst only on the heads of the present Ministry," to pay tribute to "The Liberty of the Press," "The Virtuous Few in both Houses of Parliament," and "The Arms and Manufactures of America," and to acknowledge nine prominent Englishmen who had openly and consistently opposed the administration's harsh treatment of America. The final salutes were reserved for three Americans: Benjamin Franklin, John Hancock — and Daniel Dulany, whose star had already begun its unremitting descent. Given his recent role in accelerating Dulany's decline and the enhancement of his own prospects, Charley must have found that moment of recognition ironic.[6]

Charley's nineteen-day absence in September 1774 — eleven days in Philadelphia and another eight in transit — was a distinct alteration in the normal rhythm of Carroll family life and foreshadowed the new patterns that the Revolution would bring. The familiar seasonal movement between Annapolis and Elk Ridge, whereby Papa and Mrs. Darnall spent the winters in town and Molly and little Pol enjoyed long summer days at Doohoragen, often joined by Charley for weeks at a time when business permitted, assumed different configurations

5. John Adams's Diary, Sept. 14, 1774, in Paul H. Smith et al., eds., *Letters of Delegates to Congress, 1774–1789* (Washington, D.C., 1976–), I, 69. Although the exact size of the Carrolls' fortune in 1774 is unknown, their wealth certainly exceeded the £88,380 sterling CCA recorded in 1764. CCA to Charles Carroll, Jan. 9, 1764, Outerbridge Horsey Collection of Lee, Horsey, and Carroll Family Papers, MS 1974, MdHi.

6. Caesar Rodney to Thomas Rodney, Sept. 12, 1774, Robert Treat Paine's Diary, [Sept. 16, 1774], in Smith et al., eds., *Letters of Delegates to Congress,* I, 66–67, 75; "A List of Toasts Drank at the Treat given to the Congress," September 1774, Carroll Papers, MS 206.

Scenes from a Marriage

in response to the changing times. In short, Molly began to spend more and more time with her mother and father-in-law in the country while her husband attended to political responsibilities in Annapolis and elsewhere. When Charley left for Philadelphia on September 2, 1774, for example, Molly, then about three months into the pregnancy that would produce the longed-for son, took little Pol to Doohoragen, and they stayed there until Charley came for them on his way home. Moreover, the Carrolls' post-1774 separations differed from past ones, because they were brought about by a growing public crisis rather than rounds of visits to extended family and friends. The world into which Charley was henceforth steadily drawn would be only as accessible to Molly as he chose to make it, and in this respect, as became immediately apparent, Charles Carroll of Carrollton was no John Adams. During those eleven days in Philadelphia in 1774, Charley wrote three thoughtful and informative letters to his father but contented himself with merely transmitting affectionate greetings to his wife, on the grounds that he would write "a separate letter to Molly if I had a subject to write on, but not having seen any of the ladies as yet, I want material for a letter."[7]

Contrary to the implications of this convenient rationale, Charley saw plenty of ladies during his next trip to Philadelphia early in 1776, but the encounters did not increase the frequency of his correspondence with his wife. Indeed, the manner in which he generally reported them, via Papa, likely had a negative rather than a positive effect on his spouse, who had, within a couple of weeks of his departure, begun to experience a return of the "bileous disorder" that signaled the early stages of another pregnancy. His presence in Philadelphia required by his congressional appointment as one of the three commissioners to Canada, Charley departed Annapolis on February 27, accompanied by his cousin Jack (Father John) Carroll, whose participation in the mission Congress had asked him to arrange.[8] He left his family with some trepidation: Sir Henry Clinton's arrival in Virginia presented the fearful possibility that a British man-of-war might venture up the bay to Annapolis before Molly and the children left the capital for Doohoragen. Nor did Charley's trip north go well. Bitterly cold

7. CCC to CCA, Sept. 9, 1774, Carroll Papers, MS 206.

8. Although Charley does not give his traveling companion's name, it was most likely John Carroll. Writing to his father on March 8, from Philadelphia, Charley reported that "Cousin J. Carroll has determined on going with us" to Canada. Similarly, his apology in his March 21 letter to Papa for failing to convey greetings from "Cousin Carroll" as regularly as the priest had asked him to further suggests that Father Carroll had been in Philadelphia for some time. CCC to CCA, Mar. 8, 21, 1776, ibid.

winds roughened the bay and made the travelers' crossing arduous, and the poor condition of the roads impeded them on land. As they approached Philadelphia from the Delaware River, Charley noted fortifications to protect the city already in place.

The defenses the younger Carroll inspected and described to his father during his first week in Philadelphia symbolized the changes in the city since his last visit. If the Governor's Club still existed, he did not mention it, and reports on the military situation in Boston, together with speculations about what Congress or the British might do next, dominated his letters. He wrote faithfully to his father twice a week, beginning on March 4, two days after his arrival — and four days before he first wrote to his wife. He enjoyed his initial contact with "the ladies" on March 11, when he dined at the home of merchant Reese Meredith in the company of Mrs. Meredith, their daughter Ann Meredith Hill, Margaret Allen DeLancy, and Mary Cadwalader Dickinson.[9] Although all of the women asked about Molly, Charley did not get around to conveying their regards until the sixteenth, the day after he received her first letter to him. He did, however, take care to explain when he wrote to Papa on the fifteenth that the missive was intended "for Molly as well as you, for I find she is become a politician, & has given me a good acct of the proceedings in & about Annapolis."[10]

It was not that Charley never thought of Molly. He was genuinely relieved to learn that, by the second week in March, she and the two children and "all my material papers, books of acct, Library, Plate &c" had been moved to safety at Doohoragen. Beyond that, he took her desire to have half a dozen pairs of shoes made seriously enough to apprise her regularly, albeit through Papa, of his persistent efforts to get "the rascally shoemaker" to perform.[11] Nevertheless, only

9. For Charley's description of Philadelphia's defenses, see CCC to CCA, Mar. 8, 1776, ibid.

Charley's host, Reese Meredith (1705–1777), a Welshman by birth, was one of Philadelphia's most prominent merchants. His daughter Ann Meredith Hill attended the dinner with her husband, Henry. The daughter of William Allen, Sr., Margaret Allen DeLancy had married James DeLancy (1731–1800) of New York and returned with her loyalist husband to England soon after the war began. Mary Cadwalader Dickinson (d. 1791) was the first wife of Philemon Dickinson (1739–1809), John Dickinson's younger brother. Carl Bridenbaugh and Jessica Bridenbaugh, *Rebels and Gentlemen: Philadelphia in the Age of Franklin* (New York, 1942), 187; Egle, "The Constitutional Convention of 1776," *PMHB*, III (1879), 441–442; "Notes and Queries," *PMHB*, V (1881), 480–481.

10. CCC to CCA, Mar. 15, 1776, Carroll Papers, MS 206. None of the letters Molly wrote Charley between March and June 1776 has been found.

11. CCC to CCA, Mar. 12, 15, 1776, ibid.

Scenes from a Marriage

two of the dozen or so letters Charley is known to have written Molly during the entire course of their marriage and just one of those she wrote to him have survived, so their feelings about each other and much of the substance of their relationship can only be inferred from the voluminous correspondence between Charley and his father. As recorded therein, Charley's attitudes range from a kind of intermittent, absentminded affection to a lack of sensitivity that borders on the obtuse. How else but in the latter vein can the younger Carroll's report on his March 16 dinner with the Beveridges be interpreted?

> Tell Molly I dined the day before yesterday with Mr. Beveridge, he and his lady enquired kindly after her: Mrs. Beveridge has a very pretty sister, indeed I think her charming, there was so much vivacity, and at the same time sweetness in her countenance that during the whole time of dinner I could not keep my eyes off of her: she retired soon after dinner to my regret, as her conversation, from the small specimen I had of it, would have been very entertaining, I think.[12]

Charley's demeanor toward his son, Charles, who celebrated his first birthday on March 2, the day his father got to Philadelphia, is also curious. Aside from including him in plural greetings to Molly and "the children" or "the little ones," Charley never further acknowledges the lad, nor does he even once call him by name in any of the letters he sent home during his Canadian adventure from early March through mid-June 1776. Sometimes he seems to have entirely forgotten the little boy's existence, or that the child was his: "My love to both the Mollies & Mrs. Darnall," he breezily concluded his March 21 letter to Papa, and on May 5 he advised Molly, through Papa, not to worry unduly about a rash that had appeared on "her little boy's face." His relationship with his daughter, now five and a half, had warmed up considerably, however. "Kiss little Poll for me," he instructed Papa on March 4, completely reversing the pattern of their former exchanges, and added the promise, "I will bring her some pretty thing when I return." Two weeks later, after directing his father, "Assure Molly of my tenderest affection," Charley again requested that he "kiss little Poll for me & tell her to mind her book & to be a good girl." Upon learning that his daughter had obeyed his dictum, he conceded magnanimously to Papa, "Indeed she was always a pretty good child."[13]

The questions about the quality of Charley's marital and parental connec-

12. CCC to CCA, Mar. 18, 1776, ibid.
13. CCC to CCA, Mar. 4, 21, 23, May 5, 1776, ibid.

tions raised by his letters during the spring of 1776, both from Philadelphia and later while en route to Canada, contrast sharply with the consistent affirmation of his relationship with his father revealed in that same correspondence. Unperturbed when he received news in mid-March that Molly was unwell, Charley offered advice rather than sympathy: he regretted his wife's indisposition but looked upon it as temporary and assured Papa confidently that a "change of air & exercise will I flatter myself remove her complaint." Upon learning while in Montreal in early May of "my dear Molly's recovery," Charley reiterated that curative regimen, telling Papa, "I hope with care, proper exercise, & proper diet she may be able to shake off the bileous disorder with which she has been so much afflicted of late." Toward his father, who remained hale and hearty the whole time he was away, Charley conveyed considerably more concern, emphasizing that Papa must keep him informed "of every occurrence domestic or public wh you think will be interesting to me, particularly the state of your health, wh is so dear to me, and about wh I am always sollicitous, but particularly so when at a distance from you." [14]

The frequency of Charley's correspondence tells a similar story. Having written to Molly twice during the three and a half weeks he waited impatiently in Philadelphia for Congress to finish its instructions to the commissioners, he then managed to send her only a single letter between March 26, the day he left for Canada, and June 11, the day he returned. By comparison, he wrote Papa eleven times before departing on his northern trek, and, through the ensuing nine weeks of the expedition, he composed at least one letter a week to his father and even found time to make regular entries in the journal he kept on his journey. [15]

The substance of his sole letter to Molly also merits comment. Dated April 15, 1776, and written from the home of General and Mrs. Philip Schuyler at Saratoga, New York, where Charley (according to his journal) enjoyed a memorable and "most pleasing sejour," the missive is friendly but by no means intimate,

14. CCC to CCA, Mar. 8, 25, May 5, 1776, ibid.

15. There are three published editions of the journal Charley began on Apr. 2, 1776. These are Brantz Mayer, ed., *Journal of Charles Carroll of Carrollton during His Visit to Canada in 1776, as One of the Commissioners from Congress; with a Memoir and Notes* (Baltimore, 1845, 1876) (rpt. New York, 1969, in the series Eyewitness Accounts of the American Revolution); appendix B in Kate Mason Rowland, *The Life of Charles Carroll of Carrollton, 1737–1832, with His Correspondence and Public Papers* (New York, 1898), I, 363–400; and Allan S. Everest, ed., *The Journal of Charles Carroll of Carrollton as One of the Congressional Commissioners to Canada in 1776* (Fort Ticonderoga, N.Y., 1976). The manuscript, Charles Carroll of Carrollton, "Diary of a Journey to Canada, Apr. 2–June 10, 1776," is filed in the Revolutionary War Collection, MdHi.

Scenes from a Marriage

perhaps because the writer was not alone when he wrote it. "I am writing this letter," Charley gaily informed his wife, "in company with a sweet pretty young lady Miss Peggy Schuyler. She is all life & spirits good natured & witty qualities seldom united in the same person." Notwithstanding his solemn avowal to Molly that only his determination to "render important services to my country" made "this tedious absence from my dearest connections" bearable, Charley left no doubt in either his letter or his journal that "the lively behaviour" of eighteen-year-old Peggy and her nineteen-year-old sister Betsy alleviated very pleasantly, if only temporarily, the boredom and anxiety that periodically beset him. He would leave Saratoga "with reluctance," he told Molly, "as I do not expect to meet with such agreeable company till I see my own home." [16] Two weeks later, on April 29, however, Charley's spirits received another delightful boost from the first "french Inhabitants" of Canada that he met, namely, the wives of the men who attended the dinner party given by General Benedict Arnold in honor of the commissioners on the day of their arrival in Montreal. "The french ladies, who supped with us at the General's, and who are all married to english men of our party and attached to the Colonies," were, he reported admiringly to Papa, "very agreeable, lively, and truely polite: there is an ease and Softeness in their manners wh is charming and at the first glance discovers the last polish of an excellent education." [17]

Charley's expectations about receiving mail from his wife differed markedly from his own pattern in sending it. "Molly will excuse me from writing to her from this place," he wrote Papa when the commissioners stopped in New York in late March. "I have scarce time to write this letter being engaged all day in company," but he followed by saying, "I beg she will write frequently to me & let me know how she & the children are." With unexpectedly wistful affection, he added, "I wish I could hear a little of two shoe's prattle." Complaining to Papa on April 1 that he had heard from Molly only twice since leaving home, Charley noted pointedly, "My letters to you are intended as much as for her as for you: she must not expect a separate letter by every post particularly as I shall have my hands full when I get to Montreal." A week later, he put it a little more gently: "I

16. CCC to MDC, Apr. 15, 1776, Carroll Papers, MS 206. Betsy Schuyler, who later married Alexander Hamilton, and her sister Peggy (Margarita) were the two younger of the Schuylers' three daughters. Philip Schuyler (1733–1804) and his wife Catherine Van Rensselaer (1734–1803) also had three sons. Florence Van Rensselaer and Ethel L. Fitz Randolph, *The Van Rensselaers in Holland and in America* (New York, 1956), 5–6, 8–9, 20.

17. CCC to CCA, Apr. 30, 1776, Carroll Papers, MS 206.

have not lately wrote to my dear Molly: but she must consider my letters to you as written to herself." He intended to do better in the future: "After some residence in Canada, when I get a little settled, I shall write her a long letter — I am now obliged to snatch every little leisure (& I have but little) to write to you." What was there to say, anyhow? "She must be convinced of my love, and my letters to her could only inform her of that. I may have some agreeable subjects to write on from Canada: politics certainly cannot be so to her."[18]

The "long letter" from Canada never materialized, of course, and, Charley's promises and protestations aside, the two pages to Molly on April 15 from the Schuylers — before being "called to supper" brought that effort to a close — marked the end of his direct correspondence with his wife during the spring of 1776. Nevertheless, he continued to urge Papa to "write me often & press Molly to do the same: every little incident at this distance is interesting, be it ever so trivial," and, when he found no "bulky packet" of letters awaiting him in Montreal, Charley got very specific: "I hope to receive letters from Molly," he wrote Papa firmly on April 30. "She has little to do and therefore may write long letters: the most trivial domestic occurrences at this distance coming from her will be pleasing." She was not, however, to expect the same attention in return; again Charley insisted: "She must consider my letters to you as to her self I have but little time to spare for letterwriting." That he might occasionally divide the time he did have a bit more equally between his father and his wife evidently did not occur to him, and he did not even take a moment to write to Molly that he was pleased to learn her health had improved. "I can not write to Molly by this Post — I write this before breakfast, & the hour is nigh, after that our hands will be full," he explained to Papa on May 5 after receiving three letters from her informing him that she was better. As usual, Charley left it to his father: "Assure her of my tender affection and remembrance."[19]

For the Carrolls, letters were lifelines, the tangible manifestations of the intangible ties that bound them. Whatever their contents — didactic instructions, stern reprimands, endless requests, homesickness, grief, dry legal information, or legislative reports — these missives connected Papa and Charley in ways that only death could sever. Whether separated by the expanse of the Atlantic Ocean or only by the thirty-two miles between Annapolis and Elk Ridge, Papa and Charley wove with their pens the enduring fabric of their relationship. Contrasting sharply with that reality is the desultory and haphazard way in which Charley conducted his correspondence with Molly and his insistence that

18. CCC to CCA, Mar. 29, Apr. 1, 8, 1776, ibid.

19. CCC to CCA, Apr. 15, 18, 30, May 5, 1776, ibid.

his letters to Papa would suffice for her as well. Moreover, his frequent assertions of that rationale lend credence to the suspicion that he knew better but chose not to do so. As his habits of correspondence so effectively demonstrate, the center of the son's emotional existence had, from his youth, been fixed on the father, leaving little room, need, or desire for an intimate personal connection with anyone else.

The new patterns of living that the Carrolls adopted when Charley accepted his first congressional assignment in the spring of 1776 continued with only slight variations for the next two and a half years. Cumulatively, service in Congress and in state government kept him away from his family for fifteen months of that time, and during those separations he invariably maintained contact with his "dearest connections" by writing regularly and at length to his father and only very occasionally to his wife. Because only one of her letters to her husband survives, the shape and substance of Molly's life must be recovered from what her husband and father-in-law wrote about her. The picture that emerges is not so secondhand as might seem inevitable. Through her behavior, as described by the men closest to her, Molly Carroll speaks effectively, if indirectly, for herself.

The happy reunion with Papa and Molly that Charley anticipated with increasing eagerness during the final frustrating weeks in Canada lasted only a few days. Arriving at Doohoragen about June 19, he scarcely had time to embrace his family before leaving again for Annapolis, where he took his seat in the eighth convention on June 24. Ten days later, having witnessed the departure of Governor Eden for England and played a major role in persuading his colleagues in the convention to vote for Independence, Charley found himself chosen as one of Maryland's delegates to Congress, an honor that necessitated his traveling back to Philadelphia almost immediately. Although elated by the appointment, he regarded the trip with limited enthusiasm. He was tired, he told Papa on July 5, and so "jaded with the heat & close attendance on the house" that he could not, of course, write to Molly. He and Chase set out for Philadelphia on July 12, but Charley's sojourn there lasted only four weeks, long enough for him to get appointed to the Board of War, sign the Declaration of Independence, and conduct some business for his father. He wrote Papa five letters, but he did not correspond with Molly at all, perhaps because he had to spend too much time trying to acquire the goods she wanted. Through no fault of his, he met with little success. As he explained to Papa on July 27, "Newton the shoe maker is gone to the flying camp: so no shoes for the ladies." [20]

20. CCC to CCA, July 5, 27, 1776, ibid.

Charley left the tense and sweltering city of Philadelphia for the refreshing rural charms of Doohoragen on August 10, but, again, he could not linger to avail himself of the restorative potential of the countryside. The ninth provincial convention, to which he had been elected in absentia, was due to convene within the week to devise a constitution and form of government for Maryland. But, although he bade farewell to his father and left his son behind at Elk Ridge in Mrs. Darnall's care, Charley did take his wife and daughter back to Annapolis with him. Having been apart for most of 1776, husband and wife undoubtedly wished to end their separation. Given the serious business upon which the convention was about to embark, having the mistress of the house on Duke of Gloucester Street in residence without the distraction of her eighteen-month-old son seemed desirable. At age six and as often called Molly as little Pol, Charley's daughter was far more attuned to the demands of polite behavior than her baby brother. Moreover, she had become a favorite among her parents' friends and had even worked her charms upon her own generally aloof father. "My Dear little Girl is quite well," Molly reported to her mother on August 30, and went on to confirm the child's winning ways by adding, "Mrs Ridout was in town Yesterday she put it into Mollys head to go to White-hall with her — all that I could do or say wou[ld n]ot prevent her — her Papa, was fond of indulging h[er] — so I was obliged to submit."[21]

Beyond her desire to be reunited with her husband and the demands on her as the wife of an important member of the provisional government, Molly was probably eager for a change. However much she might have enjoyed and benefited from being pampered by her mother and Papa during the nauseous weeks of early pregnancy the previous spring, Molly was at heart a social person. Notwithstanding her period of indisposition, she had been stuck in the country for five months, dependent for entertainment upon two little children and an older parent and parent-in-law and treated regularly to Charley's accounts, sent by and large to Papa, of his engagements and experiences in a wider and more exciting world. Once, before she knew she was pregnant, she had considered going to Canada with him, and although his description of the rough travel and accommodations no doubt convinced her that changing that plan had been wise, there must surely have been times when Charley's descriptions of his encounters — and his undisguised enjoyment of the winsome women he met — rankled. By August 1776, Molly wanted to be back in the swing of things, even if it meant being separated from her son.

21. MDC to Rachel Darnall, [Aug. 30, 1776], Carroll Papers, MS 216, MdHi.

The Annapolis to which she and Charley returned was quite a different place from the gay little town she had previously known, however. Even before she left for Doohoragen in March, the uncertainties of the conflict between the colonies and mother country had begun to dampen the capital's convivial atmosphere. Henrietta Ogle, one of Molly's equally social contemporaries, described the unhappy changes well in the litany of complaints she wrote to her mother-in-law that February: "Annapolis is vastly dull, many Families having left it and almost everyone preparing to go. We have neither Balls or Routs and very little Dining and Supping out. The same dull Scenes forever." By August, as the Revolution transformed Annapolis from "a town of wealthy consumers into an armed camp and distribution center for the war effort," the scene offered even grimmer prospects: batteries had been built along the shoreline near Governor Eden's house, other fortifications bristling with artillery glowered from the hilltops, and by midsummer "troops from all over the province" were arriving to join the flying camp housed in tents on the capital's perimeter. The Council of Safety advertised for laborers "to work on intrenchments at Annapolis" at wages of 3s 6d a day, and its medical adviser, Dr. Richard Tootell, commenced the task of converting the free school on State House Circle into a military hospital.[22]

In the absence of their traditional trade and former customers — some loyalists had returned to England, and many of those favorably disposed to the patriot cause moved to their country seats because of the capital's vulnerability to enemy ships in the bay — the merchants remaining in Annapolis refocused their attention on supplying the troops. There is perhaps no more graphic illustration of the war's effect on the genteel ambiance formerly enjoyed by the town's affluent elite than the resolution the Council of Safety adopted that summer prohibiting any further slaughtering of animals within the town's limits, lest "the intolerable stench arising from slaughter houses [and] spreading green hides to dry" produce "pestilential disorder and other ill consequences to the troops and others residing in the city."[23]

22. Henrietta Hill Ogle to Anne Tasker Ogle, February 1776, Ridout Papers, folder 574, MdAA, quoted in Shirley Vlasak Baltz, *A Chronicle of Belair* (Bowie, Md., 1984), 44; Edward C. Papenfuse, *In Pursuit of Profit: The Annapolis Merchants in the Era of the American Revolution, 1763–1805* (Baltimore, 1975), 78, 80, 85; *Maryland Gazette* (Annapolis), Sept. 5, 22, 1776. My descriptions of wartime Annapolis are drawn from *In Pursuit of Profit*, which is the most authoritative treatment of the town and its mercantile community during the Revolutionary period.

23. Papenfuse, *In Pursuit of Profit*, 80–81; William Hand Browne et al., eds., *Archives of Maryland* (Baltimore, 1883–), XII, 89, quoted in Papenfuse, *In Pursuit of Profit*, 91.

In the midst of such conditions even the wife of Maryland's wealthiest patriot must make do, and so Molly Carroll, contrary perhaps to her expectations, devoted much of her time during the rainy and unseasonably cool month she spent in Annapolis from mid-August to mid-September 1776 patching together as genteel a life as she could. Though limited in comparison to the past, her social life remained active enough to require that she write her mother to "look in my Trunk where I keep my Silk Gowns" for her "Brown Taffity Gown," which, with "the Stomacher & Bows," must be sent to town. The shortage of dry goods presented more of a problem since she desperately needed "a yard & three-quarters of Black gauze" from which to make a "Shade" to cover the bosom of her low-necked dresses, for, as she told Rachel candidly, she had in the final trimester of her pregnancy grown "quite too big to go with out." To make collars and "pads," the rump-furbelows or bustles so in vogue, Molly asked her mother to spare her "about 6. yards of thick linen" from what had been made at Doohoragen, hoping Rachel would "be so kind as to let us have that Quantity — for other wise I must take some linen that will make the Servants very good Shirts, & poor Creatures tis what they are in great want of." Although prepared to deprive her slaves in order to maintain herself in the latest fashion, Molly compromised readily in other areas and asked her mother to "send me down one or two of Papas old Shirts" for making "little things" like baby clothes and underwear.[24]

Enlivened briefly by the diversion of a weekend trip to the Ridouts at Whitehall to retrieve little Pol, Molly's time in Annapolis nevertheless proved generally disappointing. Preoccupied with his work in the convention and beset with deepening fears about the future of the cause to which he had committed himself and his family, Charley had neither the time nor the heart for levity, and Molly found it more difficult than she had anticipated to be separated from her son. Writing to her mother in late August, she began her letter on that note: "You cannot doubt of my Anxiety to see My dear Boy, & all of you." She returned to it in closing: "I am glad to hear that he often takes air-rings, I am sure it will be of infinite service to him — is he fatter or thinner than when I left him, I long to see the dear Creature, but I do not as yet know when I shall be so happy." A natural event during Molly's stay symbolized with uncanny accuracy the dismal public and private uncertainties with which she and Charley wrestled — lightning struck twice in Annapolis, hitting both the State House and the chimney of the home of the Carrolls' near neighbors, Dr. and Mrs. Upton Scott. Thanks to

24. MDC to Rachel Darnall, [Aug. 30, 1776], Carroll Papers, MS 216.

a lightning rod, the loyalist doctor's abode, which he abandoned in June to return to England, escaped harm altogether, but the State House, where the convention met and constitutional deliberations took place, sustained one hundred pounds of damage.[25] If an omen, it could not be read as propitious: when the opportunity to return to Doohoragen arose in mid-September, Molly took little Pol and went joyfully and with relief to be reunited with her son.

Yet, despite Molly's change of venue, the autumn still was troubled and dreary. Charley continued his struggles for a conservative constitution in the convention while Maryland, to his alarm and despair, lurched toward anarchy. At Doohoragen Papa fell ill with a cold and, even more worrisome, with so severe a recurrence of the ulcerated condition that periodically affected one of his legs that Molly feared he would not be able to walk. "I am much concerned to hear that you are indisposed," Charley wrote the old man in mid-October, and, although critically important political matters currently engaged his attention, he told his father firmly, "If you should find your health decline pray send for me." However, neither the discomforts experienced by his wife as she neared the end of her pregnancy nor the means by which she alleviated them aroused Charley to similar expressions of anxiety and solicitude. "As Molly's time approaches she is more unwieldy has frequent feavours, does not sleep well but by the help of laudanum," Papa reported in early November.[26] Little did the old man know what that brief comment, to which Charley did not respond, portended. Laudanum, a preparation of powdered opium dissolved in alcohol, was widely used in the eighteenth century not only as a cure for insomnia but also to relieve pain, treat a variety of ailments ranging from nausea, coughs, and diarrhea to diseases like smallpox, syphilis, and tuberculosis, and even to control spasms and insanity.[27] The remedy appears in the Carrolls' orders to England as early as 1772, but Papa's November 1776 reference is the first evidence linking Molly to its use. It would not be the last.

On November 11, having at last acted favorably on the constitution and form of government Charley and his fellow committeemen had devised, the convention dissolved itself. Released thereby from his public responsibilities, at least temporarily, Charley went directly to Doohoragen to see for himself that Papa

25. Ibid.; CCC to CCA, Aug. 20, 1776, Carroll Papers, MS 206.

26. CCC to CCA, Oct. 18, 1776, ibid., MS 206; CCA to CCC, Nov. 7, 1776, Etting Papers, HSP.

27. George B. Wood, *The Dispensatory of the United States of America* (Philadelphia, 1834), 486–487.

had gotten well and, though perhaps secondarily, to be on hand for Molly's delivery. That event occurred on November 23 and added to the Carroll household another little girl, who was called Nancy, the diminutive of her formal name, Ann Brooke Carroll. In deference to Molly's recovery from childbirth as well as to conditions in the capital, the family reversed its usual practice of wintering in town, and Charley settled in for an extended stay in the country, remaining at Doohoragen until late January, when preparations for the opening of the state government he had helped create demanded his presence in Annapolis. Present on February 5 for the convening of the Senate, to which he had been elected as one of nine senators from the Western Shore, he gave close attention for nearly three weeks to a broad spectrum of public business. Despite his full agenda, he made time to write one lengthy letter to his wife concerning the imminent inclusion of a new clerk in their ménage. For once, Molly turned the tables on him. "She has not," Charley told Papa irritably on February 14, "answered my letter by this day's messenger." Though he professed to recognize that "indisposition," or perhaps having "nothing to write," probably accounted for his wife's silence, he still took pains to make known his awareness that neither possibility had kept her from corresponding with others: "Her letter to Mrs. Ridout I have just sent over & suppose she will receive an answer tomorrow." [28] Whether his pique was of long or short duration is unknown, but within ten days of this incident Charley took a leave of absence from his senatorial duties to pay a short visit to his family at the manor. When he returned to Annapolis on March 1, Molly left her children — little Pol, Charles, and Nancy, barely three months old — behind to accompany him.

The revels Annapolis offered in the spring of 1777 paled in comparison with those routinely available during the golden years of the early 1770s, but, even so, they were gayer than anything the previous year had brought. The inauguration of the state's first governor, Thomas Johnson, Jr., on March 21, constituted the centerpiece of the wartime social season. The official ceremonies, held "in the presence of a great number of people who expressed the highest satisfaction on the occasion," began at noon with a procession of dignitaries. Led by the high sheriff of Anne Arundel County, the parade included a hierarchy of officeholders, with the president of the Senate and the senators, Charley among them, first in the line, followed by the governor-elect and his council, the

28. Charley was particularly concerned that the young man, William Skerrett, an Irishman recommended by Folly Quarter overseer John Flattery as William Deards's replacement, understand his duties in advance and that he "not expect to be admitted to my table." CCC to CCA, Feb. 13, 1777, Carroll Papers, MS 206.

sergeant at arms bearing the mace, the speaker and members of the House of Delegates, the mayor, recorder, aldermen, and common council of Annapolis, "Military Officers," "Gentlemen Strangers," and "Citizens." These august personages marched from the ballroom on Duke of Gloucester Street to the State House, where the high sheriff, according to his instructions from the legislature, "commanded" silence and "proclaimed the governor." After three volleys of small arms and the firing of thirteen cannon had saluted this announcement, the procession retraced its steps, but in a slightly different order that placed "HIS EXCELLENCY the GOVERNOR" and the council directly behind the high sheriff and in front of the officers and members of the general assembly.

With their ceremonial duties completed, the gentlemen adjourned to the coffeehouse for entertainment and a dinner at which thirteen toasts were drunk. Not surprisingly, the libations consumed on this occasion, unlike those Charley imbibed in Philadelphia in 1774, were not accompanied by references to the king, the queen, or any members of the royal family. Excluded, like others of her sex, from the fete at the coffeehouse, Molly could nevertheless enjoy the day's grand finale: the "elegant ball in the evening," with which the festivities concluded.[29]

Returning to her children in mid-April, Molly spent the next six and a half months at Doohoragen while Charley served two different stints away from Maryland in Congress. Although these separations were similar in form to the previous year's, with Charley again writing regularly to Papa and only rarely to his wife, they differed markedly in substance, primarily because in 1777 Molly did not become pregnant. Free of biliousness and other physical complaints, she had no difficulty finding entertaining things to do in the country, and, when necessary, she did not hesitate to contend with her absent husband in behalf of her own wishes and desires. A steady stream of visitors wound its way to the manor, beginning, a bit annoyingly, in early May, when Charley informed his family that he had offered their hospitality to Samuel Hanson of Port Tobacco, Maryland, and his bride. Recently wed in Philadelphia, the couple would, Charley told Papa, stop at Doohoragen on their way home. His eye for attractive women as keen as ever, Charley alerted his father to Mrs. Hanson's charms — "I think you will admire his lady: she is not only beautiful, but appears to be of a sweet and amiable temper" — and then, typically, went on to specify, "Molly &

29. The description of Governor Johnson's inauguration is taken from *Md. Gaz.*, Mar. 28, 1777. For the general assembly's instructions for proclaiming the governor, see *Votes and Proceedings of the Senate of the State of Maryland,* February Session, 1777, 21 (hereafter *VPS*).

Mrs. Darnall & you will do all in yr. power to make her stay at Doohoragen agreeable." More to Molly's liking, Mary and John Ridout arrived later in May for a visit that extended into June. As that month drew to a close, Molly began to plan for her attendance at the wedding of Cousin Daniel's daughter Mary and Colonel Patrick Sim, scheduled to take place at Mellwood in July.[30]

As might be expected, this round of activity scarcely left Molly any time for writing to Charley, as he duly noted in a letter to his father on June 2. The missive she penned to remedy the omission cannot have entirely pleased him, however, since it dealt with a matter he considered already closed — the shoes and tea she had asked him to buy for her in Philadelphia. "Tell Molly," he had instructed Papa on May 14, "they ask for making shoes 45/ for tea £4:15 per pound — I can not give such prices, and I am sure she will commend me for it." The considerably meeker message he asked Papa to deliver on June 10 suggests that his confident prediction was in error: "I will answer Molly's letter by the next post; she shall have her shoes by Col: Sim & some other things."[31]

Having yielded to his wife on that issue, Charley shortly found himself confronted by another, equally tricky dilemma involving her determination to be present at Mellwood for the Carroll-Sim nuptials in early July. The problem began when Charley directed that Johny (Molly's coachman and a brother of Sam, the Annapolis house slave he had taken with him to Philadelphia) be sent up with his horses so that he could "ride out & take exercise." Johny arrived on June 25, but, instead of sending him home after a day's rest as planned, Charley ordered him to assume his brother's duties as waiting man, because Sam had fallen sick. Although Charley insisted that he kept Johny "to attend Sam, as much as to wait on myself," he recognized that he risked clouds on the domestic front: as he acknowledged to Papa, detaining Molly's driver in Philadelphia might make it impossible for her to attend the wedding. Sam's subsequent improvement and the absence of any mention of Johny's presence in Philadelphia after June 28 suggest that Molly did not miss the festivities at Mellwood after all.[32]

30. CCC to CCA, May 4, 1777, Carroll Papers, MS 206. Patrick Sim (d. 1819), a lieutenant colonel in the First Maryland Regiment, was the son of Joseph Sim (d. 1793) of Prince George's County and his first wife, Catherine Murdock (c. 1735–1771). Papenfuse et al., eds., *Biographical Dictionary*, II, 736–738; Francis B. Heitman, *Historical Register of Officers of the Continental Army during the War of the Revolution, April 1775 to December 1783* (Washington, D.C., 1914), 497.

31. CCC to CCA, May [16?], June 10, 1777, Carroll Papers, MS 206.

32. CCC to CCA, June 20, 26, 1777, ibid.

The good health and consequently happy outlook that sparked Molly's active social life and her successful contests with Charley also animated her interest in the events within the larger context of her life — the ever-present war. Indeed, Papa feared that her undisguised elation over the American victory at Saratoga might well have offended the Ridouts, whose close ties to English patrons had led them to adopt a carefully neutral stance. Writing to Charley on November 7, 1777, Papa thought Molly had been "rather too insulting among Her Tory Acquaintance" concerning Burgoyne's defeat. "How," the old man wanted to know, "did Her Friend Mrs. Ridoute bear the News and Her Behaviour[?]" The high spirits evident in that glimpse of Molly render even more poignant and cruel the catastrophe that befell her two short months later: in mid-January, she became so desperately sick that Papa sent an express to York, Pennsylvania, where Congress was meeting, to summon Charley home. The nature of her illness is nowhere specified in the family's papers, but its severity and duration kept Charley at Doohoragen for three months. Her condition improved slightly in February, but she suffered a relapse of such proportions that on March 13 Papa grimly informed John Ridout, "My Son can not leave Mrs. Carroll," even to come to Annapolis to sound out the Senate on a matter as important as the repeal of the legal tender law. It was not until early April that Molly recovered sufficiently to allow her husband to return to Congress.[33]

The aftermath of this episode that very nearly cost Molly her life offers another startling perspective on the dynamics of the Carrolls' marriage and the personalities of the two individuals it bound together. What emerges most clearly from an examination of the period between April and June 1778 is that not even his wife's brush with death had the power to alter Charley. Having been at Doohoragen, ostensibly at Molly's bedside, since the middle of January, Charley left the manor for York about April 12. On April 20, several days after his arrival, he sent Papa four closely written pages about the progress of the war, various aspects of congressional business, and even a long summary of two bills currently pending in Parliament. Regarding his wife, he had only this to say: "I write this to Molly as much as to you. I hope she is assured of my affectionate love, & that she will take great care & use much industry to recover her health — I hope she will send me the thread stockings when finished; by this time I dare say Miss Betsy has finished the pair she was about when I left home." The minimal solicitude and matter-of-fact tone are surpassed only by the juxtaposition

33. CCA to CCC, Nov. 7, 1777, Daniel of St. Thomas Jenifer to CCA, Feb. 26, 1778, John Ridout to CCA, Mar. 11, 1778, CCA to John Ridout, Mar. 13, 1778, ibid.

of the comments in his April 27 letter to his father. "I wish Molly could recover faster, but her perfect recovery must be the work of time & a proper regimen — I am sorry for the death of bold Robin; his death is a real loss." The late, lamented Bold Robin was a horse.[34]

Not until May 3 did Charley finally write Molly the letter that constituted his only direct communication with her during his ten weeks at York, a period in which he wrote sixteen letters to his father. For her part, Molly wrote to Charley twice, once about May 9, and again on May 21. Neither of her letters has been found, but one of them must have apprised him of the chief reason she had recuperated so slowly after his departure. By the third week of May, Molly surely knew that once again she was pregnant.

Whatever joy the prospect of another baby brought Molly must have been considerably circumscribed by the restrictions her condition imposed. Most immediately, the pregnancy prevented her from completing her recuperation by making a trip to the medicinal springs at Bath, in western Virginia, where the Carrolls had recently constructed a house on land they had purchased the previous year. The journey would have ministered to her soul as well as her body, for, in addition to its healing waters, the spa offered a lively round of social activity.[35] In the summer of 1778, a glittering representation from the Maryland and Virginia gentry congregated there, among them the Fielding Lewises from Fredericksburg, the John Augustine Washingtons of Westmoreland County, the Thomas Blackburns of Rippon Lodge in Prince William County, and from Maryland the John Ridouts and Major Daniel of St. Thomas Jenifer and his sister-in-law, Mrs. Betty Eden. Even with Charley at Doohoragen to keep her

34. CCC to CCA, Apr. 20, 27, 1778, ibid.

35. The Carrolls became interested in acquiring property at Bath (Berkeley Springs), now in West Virginia, after Papa visited there with Major Jenifer in August 1777 in hopes of healing his recurring fistula. Although the curative properties of the waters had long been known to Indians and colonists, the town of Bath was not created until the fall of 1776, when the Virginia assembly authorized that fifty acres of land surrounding the springs be marked out in quarter-acre lots and sold at public auction. Buyers were to be encouraged specifically "to build convenient homes for accommodating numbers of infirm persons, who frequent those springs yearly for recovery of their health." The Carrolls purchased their lots late in 1777 and commenced the construction of a house in the spring of the following year. Mabel Henshaw Gardiner and Ann Henshaw Gardiner, *Chronicles of Old Berkeley: A Narrative History of a Virginia County from Its Beginnings to 1926* (Durham, N.C., 1938), 50–51; CCC to CCA, Dec. 6, 1777, Daniel of St. Thomas Jenifer to CCA, Aug. 3, 1778, Carroll Papers, MS 206. The Carrolls' copy of the town plat is filed in MS 206, oversize.

company — he had terminated his service in Congress for good at the end of June — there is little doubt that Molly knew what she was missing, and the knowledge that her best friend Mary Ridout was there enjoying it without her must have rankled even more. "Balls twice a week, besides Hops — the difference betwixt them is that at the Balls there are Suppers, at the Hops nothing but Dan[c]ing," reported Major Jenifer in a letter to Papa from the springs in mid-August. The major capped his description of the gay scene with the last thing Molly probably wanted to hear: "But every Night some entertainment or other — such as selling Pawns Blind mans Buff &c and our friend Mrs. Ridout as much the Girl as any at the Springs in promoting Mirth." [36]

In addition to affecting her spirits, Molly's pregnancy posed grave threats to her body. She had conceived during her uneven recovery from a life-threatening illness. Beyond that, the pregnancy was her sixth in ten years; allowing nine months for gestation and a minimum of three for parturition and recovery, the physical demands associated with childbearing had consumed 60 percent of her time and energy since she married Charley in June 1768. By comparison, her friends Mary Ridout and Henrietta Ogle proceeded at an almost leisurely pace, each producing three children within the first five years of their marriages and then enjoying a hiatus of ten years before adding a fourth and final child. Similarly, Molly's more casual acquaintance Elizabeth Tayloe Lloyd bore only four children during her first decade of wedlock with Edward Lloyd IV.[37] In addition, Molly had by 1778 suffered far more than any of these friends from infant mortality: although neither Mary Ridout nor Elizabeth Lloyd had buried any children, and Henrietta Ogle only one, Molly had lost her firstborn, Elizabeth, in 1769 and Louisa in 1772; on September 7, 1778, her youngest child, Nancy, died at Doohoragen at the age of twenty-two months. With the family in mourning together at Elk Ridge until mid-October, the sole hint of the toll this tragedy exacted from Molly, then in the last trimester of her pregnancy, comes from lines of condolence written to Papa by Major Jenifer: "I am exceedingly sorry for the loss you have lately sustained, & feel for Mrs Carrolls distress, whose sensibility must have greatly encreased her misery." [38]

36. Daniel of St. Thomas Jenifer to CCA, Aug. 15, 1778, Carroll Papers, MS 206.

37. Information on the children of Mary Ogle Ridout, her sister-in-law Henrietta Hill Ogle, and Elizabeth Tayloe Lloyd is found in Papenfuse et al., eds., *Biographical Dictionary*, II, 537, 617–618, 692. Between 1777 and 1784, Elizabeth Tayloe Lloyd, who had married in 1767, bore three more children.

38. Daniel of St. Thomas Jenifer to CCA, Oct. 1, 1778, Carroll Papers, MS 206.

To ease her physical and emotional distress, Molly began to rely increasingly on laudanum, but the temporary relief it afforded could not compare with its deleterious effects. The birth of another daughter — Catharine Carroll, called Kitty — on December 18, 1778, left her weak, and a disappointingly slow recovery from her confinement depressed her. Doses of bark and bitters prepared by her mother did little to help, and, when she had not materially improved by mid-April, Papa worried to Charley, "Mollys long continued complaints & indisposition make me uneasy." An examination by a physician shortly thereafter finally provided the first clear understanding of what ailed her: "Molly is much better today than she has been for several days past," Charley wrote his father on April 17. "Her disorder is partly bileous, and partly a relaxed habit, owing to too great an use of opi[um] as the Docr. thinks: a proper regimen, the bark, bitters, air & exercise & time with the help of youth, will, I hope, restore her to her usual health." Less optimistic than his son, Papa offered a more direct assessment of Molly's condition: "I wish Mollys letter to Her Mother had corresponded with Yrs to me, by the former She seems quite dispirited," he told Charley on April 22. "It is fruitless to mention what is past, but for the future let Her avoid that poison Laudanum, or any thing else wh may give only present ease." The stakes, in Papa's view, could not be higher: "Myne, Yrs, Her owne, Her Childrens Happyness require Her Strictest attention & conformity to Every thing wh may be thought condu[cive] to her health." [39]

Unlike Papa, who immediately grasped the insidious dangers of a habitual use of opium, Charley and Molly reacted more casually to that part of the doctor's diagnosis. Declaring in late April, "Nothing shall be omitted to restore Molly's health which I have the satisfaction to assure you is much mended within this day or two," Charley placed his confidence in traditional remedies and confidently predicted that further improvement would result from a trip he and his wife intended to make to the Eastern Shore the first of May. "I think," he told Papa, "the voyage, change of air, & exercise will be of great service to Molly — her disorder arises from a relaxed, bileous, & scorbutic habit." Although somewhat startled to learn that "Molly thinks Herself well enough to Cross the Bay," the elder Carroll nevertheless wished her well, but he remained unconvinced that the measures Charley advocated would by themselves effect a cure. Reiterating his earlier advice with an urgency that confirms Molly had not yet heeded it, Papa instructed Charley: "Tel Her I beg Her never to touch Laudanum wh I hear she stil takes, it is as bad as Dram drinking." Unmoved by the positive reports he received from the travelers during their journey, he repeated his in-

39. CCA to CCC, Apr. 16, 22, 1779, CCC to CCA, Apr. 17, 1779, ibid.

junction with equal fervor the day they returned home: "I earnestly beg she will entirely abstain from that Poison Laudanum wh She must be Sensible is very prejudicial to Her health." [40]

By the end of May, Papa's insistent appeals had finally begun to have the desired effect. On the eighth, the day after their return to Annapolis, Charley began a letter to Papa by emphasizing how much his wife had benefited from several episodes of violent seasickness she had suffered on the bay, but he closed his missive several pages later with a much more somber line: "Molly has set a resolution not to take any more opium." A week later, when the gains promised by the voyage had faded and those to be expected from abstinence were only barely apparent, he composed a decidedly more subdued assessment: "Molly is better than when she crossed the bay but I do not think so well as I could wish — it will take time & care to get her health again." Fully aware that perseverance alone would yield permanent results, Papa's response was calculated to strengthen his daughter-in-law's resolve. She would, he told Charley firmly, "soon recover a good State of Health if She will keep Her resolution to abstain Entirely from Laudanum, use exercise, keep regular hours & abstain from any food wh by Experience She finds does not agree with Her: beside Her owne Health, the happyness of Her Children depends on her due observance of what I advise." Steadied, perhaps, by her father-in-law's determination, Molly did not waver, and on May 22 Charley noted, "She has left off entirely the use of opium." It was a course she managed to stay for nearly two years. [41]

Once Molly had taken this essential first step toward regaining her health, the family decided that a sojourn at Bath similar to the one that had been canceled the previous year might assist substantially. Accordingly, she and Charley set off for the spa in mid-July 1779, intending to stay, at Papa's insistence, at least six weeks. "I hope Molly will not be tired with the Place," the old man cautioned Charley sternly soon after the couple left home. "She must consider She went not for Pleasure but Her Health, 6 Weeks may do what a Month may not do, & if she finds benefit in a Month, 6 or 7 Weeks may Compleat Her cure, in Short I do not wish to See Her before the 6th: or 7th: of Sepr." Papa needn't have worried about Molly, who found Bath quite to her liking. The elder Carroll should have aimed his lecture at his son, who reacted negatively to nearly everything at the springs from the moment of his arrival. Indeed, Charley and Molly experienced their stay at Bath so differently that the visit serves as a metaphor for their entire marriage. From Charley's point of view, nothing was right: the food was

40. CCC to CCA, Apr. 25, 1779, CCA to CCC, Apr. 28, May 7, 1779, ibid.
41. CCC to CCA, May 8, [14], 22, 1779, CCA to CCC, May 21, 1779, ibid.

bad and overpriced; the weather, thanks to incessant rains, turned "damp, hot, & sultry." His house, deemed "a Palece" by the carpenter who built it in 1778, did not suit him: besides being too small, it was "dark" and "inconvenient," the floors had not been laid, and the whole place was infested with fleas![42]

For the first fortnight of his stay, the younger Carroll found the clientele unimpressive. Even after the arrival of such families as the Fielding Lewises, the John Washingtons, and, most notably, General and Mrs. Friedrich von Riedesel of the Convention Army, by early August, improved the quality of "the company," Charley could still muster little enthusiasm for the chief amusements at the springs. "I hate this idle sauntering life," he wrote Papa irritably in mid-August. "Dancing & tea-drinkings take up the time of the ladies, & gaming that of the gentlemen — I mean the generality of them." Determined to leave for home by September 1, as he had planned from the moment he and Molly got to Bath, he reminded his father three or four times to be sure the slaves and horses assigned to transport them reached the spa no later than August 30. In short, he could hardly wait to quit the place.[43]

As none of Molly's letters from the springs has survived, her reactions must be inferred from those Charley wrote, and from that source an interesting picture emerges. In spite of the hardships and inconveniences of the adventure, Molly thrived. To reach Bath from Doohoragen required four days of travel over primitive, rock-strewn roads, but, although the ordeal tired her, she bore it much better than her husband had anticipated and to his further surprise had eaten heartily along the way. If she had complaints about having to occupy other quarters until their house had been altered to satisfy Charley, he did not relate them, nor is her opinion of the climate he considered so oppressive known. Her initial discouragements were different: taking the waters, the only aspect of the spa that Charley found reasonably pleasant, did not immediately remove all of her symptoms. "She still complains of the bile, pains in her stomach &c," her husband told his father on July 24. She progressed steadily during the ensuing weeks, however, and by mid-August Charley conceded: "Altho' the weather has been very disagreeable for 3 weeks past, either constantly raining, or exceedingly damp & close, yet I think Molly has her health better than at home. She eats with an appetite & what she eats agrees with her stomach."[44]

The explanation for Molly's remarkable improvement in a less than optimum

42. CCA to CCC, July 21, 1779, CCC to CCA, July 15, 24, Aug. 12, 1779, Daniel of St. Thomas Jenifer to CCA, Aug. 3, 1778, ibid.

43. CCC to CCA, Aug. 19, 1779, ibid.

44. CCC to CCA, July 24, Aug. 19, 1779, ibid.

Scenes from a Marriage

physical environment lies in the transcendent social benefits of her stay at Bath. Where Charley found only tedium — "This place affords very little variety, or to me entertainment" — Molly found welcome diversion. Amid the rounds of visiting, drinking tea, and dancing that her husband considered so idle and inconsequential, she also discovered a wonderfully engaging new friend: Baroness Frederika Charlotte Louise Massow von Riedesel. The demands of war that caused the paths of these two women to cross decreed as well that their relationship would be short, lasting at most six weeks. Nevertheless, the rapport they established was of sufficient depth for the baroness to note it warmly in the journal of her adventures in Revolutionary America.[45]

Charley's sparse description of Frederika von Riedesel as merely "sensible," "amiable," and "well bred" suggests that he did not consider her a particularly captivating representative of her sex.[46] Molly thought the baroness a thoroughly delightful companion, however, and, from the moment they met on July 31 until the end of August when they left the spa, the two were practically inseparable. Given the vast differences in the circumstances of their lives, they were in many respects an unlikely pair. Older than her new friend by only three years, Frederika had nonetheless led an exciting life, especially when compared to Molly's almost exclusively local experiences.

Daughter of a Prussian general and wife to an officer who served the duke of Brunswick, the intrepid baroness had chosen not to allow her husband's military career to keep them apart. Thus, in May 1776, several months after he departed for Canada in command of a regiment of German mercenaries sent to reinforce Carleton, Frederika set out from Wölfenbuttel with their three little girls (aged four, two, and just ten weeks) to join him. Although the practice of wives' following their husbands was relatively common in eighteenth-century armies, Martha Washington being the most notable American example, the baroness's yearlong journey encompassed an array of unusually varied adventures, ranging

---

45. CCC to CCA, Aug. 19, 1779, ibid. The first edition of Baroness von Riedesel's journal was privately published in Berlin in 1800 by her son-in-law Heinrich XLIV, count of Reuss; the modern edition is Marvin L. Brown, Jr., trans. and ed., *Baroness von Riedesel and the American Revolution: Journal and Correspondence of a Tour of Duty, 1776–1783* (Chapel Hill, N.C., 1965). In the portion devoted to her friendship with Molly Carroll, Frederika von Riedesel mentions receiving a letter from Molly after visiting Doohoragen in September 1779, so it is possible that the two women continued their relationship via correspondence, although no such letters have been found. Brown, trans. and ed., *Baroness von Riedesel*, 90.

46. CCC to CCA, July 25, Aug. 12, 1779, Carroll Papers, MS 206.

from her presentation at the court of George III to being called "a French whore" by an English crowd that took offense at her fashionable continental attire. Four months after she finally arrived in Quebec, the English were defeated at Saratoga, whereupon General von Riedesel became an officer in the Convention Army (the name given to Burgoyne's surrendered forces), and until his exchange in October 1780 he and his family traveled up and down the eastern seaboard with these troops. The Riedesels had come to Bath in August 1779 from the Convention Army's current headquarters in Charlottesville, Virginia, by special permission of Governor Thomas Jefferson, who wished to give the general an opportunity to take the waters for his health.[47]

The deep emotional attachment that characterized the Riedesels' marriage and inspired the baroness to embark upon her hard and hazardous travels must have seemed almost as foreign to Molly as the travels themselves. Although a product of parental arrangements, the union was "clearly a love match" of such mutual value that neither husband nor wife quailed at the risks they must take if they wished to remain together during the arduous American campaign. Despite the ordeals she had already encountered, like being under fire with her children at Saratoga, and those she had every reason to anticipate — by the time she reached Bath, Frederika knew she was pregnant — the baroness followed her general resolutely wherever professional soldiering led him. And though her bearing, dress, and speech unmistakably identified her as a German noblewoman, the good humor and high spirits she maintained even in the most distressing circumstances endeared her to her husband's troops and often charmed her American captors as well.[48]

The disparity of experience that makes the relationship between Molly Carroll and Frederika von Riedesel interesting renders equally intriguing the baroness's assessment of Molly's personality and the effect upon it of being married to Charley. Declaring Molly "a very pleasant woman" and "a very enthusiastic patriot, but reasonable," Frederika recorded that the two of them "became great friends" at Bath, where they spent most mornings together enjoying such pastimes as impromptu musicales, at which the baroness delighted her new companion by singing "Italian arias." However, Frederika's most telling remarks about her American friend resulted, not from their pleasant interlude at

47. Brown, trans. and ed., *Baroness von Riedesel,* 13; Louise Hall Tharp, *The Baroness and the General* (Boston, 1962), 323.

48. Tharp, *The Baroness and the General,* 1–10, 192–222; Brown, trans. and ed., *Baroness von Riedesel,* xxiii, xxv, xxix, xxxi.

the springs, but from her observations during the ten days she and her daughters spent at Doohoragen after leaving the springs in early September. Urged repeatedly by Molly to visit at Elk Ridge, the baroness accepted the invitation when negotiations for General von Riedesel's exchange required that he travel to York, Pennsylvania, ahead of her. In her journal Frederika found the Carroll estate generally impressive, particularly the "very handsome house," the "magnificent garden," and the apparently breathtaking view of the surrounding countryside afforded from the summit of Papa's hilltop vineyard. The style of life enjoyed at the manor similarly earned her approbation: "Our meals were served on silver platters, without elegance, to be sure, but prepared with taste, and nothing was lacking."[49]

And with one notable exception, she approved of Molly's family. Papa, whom she described as "an old gentleman in the best of health, and in the most charmingly merry mood, and on whose venerable face one saw the happiest contentment stamped," won her heart not only for these qualities but also because of his obvious fondness for Molly, "our amiable hostess." Molly's children she thought "darling," but, notwithstanding their previous acquaintance at Bath, Molly's husband did not enchant her. Well traveled and erudite Charley might be, but, the baroness concluded, "in other respects he was not such a lovable man, but rather brusque and stingy." Even more significantly, Frederika judged him to be "not at all a suitable mate for his wife, who, although she would not let any of this be noticed, did not seem to be very happy." By contrast, "her father-in-law loved her dearly." In the view of the happily married Mrs. von Riedesel, her "loving and affectionate" friend Mrs. Carroll would have preferred — and surely deserved — a more sensitive, warmly demonstrative spouse.[50]

The improvement in Molly's health initiated by her renunciation of laudanum and reinforced by her month and a half at Bath lasted for more than a year, withstanding even the rigors of another pregnancy beginning in late January 1780. So well was she that, this time, the indispositions of her first several months inspired solicitude but not alarm, and by mid-May she was sufficiently free of ailments that she took little Pol and Charles off on an extended visit to Sim's Delight, the home of Colonel Patrick and Mary Carroll Sim near Nottingham in Prince George's County. For once, Charley really seems to have missed her: "I recd a letter from Molly this morning," he wrote Papa from Annapolis on

49. Brown, trans. and ed., *Baroness von Riedesel*, 85, 89.
50. Ibid., 89–90.

June 11, when she was on her way home. "She got to Mr. Digge's last night — I believe I shall go to morrow very early to meet her If I can with prudence leave this place, & without running the risk of preventing the making of a Senate."[51]

Alas, the risk proved too great for Charley — June 12 found him seated dutifully in the upper house, his fleeting romantic impulses subsumed by the greater priority of assuring that body a quorum.[52] Although the quality of the welcome she received when she finally reached Annapolis on June 14 might have had little to do with it, Molly did not linger long in town. Within ten days she had arranged for the transport of considerable baggage, including her spinet, to Elk Ridge, and on June 26 she returned to Doohoragen with her two older children for a stay that ultimately lasted until March of the following year.

Until the end of her pregnancy in late October, Molly's residence in the country did not signify a health-induced withdrawal. To the contrary, she remained remarkably busy during the summer and early fall of 1780, adding to her usual round of familial responsibilities and social activity a new public role by becoming involved in a women's drive to collect money for the American troops. Initiated in Philadelphia the previous spring by Esther DeBerdt Reed (whose husband, Joseph Reed, was president of the Supreme Executive Council of Pennsylvania), the project spread quickly to other states through a network of upper-class women that included Mary Digges Lee (the wife of Maryland's governor Thomas Sim Lee and stepdaughter of Charley's cousin Mary Carroll Digges, the mistress of Mellwood, whom Molly had visited on her way back to Annapolis in early June). On June 27, the *Maryland Journal*'s reprinting of *The Sentiments of an American Woman,* a broadside published in Philadelphia on June 10, placed the cause directly before the women of Maryland. Recalling the patriotic actions of heroines like Joan of Arc, the writer asked why, given the pitiful condition of the Continental army, American women should "hesitate to wear a cloathing more simple; hair-dresses less elegant" and called upon her readers to practice self-denial in behalf of the gallant rank and file: "Who amongst us, will not renounce with the highest pleasure, those vain ornaments,

---

51. CCC to CCA, June 11, 1780, Carroll Papers, MS 206. Molly's destination in Prince George's County is assumed from the fact that Cousin Daniel, Mrs. Sim's father, accompanied her on the trip. Sim's Delight, later called Bellefield, remained in the Sim family until 1799. CCC to CCA, June 3, 1780, Carroll Papers, MS 206; Effie Gwynn Bowie, *Across the Years in Prince George's County: A Genealogical and Biographical History of Some Prince George's County, Maryland, and Allied Families* (Richmond, Va., 1947), 766n.

52. *VPS,* June Session, 1780, 97.

when she shall consider that the valiant defenders of America will be able to draw some advantage from the money she may have laid out in these[?]"[53]

With the goal of giving every Continental soldier two dollars in hard currency, Mrs. Reed, the likely author of the broadside, and the gentlewomen of Philadelphia moved beyond personal sacrifice to organize a citywide, house-to-house canvass that by July 4 had raised $200,580 in Continental money and £625.6.8 in specie. Two letters from "A woman in Philadelphia to her friend in Annapolis" dated June 20 and July 6 and published in the *Maryland Gazette* on July 21 and 28 reported the details of the collection. Undoubtedly part of a larger, not extant correspondence between Esther Reed and Mary Digges Lee, these missives were probably printed at Mrs. Lee's behest to encourage participation in the similar undertaking she had launched in Maryland. The drive was certainly under way by early July; on the fifth of that month, a Continental officer in Baltimore informed his counterpart in North Carolina that "the Examp[le]" set by the women of Philadelphia "has been spiritedly follow'd by the Ladies of this place." No information about the organizational structure of the Maryland effort has survived; nevertheless, it is clear that Molly did her part with energy, enthusiasm, and a determination that proved her patriotism equal to her love of finery and earned the approbation of her husband's political associates. Writing to Charley on August 7, congressional delegate John Hanson hoped "Mrs Carroll will Succeed to the Utmost of her Wishes in the laudable Business she is at present engaged in."[54]

53. *Maryland Journal, and the Baltimore Advertiser,* June 27, 1780. For the authorship of *The Sentiments of an American Woman,* see Mary Beth Norton, *Liberty's Daughters: The Revolutionary Experience of American Women, 1750–1800* (Boston, 1980), 178. The document, along with a plan for raising money, appeared in the *Pennsylvania Gazette* (Philadelphia) on June 21. Norton, *Liberty's Daughters,* 179; George Washington to President Joseph Reed, June 25, 1780, in John C. Fitzpatrick, ed., *The Writings of George Washington from the Original Manuscript Sources, 1745–1799* (Washington, D.C., 1931–1944), XIX, 71.

54. Sam[uel] Smith to Otho H[olland] Williams, July 5, 1780, Otho Holland Williams Papers, MdHi; John Hanson to CCC, Aug. 7, 1780, Carroll Papers, MS 206. For more extensive treatment of the Philadelphia enterprise, see Norton, *Liberty's Daughters,* 178–188; Linda K. Kerber, *Women of the Republic: Intellect and Ideology in Revolutionary America* (Chapel Hill, N.C., 1980), 99–113; Lyman H. Butterfield, "General Washington's Sewing Circle," *American Heritage,* N.S., II, no. 4 (Summer 1951), 7. The author is indebted to Jennifer A. Bryan, curator of manuscripts at the Maryland Historical Society, who, during her tenure as a research assistant on the Charles Carroll of Carrollton Pa-

Molly's well-being and the lively pursuits that flowed from it ended abruptly with her confinement. Increasingly troubled by headaches and other precursory indispositions after Charley left the manor for Annapolis in mid-October, she delivered her seventh child, Eliza, on October 26, 1780, while he awaited the opening of the legislative session in town. The birth was difficult, and Molly's recovery from it so uncertain that on two occasions, once in November and again in late December, Charley found it necessary to suspend his senatorial duties and go to Doohoragen. That his second absence left the upper house without a quorum attests the seriousness of his wife's condition. Plagued almost constantly by her old complaints — "a pain in Her Stomach & Bowells" — through the early months of 1781, Molly still managed to return to the capital with Charley and their two older children in March, but the multiplicity of stresses she encountered there contributed little either to her peace of mind or to the restoration of her health. The chief cause of her anxiety lay in the decision to inoculate little Pol and Charles against smallpox, a procedure that commenced under the careful supervision of Dr. Upton Scott as soon as they got back to town. Not even the assurances of this old and trusted friend that "every symptom attending the children is favourable" could allay Molly's fears.[55]

Several unpleasant occurrences emanating from the war undoubtedly heightened the tensions associated with the children's inoculation, despite Charley's insistence to the contrary. Upon their return to Annapolis, the Carrolls received the news that British ships, searching for provisions after an inconclusive clash with a French squadron farther down the bay, had sailed north and once again pillaged Poplar Island. Charley reacted with surprising equanimity. Magnanimously declaring that "this misfortune compared with what many others have suffered is but light," he calmly assured Papa, whose sensitivity to his daughter-in-law led him to suspect otherwise, that the incident and the losses associated with it had made "no impression on Molly's mind — that being totally absorbed by her attention & anxiety for her children." By contrast, the damage

pers editorial project, ferreted out and placed in a narrative context the sparse evidence concerning the Maryland drive.

55. John Hanson to CCC, Nov. 7, 1781, Charles Francis Jenkins Collection, HSP; *VPS*, October Session, 1780, 1, 5, 10, 23; CCA to CCC, Jan. 7, 1781, CCC to CCA, Mar. 31, 1781, Carroll Papers, MS 206. Dr. Scott returned to Maryland from England in November 1780, having secured a passport from Benjamin Franklin and given Sir Henry Clinton his parole. Rosamond Randall Beirne, "Portrait of a Colonial Governor: Robert Eden," *Maryland Historical Magazine*, XLV (1950), 298.

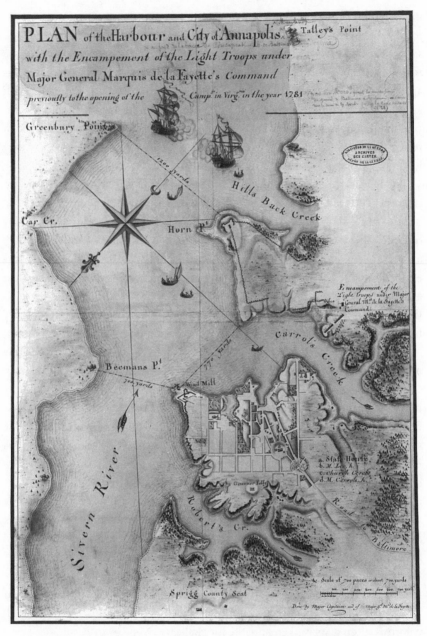

MAP 7. Plan of the Harbour and City of Annapolis. *By Major Pierre Captaine, 1781.*
Permission of the Ministry of Defense, Dépôt de la Guerre, Paris.
Photograph courtesy of the Maryland State Archives, Marion Warren
Photograph Collection, MSA SC 1890-02-3502

inflicted on Charley's property by the French troops whose arrival in town co-incided with his and Molly's produced a far less dispassionate response. "The soldiers are very troublesome," he wrote irritably to his father on April 5, noting that they had not only "stolen the Chickens that were sent down from Doohor-agen" but had also "burn[t] a great many of the rails of my lotts in town." With an impatience more reflective of the various household stresses than of his re-cent material losses, Charley unceremoniously pronounced the rank and file of his country's essential ally "a great nusance." In short: "I heartily wis[h] they were gone."[56]

But neither Molly's health, nor "the pock" that had "come finely out" to cover her children, nor even Charley's rancor over the pilfering of fence rails and poultry prevented the Carrolls from entertaining the commander of the highly objectionable troops, "the marquiss de la Fayette," General William Smallwood, and several other officers at dinner on April 4. That Molly could cope, appar-ently successfully, with the responsibilities of the hostess of such a distinguished gathering does not gainsay the physical discomfort and mental strain that con-tinued to beset her. As the children progressed steadily toward a full recovery from inoculation, Papa hoped — indeed, he expected — that their mother, "freed from the anxiety she has been under," would rapidly "recover her Spirits and perfect health." But, to his distress, the brief reports he received from Charley said only that "Molly is very indifferent." By May, the underlying cause of her lingering malaise had become apparent: at some point during the stress-ful aftermath of Eliza's birth, Molly had resumed the use of laudanum. With the same anguished affection that had infused his entreaties two years before, Papa implored his daughter-in-law to renew her pledge of abstinence. "I am very sorry to hear Molly is very indifferent," he wrote Charley on May 7. "I think she cannot hope for health, if she wil not resolve to overcome Her strange Appetite for Chalk & Opium, I earnestly begg it for the sake of Her family & Children, & as I love Her."[57] Papa's reference to chalk reveals that, besides her addiction to laudanum, Molly also suffered from chlorosis, an iron-deficiency anemia. Al-though chlorosis most commonly affects girls at the time of puberty, causing ir-regular menses and a pale or greenish complexion, the disease can also appear in married women. In the seventeenth and eighteenth centuries, women with chlorosis often displayed an appetite for chalk.

This time Papa was fighting a battle that neither his love nor his iron deter-

56. CCA to CCC, Mar. 30, 1781, CCC to CCA, Mar. 31, Apr. 5, 11, 1781, Carroll Papers, MS 206. For information on the British attacks on Poplar Island, see Chapter 10, above.
57. CCC to CCA, Apr. 5, May 2, 1781, CCA to CCC, Apr. 10, May 7, 1781, ibid.

Scenes from a Marriage

mination could win. Sometimes Molly seemed to be getting better. Although "much indisposed" during a trip to White Hall that ended on May 21, she had recovered sufficiently by May 24 to attend "an entertainment" given by Thomas Jennings in celebration of his daughter's marriage, unaccompanied by Charley, whose longstanding antipathy for the host led him to decline the invitation.[58] Within two weeks of her return to Doohoragen in early June, however, Papa could no longer deny the unpleasant truth of his firsthand observations: any improvement in his daughter-in-law's condition invariably turned out to be sporadic and impermanent. "Molly is as when She left Annapolis," he wrote his son heavily on June 16, "never quite well." Charley's reply the following day suggests that irritated weariness had overcome his shallow reservoir of husbandly concern: "Do give my love to Molly — I am very sorry to hear she is [so] indisposed. I would answer her letter, but I have been engaged all this afternoon in public business. I write this at 9 o'clock & am quite Jaded — my love to Mrs. Darnall & the Children. I would send one of my Shirts to Molly for a pattern to cut out my new Shirts by, but some of them do not fit well — I hope the Assembly will rise next Saturday — I really am quite tired & fatigued & disgusted with everything."[59]

Beset on one side by her father-in-law's relentlessly well-meaning encouragement and on the other by her husband's tired annoyance, Molly could still turn to her mother for sympathy and understanding. As unassuming a Carroll in-law as she had been a niece and housekeeper, Rachel served as an important source of maternal affection for her grandchildren, several of whom spent large portions of their young lives in her care, as well as for her daughter, who sometimes, at least in Papa's view, took that steady devotion for granted. "Molly does not

58. CCC to CCA, May 24, 1781, ibid. Held at the Paca house on Prince George Street, which Jennings had purchased in 1780, the "entertainment" marked the May 23 nuptials of Juliana Jennings (c. 1764–1837) and James Brice (1746–1801). Charley's dislike for the bride's father dated from the early 1770s when Jennings, then Maryland's attorney general, became overtly sympathetic to Ignatius Digges in the *Digges v. Carroll* case, thereby breaking his earlier promise to Papa "to serve me against Digges." Similar behavior by Jennings in May 1781 provoked Charley into boycotting the party: having talked with Charley about representing the Carrolls in a lawsuit, Jennings abruptly and without notice accepted an offer to work for the opposition. Papa was not surprised; ever since the day Jennings "forfeited His word" in the Digges case, he had, he told Charley, "looked upon Him as a Scoundrell." CCC to CCA, [Apr. 14, 1771], May 18, 1781, CCA to CCC, May 22, 1781, ibid.; Papenfuse et al., eds., *Biographical Dictionary*, I, 164, II, 488–489; Gregory A. Stiverson and Phebe R. Jacobsen, *William Paca: A Biography* (Baltimore, 1976), 43–44.

59. CCA to CCC, June 16, 1781, CCC to CCA, June 16, 1781, Carroll Papers, MS 206.

write to Her Mother," the old man wrote sternly to his son on one such occasion. "Mrs. Darnall may have foibles, but I hope they are not Such as to deserve to be Slighted by Her Daughter." In addition to emotional sustenance, Rachel bestowed upon her family her skill at concocting the various mixtures commonly used as medicines. (Mainly emetics and cathartics, they probably did more harm than good, given the nature of Molly's bodily distress in 1781.) But if Rachel could not cure her daughter, she could at least give Molly some of the warmth and comfort she so sorely needed, especially in early July when she learned that death had claimed Mary Ridout's youngest child, a little girl only two and a half months older than her own Eliza.[60]

The death of her best friend's baby was by no means the cruelest stroke in store for Molly Carroll that summer. During a visit to the home of Cousin Daniel's mother at Rock Creek in August, Rachel suddenly fell sick. Scarcely had the family at Doohoragen received news of her illness when they learned that she was dead. Even Charley found his composure shaken by the unexpected loss: long before she became his mother-in-law, Rachel had endeared herself to him forever by caring tenderly for his dying mother. Mindful of this and other debts of gratitude, Charley rode to Rock Creek himself to bring her body home, and on the morning of August 26, after Father John Carroll had performed a funeral service, the grieving family buried Rachel in the manor chapel. Writing to Governor Thomas Sim Lee that afternoon, Charley noted sadly, "This melancholy incident has thrown a great damp on all our spirits, but particularly on those of Mrs Carroll."[61]

With characteristic reserve Charley understated the case. To Molly, already physically and emotionally exhausted, her mother's sudden death at the age of fifty-one was almost insupportable, depriving her of a sure source of solace and support and at the same time thrusting upon her the household responsibilities that had formerly come under Rachel's purview. Moreover, the Carroll children, abruptly denied the comforting presence of their grandmother, now had nowhere to turn with their grief and their other needs except to their distraught and vulnerable mother. The fact that both little Pol and Charles grew "pulled downe pale & thin" that fall suggests the toll that Rachel's death and its difficult aftermath took on them. Although greatly preoccupied with the vitriolic battle

60. CCA to CCC, May 29, 1781, ibid.; Helen W. Ridgely, ed., *Historic Graves of Maryland and the District of Columbia* . . . (New York, 1908), 8. Meliora Ridout was buried at White Hall.

61. CCC to Thomas Sim Lee, Aug. 18, 26, 1781, Outerbridge Horsey Coll.; CCC, "Memorandum," 11 A-J-1, Archives, Archdiocese of Baltimore, Baltimore.

he was conducting against his one-time ally Samuel Chase in the pages of the *Maryland Gazette*, Charley did stay at Doohoragen with his wife until time for the general assembly to convene in mid-October, but his presence does not seem to have improved her condition much.[62]

On October 30, two weeks after he had left the manor, Papa wrote him hopefully, "Molly has been better for 6 or 7 days past than she has been Since Her Mothers death," but the following week the old man could report only that his daughter-in-law was "much as usual." Molly confirmed her lack of progress in a brief postscript to Papa's letter: "I have been too much indisposed My Dear Mr Carroll to Write to you. I hope you are well, & God keep you so is my very sincere prayer." At times her health seemed to fluctuate almost daily: two days after penning her morose message to Charley, she felt well enough to ride out to dine at the home of a neighbor. By the middle of November she had begun to look forward to returning to Annapolis with such enthusiasm that Papa decided not to ask her to remain at the manor until the arrival of "the Negroes clothing," although he clearly preferred that she do so. "I did not mention it to Her," he confided to Charley, "knowing how much She desires to be with You." The unusually exciting events taking place in her absence undoubtedly spurred Molly's anticipation: on October 18, her husband hosted an intimate dinner that included Governor and Mrs. Lee among the half-dozen guests. When the news of Cornwallis's surrender reached Annapolis two days later, it was Charley who, as he told Papa modestly, "had the pleasure of communicating it to the Public by turning into English Count de Grasse's letter to the Governor dated on board la ville de Paris the 18th instant."[63]

62. CCA to CCC, Oct. 30, 1781, Carroll Papers, MS 206. In May 1781, Chase, writing under the name "Censor," launched an attack on the Maryland Senate and Charles Carroll of Carrollton, whom he held individually and collectively responsible for impugning his character with regard to the 1778 rumors that he had used privileged congressional information to corner the flour market. As Chase's initially veiled accusations grew more and more explicit, Charley realized that he would have to respond to the charges. He began to compose his first reply after he arrived at Doohoragen at the close of the legislative session on June 27, and the piece appeared in the *Md. Gaz.* on August 23. For a detailed analysis of the exchanges between Charley and Chase that continued until February 1782 and a sample of the documents, see Ronald Hoffman, Sally D. Mason, and Eleanor S. Darcy, eds., *Dear Papa, Dear Charley: The Peregrinations of a Revolutionary Aristocrat, as Told by Charles Carroll of Carrollton and His Father, Charles Carroll of Annapolis, with Sundry Observations on Bastardy, Child-Rearing, Romance, Matrimony, Commerce, Tobacco, Slavery, and the Politics of Revolutionary America* (forthcoming).

63. CCA to CCC, Oct. 30, Nov. 7, 9, 10, 1781, CCC to CCA, Oct. 18, 20, 1781, Carroll Papers, MS 206.

The bitterness surrounding Charley's continuing dispute with Chase and the related inquiry into Chase's past behavior conducted by the general assembly in January 1782 probably made the Carrolls' winter sojourn in Annapolis less happy and relaxed than Molly would have liked. By the time the two antagonists finally compromised their differences sufficiently to put an end to their press war, it was late February and time for Papa to make his lonely way back to Doohoragen. Alone in the sprawling house for the first time since Rachel's death, the old man did not entirely relish his solitude. He remained at the manor until early April, long enough to check the state of his beloved vineyard, meet with the new Carrollton steward Joseph Smith, and "to make my Easter"; then, in a departure from the schedule he had kept for many years, he returned to his son and daughter-in-law and his grandchildren in town. Before he left Elk Ridge, however, Papa prepared "Instructions to be observed by Mr: Danl: Mackenzie," an agent employed to collect debts. Lucid and to the point and written boldly in his own hand, those directions show that Papa's mind was as sharp as ever and that his unprecedented springtime absence from Doohoragen did not mean he intended to relinquish his control over his family's business. He would, he told Mackenzie firmly, "be at my Manor on the 15th of Next June and continue there at least a Month." [64]

His plan was not to be realized. Indeed, by mid-June 1782, the intimate context of the Carrolls' lives had changed as radically and profoundly as had that of the larger world when the events at Yorktown turned it "upside down" the previous fall. On May 30, two and a half weeks after his eightieth birthday, Papa lost his balance and fell headfirst from the porch leading to the garden at the east end of the Annapolis house. The cause of the accident — whether "stumbling, or a sudden giddiness" — was not apparent either to Cousin Daniel or to Molly, both of whom witnessed it. Rendered unable to speak, the doughty, seemingly indestructible old man died within the next hour. [65]

The shock sent Molly to bed with a mysterious illness that did not respond to the skills of the trusted Dr. Scott. Although the limitations of eighteenth-century medical practice may partially account for the lack of progress, the patient had quite clearly given up the fight. On June 10, after telling "her Women who were

<hr>

64. CCA to CCC, Mar. 24, 1782, ibid.

65. John Carroll to Anthony Carroll, Sept. 23, 1784, Duke of Leeds Papers, DD5/XI/V/Bundle 5, Yorkshire Archaeological Society, Leeds, U.K.; J. C. Carpenter, "Historic Houses of America: Doughoregan Manor, and Charles Carroll of Carrollton," *Appletons' Journal*, XII (Sept. 19, 1874), 352–356.

Scenes from a Marriage

crying about her . . . That her God call'd & she must go & wish'd to be with him & did not desire to live," Molly died. She had remained "sensible until a little time before she breathed her last," and, as the end drew near, she seemed to an attending friend "as perfectly resign'd & compos'd as a person could be," asking the doctor several times "how long he thought she could live, or if she was dying." Following the service conducted by Father Carroll, Molly was laid to rest in the family graveyard at Annapolis quarter, four miles outside of town. Three generations of Carrolls awaited her there: Charles Carroll the Settler, his wife, and several of their infant children, Papa and Mama, and two of her own little girls, her first baby, Elizabeth, and Louisa, her third.[66]

And what of Charley, suddenly bereft not only of his thirty-three-year-old wife but also of the father who for forty-five years had ordered his existence and molded him according to the dictates of an implacable will? As he stood close by Papa's freshly covered grave in the burying ground begun by the Settler when he moved to Annapolis in 1696 and watched the earth falling upon Molly's coffin, what thoughts and memories swept his mind and filled his heart? A family friend described him as being "in great grief."[67] On June 3, four days after Papa's death and a week before Molly's, Charley wrote to Baltimore merchant William Russell for enough "superfine black Cloth as will make me a coat." Noting that his correspondent had undoubtedly "heared the melancholy occasion of my wanting black," Charley then allowed himself a brief understatement of his pain: "You, who knew, his real worth, can judge of my loss."[68]

His only other surviving mention of the wrenching events appears in a short letter he wrote to Joshua Johnson, his mercantile correspondent at Nantes, just a month after Molly's death. Placed at the end of a paragraph devoted to listing the dates of his most recent correspondence and immediately followed by his closing instructions, the reference is brief and to the point: "Since mine of the 11th. May I have had the Misfortune to lose my Father & Wife within a very little time of each other, My Father died the 30th. of may Suddenly and my wife on

66. Henrietta Hill Ogle to John Thomas [June 1782], Pennington Collection, 1713–1904, MdHi. Nancy (Ann Brooke Carroll), Molly's fifth child, died at Doohoragen and is presumed to have been buried in the manor chapel.

67. The comment about Charley was made by Henrietta Ogle, whose husband, Benjamin, served as one of Molly's pallbearers. Henrietta Hill Ogle to John Thomas, [June 1782], Pennington Collection.

68. CCC to William Russell, Collection Château Ramezay, P345, SD-1, P191, Archives Nationales du Québec, Montreal. I am grateful to Eric R. Papenfuse, who discovered this letter in the course of his research and made it known to me.

the 10th. Ultimo after a Short but very painful illness. Be pleased to carry to my Credit when paid the undernoted Bill of Exchange."[69]

Without gainsaying the effect on Charley of Molly's tragic demise, the poignancy of his dual loss inevitably juxtaposes the frequently arid context of his fourteen-year marriage to the emotional complexity inherent in his relationship with his father. Losing his wife deprived Charley of conjugal companionship and gave him the additional burden of parenting four motherless children by himself; but, if he chose to remarry, he could effectively mitigate the practical and at least some of the personal effects of those situations. His father's death, by contrast, brought him to the eminently desirable position of familial power and responsibility for which he had been bred and so carefully and painstakingly groomed. Worthy heir to the grand legacy born of the mythic memory and relentless determination of his Gaelic forebears, Charles Carroll of Carrollton had gained the summit, but he stood upon that grand pinnacle deeply and profoundly alone.

69. CCC to Wallace, Johnson, & Muir, July 9, 1782, Charles Carroll Letter-book 1771–1833, fol. 60v, Arents Collections, New York Public Library, Astor, Lenox, and Tilden Foundations, New York. Like the vast majority of correspondence contained in this journal, Charley's letter is in his clerk's hand.

Epilogue

Never remarrying, Charley remained a widower for fifty years. When he died on November 14, 1832, at the age of ninety-five, the nation mourned the passing of this last symbol of its Revolutionary birth. The headline that appeared in the *Easton Gazette* was typical: "CHARLES CARROLL IS NO MORE! *A great man is fallen in Israel!*" To mark Carroll's death, President Andrew Jackson ordered the United States government closed. Only one other Revolutionary hero had been accorded this honor — George Washington. In Maryland the Senate chamber was draped in black. Charley's funeral cortege in Baltimore stretched for blocks. National and state officials mixed with foreign dignitaries, business leaders, Revolutionary war veterans, "Invited Strangers," and ordinary citizens, among them "IRISHMEN AND THEIR DESCENDANTS" who had been called to assemble

> at Patrick Reiley's Tavern, THIS MORNING at 10 o'clock, thence to form and from thence to proceed with their fellow-citizens to the late residence of "Charles Carroll," whose death as a descendant of Ireland, and a friend of Universal Liberty they have in a peculiar manner to deplore. The Marshall will allot them a respectable and suitable place in the procession.

Charley's personal life continued to be marred by tragedy. A year after her mother's demise, the youngest Carroll child, three-year-old Eliza, died. The pain of her death, though sharp, was short. Of far greater anguish was the realization, over the course of many years, that his assiduous efforts to replicate Papa's shaping of a worthy heir had failed. Charles Carroll of Homewood, the son whose birth had been so joyfully celebrated, grew into a troubled, tormented man, a source of endless despair and heartbreak to his father. Charles Carroll of Homewood's marriage ended in a permanent separation in 1816, and in 1825 he died hopelessly addicted to alcohol. He was survived by four daughters and a son, Charles Carroll of Doughoragen, who became Charley's heir. Kitty, the third of the Carroll children to reach adulthood, married South Carolinian Robert Goodloe Harper, a debonair politician who had served several terms in the United States House of Representatives, was elected to and resigned from the United States Senate in 1816, and stood as the Federalist candidate for vice president before turning his efforts to the work of the American Colonization Society. Three of Kitty's six children died in childhood, and two others as young adults.

Papa's beloved "little Pol" led a happier life. She and her husband, Richard Caton, a handsome but chronically indebted merchant, raised four daughters, three of whom — Mary Ann, Elizabeth, and Louisa — gained entrée to the highest levels of English society. Known as the "American graces," these women married titled Englishmen, thereby fulfilling in spectacular fashion a vision of life that Molly, the sociable grandmother they never knew, would have dearly loved but could scarcely have imagined. The most illustrious of these marriages was Mary Ann's. In 1825, three years after the death of her first husband, Robert Patterson of Baltimore, Mary Ann married Richard Colley Wellesley, second earl of Mornington and Marquess Wellesley. The elder brother of the duke of Wellington, Wellesley was viceroy of Ireland, and Mary Ann returned there with him, in triumph, as vicereine. She remained in Dublin until 1828, when Wellesley resigned at the request of his brother, who had become Great Britain's prime minister and held harsher views on Ireland.

The duke of Wellington's strong affection for Mary Ann, observable and commented upon from their initial meeting during her first trip to England in 1816, made him her devoted friend and admirer throughout her life. Seemingly aware of this attachment, Charley expressed in his letters to his granddaughter his sharp dissatisfaction over Great Britain's treatment of Roman Catholics in England and Ireland. Although Wellington as prime minister personally opposed Roman Catholic emancipation, political reasons induced him to drive that measure through Parliament in 1829, in the teeth of vigorous opposition. The statute gave English and Irish Catholics virtually full access to civic participation. Securely positioned by her connections among the English aristocracy, Mary Ann became lady of the bedchamber to Queen Adelaide, the wife of William IV, and lived on in England after Wellesley's death in 1842. She died in 1853, in her grace-and-favour apartment in Hampton Court.

To the end of his days, Charley bore the stamp of Papa's molding. None of his offspring or their spouses could handle money. He capitalized their marriages handsomely, and, when they came to him to borrow more, he granted their requests but required deeds to their properties as collateral. Thus, by the end of his life, Charley had reconsolidated all the family's assets.

And, like Papa, Charley knew how to invest. Refusing President George Washington's personal request for a loan, Charley carefully scrutinized all who came to his door. Increasingly he preferred to place his money in the new instruments of the nation's expanding capitalist economy, although during the War of 1812 his holdings also included British naval stock. He remained in full command of all his faculties until his death, and, even when he surrendered power of attorney in 1831, at the age of ninety-four, he made sure that the document contained a clause that allowed him to revoke the arrangement if he became dissatisfied with the way his affairs were being managed. To the last Charley was Papa's worthy heir.

A Poem about the O'Carroll Forces after the Battle of Aughrim

I am indebted to Paddy Heaney of Cadamstown, County Offaly, for the following poem recounting the experience of the O'Carroll forces after the Battle of Aughrim, July 12, 1691. In forwarding the poem Mr. Heaney wrote as follows:

> I am sending on three verses of that famous poem I heard recited when I was a young fellow. There are many more verses; unfortunately they are lost. The old people always referred to the battle of Aughrim and talked about the local connection. As you see by the poem, O'Carroll was wounded. O'Gorman was second in command. He fought a rear-guard action and protected the wounded and brought them safely to Doohoragen Valley.

LET GORMAN STAY BEHIND

We crossed the Silver River, as the sun rose o'er the hill,
We galloped o'er the heather, through the valley calm and still,
With twice a hundred horsemen, to the mountains we were bound
With our wounded close beside us; there was silence all around.
At the battle-field of Aughrim, we left our slain behind,
We retreated o'er the Shannon and gained the other side;
Our horses they were weary, as we urged them on again
With the Slieve Blooms in the distance and Doohoragen glen.

O'Carroll he was our Captain, he was wounded on that day;
He urged us into battle, with our war cry's loud "Hurraugh!"
With the thunder of the cannon, we charged their lines again;
As the grape-shot fell around us, we gained the higher ground.

O'Carroll and Kelly fell that day, O'Dunne and Daly too;
We were now without a leader, o what were we to do?
We left the field of battle and faced the Shannon Tide;
The cry went up around us, "Let Gorman stay behind,"
"O brave and dauntless soldier, let Gorman stay behind."

O'Gorman was a mountain man and proud to be the same;
He joined O'Carroll's regiment, to strike a blow again.
He left his native Slieve Blooms, its hills and valleys fair,
And bade farewell to all his friends he might never see again.
"We are safe in Doohoragen," said O'Gorman to his men,
"We'll rest until tomorrow, then we'll join the fight again."
They rose at early morning and formed into a line,
Then they cry went up around us, "Let Gorman stay behind!"
"O brave and dauntless soldier, let Gorman stay behind!"

Mr. Heaney added this note:

O'Gorman was born in the Slieve Blooms, according to local historians. After the Treaty of Limerick in 1691, he went with the "Wild Geese" to France. He fought with Dillon's regiment, and was killed in the "Lowlands." There is a hill in the Cadamstown area still called Gorman's Hill, after that great man.

The O'Carroll Forces after the Battle of Aughrim

APPENDIX 2

Ely-Éile

"Ely," an anglicized version of the Gaelic toponym Éile, was introduced by the English at least as early as the fourteenth century.[1] Historians of ancient Ireland disagree about the origin of the word. Some have suggested that it is taken from Eile Ridhearg, a fifth-century descendant of Olioll Olum, king of Munster (d. 234), whose son Cian (Kean) is held to be the progenitor of the O'Carroll sept. Others argue for an even older derivation from Eli, a daughter of Eochaidh, who ruled Munster at the beginning of the Christian era, or support the tradition that claims an Iron Age tribe known as the Eile gave its name to the territory. After setting forth several conflicting possibilities, one evidently well respected nineteenth-century scholar concluded that the question was actually of "little consequence" and asserted, "It is indisputable that they [the Munster O'Carrolls] were, in very early ages, the Supreme Princes of the entire district; and in more modern times when surnames became hereditary gave their patronimic name to that part of the district which they then possessed."[2]

One of the first official uses of the term to designate the O'Carroll territory occurred in 1538 when Fearganainm O'Carroll, the current chief, agreed that he and those who succeeded him would pay Henry VIII "12d for every carucate of land within Eile . . . supply soldiers and victuals for the King's military expeditions," and allow the lord deputy of Ireland, Leonard Grey, free passage through "O'Carroll's country." In return, the king designated Fearganainm "Captain of Ely."[3]

1. Indenture between the earl of Ormond and Rory O'Carroll, June 8, 1361, in Edmund Curtis, *Calendar of Ormond Deeds,* II, *1350–1413* (Dublin, 1934), 65.

2. Edward O'Reilly, quoted in John O'Donovan, "Ordnance Survey Field Name Books of the King's County, 1837–1840," II (typescript, Offaly County Library, Tullamore).

3. Elizabeth FitzPatrick, "Towards an Understanding of the Aristocratic Elements of the Sept of Uéı Cearbhaill," lecture delivered to the Irish Genealogical Research Society, Mar. 11, 1992, printed in the Carroll Institute Report for March 1991, 49.

Incomes of the Wealthy in Early Maryland

Calculating the incomes of Maryland's wealthiest men for the last decade of the seventeenth century and the first decade of the eighteenth is extraordinarily difficult, but, if I have erred, I believe I have done so on the conservative side. Gloria Main cites one wealthy planter, Joseph Chew, who in 1705 shipped two years' production of tobacco, 150 hogsheads, and received a price in England of £449 sterling (Main, *Tobacco Colony*, 84). Certainly, the incomes of Maryland's greatest planters whose slaveholding and servant assets exceeded Chew's — he died in 1705 with 20, whereas seven years later Henry Darnall's estate contained more than 100 — suggest that there were men who could produce more than 75 hogsheads annually. Further, since most wealth estimates for the colonial period are based on probate records, no hard figures exist for planters' yearly earnings from their mercantile pursuits. One way to approximate annual income from retailing in Maryland is to multiply capital investments in merchant goods as listed in probate inventories by a conservative rate of return — 8 percent, a figure 2 percent higher than the legal interest rate. Thus planter-merchant Philemon Lloyd, the richest man of his time, who died in 1685 possessed of an inventory of mercantile goods worth £751, probably received a net return of at least £60 annually. The net return Lloyd earned through exporting tobacco — the year of his death he shipped nearly 200 hogsheads that he acquired through trade — certainly equaled his domestic business and probably exceeded it. The money owed Lloyd's estate in 1685 approximated some £1,900 sterling, the interest on which probably returned him £100 a year. Talbot County, Inventories, liber J.R. no. 1, fols. 324–327, and Prerogative Court, Inventories and Accounts, liber 9, fol. 244, both at MdAA.

Regarding planters who were also lawyers, William Stone of Prince George's County earned nearly £100 annually in the mid-1690s by practicing in three county courts (Lois Green Carr, "County Government in Maryland, 1688–

1709" [Ph.D. diss., Harvard University, 1968], 505–507). Lawyers plying their trade in higher courts presumably collected a minimum of £150 a year. A lawyer's income, it should be noted, was especially high because lawyer's fees represented net profit, whereas a planter's return consisted of gross earnings minus his costs of production and shipping. Finally, the highest proprietary office-holders, who were expected to pay a percentage of their income to their patrons, could expect to earn anywhere from £200 to £300 or more from their posts. Donnell MacClure Owings, *His Lordship's Patronage: Offices of Profit in Colonial Maryland* (Baltimore, 1953), 23–24, 34, 79.

Nineteenth-Century Accounts of Charles Carroll of Carrollton's Birth

Although Charles Carroll of Annapolis and Elizabeth Brooke made no attempt to hide the common law status of their relationship from either their son or their contemporaries, their extramarital union had, by the nineteenth century, become a source of embarrassment to their descendants and friends. One of the earliest indications that the Carroll-Brooke cohabitation remained a topic of gossip long after both of them were dead is found in a letter written in 1814 by Rosalie E. Stier Calvert (1788–1821) of Riversdale, a plantation located near Bladensburg, in Prince George's County, to her father. After reporting critically on recent activities of several children and grandchildren of Charles Carroll of Carrollton that she knew had displeased the man she called one of "our old friends, the venerable Carroll," Mrs. Calvert proceeded to relate the following vignette: "I don't know if you knew that the older Carroll is an illegitimate son, and when he returned from Europe at the age of twenty, he refused to return to his father's house unless his father would marry his mother, who was a woman of the lowest class. What an idea to say that the nobility is an imaginary good!" [1] Given her own proximity to illicit relationships, this lady's interest in the story might have been sympathetic rather than malicious: her husband, George Culvert (1768–1838), himself a grandson of "an illegitimate but acknowledged son of Charles Calvert, the fifth Lord Baltimore," began an alliance with a slave mistress in the late 1780s that had, by the time he married Rosalie Stier in 1799, produced several children for whom he openly took legal responsibility.[2]

1. R. E. Calvert to H. J. Stier, June 10, 1814, in Margaret Law Callcott, ed., *Mistress of Riversdale: The Plantation Letters of Rosalie Stier Calvert, 1795–1821* (Baltimore, 1991), 267–268.
2. Ibid., 17, 378–379. Callcott assumes that Calvert "probably" had more than one slave mistress and that, while his wife never mentioned his liaisons in her letters, "it is

By contrast, Anna Hanson McKenney Dorsey, a noted Roman Catholic author who repeated the same tale almost verbatim in 1892, sixty years after Charles Carroll of Carrollton's death, seems to have regarded her knowlege of it as proof of the caliber of her social connections.[3] In her letter of February 27, 1892, to Notre Dame University's Father Daniel Hudson, editor of *Ave Maria*, a periodical to which she frequently contributed, Mrs. Dorsey wrote:

> I know my friend that you are weary and yawning over my babble but I'll risk a *coup de grace* to "murder sleep." I will tell you of the scrap of private history about Charles Carroll of Carrollton, known only to some of the Carrolls, one or two of the clergy, and some old friends of the family, and which I think redounds to his honor. Charles Carroll of Carrollton was an *illegitimate son* of his father Charles Carroll of the Manor. His mother was his Father's housekeeper, and he had never married. When his son was of the proper age, he sent him abroad to be educated at the English college at St. Omers, Belgium (where by the way my grandfather was educated). When young Carroll's course was finished, he having gained high honors in his classes, his father who loved him and was very proud of him wrote him word to travel a few months and come home — The young fellow travelled but failed to obey his fathers summons home. He received a more peremptory mandate "to return immediately." To this he returned answer: "I will never return home unless you legitimize my birth by marrying my mother, wiping dishonor from her as well as myself."
>
> The next letter he received announced the marriage and he returned home where he was received with festivities and attention on every hand, and by his parents with the greatest pride and affection. Is not life made up of facts stranger than fiction?

---

difficult to imagine" her not knowing of them: "Her slaves knew, and for a number of years Calvert's wife and his mistress lived on the same plantation" (379). For full details, see Callcott's fascinating account "George Calvert's Other Family" (378–384) in her gracefully edited collection of Rosalie Stier Calvert's correspondence.

3. Anna Hanson McKenney Dorsey (1815–1896) was a native of Washington, D.C. Raised as a Protestant, she converted to Catholicism in 1840 and by 1847 had published her first novel, *The Student of Blenheim Forest; or, The Trials of a Convert.* In 1889 James, Cardinal Gibbons presented to Mrs. Dorsey the Laetare Medal, the church's highest lay award, in recognition of her contribution to the development of American Catholic literature. Among her numerous publications are such titles as *Guy, the Leper; Conscience; or, The Trials of May Brooke; Coaina, the Rose of the Algonquins;* and *The Old Gray Rosary.*

Burn all my letters dear Friend sometime before you die — on account of the personalities in them.[4]

Six months later Mrs. Dorsey returned to this theme in another letter:

The little scrap of secret history I imparted to you about Charles Carroll of Carrollton I first heard 40 years ago from a dear and venerable old lady who in her youth and up to that date was and continued to be the intimate friend of Mr. Carrolls daughters Mrs. Caton (the mother of the three English peeresses: the Duchess of Leeds, Lady Stafford, and the Countess of Wellesley): and Mrs. Gen. Harper, the mother of Miss Emily Harper who died recently. She told me many interesting things about the Carrolls. I am glad to say that Mrs. Caton, Mrs. Harper and Miss Emily Harper were my dear friends altho' the two first named were very much older than myself. The fact I related, was one well known in Maryland but never commented on, and was considered rather the glory (I mean his action about his mother's marriage) than the shame of his noble life. I never alluded to it except once, until I told you, and then about 12 years ago, the Rev. Father Griffin of St. Charles Borromea, who is almost a life long friend of mine, and has been for many years Chaplain at Mr. Carrolls seat, "Dohoregan Manor" near St. Charles; called to see me in Washington. We were alone, and I took the opportunity to ask him if the story I had heard was true. He hesitated a moment before answering, then said: "it is true, but people revere the memory of the old signer so deeply, and have such respect for his family, that no one ever speaks of it, in fact it is unknown to the present generation.[5]

The most fanciful — and hopelessly garbled — nineteenth-century account of the circumstances of Charley's birth is contained in an undated letter written to J. K. Harwood (1824–1895) at the city tax office in Baltimore by his wife, Henrietta G. Harwood (by 1852–1885) on a Tuesday in August sometime during the 1870s or early 1880s:

I want to tell you a game story that Mrs. Porter vouches for. The old Harry Dorsey had been away from home a day & a night & was riding home early in the morning, when he saw a bundle hanging on a fence rail. He rode up to

4. Anna Hanson McKenney Dorsey to Father Daniel Hudson, Feb. 27, 1892, University of Notre Dame Archives, Notre Dame, Ind. Father Daniel Hudson was a member of the Notre Dame faculty and edited *Ave Maria* from the 1860s until his death in 1918. Biographical Files, University of Notre Dame Archives.

5. Dorsey to Hudson, July 21, 1892, University of Notre Dame Archives.

Charles Carroll of Carrollton's Birth

it & took it off, when it proved to be a new-born baby. His home was near this Poolesville, and his wife was a Worthington with the uncertain temper of her family. He took the little thing home in his arms, and as his wife come out to greet him, handled the bundle to her. She went into the house, seized a broom stick & proceeded to lay it stoutly upon his head & neck, ordering him to quit the house nor dare bring his children to *her* to care for, that it was easy to see where he had been all night. These circumstances were against him — so he rode disconsolately away, baby in arms. He went to Annapolis — he started inquiries, he paid counsel — he left no stone unturned until he discovered the mother of the child — her name was Nell Darnell (the family still lives here) he went to her — she acknowledged that the child's father was Mr. O'Carroll. Dorsey took the child to its father, telling him all the circumstances & so worked upon the gentleman's mind that he acknowledged the baby, took him to his own house, & sent him to Italy to be educated. The baby was Charles Carroll of Carrollton![6]

Upon ending her letter, Henrietta Harwood found that she had omitted a final bit of information, so she added it after her signature: "I forgot to tell you that the unfortunate Dorsey was an absentee from his own house for 5 months until he could clearly demonstrate the parentage of the baby. Hurrah for Mrs. Dorsey!"

Although imaginatively and incorrectly embellished, the central truth of these narratives graphically demonstrates the persistent influence of lineage, Even during the early decades of the twentieth century, the presence of the bar sinister in the Carroll past led a prominent patriotic society to refuse membership to women who claimed descent through Charles Carroll of Carrollton's line.[7]

6. Henrietta G. Harwood to James K. Harwood, Harwood Family Papers, MS 1022, MdHi. I am grateful to Karen Stuart of the Manuscripts Division, Library of Congress, Washington, D.C., for bringing this missive to my attention during her tenure as Manuscripts Librarian at the Maryland Historical Society.

7. I wish to thank Minnie Hill of Washington, D.C., a direct descendant of Daniel Carroll of Duddington, for this information.

Carroll Real Estate Transactions, Baltimore Town, 1745–1763

APPENDIX 5. Carroll Real Estate Transactions, Baltimore Town, 1745–1763

Year	Amount Sterling	Acres	Number of Lots	Unspecified
1745	£ 25.00.00		5	
1746	20.00.00		4	
1747				
1748	30.00.00		6	
1749	5.00.00		1	
1750	15.00.00		3	
1751	20.00.00		1	
1752	5.05.00			part of Coles Harbour
1753	18.00.00	3		
1754				
1755	6.00.00		1	
1756ᵃ				
1757	61.15.00	43 ¾		
1758	10.00.00		2	
1759	146.03.00 ½	150		
1760	18.00.00		2	the Island
1761	38.00.00		4	
1762	19.14.09		2	
1763	153.06.04	26		
Total	591.04.01 ½	222 ¾	31	

Source: Baltimore County, Deeds, and Provincial Court, Deeds, MdAA. The deeds specify that the property being sold belonged to Daniel Carroll's heirs and reiterate the authority of Charles Carroll of Annapolis to sell it under the provision of his brother's will directing the disposal of all tracts containing fewer than five hundred acres. The lots involved in these sales were located in the original sixty-acre town tract as well as in the subsequent additions to it.

   [a]Although no sales were made during 1756, Charles Carroll of Annapolis accepted lots 63 and 64 as security for a loan of £150 sterling in March of that year.

APPENDIX 6

Genealogical Charts

CHART A: IRISH ANCESTRY OF THE CARROLLS
(DESCENDANTS OF DANIEL CARROLL OF BALLYMOONEY)

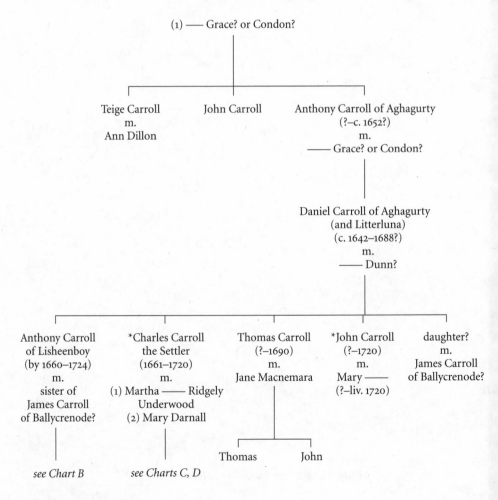

(1) —— Grace? or Condon?

Teige Carroll
m.
Ann Dillon

John Carroll

Anthony Carroll of Aghagurty
(?–c. 1652?)
m.
—— Grace? or Condon?

Daniel Carroll of Aghagurty
(and Litterluna)
(c. 1642–1688?)
m.
—— Dunn?

Anthony Carroll
of Lisheenboy
(by 1660–1724)
m.
sister of
James Carroll
of Ballycrenode?

*Charles Carroll
the Settler
(1661–1720)
m.
(1) Martha —— Ridgely
Underwood
(2) Mary Darnall

Thomas Carroll
(?–1690)
m.
Jane Macnemara

*John Carroll
(?–1720)
m.
Mary ——
(?–liv. 1720)

daughter?
m.
James Carroll
of Ballycrenode?

Thomas   John

see Chart B   *see Charts C, D*

* Immigrated to Maryland.

Donnell McTeige Oure O'Carroll
of Kenechane and Ballymooney
(?–liv. 1642?)
m.
──── Grace?

Daniel Carroll of Ballymooney
(?–by 1661?)
m.

(2) ?

Owen Carroll of Kilmaine
(c. 1653–1723)
m.
(1) Eleanor Coughlan (2) ──── Tunstal

Keane Carroll of Aghagurty
(?– liv. 1700)

Barnaby Carroll
(c. 1690–by 1758)
d.s.p.

daughter
m.
──── Grace

*Daniel Carroll I of Upper Marlboro
(1696–1751)

see Chart E

Owen Grace   Oliver Grace   Elizabeth Grace   Elinor Grace
(minor in 1730)

CHART B: DESCENDANTS OF ANTHONY CARROLL OF LISHEENBOY

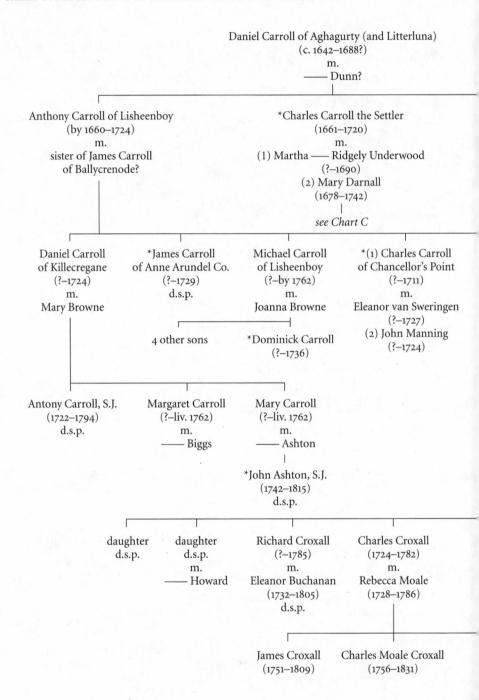

Daniel Carroll of Aghagurty (and Litterluna)
(c. 1642–1688?)
m.
—— Dunn?

Anthony Carroll of Lisheenboy
(by 1660–1724)
m.
sister of James Carroll
of Ballycrenode?

*Charles Carroll the Settler
(1661–1720)
m.
(1) Martha —— Ridgely Underwood
(?–1690)
(2) Mary Darnall
(1678–1742)

see Chart C

Daniel Carroll
of Killecregane
(?–1724)
m.
Mary Browne

*James Carroll
of Anne Arundel Co.
(?–1729)
d.s.p.

Michael Carroll
of Lisheenboy
(?–by 1762)
m.
Joanna Browne

*(1) Charles Carroll
of Chancellor's Point
(?–1711)
m.
Eleanor van Sweringen
(?–1727)
(2) John Manning
(?–1724)

4 other sons

*Dominick Carroll
(?–1736)

Antony Carroll, S.J.
(1722–1794)
d.s.p.

Margaret Carroll
(?–liv. 1762)
m.
—— Biggs

Mary Carroll
(?–liv. 1762)
m.
—— Ashton

*John Ashton, S.J.
(1742–1815)
d.s.p.

daughter
d.s.p.

daughter
d.s.p.
m.
—— Howard

Richard Croxall
(?–1785)
m.
Eleanor Buchanan
(1732–1805)
d.s.p.

Charles Croxall
(1724–1782)
m.
Rebecca Moale
(1728–1786)

James Croxall
(1751–1809)

Charles Moale Croxall
(1756–1831)

*Immigrated to Maryland.

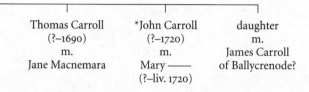

Thomas Carroll
(?–1690)
m.
Jane Macnemara

*John Carroll
(?–1720)
m.
Mary ——
(?–liv. 1720)

daughter
m.
James Carroll
of Ballycrenode?

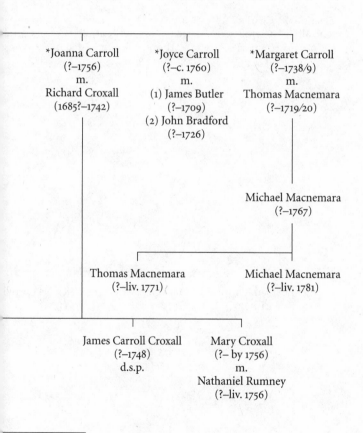

*Joanna Carroll
(?–1756)
m.
Richard Croxall
(1685?–1742)

*Joyce Carroll
(?–c. 1760)
m.
(1) James Butler
(?–1709)
(2) John Bradford
(?–1726)

*Margaret Carroll
(?–1738/9)
m.
Thomas Macnemara
(?–1719/20)

Michael Macnemara
(?–1767)

Thomas Macnemara
(?–liv. 1771)

Michael Macnemara
(?–liv. 1781)

James Carroll Croxall
(?–1748)
d.s.p.

Mary Croxall
(?– by 1756)
m.
Nathaniel Rumney
(?–liv. 1756)

8 other children

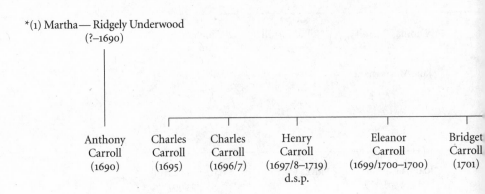

*(1) Martha — Ridgely Underwood
       (?–1690)

| Anthony Carroll (1690) | Charles Carroll (1695) | Charles Carroll (1696/7) | Henry Carroll (1697/8–1719) d.s.p. | Eleanor Carroll (1699/1700–1700) | Bridget Carroll (1701) |

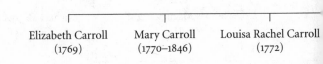

| Elizabeth Carroll (1769) | Mary Carroll (1770–1846) | Louisa Rachel Carroll (1772) |

*Immigrated to Maryland.

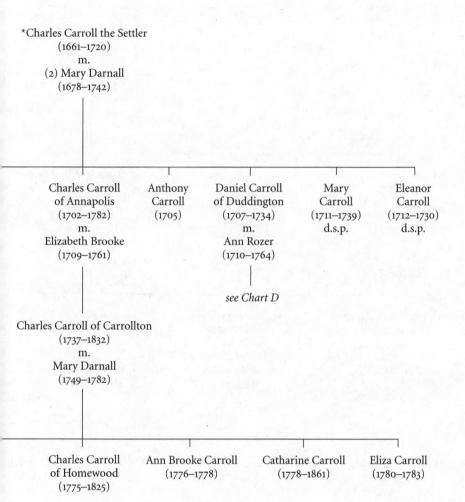

*Charles Carroll the Settler
(1661–1720)
m.
(2) Mary Darnall
(1678–1742)

Charles Carroll
of Annapolis
(1702–1782)
m.
Elizabeth Brooke
(1709–1761)

Anthony
Carroll
(1705)

Daniel Carroll
of Duddington
(1707–1734)
m.
Ann Rozer
(1710–1764)

see Chart D

Mary
Carroll
(1711–1739)
d.s.p.

Eleanor
Carroll
(1712–1730)
d.s.p.

Charles Carroll of Carrollton
(1737–1832)
m.
Mary Darnall
(1749–1782)

Charles Carroll
of Homewood
(1775–1825)

Ann Brooke Carroll
(1776–1778)

Catharine Carroll
(1778–1861)

Eliza Carroll
(1780–1783)

CHART D: DESCENDANTS OF CHARLES CARROLL THE SETTLER:
DANIEL CARROLL OF DUDDINGTON'S LINE

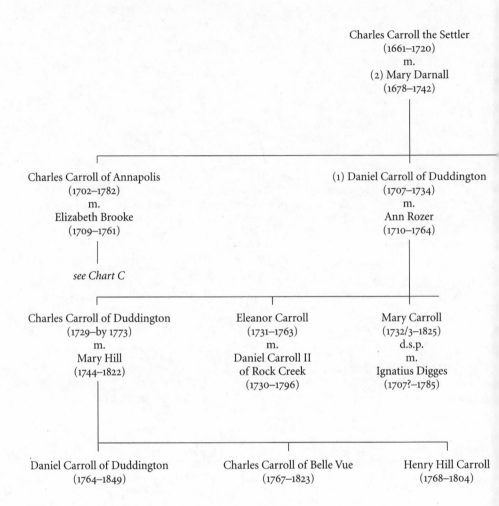

Charles Carroll the Settler
(1661–1720)
m.
(2) Mary Darnall
(1678–1742)

Charles Carroll of Annapolis
(1702–1782)
m.
Elizabeth Brooke
(1709–1761)

(1) Daniel Carroll of Duddington
(1707–1734)
m.
Ann Rozer
(1710–1764)

see Chart C

Charles Carroll of Duddington
(1729–by 1773)
m.
Mary Hill
(1744–1822)

Eleanor Carroll
(1731–1763)
m.
Daniel Carroll II
of Rock Creek
(1730–1796)

Mary Carroll
(1732/3–1825)
d.s.p.
m.
Ignatius Digges
(1707?–1785)

Daniel Carroll of Duddington
(1764–1849)

Charles Carroll of Belle Vue
(1767–1823)

Henry Hill Carroll
(1768–1804)

8 other children

(m. 2) Benjamin Young
(?–1754)

Notley Young
(1736/7–1802)
m.
(1) Jane? or Eleanor? Digges
(2) Mary Carroll
(1742–1815)

CHART E: DESCENDANTS OF DANIEL CARROLL I OF UPPER MARLBORO

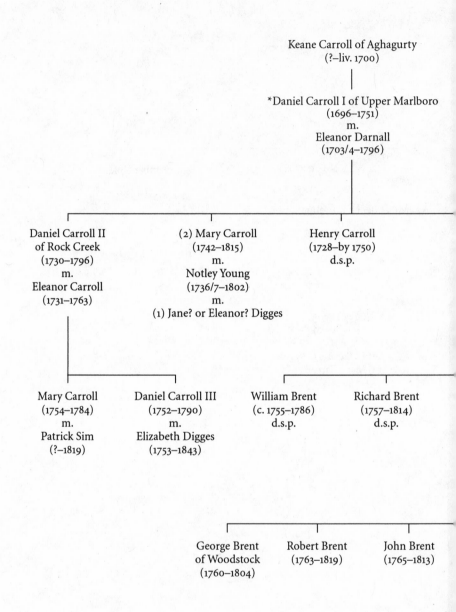

Keane Carroll of Aghagurty
(?–liv. 1700)

*Daniel Carroll I of Upper Marlboro
(1696–1751)
m.
Eleanor Darnall
(1703/4–1796)

Daniel Carroll II
of Rock Creek
(1730–1796)
m.
Eleanor Carroll
(1731–1763)

(2) Mary Carroll
(1742–1815)
m.
Notley Young
(1736/7–1802)
m.
(1) Jane? or Eleanor? Digges

Henry Carroll
(1728–by 1750)
d.s.p.

Mary Carroll
(1754–1784)
m.
Patrick Sim
(?–1819)

Daniel Carroll III
(1752–1790)
m.
Elizabeth Digges
(1753–1843)

William Brent
(c. 1755–1786)
d.s.p.

Richard Brent
(1757–1814)
d.s.p.

George Brent
of Woodstock
(1760–1804)

Robert Brent
(1763–1819)

John Brent
(1765–1813)

*Immigrated to Maryland.

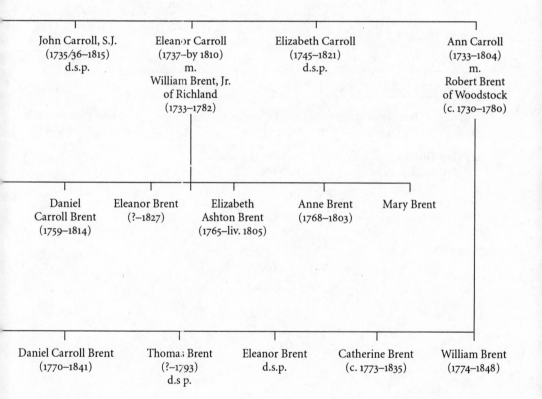

John Carroll, S.J.
(1735/36–1815)
d.s.p.

Eleanor Carroll
(1737–by 1810)
m.
William Brent, Jr.
of Richland
(1733–1782)

Elizabeth Carroll
(1745–1821)
d.s.p.

Ann Carroll
(1733–1804)
m.
Robert Brent
of Woodstock
(c. 1730–1780)

Daniel
Carroll Brent
(1759–1814)

Eleanor Brent
(?–1827)

Elizabeth
Ashton Brent
(1765–liv. 1805)

Anne Brent
(1768–1803)

Mary Brent

Daniel Carroll Brent
(1770–1841)

Thomas Brent
(?–1793)
d.s p.

Eleanor Brent
d.s.p.

Catherine Brent
(c. 1773–1835)

William Brent
(1774–1848)

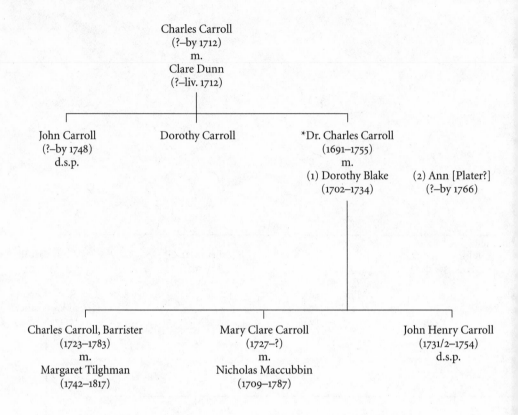

Charles Carroll
(?–by 1712)
m.
Clare Dunn
(?–liv. 1712)

John Carroll
(?–by 1748)
d.s.p.

Dorothy Carroll

*Dr. Charles Carroll
(1691–1755)
m.

(1) Dorothy Blake
(1702–1734)

(2) Ann [Plater?]
(?–by 1766)

Charles Carroll, Barrister
(1723–1783)
m.
Margaret Tilghman
(1742–1817)

Mary Clare Carroll
(1727–?)
m.
Nicholas Maccubbin
(1709–1787)

John Henry Carroll
(1731/2–1754)
d.s.p.

*Immigrated to Maryland.

Index

Abraham (Carpenter Harry's son), 251
Acadians, 277n
Acquaviva, Father Claudius, 153n
Adams, John, 299, 301, 309, 315, 353–354
Adams, Samuel, 315
Administration of Justice Act, 294
Adventurer's Act, 26
Aghagurty, 37, 53
Alcock, Miss, 157n
Alexander, Robert, 308
Allen, Rev. Bennett, 290n
Allen, William, 352
Allen, William, Sr., 356n
Anderson, Joseph Horatio, 250
Anglo-Irish. See Anglo-Normans
Anglo-Normans: and invasion of Ireland, 3–4; and Gaelic Irish, 3–5, 26; and Nine Year's War, 14; culture and acculturation of, 20; under penal laws, 21, 48, 49
Annapolis: as new seat of government, 71–72; merchants in, 75–76; and CCS's land, 101n, 102; architecture in, 103–104, 186, 212–215; in 1765, 186; social life in, 211–213, 215–217, 363, 381; radical meeting in, 295–296; during Revolution, 363, 366–367, 381; State House in, 365, 367
Annapolis quarter, 71–72, 76–77n, 237, 241–242; slaves at, 246, 252; family graveyard at, 387
Anne (queen of England), 78–80
Anne Arundel County, 69n, 72, 310–313
"Antilon," 287–288, 291–292
Arbuthnot, Adm. Marriot, 338
Architecture, 62, 66; and status, 77, 103–104; in Annapolis, 103–104, 186, 212–215; of Doohoragen, 115, 250; Georgian, 212–213
Arnold, Benedict, 338, 359

Arundell, Henry, third Lord, of Wardour, 39–40n
Arundell, Mary, 39–40n
Ashe, Sir Thomas, 16
Ashton, Father John, 240, 255
Athlone, 49
Aughrim, Battle of, 393–394
Aunt Jenny, 165

Baker, John, 176–181
Baker, Louisa, 175–182, 197, 208
Baker, Mary Ryan, 179–181
Ballybritt, barony of, 2, 10
Ballymacadam Castle, 2–3, 16–17
Ballymooney Castle, 24–25
Baltimore, Lords. See Calverts
Baltimore, Md., 120–122, 337, 347, 402
Baltimore Company, 108–110, 120–123; Carrolls' share in, 179, 229–234; location of, 188–189; during Revolution, 345–349. See also Ironworks
Baltimore County, 69n, 72, 76n, 120
Banks Nanny, 251
Barrington, Daines, 174
Bashford Manor, 68, 72n, 107–108, 188–189; collection of rents at, 107–108, 223–228
Bastardy, 80–81n, 142-143, 155n, 398–401
Bath, Va., 188–189, 327, 370, 373–376
Battle Creek Nanny, 251
Beake, Thomas, 80, 83
Bedlam Neck, 223
Belisle, Magdalen, 240, 334
Bellingham, Sir Edward, 16
Bennett, Henry, 34
Bennett, Richard, 186n
Berkeley Springs, Va., 188–189, 327, 370, 373–376
Berruyer, Isaac Joseph, 155, 281
Berry, Jeremiah, 229

Beveridge, David, 353, 357

Bibber, Abraham van, 349n

Bibber, Isaac van, 349n

Bird, Christopher, 172, 192, 194–196, 198, 218

Bird, Esther, 196, 199, 202

Birr Castle, 2, 10n, 16, 22–23, 57

Blackburn, Thomas, 370

Blackstone, William, 142, 164

Bladen, William, 83

Blake, Sarah Darnall, 185–186n

Blakiston, John, 225

Blakiston family, 224

Board of War, 340

Bolling, Robert, 140

Bond, John, 225–227

Bookkeeping, 167, 169–170

Bookplates, 54, 55, 170

Boston Port Act, 294–295

Boston Tea Party, 294–295

Boucher, Rev. Jonathan, 212

Bourdaloue, Father Louis, 155

Bourges, 151–152

Boyne, Battle of the, xxi, 47–48

Bradshaw, Thomas, 175, 192, 194–195

Brashears, Thomas, 118, 221–222n

Brerewood, Thomas, Sr., 116n

Brice, James, 213, 383n

Brice, John, II, 192n

Brooke, Clement (Baltimore Company), 231–232, 345–346, 348–349

Brooke, Clement (ship captain), 103

Brooke, Clement, Sr., 131, 139

Brooke, Elizabeth, 131–132; portrait of, 133. *See also* Carroll, Elizabeth Brooke

Brooke, Jane Sewall, 131–132, 138–139, 195

Brooke, Nicholas, 131–132

Brooke, Dr. Richard, 273

Brooke, Maj. Thomas, 139

Brown, John, 196

Brown, William, 202

Buchanan, John, 261–262

Burgess, Joseph, 240

Butler, James, twelfth earl of Ormond, 33n, 78

Butler, Theobald, 9, 15n

Butler family (earls of Ormond), 5, 10–13, 16

Byrd, William, II, 140

Cadwalader, Dr. Thomas, 352

Calvert, Benedict Leonard, fourth Lord Baltimore, 79–80, 103n

Calvert, Cecilius, 173, 268–270, 277

Calvert, Charles (Maryland governor), 103, 110

Calvert, Charles, third Lord Baltimore, 139; as proprietor of Maryland, 39–40; and control over Maryland government, 44–45; and CCS, 46, 67, 72–73; and Robert Harley, 78–79; and son, 79–81; and Carroll family, 86–87

Calvert, Charles, fifth Lord Baltimore, 398; and selection of guardian, 80; and Carrolls, 91, 173–174, 269–270; and anti-Catholic measures, 273

Calvert, Charlotte Lee, 80–81n, 87, 116

Calvert, Frederick, sixth Lord Baltimore, 287n

Calvert, George, 398

Calvert, Margaret, 87

Calvert, Rosalie E. Stier, 398

Calvert County, 68

Canada: and Quebec Act, 294–295; diplomatic mission to, 299–300, 304, 307, 355, 358–360

Carberry, John Baptist, 224n

Carew, Sir George, 15

Carmichael, William, 331

Carmichael, William, Sr., 185–186

Carpenter Harry, 251

Carroll, Alexander, of Kilfadda, 54, 56, 58

Carroll, Ann Brooke (Nancy), 366, 371

Carroll, Ann Rozer, 104–105, 114

Carroll, Anthony (son of CCS), 65

Carroll, Anthony (son of Michael of Lisheenboy), 54

Carroll, Anthony, of Aghagurty, 32–33, 36

Carroll, Anthony, of Lisheenboy, 36–38,

Index

186n; and Stuarts, 38; at Limerick, 51; and Lisheenboy, 52; and sons, 54–55; death of, 56

Carroll, Anthony, S.J. (1722–1794), 56–59, 153

Carroll, Barnaby, 57–58

Carroll, Caesar, 58

Carroll, Catharine (Kitty), 372, 389–390, 400

Carroll, Dr. Charles, 109, 229–230, 269–273

Carroll, Charles, Barrister, 229, 231, 293, 296; and Maryland constitution, 311–313; and Baltimore Company, 346; death of, 349

Carroll, Charles, the Settler, xxi–xxiii, 30, 321–322; Catholicism of, xxiii–xxiv, 37–38, 82–83, 269; emigration of, to Maryland, 36; education of, 37–38; defiance of, 44; imprisonment of, 45–46; and family responsibilities, 53–54; portrait of, 60; marriages of, 64–66; estate of, 68, 76–77, 99–101; and acquisition of land, 70–73, 223–224; as merchant, 75–76; and political power, 77–79; and proprietary officials, 82–83; and John Hart, 83–86, 89–95; and oath of abjuration, 85–86, 88; death of, 95; slaves of, 111, 115

Carroll, Charles, of Annapolis, xxii–xxiii; wealth of, xxiii, 120, 122–123, 176; portraits of, 96, 134; and study of law, 101, 166; genteel identity of, 139–140; emotional reserve of, 166, 210–211; frugality of, 191–192, 215–216; self-sufficiency of, 241–242; and slavery, 253–257; and treatment of servants, 258–259; trip of, to London, 275–276; Enlightenment ideals of, 281–282; life experience of, 322; death of, 386

— advice: on manner and dress, 150–152, 184; on money and frugality, 151, 191–192, 215–216; on religion, 154–155; on women and marriage, 157–163, 178, 182, 205, 211; on education, 163–164, 166–170; on

socializing, 172; on plantation management, 246–247; on merchants, 260–261; on laudanum, 372–373, 382

— agriculture, 235–264: estate income of, 107–108; and tenancy, 111–113; as landlord, 224–225; and Doohoragen Manor, 242–243, 334, 339; as agricultural experimenter, 247–248

— business life: cashbook of, 103–104, 113n, 117–118n; as estate agent, 108–109; and Baltimore Company, 109–110; as moneylender, 114, 122–123, 262–264; and tobacco merchants, 261–262

— family relationships: and translation of genealogy, xxiv–xxv; and family memory, 29, 269–270; and father's estate, 76n, 101, 108; house of, in Annapolis, 103–104; and family responsibilities, 114, 125, 129–130; family lawsuits against, 123–130, 218–219; common law relationship of, 136–142, 161, 398; marriage of, 138, 398–401; will of, 142–144; and plan for Charley, 144–148; as grandfather, 207–208, 210–211; and fight over James Carroll's will, 271–272

— political life: and tobacco bill, 106–107; and Stamp Act, 285; and political office, 291–293, 317; and opposition to Great Britain, 300; and legal tender act, 318–330; and petition to assembly, 326–327; on taxation, 335

— religion: Catholicism of, xxiv, 279–281; importance of, 154–155; and Catholic repression, 266–267; plan of, to move to Louisiana, 275–278

Carroll, Charles, of Carrollton: Catholicism of, xix–xx, xxiv, 265–266, 281–282; Enlightenment ideals of, 155–156, 314; and view of women, 157n, 162, 194–196, 201–202; portraits of, 170–171, 199–200; emotional reserve of, 182–183; and adoption of appellation "of Carrollton," 188–190; adjustment of, to Maryland, 191–194; correspondence of, with English friends, 192–194; library of, 193; and slav-

ery, 254–255; life experience of, 322–323;
as aristocrat, 323–324; and family wealth,
327–329, 390; death of, 389
—business life, 218–234; and management
of manor lands, 223–229, 334–336, 339;
and Baltimore Company, 229–234, 345–
350; as moneylender, 262–264
—family relationships: courtships of, 195,
200–201; marriage of, 204–205, 351–388;
relationship of, with children, 208–211;
correspondence of, with wife, 355–356,
358–360, 369–370; correspondence of,
with father, 357, 360–361; and visit to
springs, 373–376; on death of father and
wife, 387–388
—political career: and Whig republican
rhetoric, 283; as "First Citizen," 287–288,
291–292; duel of, with Lloyd Dulany,
289–290; and Committee of Correspondence, 297; and public office, 297, 366;
and diplomatic mission to Canada,
299–300, 304, 307, 355, 358–360; and Second Continental Congress, 299, 308; on
government, 300–301, 312–314; and signing of Declaration of Independence, 301,
308–309; and Samuel Chase, 304–305,
330, 385–386; and notion of public service, 306–307; apprehensions of, over
Independence, 314–316; and legal tender
act, 318–330; on taxation, 335–336; social
life of, in Philadelphia, 351–355
—youth: description of, xxiii, 200, 377;
birth of, 132; illegitimacy of, 134–136,
141–142, 398–401; education of, 143–145,
150, 153–154, 163–164; and mother, 144,
146–147, 165; and the law, 163–168, 306;
bookplate of, 170; and geneaologist, 170;
negotiations of, with John Baker, 177–
181; return of, to America, 183–185
Carroll, Charles, of Doughoragen, 389
Carroll, Charles, of Duddington, 123–132,
169, 187, 218–219, 229, 231, 274–275
Carroll, Charles, of Homewood, 209, 211,
357, 380, 384, 389
Carroll, Daniel (son of Anthony of

Lisheenboy). *See* Carroll, Daniel, of
Killecregane
Carroll, Daniel, I, of Upper Marlboro, 53,
101n, 269
Carroll, Daniel, II, of Rock Creek, 53n, 125,
130, 187, 190, 239, 283, 332, 386; portrait
of, 190
Carroll, Daniel, of Aghagurty (and Litter-
luna), 35–36, 51–52, 54–55
Carroll, Daniel, of Ballymooney, 24n, 25,
29–32, 36
Carroll, Daniel, of Duddington (1707–
1734), 97, 101, 104, 108–109, 114, 123
Carroll, Daniel, of Duddington (1764–
1849), 130
Carroll, Daniel, of Killecregane, 37n, 51,
53–54, 56
Carroll, Daniel, of Litterluna. *See* Carroll,
Daniel, of Aghagurty
Carroll, Dominick, 56, 186n
Carroll, Eleanor (1712–1730), 86, 99–100,
103, 108, 131
Carroll, Eleanor Carroll (1731–1763), 105,
124, 127, 130, 187, 276n
Carroll, Eliza, 380, 389
Carroll, Elizabeth (Charley and Molly's
first child), 206, 371
Carroll, Elizabeth Brooke, 131–142; mar-
riage of, 132, 275, 280, 289; portrait of,
133; common law relationship of, 136–
142, 161, 398; family of, 139; relationship
of, with son, 144, 146–147; death of, 165,
187, 199
Carroll, Henry (1697–1719), 87n, 97, 100–
101, 185
Carroll, Henry (ship captain), 172
Carroll, James, of Anne Arundel County,
37–38n, 53, 56, 76, 101–102, 108, 271–272
Carroll, James Maccubbin, 349
Carroll, Jane Macnemara, 51n
Carroll, Joanna, 53
Carroll, John (son of Daniel of Agha-
gurty), 36
Carroll, John (son of Thomas), 51
Carroll, John, S.J. (Cousin Jack), 144, 152,

175, 355; as first Catholic bishop in U.S., 53n; and diplomatic mission to Canada, 304; and family funeral, 384, 387

Carroll, Joyce, 53

Carroll, Keane, 53

Carroll, Louisa Rachel, 207–208, 371

Carroll, Margaret, 53

Carroll, Martha Ridgely Underwood, 64–67, 71n

Carroll, Mary (1711–1739), 99–100, 103, 108, 131

Carroll, Mary (1732–1825), 105, 124, 126, 128, 130, 332n, 378

Carroll, Mary (1754–1784), 368, 377

Carroll, Mary (little Pol, little Molly), 207–208, 210, 355, 357, 362; inoculation of, 380, 382; and grandmother's death, 384; adulthood of, 390

Carroll, Mary (widow of John), 51

Carroll, Mary Browne, 54, 56

Carroll, Mary Darnall (Molly): and Papa's household, 187, 198–199; relationship of, with Charley, 200–201; marriage of, 202–206, 351–388; and visit to springs, 327, 370, 373–376; and time with Papa, 354–355, 362; correspondence of, with Charley, 356, 358–360, 369–370; pregnancies of, 364–366, 370–371, 377; and laudanum, 364–365, 372–373, 382; and Revolution, 369; health of, 369, 380–387; and Frederika von Riedesel, 375–377; death of, 387. *See also* Carroll, Charles, of Carrollton

Carroll, Mary Darnall (wife of CCS), 67, 99, 104, 108, 111n

Carroll, Mary Hill, 128n, 129, 231–232n, 346n, 349

Carroll, Michael, of Lisheenboy, 53–54, 56, 58, 186n

Carroll, Nicholas Maccubbin, 349

Carroll, Owen, of Kilmaine, 36, 57–58

Carroll, Thomas (son of Daniel of Aghagurty), 36, 51

Carroll, Thomas (son of Thomas), 51

Carroll's Delight, 264

Carrollton Manor, 68, 112–113, 188–189; leases at, 116–119, 340–345; rents at, 118–119, 342–345; acreage of, 122n; tenants at, 220–222; as managed by Papa, 342–343

Carter, Robert (of Nomini Hall), 231–232, 345

Castles: of the O'Carrolls, 2–3, 10n, 16–17, 22–25, 57

Caton, Elizabeth, 390, 400

Caton, Louisa, 390, 400

Caton, Mary Ann, xxvi, 390, 400

Caton, Richard, 390

Cecil County, 68

Challoner, Richard, 267n, 278–279, 281

Champion, Anthony, 174–175

Chance (tract), 124, 179, 235

Charity (wife of Johnny), 254

Charles I, 19–21, 26–27, 30, 41

Charles II, 28, 33–34, 87

Chase, Samuel, 215, 305–306; and Charley, 292–296, 330, 353–354; and diplomatic mission to Canada, 299, 304, 307; and John Adams, 301, 353–354; and Second Continental Congress, 308, 313; and Maryland constitution, 311–313; Papa's anger at, 325–326; and purchase of Carroll tobacco, 337; as "Censor," 385–386

Chase, Rev. Thomas, 304–305

Cheseldyne, Kenelm, 228

Cheseldyne family, 224

Chew, Joseph, 396

Chew, Samuel, 76

Chlorosis, 382

Christie, James, 192n

Christie, Robert, 347

Clandestine marriage, 137–138

Clarendon, Edward Hyde, second earl of, 38

Clarke, Cuthbert, 248

Clarke, Edward, 239

Class, 62, 63, 138; and religion, 63–64n, 267–268; upper, in Annapolis, 186, 217, 272; and merchants, 260–261; Charley's sense of, 282, 323–342; Revolution as threat to, 301, 316, 320, 329; and women, 378

"Clericus Philogeralethobolus," 291n

Clifton, William, 128–129

Climacteric, 163

Clinmalira, 87n, 101n, 115–116, 219

Clinton, Sir Henry, 355

Clonlisk, 2, 10, 16

Cloth and clothing: as measure of wealth, 77, 105; Charley's purchase of, 150, 152, 170; and social impressions, 184–185; nuptial, 196, 202; weaving of, 241, 244, 339–340; of slaves, 339

Clouen Couse, 113n, 219

Coercive Acts, 294–296

Coles Harbour, 120–121, 402

Collège Louis-le-Grand, 276

Colmore, Thomas, 101n

Compton-Bassett, 274n

Concord. See Western Branch

Condon, Eleanor, 23n

Condon family, 23

Confiscation: in Ireland, xxi, 6–7, 19, 27, 50; in Maryland, 330–332

Connacht, 1–2, 6, 27

Considerations on the Propriety of Imposing Taxes (Dulany), 284n

Continental army, 336n, 352

Continental Association, 298

Continental Congress: First, 296, 354; Second, 299, 308, 329

Convention army, 375–376

Conversion, partial, 269, 281

Convicts, 231–232, 258

Coode, John, 43, 63, 139, 224

Cooke, John, 195

Cooke, Rachel, 195–198, 208

Cooke, Sophia Sewall, 195

Cooke, William, 128–129, 185-186n, 195, 218

Cranch, Richard, 309

Cromwell, Oliver, xxi, 27–28

Cromwellian settlement, 27–29, 47

Crookshanks, Alexander, S.J., 175–176, 181, 277

Crops: diversification of, 237; for food, 240–241; at Doohoragen, 243–245, 247

Croxall, Richard, 110n, 168

Curtis, Michael, 223–224, 228

Curtis, Sarah, 223

Darnall, Col. Henry: as Catholic in upper house, 43; and CCS, 45, 70, 97; as proprietary official, 67, 70; marriage settlement of, with CCS, 68–69n; death of, 73; slaves of, 396

Darnall, Henry, II, 101n, 103, 269

Darnall, Henry, III, 169–170

Darnall, Henry, Jr., 170, 198–199, 202n, 203–204

Darnall, John, 119n, 169–170

Darnall, Mary (Molly). See Carroll, Mary Darnall (Molly)

Darnall, Rachel Brooke, 167, 187, 259; marriage of, 198–199; and petition to assembly, 202n, 203–204; move of, to Doohoragen, 205; and grandchildren, 362, 383; as nurse to daughter, 383–384; death of, 384–385

Darnall, Robert, 203–204

Darnall's Goodwill, 113n

Deards, John, 216

Deards, William, 212, 216n, 241–242, 335, 366n

Declaration of Independence, 301, 308–309

Dederick, Bernard, 240

DeLancy, James, 356n

DeLancy, Margaret Allen, 356

Dennis, 251

Dick and Stewart (merchants), 299

Dickinson, John, 353

Dickinson, Mary Cadwalader, 356

Dickinson, Philemon, 356n

Digges, Charles, 197

Digges, Ignatius, 124, 128–129, 140, 187, 192n, 218, 383n; and double-tax bill, 274–275

Digges, Mary Carroll, 105, 124, 126, 128, 130, 332n, 378

Digges, William, 43

Dilling, James, 264
Dillon, Ann, 23n
Dillon family, 23
Dominicans, 37
Donaldson and Roe (merchants), 347
Donnington, James, 240
Doohoragen Manor, xxv, 69n, 72, 101n, 132, 188–189, 235–236; as managed by Papa, 111, 115; architecture of, 115, 250; slaves at, 120, 339, 350; acreage of, in 1764, 122n; in settlement with Charles Carroll of Duddington, 124, 220; Papa's move to, 205; organization of, 237, 241–242; artisans at, 240, 242; weaving operations at, 241, 244, 339–340; vineyard at, 248–249; livestock at, 340; at close of American Revolution, 350; von Riedesels visit to, 377
Doohoragen Valley (Ireland), xxv, 393
Dorchester County, 68
Dorsey, Anna Hanson McKenney, 399–400
Dorsey, Edward, 347
Dorsey, Samuel, 347
Dorsey's Forge, 347
Douai, Jesuit school at, 100n, 101
Douglas, James, 49
Dower right, 141–142, 160, 202–203
Doyne, Joshua, 107, 224–225, 226
Duddington Manor, 104–105, 114, 188–189
Duke of Gloucester Street (Annapolis), 211–212, 214, 350
Dulany, Daniel (son of Walter), 348
Dulany, Daniel, Sr., 108–109, 348
Dulany, Daniel, Jr., 123, 206; as deputy secretary, 173–174; opposition of, to private petition, 204, 289; and Baltimore Company, 229-230, 232n, 233, 346n, 348; and Stamp Act, 284; and officers' fees, 286–287; as "Antilon," 287–288, 291–292; and Dr. Charles Carroll, 288; and duel with Charley, 289–290; and Revolution, 299–300, 321; toast to, in Philadelphia, 354
Dulany, Daniel, III, 231, 348–349n
Dulany, Lloyd, 206, 212–213, 289–290
Dulany, Rebecca, 288n
Dulany, Walter, 123, 229–231, 233, 286
Dunlap's Maryland Gazette, 300–301
Dutch East India Company, 294
Duvall, Lewis, 66n
Duvall, Martha Ridgely, 66n

Eastern Branch, 113n, 219
East India Company, 294
Eddis, William, 212
Eden, Betty, 370
Eden, Sir Robert: as colonial governor, 212, 219, 361; and fee schedule, 286–288; and Carrolls, 291–292; house of, 331, 363
Education, 100n, 101, 163–166; of women, 103–104, 211. See also St. Omer, College of the English Jesuits at
Edward VI, 11, 24n
Elisha, 251
Elizabeth I, 11, 13, 20
Elk Ridge. See Doohoragen Manor
Ely (Éile), 395
Ely O'Carroll (Baltimore County tract), 116, 219
Ely O'Carroll (Ireland), 1–3, 7–16, 21–25
Enfield Chace, 76n, 99, 111
English Civil Wars, 26–27
Enlightenment, 155–156, 281–282
Explanation, Act of (1665), 29n, 33n
Eyre, John, 34n

Fahy, Edmund, 16–18
Fee controversy, 285–288, 293
Fenwick, Ignatius, 349
Field, Thomas Meagher, 147n, 192n, 283n
Fifteen Rebellion, 78, 81, 88
"First Citizen," 287–288, 291–292
Fitzgerald, Gerald, eighth earl of Kildare, 7n
Fitzgeralds (earls of Kildare), 5, 12, 16
Fitzhugh, William, 327
Fitzredmond, William, 84
Flanigan, Dennis, 260
Flattery, John, 239, 340, 366n
Flour scandal, 330, 385n
Folly Quarter, 238, 252

Forensic Club, 191, 212, 304
Frank, 338n
Franklin, Benjamin, 304, 354, 380n
Frederick County, 122n
Frederick Town, 188–189
Frost, James, 238, 248, 252, 254–255

Gaelic Irish, 3, 6–7, 9–14, 19–20, 22
Galloway, Samuel, 192n
Gardens: in Annapolis, 213–214, 350; kitchen, 241; at Doohoragen, 249–250; of slaves, 255
Garrett, Amos, 76
Gates, Horatio, 308n
Gavelkind, 7n, 23–24
Geffes Increase. *See* Annapolis quarter
Genealogy: and Carroll family identity, xxiv–xxv, 9, 56–59, 138–139, 170, 279
Gentility, 77, 139–140, 164, 217, 306. *See also* Class; Cloth and clothing; Wealth
George, James, 240, 249
George, John, 240, 249
George I, 78, 80
Gerard, Thomas, 223, 228
Germanna, Va., 112n
Germans, 111–112, 259–260
Gibbons, James, Cardinal, 399n
Gibson, John, 227
Ginkel, Godard van Reede, baron von, 48
Girles Portion, 113n, 219
Glen and Organer's quarter, 237, 252
Glorious Revolution, xxii, 40–41
Godman, Samuel, 312n
Goldsborough, Robert, 296n, 311
Gordon, Thomas, 240
Goslin Kate, 251
Governor's Club, 352–353
Grace, John (Richard's nephew), 49
Grace, John, of Courtstown, 33n
Grace, Richard: and Carrolls, xxi, 34–35, 37–39, 88; and Stuarts, 20, 33; in confederate army, 32; death of, 49–51
Graiden, 195
Graves, William, 187; as Charley's friend and correspondent, 174–175, 192–194,

201, 208–209, 220, 249, 282, 296–297; legal counsel of, 203; and Papa, 205, 209–210, 235, 285
Gray, Leonard, 395
Gray's Inn (Inns of Court), 100n, 101
Great Britain: Civil Wars of, 26–27; and Glorious Revolution, 40–41; and oath of abjuration, 141. *See also* Ireland; Penal laws; Roman Catholics
Grenville, George, 265
Griffin, Father, of St. Charles Borromea, 400
Grove, Mrs., 80n
Grove Place, 177, 179
Gunpowder Plot, 197
Guy Fawkes Day, 197n

Halifax, earl of, 273
Hall, Benjamin, 101n
Hall, Francis, 185
Hall, John, 227, 295–296, 305–306, 313
Hall, Martha Neale, 185
Hamilton, Alexander, 359n
Hamilton, James, 352
Hammond, John, 305
Hammond, Matthias, 213, 295
Hammond, Rezin, 311–313
Hancock, John, 354
Hanley, Thomas O'Brien, 136
Hanson, John, 327, 329, 379
Hanson, Samuel, 367–368
Harford, Henry, 287n
Harley, Robert, earl of Oxford, 78–79
Harper, Catharine Carroll, 372, 389–390, 400
Harper, Emily, 400
Harper, Robert Goodloe, 389
Harris, Edward, 107
Harrison, Thomas, 121
Harry (Carpenter Harry's son), 251
Hart, John, 78–80, 82–85, 89–95
Harwood, Henrietta G., 400–401
Harwood, J. K., 400
Head of Elk, 185n, 188–189, 338
Health: and malaria, 190–191; and fever,

195; of slaves, 256; and smallpox, 256; of women, 358; and laudanum, 364–365, 372–373, 382; and infant mortality, 371; and chlorosis, 382

Hearne, Thomas, 80n

Heart's Delight, 274n

Heath, James Paul, 288n

Heeson, John, 238–239

Heinrich XLIV, count of Reuss, 375n

Henny, 255–256

Henry II, 3–4n

Henry VII, 5

Henry VIII, 4n, 5–6, 395

Herne, Daniel, 53n

Hill, Ann Meredith, 356

Hill, Clement, 43, 124–129n, 169, 274–275

Hill, Henry, 353, 356n

Hill, Richard, 353n

Hockley Forge, 229, 345, 347–348

Hollyday, Henry, 272

Hollyday, James, 107

Homony Club, 212

Hooe, Robert T., 313

Horace, 323

Horse racing, 127n, 212, 217

Horses, 56-57n, 104, 171, 370

Housing. *See* Architecture

Howard, Dr. Ephraim, 347

Howard, James, 337

Howe, Sir William, 338

Hoxton, Watty, 144

Hudson, Father Daniel, 399–400

Hunter, George, S.J., 275, 277

Hunter, James, 347

Hussey, Richard, 174

Hutchinson, Thomas, 294

Hutton and Maire, Messrs., 172

Hyde, John, 73–74

Ignatius of Loyola, St., 153n

Illegitimacy: of Charley, 134–136, 141–143, 191, 398–401

Indentured servants, 240, 258–260

Index Librorum Prohibitorum, 281

Infant mortality, 371

Inflation: and ironworks, 346

Inheritance: of land by marriage, 65–68, 71, 141

Inner Temple, 38, 163, 170

Inns of Court, 100n, 101, 163

Intolerable Acts, 294–295

Ireland, Capt. John, 132, 239, 252

Ireland: confiscation of land in, xxi, 6–7, 19, 27, 50; provinces of, 1–2, 6; clan warfare in, 4–5; British seizure of land in, 5–6; and Parliament, 54; and tenant labor for America, 111–113

Ireland, Act for the Settlement of (1652), 27

Ironworks, 109–110, 229–234. *See also* Baltimore Company

Jackson, Andrew, 389

Jacob's quarter at Doohoragen, 237, 252

James, duke of York, 33

James's, Mayara, quarter at Doohoragen, 237, 252

James I, 19–21, 197n

James II, 33n, 38–40, 46–48, 51–52n

James III (Old Pretender), 78, 81n, 293

Jay, John, 331

Jefferson, Thomas, 140, 376

Jen(n)ings, Edmund, 174, 192–193, 195, 197, 200, 282, 284

Jenison, Father John, 153–154

Jennings, Juliana, 383n

Jennings, Thomas, 383

Jesuits: and Anglo-Normans, 37; educational system of, 86-87, 100n, 143–145, 153-154; and tenancy, 112–113; in Maryland, 136, 138; Carrolls' reaction to suppression of, 156, 280

Johnny, 254, 368

Johnson, Joseph, 220–221, 343–344

Johnson, Joshua, 298–299, 331, 341–342, 387

Johnson, Thomas, Jr., 295–296, 308, 311, 313, 366; and Carrolls, 128–129, 218–219, 293, 328, 351

Jointure, 176, 179, 203

Jordan, James, 227

Joseph, William, 43

Kent County, 68
Kent Island, 185
Key, Edmund, 192n
Kildare, earls of. *See* Fitzgeralds
King George's War, 272
King's County (Ireland), 7, 12, 29
Kinsale, Battle of, 16, 18, 279
Kinship among slaves, 250–252

Laborers: Irish immigrants as, 111– 113; Germans as, 111–113, 259–260; convicts as, 231–232, 258; indentured servants as, 240, 258–260; prisoners as, 340. *See also* Slaves
La Fayette, marquis de, 382
La Rue, Pierre de, 276–277
Laudanum, 364–365, 372–373, 382
Law: study of, 101, 163–168, 306; and gentility, 164
Laws, Timothy, 240
Lawyers, 75, 397
Leap Castle, 16–17
Le Blanc, Ann, 240
Lee, Arthur, 352
Lee, Francis Lightfoot, 352
Lee, Mary Digges, 378–379, 385
Lee, Richard Henry, 352
Lee, Thomas Sim, 332, 378, 384–385
Lee, William, 352
Leeds, Louisa, duchess of, 390, 400
Legal tender act, 318–330
Leinster, 1–2, 5–6, 29n
"Leixiphanes," 291
Le Normant de Mézy, Sébastien-François-Ange, 276
Lewellin, John, 228
Lewis, Fielding, 370, 374
Limerick, articles of, 48, 51–52
Lineage, 138–139, 279
Lisheenboy, 53–54
Litterluna (Baltimore County tract), 101n, 116, 219
Litterluna (parish in Ireland), 1
Little Bellean, 64, 66
Lloyd, Col. Edward, III, 185

Lloyd, Edward, IV, 185–186n, 215, 371
Lloyd, Elizabeth Tayloe, 371
Lloyd, Philemon, 85, 396
Locke, John, 156
Louis XIV, 40, 47, 293n
Louisiana, 275–278
Lowe, Charles, 83, 88
Lowe, Vincent, 43
Ludwell, Philip, III, 174, 193
Lythe, Robert, 7–8

Maccubbin, Nicholas, Sr., 350
McGrath, Milerus, 14
Mackenzie, Daniel, 386
Macnemara, Margaret Carroll, 92
Macnemara, Michael, 132n
Macnemara, Thomas, 92–94
Malvell, Alexander, 240
Maners, Mat(t)hias, 132, 138
Manning, Robert, 155
Marriage. *See* Carroll, Charles, the Settler; Carroll, Charles, of Annapolis; Carroll, Charles, of Carrollton
Mary I (queen of England), 6–7, 12
Maryland: governor's council of, 41, 45–46, 270; charter of, 41–42; and plantation duty, 42n; assembly in, 42–43, 72n, 75, 81; franchise in, 42–43n, 81, 94–95; administrative structure of, 44; annual income in, 62; land office of, 70n; restoration of proprietary government in, 78–80; official seals in, 82n; marriage in, 136–138; anti-Catholic legislation in, 141, 273–274; map of, 188–189; currency of, 263; political climate in, 272–273; and Committee of Correspondence, 295–297, 304; and Declaration of Independence, 299n; conventions in, 301, 309–310; constitution of, 311–316; and legal tender act, 318–330; ironworks in, 346–347
Maryland assembly: and act against Catholics, 90, 94–95; and tobacco bill, 105–107; and Baltimore Town, 120–121n; and law of descents, 143; and Carrolls'

petitions, 202–204, 225; and black regiment, 257; anti-Catholicism in, 270, 273–274; and double-tax bill, 274; and officers' fees, 286

Maryland Gazette, 268–269n, 275, 286–287, 311, 379, 385

Meara, John, 239, 255

Mellwood, 124, 130, 188–189, 274n, 368

Memory: and family history, xx–xxii, 88, 95–96; transmission of, xxiii–xxiv; and Irish tract names, xxiv, xxv; Papa's, of Catholic repression, 265–266, 270, 309–310; and Charley, 266, 279–280; of ill-treatment by Calverts, 269; in family rivalries, 288

Mercantilism, 126, 167, 169–170

Meredith, Reese, 356

Middle Temple, 57–58

Mills, William, 227

Money lending, 73–75, 262–264

Monmouth, duke of, 38

Monocacy (Carrollton Manor), 113, 119, 222–223, 343–344

Monocacy River, 112

Montesquieu, 156

Moravians, 341

Morris, Robert, 315

Mortgage loans, 73–75, 264

Moses' quarter, 237, 252

Moylan, Stephen, 353n

Munster, 1–2, 5–6, 13n, 29n

Murdock, Catherine, 368n

My Lady's Manor, 87n, 115–116

Nan Cook, 251

Neale, Raphael, 226–228

New English, 20

Newton, Sir Isaac, 156

Nine Years' War, 4–16, 19

North, Francis, second Baron Guilford, 80, 83, 86, 88

Notley, Thomas, 104–105n

Oates, Titus, 38–39

O'Carroll, Sir Charles, 12–15, 18

O'Carroll, Daniel, 1–3

O'Carroll, Donnell McTeige Oure, 23–25

O'Carroll, Fearganainm, 395

O'Carroll, John (great-nephew of Sir Charles), 15

O'Carroll, John (son of William), 12n, 15–16

O'Carroll, Sir Maolroona, 156

O'Carroll, Teige (d. 1553), 11, 13, 18

O'Carroll, Teige McCallagh, 22–23

O'Carroll, Sir William Odher, 11–12, 13, 18, 24n

O'Carrolls (of Litterluna), 17–18, 23

O'Dempsey clan, 5

O'Dunne clan, 5

Offaly, 1, 7, 12

Ogle, Anne Tasker, 212–213n, 321

Ogle, Benjamin, 387n

Ogle, Henrietta Hill, 363, 371, 387n

Ogle, Samuel, 212n, 225n

O'Kennedy clan, 10

Old English, 20, 25–27. *See also* Anglo-Normans

Olum, Cian (Kean), 395

Olum, Oliol, 395

O'More, Rory, 26, 31–32

O'More clan, 5

O'Neill, Hugh, earl of Tyrone, 14–16, 18, 19n, 279

Organer's, Glen and, quarter, 237

Ormond, earls of. *See* Butler family

Ormond, Eleanor, 16

Outlet (Prince George's County). *See* Western Branch

Paca, William, 213, 292–296, 308, 311, 313; and Forensic Club, 191

Paine, Robert Treat, 354

Pale (Ireland), 4–6, 13n, 16

Paris, xxv, 142, 150, 152, 275–277

Parliament, 283–284n, 294–295

Parsons, Sir Laurence, 22–23, 57

Parsons, William, 22–23, 31

Patapsco River, 120, 245, 346–347

Patterson, Robert, 390

Patuxent River, 113, 248

Pearle, Basil, 221

Pearle family, 221n–222n

Peggy Stewart, 299

Penal laws: in Great Britain, xx, 27–28, 197n, 272–273; in Maryland, xx, xxii, xxiv, 44, 141, 270–271; in Ireland, xx, 21, 48, 49, 56–57

Penet, Pierre, 337

Penn, John, 353

Penn, Richard, 353

Pennsylvania, 263, 352

Perkins, William, 172–173, 202

Persons, Ralph, S.J., 143n

Peters, Richard, 339–340

Petre, Edward, S.J., 39n

Petty, Sir William, 27

Philadelphia, 308, 337, 351–353. *See also* Continental Congress

Philips, Bartholomew, 223

Philpot, Thomas, 248, 261

Pitt, William, 291

Plantation: of Leix-Offaly, 12–13; of Ulster, 21; of Ely O'Carroll, 21–25

Plater, George, 311

Popish plot, 38–39

Poplar Island, 76n, 111, 122n, 236, 241–242, 254–255; crops at, 120; location of, 188–189; slaves at, 252, 258; British raids on, 337–338, 380

Potatoes, 243, 245, 247

Potomac River, 341

Powis, Lady Elizabeth Somerset, 40n

Powis, William Herbert, earl of, 39–41

Pratt, Robert, 174

Prince George's County, 68, 76n, 113, 118, 122n. *See also* Clouen Couse; Compton-Bassett; Enfield Chace; Girles Portion; Graiden; Heart's Delight; Mellwood; Western Branch

Principio Company, 109n

Proprietary government, 285–288, 397

Prostitutes, 158, 201

Protestants: in Ireland, 21–26, 48; during civil war, 26–27; rebellion of, 38, 43, 63,

139, 224; and William of Orange, 40; in Maryland, 42–44, 63–64n, 81, 212. *See also* Ireland; Roman Catholics

"Protestant Whig, A," 291

Pye, Edward, 43

Quartering Act, 295

Quebec Act, 294–295

Queen Anne's County, 68

Queen's County, 12

Rachel, 251

Ratio Studiorum, 144, 153n

Rebellion of 1641, 26–29, 305

Redor, Thomas, 227

Reed, Esther DeBerdt, 378–379

Reed, Joseph, 378

Religious toleration, 38–39, 309

Renzi, Mathew de, 8–9

Republican ideology, 266, 283, 287

Restoration settlement, 28

Revolution, American, 299, 301, 303–317

Reynolds, Sir Joshua, 170–171, 200

Rheims, Jesuit college in, 153

Ridgely, Charles, 66n

Ridgely, Robert, 64, 66n

Ridgely, Robert, Jr., 66n

Ridgely, William, 66n

Ridgely-Underwood plantation, 64, 66, 72n

Ridhearg, Eile, 395

Ridout, John, 212–213, 217, 242, 321, 323, 368–371

Ridout, Mary Ogle, 212–213, 217, 362, 368–371, 384

Ridout, Meliora, 384n

Riedesel, Frederika von, 374–377

Riedesel, Friedrich von, 374–375

Riggs, James, 237–240, 246, 248

Rock Creek, 188–189

Rodney, Caesar, 315n

Roe, Walter, 347n

Roman Catholics: and penal laws, xx, xxii, 21, 27–28, 44, 48–49, 270–271; and laws on marriage, 136–138

—in Ireland and England: proportion of, in Irish population, 19n; divisions between, 20; and attack on Protestant settlers in Ulster, 26, 305; lands and civil rights of, 27–29, 48–49; under James II, 38–39; appointment of, 46–47; under articles of Limerick, 48; proportion of land held by, 49–50; and entry to professions, 54–55, 163–164; conversion of, 58; as gentry, 177

—in Maryland and America: marginalization of, xx, 282, 284–285; wealth of, xx; in upper house, 42; and proprietary patronage, 43; and oaths for public office, 44, 84–85, 90; and first bishop, 53n, 278–279; and office holding, 63, 81; and entry to professions, 81, 163–164; voting rights of, 94–95, 268–269n; education of, 143; and anti-Catholicism, 226, 293, 265–270; families of, 267n; conversion of, 269, 281; taxation of property of, 273–275, 279

Roundheads (Parliamentarians), 26
Rowland, Kate Mason, 136, 154n
Royalists (Cavaliers), 26–27
Rozer, Ann, 104–105, 114
Rozer, Henry, 124
Rozer, Jane Digges, 104
Rozer, Notley, 104
Rozolini, Onorio, 132–135
Rudyard, Richard, 88n
Rudyard, Richard, Jr., 88n
Russell, William, 387
Rutledge, Edward, 315n
Ryan, Thomas, 179–180

Sacramental marriage, 137–138
St. Anne's Church, 212, 271, 290n
St. Clement's Manor, 68, 72n, 107–108, 188–189, 220, 223–228
St. Croix, 176
Saint-John, Henry, Viscount Bolingbroke, 78
St. Mary's City, 42, 62, 188–189
St. Mary's County, 68, 72n, 107–108. See

also Bashford Manor; St. Clement's Manor
St. Omer, College of the English Jesuits at, 86–87, 100n, 143–145, 153–154
St. Thomas Jenifer, Daniel of, 192n, 292, 317, 326, 370–371
Sales, Francis de, 281
Sam's quarter at Doohoragen, 237, 252
Sam's Sue, 251
Saratoga, Battle of, 376
Sarsfield, Patrick, 48
Schuyler, Betsy, 359
Schuyler, Catherine Van Rensselaer (Mrs. Philip), 358
Schuyler, Peggy (Margarita), 359
Schuyler, Gen. Philip, 358
Scott, Dr. Upton, 213, 364, 380, 386
Scott, Mrs. Upton, 364
Sears, William, 254–255, 338
Seirkieran Parish, 23–25, 29
Servants, white, 258–260
Settlement, Act of (1662), 28–29, 33n, 36n
Settlement of Ireland, Act for (1652), 27
Seven Years' War, 186, 212, 268, 272, 274
Sewall, Nicholas, 43, 139, 186n
Sharpe, Horatio: as governor of Maryland, 204, 212, 267–268, 270, 275–276; departure of, 321
Sharpe, William, 173, 276
Sharper, 339
Shippen, Dr. William, 352
Sibthorp, William, 240
Sidney, Sir Henry, 11n–12n
Sidney, Sir Philip, 193
Sim, Joseph, 368n
Sim, Mary Carroll, 368, 377
Sim, Col. Patrick, 368, 377
Sim's Delight, 377–378
Skerrett, William, 255, 366n
Slaves: held by CCS, 73; trade in, 76; of Daniel Carroll of Duddington, 105; of tenant farmers, 113; at Doohoragen, 115, 120, 238, 250–252; in Annapolis, 217; and Baltimore Company, 230–232, 345–346; as head of Doohoragen quarter, 237; and

food supply, 240–241; organization of, 250–251; as artisans, 251; punishment of, 253–255, 258–259; spiritual life of, 255; and health, 256–257; clothing for, 339; transfer of, from Poplar Island, 339; as measure of wealth, 396; and relationships with masters, 398–399n

Slieve Bloom Mountains, xxv, 1, 10, 393–394

Slye, George, 227–228

Smallpox, 169, 256, 365, 380

Smallwood, Gen. William, 382

Smith, Ellen Hart, 136

Smith, Joseph, 345–346, 386

Smith, William, 349n

Society of Jesus. *See* Jesuits

Somerset, Edward Maria, 87

Somerset, John, 39–40n

Somerset County, 307–308

Spotswood, Alexander, 110, 112

Squiers, Daniel, 259

Stafford, Elizabeth, Lady, 390, 400

Stamp Act, 192, 265, 283–285, 304

State House (Annapolis), 365, 367

Steuart, Dr. George, 192n

Stone, Thomas, 308

Stone, William, 396

Stuart, Charles Edward (the Young Pretender), 268, 272, 293n

Stuart, James Edward Francis, 78, 81n, 293

Suckey, 251, 339

Sucky at Poplar Island, 339

Sukey's quarter at Doohoragen, 237, 252

Surrender and regrant, 5–7, 10–14

Swinburne, Henry, 197n

Talbot County, 68. *See also* Poplar Island

Tametsi, 137–138

Tasker, Benjamin, Sr., 109, 111n, 229–231, 233

Taxation: and the American Revolution, 317–325, 329; and Carroll fortune, 328, 335

Taxes, 42n, 273–275, 279, 294, 317–325, 328–329, 335

Tenantry in Maryland, 112–113, 115–119, 219–225

Tender act, 320–332

Thomas, John, 387n

Tilghman, Edward, of Wye, 185

Tilghman, James, 319

Tilghman, Julianna Carroll, 185–186n

Tilghman, Matthew, 219, 293, 308, 311, 352

Tilghman, Richard, 352

Tilghman, Col. Richard, III, 185

Tilghman, Richard, IV, 185

Timothy, 242, 250, 259

Tipperary, County, 7–8, 10

Tobacco, 105–107; depression of trade in, 109; as rent, 118, 220, 222, 225–226, 228, 341–343; in Baltimore, 121; planting and cultivation of, 243–246; marketing of, 260–262, 328; and inspection act, 285–286; and nonexportation laws, 298–299; and wartime gains, 336–337; profits from, 342n; as measure of wealth, 396

Tootell, Dr. Richard, 363

Townshend, Charles, 294

Townshend Acts, 294

Trent, Council of, 137, 280

Tuesday Club, 212

Tuite, Nicholas, 176n

Turnbull, John, 240, 258–260

Tyrconnell, Richard Talbot, earl of, 38–39, 46–47

Tyrone, earl of. *See* O'Neill, Hugh, earl of Tyrone

Ulster, 1–2, 6, 13n, 21

Underwood, Anthony, 64–66n

Underwood, Thomas, 66n

Villiers, Barbara, 87

Voltaire, 155, 281, 284–285

Wallace, Charles, 212, 341

Wallace, Davidson, and Johnson (Wallace and Company), 261–262, 298, 341

Ward, William, 240

Waring, Basil, 125–129n, 169, 274–275

Washington, George, 217, 307, 389–390
Washington, John Augustine, 370, 374
Wealth: and material culture, 62–63, 77, 105, 170–172; protection of, 161, 203, 313–314, 316; and social position, 170–172; of Carroll family, 187, 350; among Catholics in Maryland, 267; and threat of Revolution, 299, 301; in Maryland, 396–397
Webster, Daniel, xix
Wellesley, Mary Ann, Lady, xxvi, 390, 400
Wellesley, Richard Colley Wellesley, second earl of Mornington, first Marquess, xxvi, 390
Wellington, Arthur Wellesley, first duke of, xxvi, 390
West and Hobson (merchants), 216, 260–261
Western Branch, 76n, 111, 113, 120, 219, 228–229
Westwood Manor, 68
Whetcroft, William, 346

White, Edward, 53
White, Harry (Henry), 258, 260
William III, xxi, 40–41, 47–48
William IV, 390
Williams, Rev. John, 249
Willoughby, Mr., 157n
Wine, 127–128, 173, 217, 241, 248–249, 353n
Wollaston, John, 139
Women: education of, 103–104, 211; and health, 358, 382; and pregnancy, 364–366, 370–371; and class, 378; and support of troops, 378–379
Woolsey, George, 336
Woolsey and Salmon (merchants), 336
Worth, William, 54
Worthington, Brice T. B., 311–313

Young, Mr., 246–247
Young, Ann, 104–105, 114; children of, 105, 114
Young, Arthur, 247
Young, Benjamin, 114
Young, Notley, 114n, 129n